AF469920

SCOTLAND: FIVE DECADES

Acknowledgements

With special thanks to Clare Crawford for believing that I should write this myself, along with her inspirational editing; to Mark Bennett for his extreme patience and sensitive layout and to publisher Trevor Maher for his faith in the three of us.

First published in Great Britain in 2012 by
Lomond Books Ltd.
14 Freskyn Place
East Mains Industrial Estate
Broxburn EH52 5NF
www.lomondbooks.com

A CIP catalogue record for this book is available from the British Library

ISBN 978-1-84204-296-0

Printed in China

Front cover images, top left, clockwise:
Wee Janie, Maryhill;
Bells' Bridge, Glasgow;
Provost Bobo, Inverness;
The Lonach Gathering;
Boness and Kinneil Steam Railway;
Suilven;
Newhaven ladies.

(Right) I ♥ topiary, Caithness.

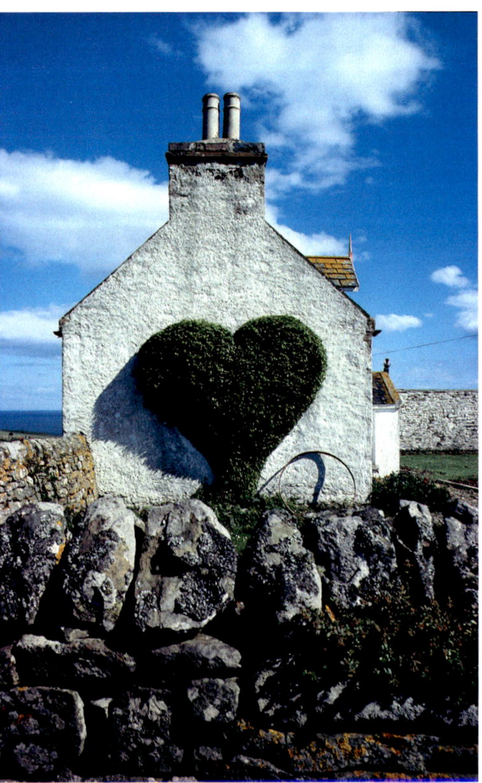

Back cover images, top left, clockwise:
St Margaret's Loch, Edinburgh;
The Falkirk Wheel;
Boys' Brigade Sunday parade in Dunfermline;
Cawdor Castle;
Glasgow Cathedral;
Speaker at the Mound, Edinburgh;
Roughpark, Aberdeenshire.

SCOTLAND: FIVE DECADES

of Photographs by

DOUGLAS CORRANCE

LOMOND

Foreword

I was fortunate enough to work alongside Douglas Corrance, albeit briefly, at *Scotland on Sunday* in 1991. The paper was blessed in having two fine young photographers in Ian Rutherford and Adam Elder, both multiple award winners later in their careers, but we had set the bar high and recruited two more classy performers in young Paul Hackett, who went on to work for *The Sunday Times*, and not-so-young Doug Corrance.

Doug soon settled in as the 'guvnor', and we all learned from his presence. I had worked in London for most of my career and had admired Doug's work from afar when he was official photographer for the former Scottish Tourist Board, and as regularly as the Scarista House Hotel appeared in the pages of the metropolitan press as the best in Scotland at the time so did the byline 'Douglas Corrance' – the latter probably photographed the former. In my experience, no two photographers are the same, and although the machinery inside their heads is best kept a mystery we had at *Scotland on Sunday* the best team in the country.

Apart from routine news, sport and feature coverage, competition was fierce to bag the front page. It has always been a challenge to get a good Saturday picture for a Sunday paper with nothing much apart from sport going on. Some of Doug's pictures from *SoS* appear in this volume, and the one that stands out in my recollection is of Ravenscraig and how he captured the scourge of unemployment there after the steel works closed. The picture on page 34 epitomises the qualities that define Doug's class. The composition is pure and simple, but the rawness of black and white imagery doesn't happen by chance. The lowering sky catches the mood of despair, and the hunched posture of the man, and the dogs, speaks for a whole blighted community. Patience, possibly the finest quality in any photographer, is Doug's hallmark.

I looked at every picture on these pages and remember many of them – some of the portraits are sweetly divine: James Kelman, Billy Connolly, the three wifies from Newhaven in their furry finery, Wee Janie in Glasgow. Don't go looking for them – just wait as you turn the pages and enjoy. This is a book that describes Scotland over fifty years and every diasporic Scot should own it, all 30 million of them at the last count. Respect.

Graeme Murdoch
January 2011

Contents

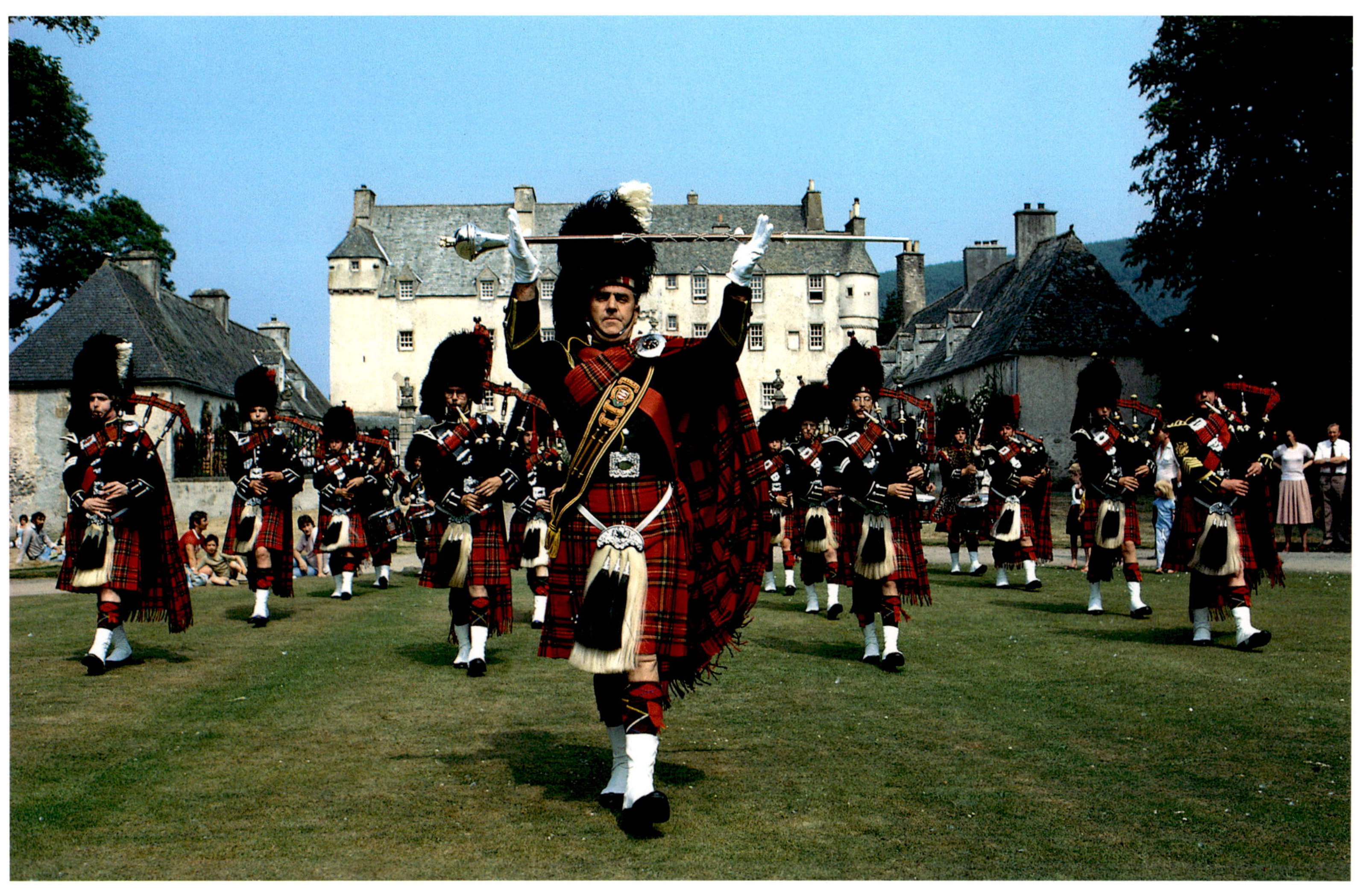

Peebles Pipe Band in front of Traquair House, one of Scotland's finest mansions. It is also reputed to be Scotland's oldest inhabited house.

'Photography is serious, everything else is fun.'

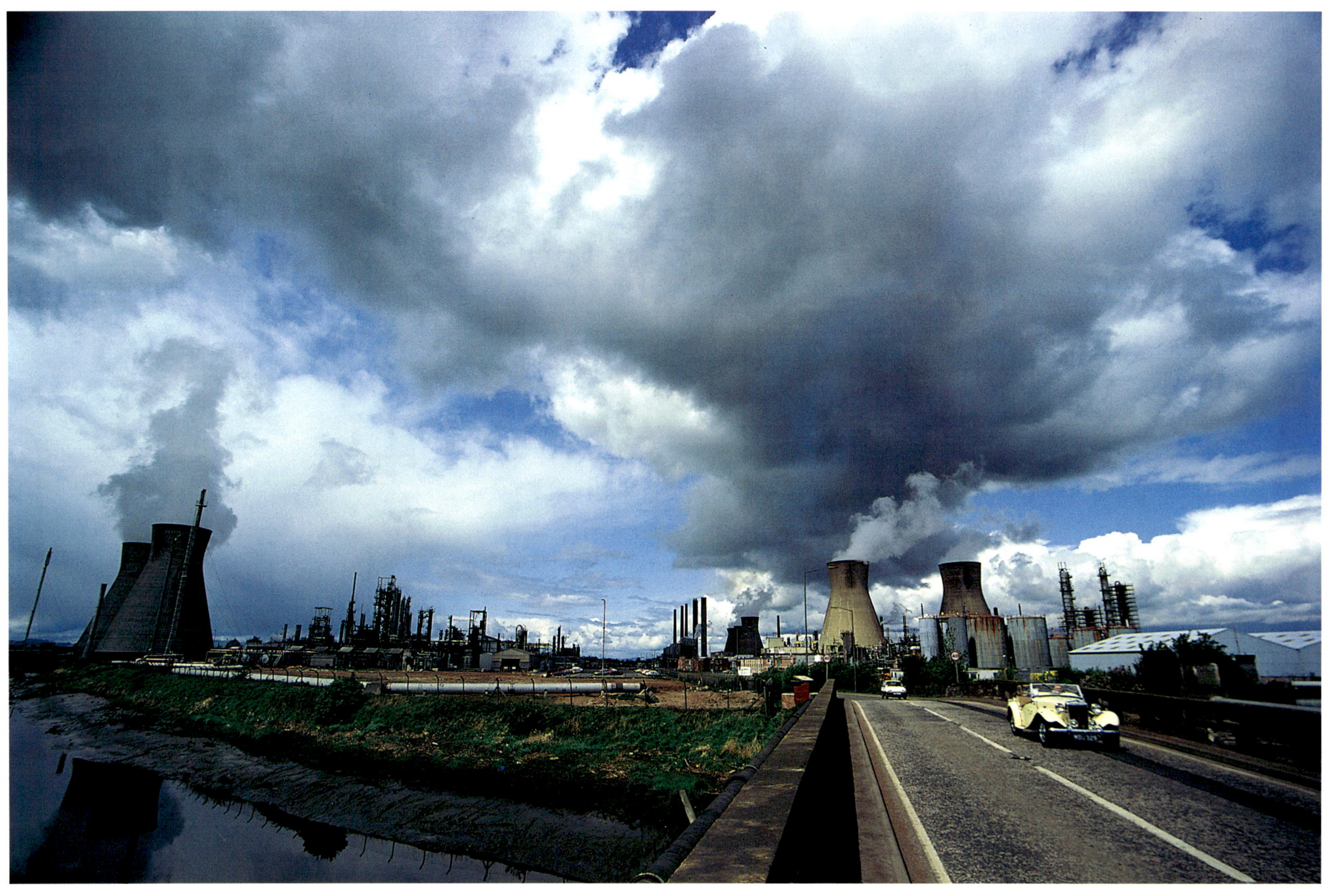

Chemical works and oil refineries are my earliest olfactory memories. I spent the first six years of my life in Grangemouth, and I still enjoy industrial odours, although perhaps not as much as the tang of a west coast beach or the scent of a pine forest. I also like the smell of fermentation from whisky distilleries.

I was born in Falkirk in 1947, the so-called baby-boomer year, which was also the beginning of the welfare state, an important event that sadly at the moment seems to be a victim of its own success. Our parents were war-weary and wanted a lot for their children, not material wealth but security and fulfilment. We still had defined communities – not that I was always happy to be part of them. I had to attend the Boys' Brigade each week and church every Sunday. At a parents' evening during a marching display I went left when the order was right, to my parents' double embarrassment. It caused a laugh and the spectators thought I was a bit of light entertainment, thus setting an unconscious pattern for my life. What I really wanted was to build a kayak and paddle my own canoe.

Scotland has a very identifiable image because of its unique and beautiful scenery and its romantic and colourful heritage. I was seven when my family moved from the industrial south in Grangemouth to Inverness, so my earlier years were spent looking on to an oil refinery and then changed to seeing wild salmon being netted at the mouth of the River Ness. Once, on a picnic with my mother on the side of Loch Ness, we witnessed the loch's phenomenon. We watched, for approximately ten minutes, a large hump with a wash like that of a small motorboat. I have never doubted what we saw, even when my account is met with derision from people who have made no study of this fascinating occurrence. Scotland has many myths that are believed in but where undeniable proof is given, many scoff. I was nine at the time and did not have a camera.

After a less than glorious period at school I could draw and paint and was good with my hands, but sums and spelling were not my bag. My future looked like tedium beyond belief. My childhood ambition was to be an artist in a garret in Paris, although by that time the scene had decamped to Greenwich Village, New York.

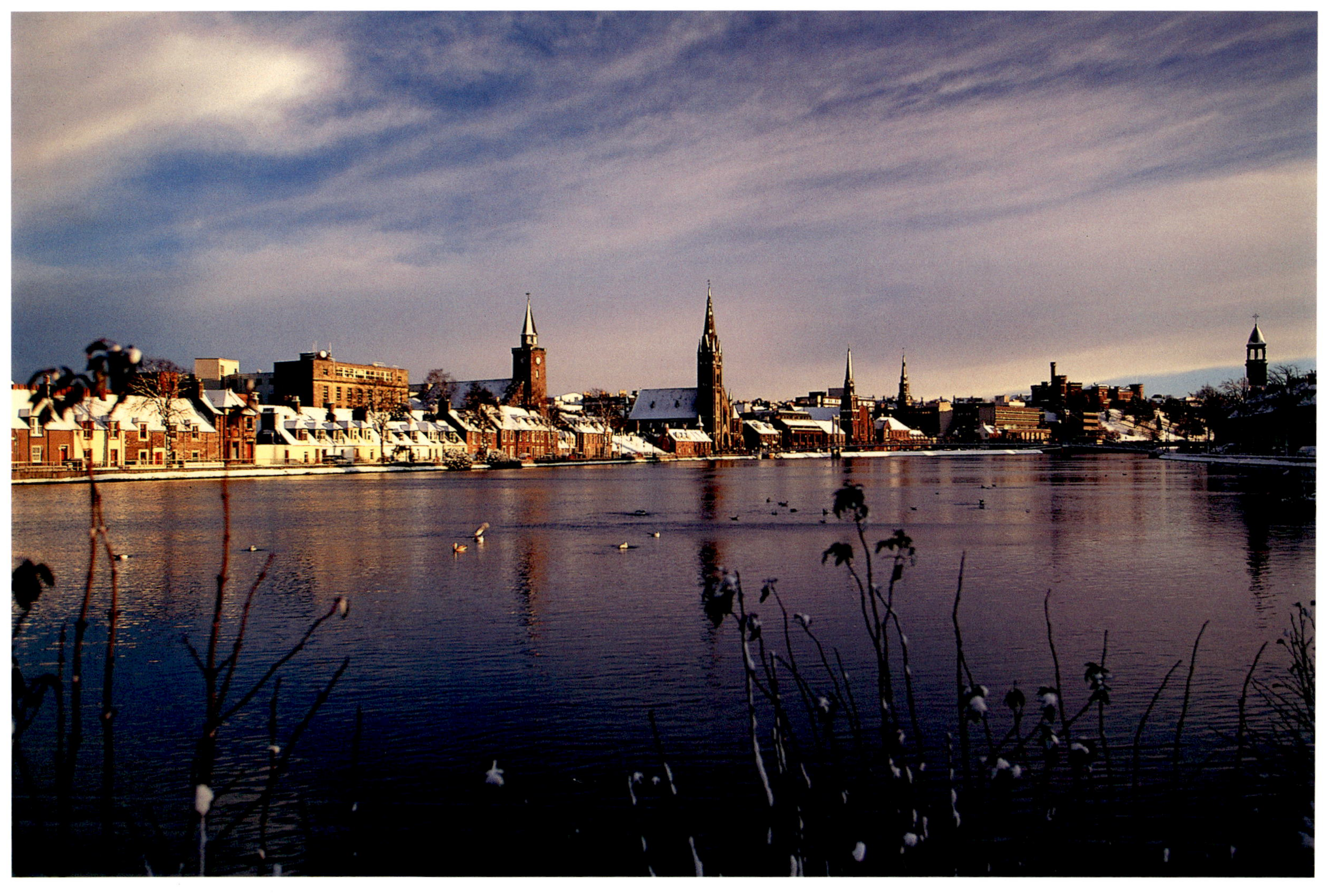

I would have had to have read the Beat poets to have known that, but they were not available in Inverness library to a twelve-year-old.

The 'promotion' examination to secondary school at age eleven ludicrously decided a child's whole future and did not recognise individual talent. At primary school the headmaster would turn on his valve radio and relay BBC schools programmes to each class through the Tannoy system. We had illustrated pamphlets to complement these broadcasts. One of these was on Africa, with accompanying photographs by George Rodger. I was totally transfixed, as I was when I saw Elvis in *Jailhouse Rock* at the Inverness La Scala cinema. Suddenly there was more to life than that classroom with its high windows through which all I could see was grey skies. Those images changed me. I knew why they stood out and why they were so special. Thirty years on I met George Rodger, a British photographer and co-founder of Magnum Photos, the famous international photographic cooperative, and was delighted to be able to tell him my tale, but unfortunately I never saw Elvis Presley live. I suffered from a primary teacher who had little imagination and tried to teach us her prejudices, which I hope have not stuck. She also had the wrong heroes – John Bunyan, self-denial and misery for nine-year-olds – and Elvis did not touch people like her. Secondary school was just a waiting room for life, except for a couple of excellent teachers. One was my first form teacher, Brian Denoon, in his first job. I had the dubious honour of giving him his long-lasting nickname, 'Hiram', after a well-known television character. I recently received a copy of his book, *Do You Say 'Sir' To Your Father?* (about his upbringing in the Highlands). It's good to still be in touch. Art teachers were usually pretty good as well. Miss MacKechnie was a great encouragement, and her beatnik appearance brought a touch of the exotic to the art class. Some of the others seemed

Near the mouth of the River Ness was where salmon were once netted. The church spires dominate what is now the cityscape of Inverness, equalled only by the number of public houses.

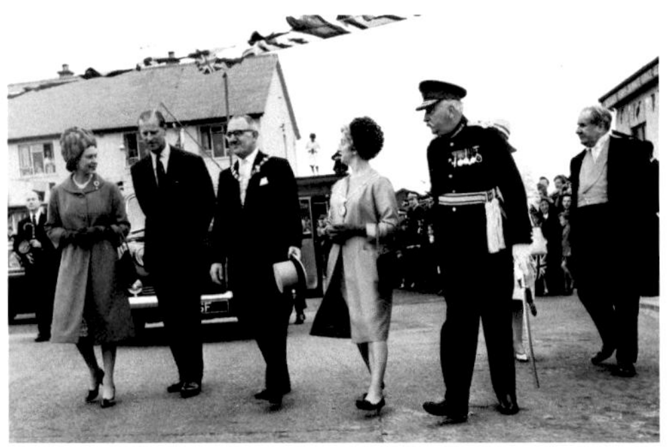

(Right) Inverness Provost Bobo MacKay opens a Scout fête. This was one of my first front page pictures for the *Highland News* in 1963. Bobo was refreshingly down-to-earth compared with some other incumbents of the office. He would give football commentaries for the blind at Highland League football matches and was always a great subject for a photograph. (Above) This photograph shows Bobo escorting Her Majesty the Queen when paying a visit to Inverness in the early 1960s. Immediately after this photograph was taken he made a remark that had everyone in stitches, even the Lord Lieutenant (on the right). I caught the action, and it was reckoned that I had the best shot of the royal visit. Sadly, the negative and the prints have disappeared.

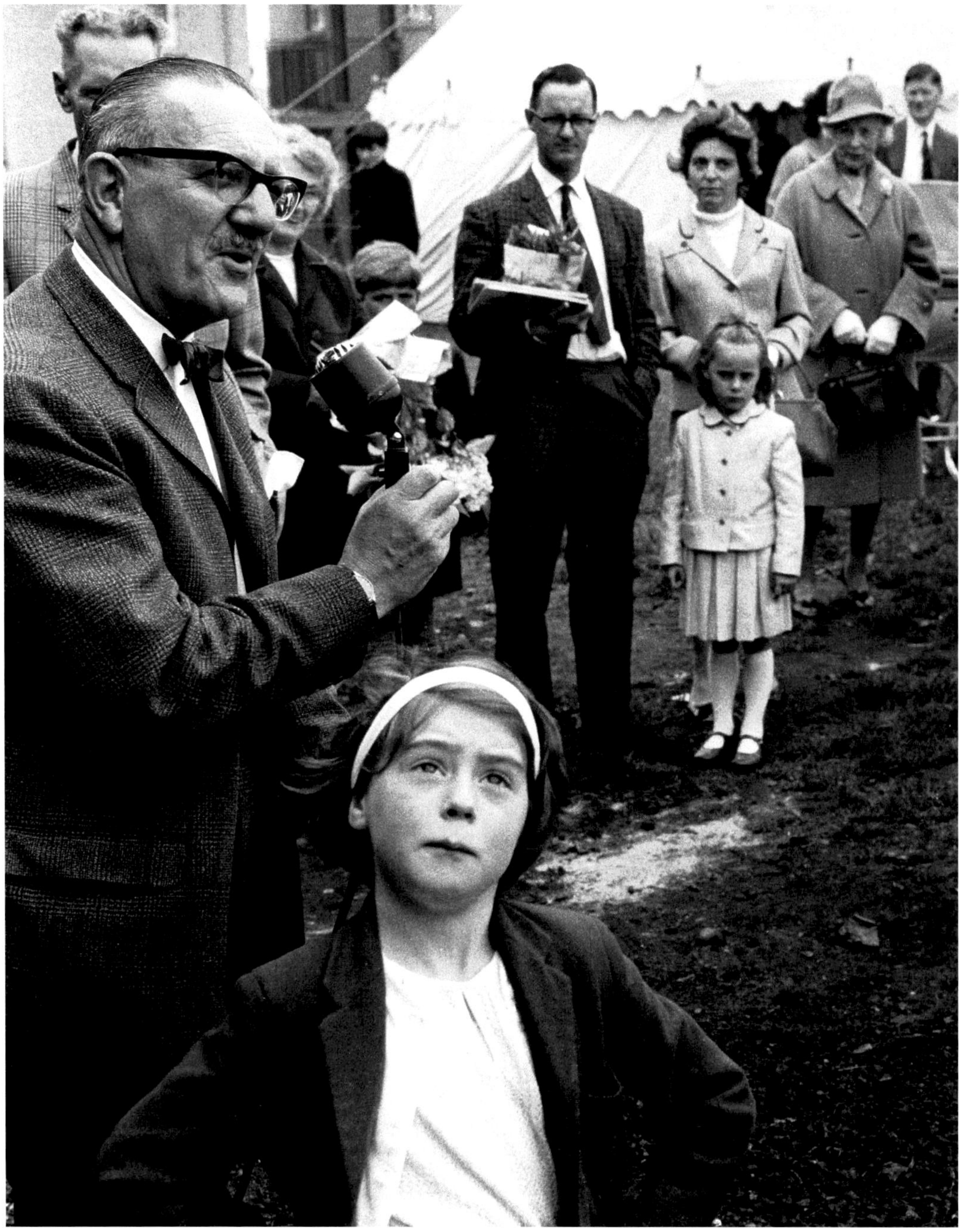

to take pleasure in putting fear into us, but we had the sixties waiting for us.

My saving was getting a job, aged fifteen, as an indentured photographer on the *Highland News*. Harvey Grainger, now a retired Church of Scotland minister, was my boss, and what a great way to enter the world of work – no regular hours and colleagues enjoying what they did. I was given responsibility immediately. By the time I was sixteen, Harvey had become the editor, I had a Rollieflex and a pushbike, and my brief was to take pictures for the *Highland News*, *Chronicle* and *Football Times*. Saturdays were hell and have put me off soccer forever. I had to snatch a goal before half-time and cycle back through sometimes near gale-force winds with horizontal rain, then process and print the image, make the metal printing block and run out to the stone (the composing bench), to be met with 'Where the bloody hell have you been? You'd better have a goal.'

Growing up in a small town gives you a different perspective from the one a city child would have, and working for the local press gave me access to everything that was going on. When I ventured into the wider world I had an attitude of perhaps going where angels fear to tread, along with an obvious naïvety. I had to photograph dinner dances, sometimes four a night, but by this time I had graduated to a motor scooter. Having to organise groups of sometimes up to one hundred people, while making sure all their faces were visible in the picture, was quite a task. I was very shy, but in photography this can work to your advantage. People can sense your shyness, and most want to

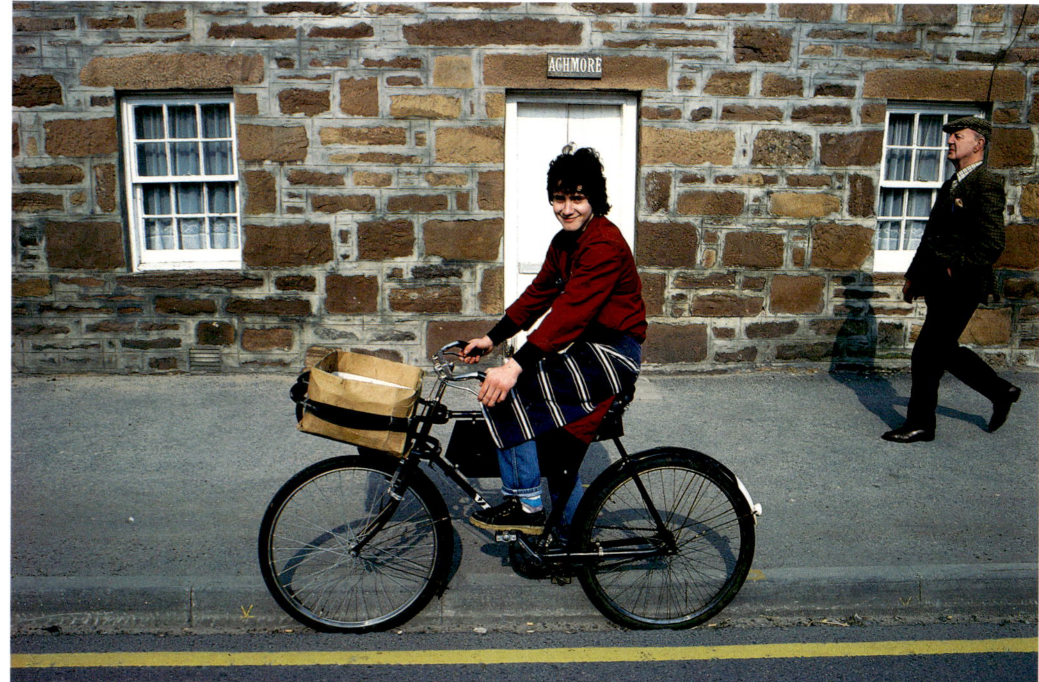

From the age of twelve, after school and all day Saturday, I was the message boy for the local grocer. I had to make a twice-weekly delivery with up to one hundredweight of provisions to the school hostel, where pupils from the islands and remote Highland regions, lodged during term time. The bike had no gears, and pushing it up Stratherrick Brae was a real challenge, especially in sideways rain or on ice. Seeing this butcher's boy in Golspie on a similar bike in the mid-1970s transports me back to that time.

make things easier for you. The copies of *Picture Post* and *Life* magazines that Harvey left in the department were an inspiration.

My indentures finished when I was eighteen and a half, and I decided to take some time out. I spent two years in Australia where I did mundane commercial photography. I carried on doing this on my return to London, but in both places my spare time was spent doing street photography, never thinking I could make a living out of it. I was becoming a *flâneur*, the impassioned observer who is most at home with the movement of people. I was also having fun, but my adventures were curtailed when I was robbed in Marrakesh. My father's philosophy was that there are more good people in the world than bad, that's how we survive. I ended up back in Inverness doing freelance press work and weddings, but no babies.

The town, now a city, had changed. A lot of people had been away, had done a lot of travelling and were now back. There was a commune in the hills around Loch Ness, and one of its residents, David Larcher, a photographer, came into my studio with what seemed to be a blank sheet of photographic paper. 'Can you mount this on board for me?' he asked and explained, 'You have to look at it for thirty minutes to see it.' I found this intriguing.

David's home was a silver-coloured furniture removal van high in the hills. He used a daylight enlarger and washed his films in a Highland stream, the grit scratching the surface and adding texture. On the face of it, this sounded like the antithesis to my way of working. I discovered later that David had been a top fashion photographer in London, working for *Vogue*, and he was also responsible for some brilliant wildlife photography in *National Geographic*. I admired his audacity. David is someone who is highly creative, and this raises the question of whether photography is an art.

We had a resident rock star in Jimmy Page of Led Zeppelin, who had bought Boleskine House, the former home and temple of Aleister Crowley, the practitioner of 'magick'. I worked with Jimmy on a successful campaign to prevent pylons being placed along the shores of Loch Ness. This led to a few landmarks in the area being saved. On one occasion Jimmy came into my office for a cup of tea, dressed in his coat, which I remember had only one surviving button, and the scruffiest of trainers (but I believe we called them plimsolls in those days). I showed him proofs of the photographs of the Inverness Police pantomime, with the local Old Bill in tutus. As chance would have it, the very subjects came in to order prints – Jimmy was convulsed with suppressed laughter. Pity I no longer hold the negatives.

At that time the local police thought everyone under a certain age and with a certain length of hair was up to some nefarious business and gave me some grief. The most ridiculous incident was when I picked up a rusty bicycle wheel and an old kettle with a hole in it that had been discarded by the side of a field. I had intended photographing some local craft jewellery against this textured background. To cut a long story short, I had been seen and reported to the police. After this, the farce started, resulting in my arrest, a night in a

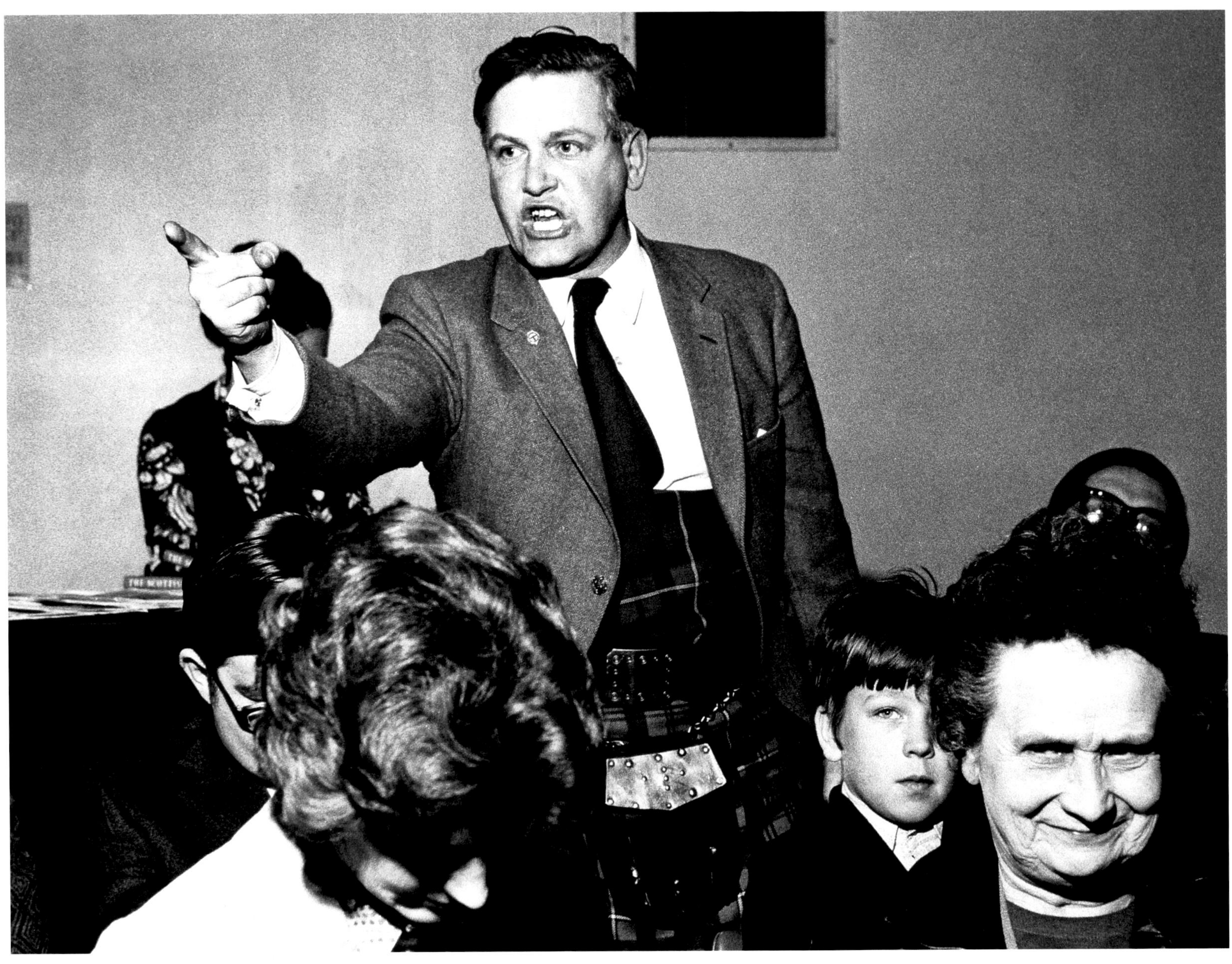

A Scottish Nationalists' meeting where strong opinions and words were being expressed. Willie Bell was a well-known character in Inverness from the 1960s and always stuck to his entrenched nationalistic views but didn't live to see his party's position of power in the Scottish parliament.

cell, release on bail and then appearance in court. I was given an absolute discharge, a thank-you from the judge for cleaning up the countryside, and his assurance that he would be complaining to the Chief Constable as to why his officers had wasted the court's time. The next day on the front page of the *Press and Journal* was the headline 'The Trials of being an Artist'.

Reay MacKenzie, the subeditor of the *Highland News*, was a delightful person who was oblivious of being an eccentric. He put a lot of work in my direction and helped further my passion for the preservation of historic buildings and landmarks. He also had an interesting method of filing of which I'll give you an example. I overheard a reporter, Darry MacKay, ask Reay, 'Where can I find the file on the Loch Ness Monster? I've looked under M for monster, L for Loch Ness, N for Nessie, and I still can't find it, so where is it?' Reay's reply was, 'Under P for phenomenon, of course!' Reay was also instrumental in my joining the Scottish Tourist Board as he saw my future position advertised and insisted that I apply for it.

The then Scottish Tourist Board (now Visit Scotland) was my next stop for eleven years, but not without its frustrations. I was aided by the fact that Richard Demarco had given me an exhibition in his Edinburgh gallery at the time of my interview for the post. On my first day at work, Lester Borley, the chief executive, called me to his office. I could honestly tell him that I could not think of any other job I'd rather be doing. The tourist boards had been set up after the Second World War to promote tourism and help the economy. Part of the constitution of the British Tourist Board was to promote world peace, but there was, and still is, a sector that sees tourism as 'bums on seats' and would have Blackpool-style holidays as a goal. Scotland should cater for all tastes, and if elitism means higher standards that you can depend upon,

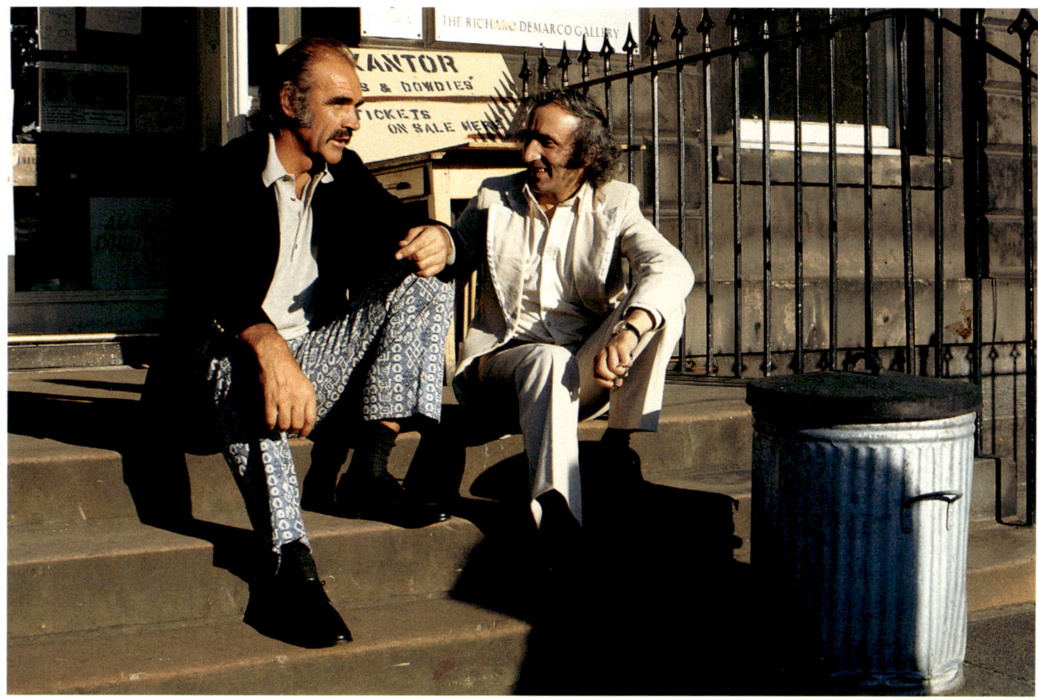

I was photographing Richard Demarco in his gallery in Edinburgh while he was holding court for a group of cool and arty American students when Sean Connery appeared. Immediately, the students were reduced to behaving like thirteen-year-olds meeting their favourite pop star. I often feel for famous personalities who have to endure such behaviour, although I suppose it does come with the territory. In the background is a poster advertising the Polish theatre director Tadeus Kantor, one of many artistic talents whom Richard has brought to prominence.

instead of an over-emphasis on commercialism (stag and hen weekends), then so be it.

My skills in dealing with bureaucracy were inadequate as I knew only the direct approach, and line management was a mystery. Despite this, I managed to raise the profile of our small photography department and received the highest Scottish tourism award, the Bill Heron Trophy, for producing books documenting Scotland. I'm also proud of the publications and posters I worked on with some very talented graphic designers. When I left the board, the exuberant chairman, Allan Devereaux, gave a farewell speech. He said, 'When I arrived I said to the staff that my door is always open. Douglas took this to heart.' (Was this what I hadn't understood about line management?) He continued, 'When I first became chairman, when attending tourism events, I'd be asked, "Do you work with Doug Corrance?"'

For a period my books received a lot of coverage on television and radio and in the press. While I was with the board I published several books. *Edinburgh* and *Glasgow*, first published in the 1980s, are the ones I am most pleased with. I believe I caught the cities at their most natural, before they put on a swank, like many other British cities trying to emulate New York or Paris. The international chains of eateries and coffee houses that pretend to be individual have been grafted rather uncomfortably on to our cityscapes. A lot of our cities should not be changed but just kept in good order. They are our past. When my *Edinburgh* book was published I received a phone call from an elderly lady: 'Hello, son, are you the laddie that did the Edinburgh book? I'm housebound and thought I'd never see my toon again. Well, my son gets the book oot the library every two weeks for me, and I can look at my toon. Well, son, all I can say is that you have created delightful nonsense.'

On the *Glasgow* book, I persuaded my editor, Clare Crawford, to include an image of a brass door bell with the number nine above it. Nine is my lucky number, I told her. The bell was on a large Victorian house in the city centre. I received a letter from a lady whose son had given her the *Glasgow* book for Christmas. She explained: 'I was glancing at the book while preparing dinner. I suddenly burst into tears, making my family rush through to the kitchen. The book was open at the page with the doorbell on it.' She told me that she had been an orphan and at fourteen was being sent into service with a doctor and his family. 'I was terrified,' she continued. 'I rang that very doorbell and was given a wonderful welcome. I spent some of the happiest years of my life with the family, which I am still close to.' A colleague said to me: 'Your *Edinburgh* and *Glasgow* books are like being eleven years old and going through the city on the top deck of a bus.'

We have lost some of our wonderment – where books, cinema and television once gave us our view of the world, now we can travel to places we could only have dreamed of, and these experiences alter our visual and social outlook, sometimes at the expense of our own image. Scotland's landscape when seen at its best is worthwhile and rewarding. I overheard an American lady, standing on the shore at

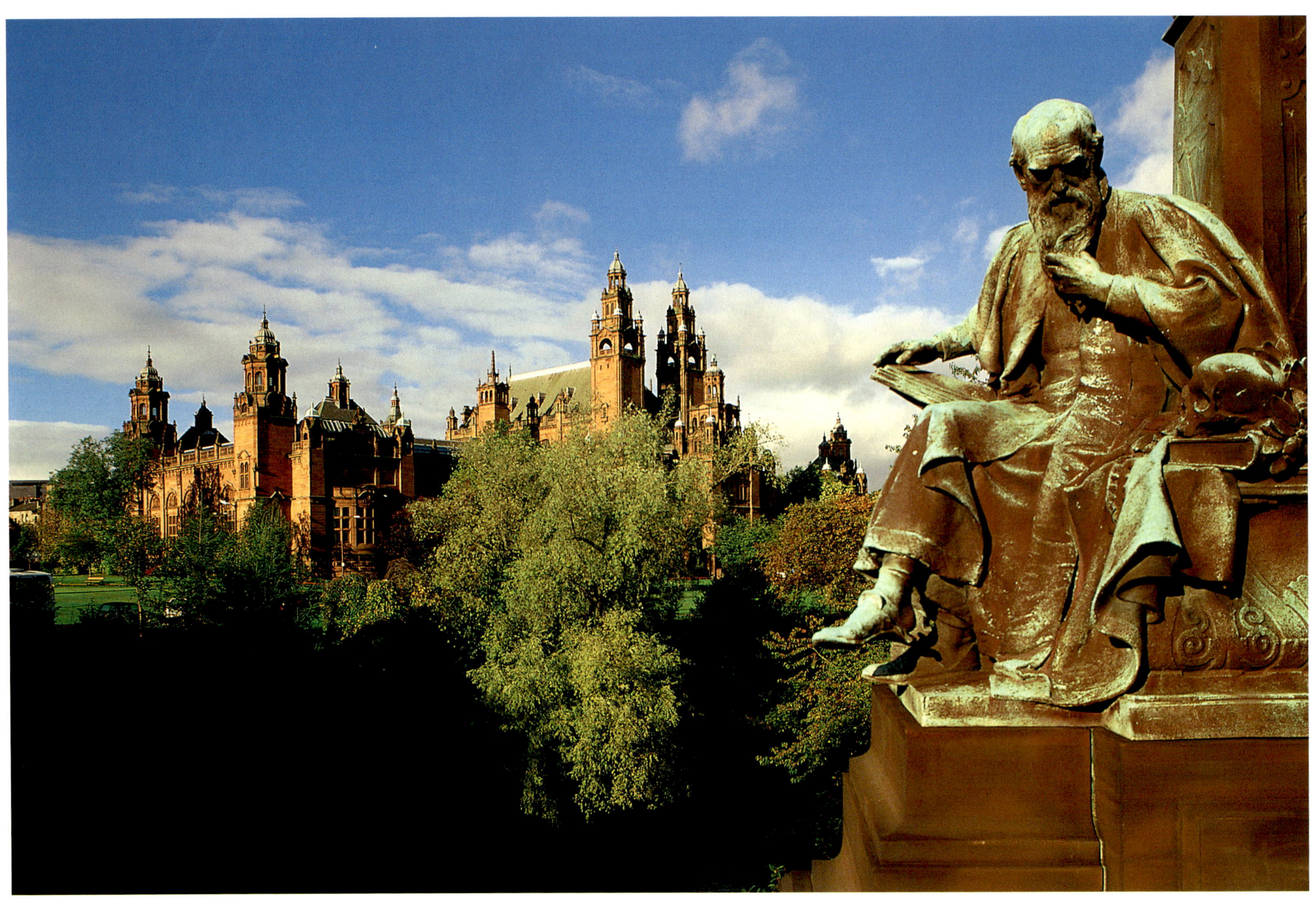

Kelvingrove Art Gallery and Museum is Scotland's most visited attraction. It has Salvador Dalí's masterpiece, *Christ of Saint John of the Cross*; two Rembrandts: *A Man in Armour* and *The Slaughtered Ox* – how good is that for a municipal gallery? The recent refurbishment has brought the magnificent main hall back to life. Glasgow folk are justifiably proud of their galleries and museums. Most of the gallery staff want visitors to get a lot out of their experience, and they have knowledge and enthusiasm about the exhibits.

Ullapool, say: 'How could my ancestors have left this beautiful place?' My response would have been perhaps because of the clearances or other hardship or perhaps just for adventure. Final year students from Singapore, studying at Edinburgh, were on Sligachan Bridge, watching the mist lift over the Cuillins, and asked, 'Why did no one tell us how beautiful Scotland is?' A young American told me: 'Gee, you've got so many castles.' We also have other great buildings: the Border Abbeys, Georgian and Victorian cities, country houses, still intact east-coast fishing villages, the buildings of Charles Rennie Mackintosh ('the poet of pure perfection') along with Neolithic sites and standing stones throughout the country. Glasgow and Edinburgh have some of the finest galleries outside London, with Rembrandts and Titians as well as one of the largest collections of Whistlers in the world and some great collections of contemporary art. That is my tourist hat speaking. I think I'm a realist, and I believe in the value of tourism, which I like to think breaks down barriers and helps towards greater understanding of other cultures. At school we were taught that Scotland played a large part in inventing the modern world, which to a great degree we did. We also have our fair share of literary giants. And we gave the world the game of golf, which caters for the snobbish and elitist but is also accessible and affordable to the hoi polloi.

Personally I must have missed out on the competitive sport gene. I love kayaking, walking and swimming, and just being. I can remember those frozen playing fields, with me and John Urquhart being the last to be chosen for a team. The other day someone said to me: 'Why is it that you always remember the other guy's name?"

I took Rik Rue, an Australian friend and avant-garde musician, to Linlithgow Palace and told him about our part in the Renaissance and how it would have looked in Mary, Queen of Scots' time. He replied, 'Jeez, Doug, wasn't it like *Braveheart*?' (the film made by his countryman, in which historical fact is noticeable by its absence – if we are to get our future right let's be accurate about our past). Architecture should take into consideration climate, light, balance with other structures and landscapes, and make more of locally sourced building materials. If you

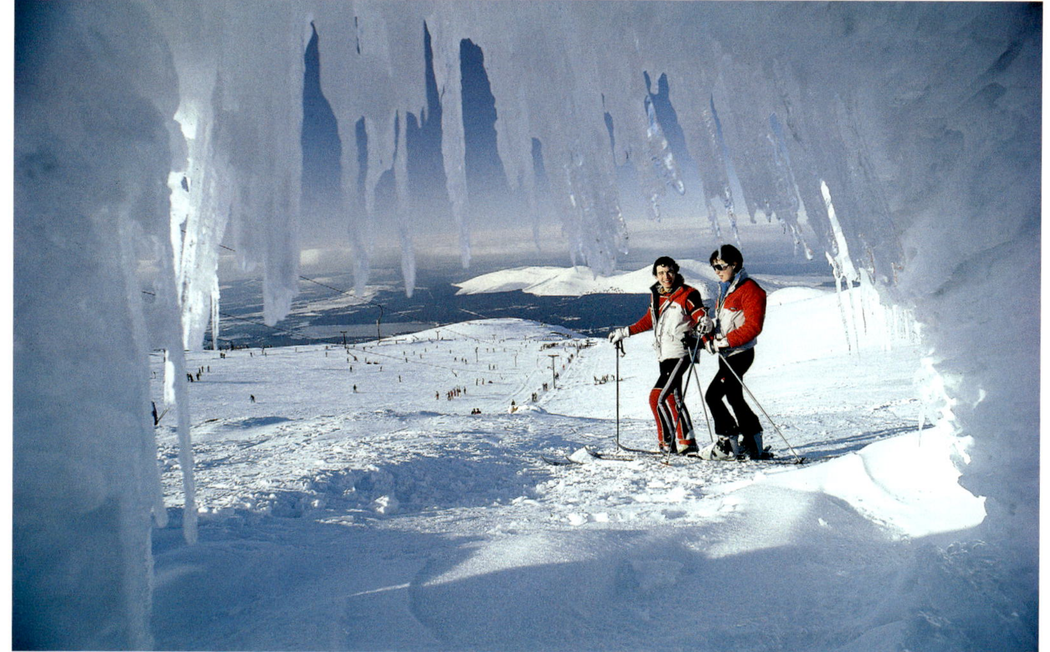

It was a perfect day for skiing in the Cairngorms. I hadn't realised how much of a fashion parade skiing was. The outfits on my models for the day, Alan and Gillian, make it so early eighties.

live in the Lowlands and want a Highland dress wedding, please get it right. The same applies to pipe bands. Cut down on trash souvenirs. Every piece of recent street furniture seems to be at odds with its surroundings.

After eleven years with the Tourist Board I became a freelance photographer. I left on the Friday and on the Monday was shooting for a guide book in New York. This was followed by books on India, Japan, France, as well as many UK guides. Along with travel I did a lot of corporate work, such as annual reports and school prospectuses, which were a challenge and could offer a lot of creative freedom. I enjoyed my very mixed assignments. One of my oddest assignments was to photograph a casket in the Collège des Ecossais in Paris, which was believed to contain the genitalia of King James VII of Scotland, the 'Old Pretender'. A more sensitive version of the story has his brain in the casket. The chapel is now part of a convent, and I was met by an Irish nun, who greeted me: 'Sure, you'll be the gentleman from Scotland to photograph James's private parts.' After being taken up a massive staircase and along seemingly endless corridors, she left me to take the picture, saying, 'I'm sure they aren't there any more – they were probably thrown into the Seine during the revolution.'

In the early 1990s I went back to press work as staff photographer with *Scotland on Sunday*. It wasn't for me and lasted for only three months although I worked for a brilliant and enthusiastic photo editor, Graeme Murdoch, who had the rare gift of completely understanding what makes a good picture. I had been out on my own too

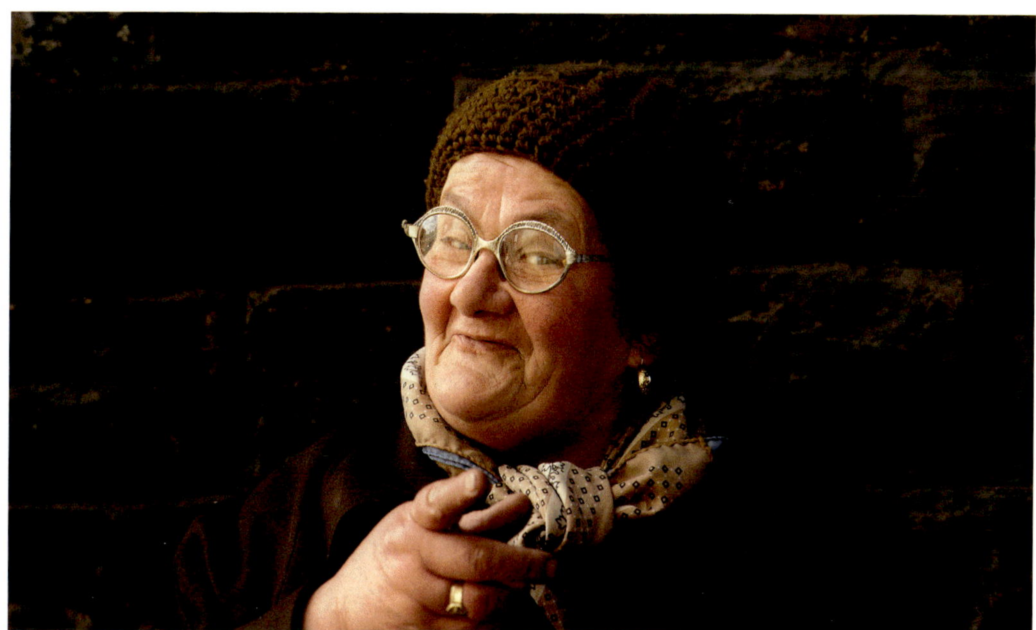

She was on the cover and on the last page of my *Glasgow* book. Eddie Boyd's brilliant poem was:

Ah'm jist a Glesca wumman,
An ordinary wife,
Nuthin' much has ever happened
Tae me a' ma life.
Ah niver got a prize at school,
Ah niver won a footba' pool,
Ah niver won at bingo no' even by a fluke.
But yin thing Ah'm determined,
Aye, that's the word, determined,
BY HOOK OR BY CROOK
AH'LL BE LAST IN THIS BOOK!

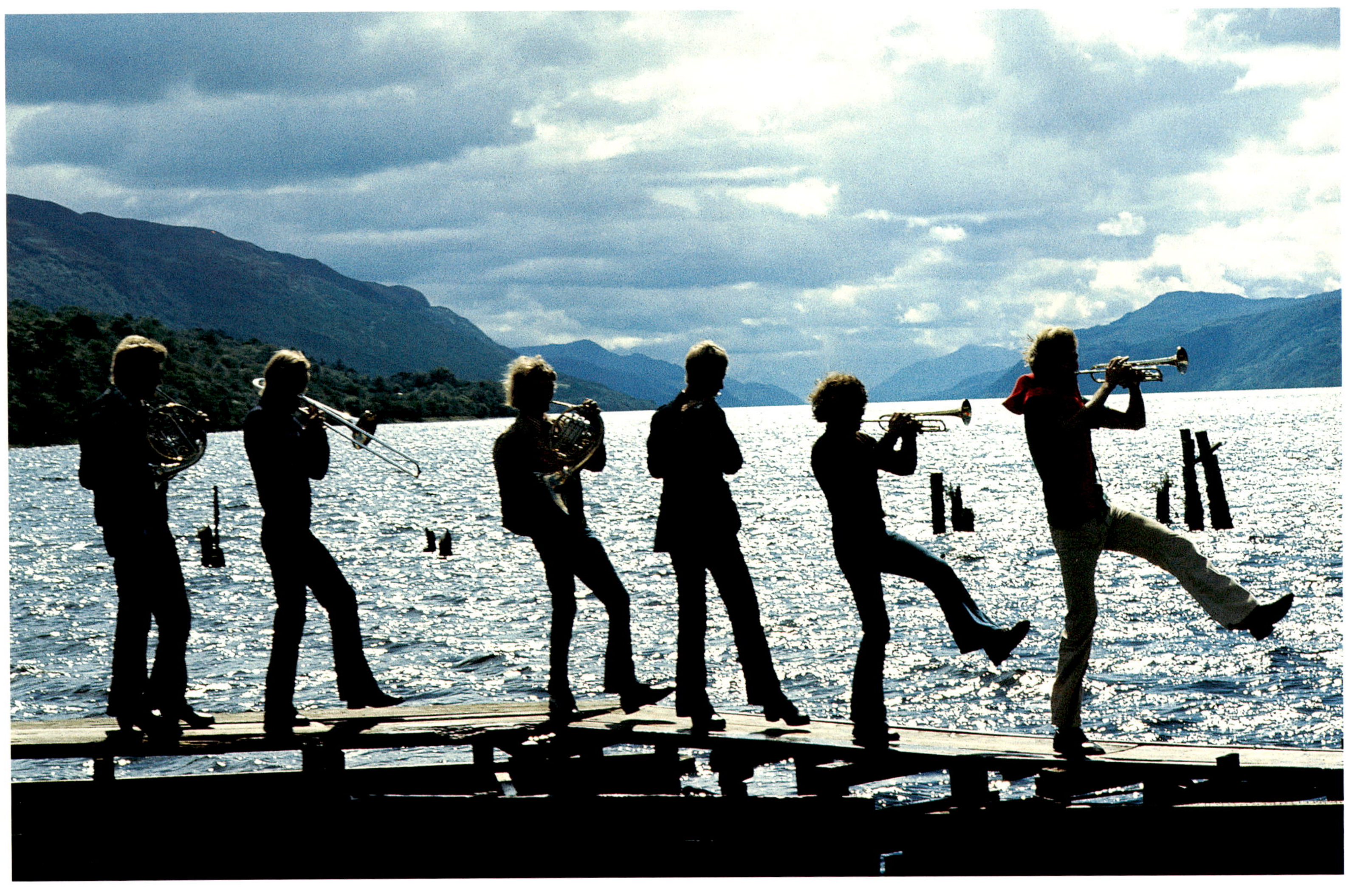

To promote a music festival in Inverness in the 1970s, I took this Swedish brass band to Loch Ness. It took considerable effort to set up this picture while two national newspaper photographers shot over my shoulder and got full-page spreads the next day. I got a single column in a flyer.

long and found the small acts of bureaucracy and the hierarchy of the pecking order too much to take. I also believed I could make a better contribution than being inside a football stadium every Saturday afternoon.

Photography is a craft and can be self-taught. Anyone with a level of visual literacy can produce good photographs, and, properly presented, they can look fine, but so many are just wallpaper – my apologies to William Morris. Think about the truly great photographs taken by some of the great photographers: André Kertész, Henri Cartier-Bresson, Arnold Newman, Bill Brandt and Ernst Haas, to mention just a few. Now compare these with some contemporary art photographs, selected by so-called experts, where any sort of ability seems to be lacking. I find this a grave cause for concern for my craft. They say luck happens to the prepared mind, and this is never more true than in photography.

The work I admire has perfect composition and can relate to the viewer in a completely literal way. You have to be a voyeur to achieve detachment as well as closeness, akin to the excitement of a hunter, taking in every part of the image, and, in the words of Henri Cartier-Bresson, 'shoot at the decisive moment'. One of my favourite pictures was taken by him and is of a small boy in Paris, carrying wine bottles. The child's joy at being entrusted to shop for the family wine, the total spontaneity of the incident and its energetic composition, make it a classic example of street photography. In what some see as our currently overprotective days a child is never allowed to shop for wine.

I have photographed in ordinary and extraordinary surroundings, and most of the time I want to avoid the ugliness of the everyday world, but it can take a lifetime to capture certain moments of spontaneity. Sadly, some people look upon 'street photography' as predatory, and they have a point, although I have never intended to be cruel but only to celebrate a moment in time. I think to record everyday people and life is important, but a shift in people's perception and recent legislation in particular have made this much more difficult for photographers in general.

I was driving to the south of Belgium in a van to set up an exhibition, with a friend, Graham Potter, accompanying me for the ride. 'You know,' he said. 'It's all very romantic, what you do.' It made me think, as all I seemed to experience was

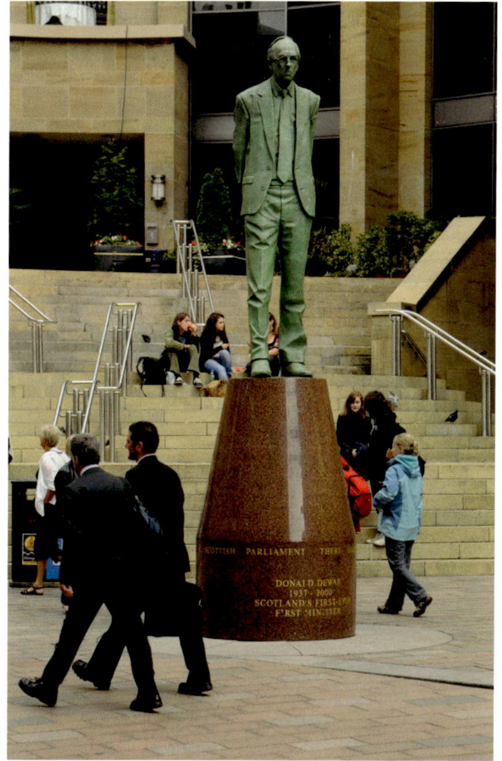

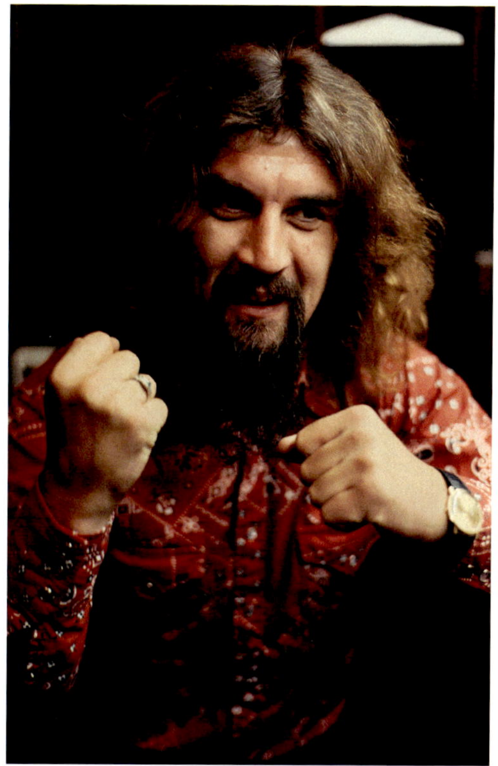

(Far left) While queuing in a Glasgow bookshop in the early 1990s, I noticed Donald Dewar, later the first First Minister of Scotland's newly refounded parliament, buying one of my books. When I looked up the catalogue of the Dewar Collection of books, which was gifted to the Scottish parliament after his death in 2001, it contained several of my books. I was a bit chuffed that such a bibliophile's collection included my work. This statue is in a prominent position below the entrance to the Royal Concert Hall in Buchanan Street, Glasgow.

(Left) For his originality and delivery, Billy Connolly could be said to have reached the status of comic genius. He was one of the most accommodating personalities I have photographed, here in the Pavilion Theatre in Glasgow in 1980. I even had him laughing when I told him a personal anecdote about a mutual friend.

anxiety. Romantic? I get paid for what I love to do, maybe not the most stressful aspect of being a photographer. One shoot involved the Chairman of the Tourist Board and the late Rod Hull and Emu, fresh from his outrageous behaviour on Michael Parkinson's TV chat show and being very uncooperative, six dancing girls and four complaining London cabbies. I had ferried them to Piccadilly Circus to photograph them against the statue of Eros. Just as I was about to shoot, the heavens opened. Somehow I managed to get a shot, which made the front page of the *Scotsman*. A colleague asked me how I kept my cool so well, and I used the analogy of the swan: serene on the surface but paddling furiously underneath. Another scary moment was seeing two months' worth of work on exposed film being further exposed on an ancient X-ray machine in Delhi airport for ten minutes. Working in Harlem, New York, all my pre-digital worries were camera settings – exposure, sharpness and colour balance – rather than my physical safety, some examples of which were being attacked by monkeys in India, caught up in a bombing in Sri Lanka, being shot at in Israel, mugged in Manhattan, narrowly avoiding miscellaneous missiles during heavyweight events at a Highland Games, being stuck on an icy ledge twenty feet above a river in spate with jagged rocks, or having my waders fill up with water and being swept down river with my Nikon held aloft like Excaliber in the vain attempt to save it, not to mention hair-raising flights, taking shots from the tops of ships' masts and some car and rickshaw rides that certainly tightened my rectum – these were all part of my working life.

A good moment was Clare Crawford handing me a copy of my first book, *Edinburgh*, hot off the Collins press. Billy Connolly told me that one of his magic moments was first seeing someone carrying his *Humblebum* album under his arm. Other good moments for me were driving along the Cote d'Azur in a BMW Cabriolet with the roof down while working on a guide; dining with a maharajah in his palace in the Rajasthan desert; attending a Shinto ceremony at the base of Mount Fuji in Japan; in New York, walking across Central Park with one of my heroes, Arnold Newman, one of the twentieth century's great photographers. Arnold had seen my work courtesy of Barry Hicks, the 'father of tourism photography in Britain' and my mentor, and had called me to ask if I would get in touch when I was next in the Big Apple. A week before he had been walking along the same path with Henri Cartier-Bresson.

I was also fortunate enough to be commissioned to do portraits of two photographers whom I admire: Bert Hardy of the *Picture Post,* who took the wonderful image of two young boys in the Gorbals in 1948, and Angus McBean, the master of theatrical and surrealist portraiture. Angus's parting lines to me were, 'Remember, Douglas, that photography is serious and everything else is fun.'

I had been away from the Tourist Board for several years when I was asked to photograph the

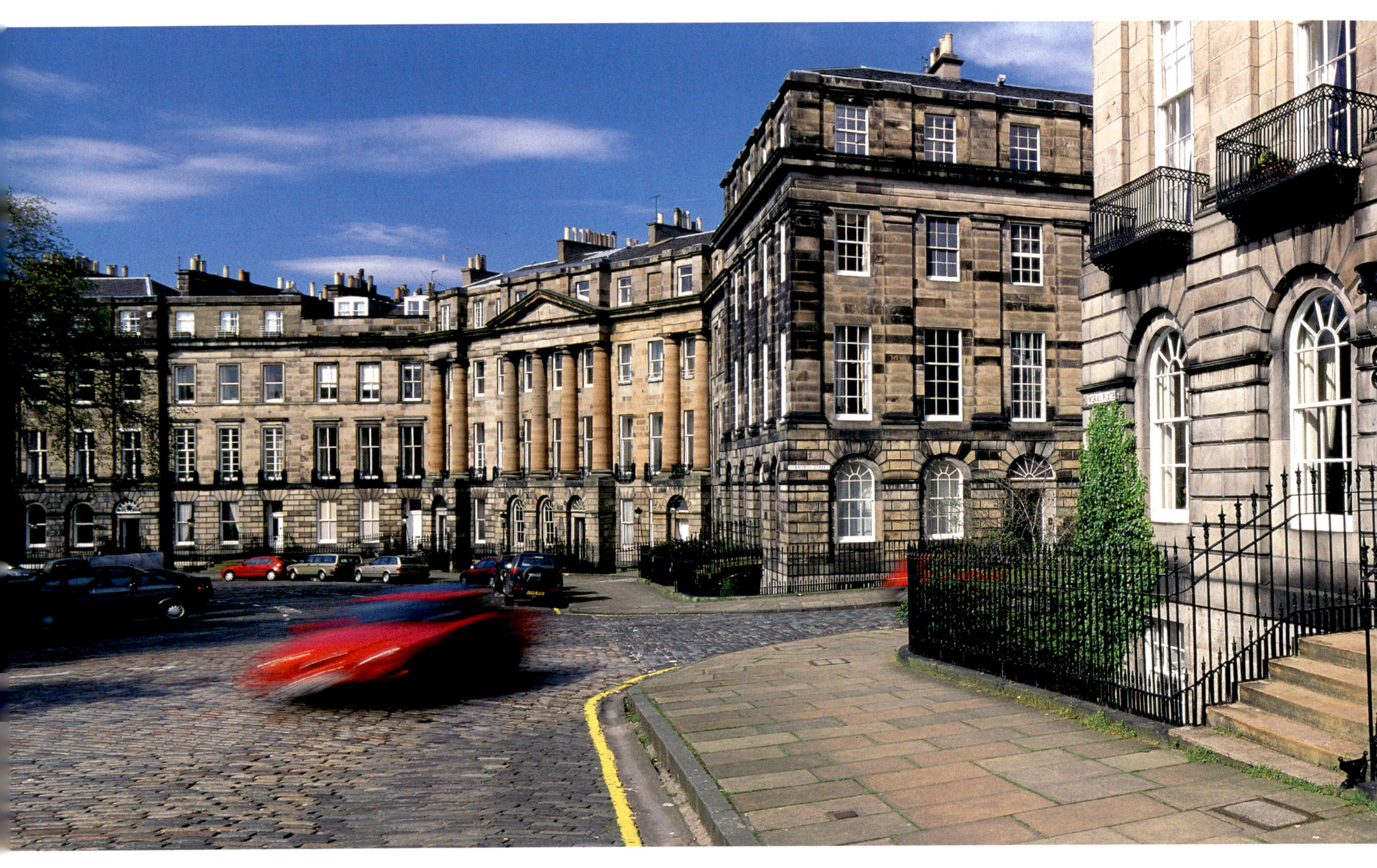

Edinburgh New Town is the world's largest Georgian city development. The earliest designs were by James Craig in 1767. My favourite area of the New Town is this great sweep on the east side of Moray Place. Charlotte Square by Robert Adam is more lauded by architectural historians, and I'm sure they are right, but it is hard to appreciate because of the volume of traffic and parked cars. I think the square was meant to be viewed and enjoyed from the first floors of the magnificent town houses.

board members, the venue a posh five-star hotel. I shot them in the lounge bar with a world-famous golf course as a backdrop. Waiting for my sitters to arrive, I had a pleasant chat with the lady behind the bar who, afterwards, when I was packing my gear, called me over and laughingly said, 'This will amuse you. After the picture was taken, I overheard a board member say, "That was Doug Corrance; he used to be a STB photographer and is a bit of a free spirit."' If I had philosophy for life and work it would be regret only what you haven't done and get paid for what you like to do.

I wonder if future decades will witness as much change as these last five have. What may make this book unique is the breadth of my work: from local to national press, from tourism to commercial commissions and other more personal work that has never before been published. Surprisingly there are some images that appear timeless, whilst in others the fashion of clothing and cars gives away the period.

I doubt whether photographers in the future will have such easy access to people, places and events as I have in my job. Hence the three main sections of the book; People, Places and Events.

It surprised me while trawling through my photographic library just how many significant events and people in the public eye that I have photographed.

This selection was never intended to be a comprehensive one but instead this is a personal view which I hope can still be entertaining, informative and objective. Some readers will recognise some notable omissions, as in the case of Scotland's former First Minister, Jack McConnell who told me he was justifiably a bit miffed at the Isle of Arran, his childhood home, being excluded from a previous book of mine on Scotland. He may be glad to know that I have included two images of Arran in this book. I feel guilty that I haven't bagged enough Munros but as the mist descended I would automatically turn back as the view was my primary purpose.

This book is very important to me as a collection of my work. I believe that all ordinary events and what is seemingly commonplace should be recorded well and nothing should be dismissed as being too trivial a subject matter. The key phrase here is 'recorded well' that is, treating the subject with consideration and capturing the moment which hopefully will

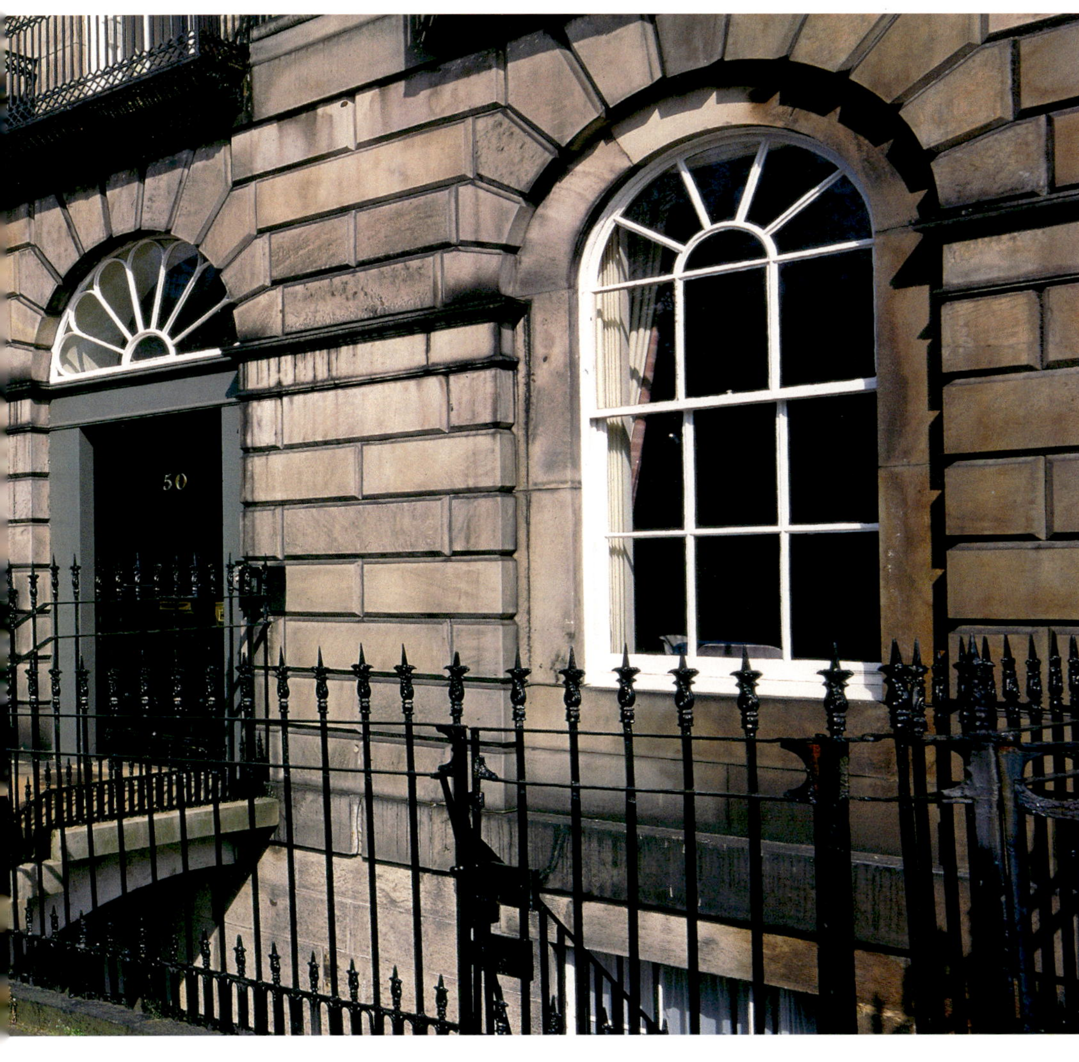

A croft on the banks of Loch Duich, which was being used as a store for fishing gear. This scene has a timeless air, and this picture, shot in the 1980s, is reminiscent of an earlier era of photography. The American photographer Paul Strand spent three months in 1954 capturing the Outer Hebrides. To my mind his are some of the finest images of Scotland.

continue to give pleasure and hold meaning in future decades.

I didn't begin to employ digital imaging until I was satisfied that it could match film in larger-sized reproduction in magazines and brochures. Had it been available in the past it would have saved me much anxiety, knowing that I had the image in the can. With my background, knowledge and experience, in certain situations and circumstances I can now work faster and be more creative. The late John Hedgecoe, in his last ever interview in *Amateur Photographer*, said, 'The changes to the medium brought on by digital photography have opened up photography to a lot more people and made it easier for people to produce good images. But I think in some ways photography has become too easy – many people don't really know how to make creative decisions – and I think that has taken some of the magic and mystery out of photography.'

I think I'll just keep taking pictures – they may not be valuable to the world, but they are important to me and I still enjoy my work.

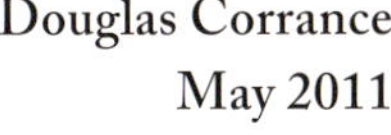

Douglas Corrance
May 2011

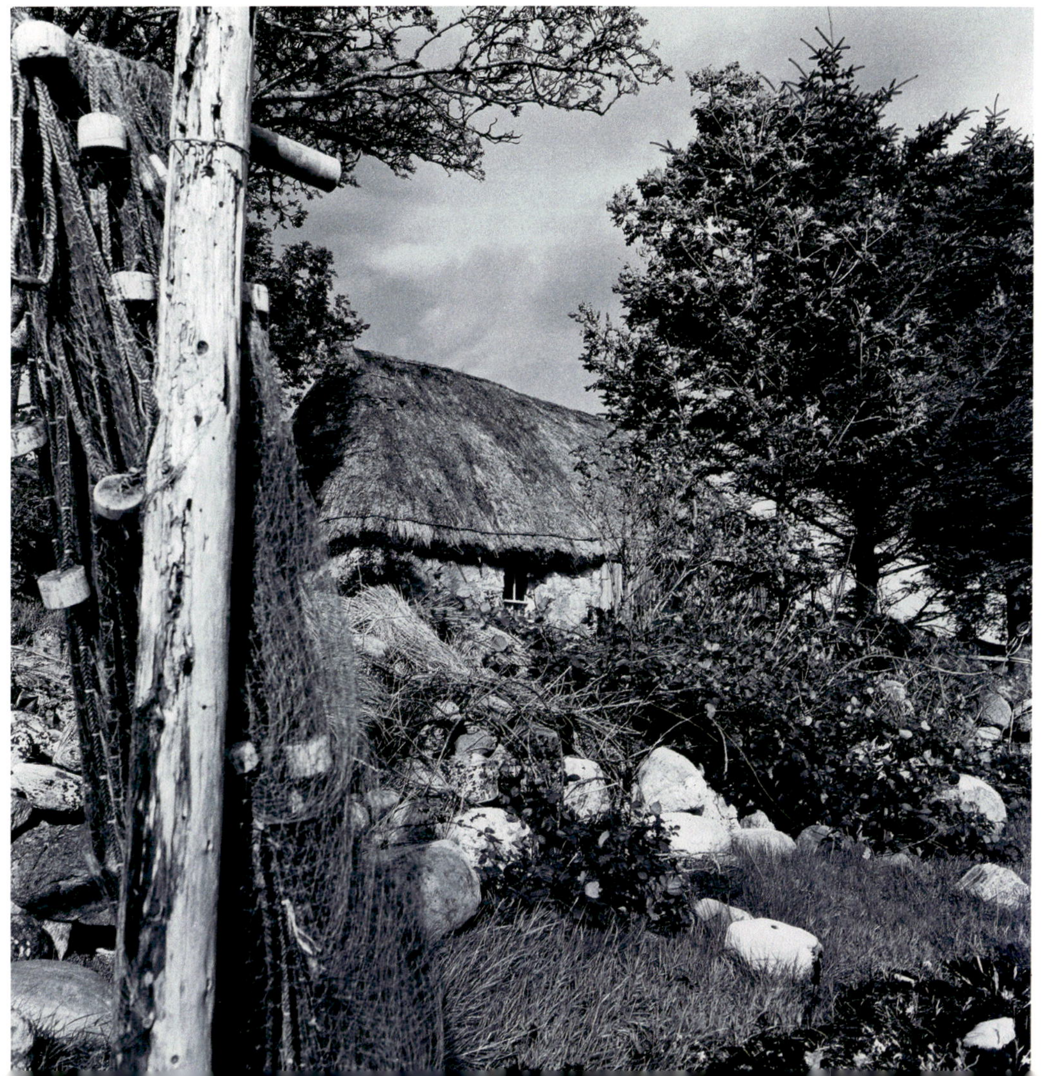

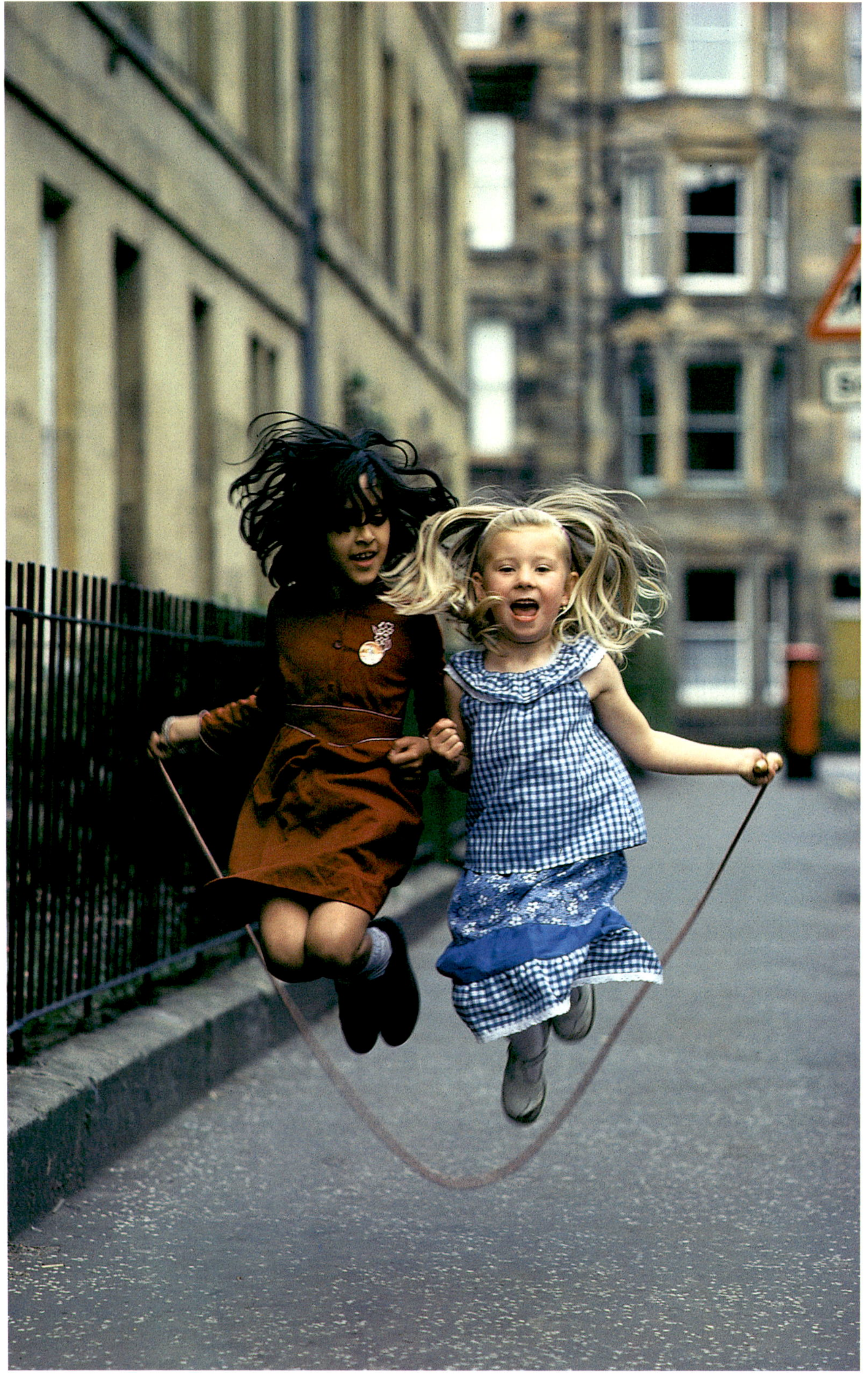

Children share a skipping rope, taken just outside the door of my first flat in Edinburgh in the 1970s. I don't even go to the post office without my camera. This picture won a national photographic award.

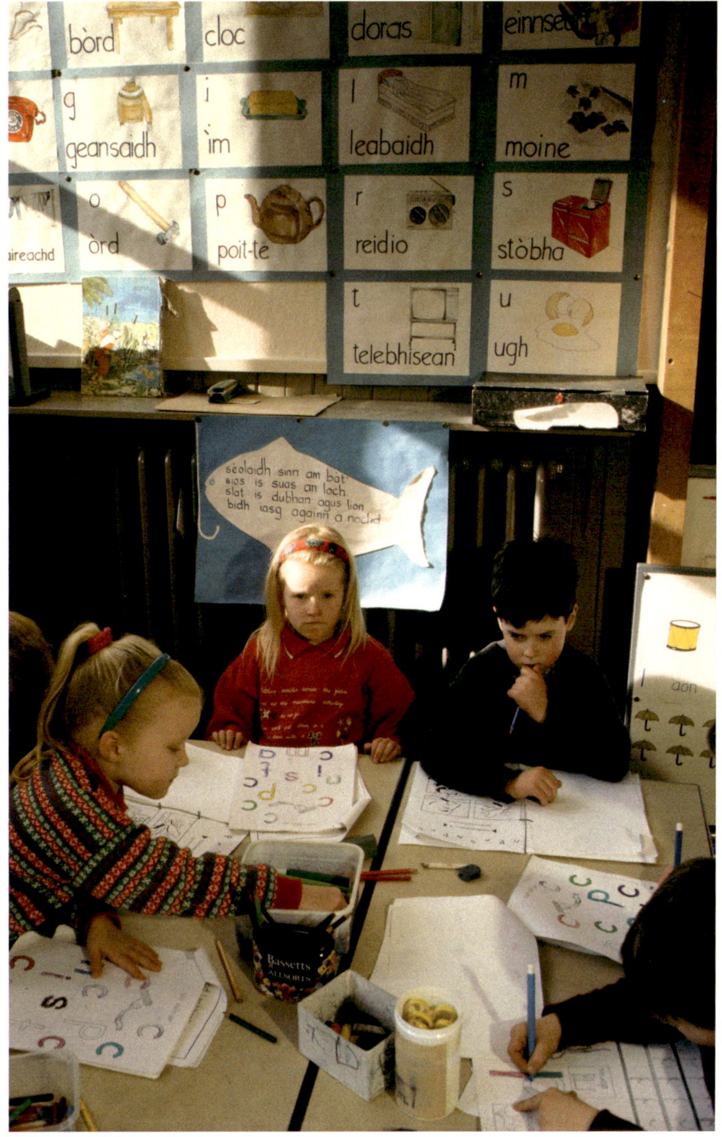

Gaelic is the native language of the West Highlands and Islands. It is alive and well on the Isle of Lewis and is part of everyday life. The more remote communities' identities are important and language is fundamental to this.

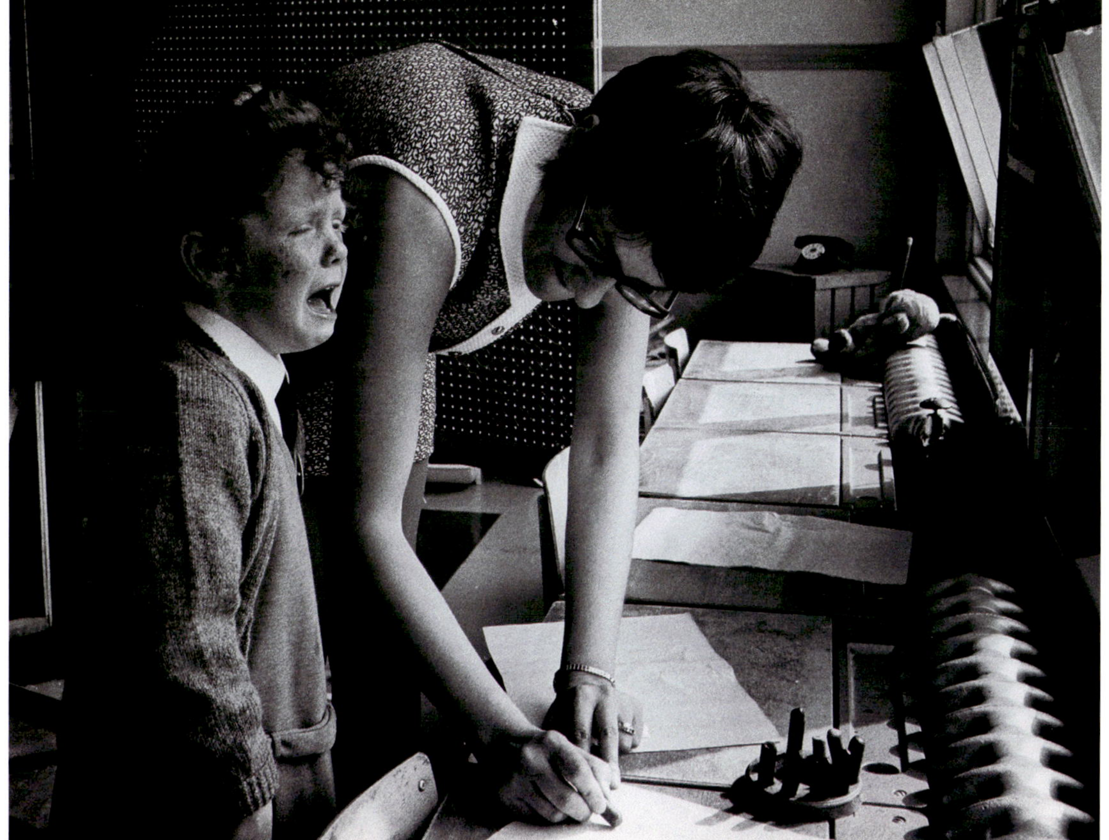

As a photographer on a local paper, you are sent along to photograph events such as a child's first day at school, the first step into the real world. There was always, at least, a couple of kids who bawled the whole day. A friend of mine's wee boy, on being taken to school on the second day, said, 'But I've been to school!' I seem to remember that most days started in the infant class with the hymn 'All things bright and beautiful'.

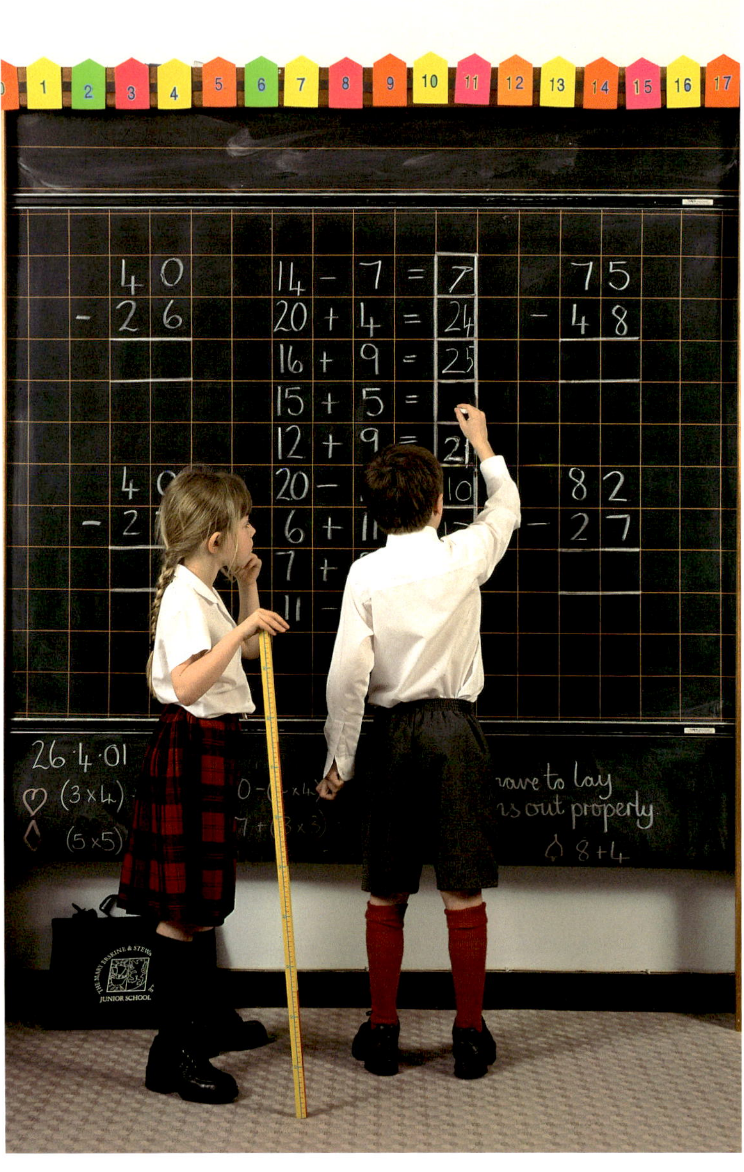

Norman Rockwell had illustrated covers for *The Saturday Evening Post* in America that were quirky and idealistic, but he could also be very political. I set this picture up while working on the prospectus of Stewart's Melville College, but later I recognised a faint nostalgia and an air of innocence reminiscent of the lighter side of Rockwell's work.

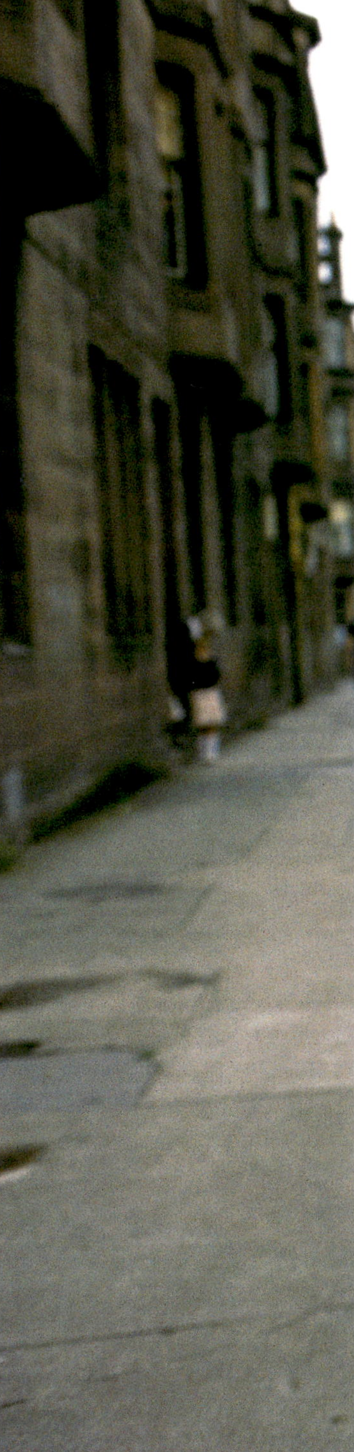

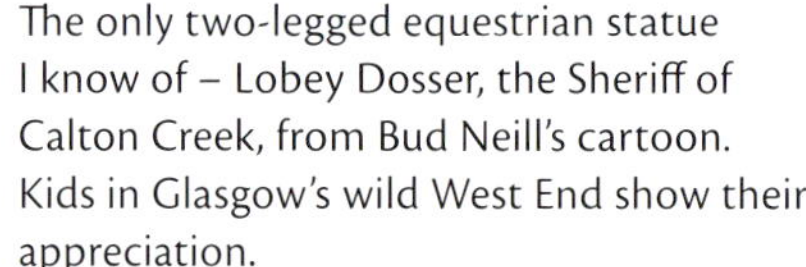

The only two-legged equestrian statue I know of – Lobey Dosser, the Sheriff of Calton Creek, from Bud Neill's cartoon. Kids in Glasgow's wild West End show their appreciation.

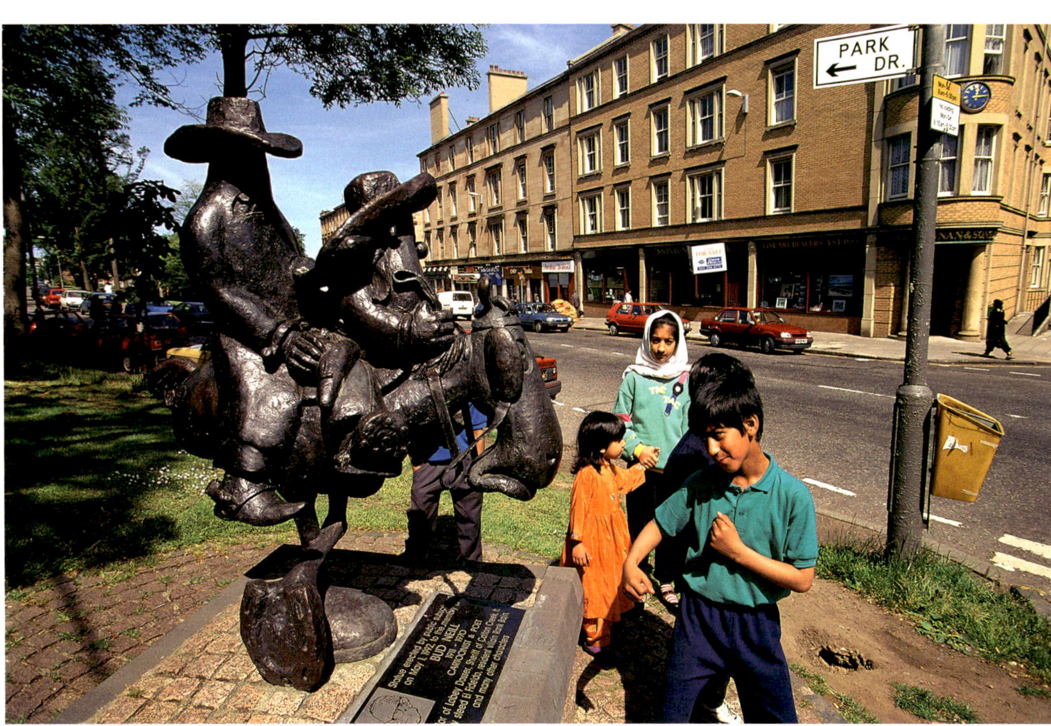

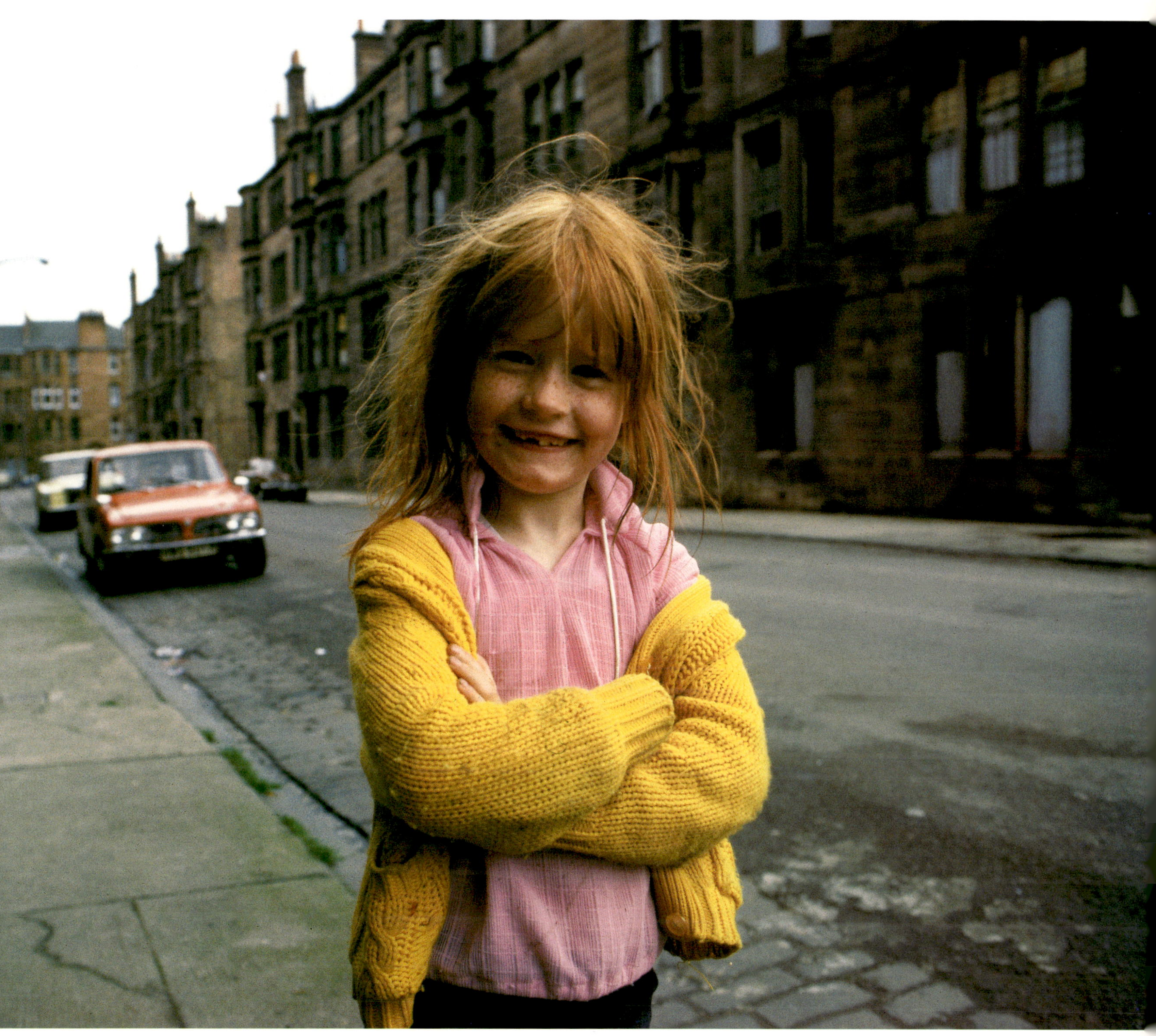

Wee Janie was in my *Glasgow* book. This is my favourite child picture by far and won an award from the *Telegraph* newspaper in 1979. I met her twenty years on – she was a mother and a delightful person. We were photographed for the Glasgow *Evening Times*. This had been the top-selling postcard in Glasgow for two decades.

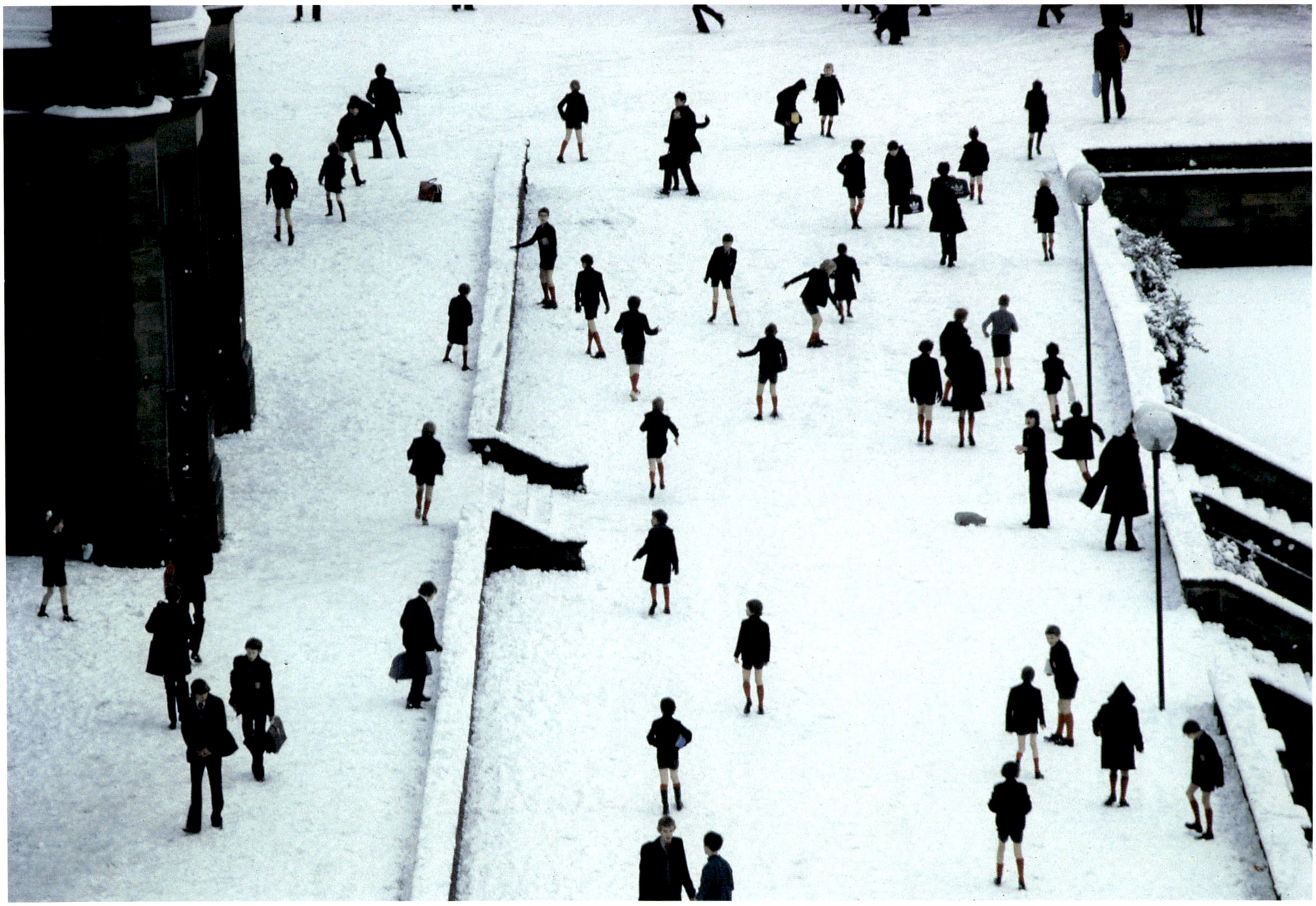

Stewart's Melville College, shot from my office window while I was with the Scottish Tourist Board in the early 1980s. Twenty years on it was used for the school prospectus. Yes, I know, matchstick men, Lowry and all that.

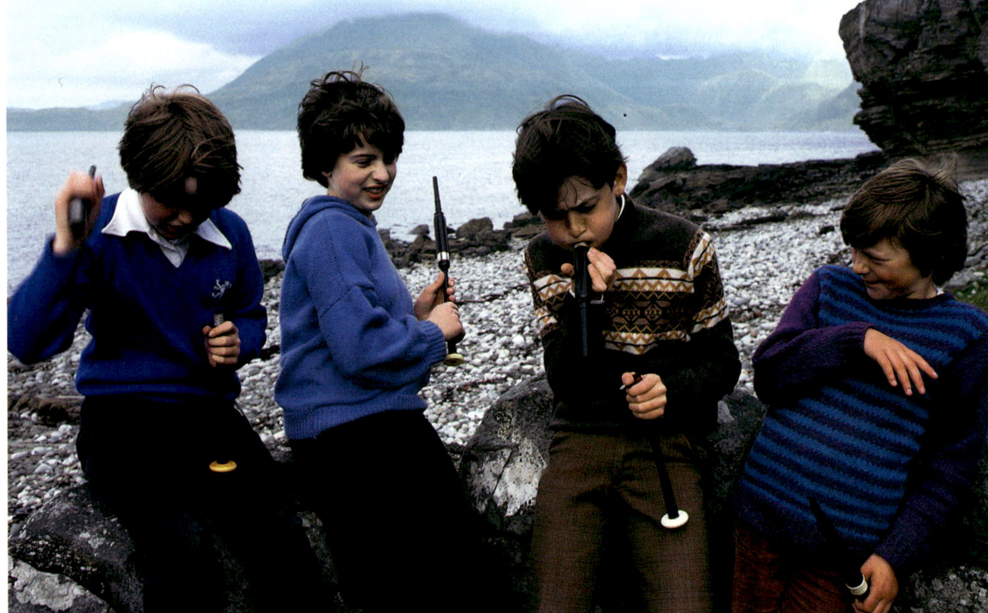

When learning the bagpipes you start with the chanter. The pupils in Elgol on Skye have the most magnificently sited school in Scotland. The boy in this class is outnumbered by the girls, and he is oblivious of his fellow students as he cleans his instrument of spittle.

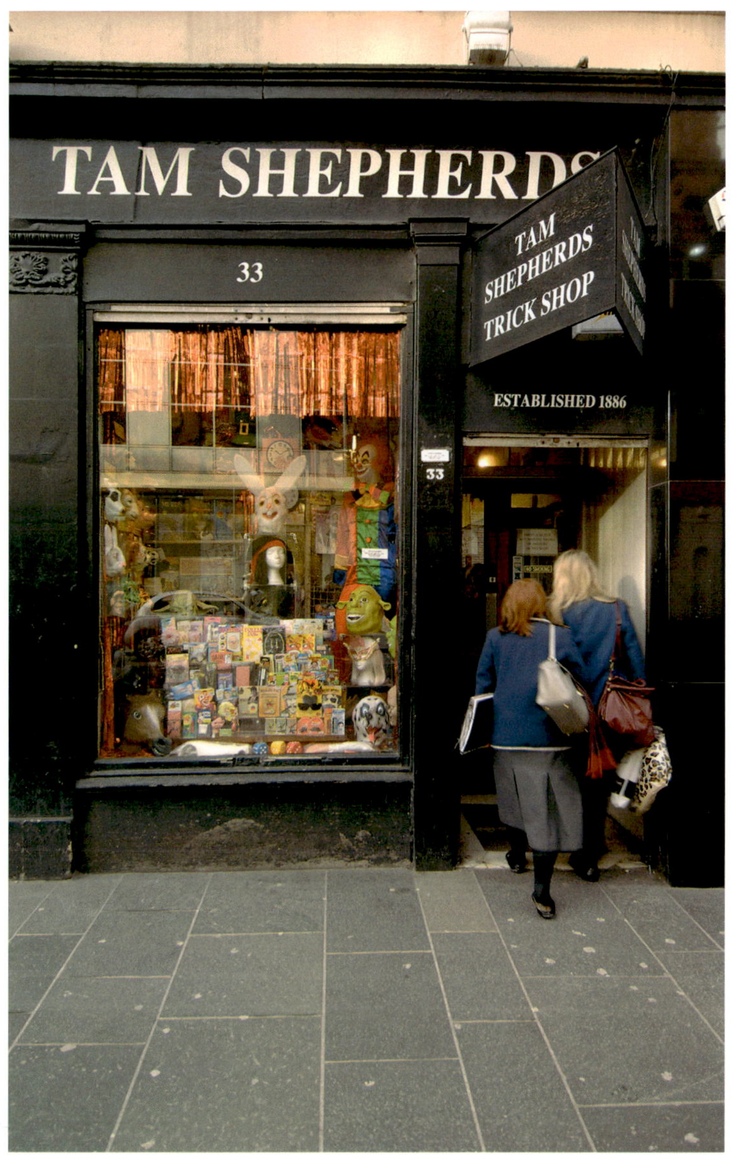

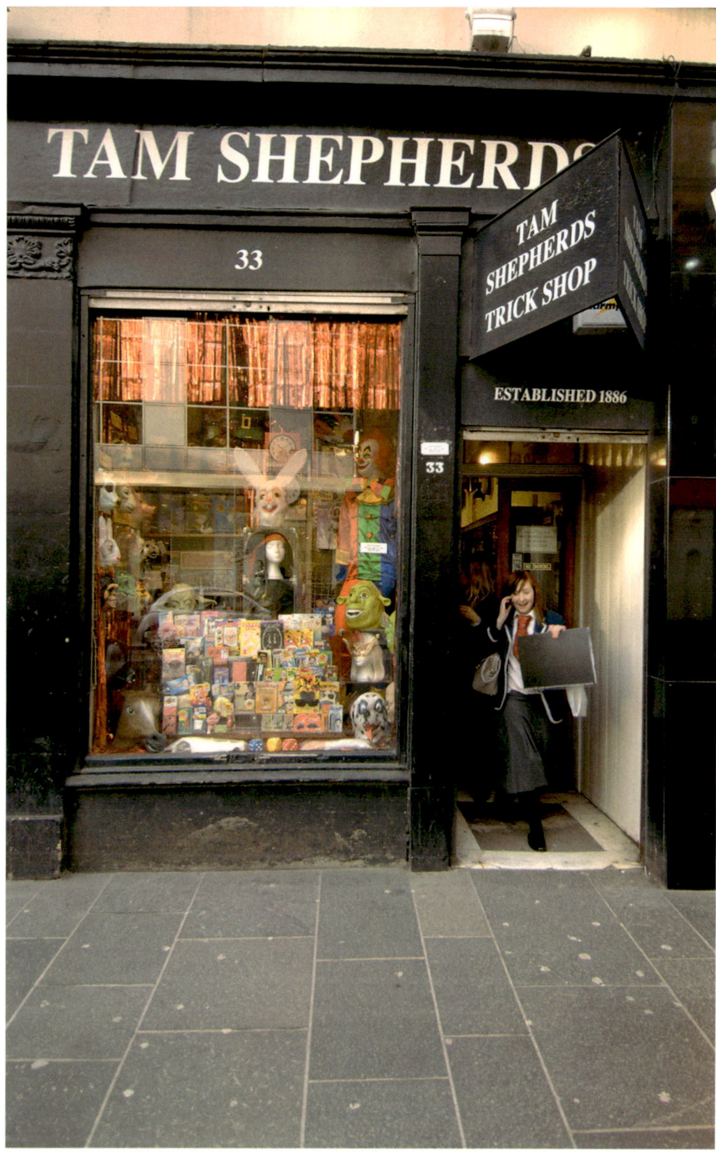

Glasgow without Tam Shepherds would be like India without the tiger. This joke shop has been part of every Glaswegian's childhood since 1886. Magic still exists here. Wee shops have to stay – supermarkets don't sell whoopee cushions or fake nails through the finger.

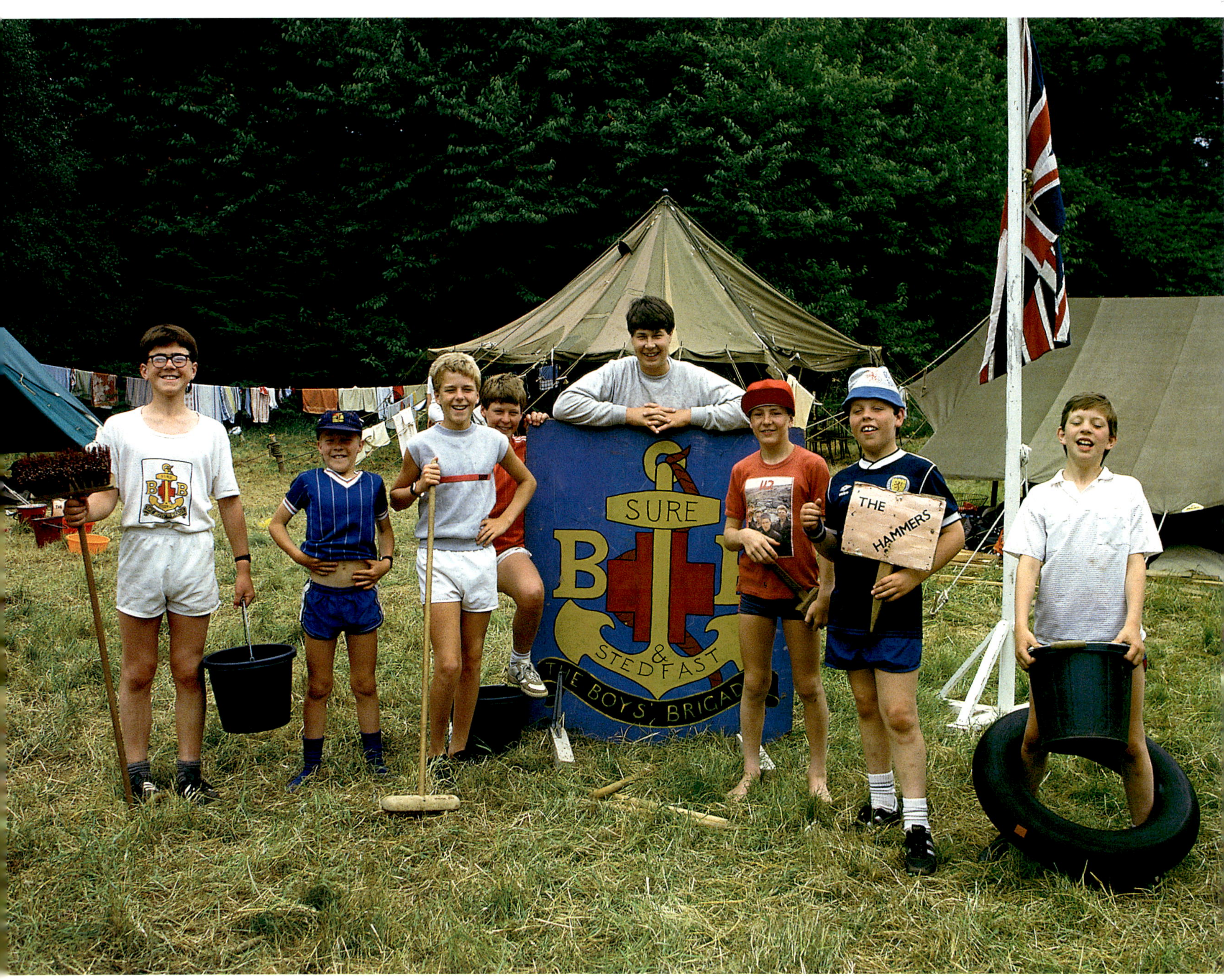

A Boys' Brigade camp shot in the 1980s. The atmosphere was very relaxed, and they were having a good time. What a contrast to my more rigid experience in the 1950s.

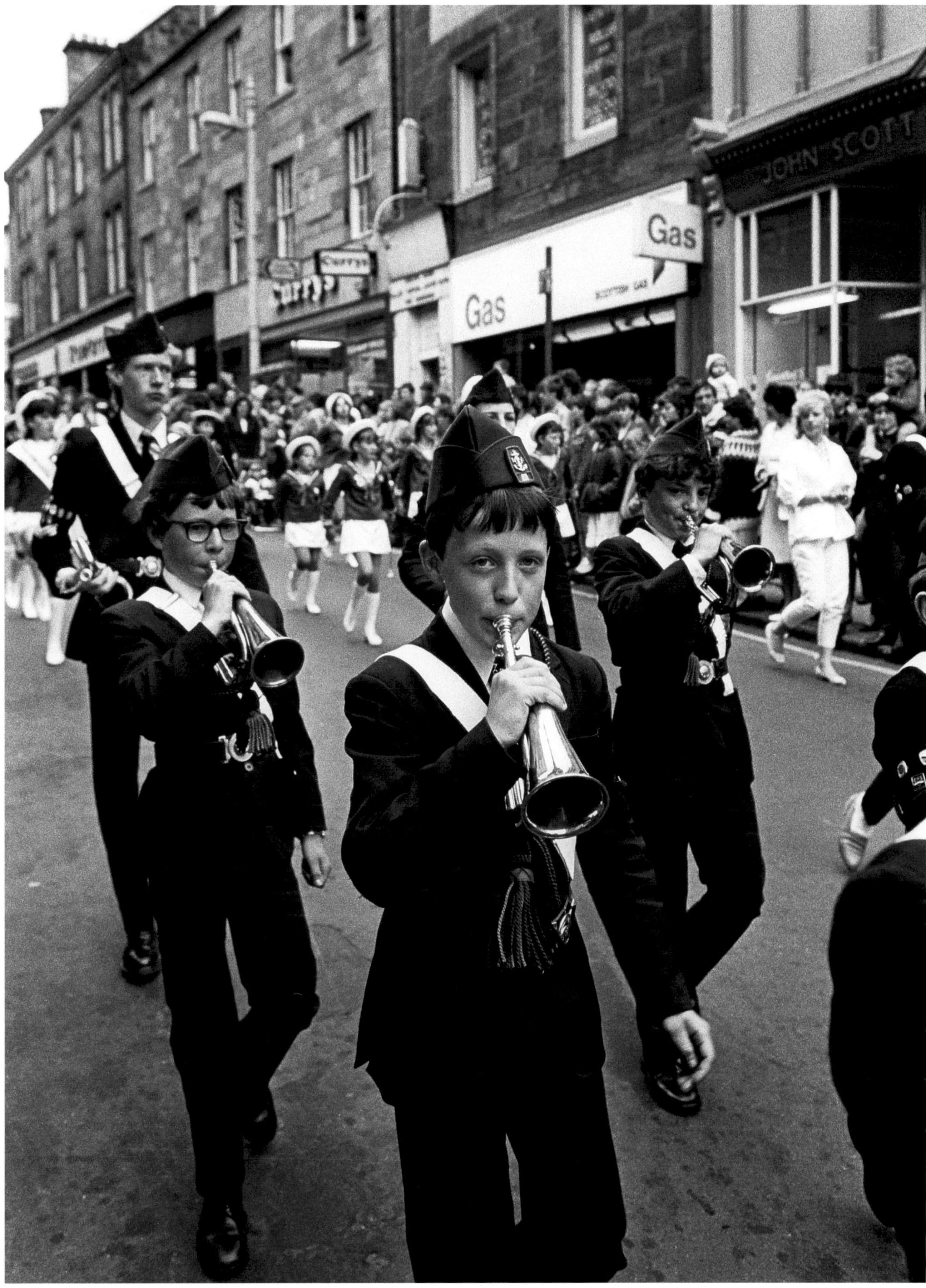

They still have the belt and lanyard but the ridiculous pillbox hat has thankfully vanished. My own Boys' Brigade career was short-lived. To spend Friday evening marching and doing physical training was not my idea of a good night, especially when I sometimes got my right foot mixed up with my left, sending the whole company into confusion during formation marching. Founded in Glasgow in 1883, predating the Scouts by 25 years, the Boys' Brigade has been a positive force for a lot of youth. Perhaps the organisation has adapted to the needs of new generations.

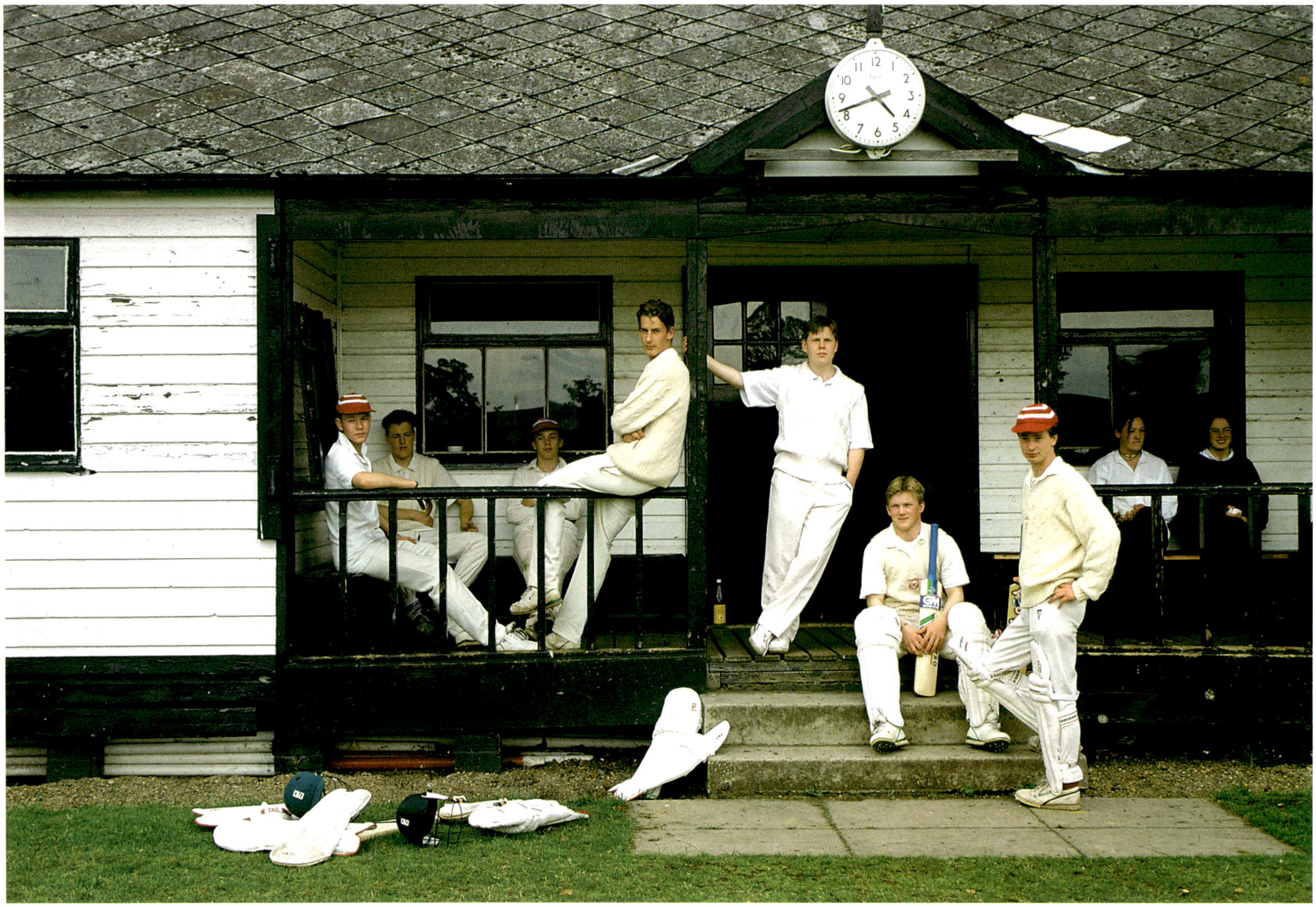

Loretto School is sometimes referred to as Scotland's Eton. Certainly, the cricket team presents a very timeless English-looking scene. Having photographed for school prospectuses throughout Britain, I like to think the Scottish ones have a less elitist ethos.

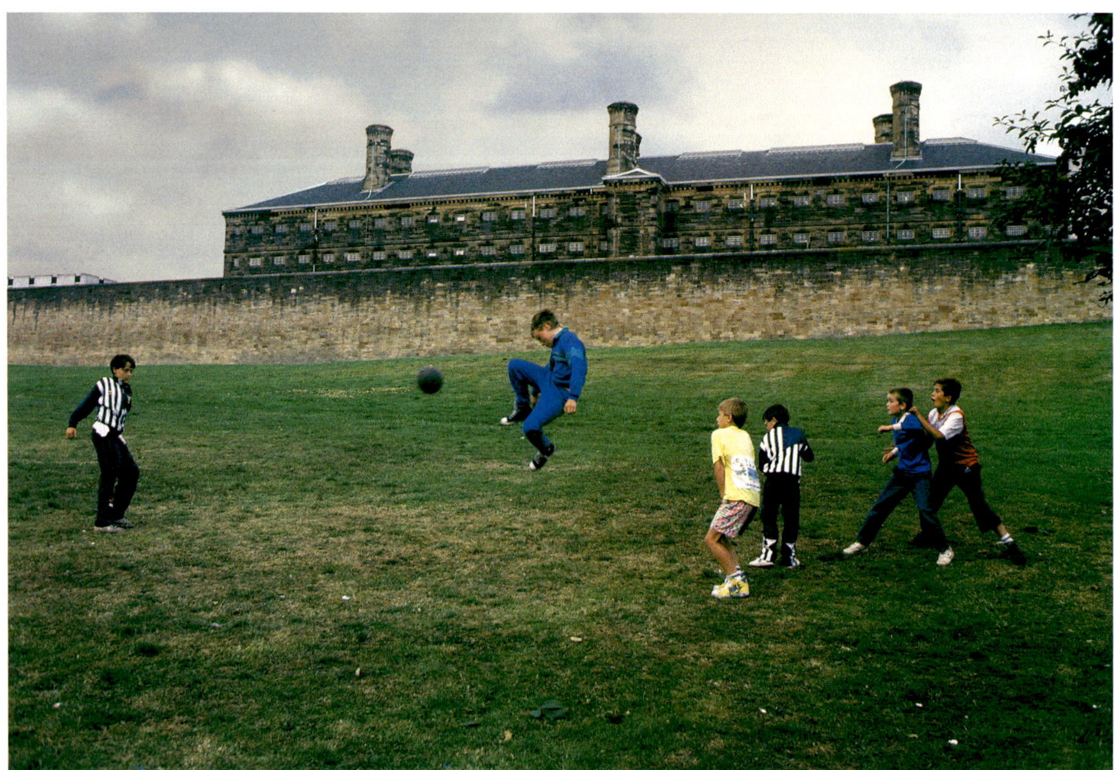

Barlinnie Prison is the backdrop for these youngsters with dreams of Ibrox or Parkhead and Hampden. The inmates would shout out to them, which I hope has had a positive effect.

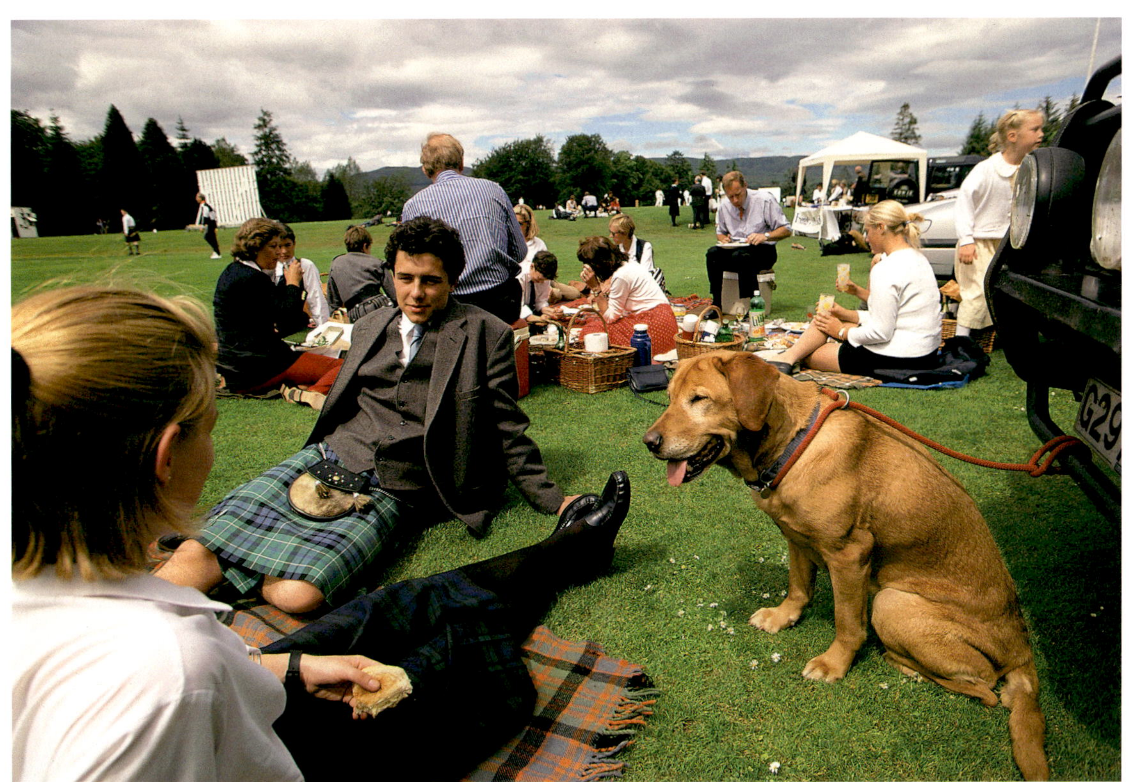

Glenalmond College parents' day. Set in the beautiful Perthshire countryside, the school building is like a mini Oxford or Cambridge college. Actor, comedian and author Robbie Coltrane is a former pupil.

Schoolchildren on an adventure course in Glencoe. Do they appreciate what an amazing country we live in? It was by travelling to other countries that I began to understand the beauty of Scotland. A book, *A Thousand and One Natural Wonders of the World*, lists 22 sites in Scotland. This bright cloudless morning belies the dark history of the infamous massacre of the MacDonalds by the Campbells in 1692.

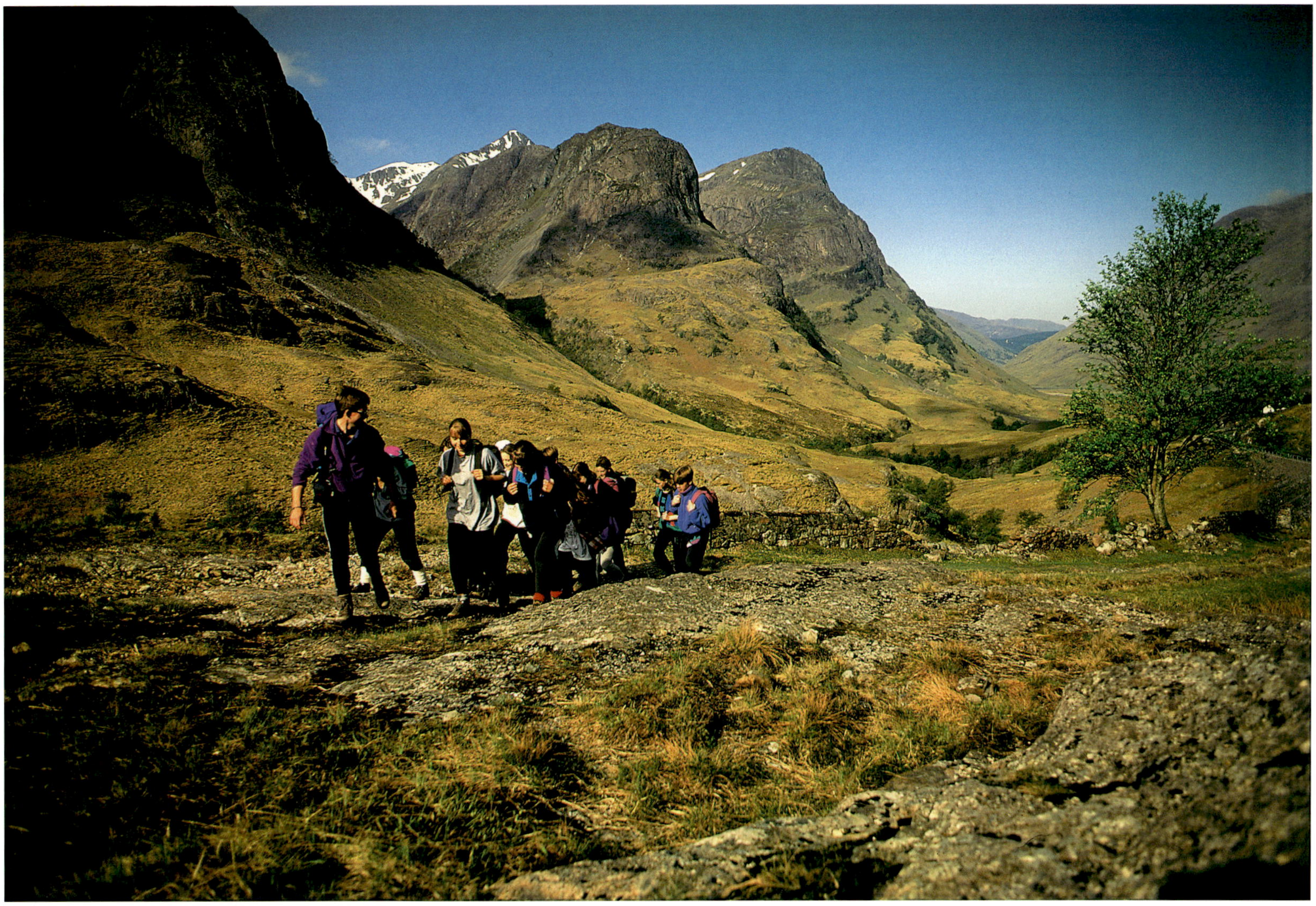

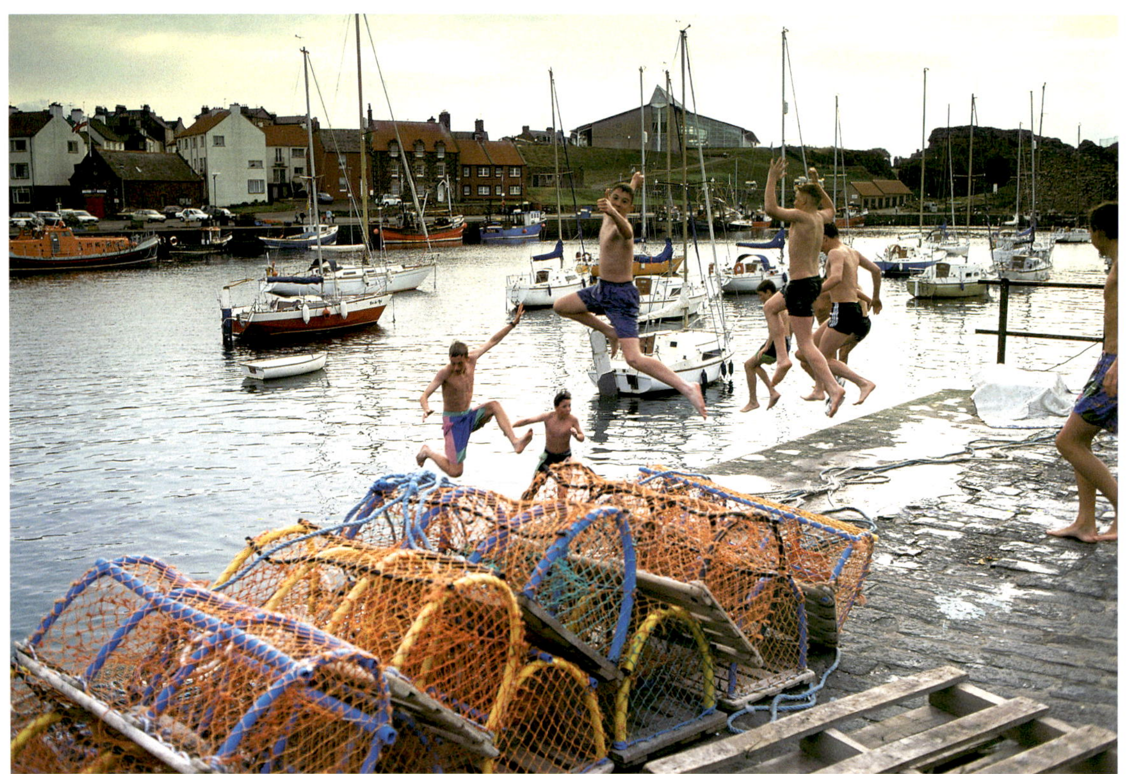

Schoolboys jumping into chilly Dunbar harbour despite having a heated swimming pool with a wave machine on the headland above. Maybe it's about freedom after school and because the pool doesn't allow dive-bombing.

St Andrews University is where Prince William studied. It is the third oldest university in the English-speaking world, founded in 1415. This is a traditional walk, held on a Sunday after church. I can't see any of the students I know being up for this.

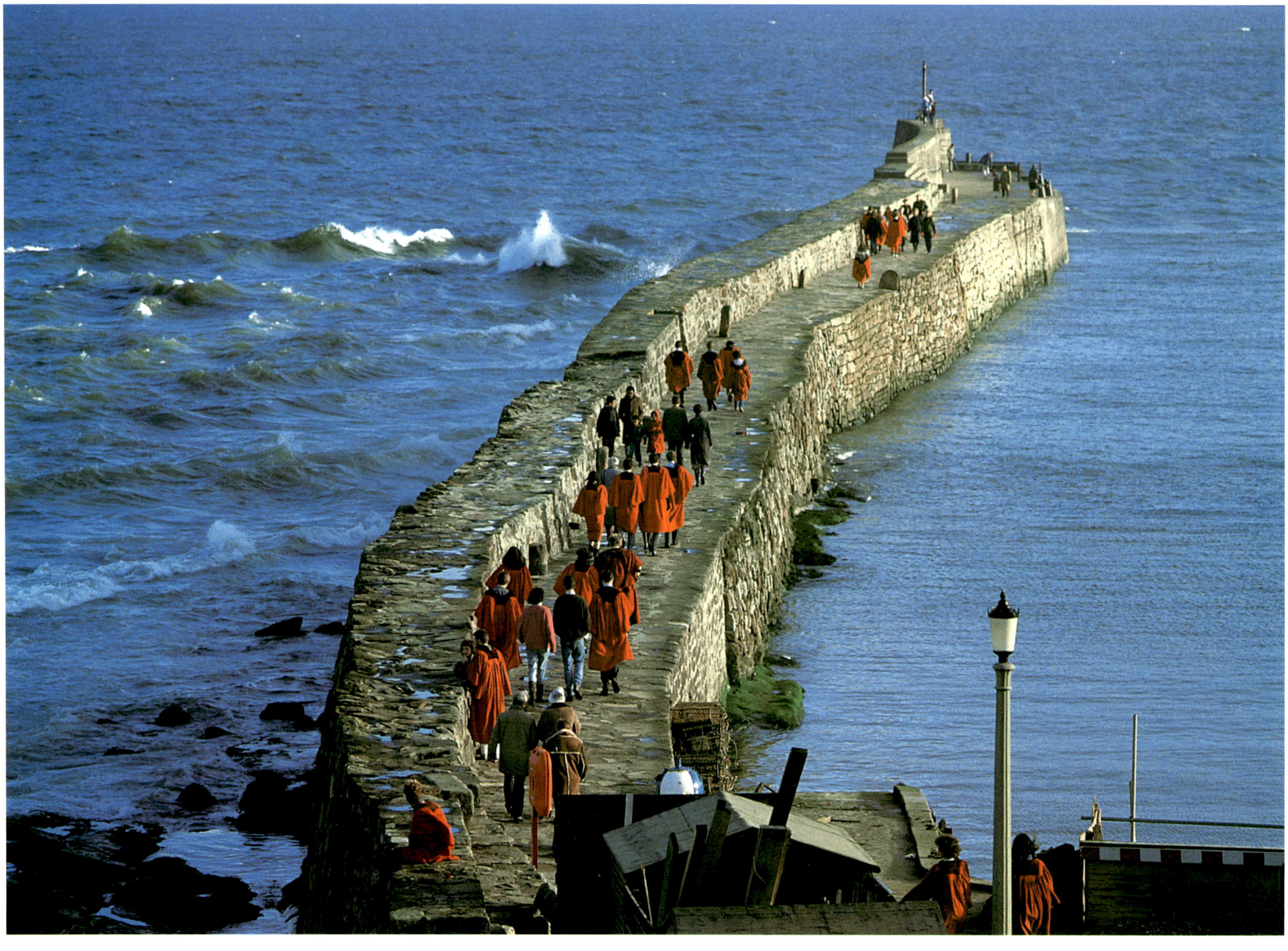

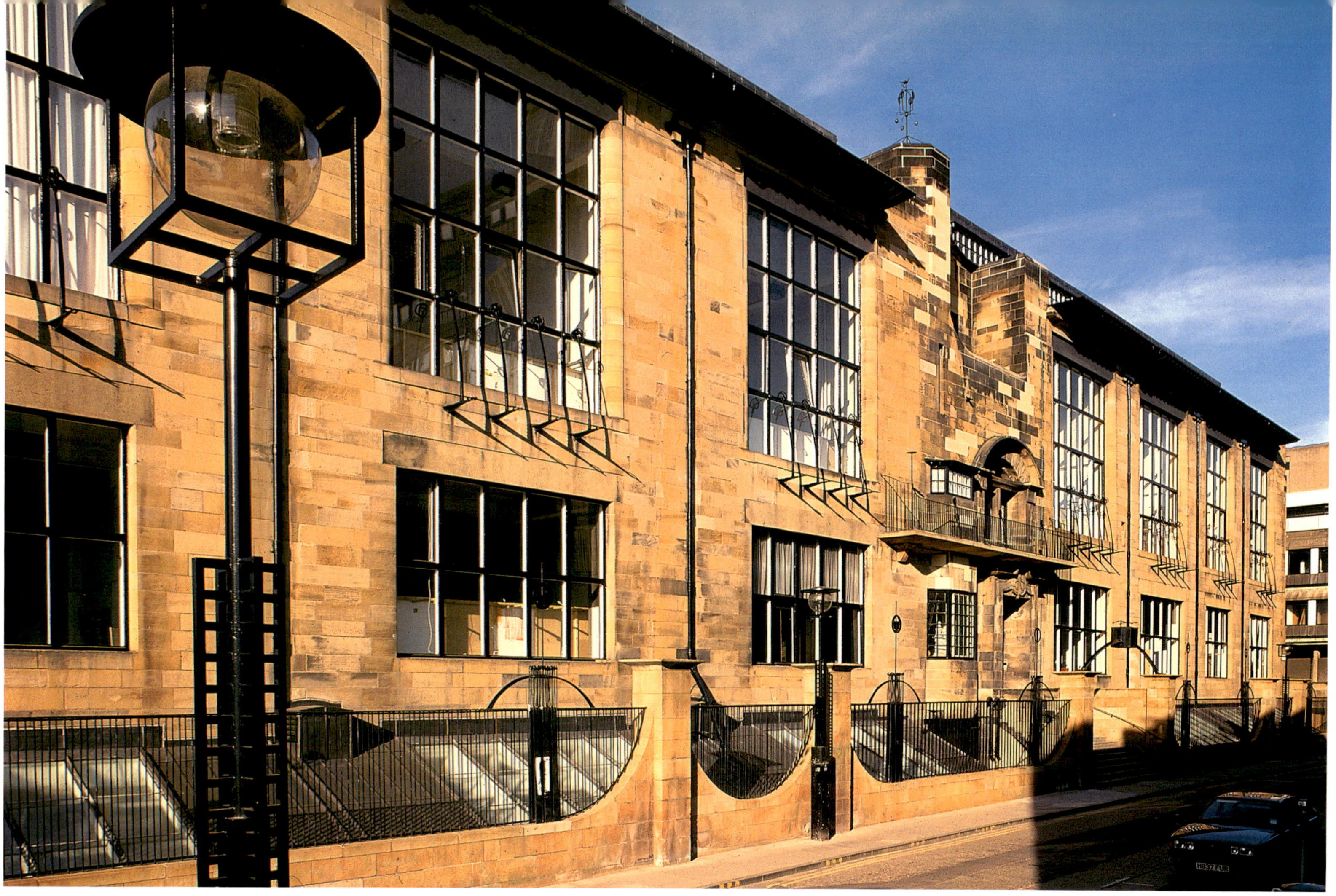

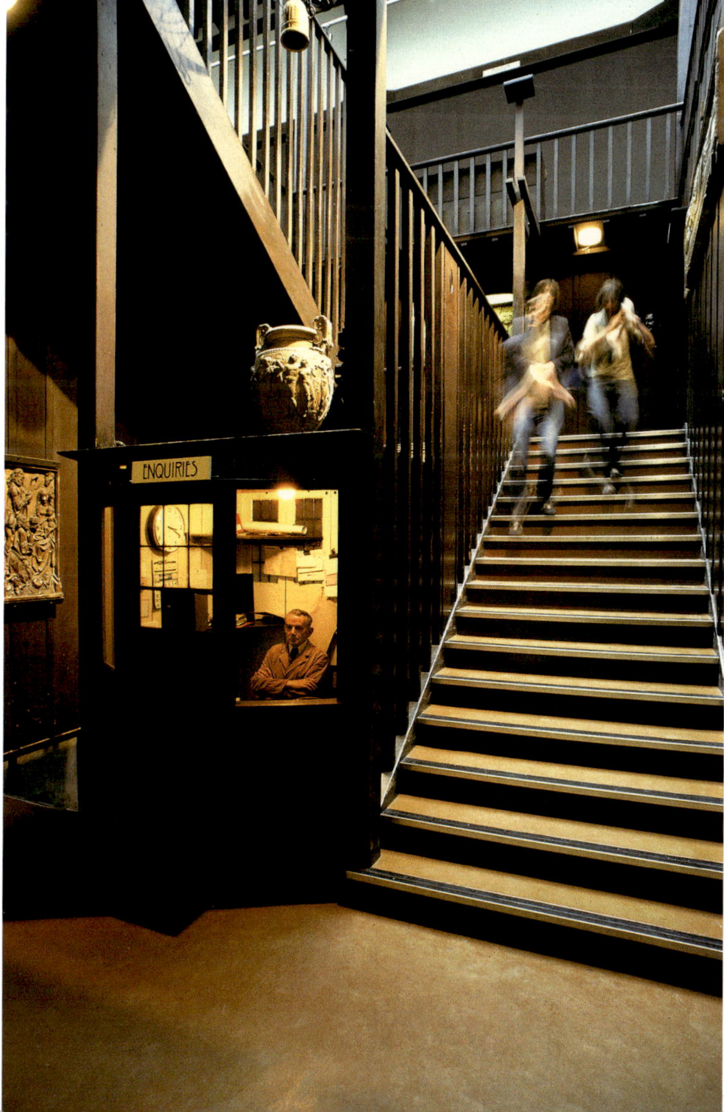

An American arts magazine described Charles Rennie Mackintosh as 'the prophet of pure perfection'. The Glasgow School of Art is internationally recognised as his masterpiece. The north façade catches the sun only in midsummer early mornings. My brother Gordon was a student there during the 1970s. He and some other students occasionally found working within a masterpiece a bit overwhelming.

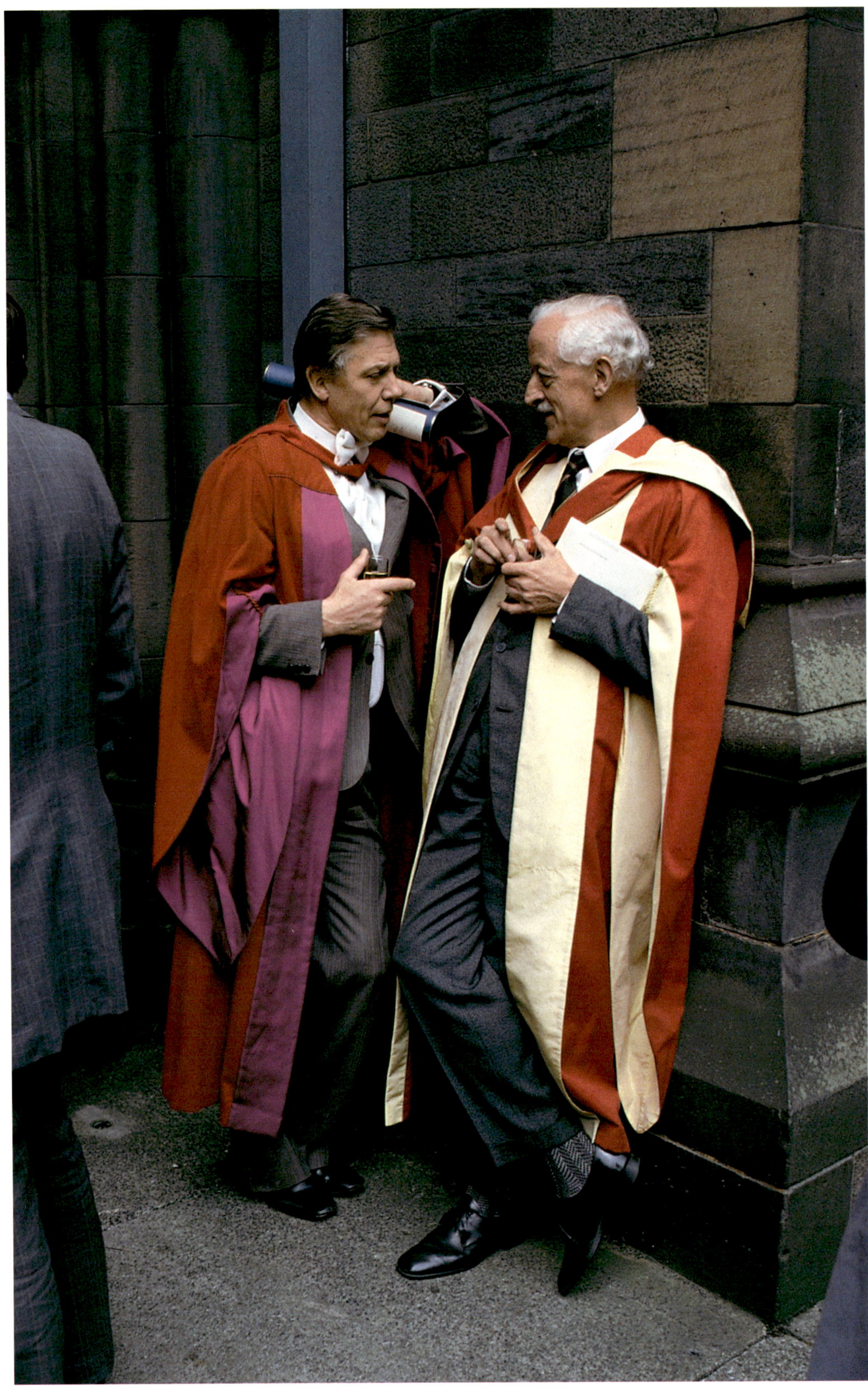

Sir David Attenborough, the much loved and respected face and voice of natural history on television, had just been awarded an honorary degree from Glasgow University in the 1980s. It was 1958 before my family got television – one channel and black and white, with *The Billy Cotton Band Show* and *The Lone Ranger*. My favourite show was *Zoo Quest*, with David Attenborough dressed in khaki shorts and shirt in search of the Komodo dragon or in caves filled with millions of bats. His influence on our appreciation and respect for wildlife and nature has been justifiably recognised by the many accolades he has received.

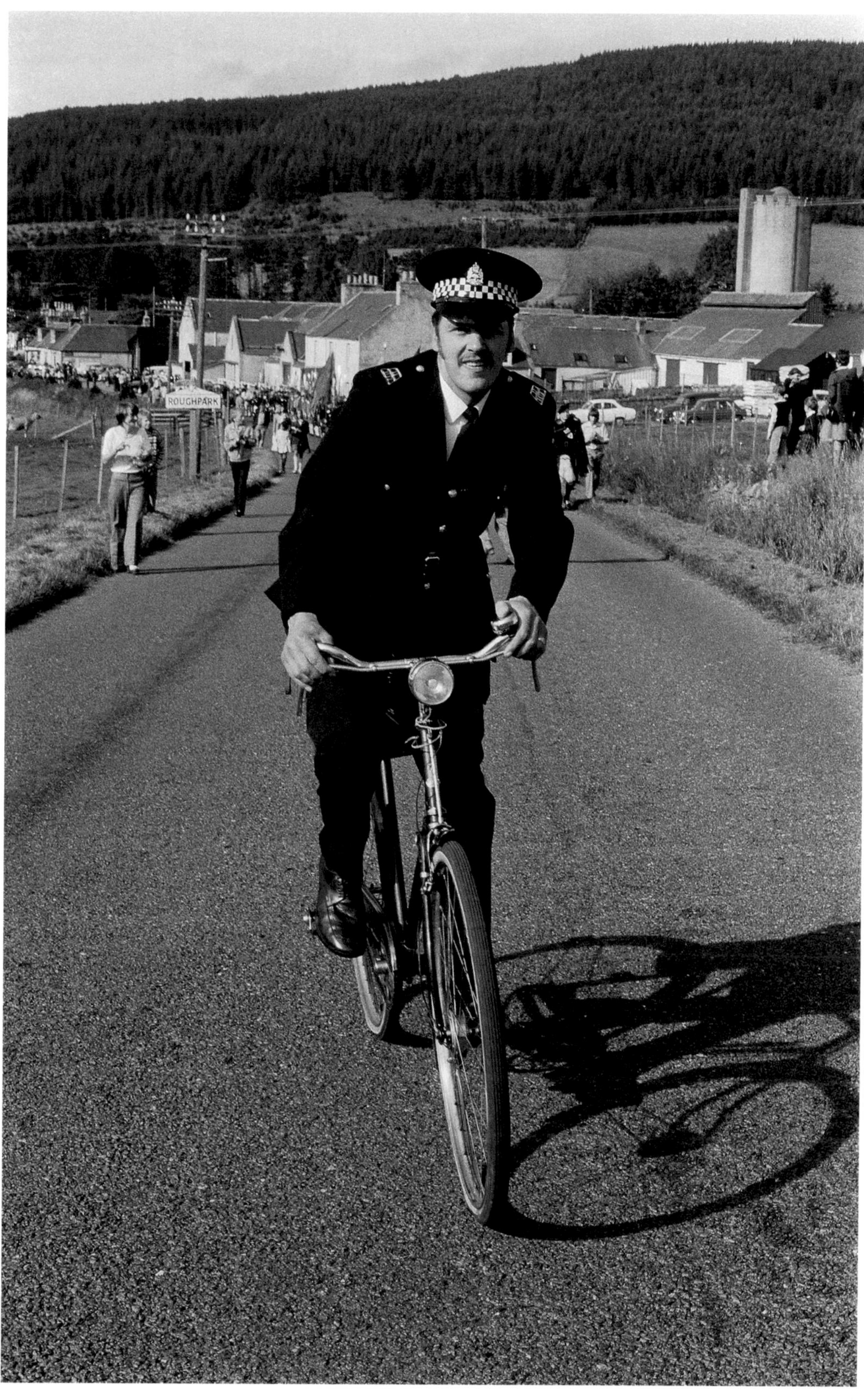

The local bobby leads the Lonach Gathering through the village of Roughpark in the parish of Strathdon in the late 1970s. This is my childhood image of the police, respected and known by everyone. Seeing an approaching bobby on his bike would put a halt to cycling on the pavement and other minor misdemeanours. This was a period of more benign policing.

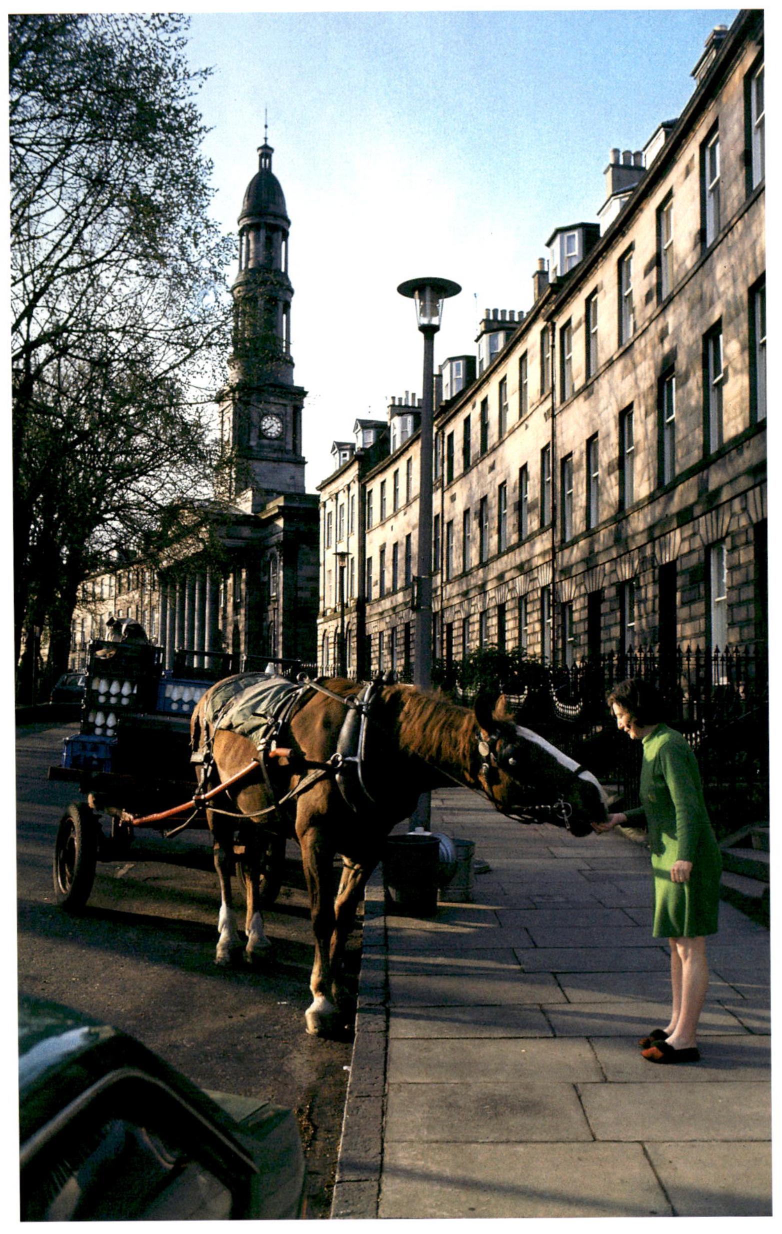

In the 1970s the local Co-op still used working horses – here in the gentle curve of Bellevue Crescent, with the clock at twenty to eight. A lady brings out some breakfast, giving the horse a break from pulling heavy milk crates over hilly cobbled streets.

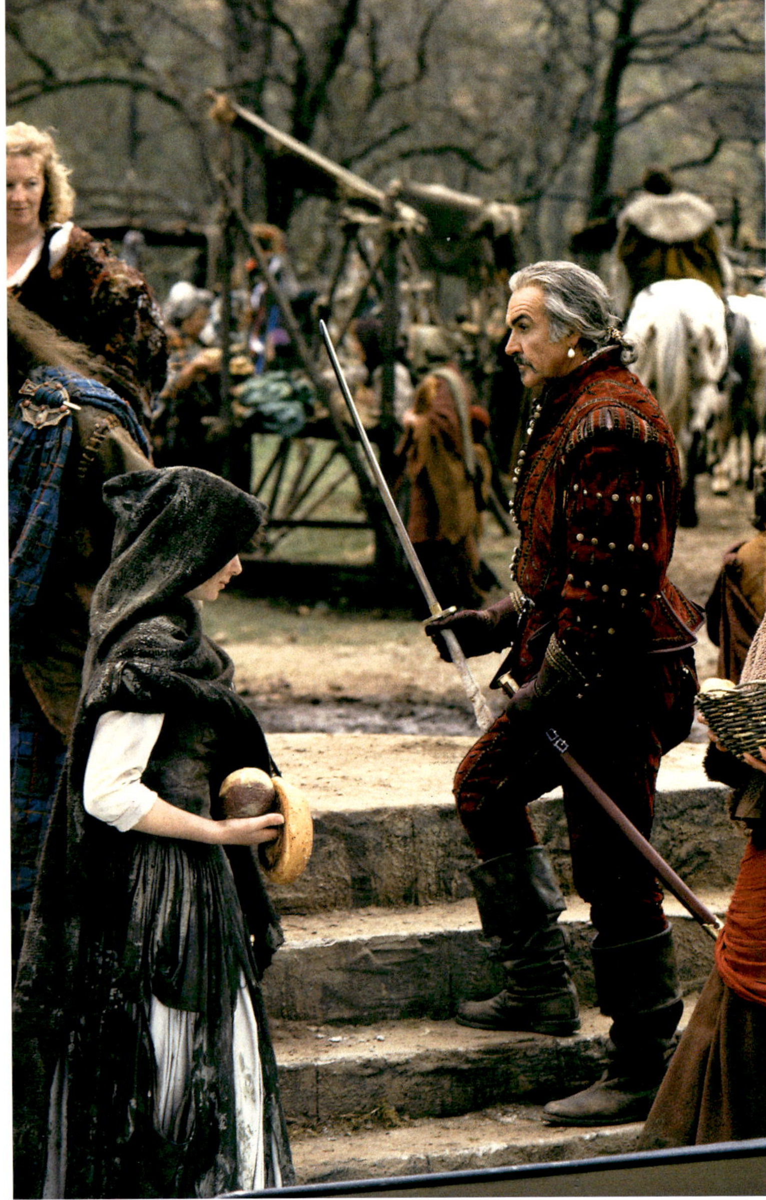

Sean Connery at work on the set of the film *Highlander*. A few months before he had complimented me on my *Edinburgh* book, which he had been presented with at an Edinburgh International Film Festival event. He was the best James Bond.

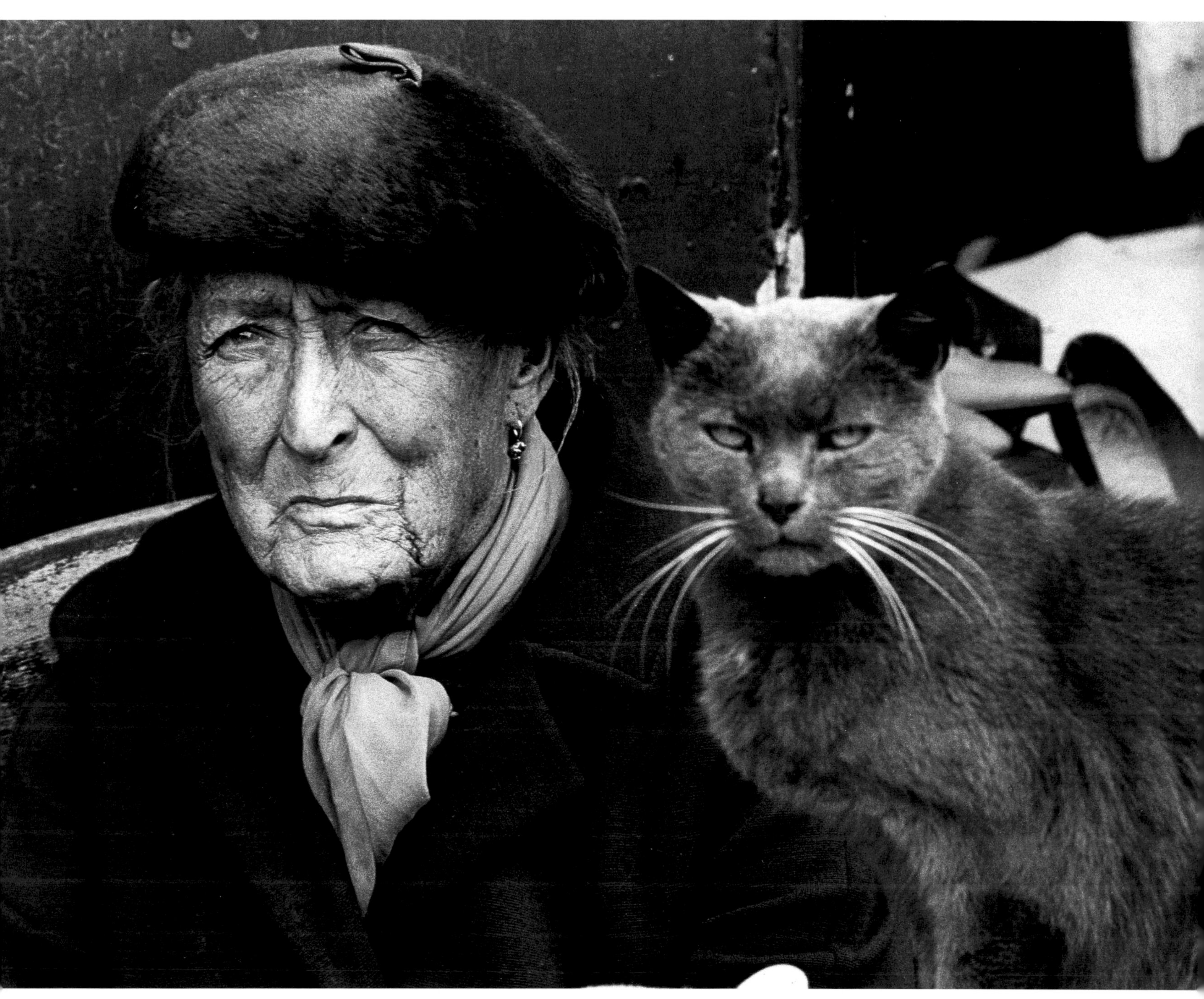

Anne Fine published her best-selling novel *Madame Doubtfire* in 1987 (later turned into a very successful film, *Mrs Doubtfire*, starring Robin Williams). She got the inspiration for the title of the book from a second-hand clothes seller who lived in the 1970s in a basement in Edinburgh's New Town, which she shared with a large coterie of cats. Madame Doubtfire was a formidable character. While I was photographing her, she was having good-natured banter with a local constable: 'I've known him since he was a bairn'. He obviously had respect and affection for her while using great diplomacy to persuade her to tidy the disorderly exterior of her shop.

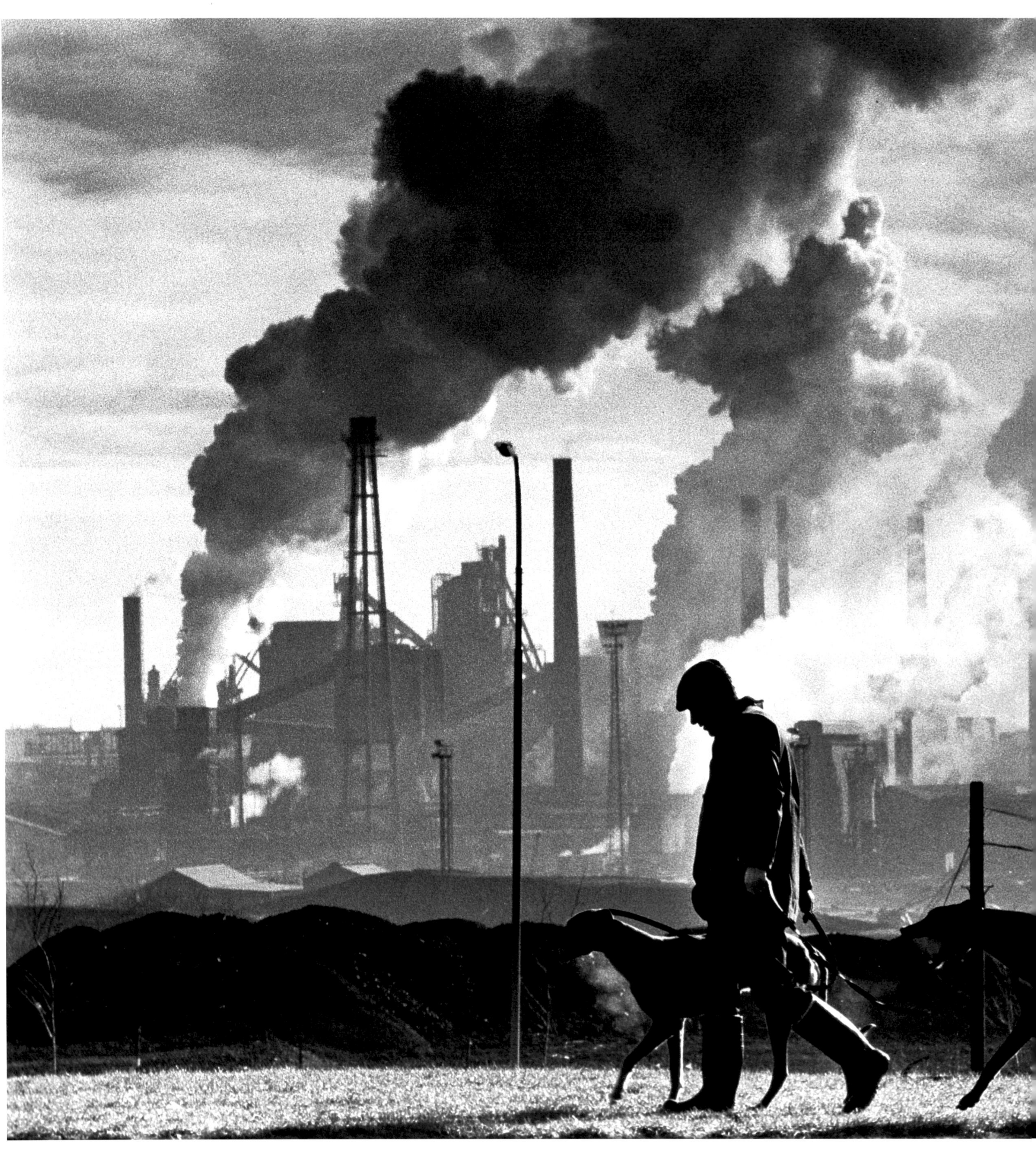

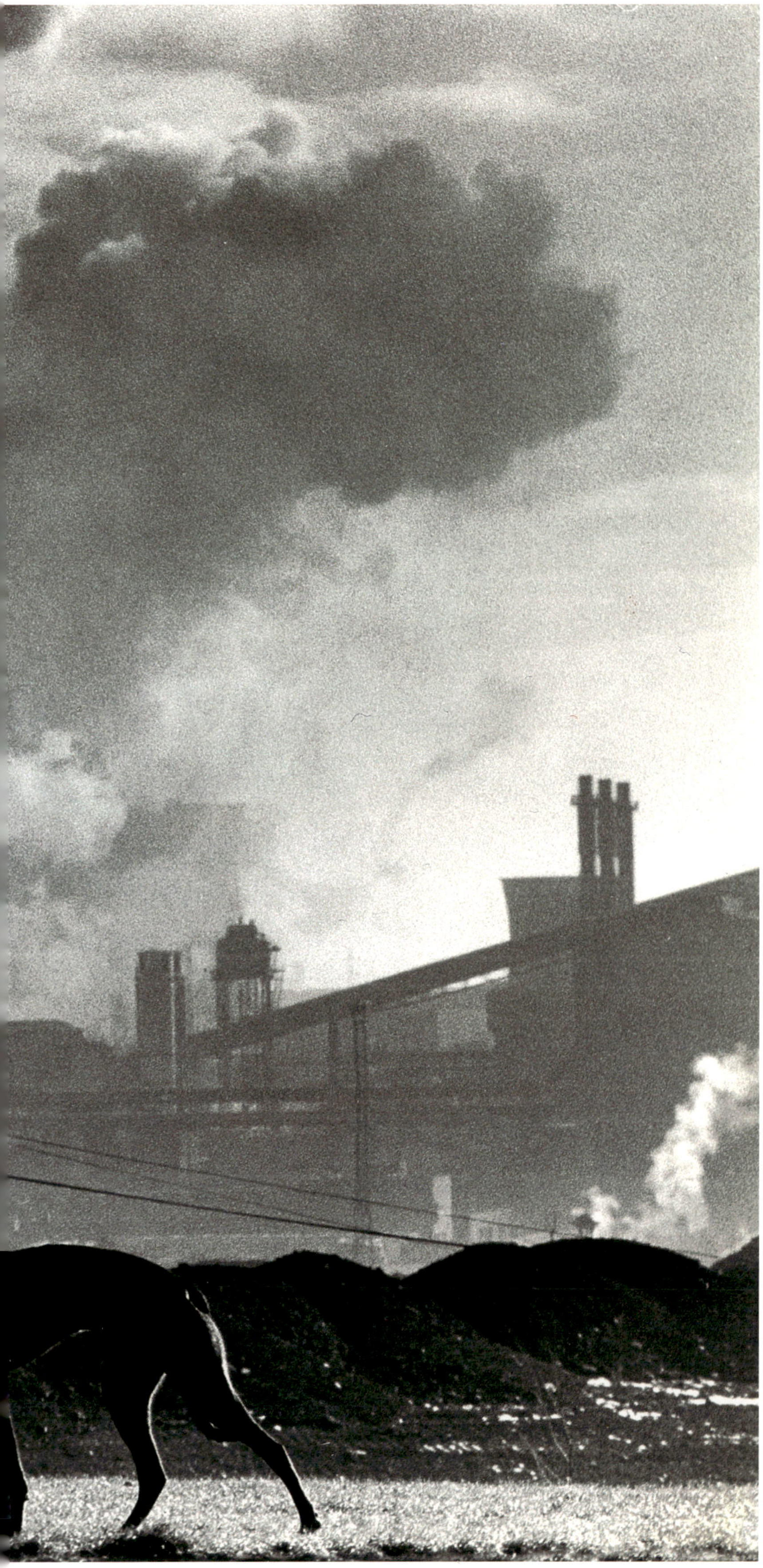

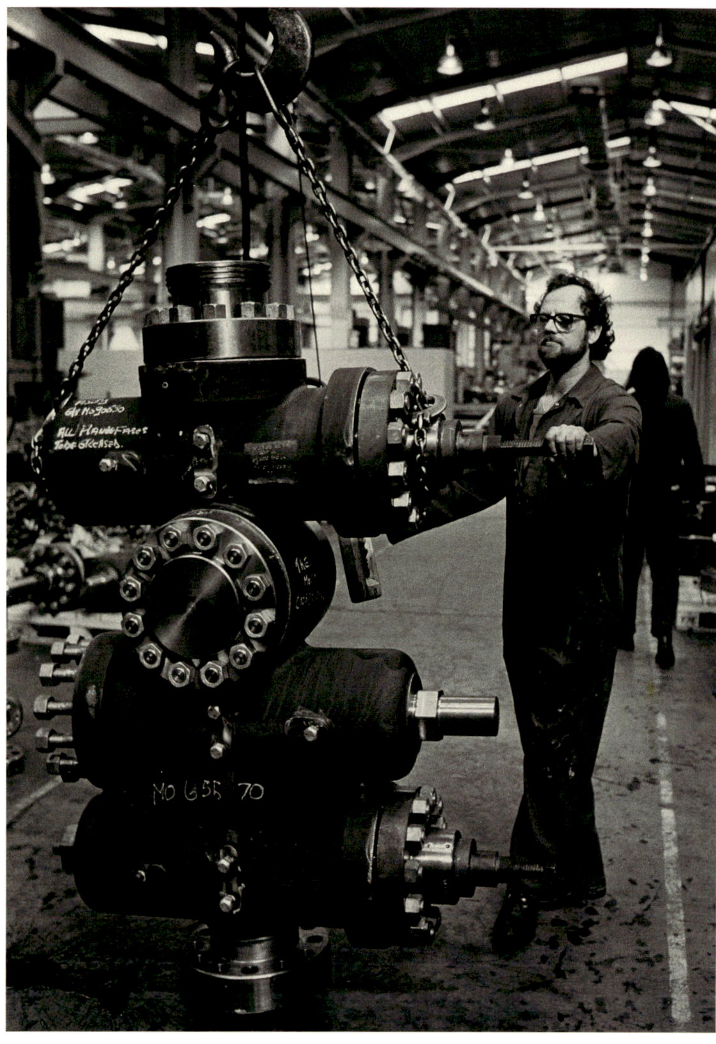

Ballet in overalls, partnered by a robotic-looking piece of heavy engineering. The 1980s was a time when we were told we were no long a manufacturing nation. Service industries – banking and insurance – were the future, where we were all expected to learn to be good at sums.

This was shot for *Scotland on Sunday* – Ravenscraig steelworks, North Lanarkshire, in the week of its closure. He had just been paid off. Like a candle, the last burst of power, a protest before dying. The site of the former steelworks (the size of 700 football grounds) has become one of the largest regeneration projects in Europe.

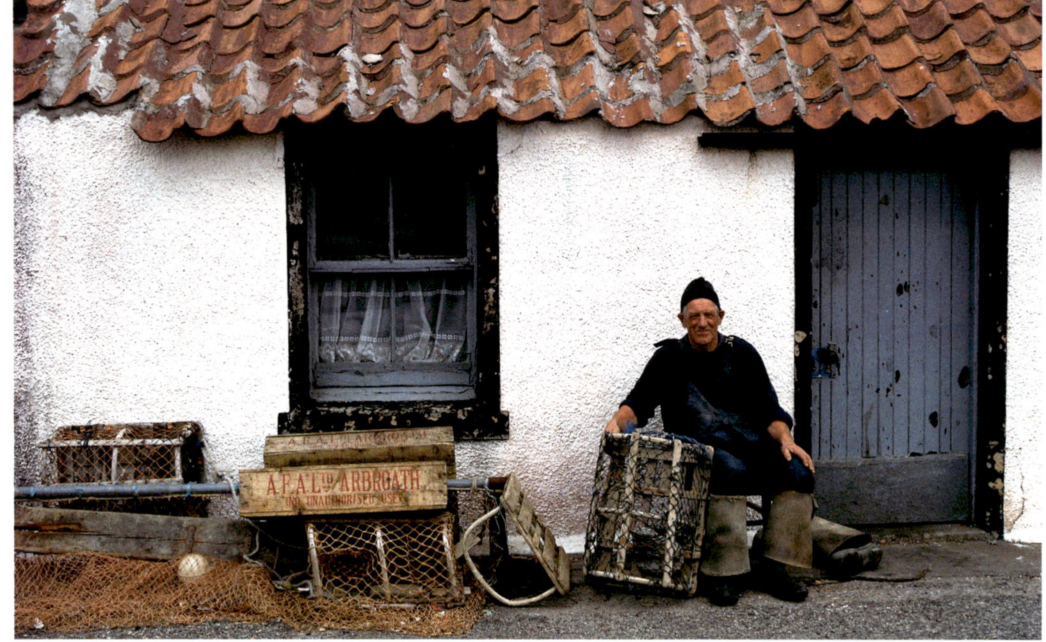

Johnshaven is a small fishing village in Aberdeenshire, which has a successful seafood festival. This fisherman has experienced the best and the worst the North Sea can throw at him. I have great respect for their skill and bravery.

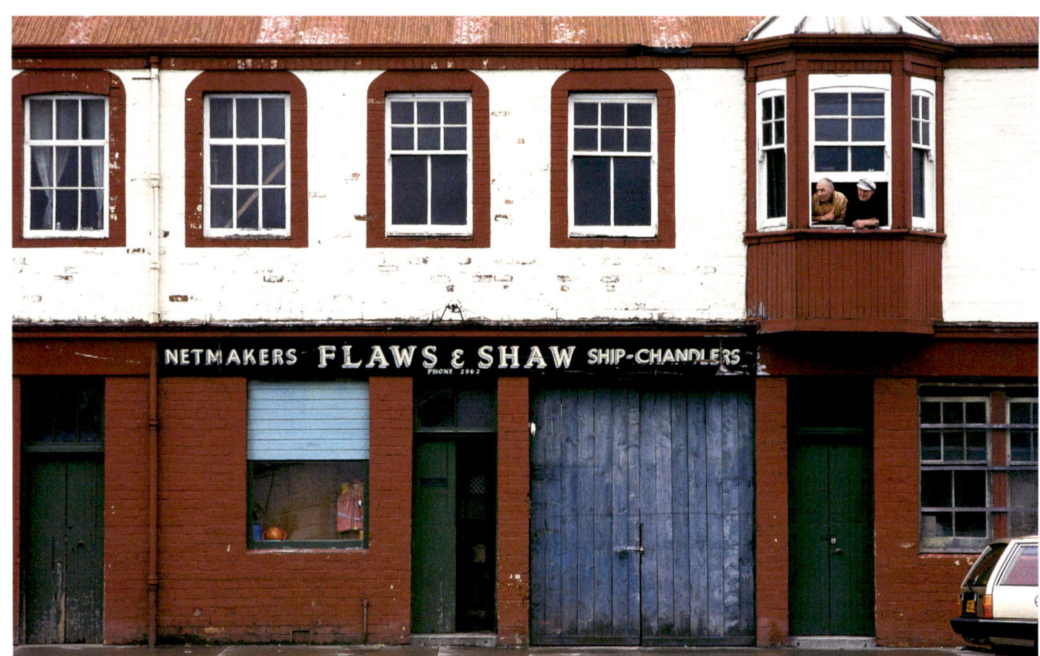

In 2010, Mr Flaws came across this shot of his grandfather's ship chandlers in Campbeltown, which was first published in one of my earlier books, *Strathclyde*. He ordered prints for his grandmother, who was delighted to see this picture for the first time. There are rewards to be found from photographing apparently ordinary scenes.

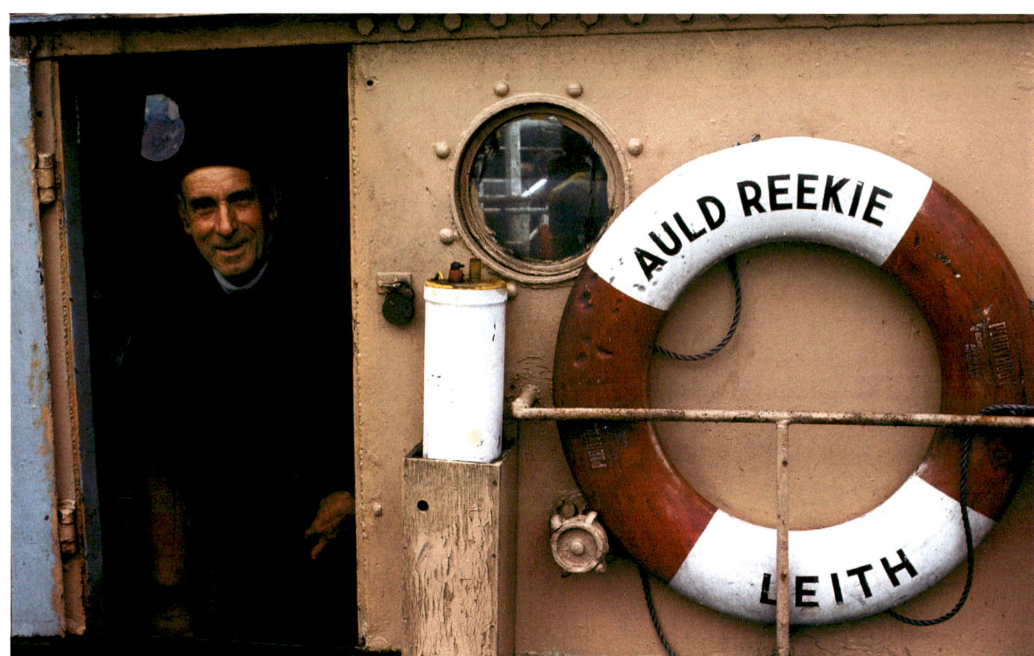

I photographed *Auld Reekie*, the last of the Clyde puffers, when she was based in Leith in the 1970s. She went on to star as the *Vital Spark* in the third *Para Handy* television series. Currently she is still playing that role while berthed at Inveraray as part of their Maritime Museum.

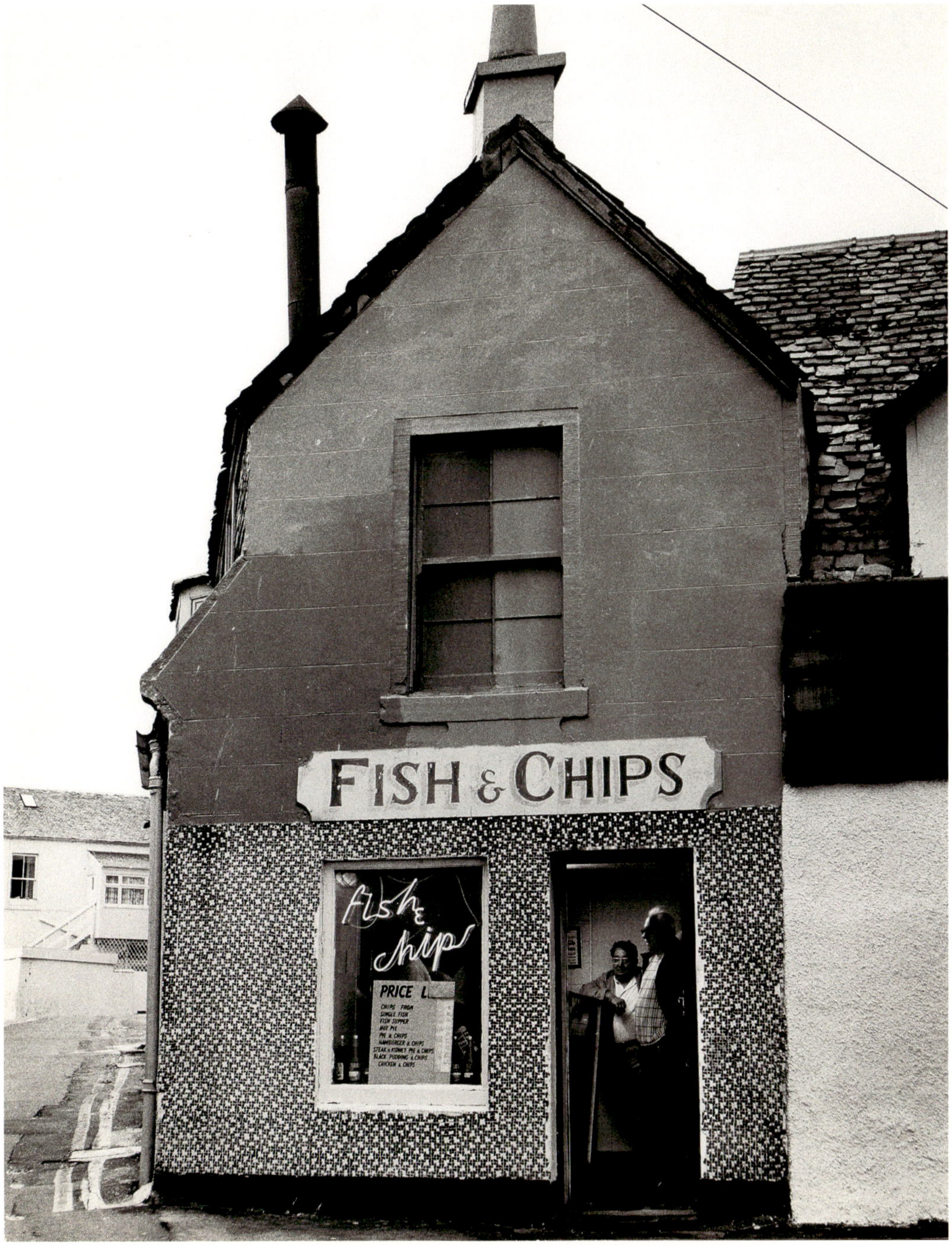

In the National Gallery of Scotland there is a painting by Sir David Young Cameron, of which the location of the scene is unknown. I think I know the place that the painting is depicting, yet I can't remember where I shot this classic-looking fish and chip shop in the 1970s. I think it was southwest of Glasgow. Does anyone know where it is or was?

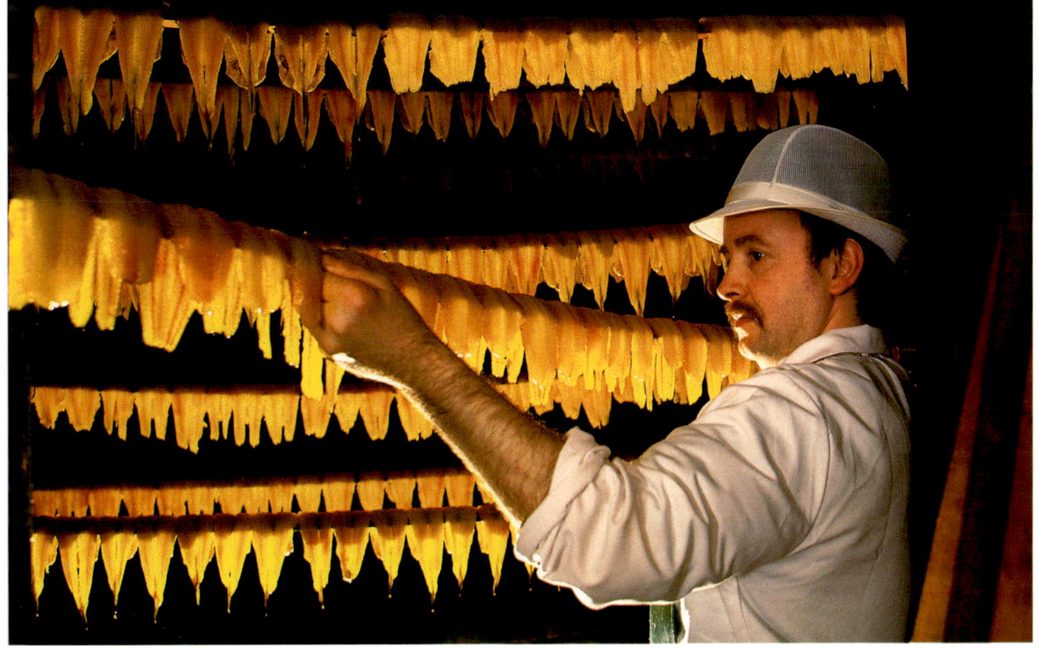

The east coast of Scotland still uses traditional methods for smoking fish. In particular the Arbroath Smokie is well lauded by the likes of Rick Stein as a classic British dish. It has received the Protected Geographical Indication, which ensures that this unique product can only be called a smokie if produced within eight kilometres of Arbroath. A similar protection is awarded to the likes of Champagne and Parma ham. Personally I love smokies but they don't make as attractive a picture as these golden haddies.

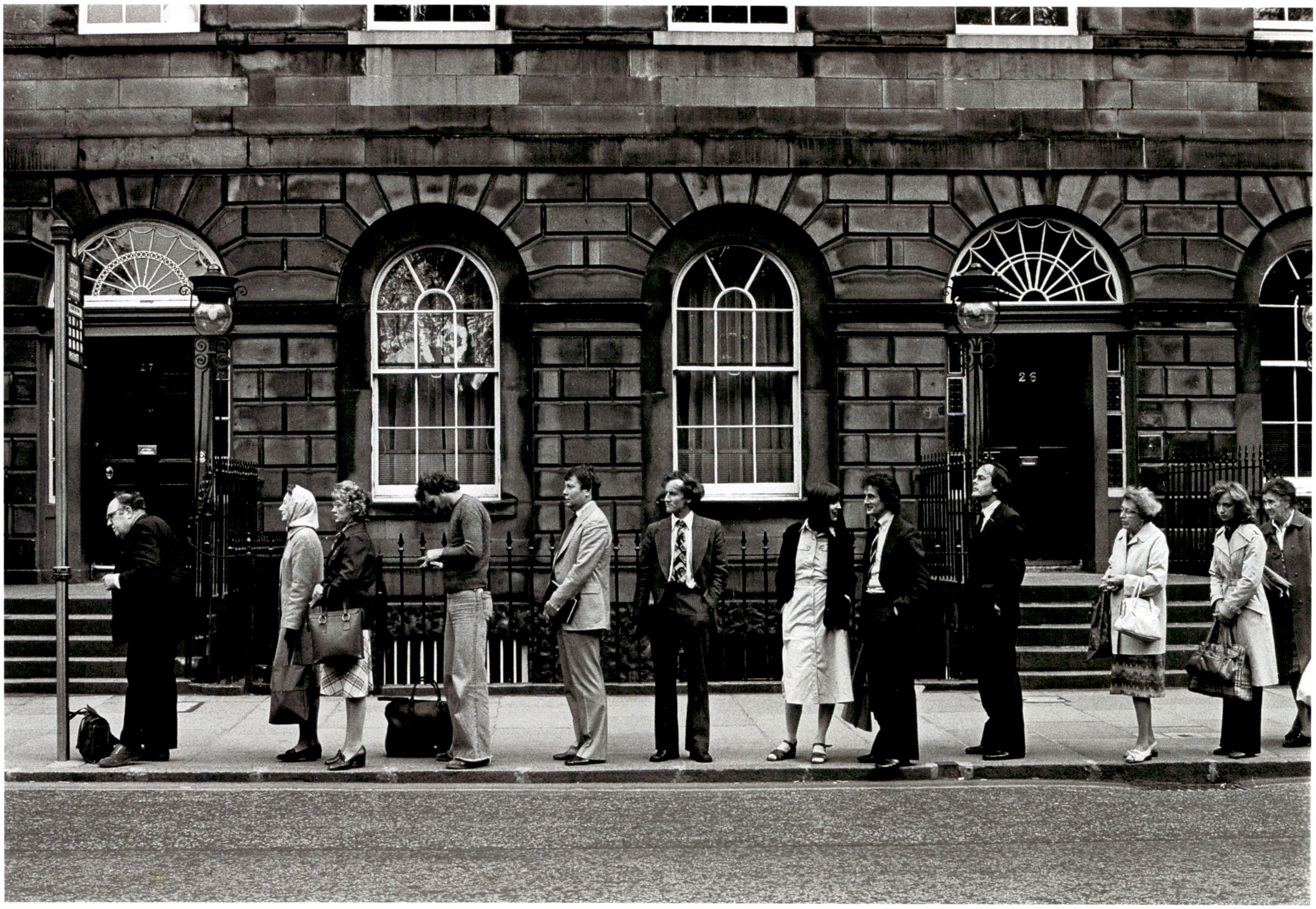

An orderly queue in Charlotte Square, Edinburgh, arranged with almost military precision spacing, in the 1970s. Along with red telephone kiosks and black hackney taxis, queuing was a part of the image we portrayed abroad, all of which now seem diminished in some way or other.

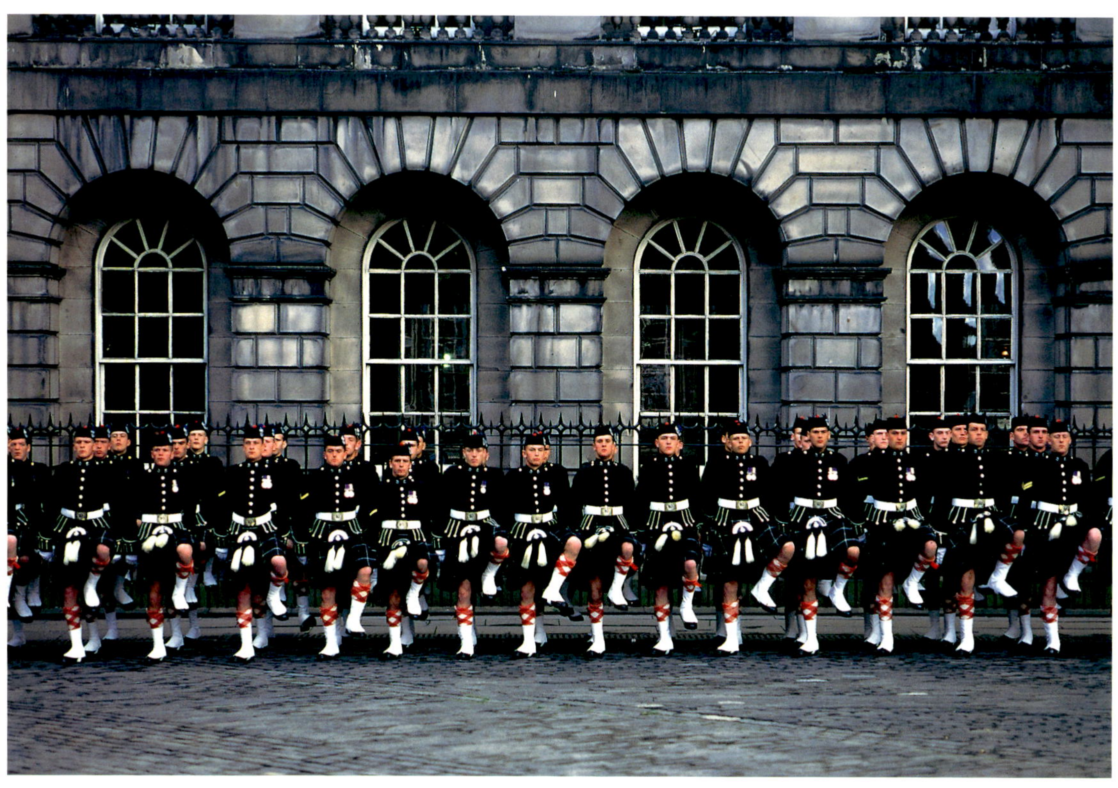

The military wear the kilt on ceremonial and official occasions. It does give a very individual and strong identity to the troops. The services' pipe bands in full dress uniform make an amazing sight. I have witnessed the delight they can bring to crowds around the world.

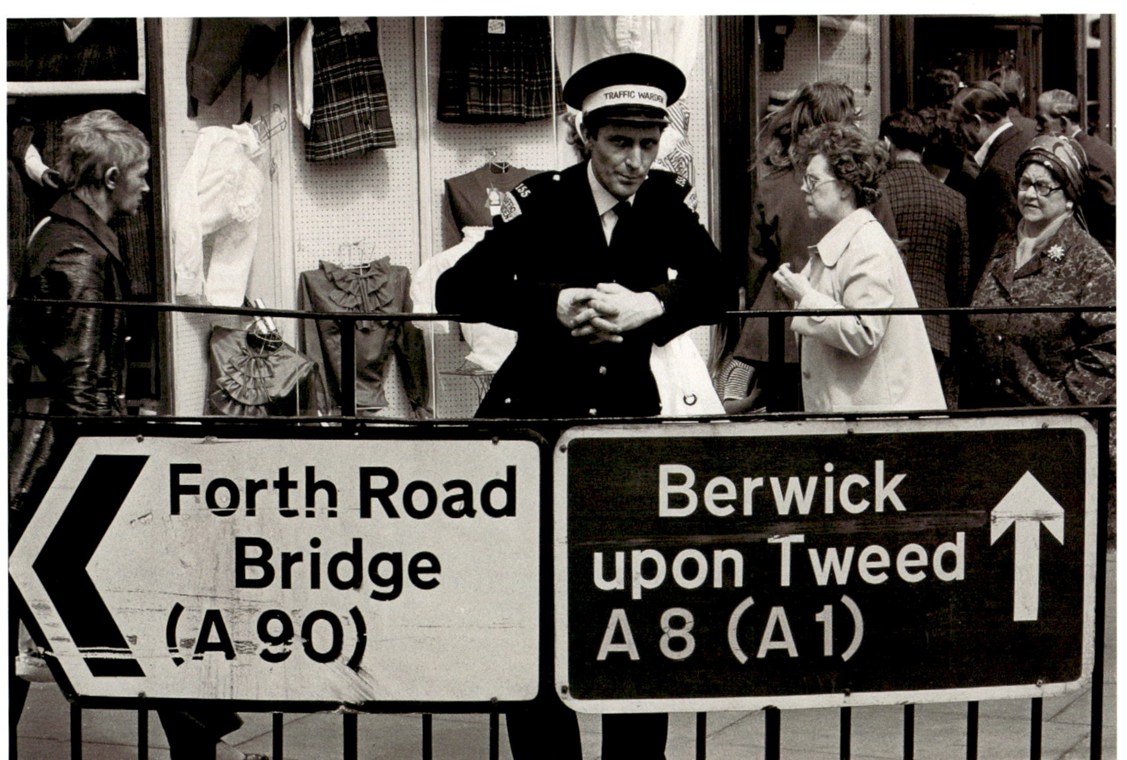

Traffic wardens in the 1970s – I'm sure their mothers loved them. Nowadays, car owners have to contend with the added imposition of the parking attendant.

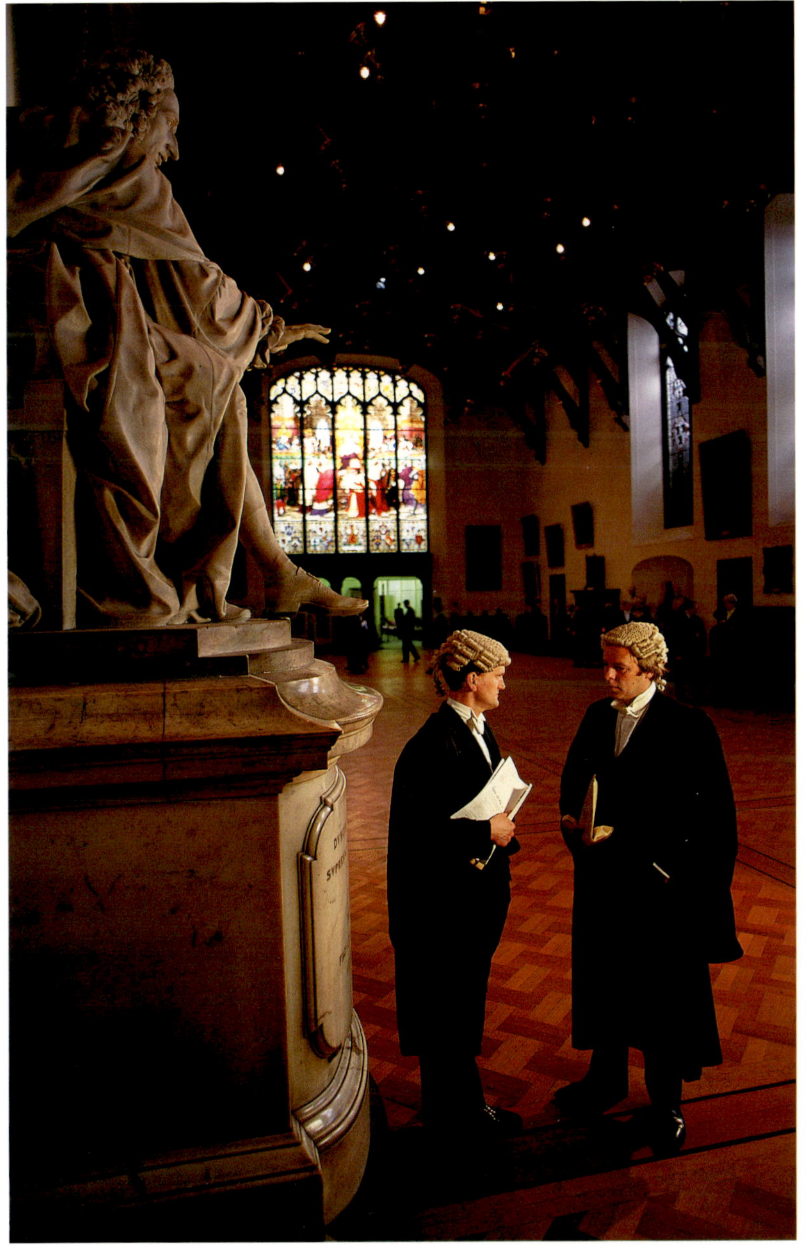

The old parliament building of Scotland, Parliament House, off Edinburgh's Royal Mile, brought solemnity to its function as the supreme court of Scotland. Duncan Forbes of Culloden, Lord Advocate from 1725-1737 waves a calming hand over proceedings. He was one of Scotland's most trusted judges who advocated leniency for the Jacobite rebels. This was ignored by the vindictive Duke of Cumberland.

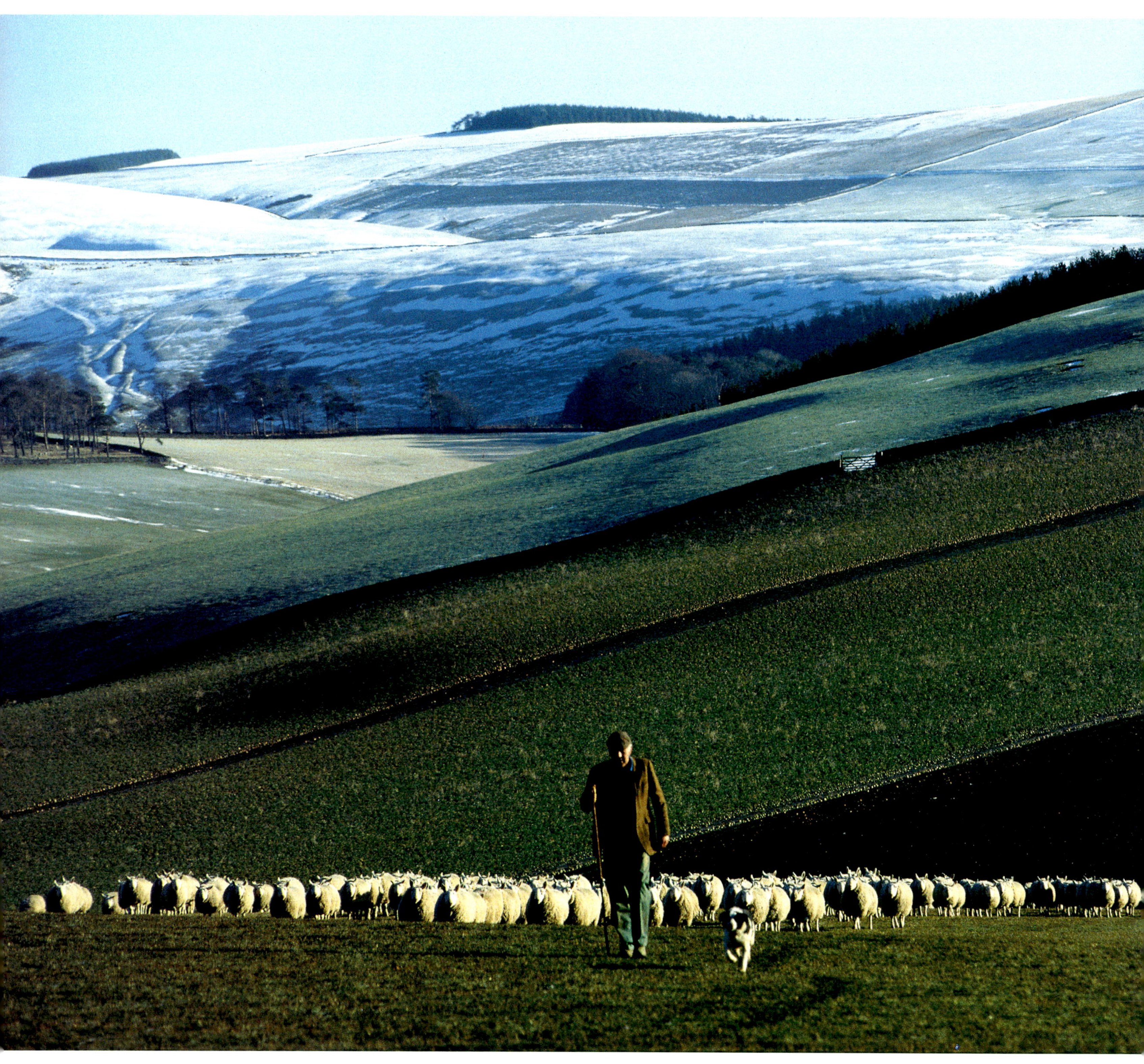

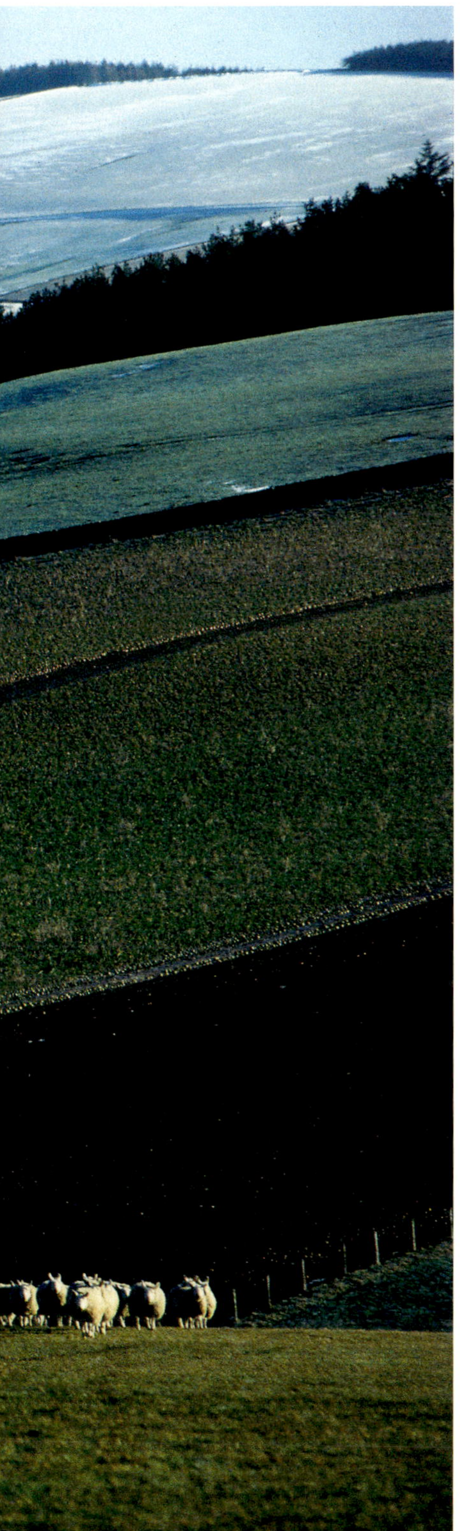

An Australian financial magazine commissioned me to photograph a Borders shepherd in the 1980s. They were delighted with this shot and used it over a double page spread. I will never stop getting a buzz when I know I have taken a good shot, the client likes it and uses it well.

Sheep-shearing in Glencoe. I hope the collie dog isn't in danger of getting his tail docked. The Border collie is an intelligent breed, a famous example of which was *Black Bob*, who appeared as a popular comic strip in *The Dandy* from 1944 until 1982. His creator, Jack Prout, shortly before retirement, acquired such a collie. Prout's colleagues at D. C. Thomson presented him with a special dog licence that allowed the dog to keep the artist as a pet.

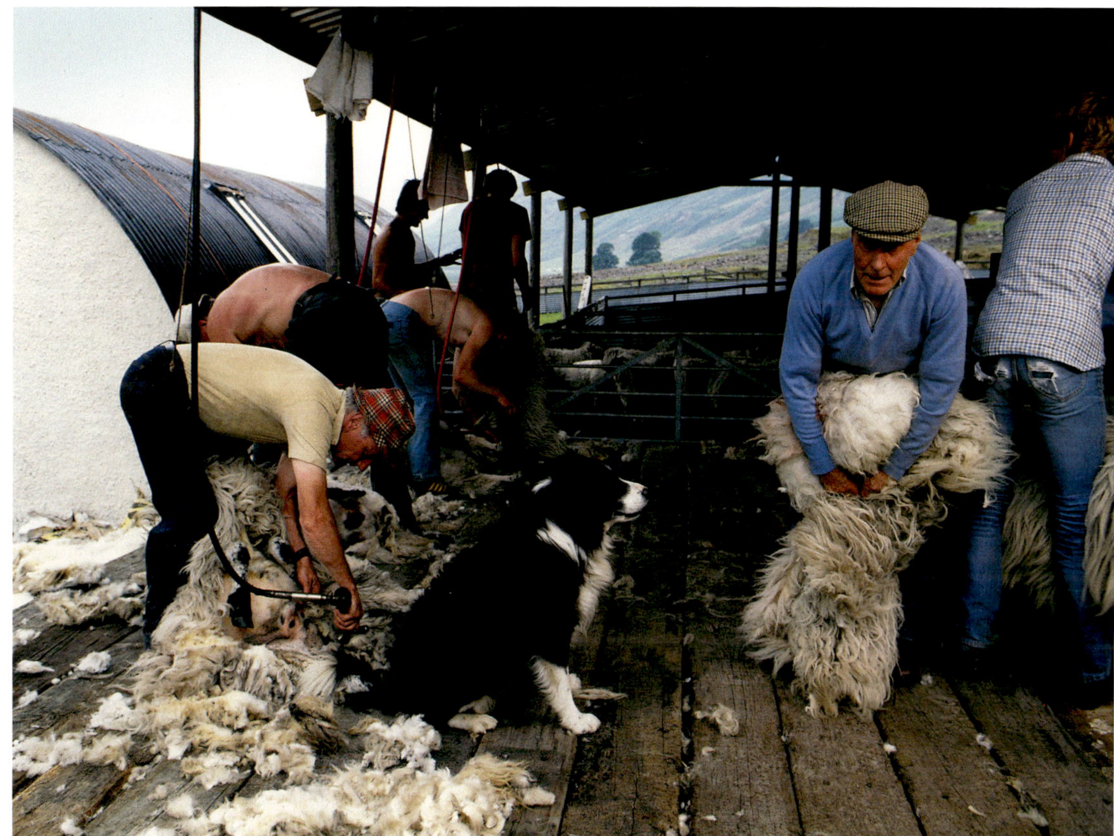

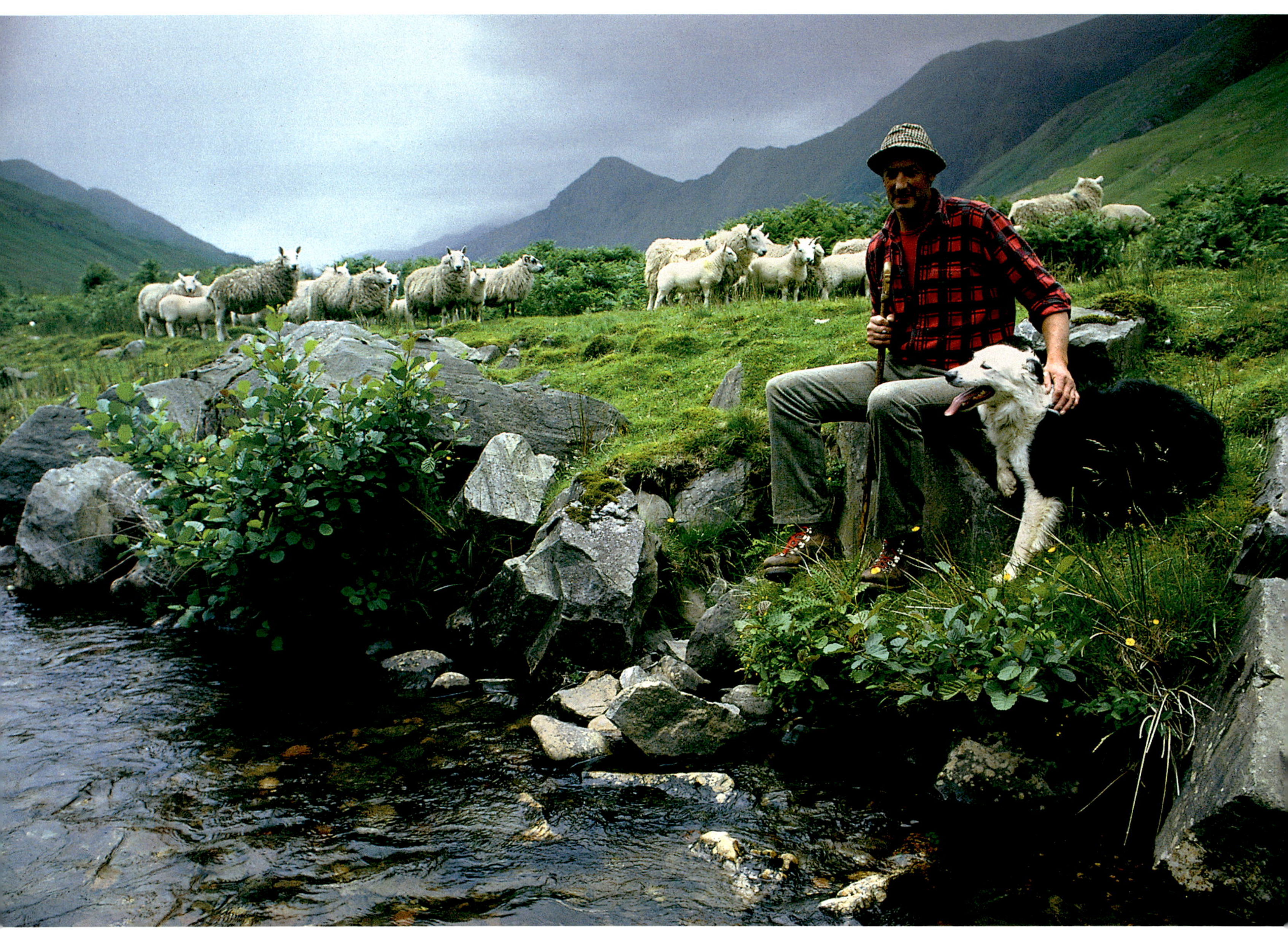

The shepherd in Glen Shiel, Kintail, in the early 1990s told me that although the golden eagle would take the odd lamb, it would be balanced out by the vermin that it killed. Not everyone is as enlightened. Kintail, in the care of the National Trust for Scotland, has six Munros (mountains over 3,000 feet) of which three make up the famous Five Sisters ridge.

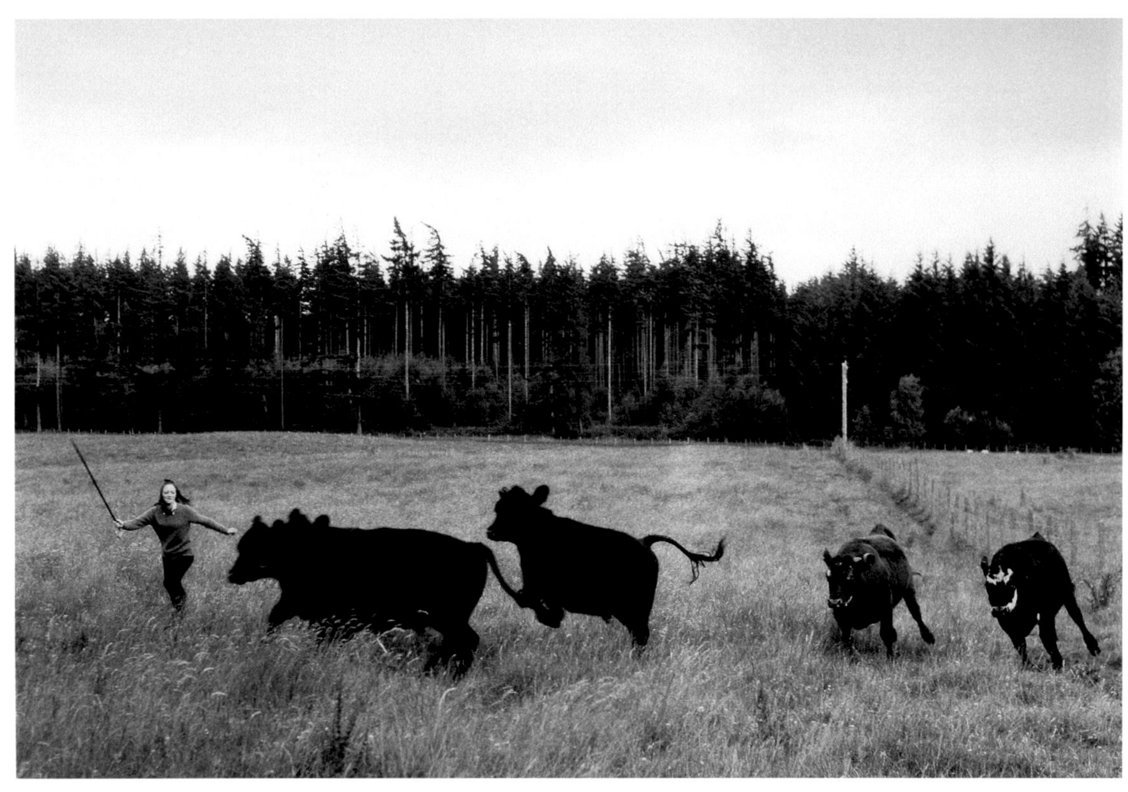

This enterprising young lady was a part-time breeder of cattle on the outskirts of Inverness. She seems to be choreographing some sort of balletic performance. This is the sort of picture I delight in – where the unexpected happens.

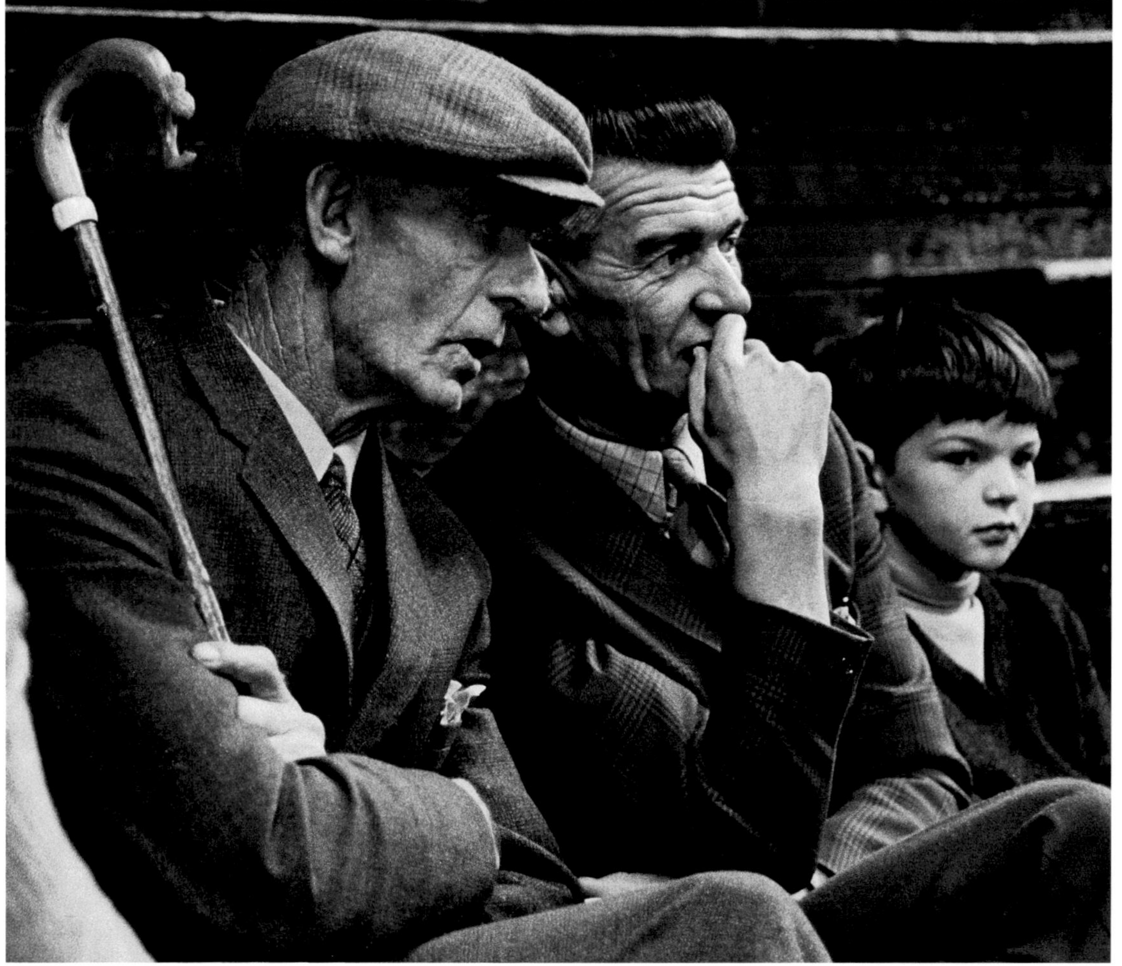

The concentration shows on the faces of these farmers at a cattle mart in the early 1970s. One of my *Highland News* weekly tasks was to photograph the highest priced beast at the market. I had to shoot it from a slight angle to show the rump to its best advantage. The auctioneer's speech is unintelligible to the unaccustomed ear – I'm sure they could make great rappers.

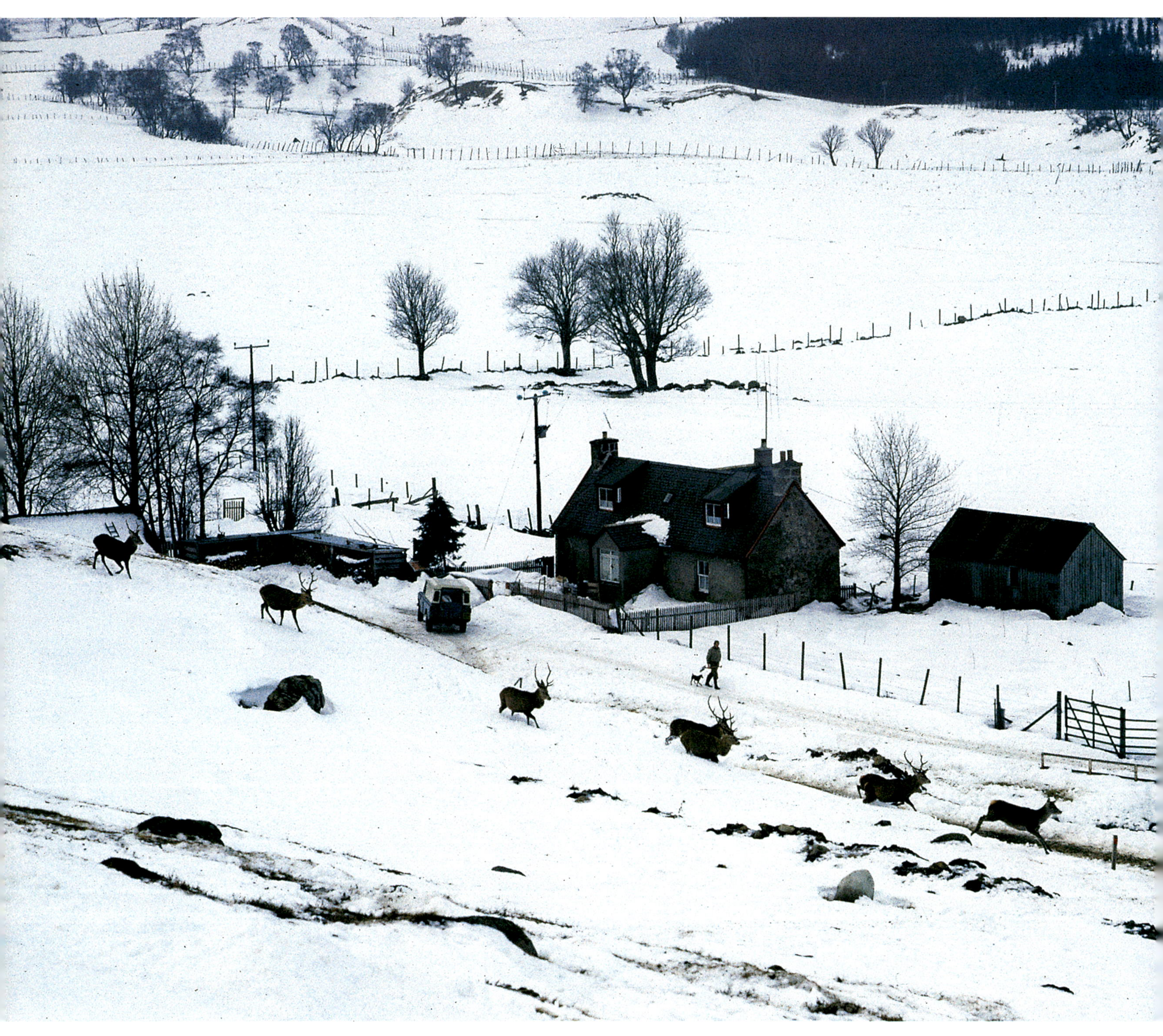

Black and white, shot in colour – Glenshee. You only get a picture like this by having your camera constantly at the ready. My first boss on the *Highland News*, Harvey Grainger, always had his camera with a telephoto lens on the passenger seat whenever he drove alongside Loch Ness. I do the same.

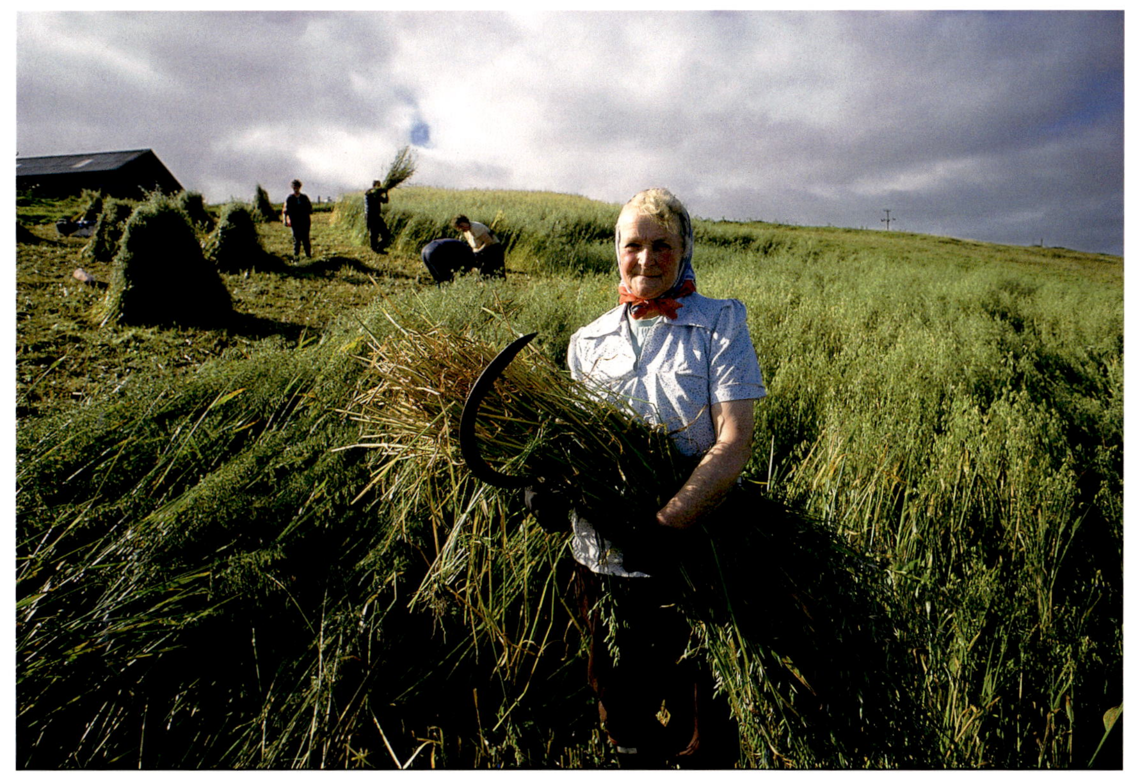

Shetland is the most northerly part of the United Kingdom. I thought this lady I photographed in the 1980s portrayed a Norse ancestry. The islands' history and culture relate more to Scandinavia than Scotland. The summer is short, but the 'simmer dim' gives a night of no blackness. Even in Inverness my parents and their neighbours would be gardening late into the evening but more often chatting over the garden gate.

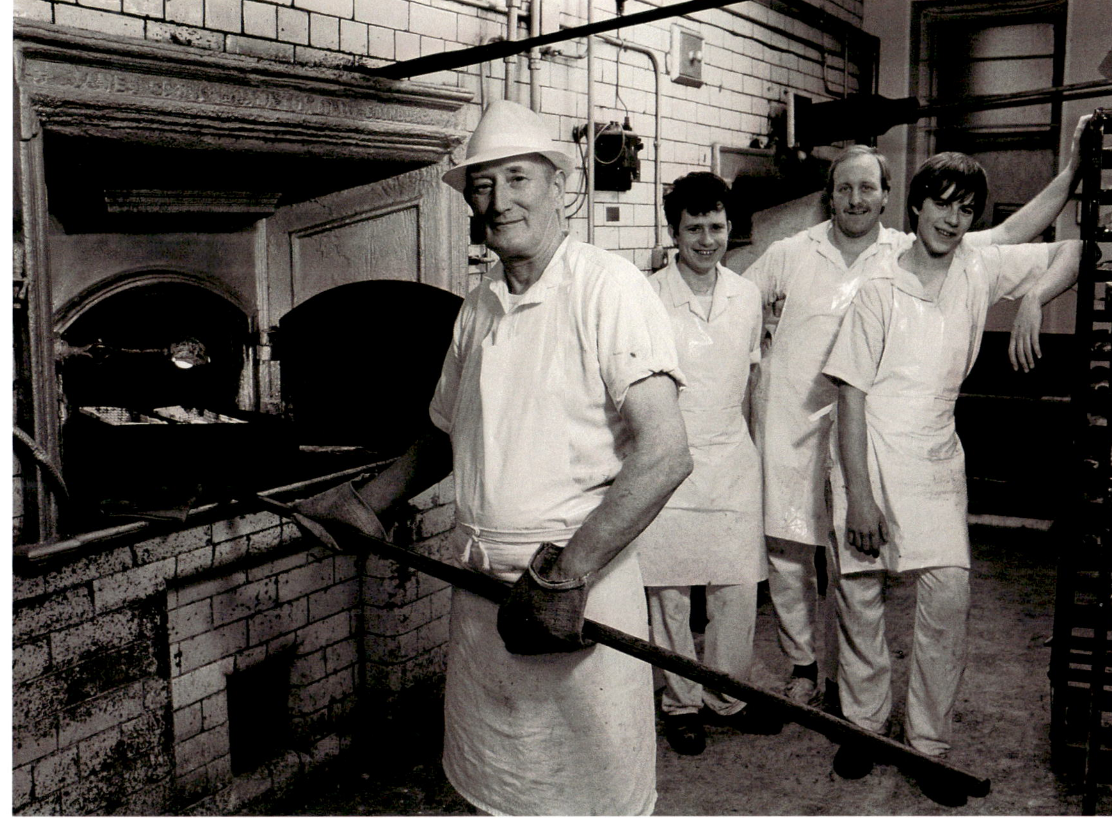

Their faces reflect the pride and skill of these craft bakers – one of the pictures taken as part of a commission for the Carnegie Trust to photograph Dunfermline in the 1980s. Somehow I can't see these guys baking sun-dried tomato and olive-flavoured bread when a good Scotch morning roll is hard to beat.

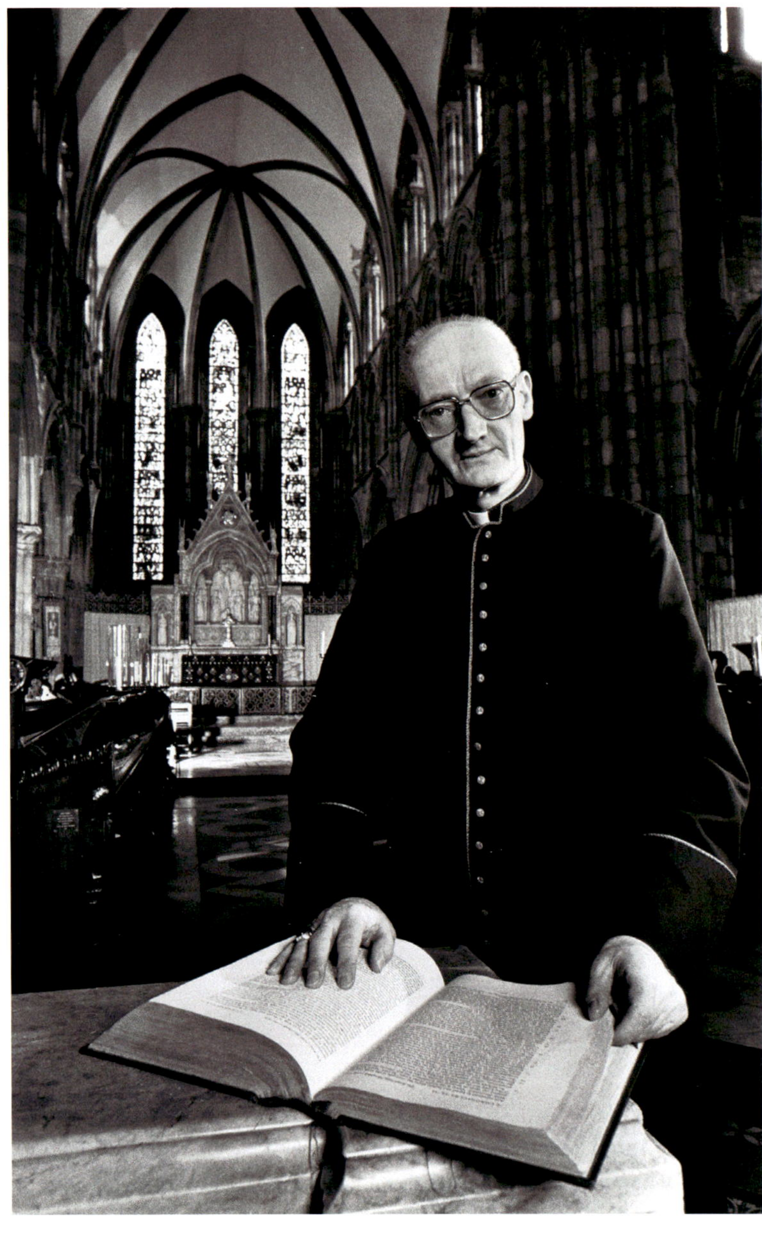

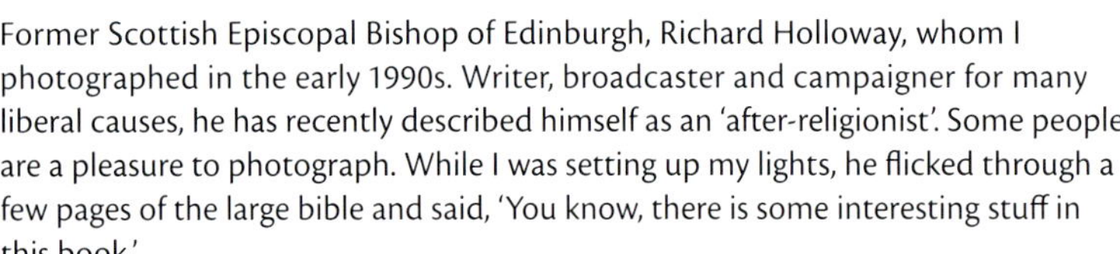

Former Scottish Episcopal Bishop of Edinburgh, Richard Holloway, whom I photographed in the early 1990s. Writer, broadcaster and campaigner for many liberal causes, he has recently described himself as an 'after-religionist'. Some people are a pleasure to photograph. While I was setting up my lights, he flicked through a few pages of the large bible and said, 'You know, there is some interesting stuff in this book.'

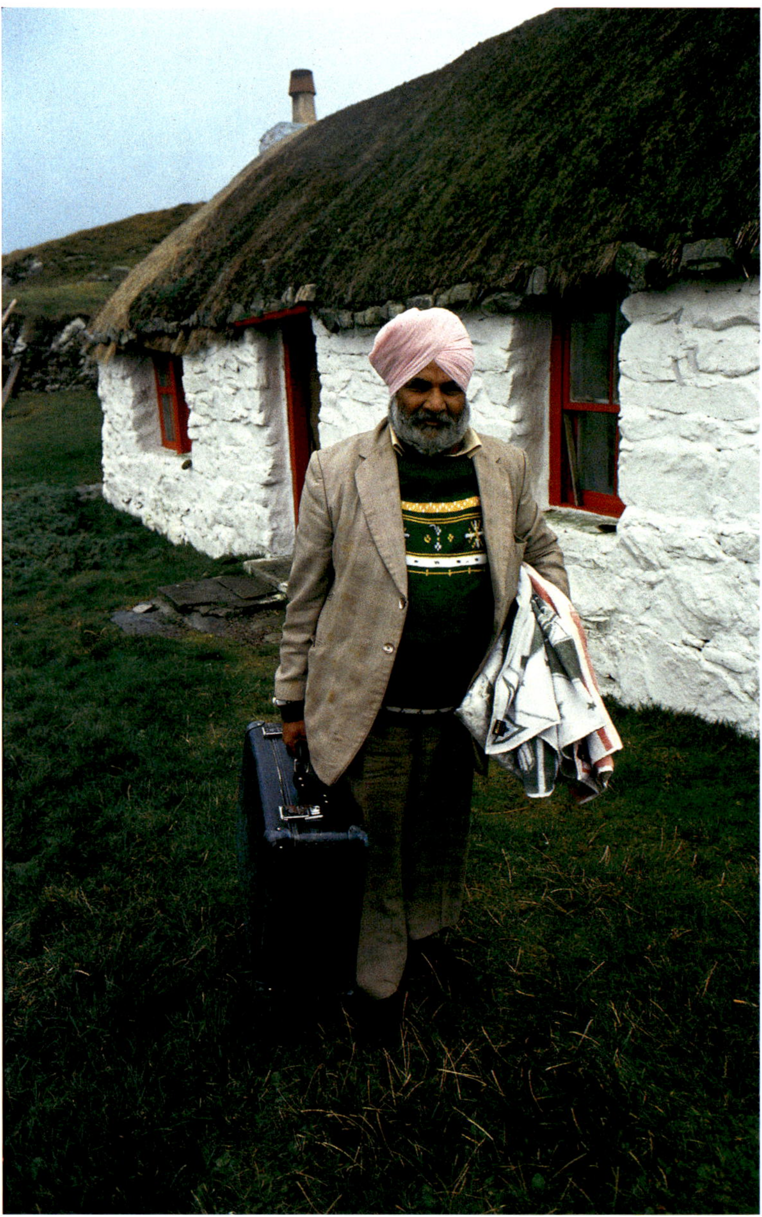

On Colonsay, the small Inner Hebridean island in the 1980s. At the ferry harbour the night before, I shared a fine malt whisky along with a very enjoyable chat with this commercial trader. He was based in Glasgow and drove his Transit van throughout the Highlands.

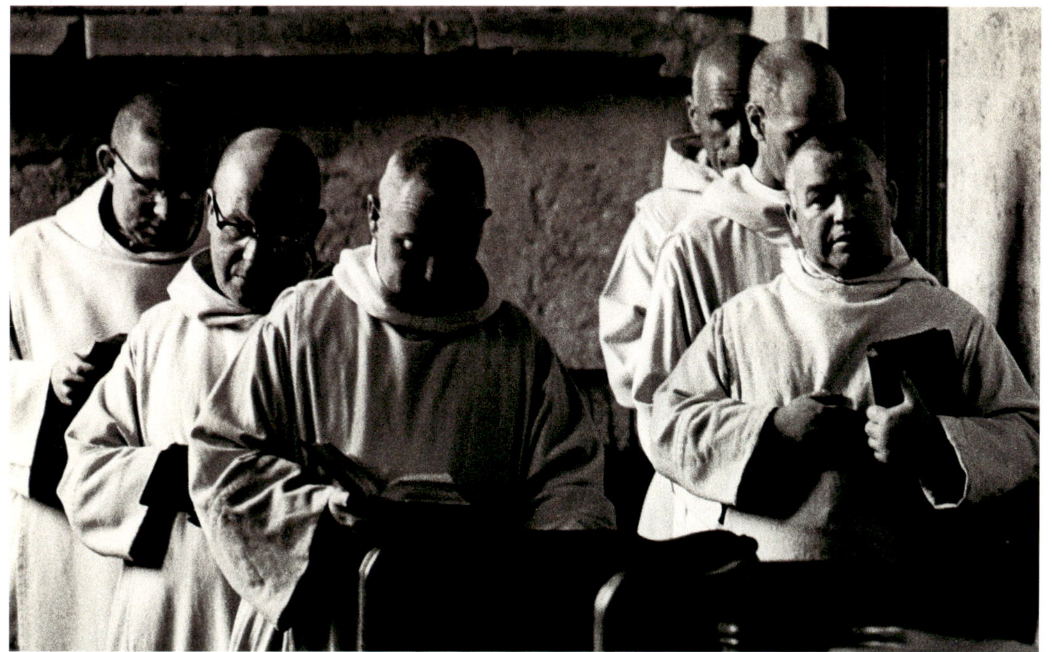

The 13th-century medieval Benedictine monastery at Pluscarden Abbey, Elgin, in the 1970s. Father Benedict, on the right, had been a stained glass window artist. In this retreat, where you share your meals with the monks in the refectory, having a bowl of tea with the excellent bread and jam produced in the abbey is one of life's simple pleasures that no chain of coffee shops can offer.

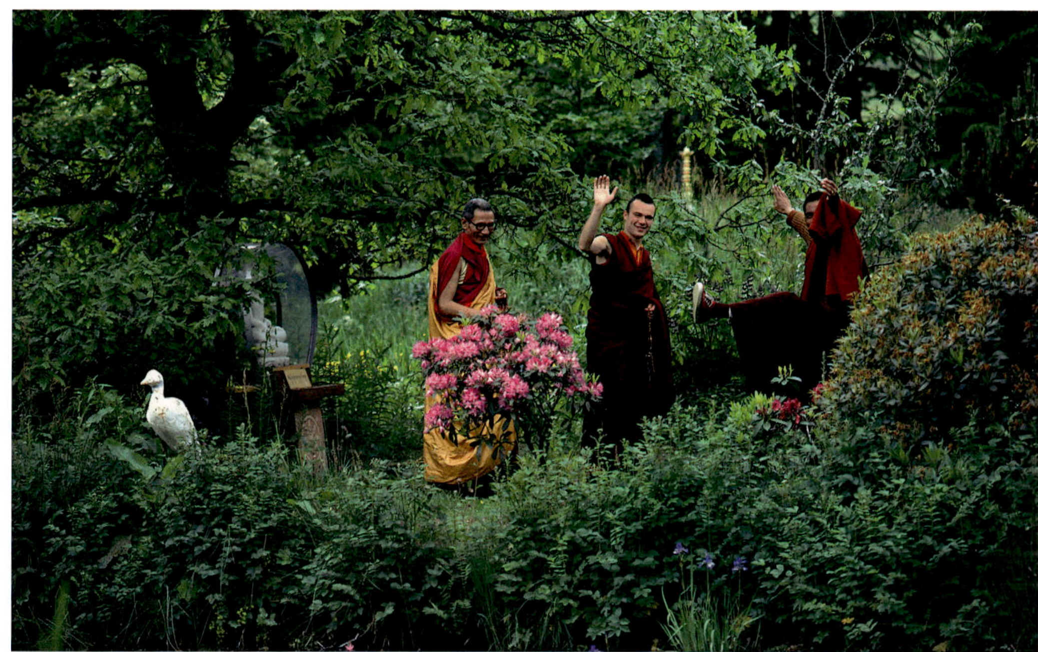

The Buddhist temple and retreat, Samye Ling in Eskdalemuir, in the 1980s. The monk on the right is imitating me falling into a wheelbarrow while walking backwards to capture this image. Nirvana is the state of perfect bliss achieved when the soul is freed from craving, anger and suffering. We could all do with a bit of bliss.

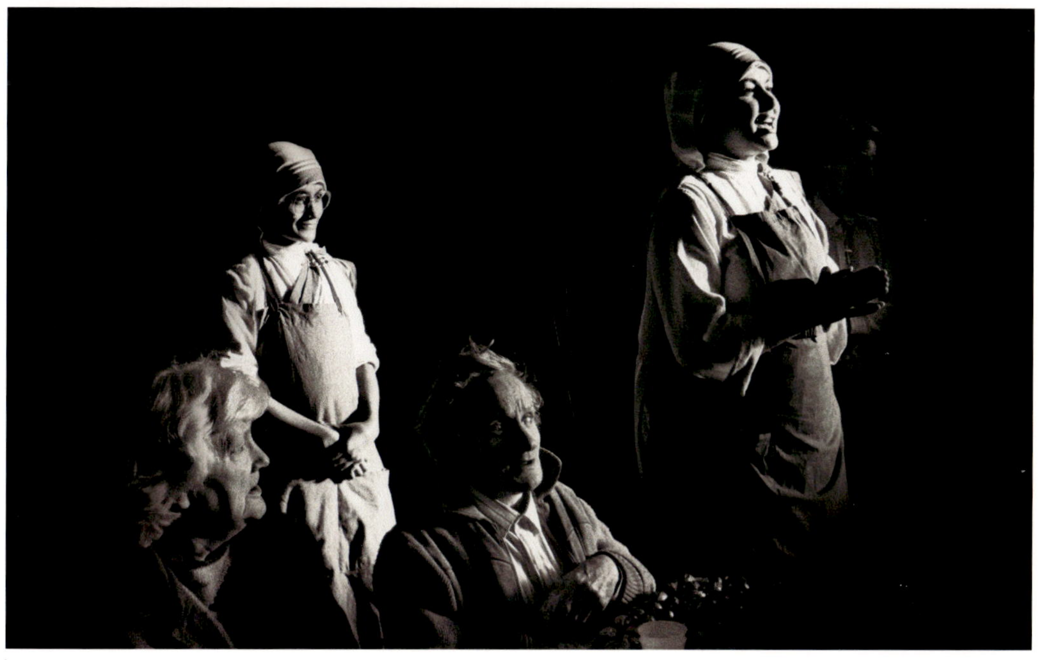

Mother Theresa's Missionaries of Charity provide meals for the more unfortunate members of society in the west as well as the east. I didn't know this place existed in a part of Edinburgh dominated by the university in the 1990s. My job has given me access to seeing all aspects of Scotland.

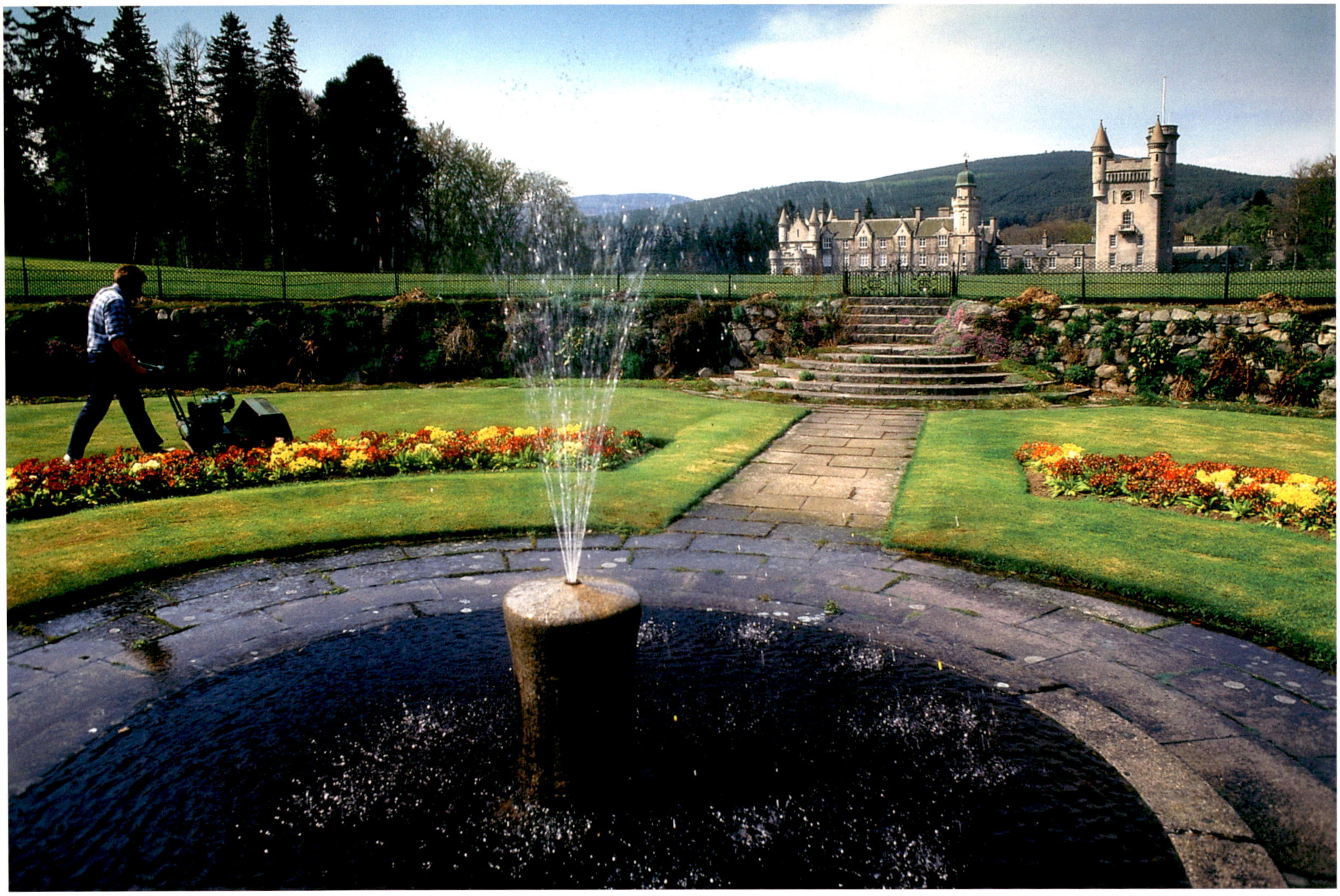

Balmoral, the Highland residence of the royal family. It was bought by Queen Victoria in 1848, rebuilt in the Scottish neo-baronial style and first occupied by the royal family in 1855. The tidy flower beds give a suburban look amidst the grandeur of the surrounding rugged landscape. *The Phrontistery* – an online dictionary of obscure words – describes Balmorality as a 'superficial enthusiasm for Scottish culture'.

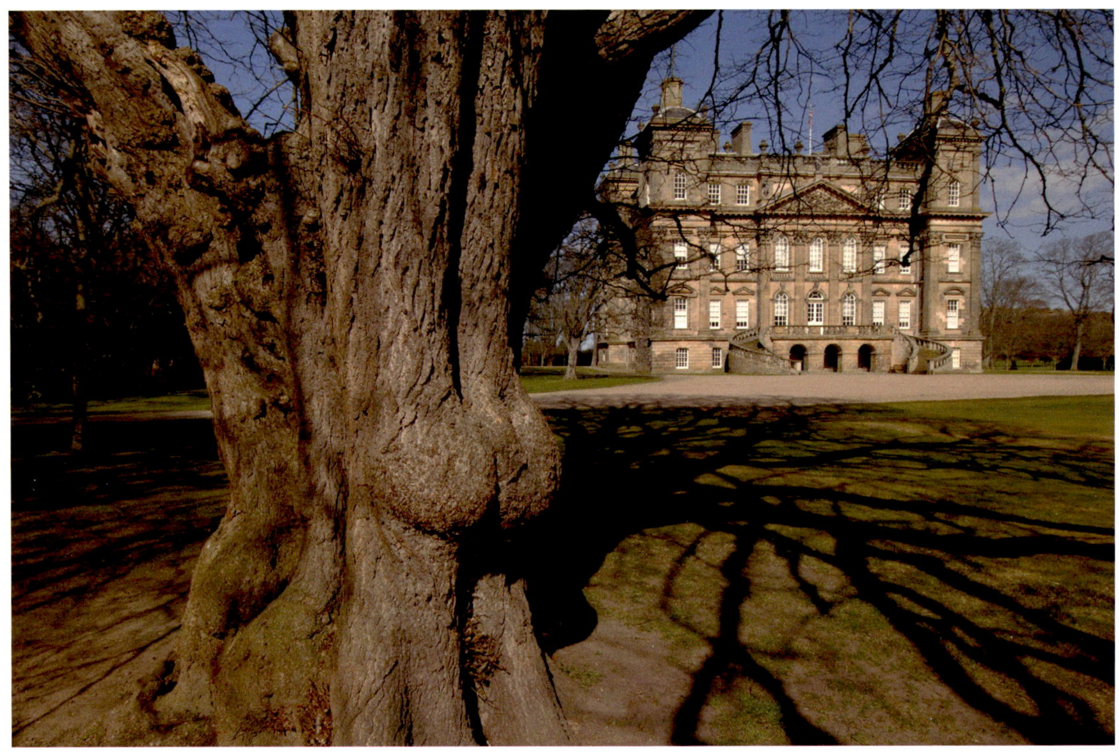

Duff House in Banff in the northeast of Scotland, designed by William Adam, is considered to be one of Britain's finest Georgian mansions. William Duff of Braco, who was responsible for building it, never had the pleasure of living there because of acrimonious disputes. In recent times the house has gone through various guises and is now part of the National Galleries of Scotland, which hosts numerous artistic events along with a permanent collection of paintings and furniture. In the foreground is an example of a natural form of simulacrum.

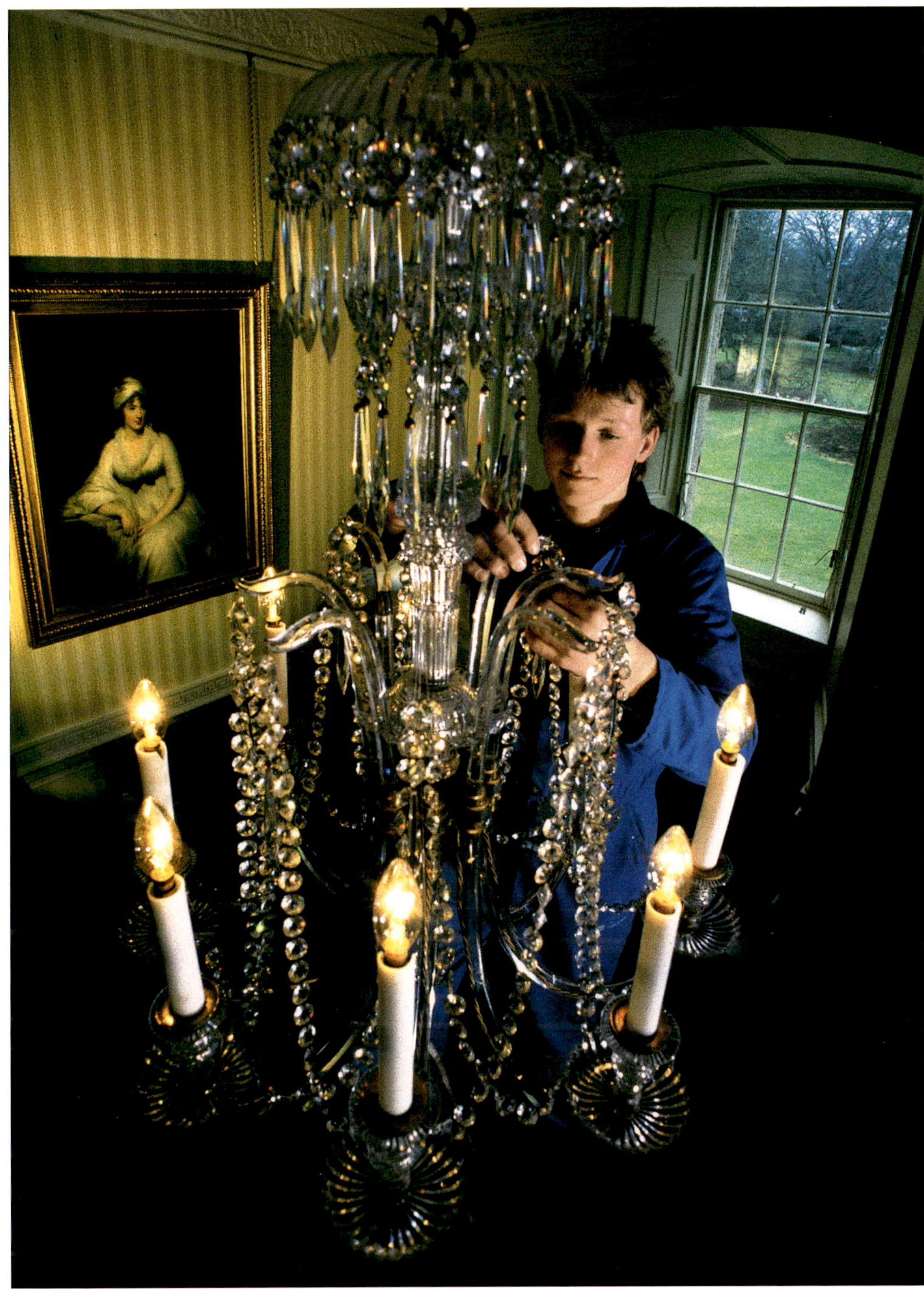

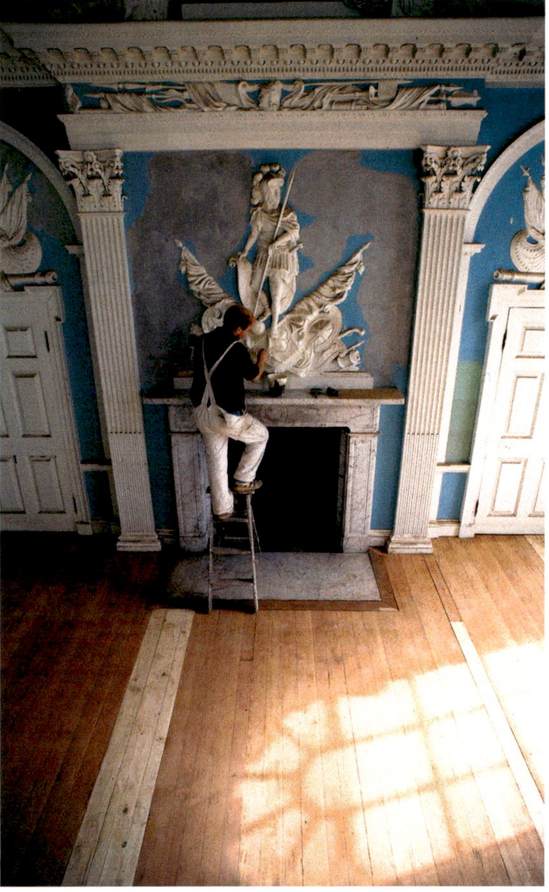

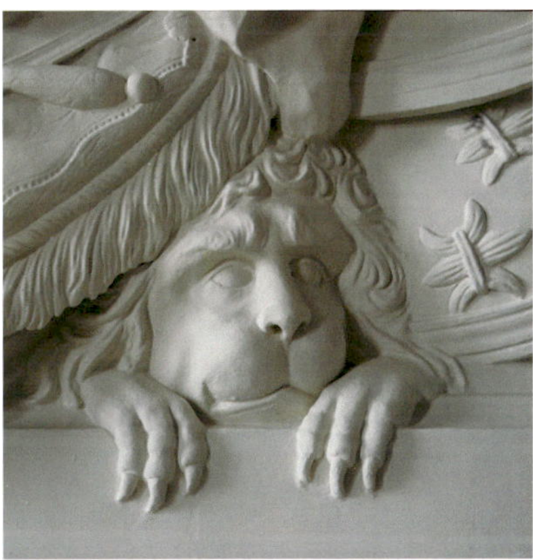

House of Dun, near Montrose, built by William Adam in 1730. The historic plasterwork by Joseph Enzer was brought back to its full glory during the house's complete renovation in the 1980s. This detail has a vitality about it and looks about to create some mischief. Is it more lion than human?

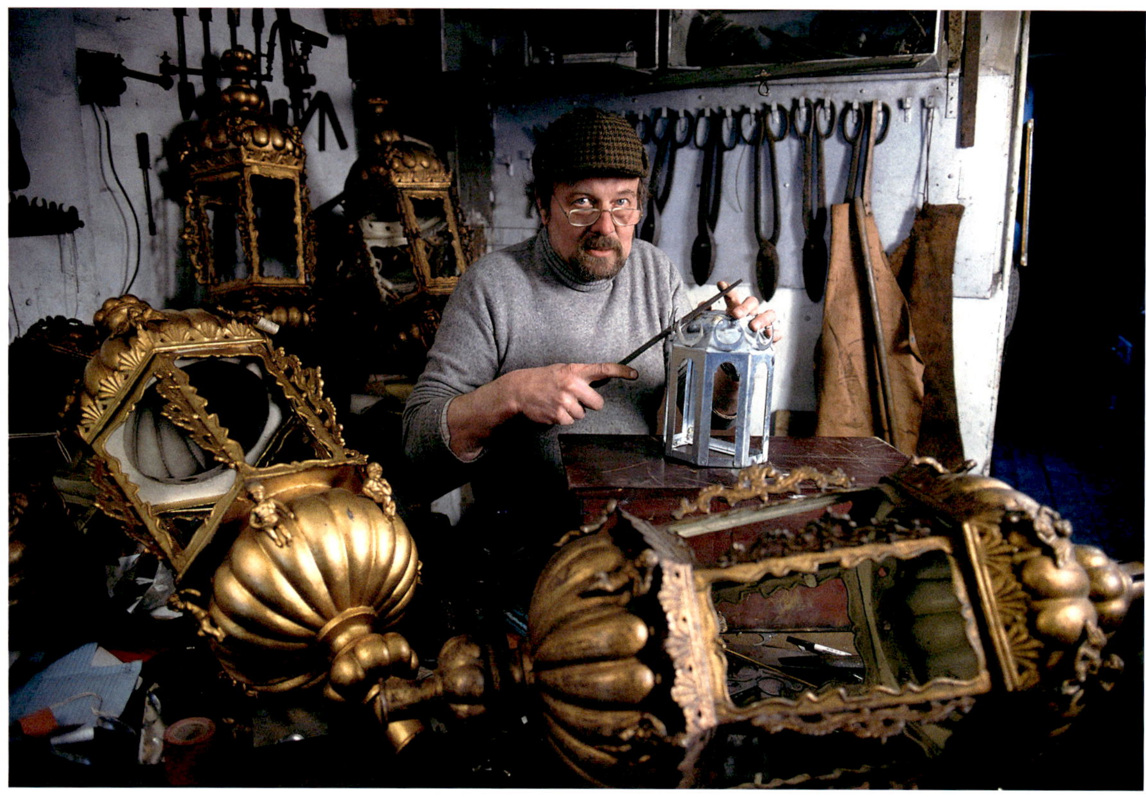

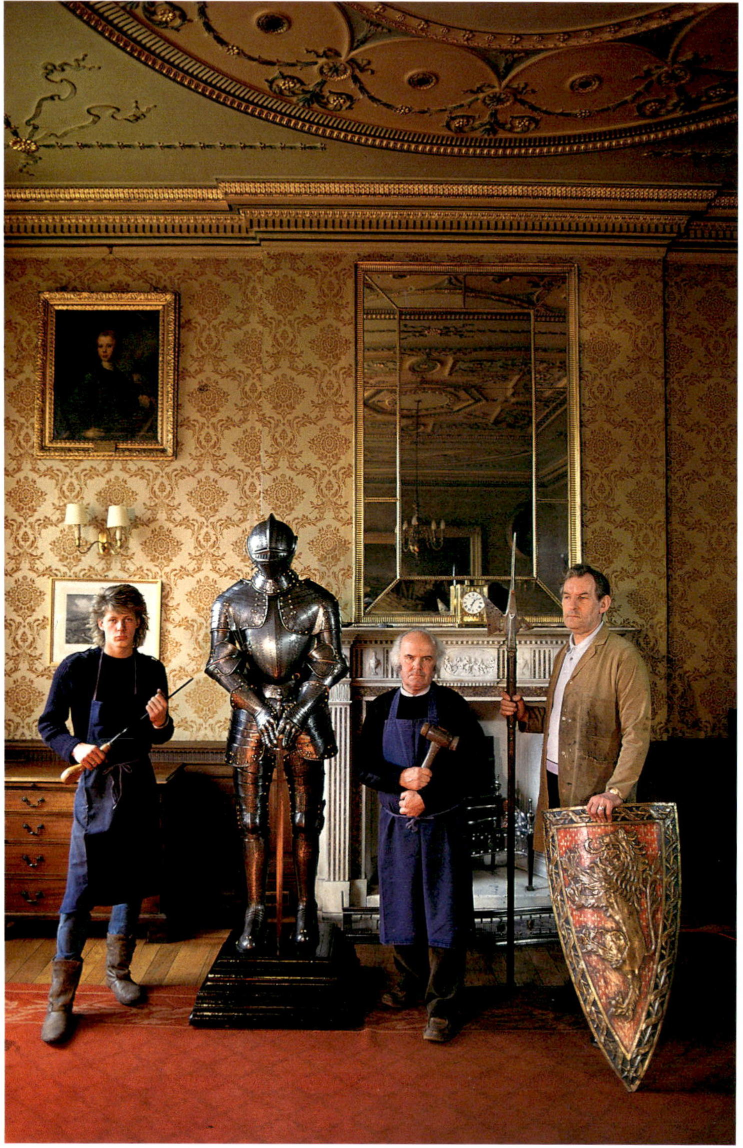

The National Trust for Scotland features a lot in my work and my leisure time. These craftsmen work behind the scenes in Edinburgh, keeping the nation's treasures in good shape for us to enjoy. The trust receives no government finance. Without the public's support through the trust so much could have been lost.

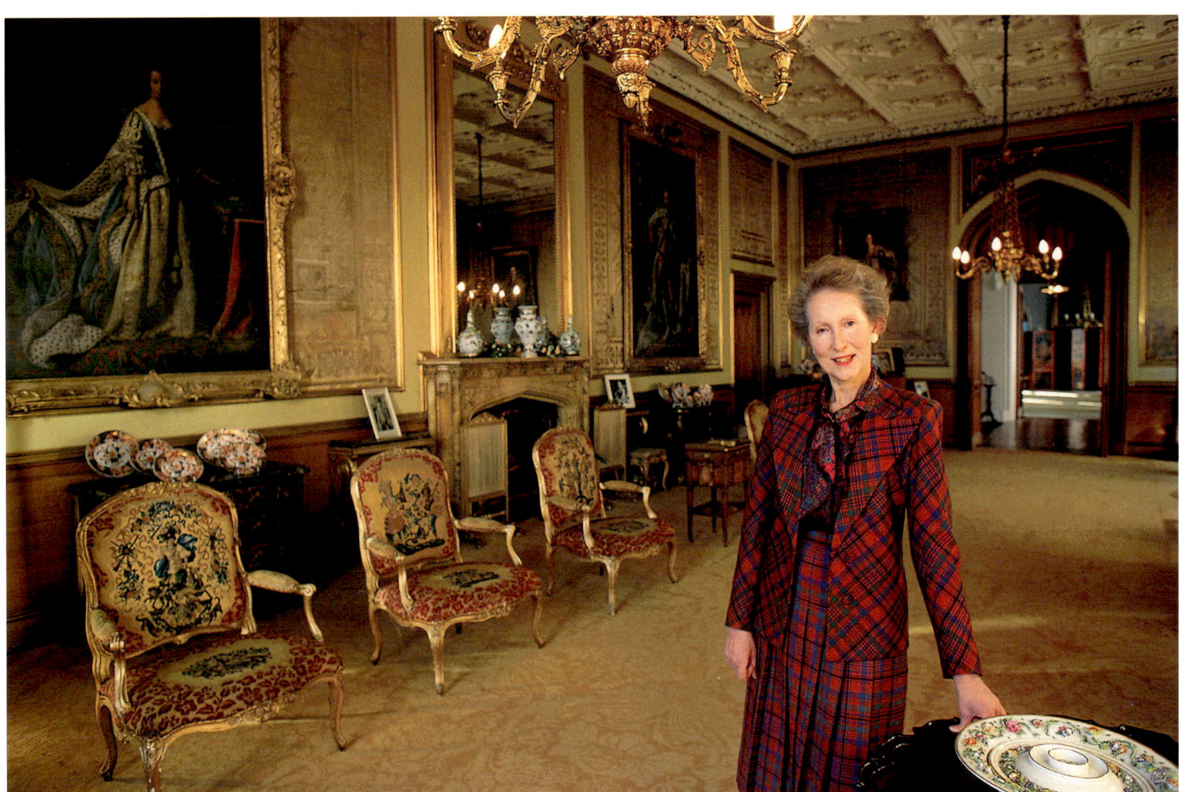

The grand interior of Scone Palace, Perthshire. It was a Sunday morning in 1990, and I was thanking the charming Countess of Mansfield for giving me her time, especially as I assumed she was missing *The Archers* on BBC Radio 4. 'How did you know?' she replied as we discussed Joe and Eddie Grundy's latest scam. You can always tell an *Archers'* fan.

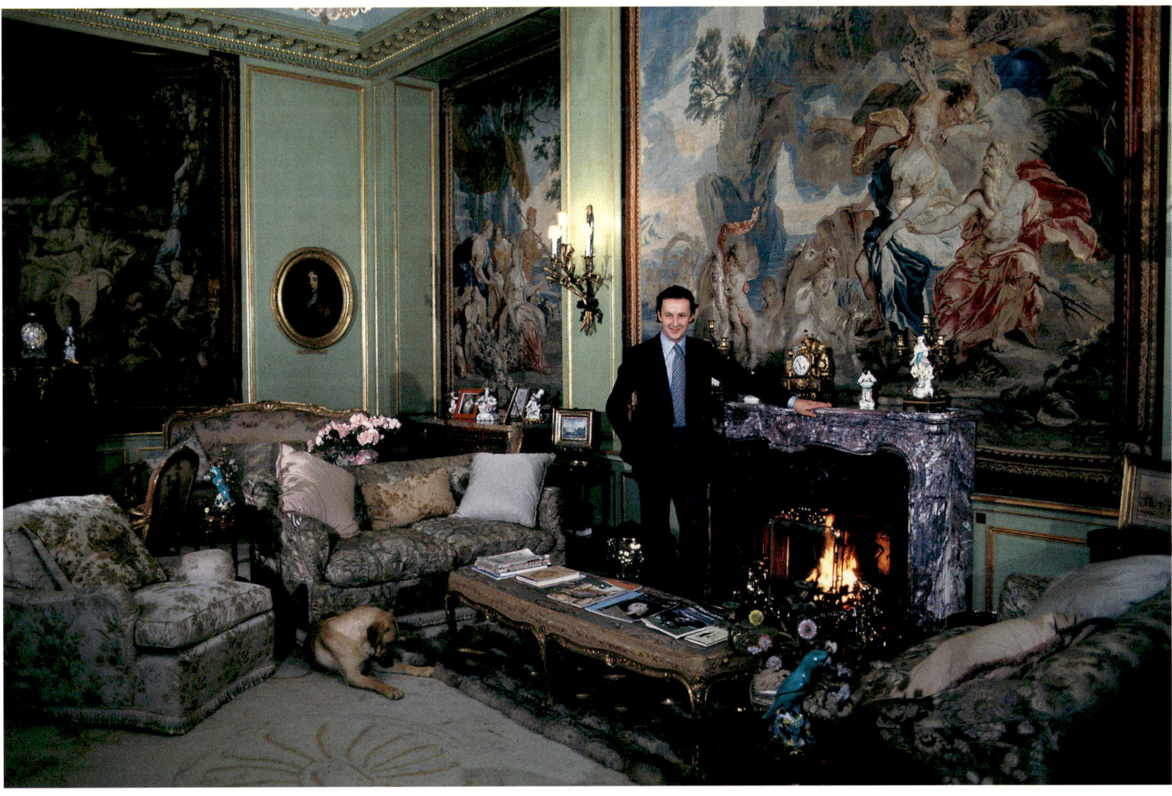

A youthful Duke of Roxburghe in his family home, Floors Castle, Kelso, in the 1980s. Here, I was interrupted by someone slamming a door, which distracted the dog's attention. My cheeky reply to the culprit was, 'You should know better than that!' The culprit who took it in good form, was the aristocratic top-flight photographer Patrick, Earl of Lichfield. It was all very good-humoured, and the Duke's retort was, 'I'll get a laugh at dinner with this.'

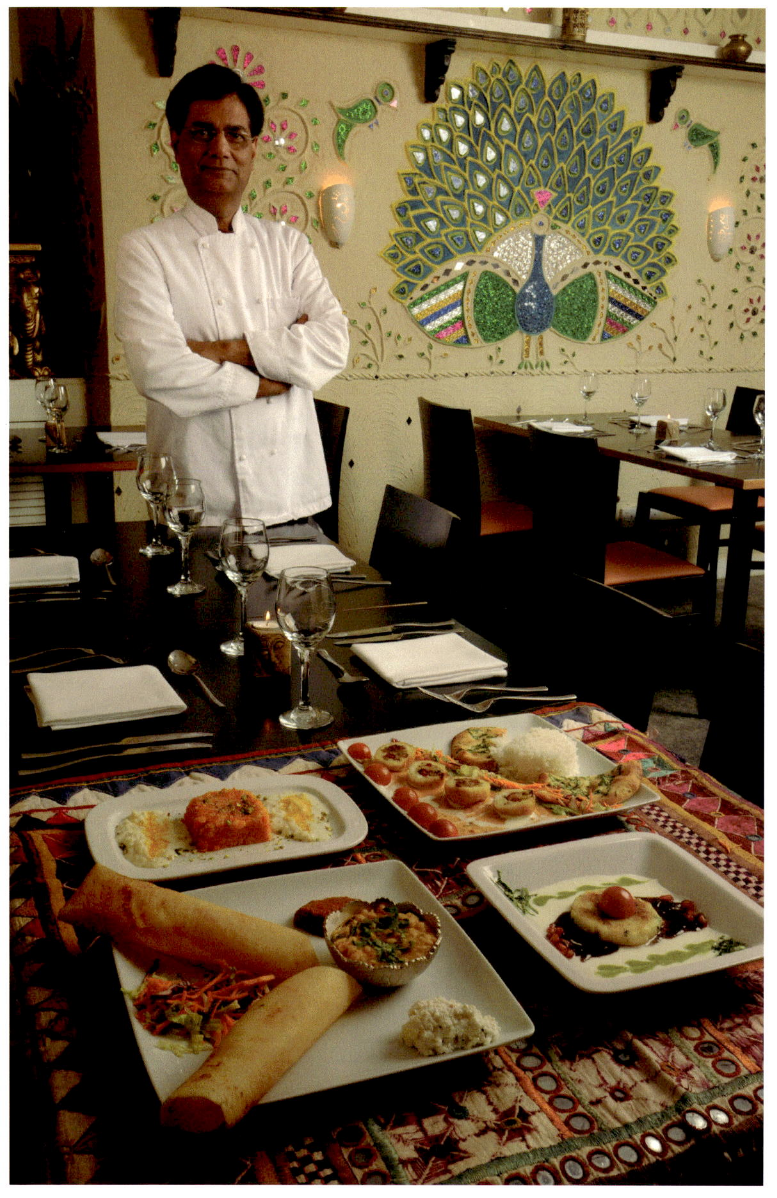

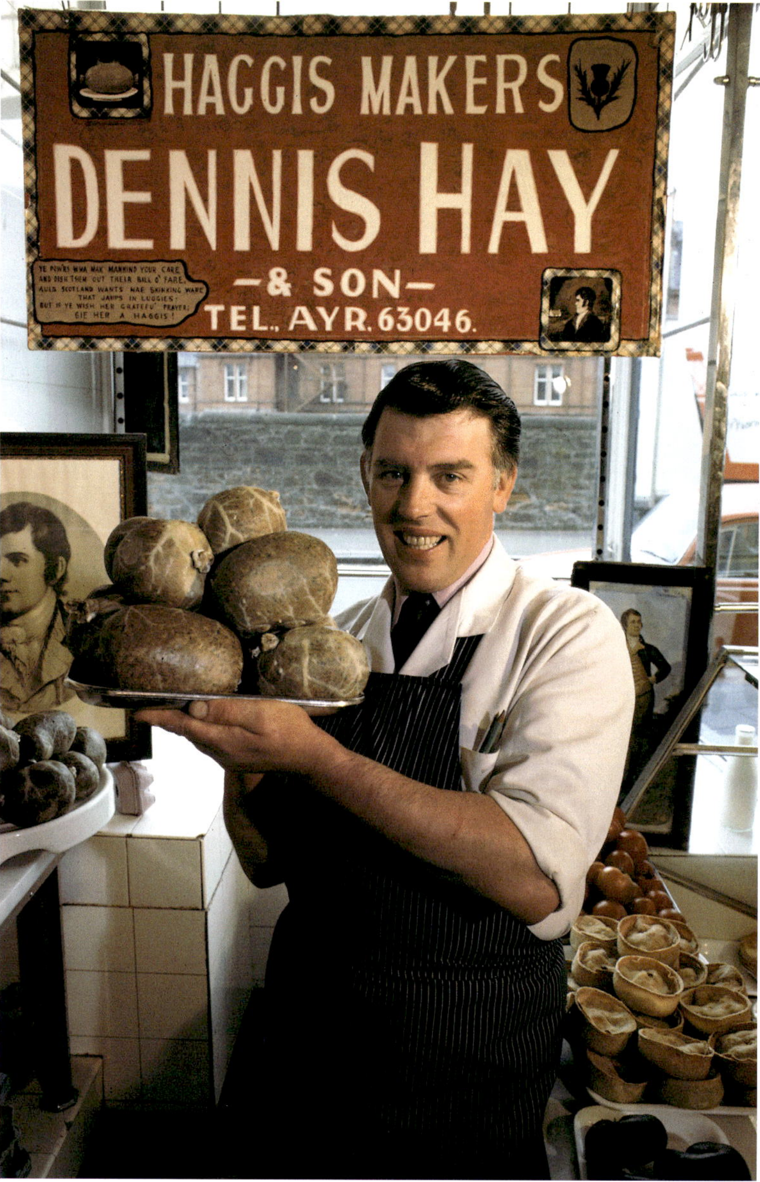

(Above) Curry is sometimes said to be Scotland's other national dish. Kalpna has been an Indian vegetarian restaurant in Edinburgh since the 1980s, whose owner and head chef, Ajay Bhartdwaj, I have been a customer of since the 1970s when he worked in London.

(Above right) Mr Hay of Ayr selling very non-vegetarian fare in the 1980s:

'Some hae meat and canna eat,
and some wad eat that want it,
but we hae meat and we can eat,
and sae the Lord be thankit.'

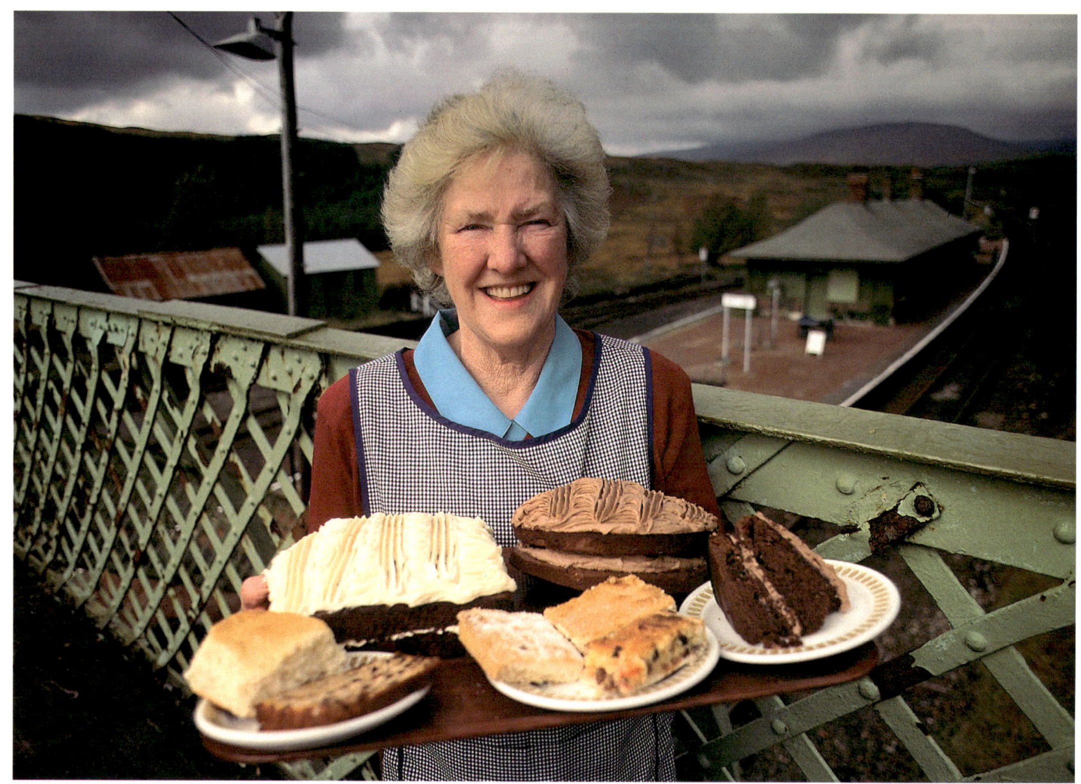

(Right) Rannoch Station is the end of the line for cars, where Mrs Eunice MacLelland had her café in the 1990s. In the 1950s most Scottish mothers were great bakers, and trays of fairy cakes, party slices and pancakes filled the kitchen on a Saturday afternoon. My father would also make excellent tablet and toffee, but to our annoyance most of it went to the church sale of work.

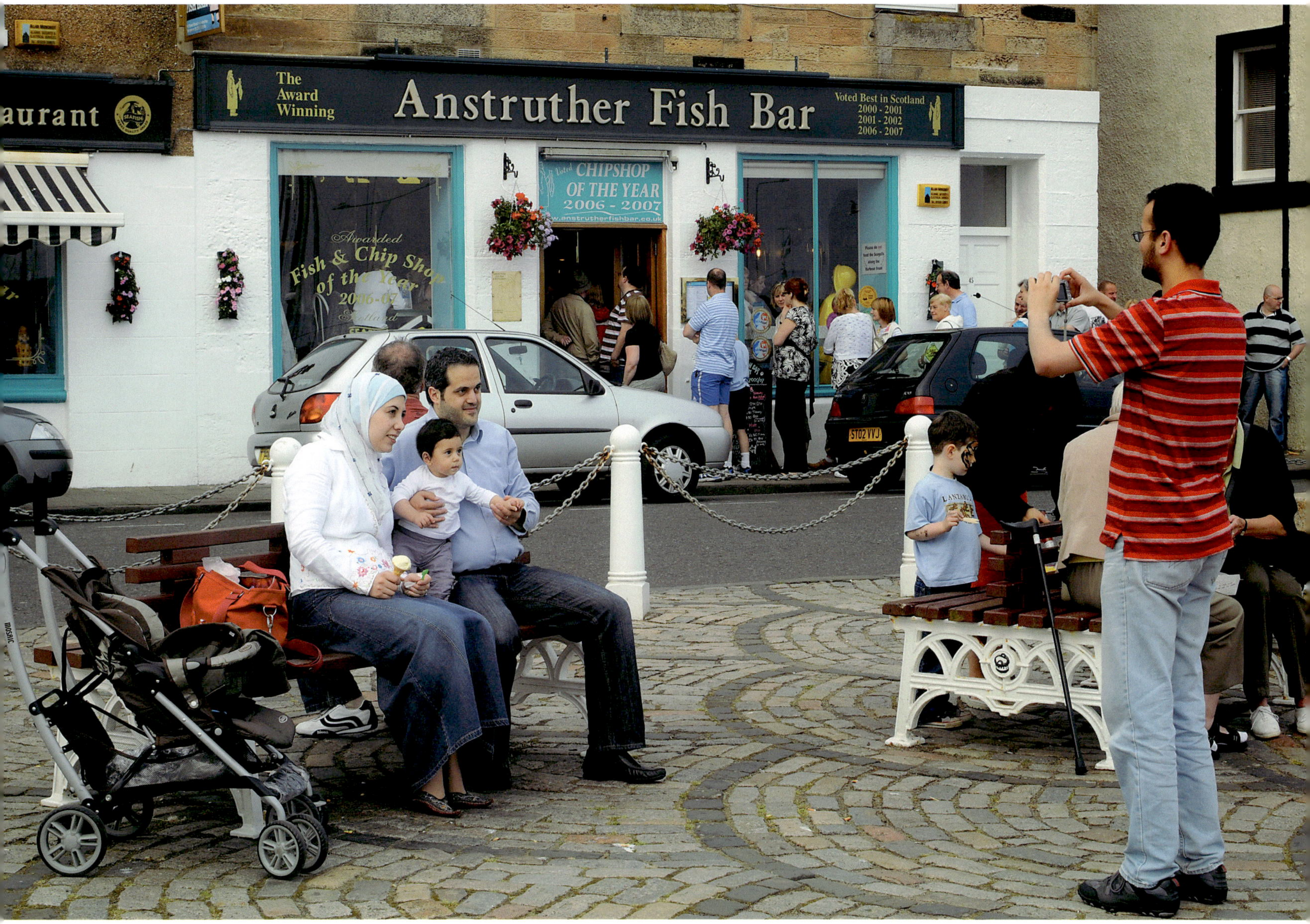

You can queue for up to an hour at Anstruther's award-winning fish bar or take family pictures while someone else does the waiting for you. This was not the case for a royal personage in 2000 whose chauffeur jumped the queue. Could this become the first chippie to receive a royal warrant?

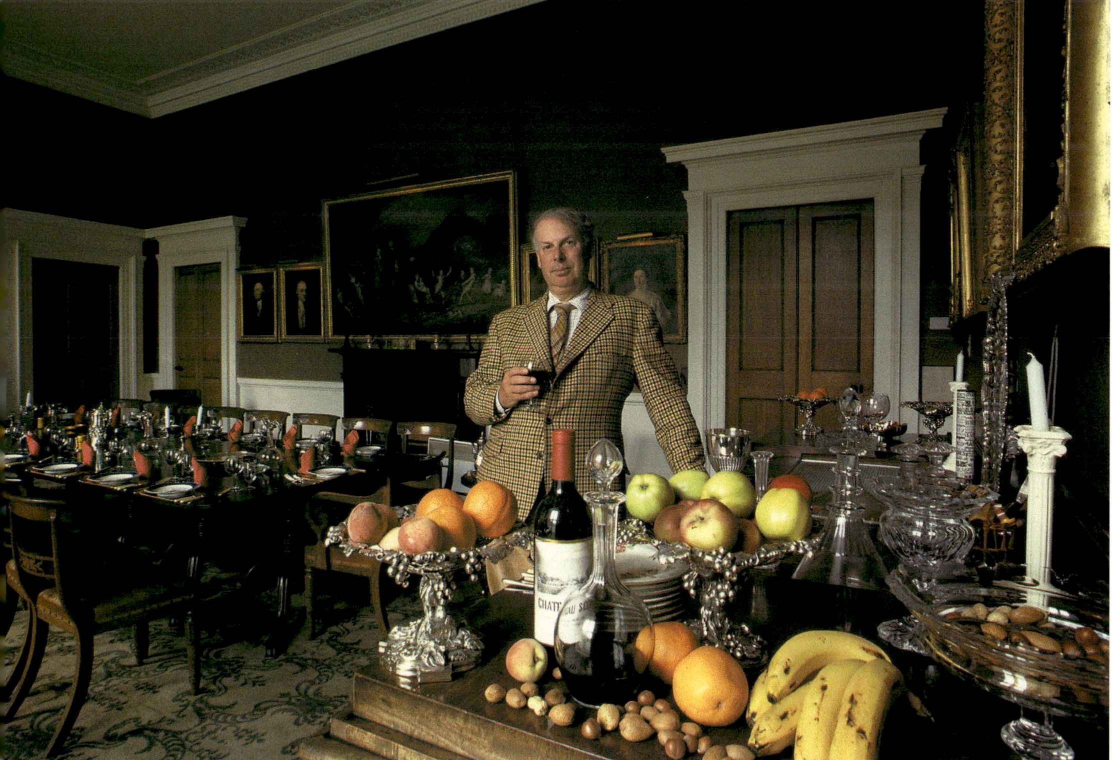

When I arrived at Blairquhan Castle, Ayrshire, in the 1980s, James Hunter Blair was whooping around the lawn on his motor mower. I thought of *The Wind in the Willows* and my favourite character, Mr Toad. The castle is now a corporate venue for conferences and weddings.

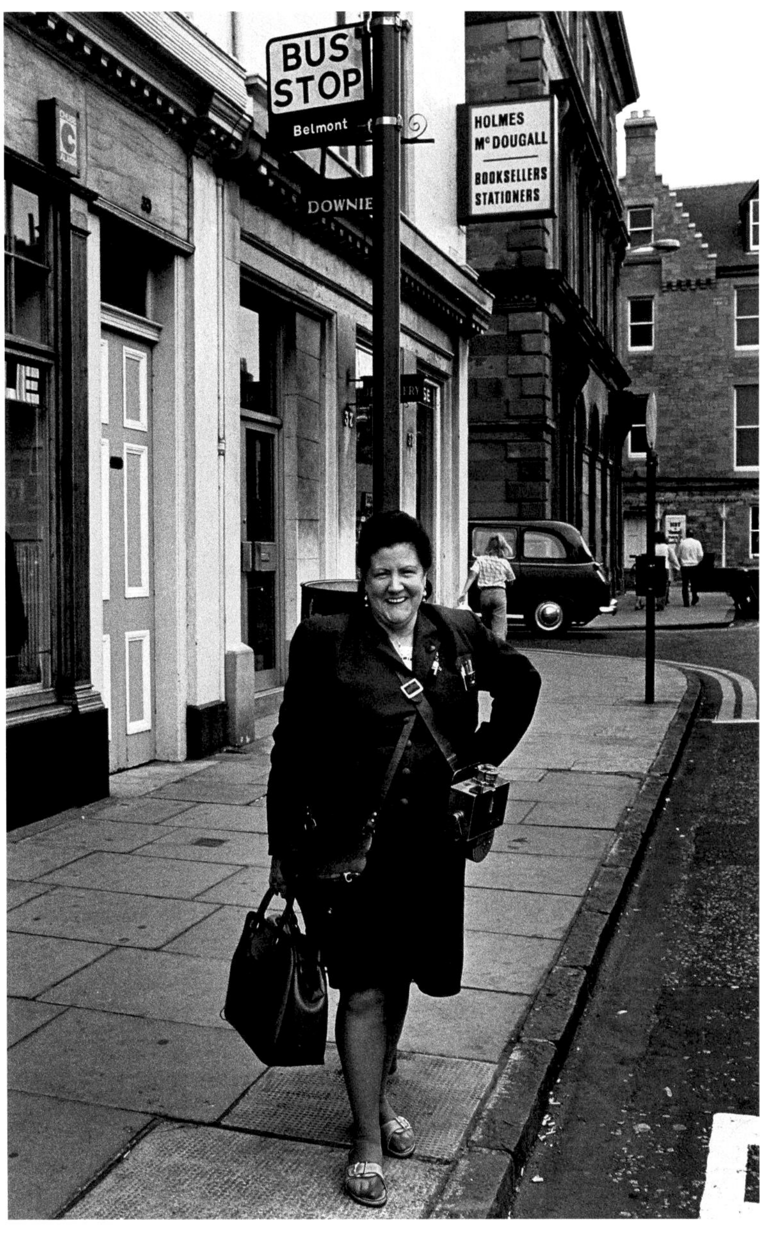

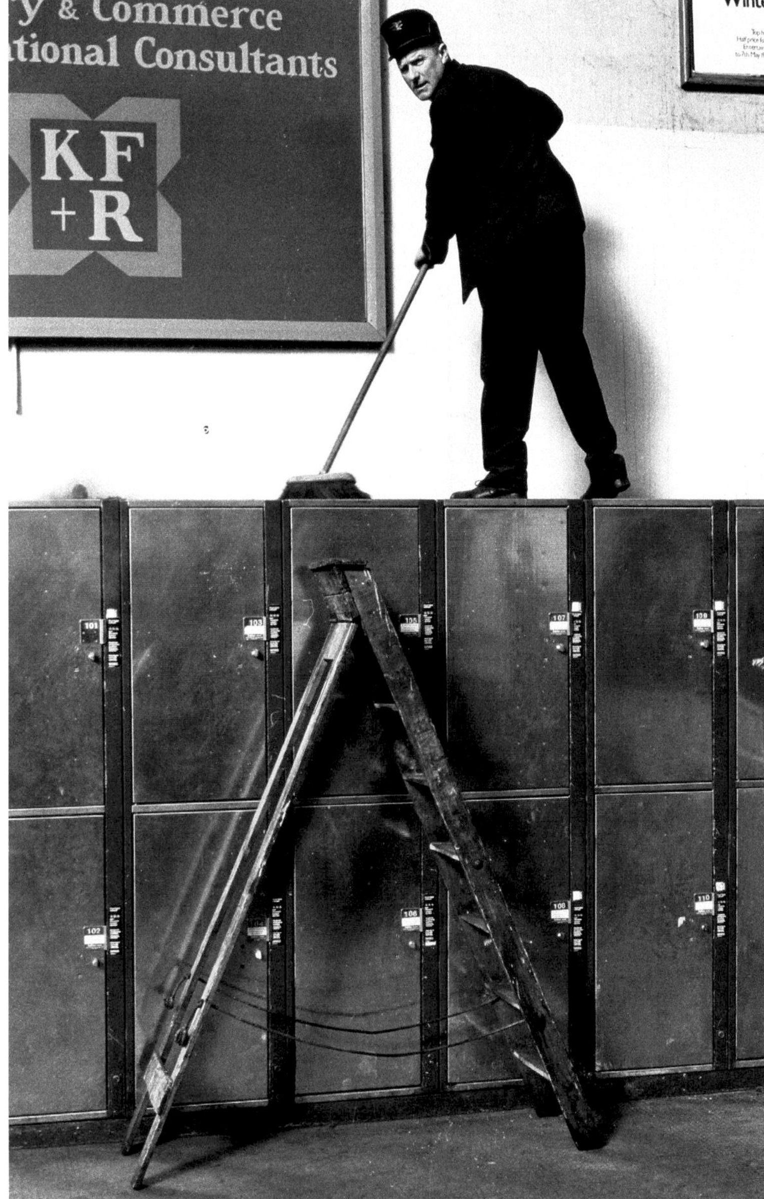

You could tell that there would be no nonsense on this clippie's bus in the 1970s and she would be able to outwit any smart alec.

She's just a Kelty clippie, she'll no tak' nae advice,
It's, 'Ach drap deid or Ah'll bile yer heid
Or Ah'll punch yer ticket twice.'

From the folk song written by John Watt and sung by Hamish Imlach, Barbara Dickson and others.

Inverness railway station in the pre-Health and Safety days of the 1970s. Would this employee have passed his ladder training? I'm sure I'm right in thinking that Scotland was then noted for its clean public spaces and towns. How would this gentleman have dealt with the patina of chewing gum that scars so many pavements today?

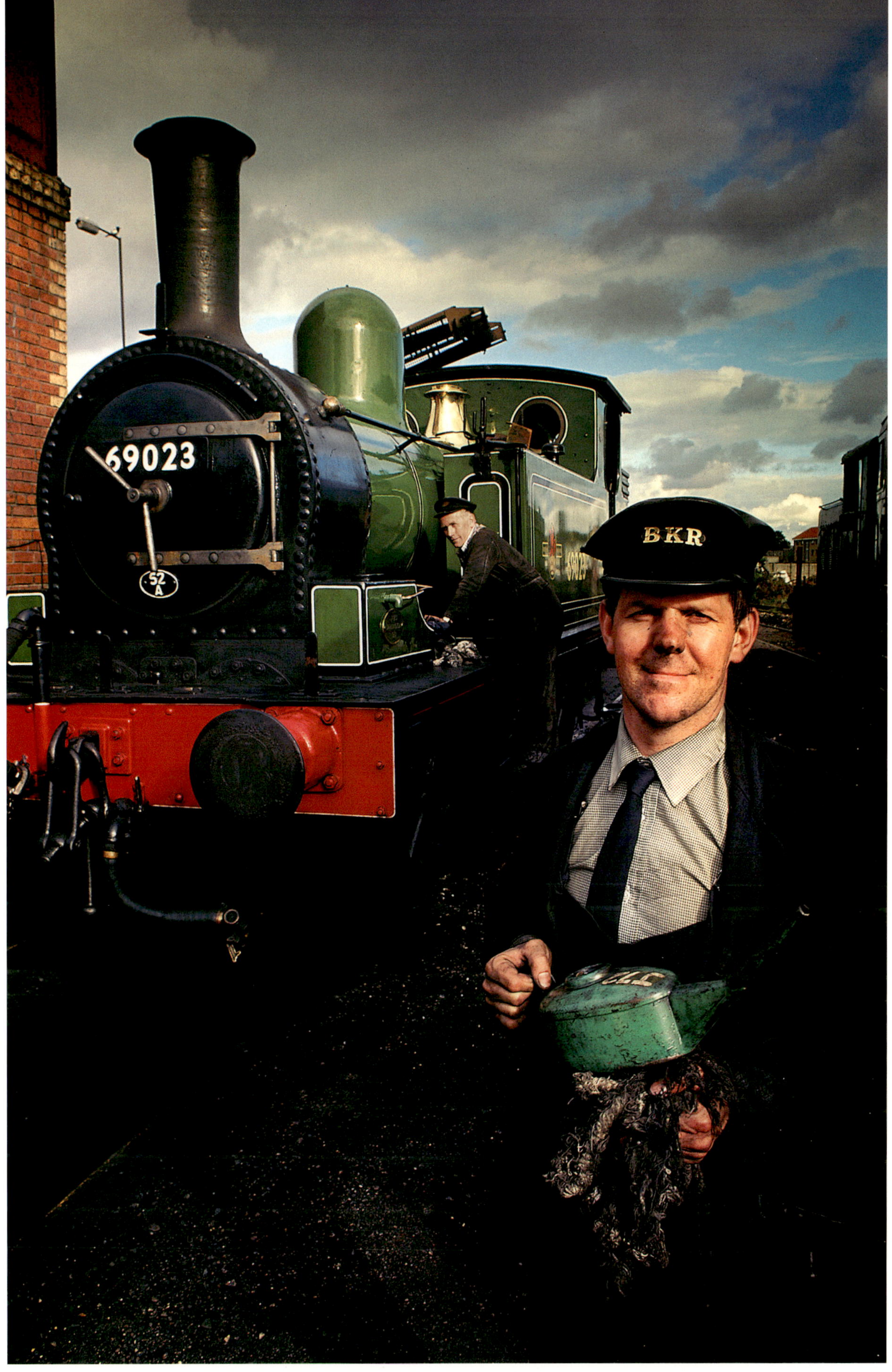

Steam engine enthusiasts at Boness spend their free time scraping rust off boilers and polishing brass, and, if you don't have an engine driving licence, the reward seems to be shovelling coal. It's fortunate for us that there are such dedicated people. What a loss it would be if these locomotives were never to run again. One of my favourite poems, W. H. Auden's *The Night Train*, has a metre in sync with the rhythm of the glorious sound steam trains make. Could a diesel train match this?

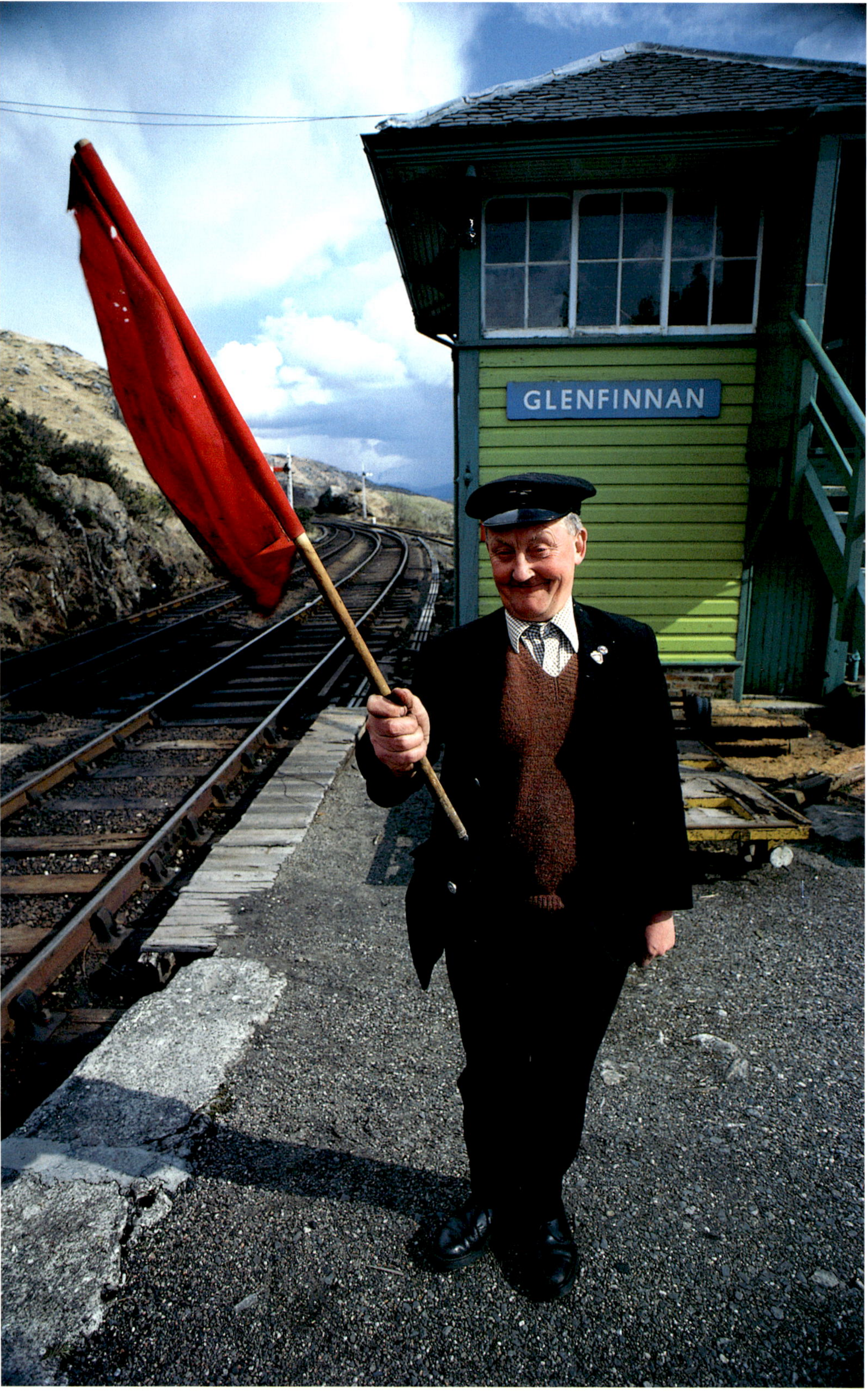

The station master at Glenfinnan on the Fort William to Mallaig line in the 1980s, arguably the most beautiful and scenic route in Britain and used in several *Harry Potter* films. On one occasion I had arranged for a steam train to puff some steam at Loch Eilt. To my dismay, the driver did it too soon. Nowadays, a client would say, 'Don't worry, we can sort that digitally.' I'm not always convinced – could I be a dinosaur or maybe just a purist?

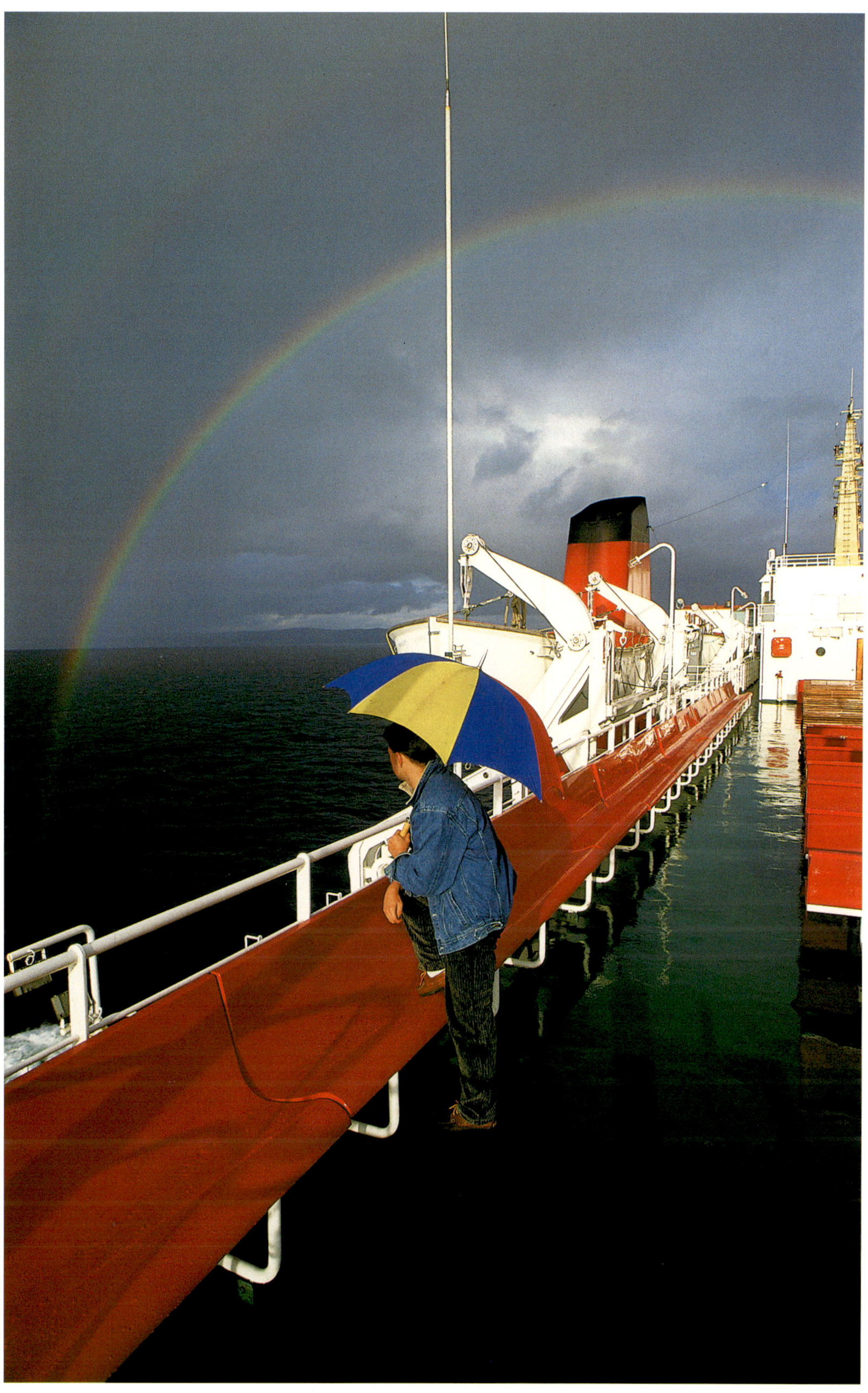

Honestly, I didn't place this passenger with his golf brolly against the rainbow on the Oban to Mull ferry.

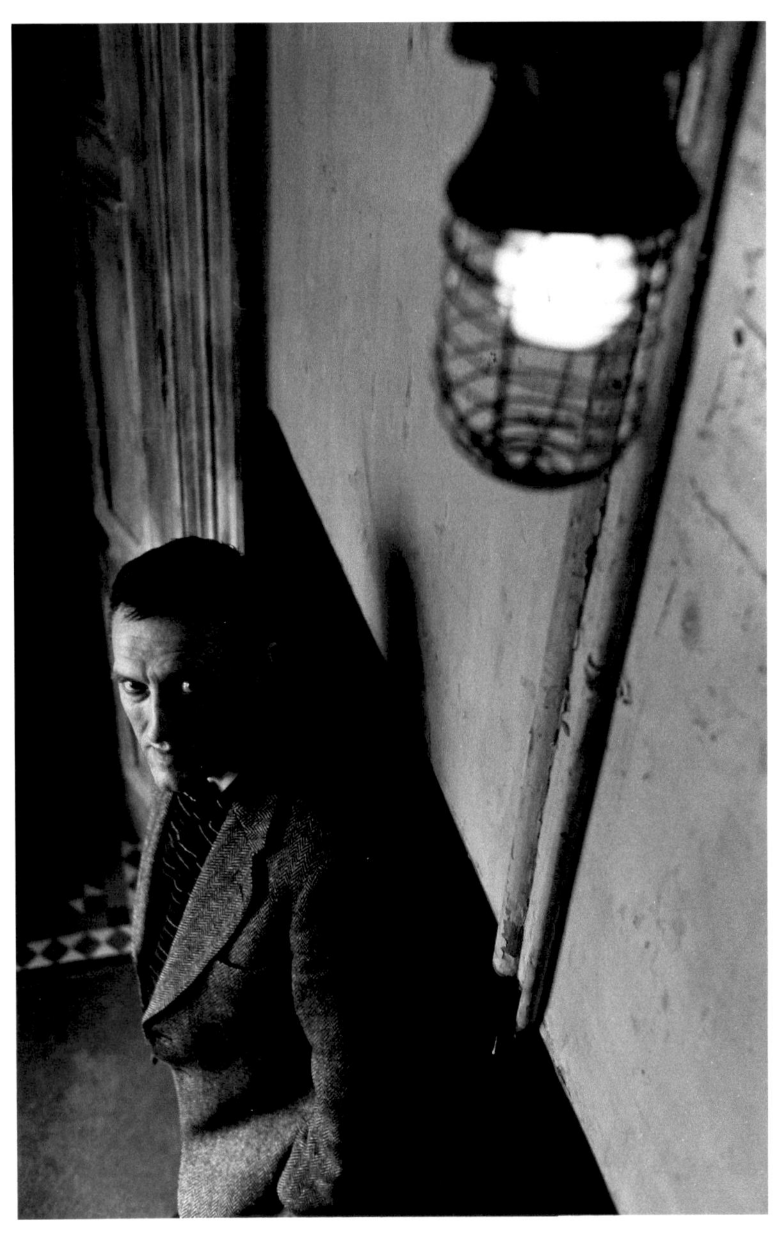

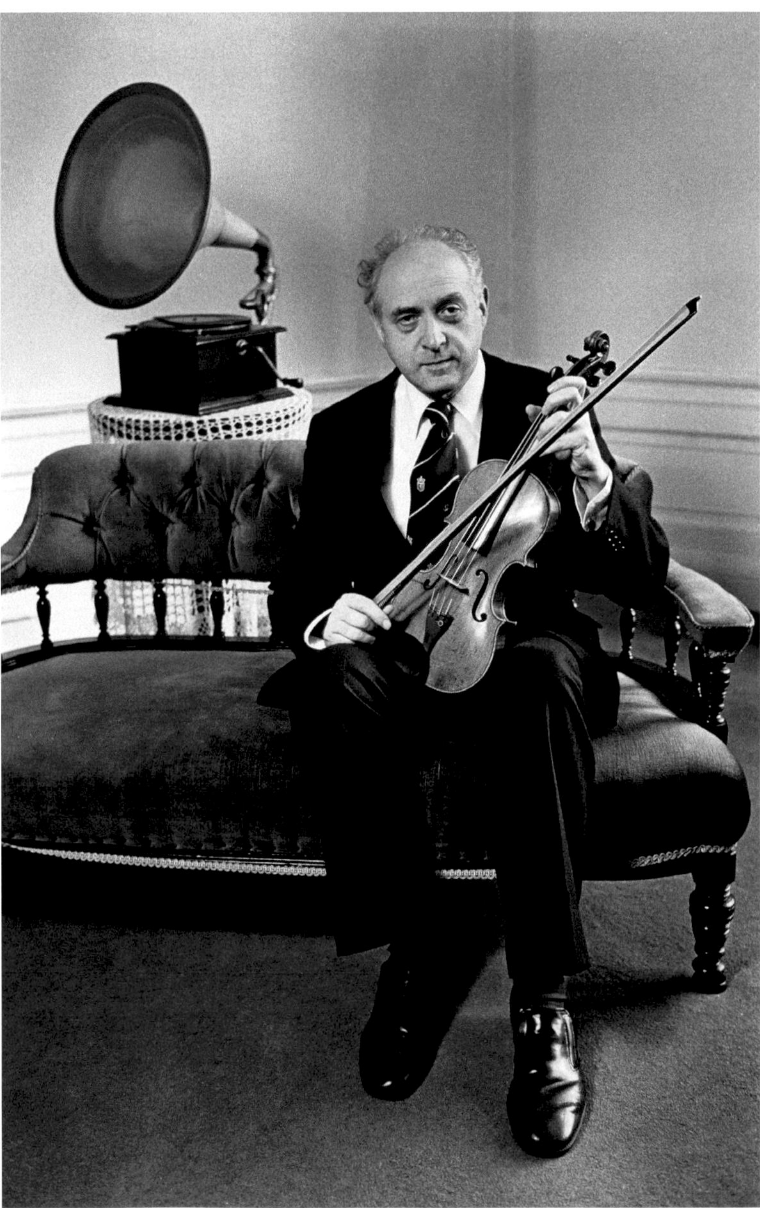

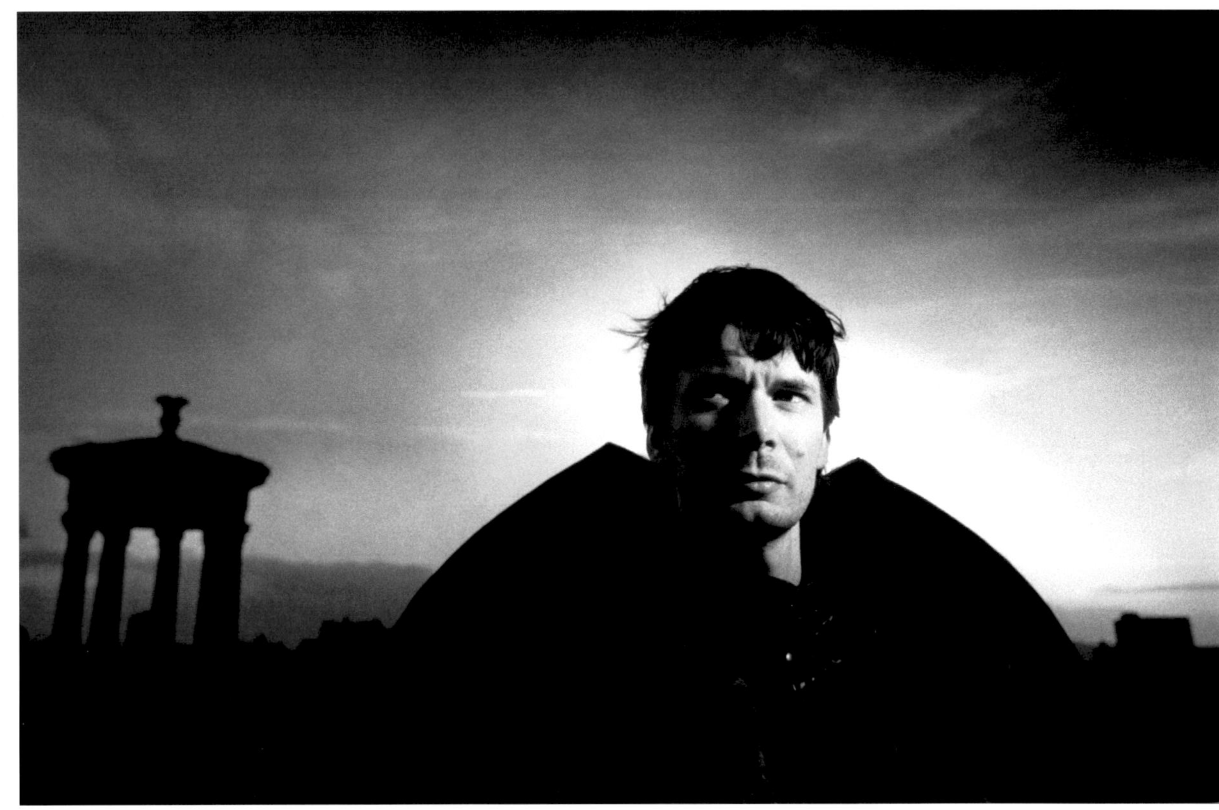

(Far left) Controversial Booker Prize-winner James Kelman was a somewhat reluctant sitter. When I suggested photographing him in the stairwell of his Glasgow tenement in 1990, he didn't seem to understand that I was trying to capture an atmosphere and had no intention of making any kind of social or political comment.

(Centre left) Leonard Friedman, violinist and founder of the Scottish Baroque Ensemble, photographed in 1980. Nothing was too much trouble for him, and he was amused by my rearrangement of the furniture in his sitting room. He was a truly brilliant performer and will be remembered as one of the great musical eccentrics.

(Below left) Ian Rankin, author of the Inspector Rebus novels, which are set in Edinburgh and account for 10 per cent of all the crime books sold in the UK and are translated into 25 languages. I took this picture on Calton Hill in 1990, with his head framed against a contemporary Italian chair I used as a prop, which helped achieve a more dramatic look.

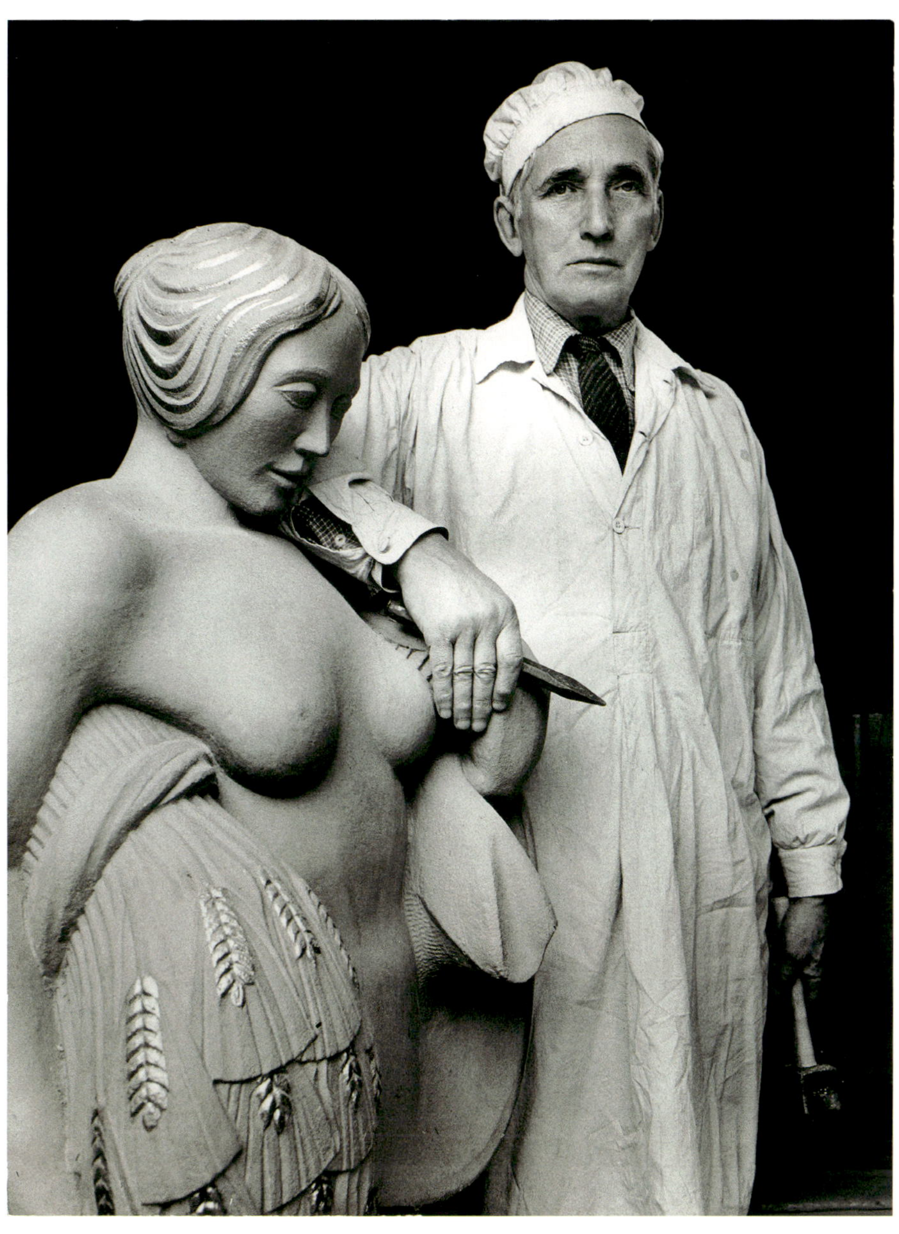

(Left) Hew Lorimer, son of the architect Robert Lorimer, studied under the sculptor Eric Gill and his work can be seen in the façade of the National Library of Scotland in Edinburgh. Probably his most famous piece, *Our Lady of the Isles*, is a prominent feature on South Uist. I photographed him in his studio at Kellie Castle, Fife, in 1980 with a work that became part of the Glasgow Garden Festival in 1988. I recently gave to the trust a print of this portrait, which I'm pleased to say is on display in the castle.

(Below) Kellie Castle was restored by the architect Robert Lorimer and became the family home. It dispels the idea of castles being cold and draughty. I find it welcoming and could imagine myself being very happy living there. Now owned by the National Trust for Scotland, its walled garden is lush and productive. You can even buy fresh vegetables.

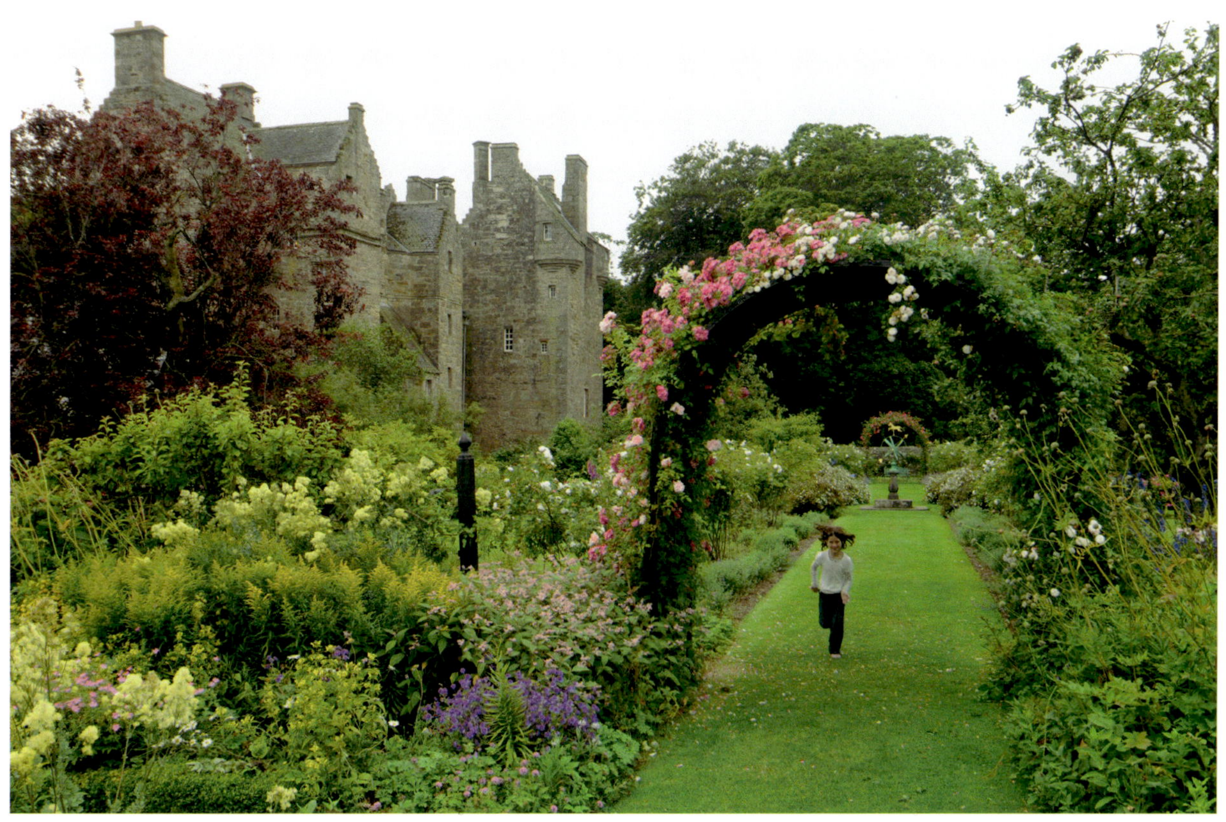

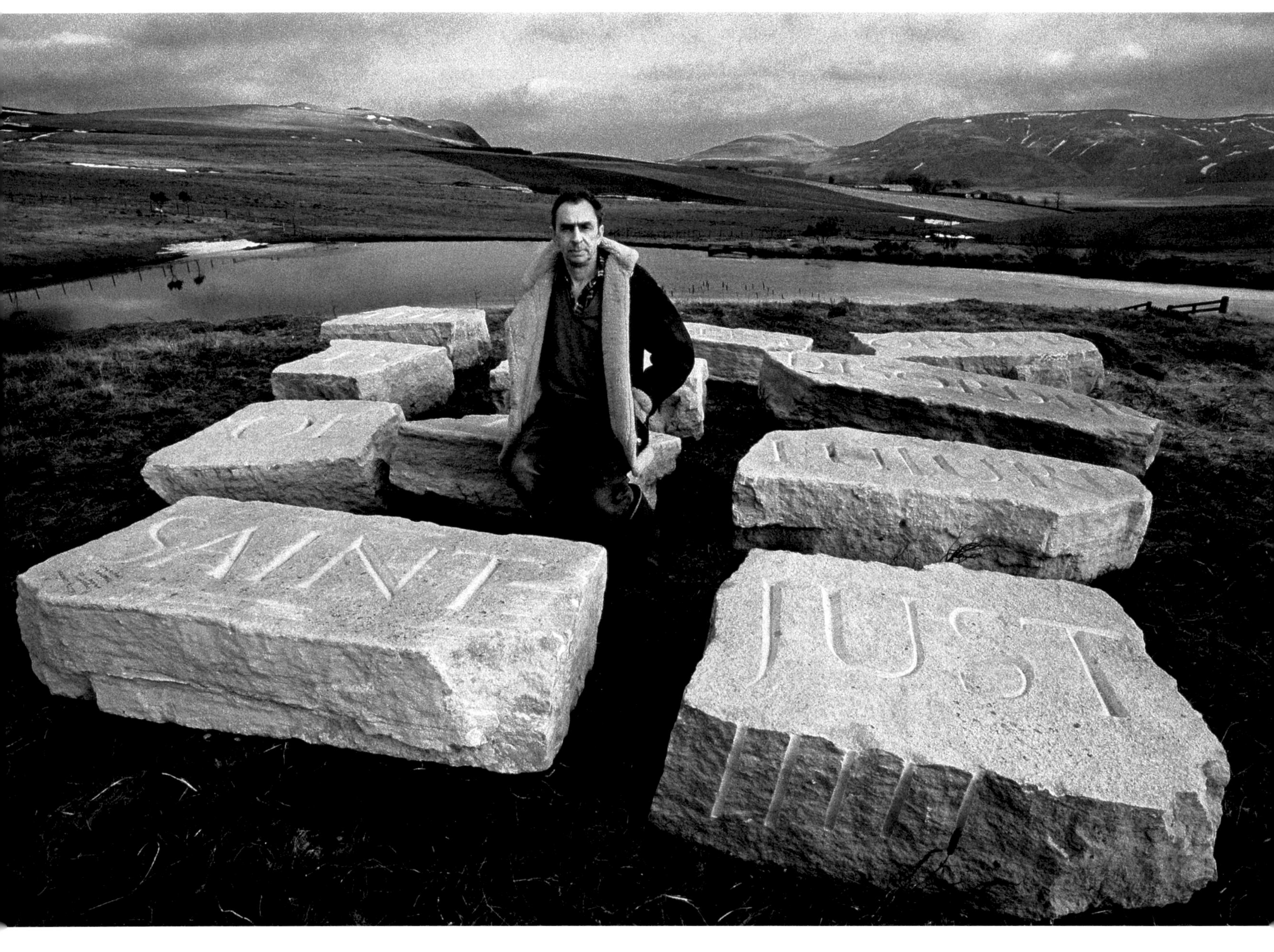

In 1966, artist, poet, gardener and writer Ian Hamilton Finlay began to transform the rundown farmhouse called Stonypath into Little Sparta, his four-acre masterpiece near Dunsyre in Lanarkshire. He was a prophet more honoured outwith his native land where he was better known for his long-standing war with Strathclyde Regional Council. He was a great talker, and I felt privileged to spend some time in his company in 1990, listening to original ideas from a genuinely free spirit.

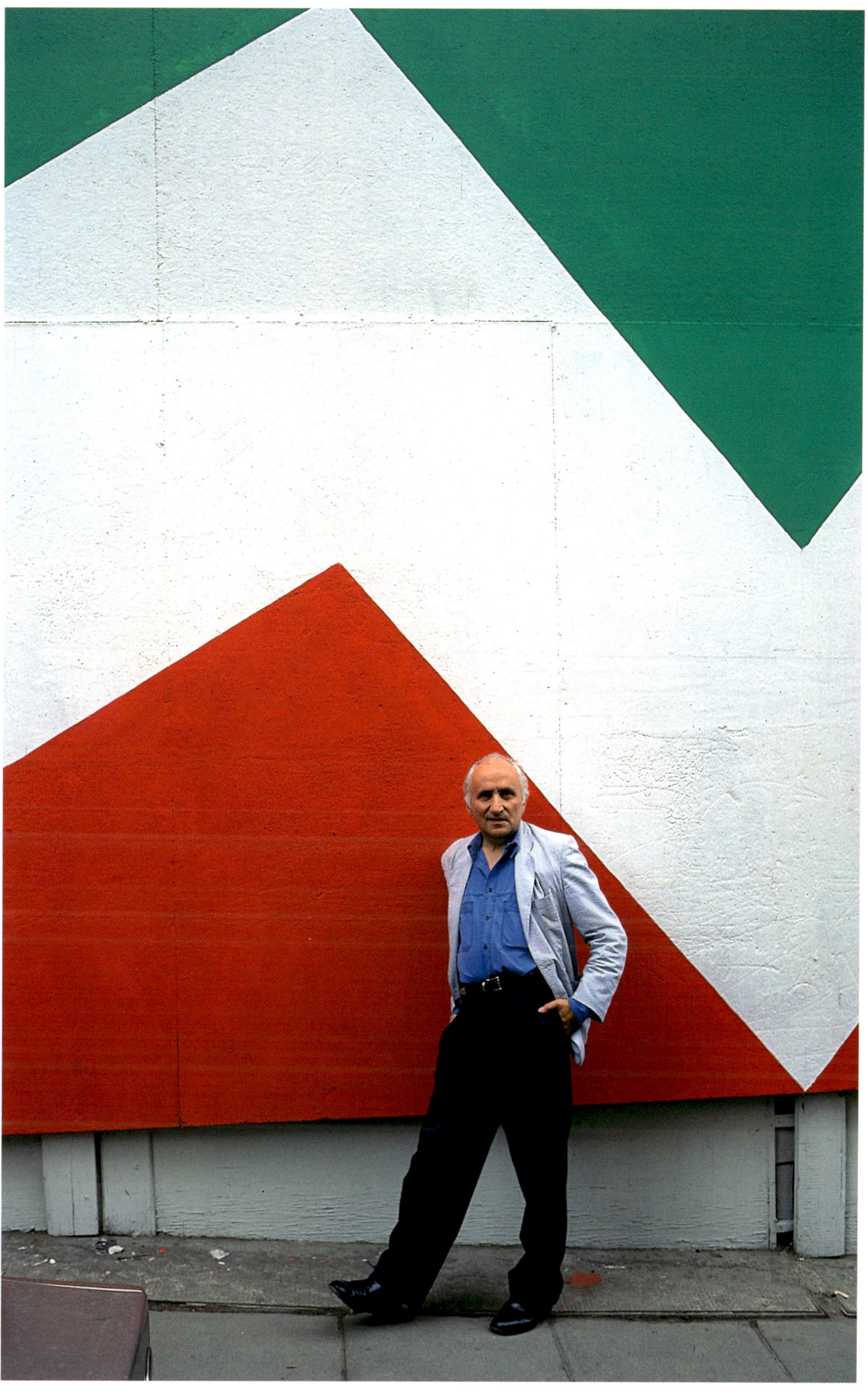

Describing himself as an artist, a promoter of the visual and performing arts and a teacher, Richard Demarco, photographed in the 1990s, is a one-off and has done much for the arts in Scotland and in Europe. Everyone he has helped has his or her own tale, which is always one of enthusiasm and encouragement. Ricky brought many international artists including Joseph Beuys, Tadeus Kantor and Paul Neagu and many more to Edinburgh, to what was Demarco's own arts festival.

Led Zeppelin had reached world domination in rock music when I photographed guitarist Jimmy Page, who was remarkably down-to-earth and a very pleasant guy to be around. This picture was taken in the early 1970s in front of Boleskine House, on the banks of Loch Ness, which was the former home of the mystic Aleister Crowley. Jimmy had recently bought the house and had started a campaign to prevent pylons scarring the landscape of Loch Ness. He was instrumental in getting the support of the local community and was successful in his protest. In 2010, a limited-edition picture-based biography of his career, compiled by Jimmy himself, used this image over a double page spread.

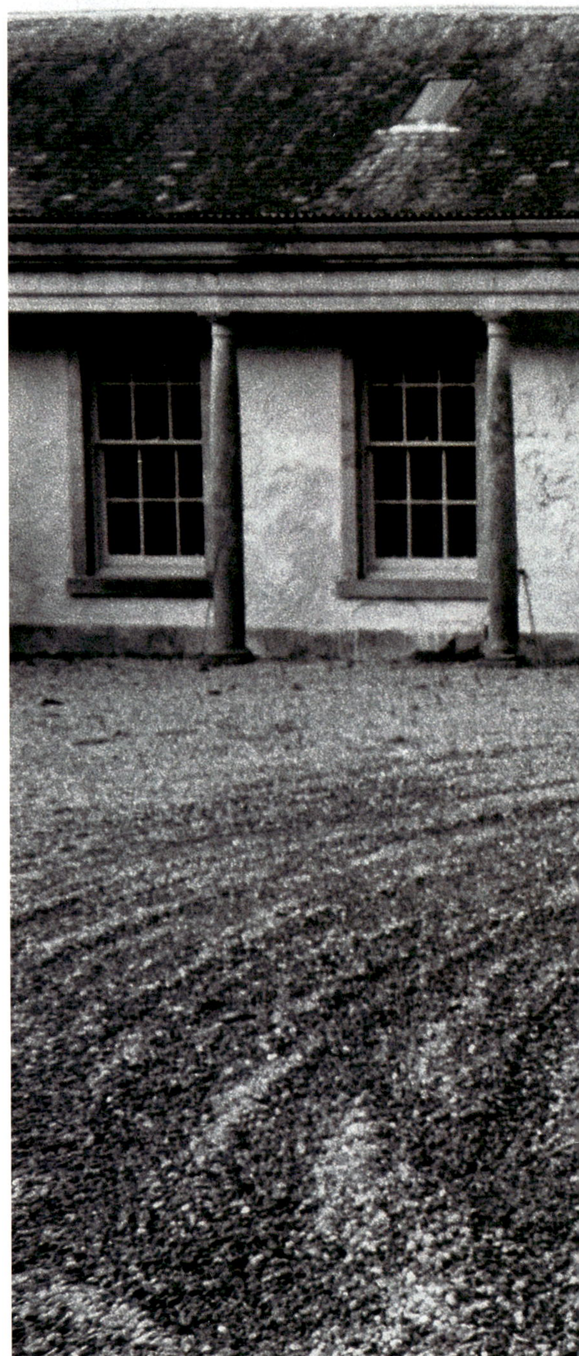

Campbeltown music shop window, with sheet music by Wings and Andy Stewart. Paul McCartney had a farm nearby and had a massive world-wide hit with 'Mull of Kintyre'. Campbeltown Pipe Band featured prominently in the recording, which provided them with new uniforms. Andy Stewart will be remembered as the host of the 1960s' TV song and dance programme *The White Heather Club*. He also had a hit with 'Campbeltown Loch (I wish you were whisky)'.

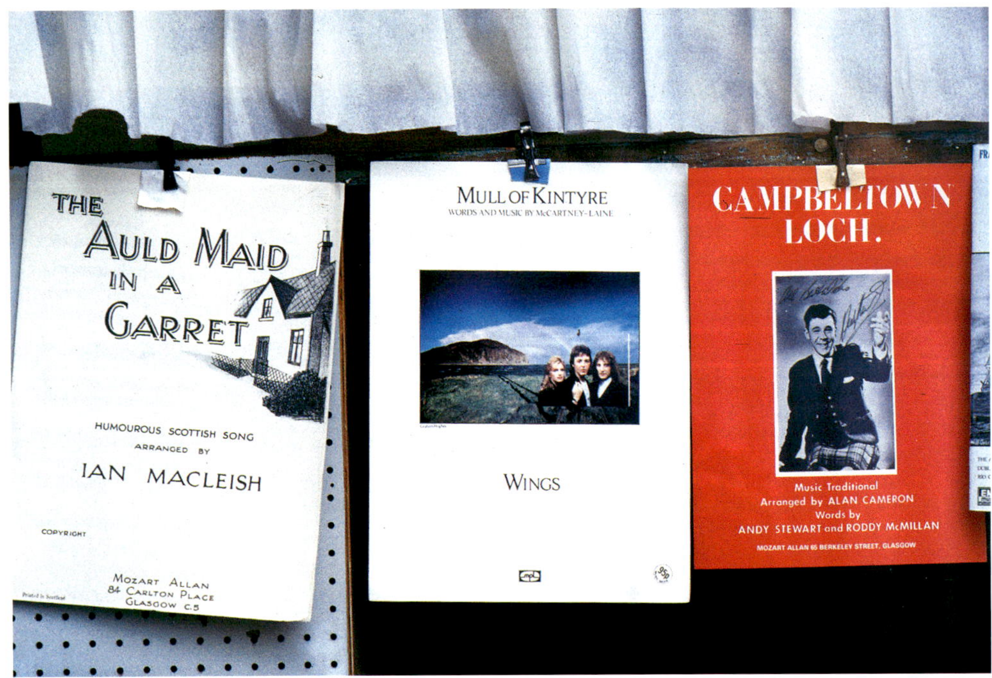

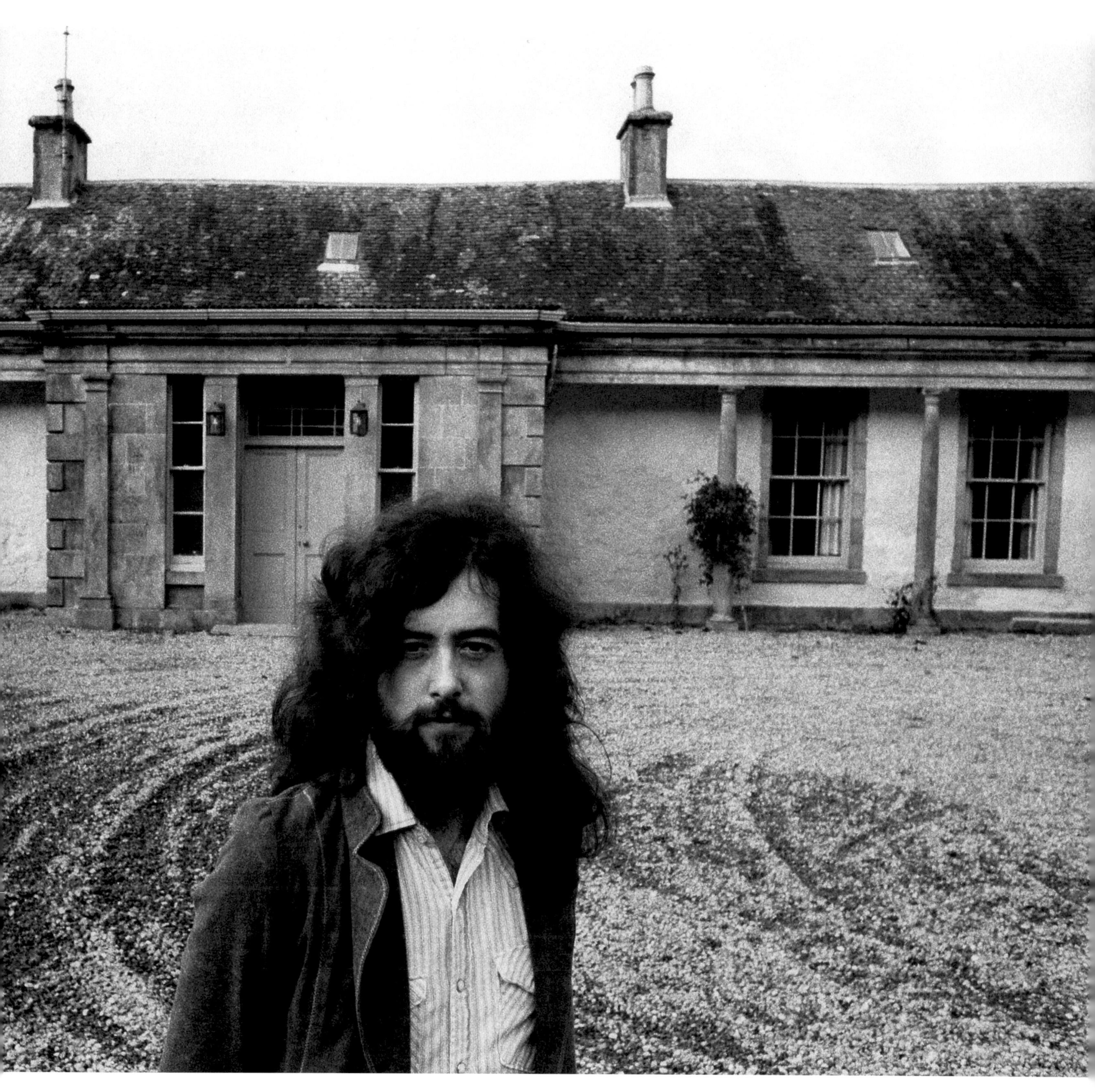

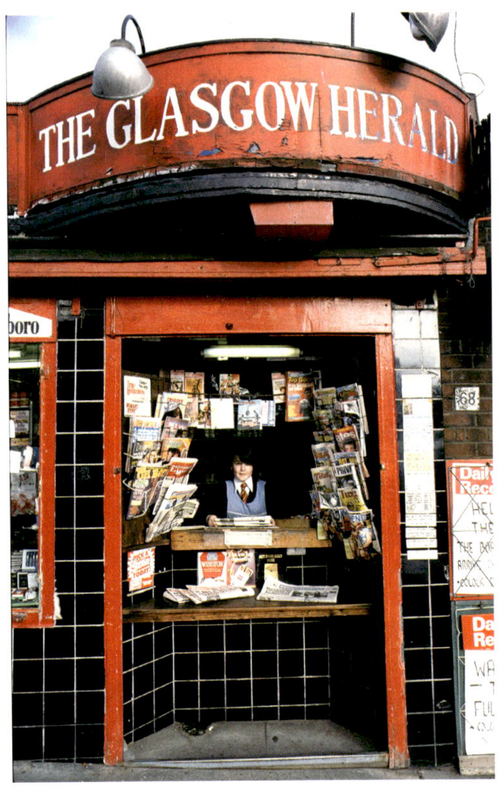

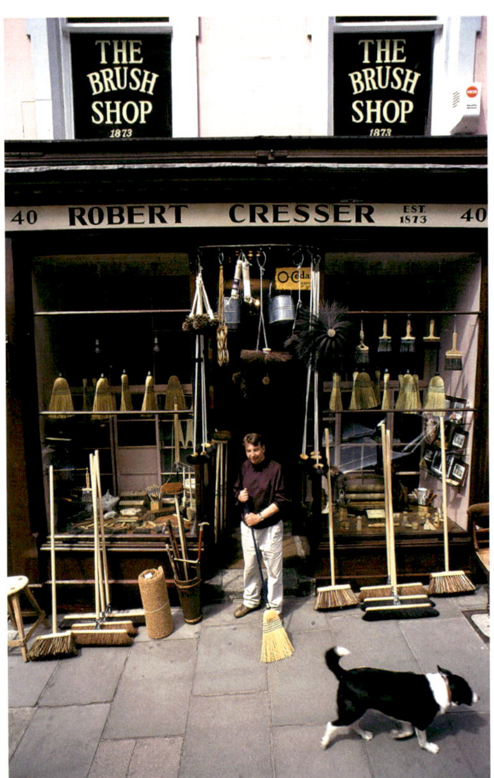

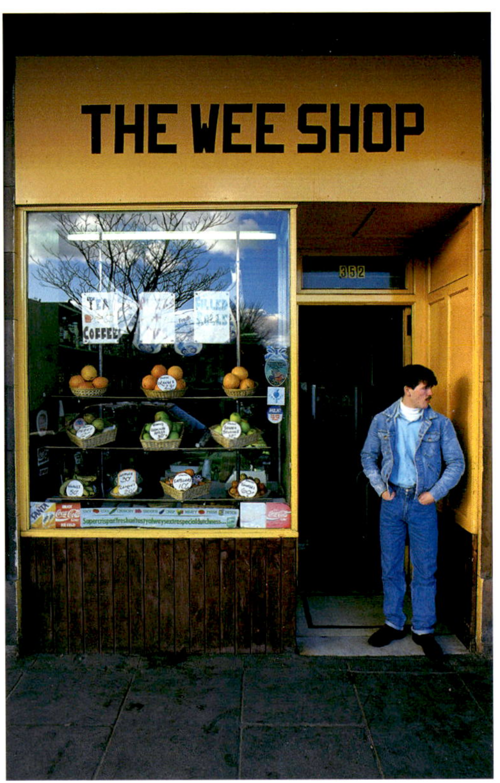

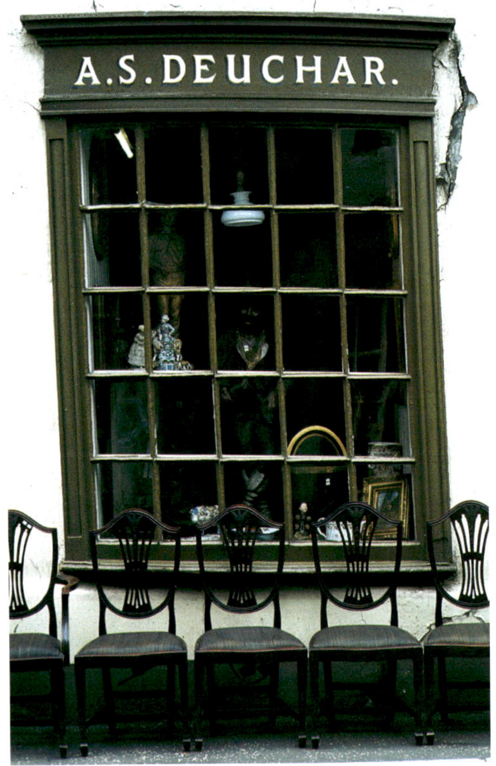

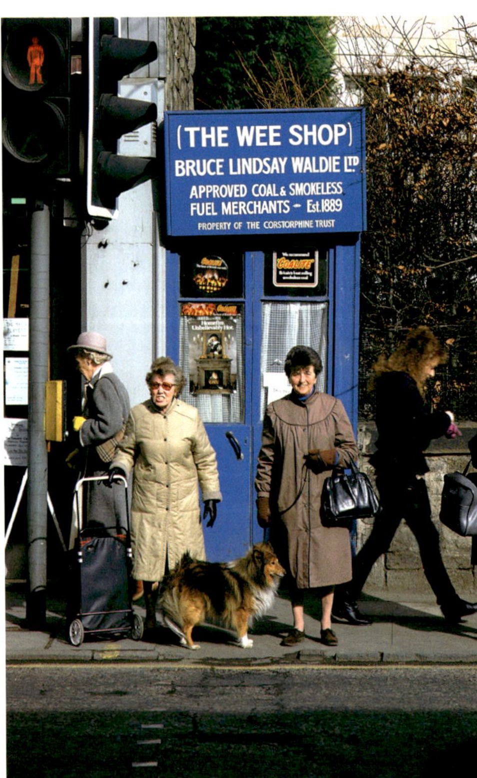

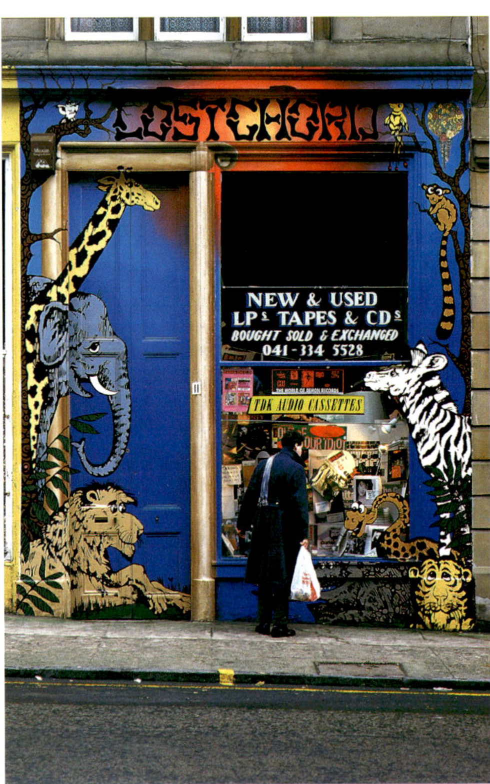

Wee shops are an important part of the local community and need all our support to survive in our increasingly homogenised high streets – think globally, act locally is a good sentiment. From left to right and top to bottom: Glasgow; Edinburgh; Edinburgh; Perth; Edinburgh; Glasgow.

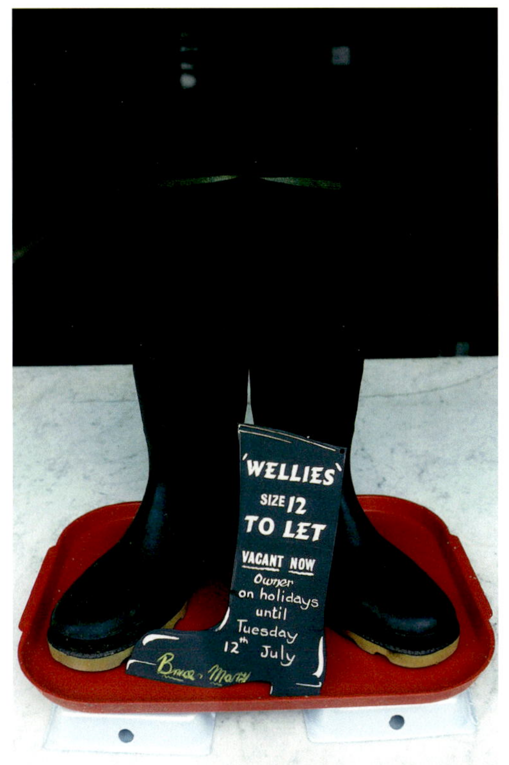

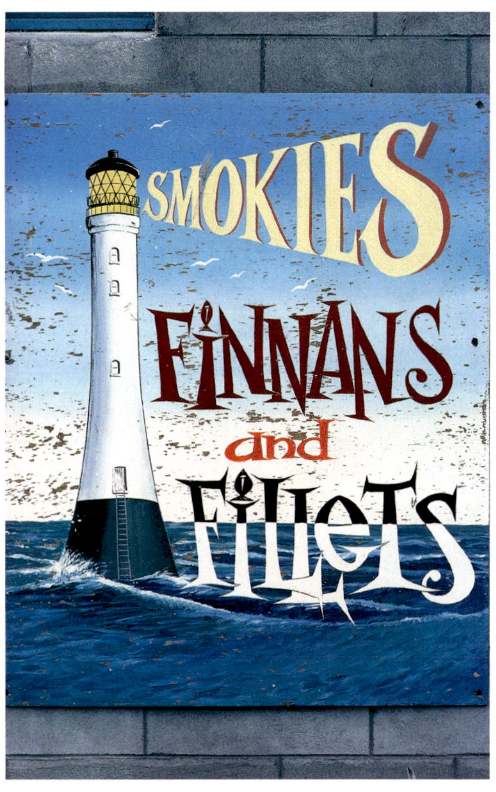

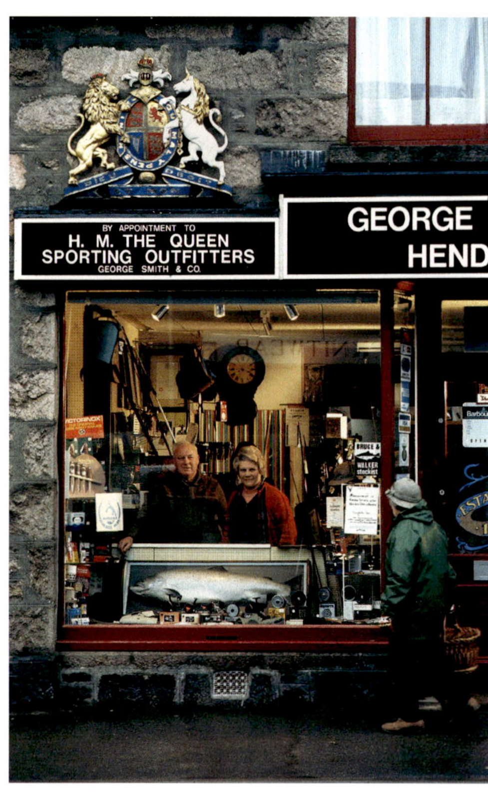

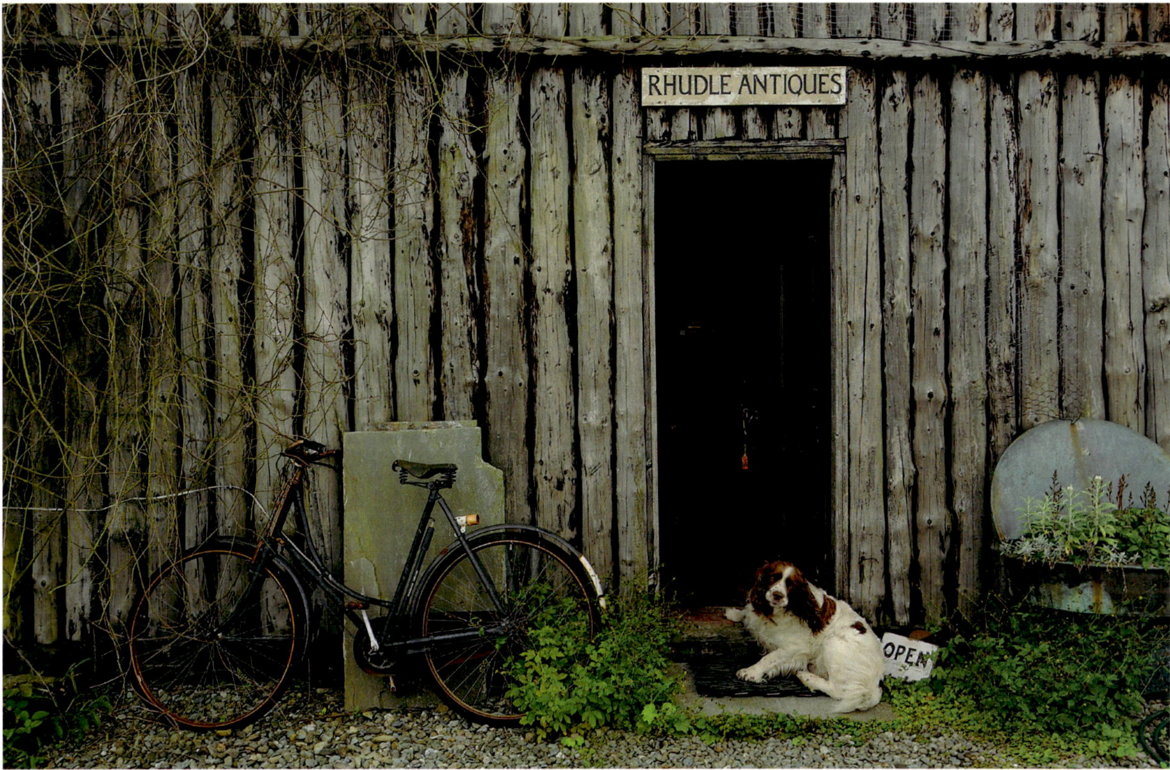

Top row, from left to right: Edinburgh; East Neuk; Ballater. (Bottom) This is the sort of place I just can't pass. I can usually find something completely impractical. On this occasion it was a tin Victorian hat box – just what I needed.

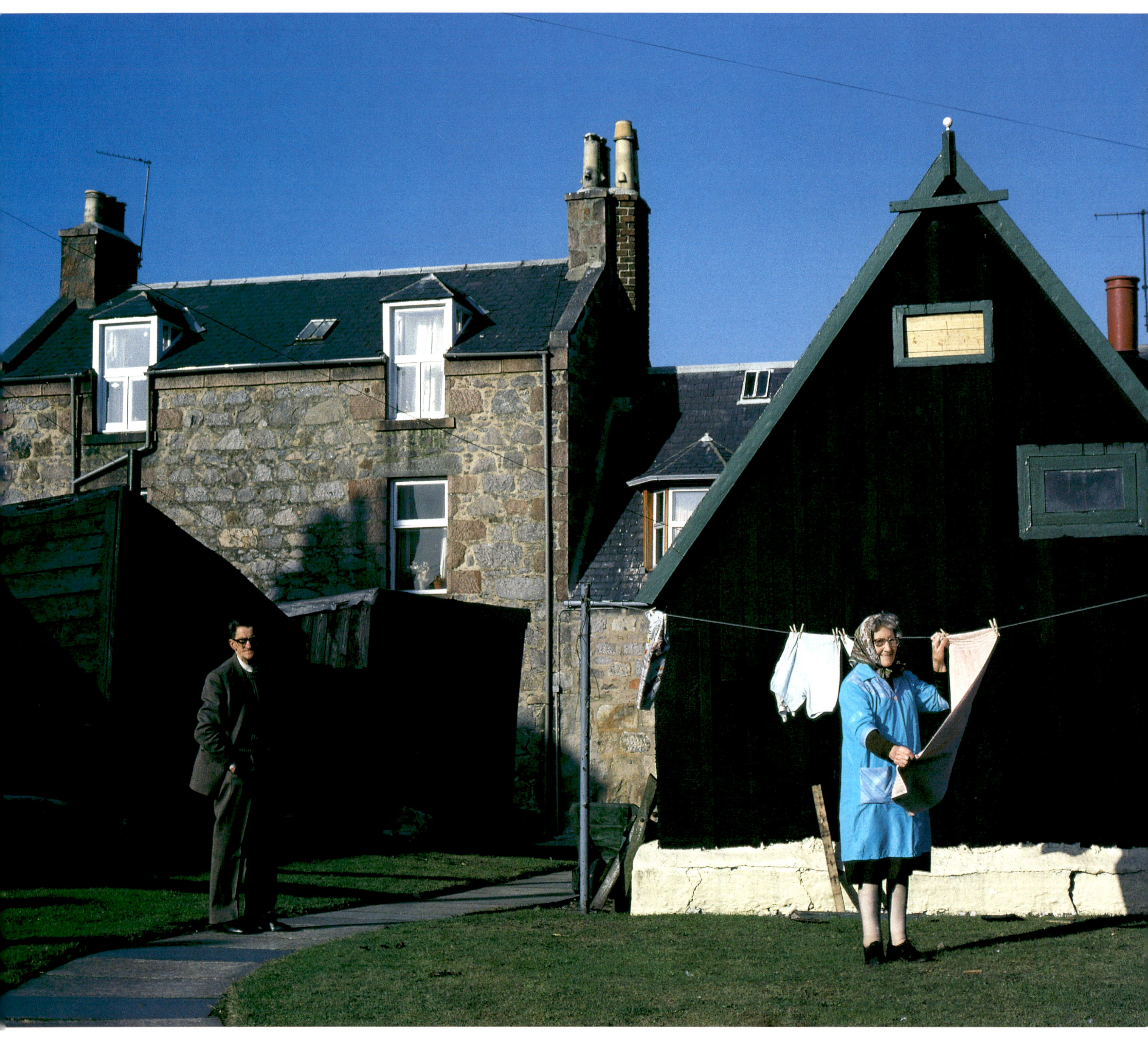

Footdee, once a fishing village on the edge of Aberdeen, is pronounced 'Futty'. I don't think it receives the interest it deserves. While I was with the Scottish Tourist Board I took some Italian travel journalists to visit it when we had time to spare from a full itinerary. They loved it and got as much from it as they had from Aberdeen's spectacular granite edifices. Sadly, ugly, unsympathetic double glazing is encroaching.

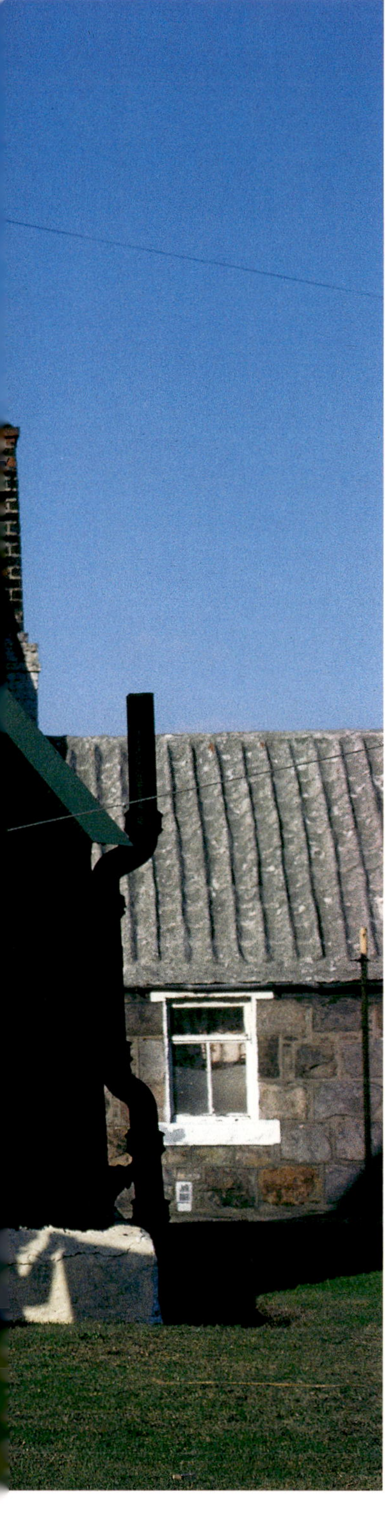

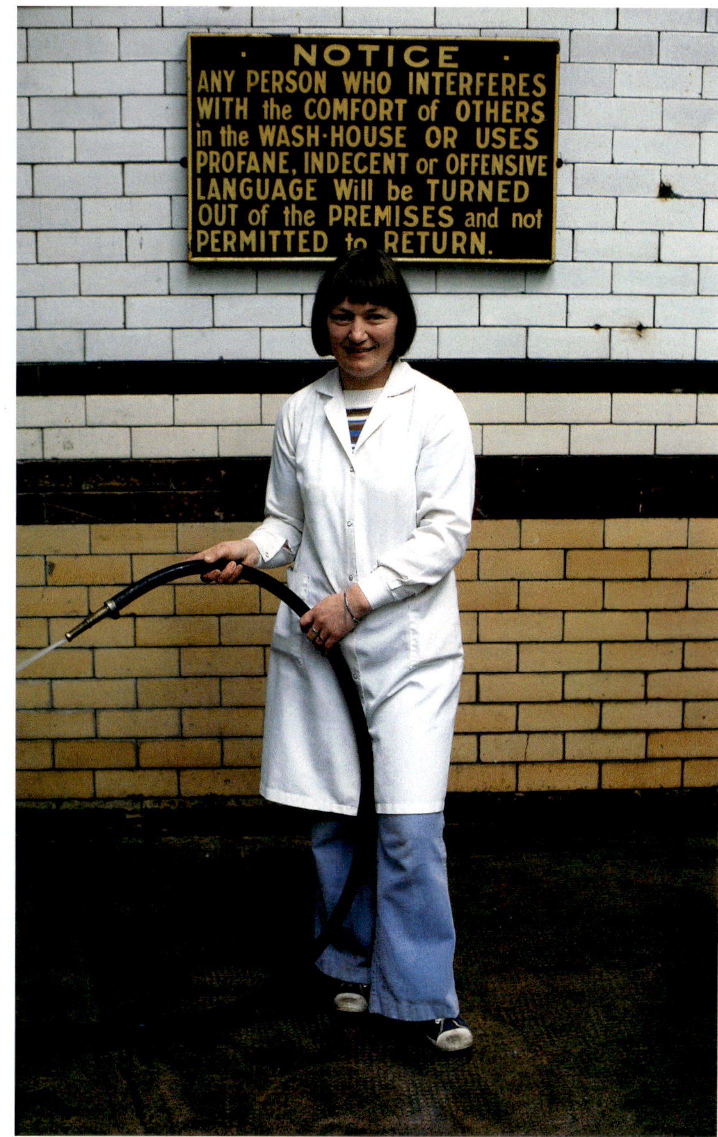

This was the last day of the last Glasgow steamie (wash-house) in Partick in 1982, the end of a tradition that began in 1732. The good nature and humour of customers and staff belies the loss of a sociable and practical amenity. We lose sensible community activities, and social planners replace them with classes in crochet, web design and the study of the social effects of the demise of the steamie in the 20th century.

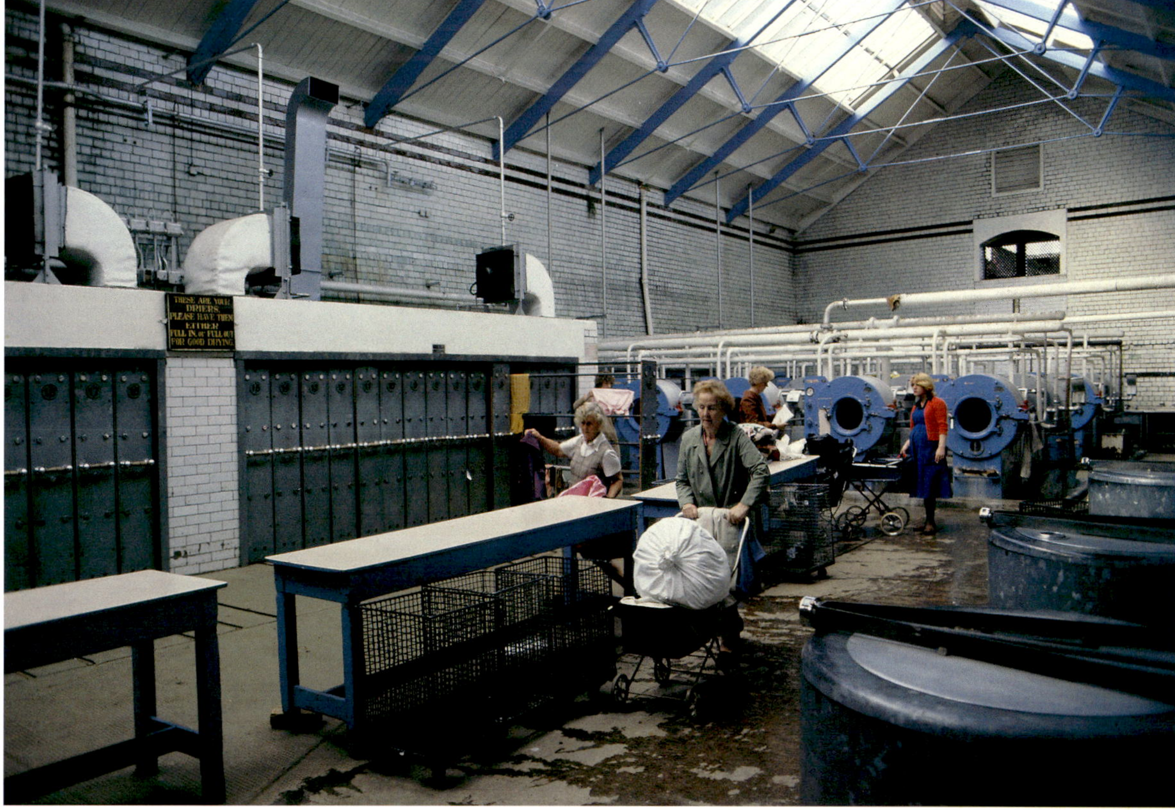

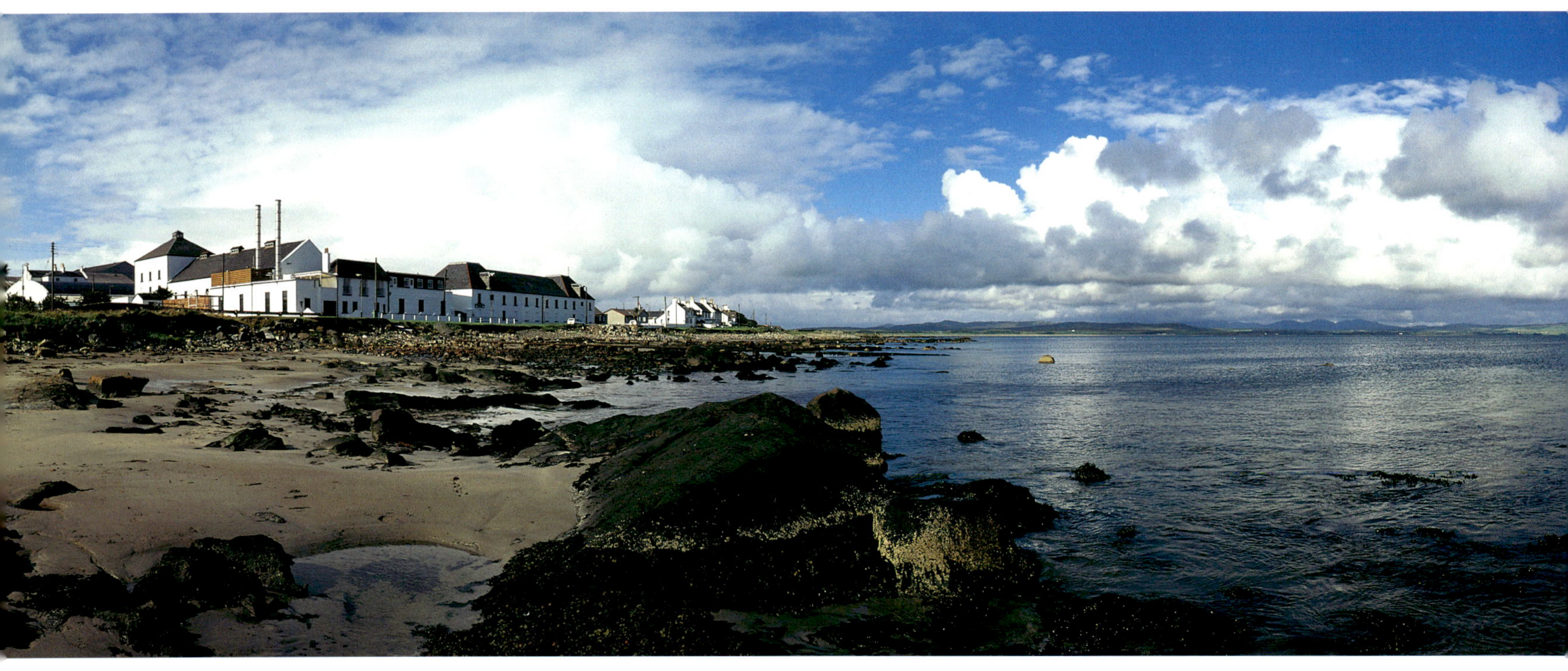

Bruichladdich distillery on Islay was closed for six years from 1994. Thankfully, it was reopened by independent bottler Murray McDavid in 2000. It would have been tragic to have lost such an exceptional example of a unique island malt. Distilleries can be beautiful industrial buildings – many seem to have evolved from the landscape.

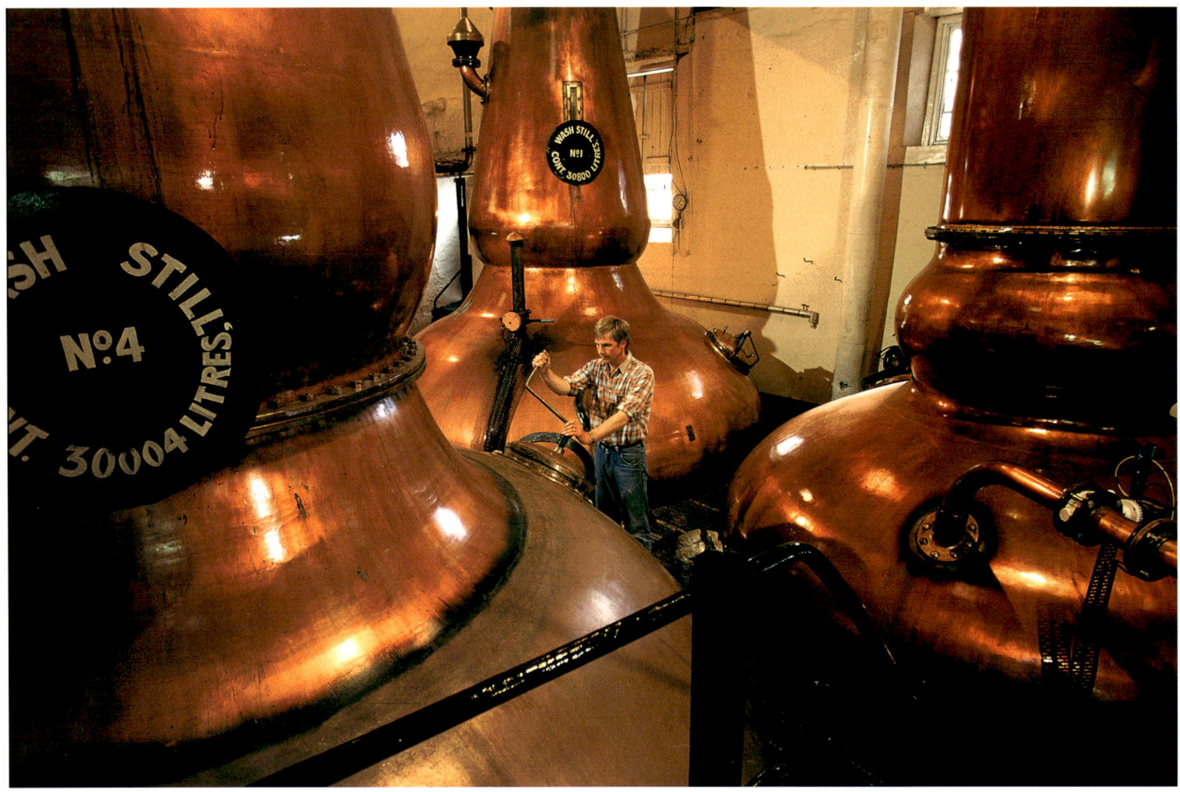

The fermentation stills at the Dalmore distillery in Alness, which produces a Highland single malt, look great after their annual clean. A visit to a distillery can create a loyalty to a particular malt or blend. This is the best kind of marketing.

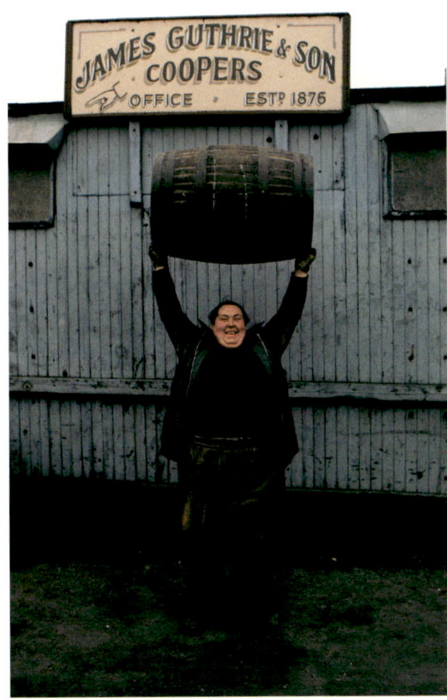

If barrel tossing were an Olympic event we could have a gold medallist in this cooperage in Govan, Glasgow.

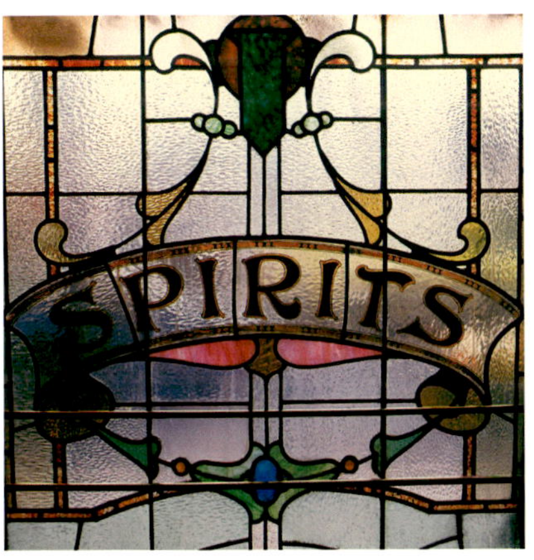

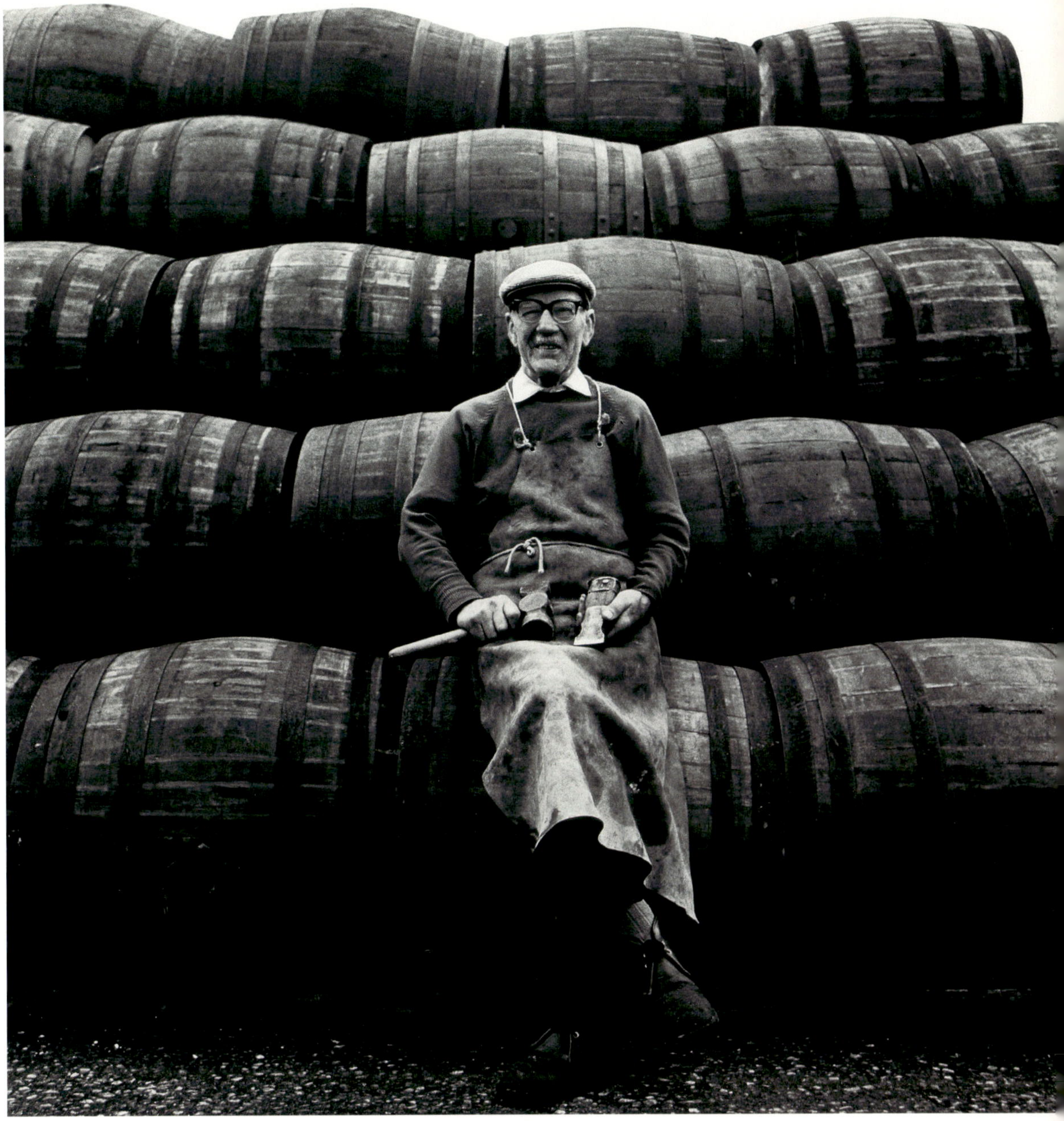

I've photographed in many distilleries, and after a day's work I'm sure the feeling of contentment I get is from the 'angel's share' (natural evaporation of the spirit in the air). A cooper on Islay still practises his highly skilled and strenuous trade when most of us are thinking of taking things easier.

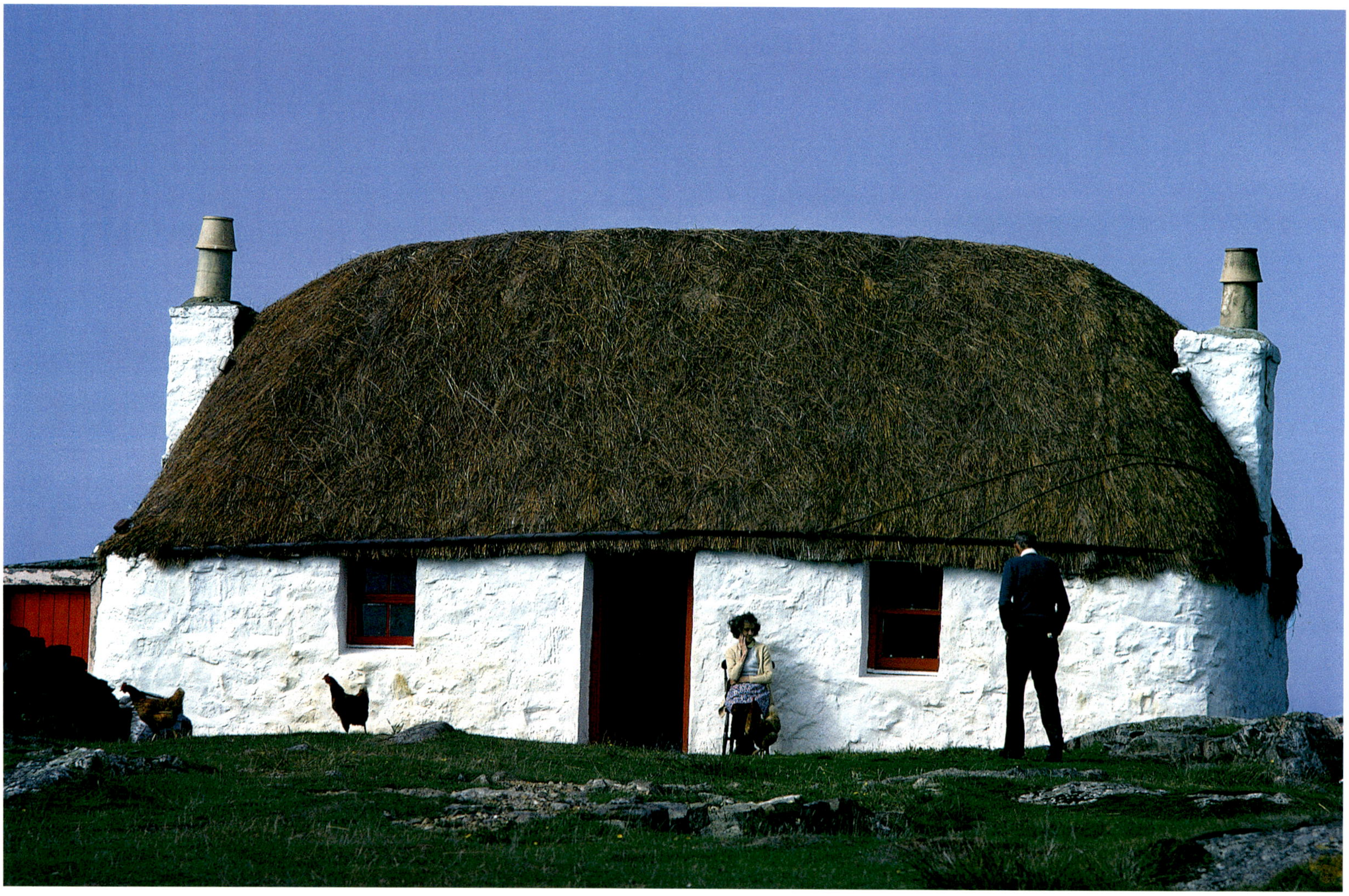

Some buildings are where they belong. I get the same satisfaction from this croft on North Uist as I do from seeing the Sydney Opera House, the Empire State Building and Taj Mahal, places that cannot be improved and any alteration to which would be wrong. Bland kit houses and even plastic houses proliferate in the Highlands and Islands. How do they get passed by the planning authorities?

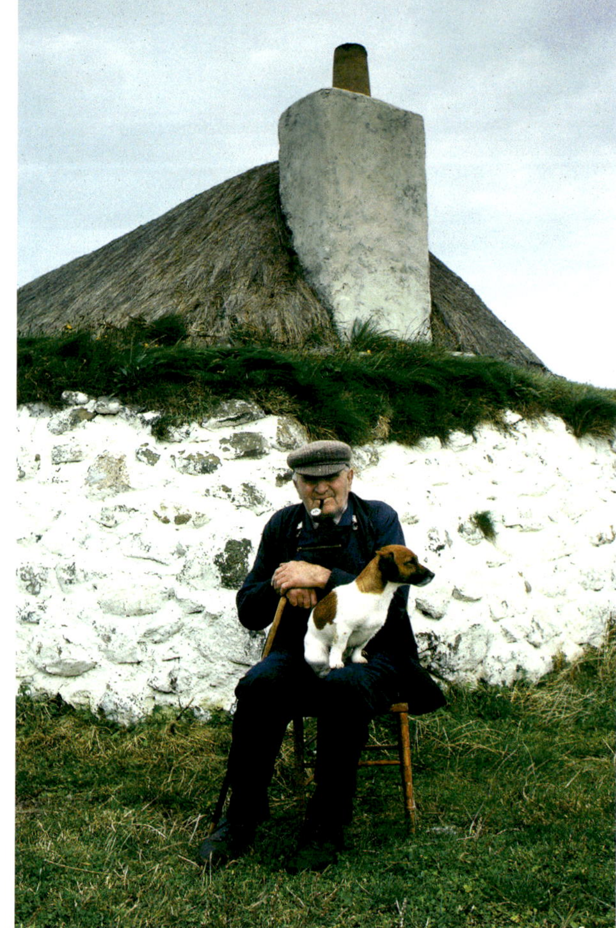

When I approached this crofter on Tiree, he didn't question why I wanted to take a photograph but asked if his dog could be in it. It is in this quiet way that some island folk react. He didn't need instruction – he positioned himself and I had what I wanted in my first few exposures. Tiree has been called 'the granary of the Hebrides', owing to its fertility. Now Tiree is where the world's best windsurfers compete in the Tiree Wave Classic competition.

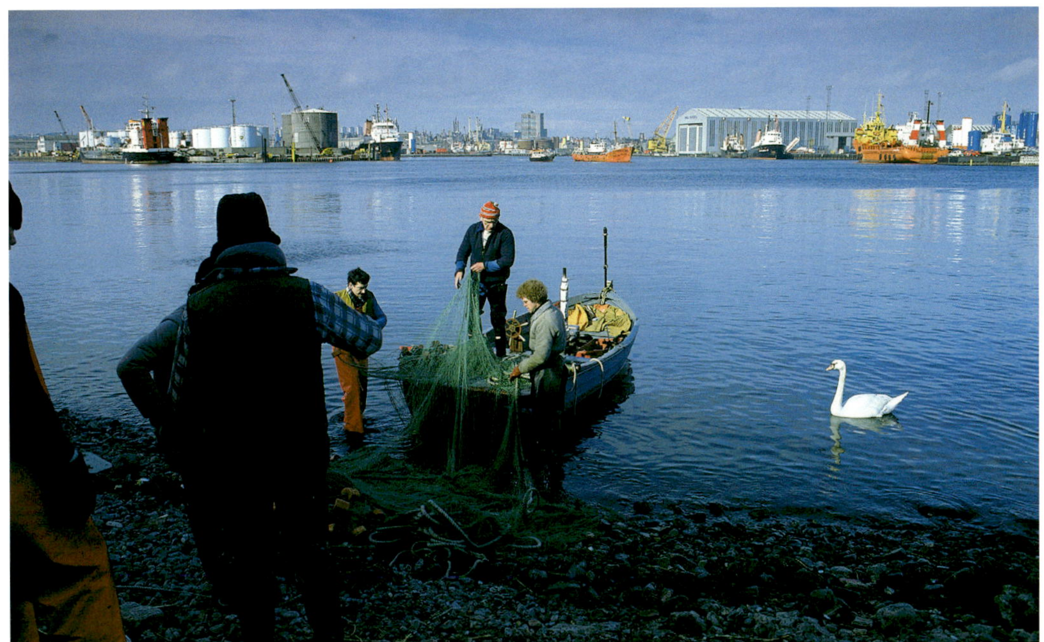

Salmon net fishing no longer exists on the River Dee (and likewise on the River Ness). It used to be quite a sight at the mouths of many rivers. My father would troop our guests from the south to witness the daily catch being hauled in. Before fish farms most people only tasted salmon out of tins.

A very popular TV programme, *Monarch of the Glen*, which ran for seven series between 2000 and 2005, was shot at Arverikie Lodge and was called Glenbogle in its fictional form. It was based on a 1941 novel by Compton Mackenzie, author of *Whisky Galore*. Queen Victoria was keen to make the lodge her Highland home but the story goes that midges drove her to Balmoral.

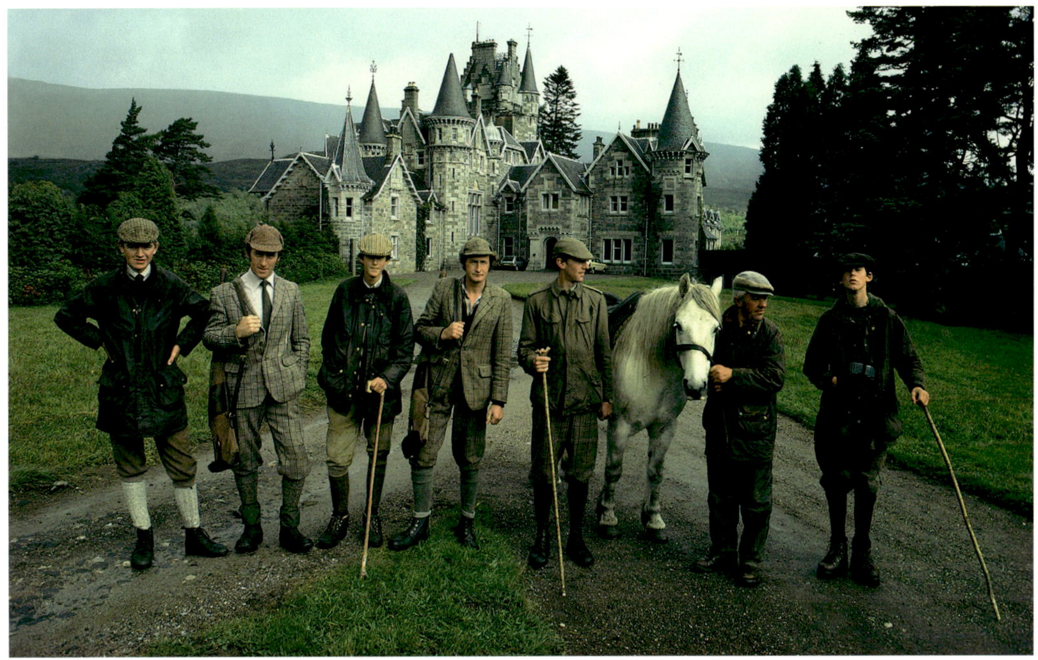

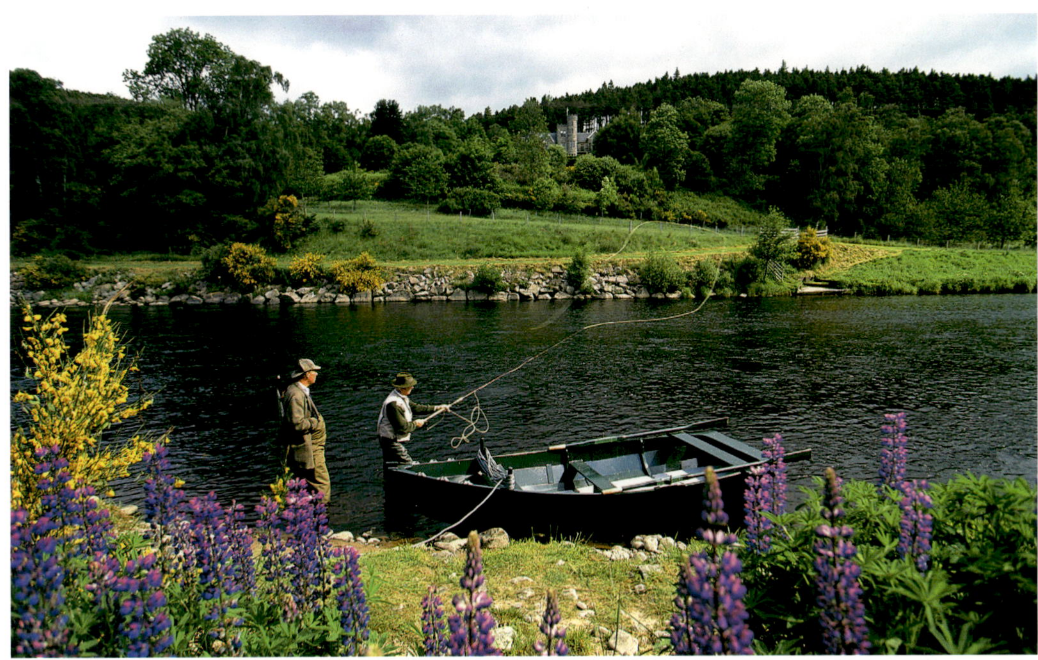

A beat on the River Spey. The guests stay in a Victorian pile, built purely for hunting and fishing, and a personal ghillie is on hand. Lunch is served in a beautifully appointed lodge on the riverbank. These anglers didn't mind me disturbing their idyll when I told them I was shooting for the *National Geographic Traveller*.

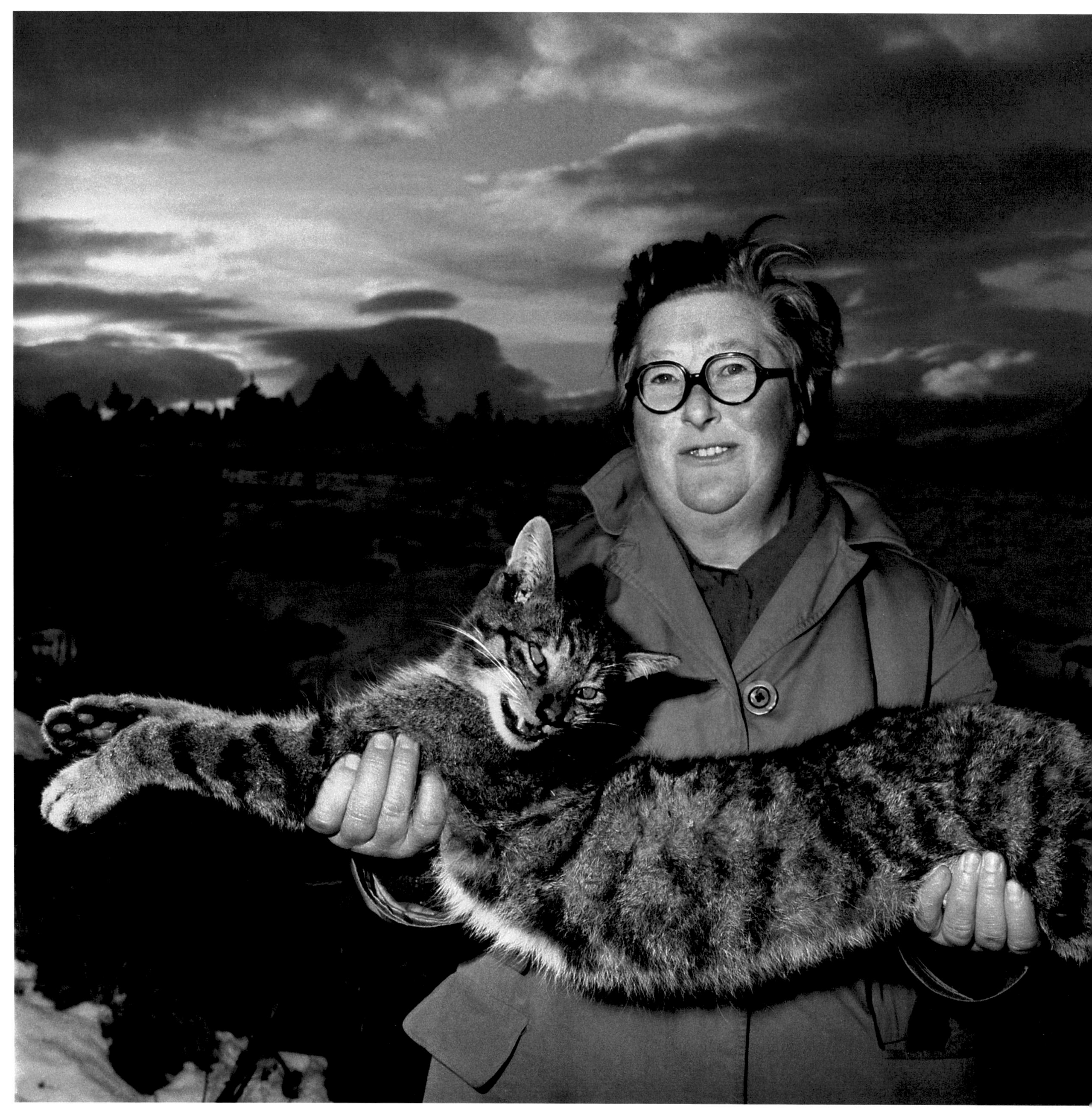

This lady was a farmer near Inverness in the early 1970s, who had saved her chickens from the wildcat by killing it with a spade. A somewhat gruesome picture takes on a theatrical and surreal look when lit with fill-in flashlight, a much favoured technique by many of today's photographers.

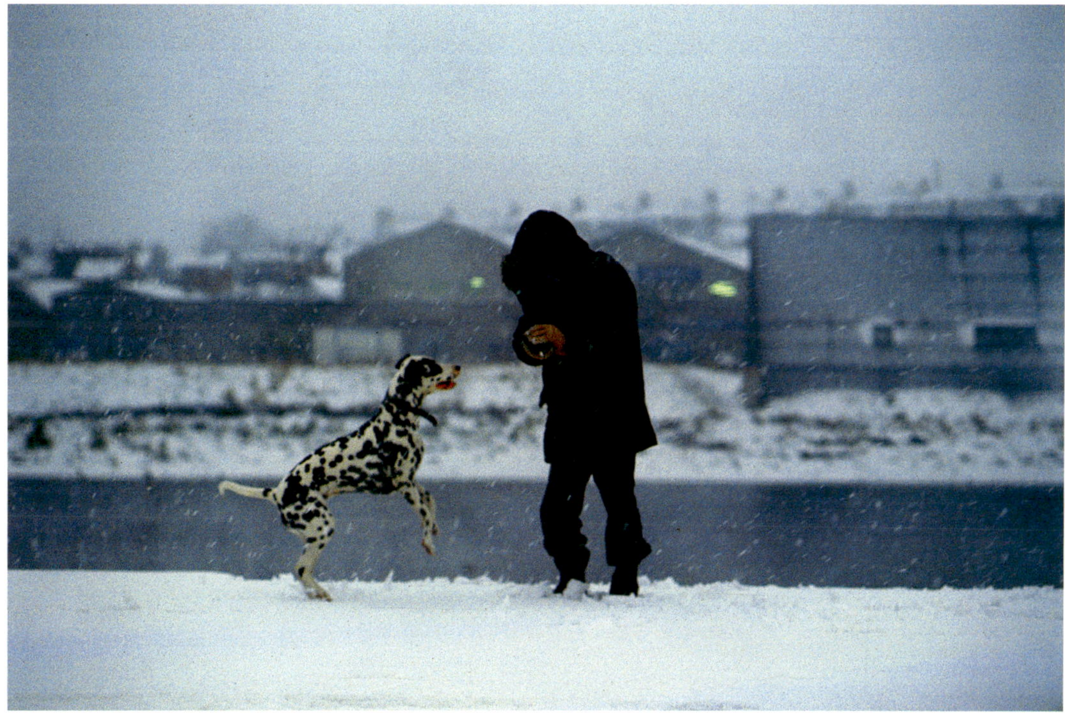

On the banks of the River Dee a dalmatian fetches snowballs – a pointless task I would have thought.

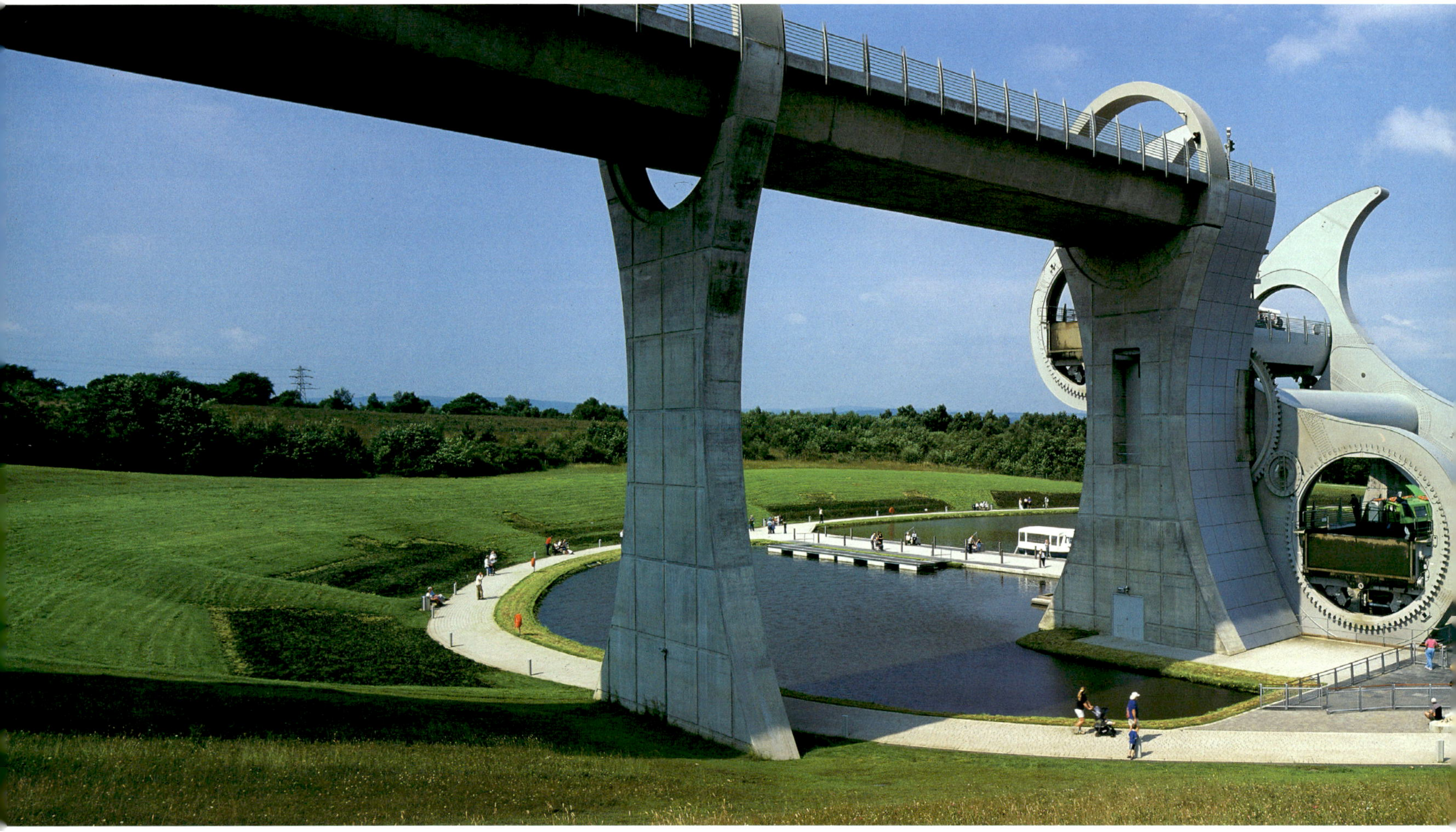

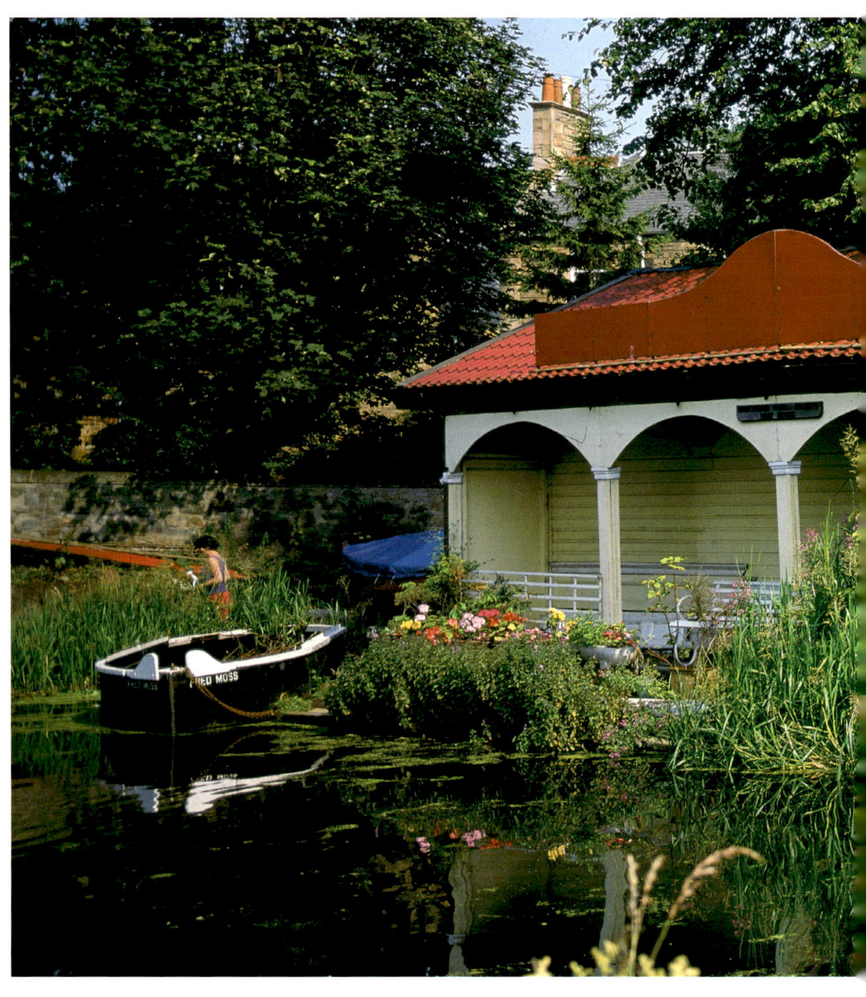

British Waterways has an ambitious plan to have a greater use of its canals for recreation. This quaint boathouse on the Union Canal in Edinburgh contrasts with the stark modernism of the Falkirk Wheel.

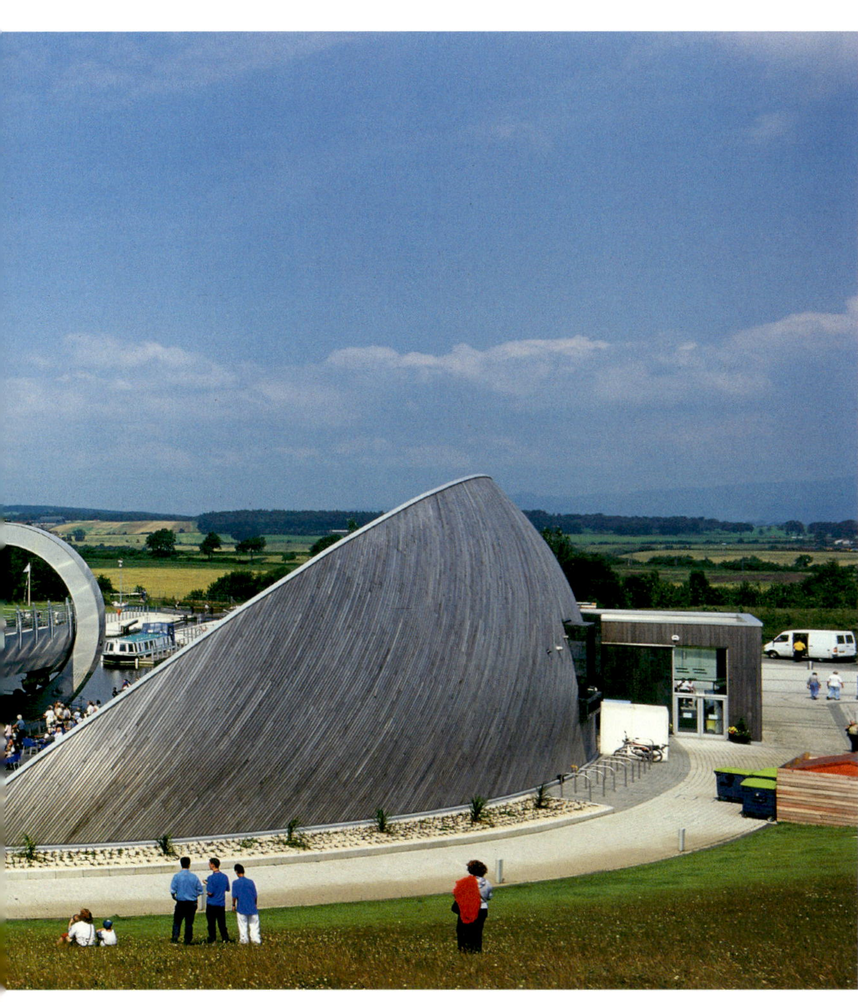

I was pleasantly surprised when a visiting Canadian friend had the Falkirk Wheel high on his itinerary. It showed that Scotland could still produce innovative and original engineering solutions to problems such as raising and lowering boats twenty-four metres from the Union Canal to the Forth and Clyde Canal. It is hoped that the canal can become the recreational amenity that the wheel was built serve.

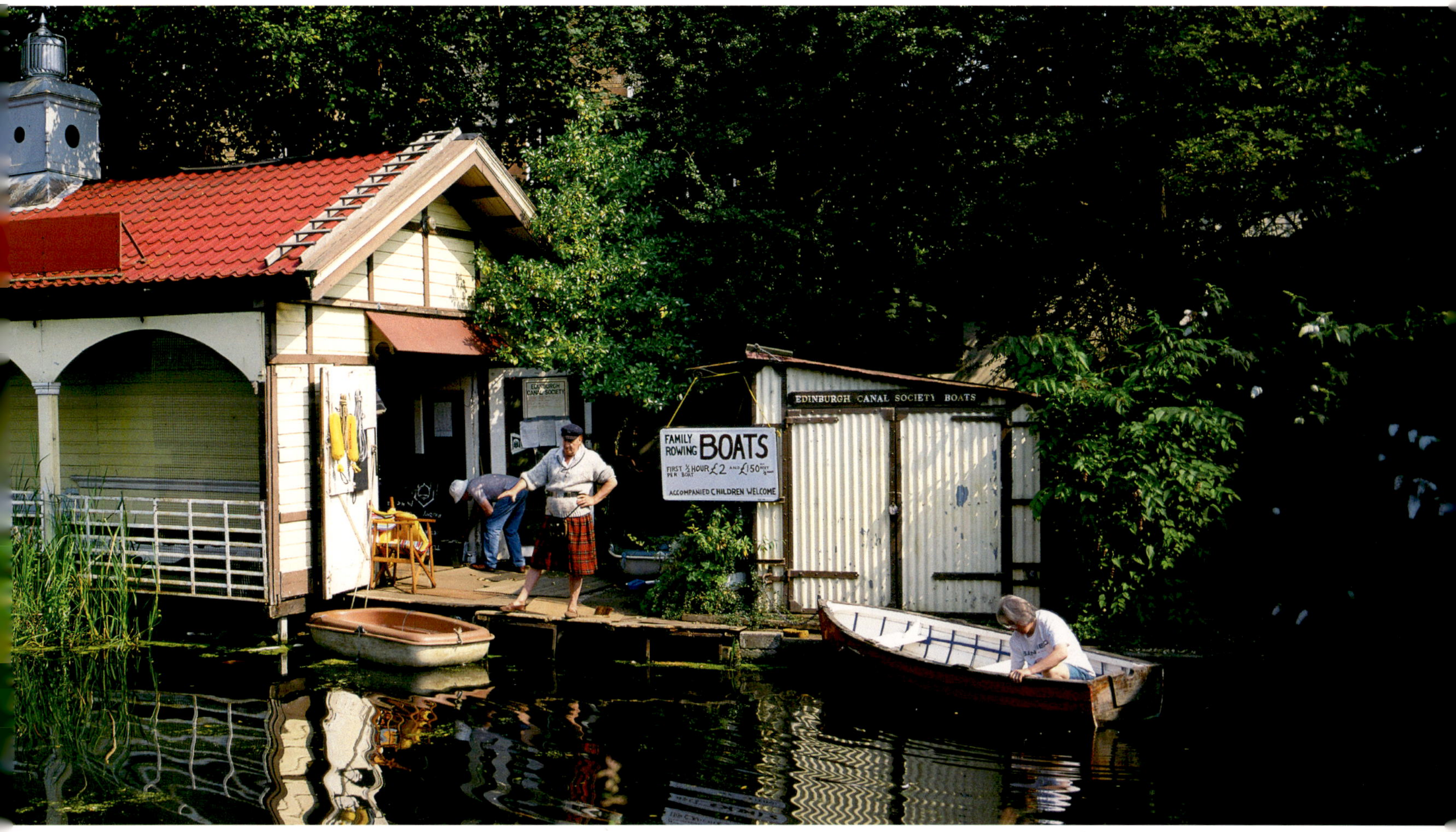

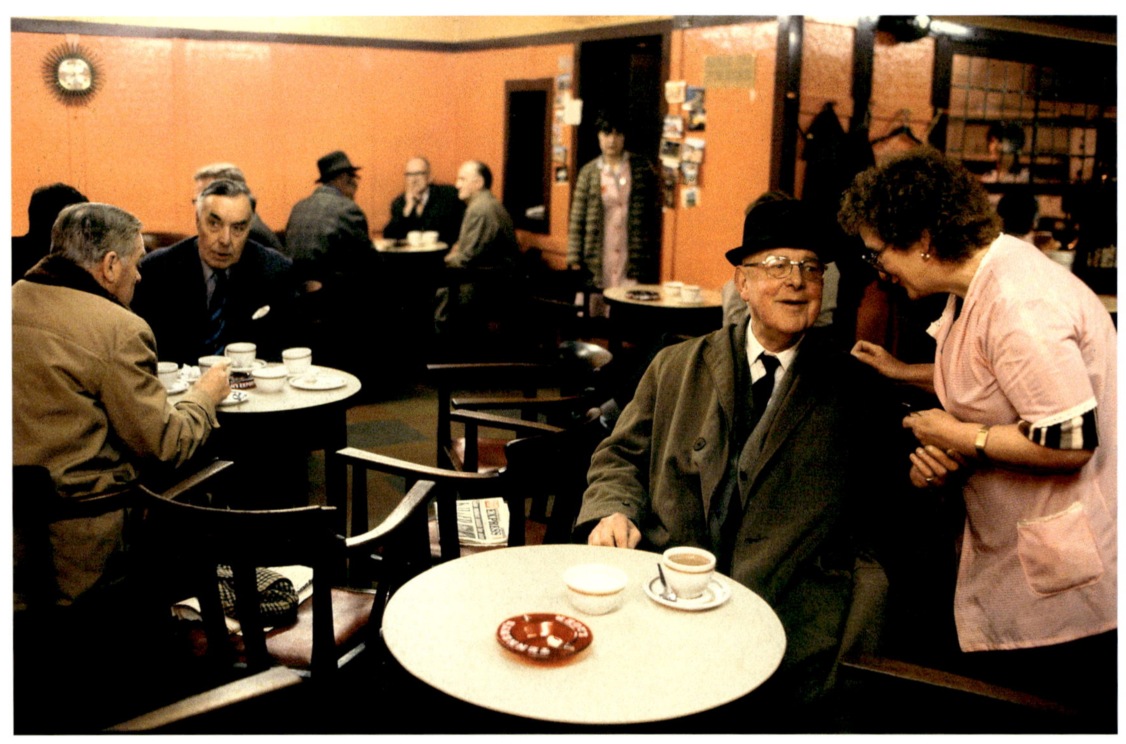

(Left) Glasgow's coffee houses of the 1970s are not to be confused with the later infiltrators from Seattle. They had many traditions, of which one was keeping your hat on. There was a pretence that business was transacted in them, but, as in pubs, the usual discussion was football, the previous evening's television and other mundane topics.

(Below left) Every day in the 1970s these ladies served sustenance and the Lord to the needy folk of Glasgow. The Tent Hall off the Saltmarket, as its name suggests, was originally a tent on Glasgow Green. The Glasgow United Evangelistic Association built this more permanent structure in 1876.

(Below) The Salutation Hotel, Perth, has a brass plaque that records its association with Bonnie Prince Charlie during the 1745 Jacobite rising. Etienne Melville, an engineering student, said he enjoyed his holiday job in 2010 as a cycle-sandwichboard man. He said he was also used as an unofficial tourist information officer.

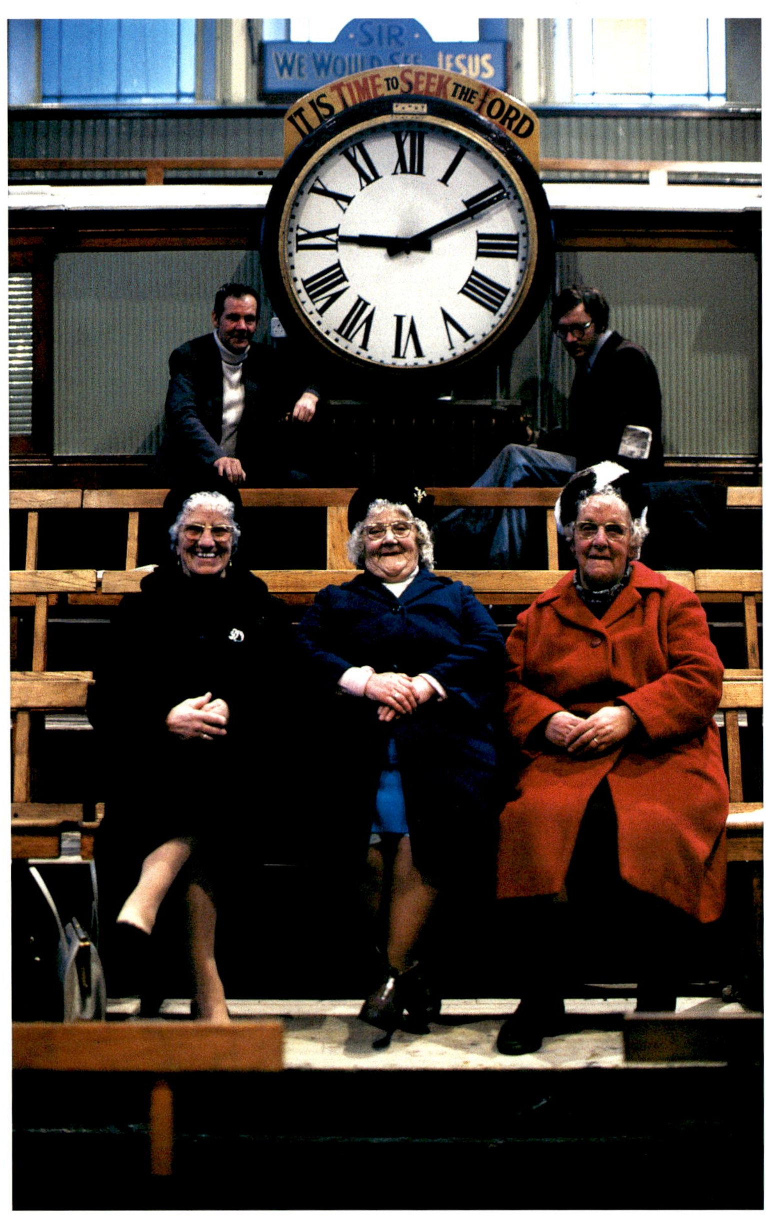

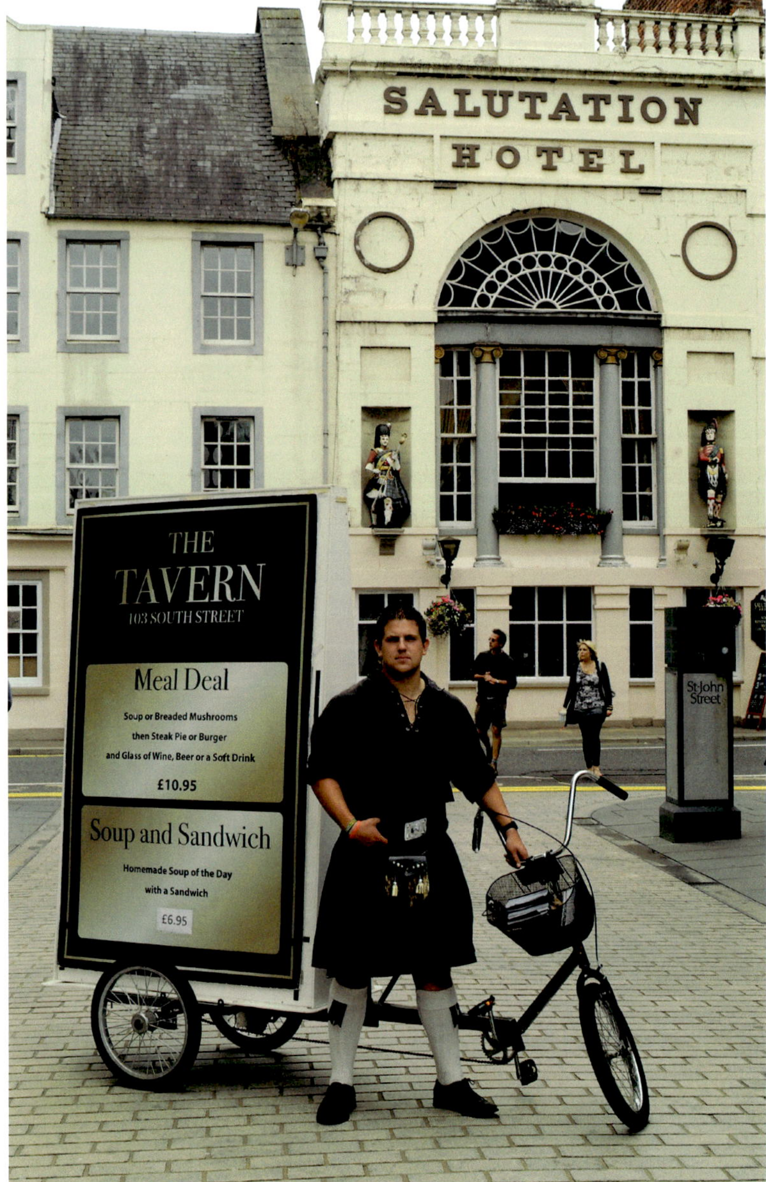

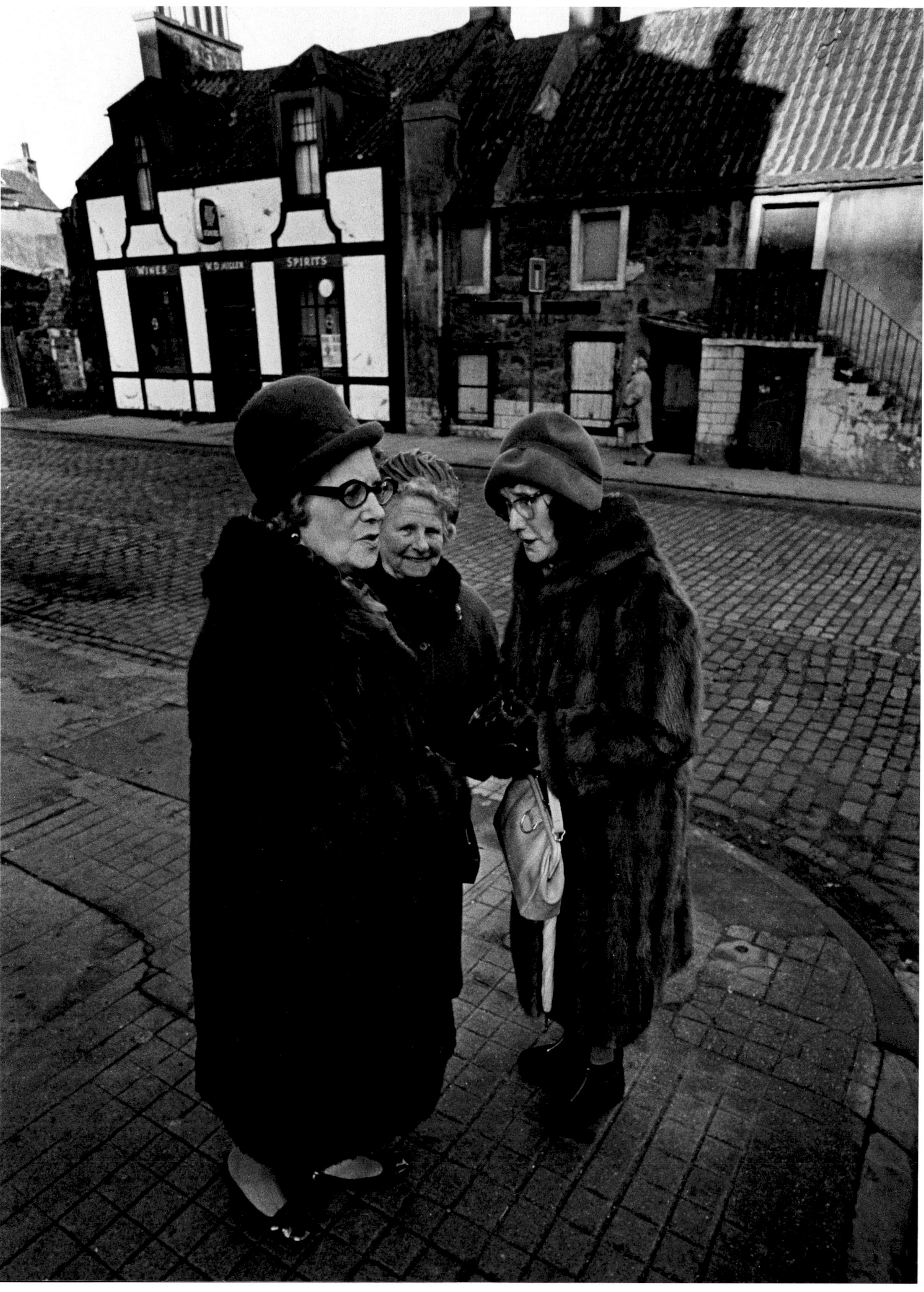

Three immaculately attired Newhaven ladies in the 1970s. Newhaven had been Edinburgh's fishing village on the Firth of Forth and was in great danger of being lost, but thankfully the buildings in this picture have been saved. This street scene would have been very different one hundred years earlier: the Newhaven fishwives in their distinctive dresses would have been preparing their willow baskets for selling the catch in the city. A description in *Blackwood's Magazine* in 1826: 'I like to see the well-shaped shanks aneath their short yellow petticoats. There's something heartsome in the creak o' their creeshy creels on their braid backs.'

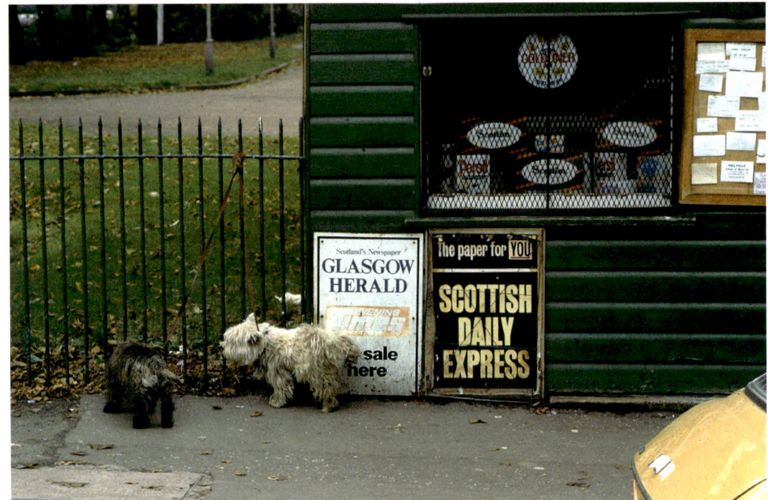

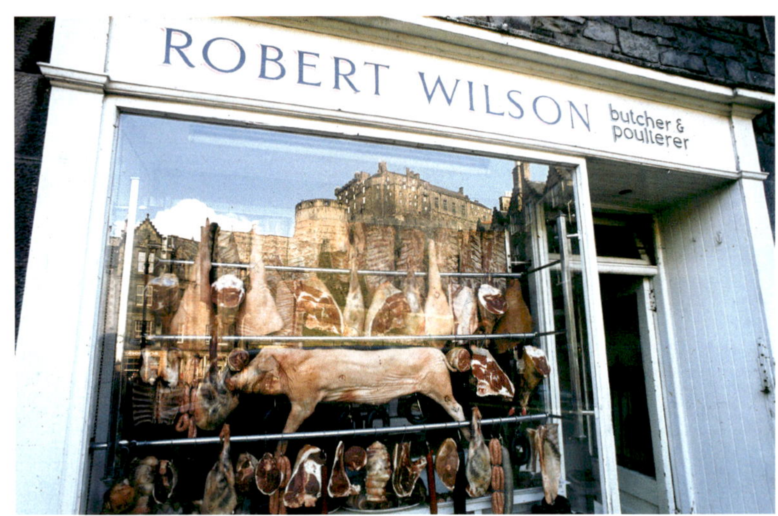

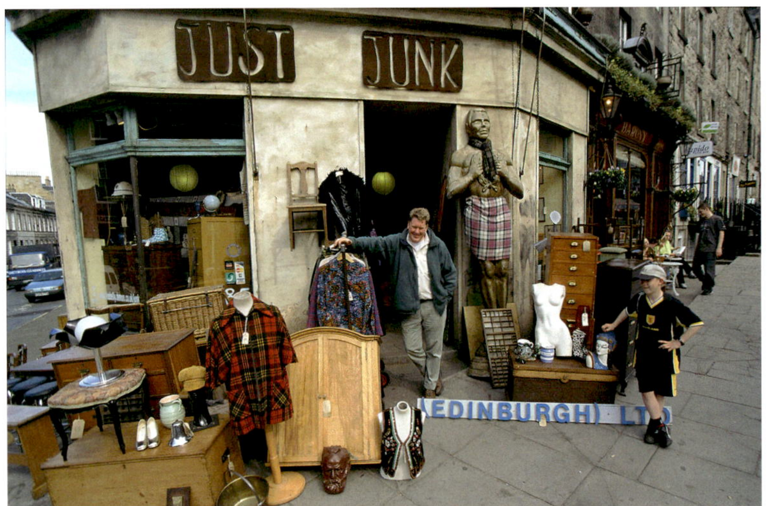

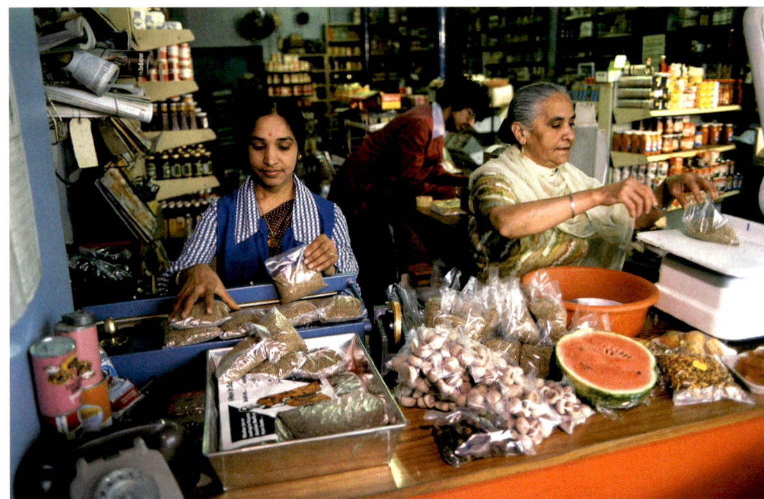

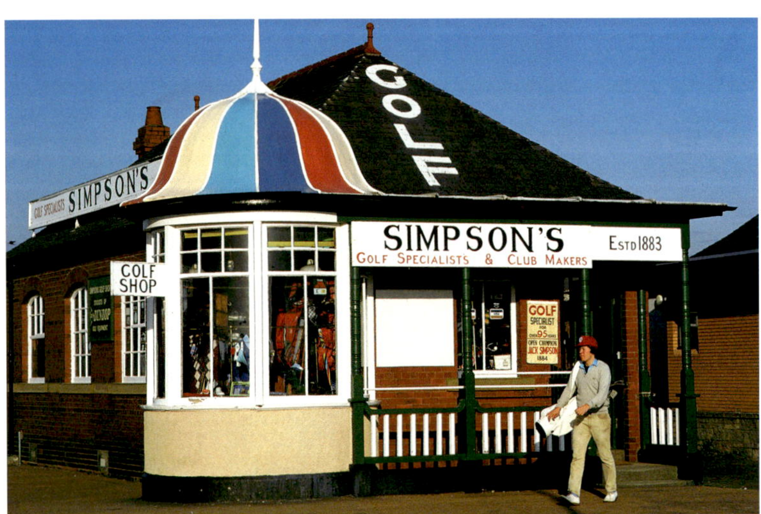

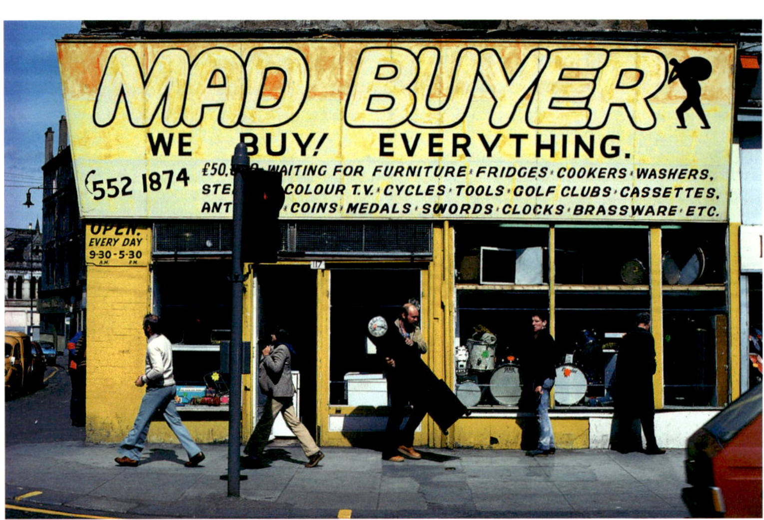

A great number of beautiful Victorian, Art Nouveau and Art Deco façades have been replaced by homogenised shopfronts, destroying the character of our high streets. Bring the fun back to shopping. Some of these pictures go back to the early 1970s. (Top left) This image was in my *Glasgow* book, and the *Scottish Daily Express* ordered a large print of it for the editorial office. From left to right, top to bottom: Glasgow; Edinburgh; Edinburgh; Glasgow; Carnoustie; Glasgow.

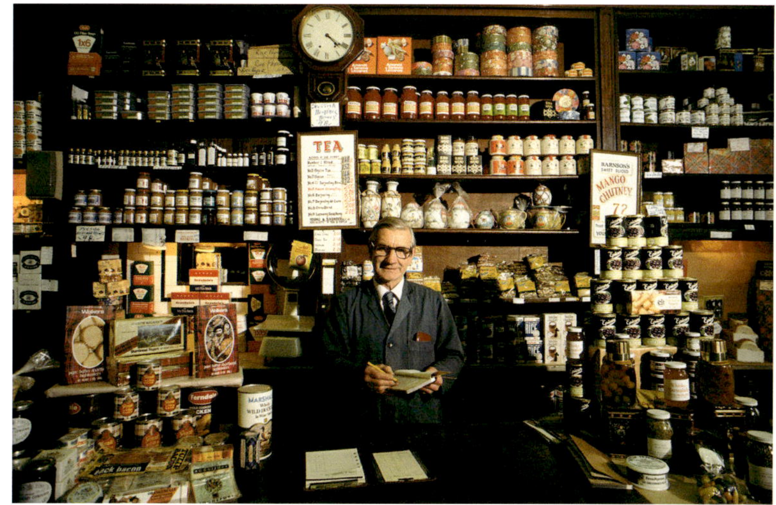

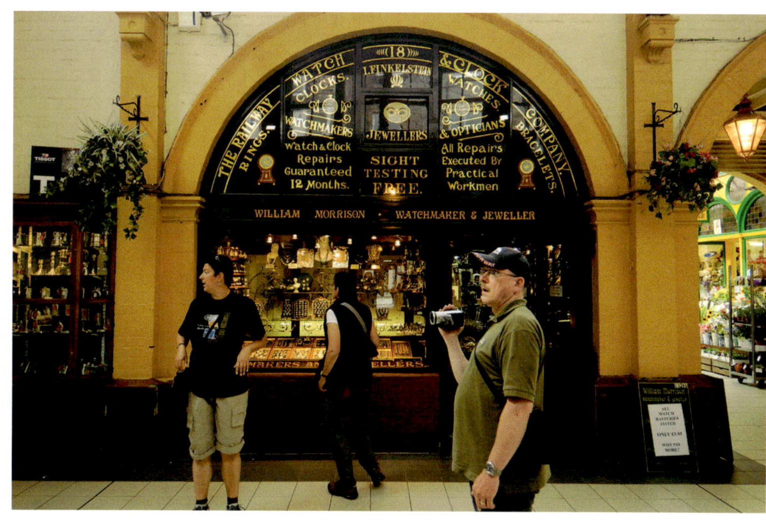

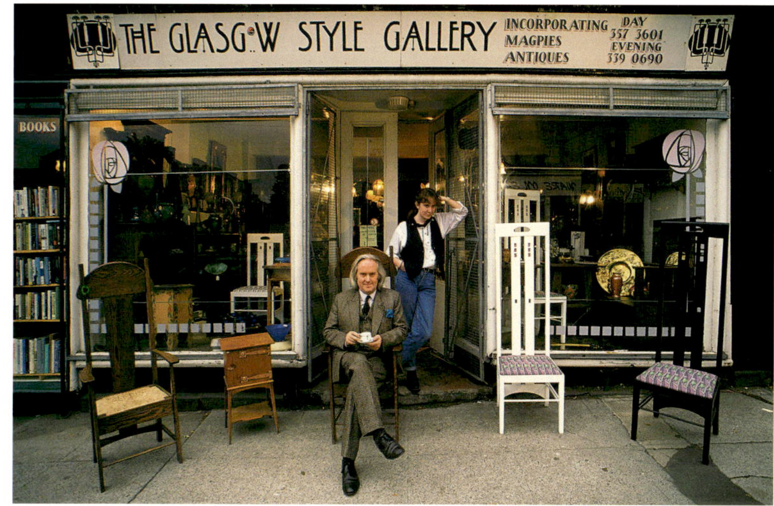

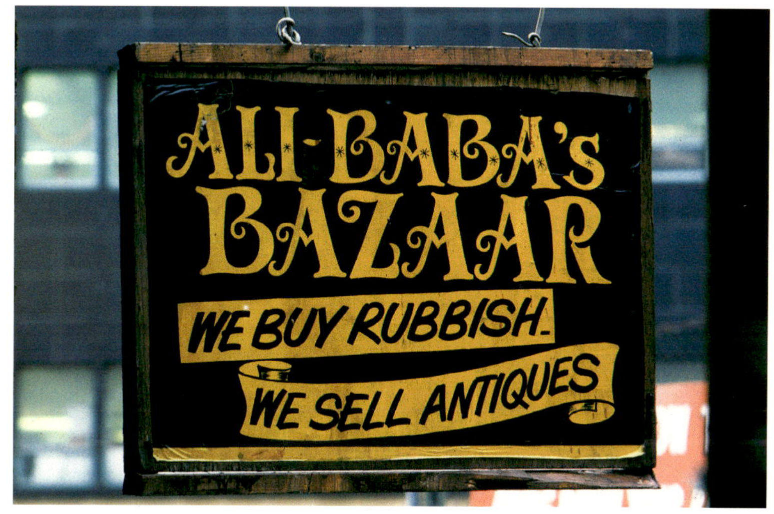

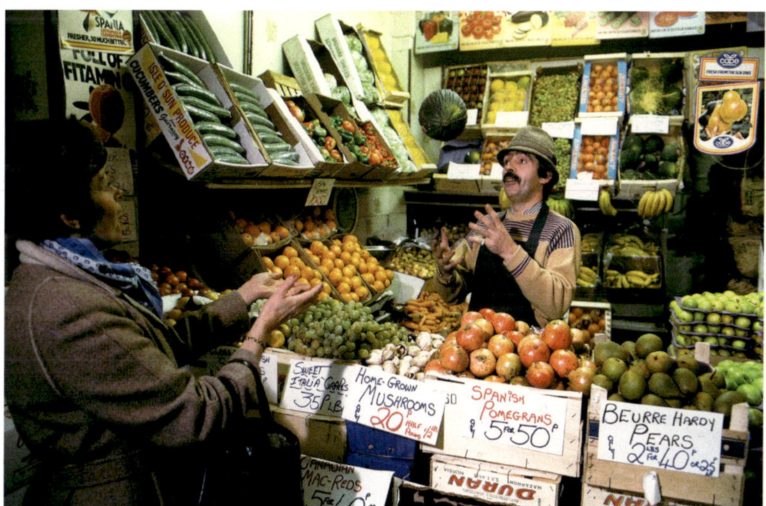

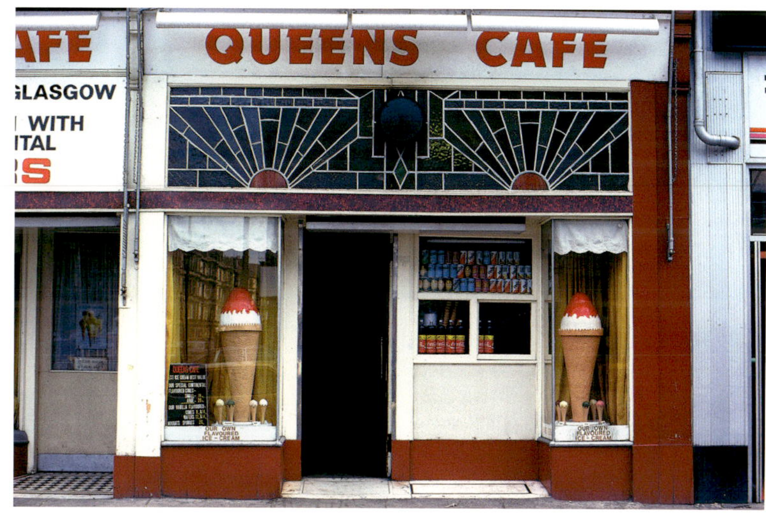

(Top right) I was innocently snapping this wonderful shopfront in Inverness Arcade when I was approached by a police officer who said, 'Photographing the jeweller's shop, sir?' I thought, 'Here we go again.' See my introduction, page 10. From left to right, top to bottom: Edinburgh; Inverness; Glasgow; Glasgow; Glasgow; Glasgow.

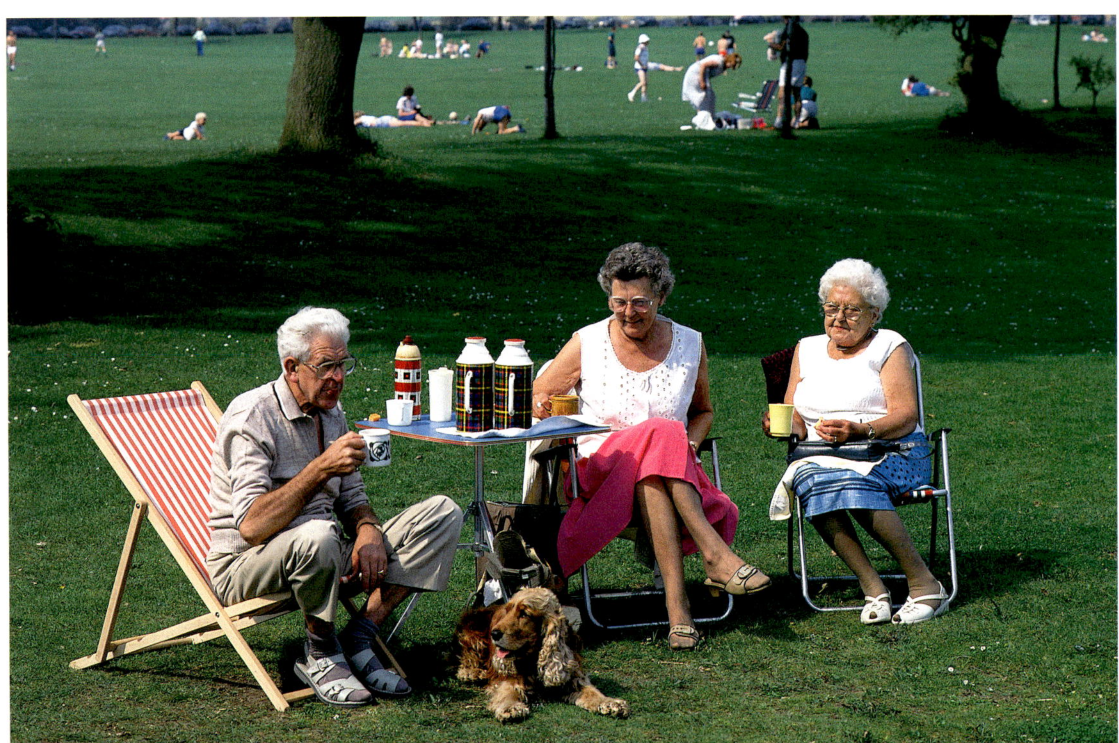

Two contrasting picnics in Fife: the one on the right, Burntisland Links with tartan flasks, is more my cup of tea. The equestrian event below, where the fare was of the order of caviar, quails' eggs and Bollinger, is still a wee bit out of my league.

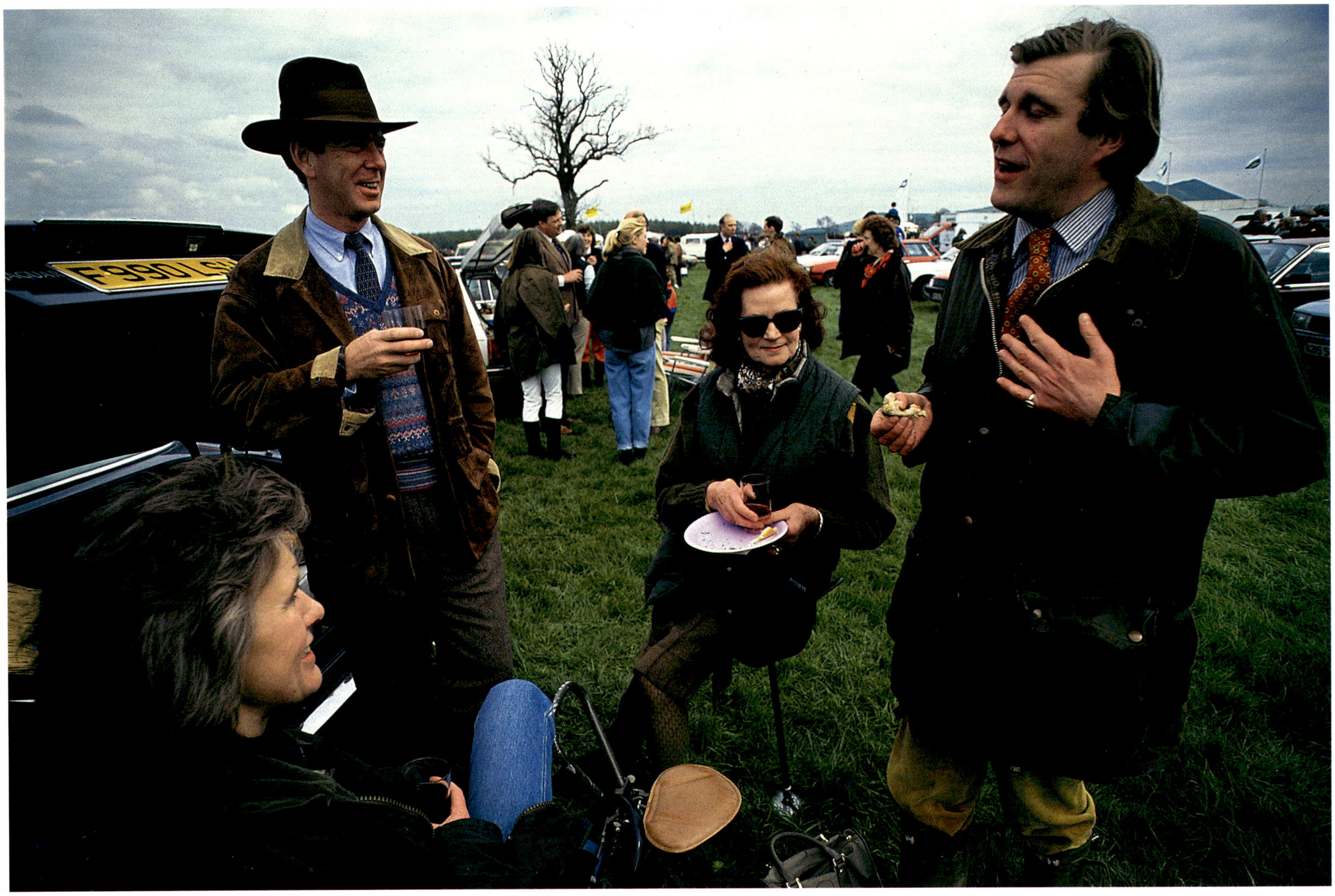

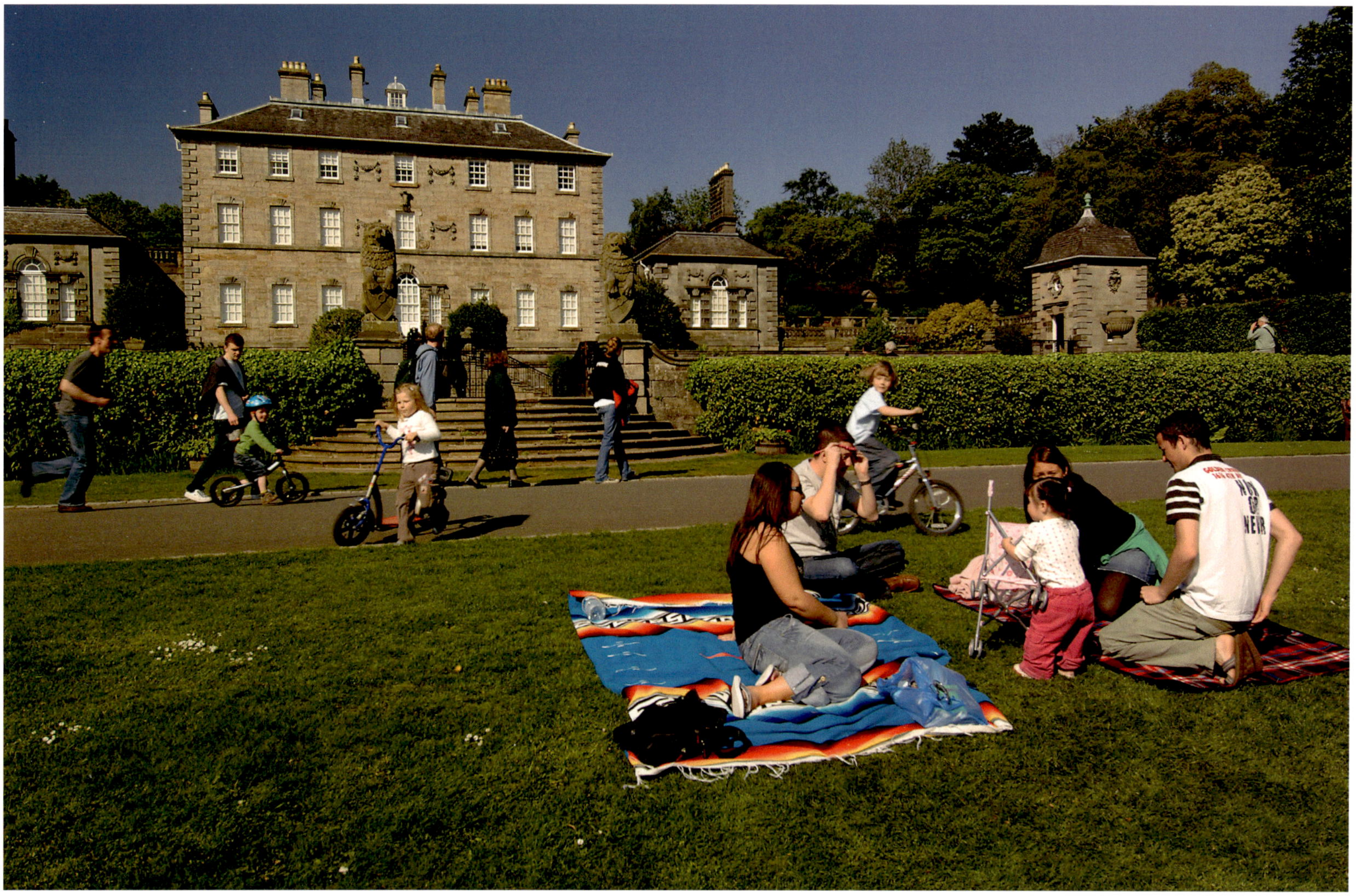

Glasgow, known as 'the Dear, Green Place', certainly lives up to its name with its many fine parks. Pollok Country Park, voted Best Park in Europe in 2008, is outstanding and includes the magnificent Burrell Collection. Pollok House, an 18th-century mansion designed by William Adam and contained within the park, is a backdrop to Glasgow folk making full use of a sunny Sunday afternoon. The house and grounds were gifted to the city by the Stirling Maxwell family in 1966.

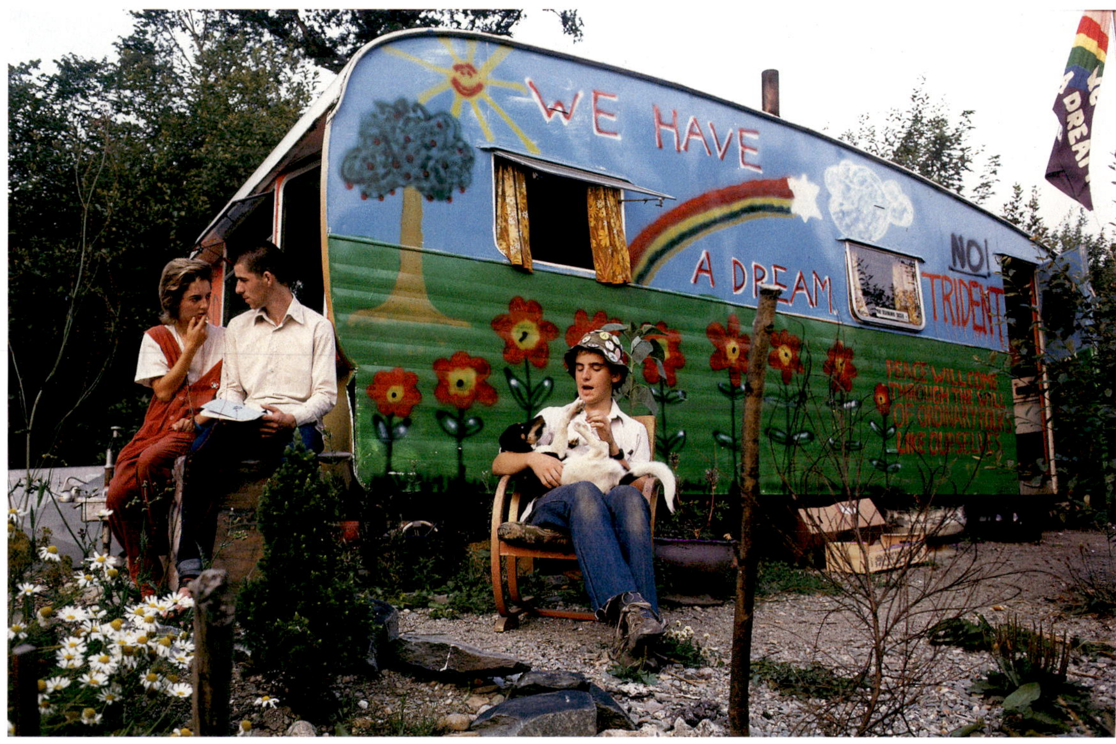

The message of peace and the prevention of the proliferation of nuclear weapons still goes on at Faslane Naval Base near Helensburgh.

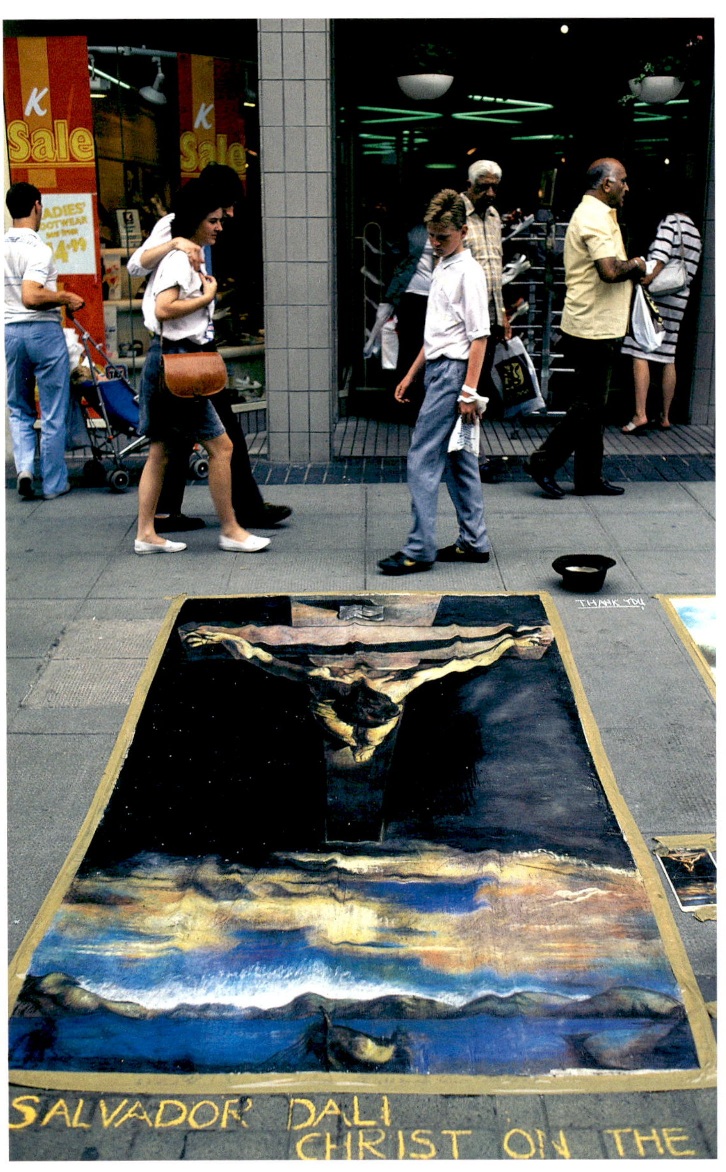

A 'pavement art' version of Salvador Dalí's *Christ of St John of the Cross* in Buchanan Street, Glasgow. The real thing was bought by the city of Glasgow for £8,200 in 1952. The price was considered a lot at the time, but the Spanish government was reported by the *Sunday Herald* to have offered £8,000,000 early in this millennium. It hangs in the Glasgow Art Gallery and Museum at Kelvingrove.

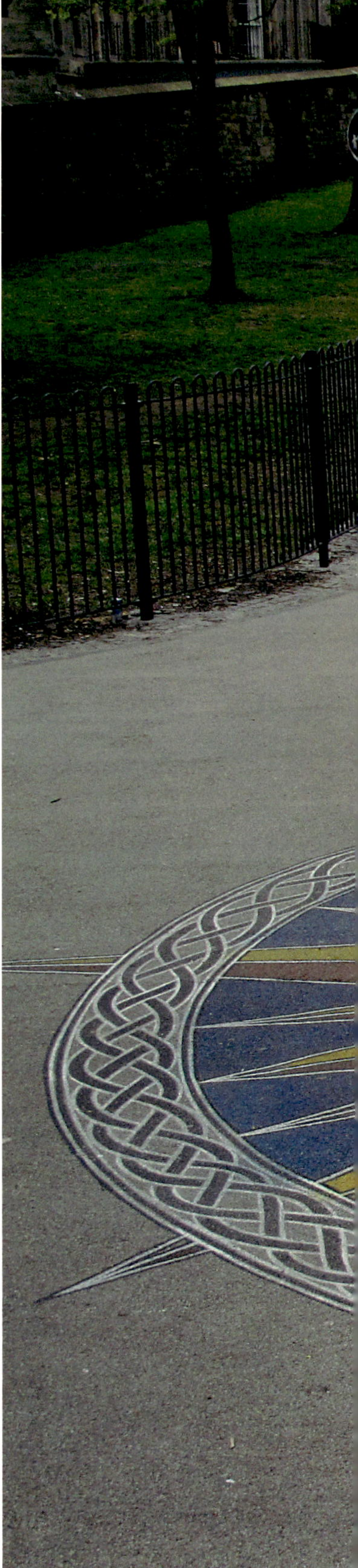

Painted on the back of Glasgow's Western Baths in 2009 is a piece of graffiti that to me shows the exuberance of the city. Sadly, part of it is obscured by wheelie bins. Some graffiti is good and could be considered as a community mural. This is not to be confused with the indiscriminate, moronic spraying on fine stonework and public transport.

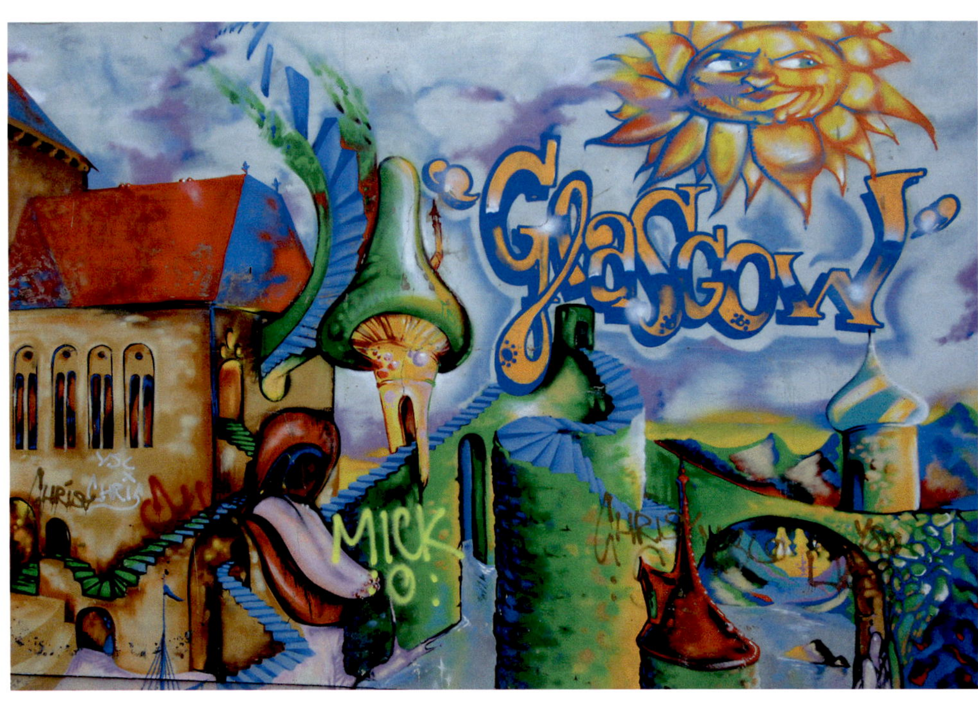

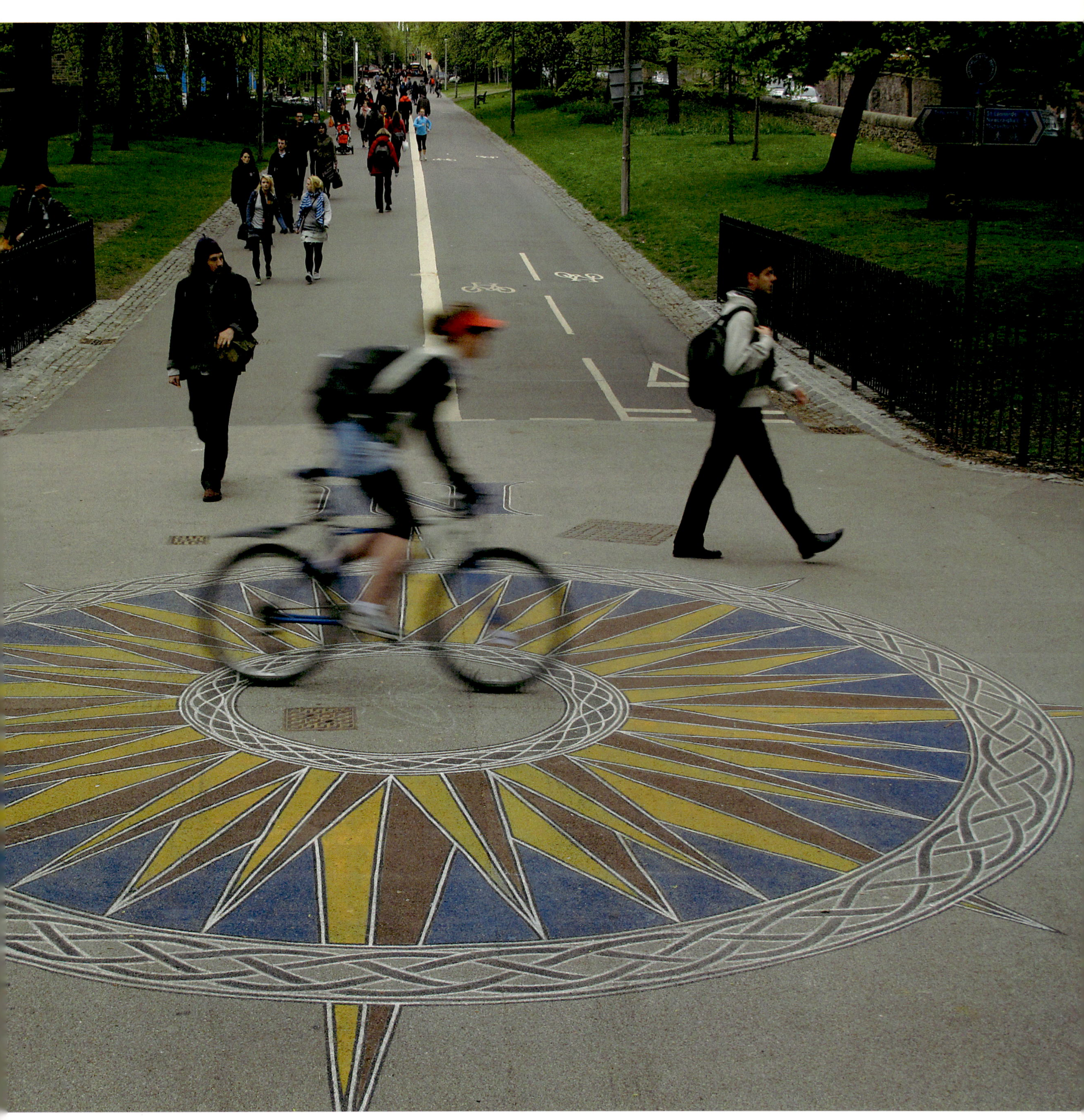

A recent picture taken not far from where I live beside the Meadows in Edinburgh. The work by Victor Fraser, a Canadian street artist, miraculously survived a week of charging cyclists. Cycle paths are a sensible addition to our parks, but when you are confronted by four bikes abreast and ten deep of joggers it all becomes a bit hazardous.

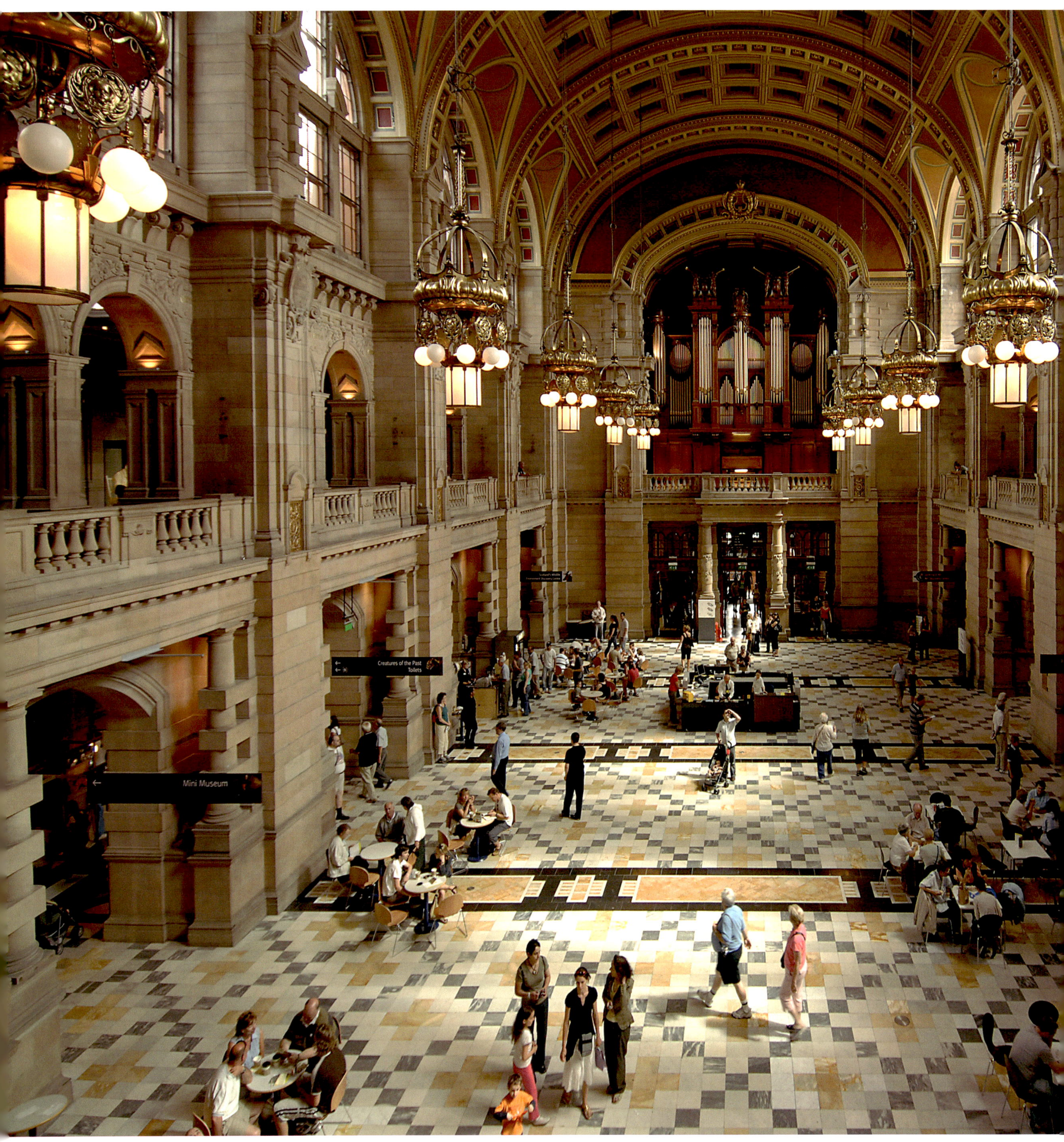

The refurbishment of the Glasgow Art Gallery and Museum at Kelvingrove in the mid-2000s has brought the magnificent interior back to life. Built in 1901, the building houses a superb collection of art and objects. No museum or gallery I have ever visited is so wholly embraced by its citizens, and there is no aloofness or elitism. To see people spell-bound by a free recital on the great organ in the main hall gives you a lift, which is the whole point.

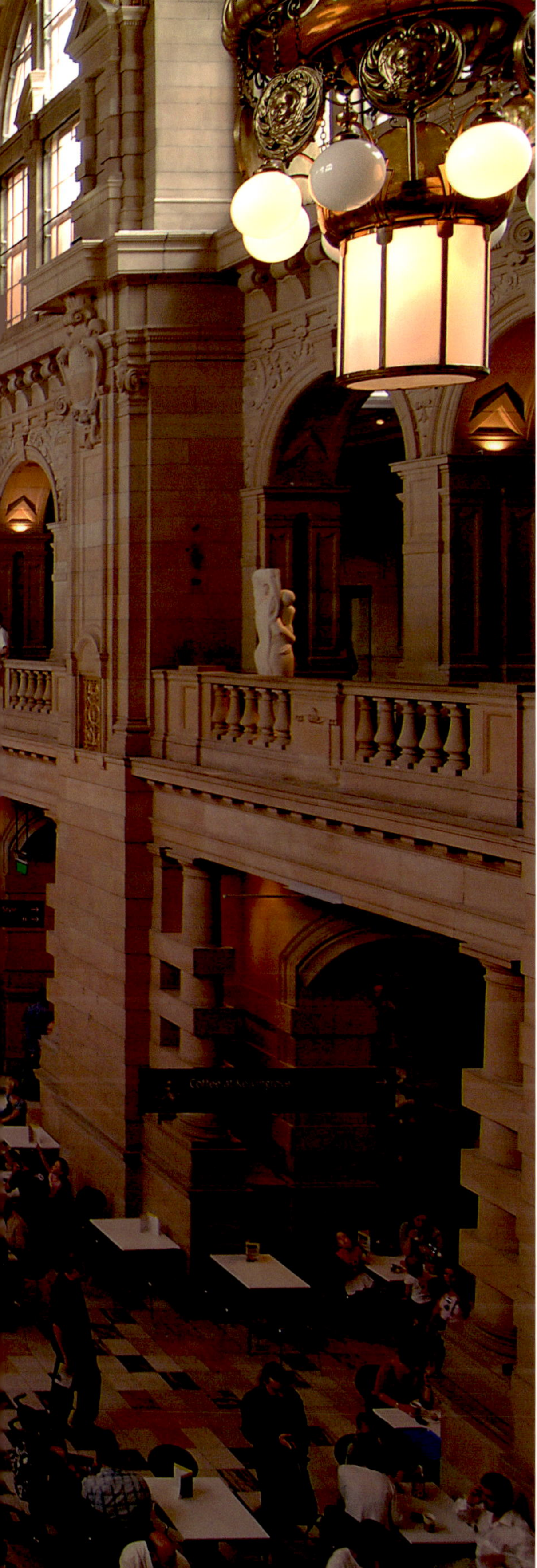

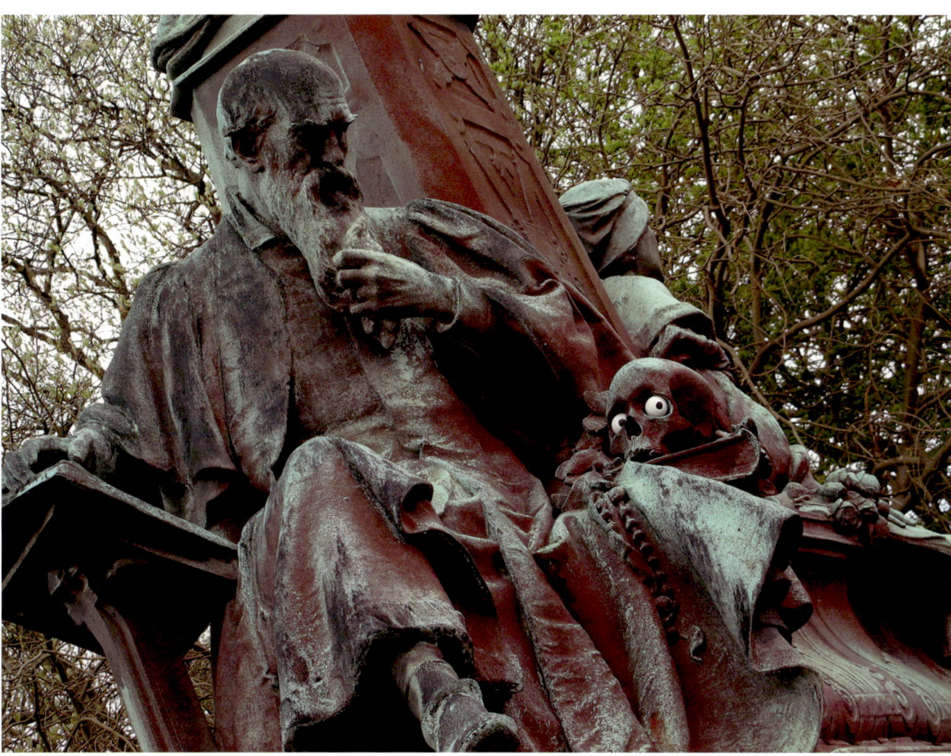

Did the prankster who first put a traffic cone on top of an equestrian statue ever realise how boring this would become? Using customised ping-pong balls shows a spark of originality and humour on the bridge over the River Kelvin at Kelvingrove. This statue of Philosophy and Inspiration is one of several statues I have scaled to find a new angle on a familiar scene, often followed by a warning from the police, but I normally have achieved my picture by then.

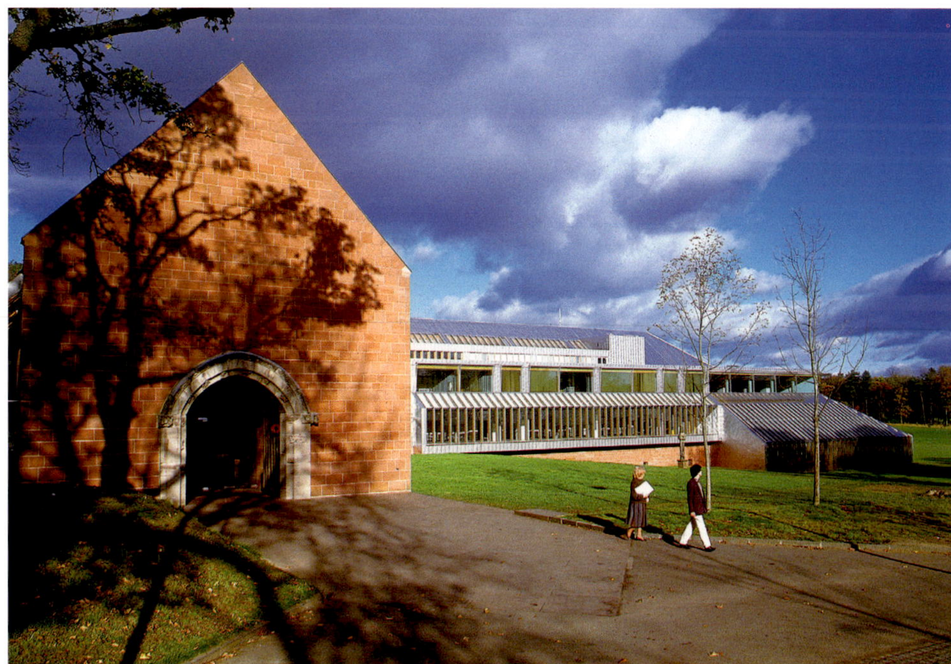

The Burrell Collection in Pollok Park, Glasgow, is an eclectic mix of sculpture, paintings, tapestries, ceramics, Jacobean interiors, and the list goes on, of which only a quarter can be on show at any one time, and adds to Glasgow's wealth of museums and art galleries. Sir William Burrell, a wealthy shipowner, donated his collection to the city in 1944, and finally housed in 1983. He amassed his fortune by ordering ships cheaply during periods of depression and making large profits when the market recovered, including selling to the government during the First World War.

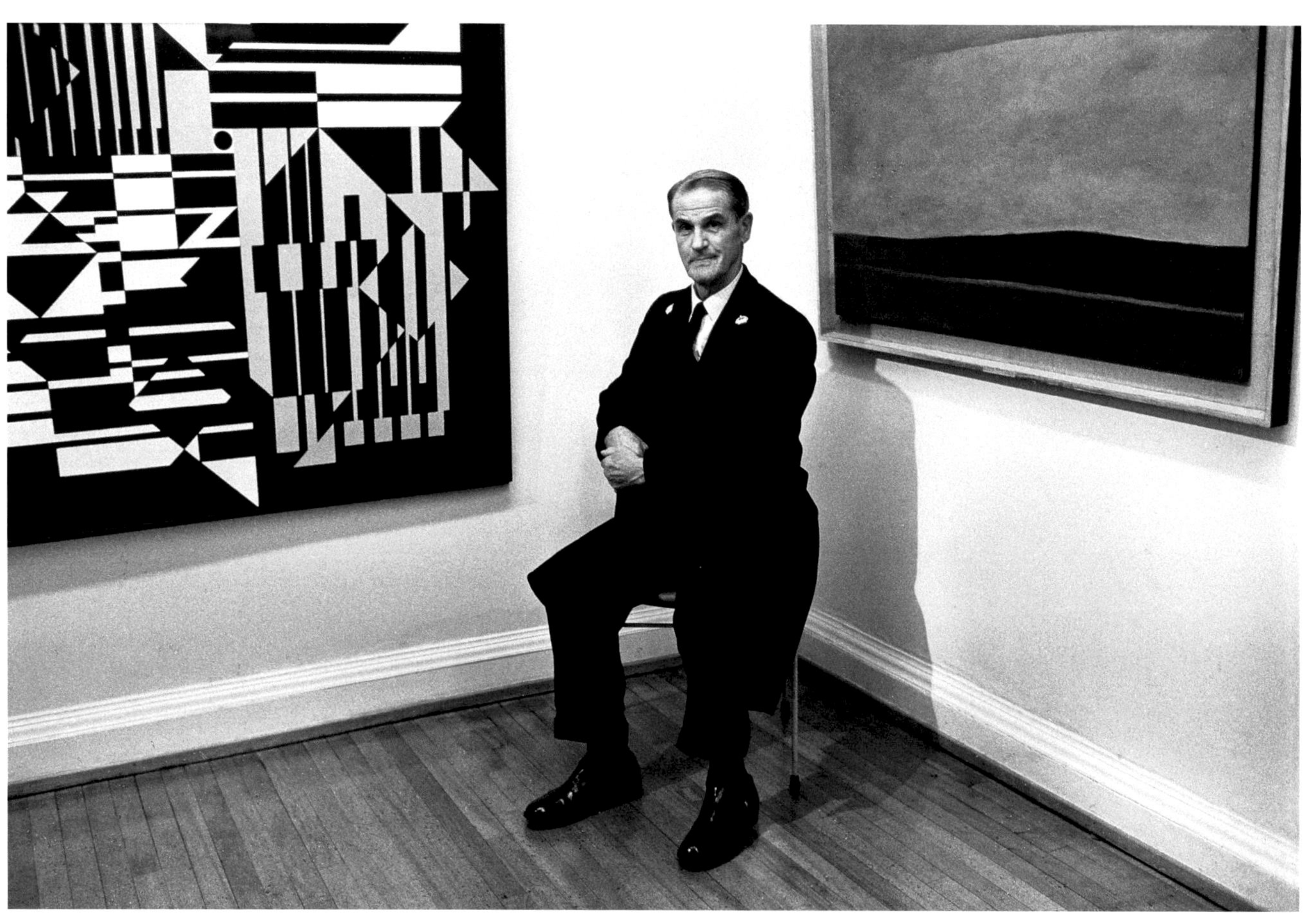

The above shot was taken in the 1970s when the Gallery of Modern Art in Edinburgh was in Inverleith House in the Royal Botanic Gardens and before the wardens were attired in questionable tartan trousers. (Below) A Henry Moore sculpture in the Royal Botanic Gardens, framing Edinburgh's classic skyline. The artist's forms seem to be inspired by the natural erosion of wind and water. I enjoy the gardens at any time of year.

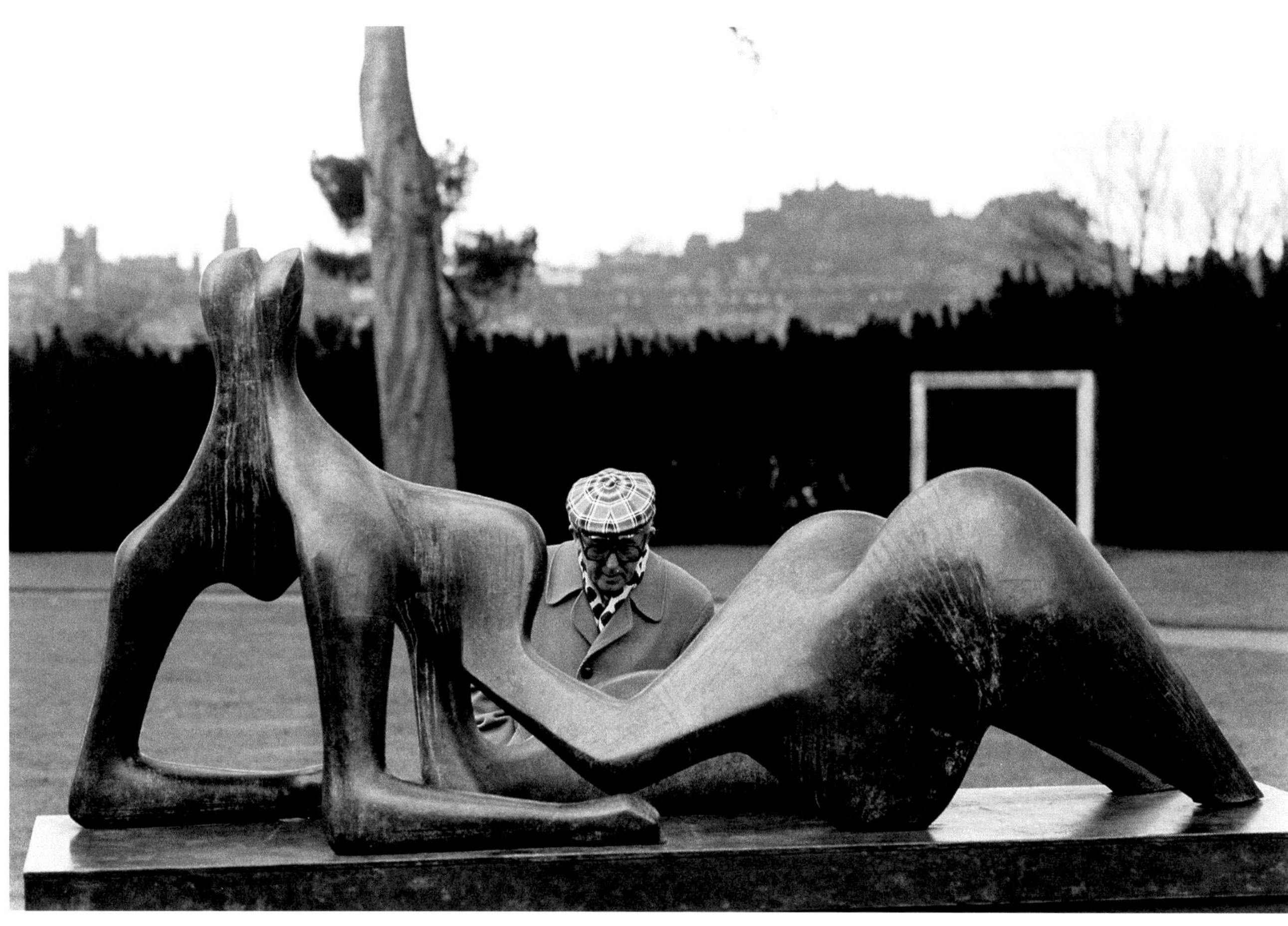

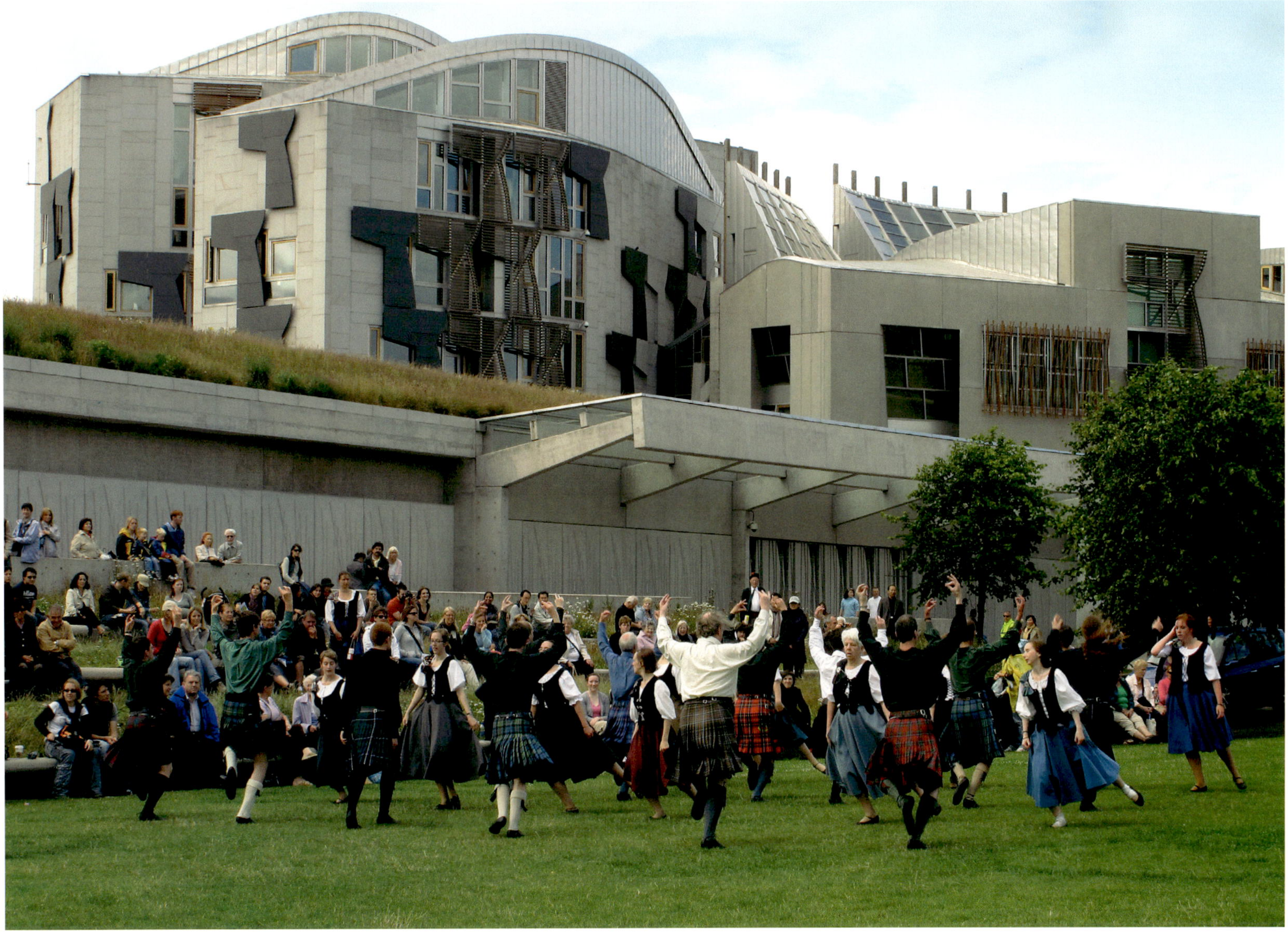

We are told that most great buildings are ahead of the public and that we have to learn to grow into them. Will this be the case with Catalan architect Enric Miralles's 2004 Scottish Parliament building in Edinburgh? Some people think the motifs on the exterior were inspired by Henry Raeburn's *The Reverend Walker skating on Duddingston Loch*. Others liken them to anvils, hairdryers and even hammers and sickles. I don't know how easily traditional Scottish country dancing lies with this façade.

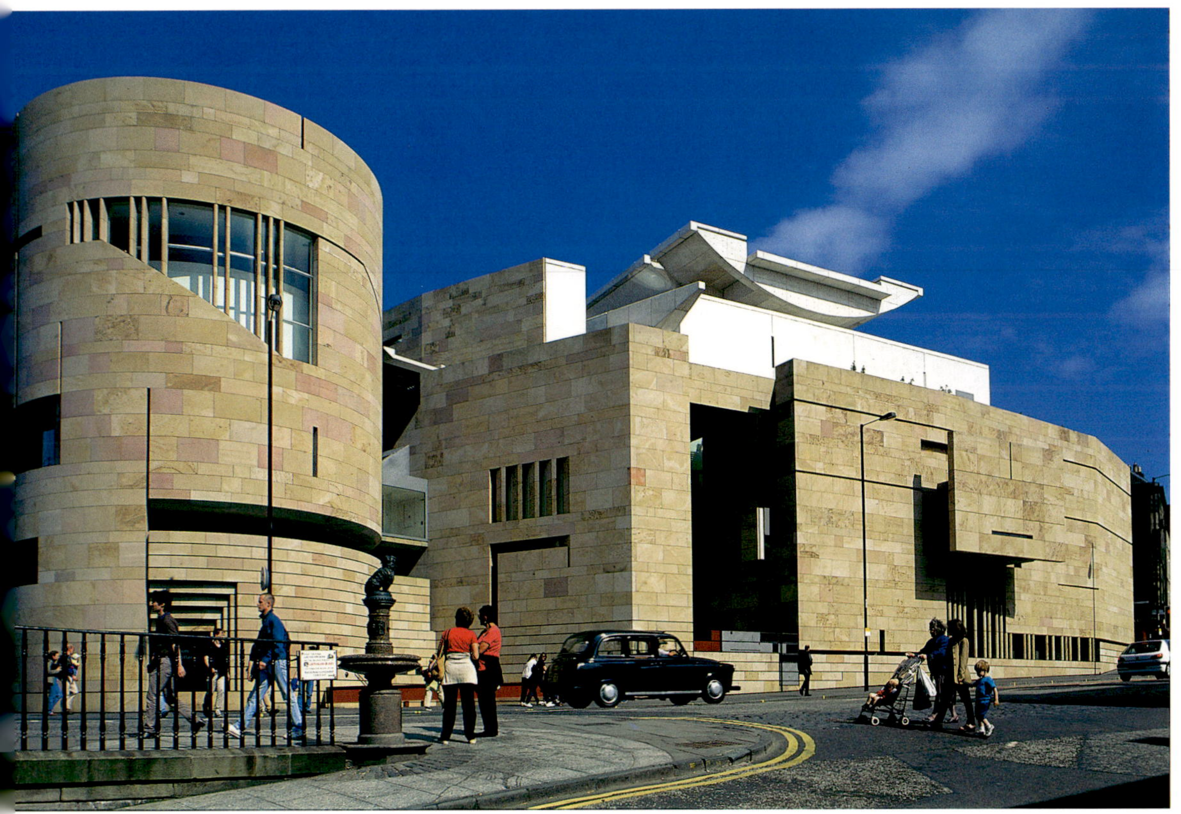

Greyfriars' Bobby dwarfed by the 1998 National Museum of Scotland in Edinburgh. The faithful dog was given the freedom of the city and immortalised by Walt Disney. On a visit from Inverness, my mother was incensed to find vandals had poured yellow paint over the statue. It took all my persuasion to stop her taking a scrubbing brush and turpentine to it. I wouldn't have given the perpetrators much hope had my mother caught them in the act.

Mercifully, the Forth Rail Bridge was free of scaffolding when I photographed Bill Stein, the oldest disabled English Channel swimmer, in the 1980s. It was November, and in order to get this angle I was up to my chest in the Firth of Forth – I didn't have a wetsuit so it was a bit chilly. An acquaintance who witnessed my endeavours during her Sunday walk commented, 'I knew you went to great lengths to get a picture but this is ridiculous.'

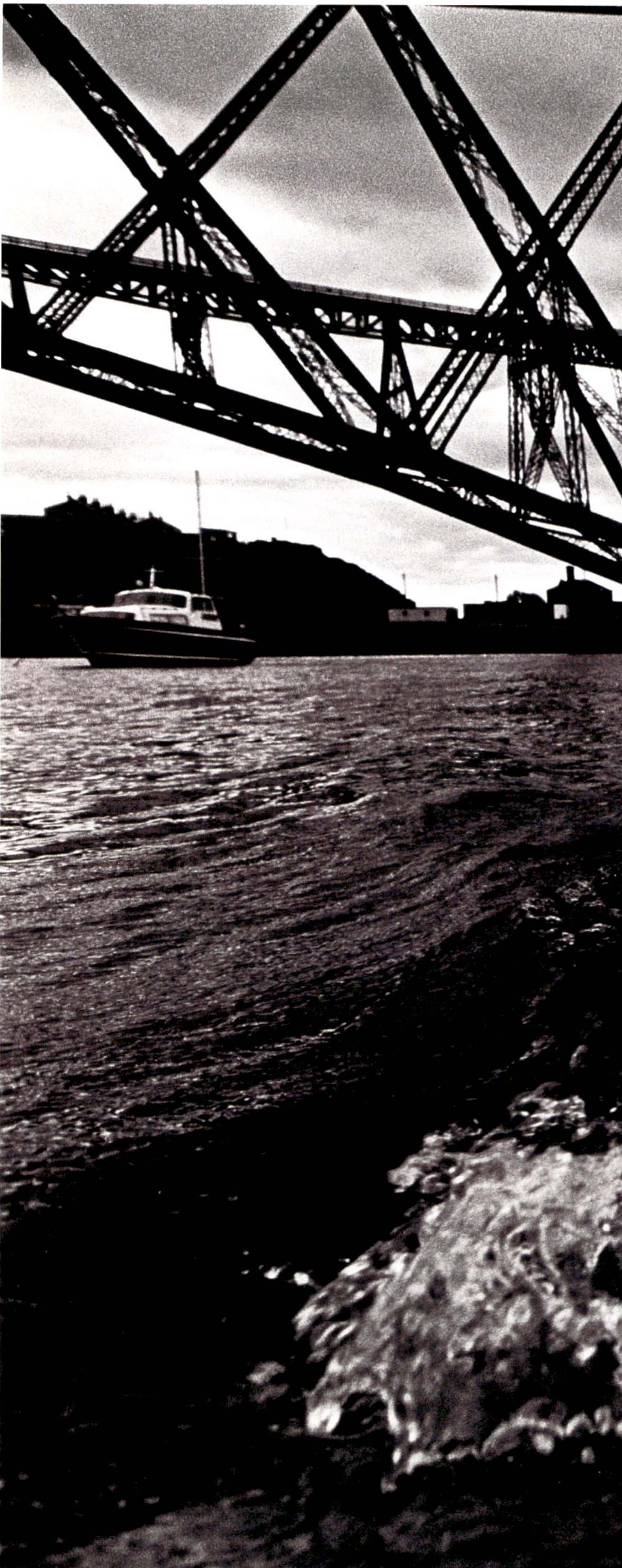

Glasgow University Rowing Team has a Saturday morning practice on the Clyde in the 1980s.

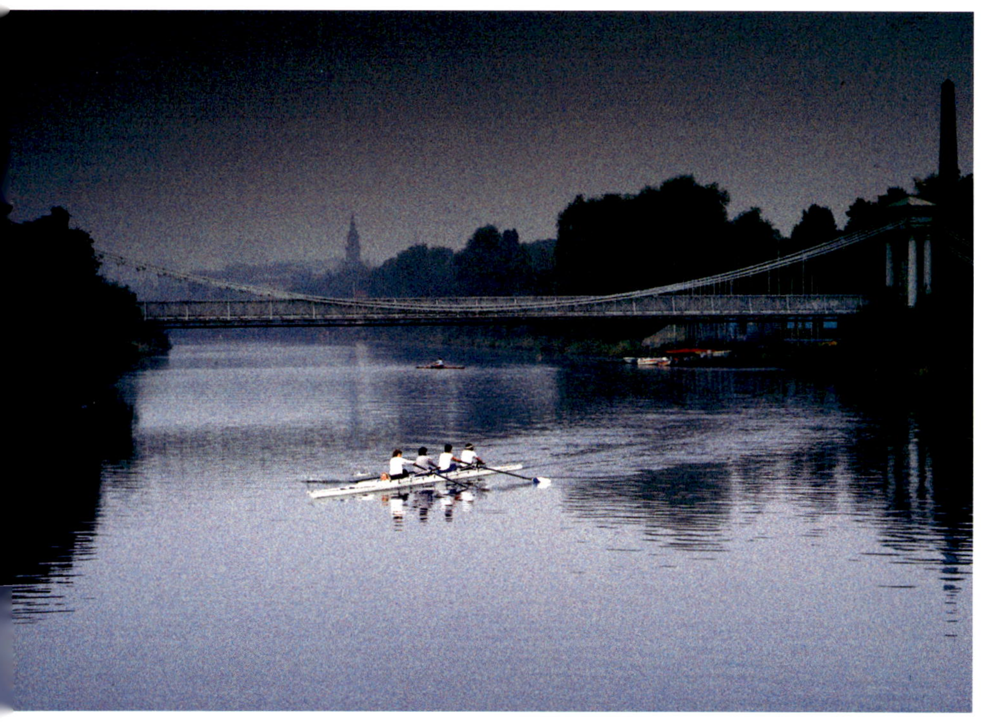

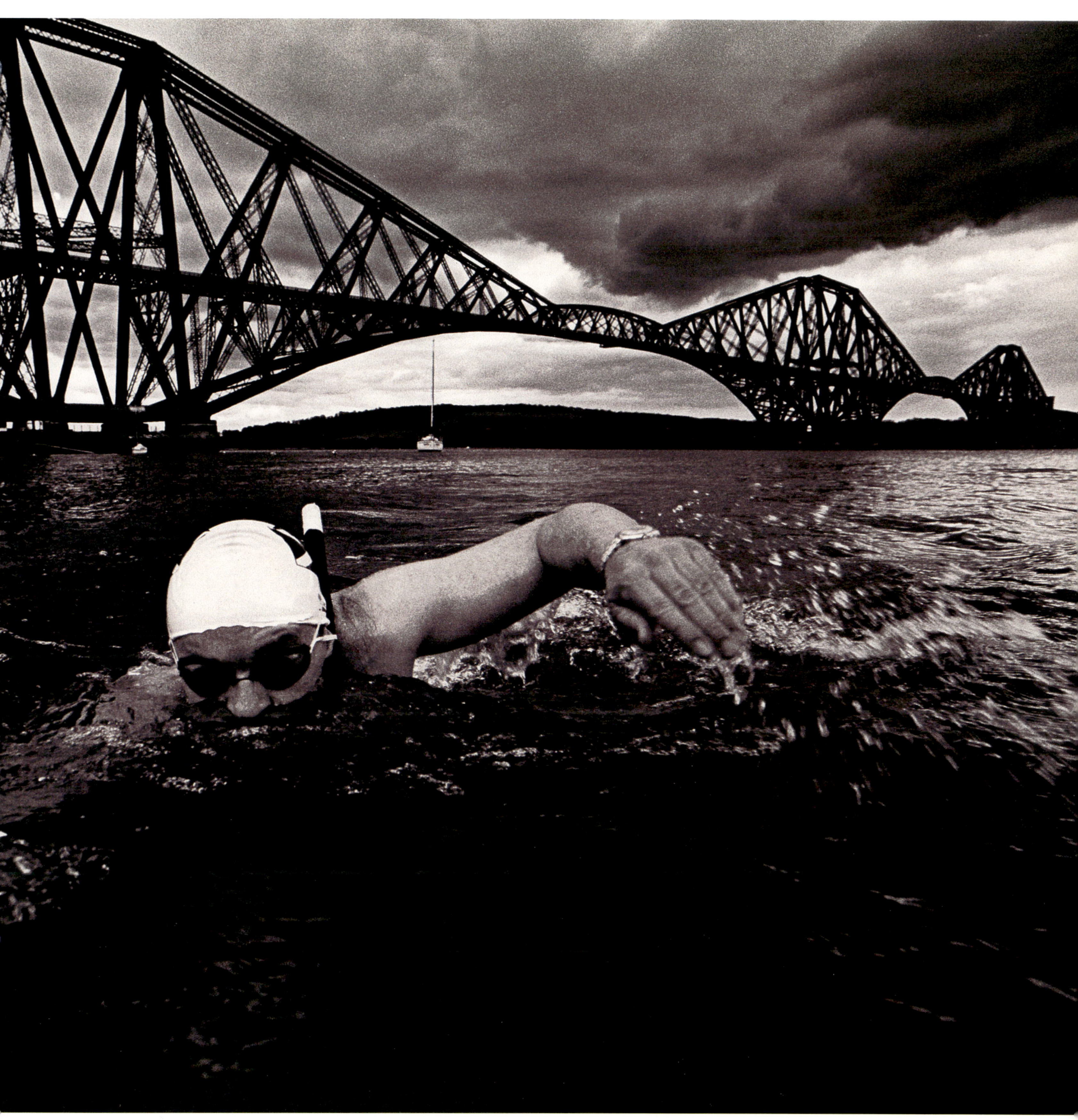

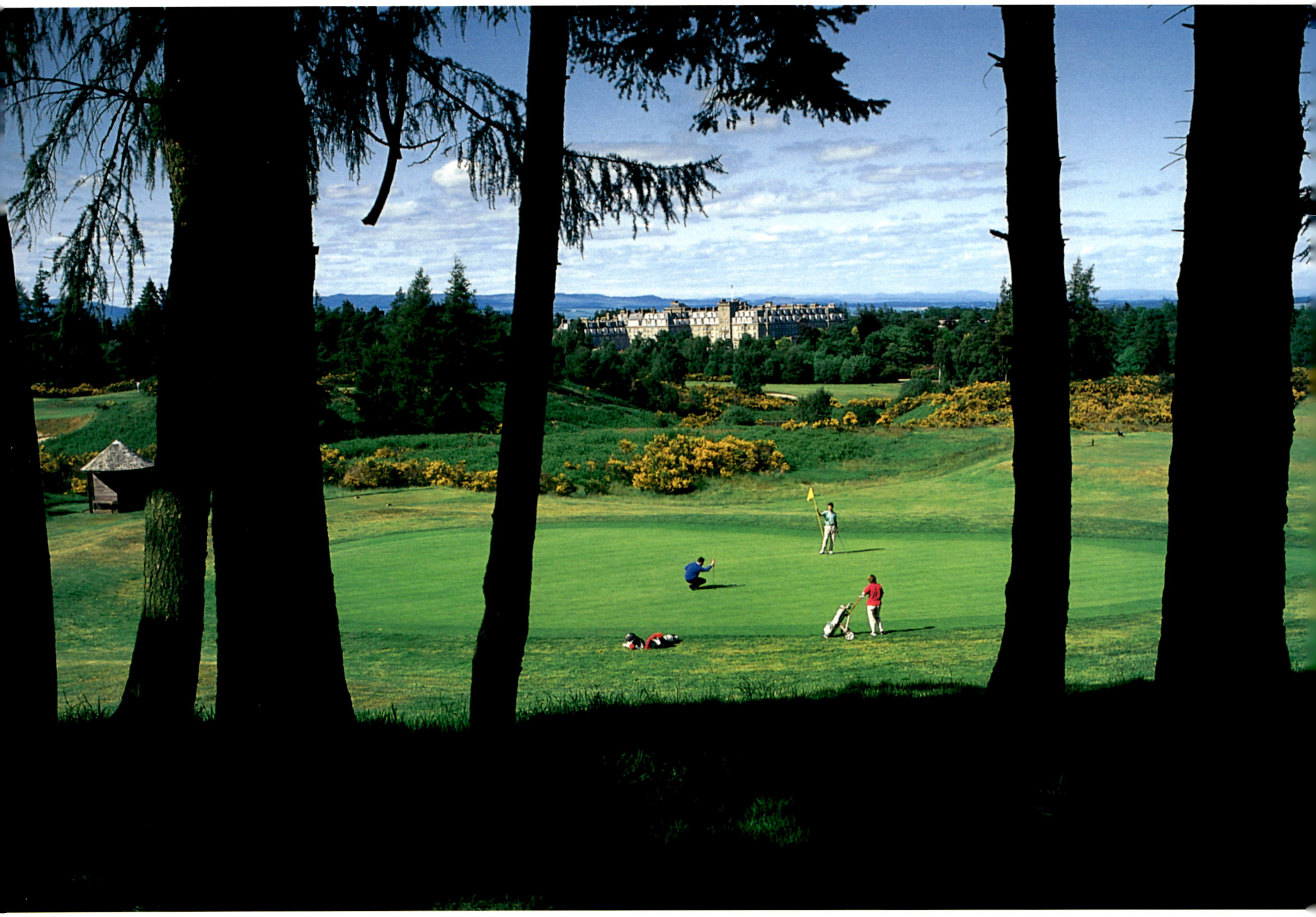

If I was ever to take up golf, then the beautifully scenic course at Gleneagles might tempt me. That's if I could afford the five-star prices. I once had to receive an award at the famous hotel, which occurred on the same day as a pro-am golf tournament. Seated beside me was my editor, Clare Crawford, and between us we had counted thirteen celebrities, such as Terry Wogan, Bruce Forsyth and Sean Connery, when I said to Clare, 'Behind you! Dracula!' and looming behind her was Christopher Lee.

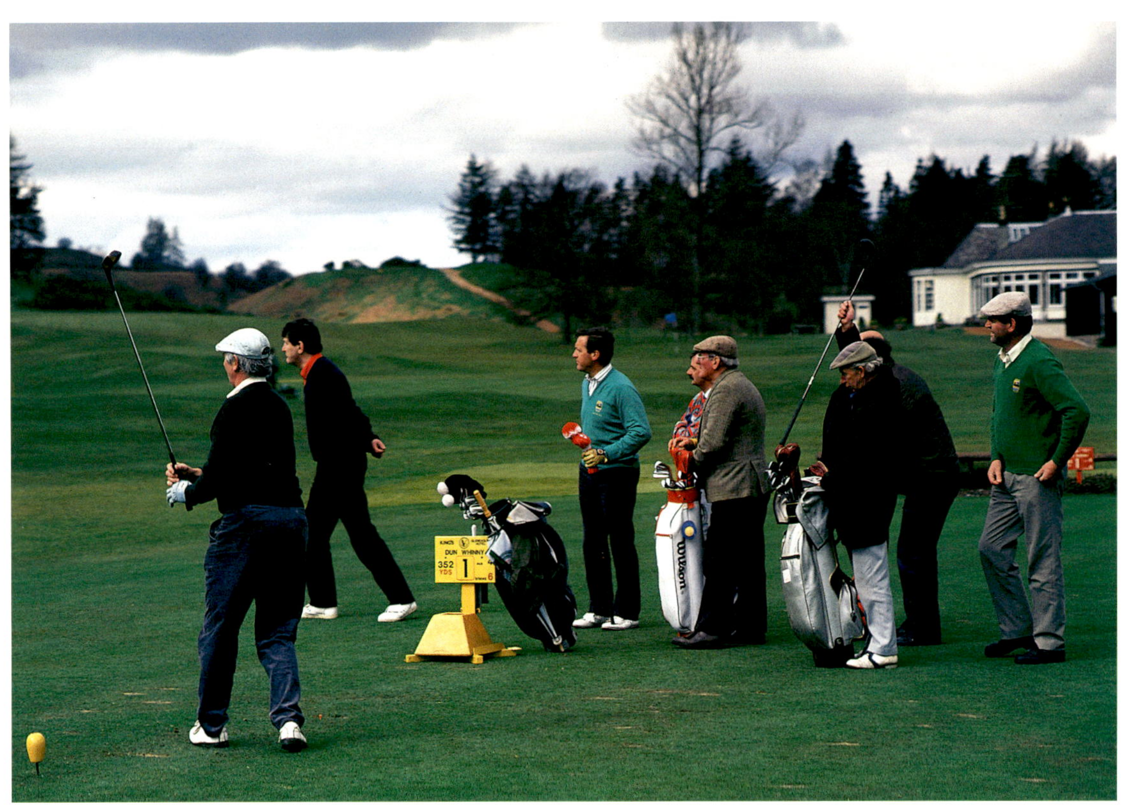

Golfers at Gleneagles get a richer experience when using caddies, who impart an intimate knowledge of the course and the surrounding area. You don't get advice from an electric caddie or a buggy.

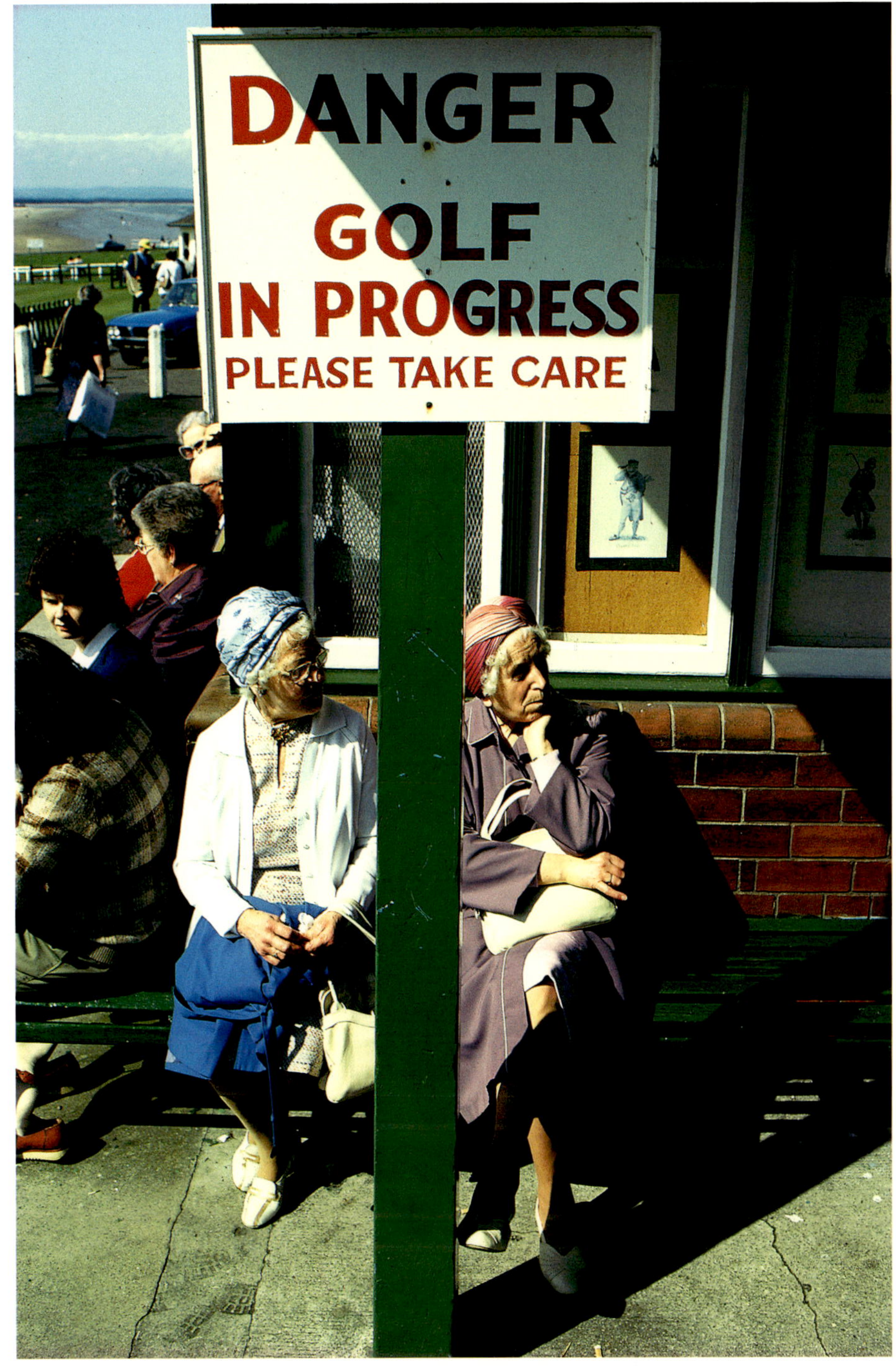

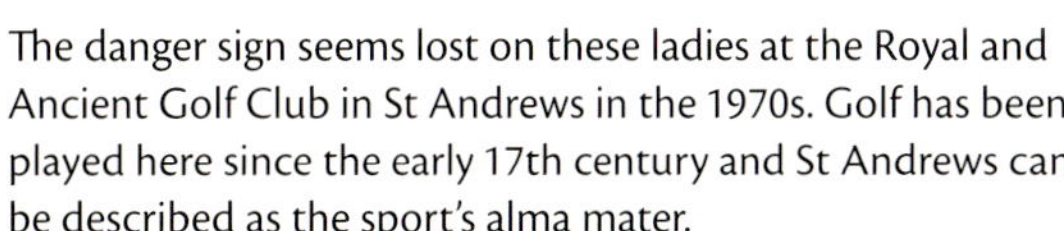
The danger sign seems lost on these ladies at the Royal and Ancient Golf Club in St Andrews in the 1970s. Golf has been played here since the early 17th century and St Andrews can be described as the sport's alma mater.

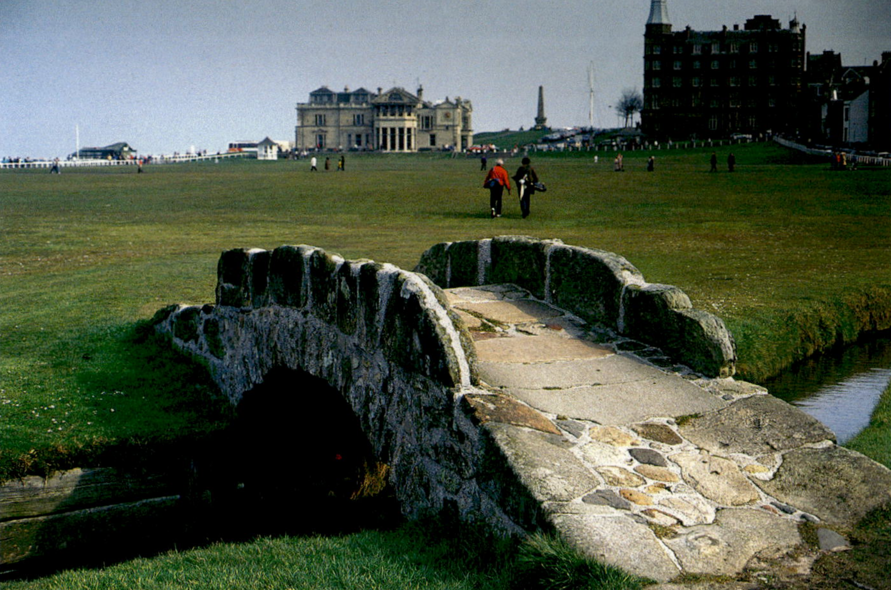

The Swilcan Bridge on St Andrews Old Course could well be the most famous small bridge in the world. I was thinking of a caption when I picked up the *Scotsman* newspaper, which had a picture of Tom Watson, the retiring five-time winner of the British Open, kissing it goodbye.

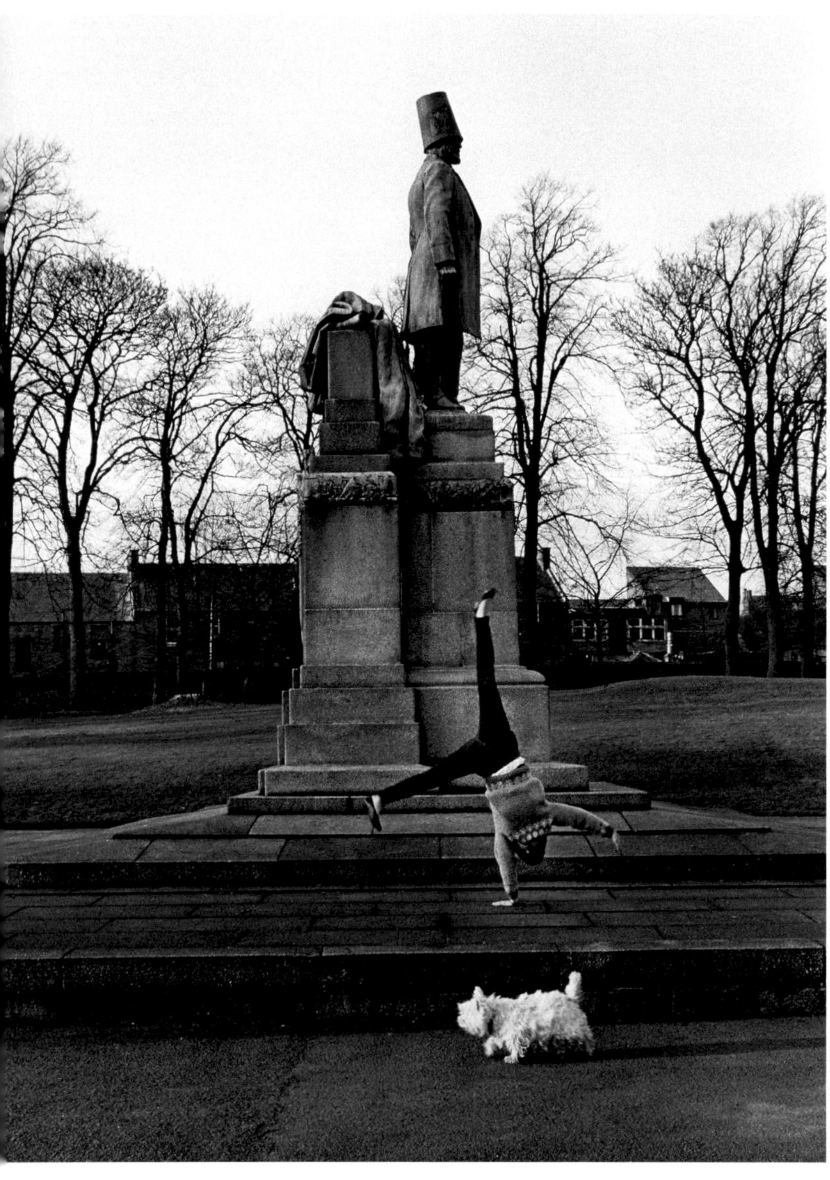

Andrew Carnegie's statue in Pittencrieff Glen, Dunfermline. At one time he was the world's richest man, his fortune generated by his steelworks in the United States. He wasn't always honourable in his dealings with his workers, but he did improve his reputation by building 2,509 public libraries internationally along with this park in his native town.

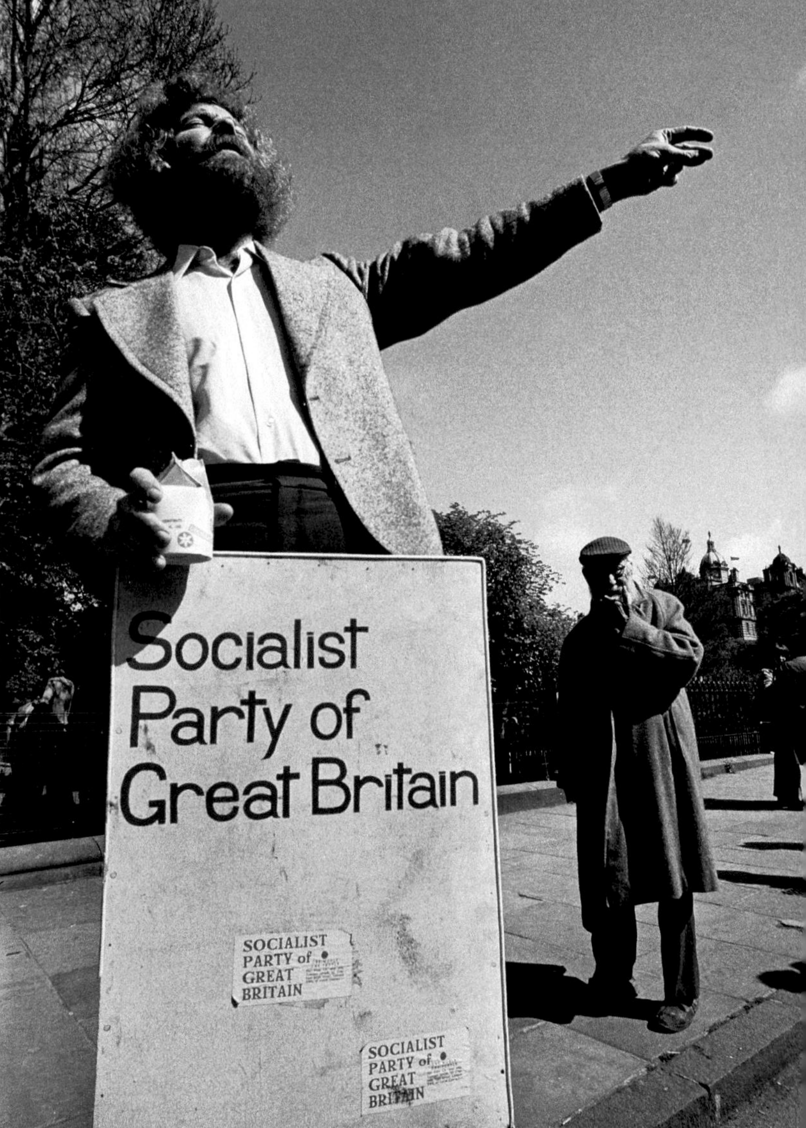

The Mound in Edinburgh was as close as the city got to having a Speakers' Corner in the 1970s. It is now more frequently used by buskers and the ubiquitous hairbraiders, face-painters and sellers of ethnic jewellery. Apart from his animation, this figure bears a resemblance to Karl Marx's memorial in Highgate Cemetery in London.

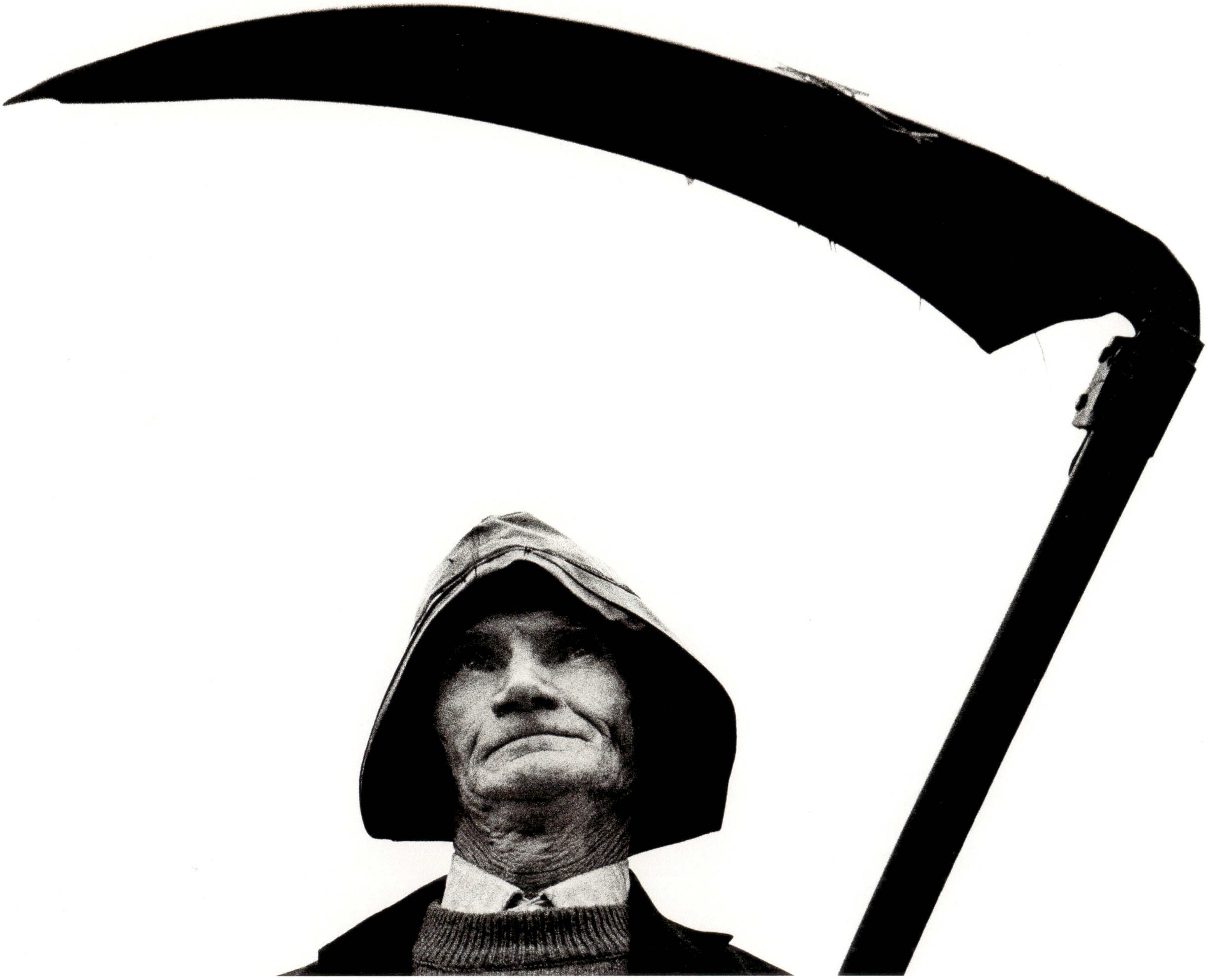

A local authority gardener cutting the grass at Kilmartin graveyard in Argyll. Although this image was taken in the 1980s, it has an almost medieval look that wouldn't be out of place in a film by the great Swedish director Ingmar Bergman, who has always been a source of inspiration to me.

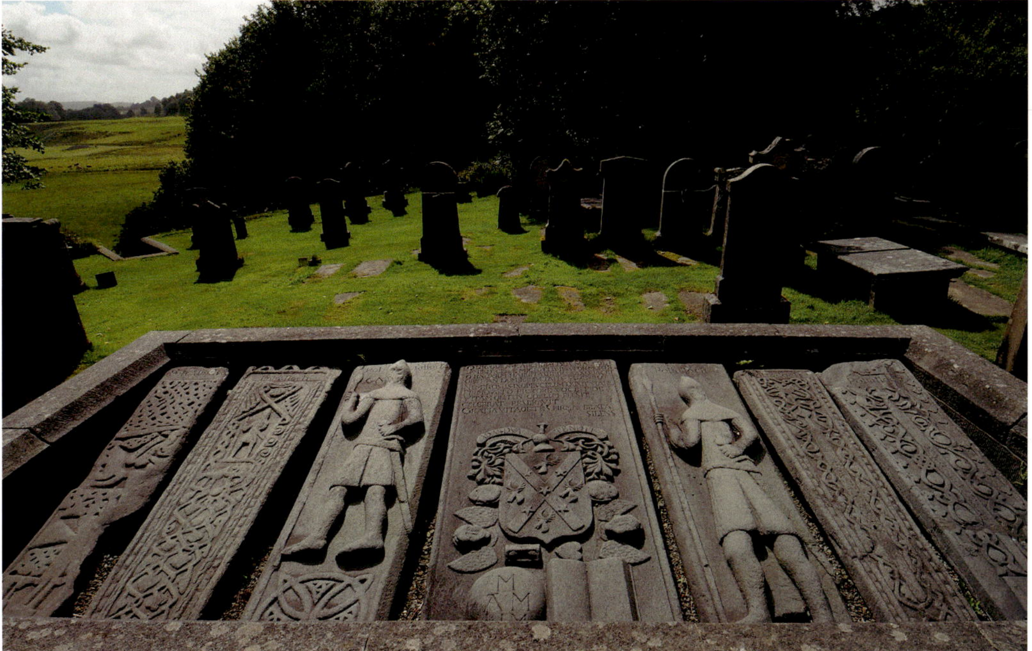

Kilmartin Churchyard, Argyll, is home to the famous Kilmartin Cross. These richly carved grave slabs show warriors dating from between the 14th and the 16th centuries and to me evoke an image of knights and chivalry that seems almost Arthurian. Nearby are chambered cairns and various groups of Bronze Age cup and ring-marked rocks.

Lord Cockburn wrote, in 1849, a letter to the Lord Provost about the best ways of spoiling the beauty of Edinburgh. Cockburn was a serious pain in the neck to all who, through ignorance, apathy, vanity or greed, threatened the unique beauty and character of his beloved city. He disapproved of the view from the west of the Castle, showing the tenement-like structure of the barracks. What would he have thought of some of the more recent additions to the city? The low light subdues the incongruous 1960s' office block on the right.

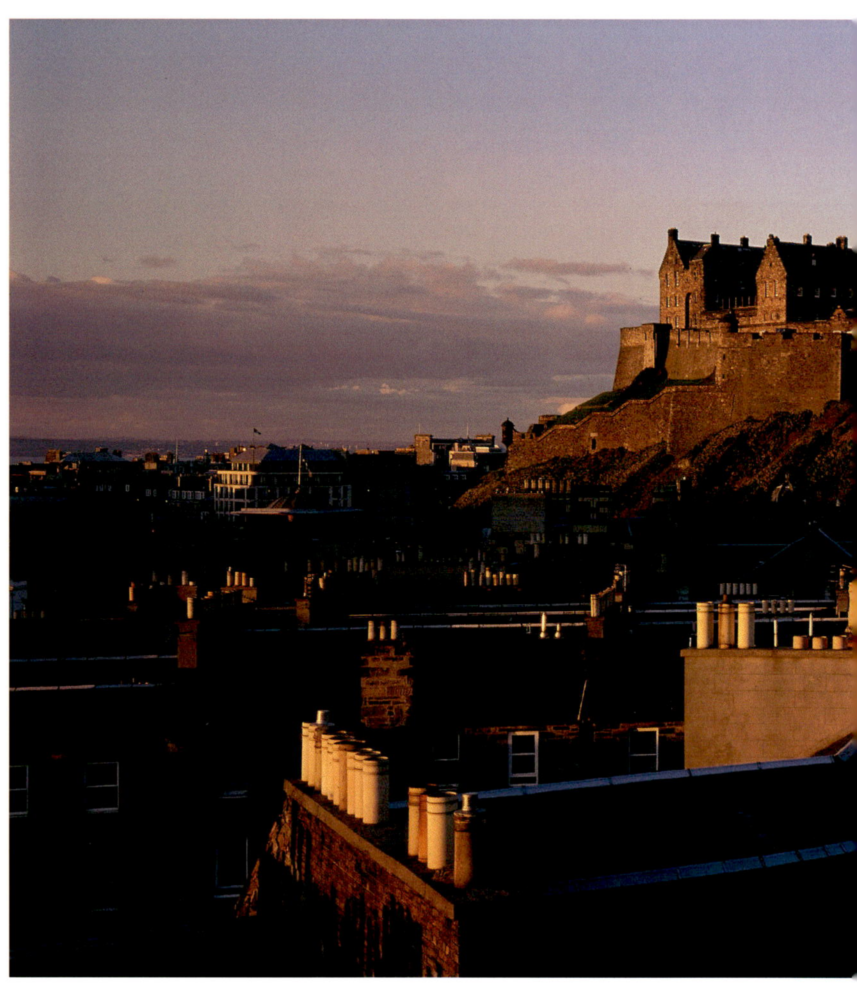

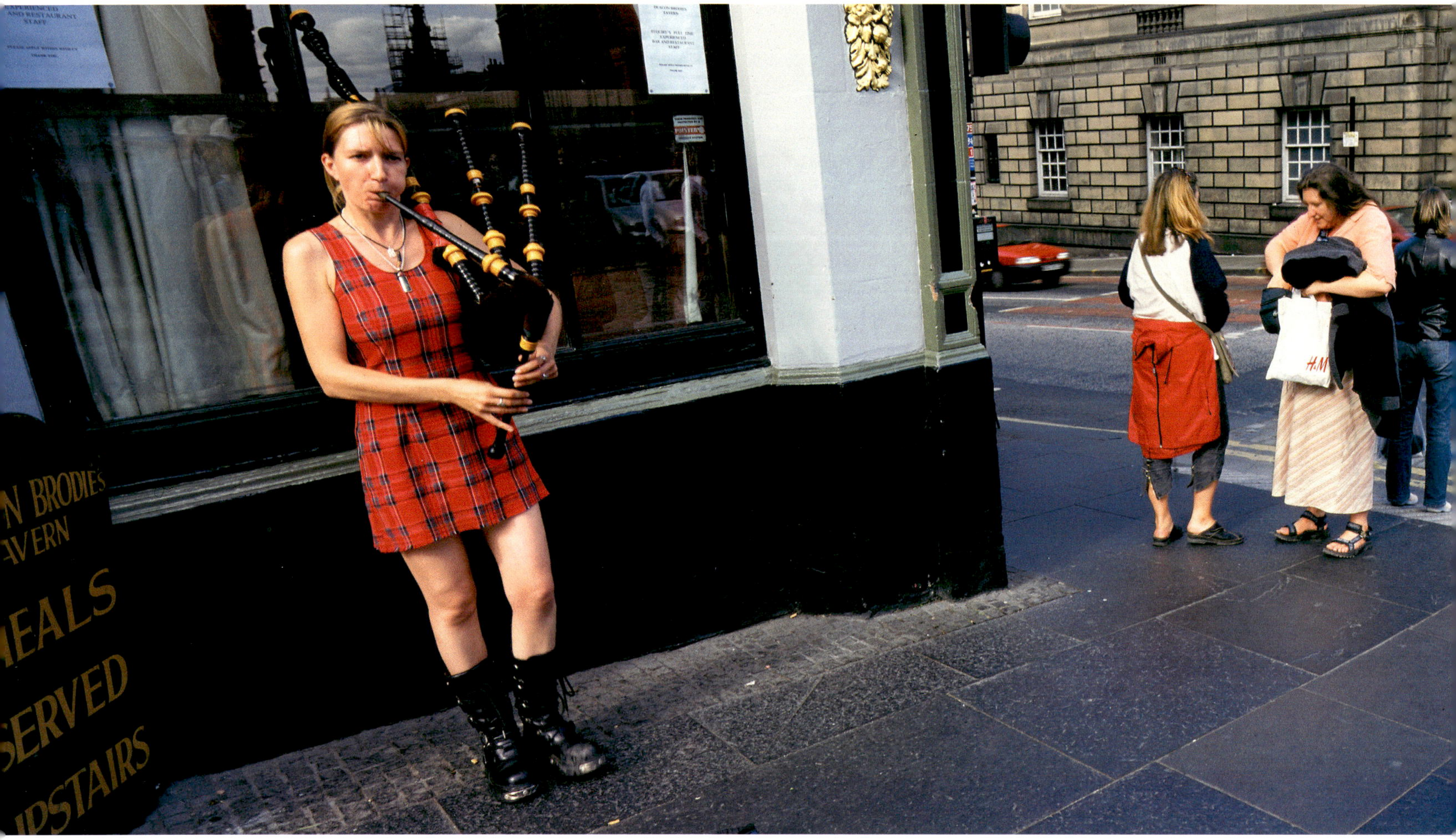

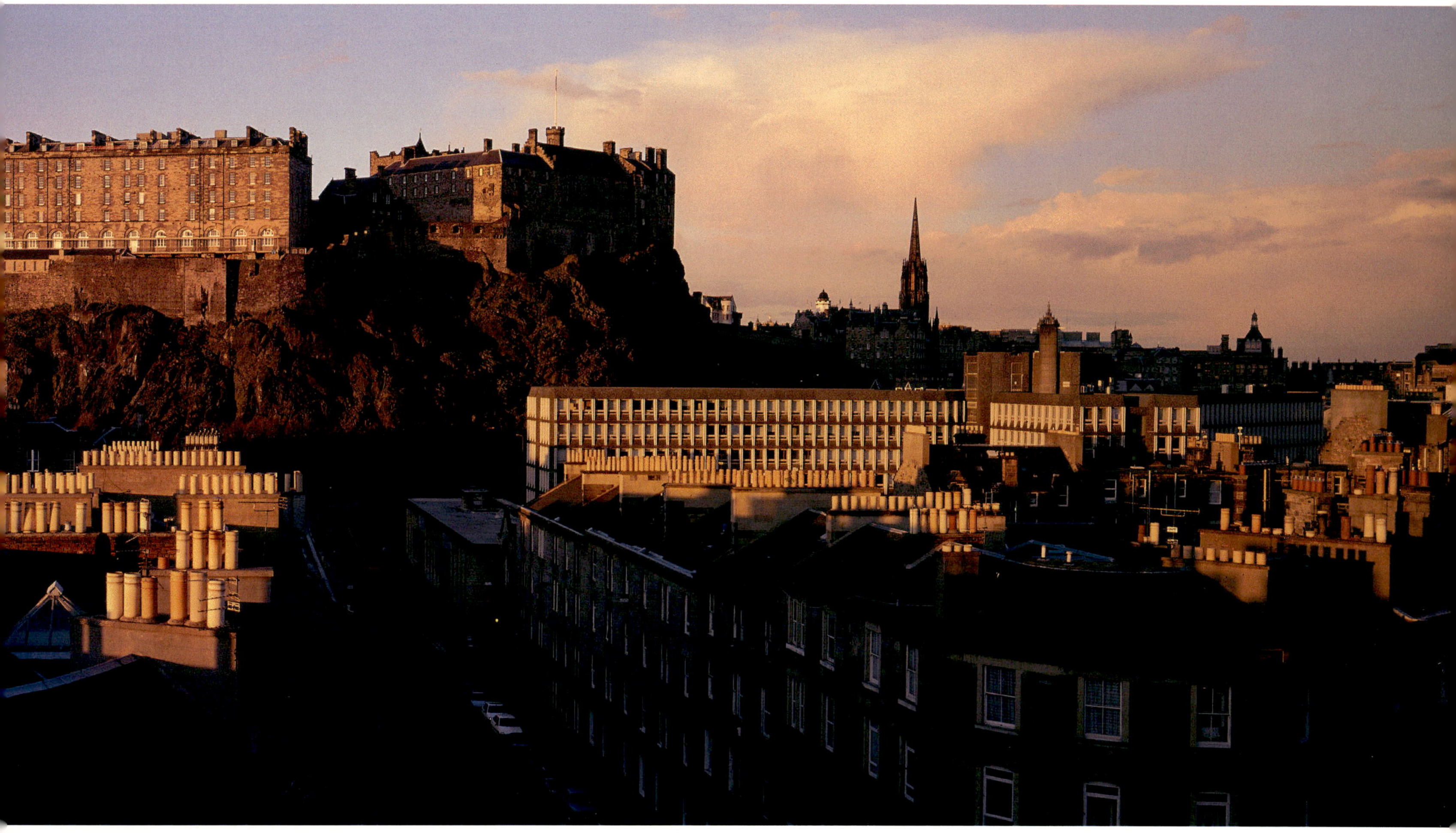

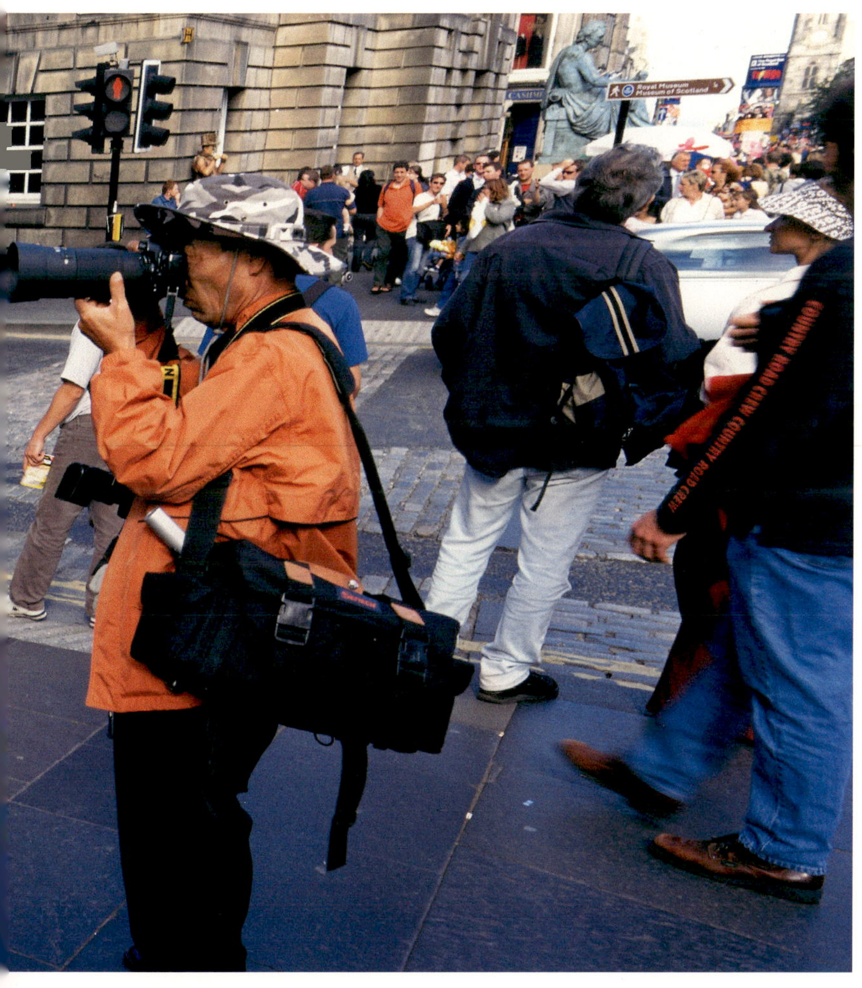

Deacon Brodie's Tavern on the Royal Mile is named after the historical figure that Robert Louis Stevenson based his character of Jekyll and Hyde upon. This Edinburgh city councillor was by day a respectable business man who used the knowledge gained in his job as a cabinet maker and locksmith to burgle his clients by night. There's no escaping the sound of the bagpipes in Edinburgh, and this unconventional piper's outfit certainly catches the attention of another photographer.

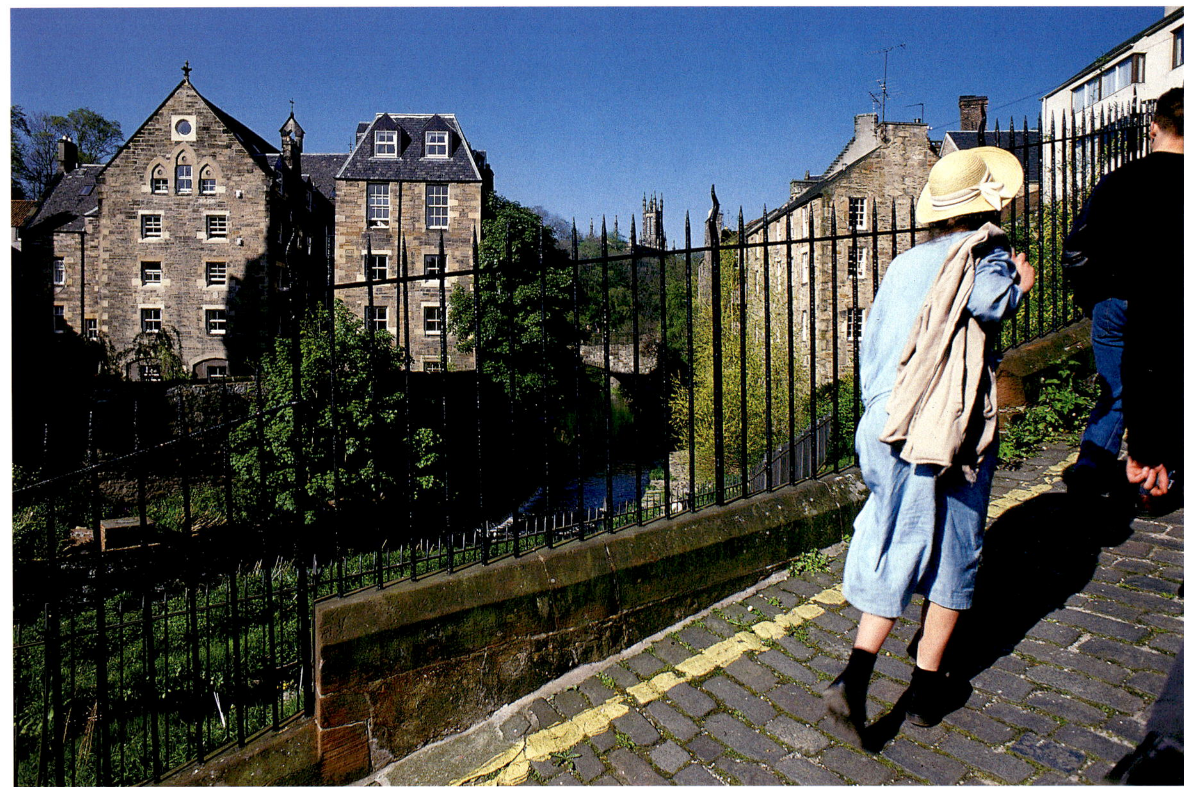

As a photographer I have an unusual complaint – people won't walk in front of me, out of politeness. This can be frustrating, as I often like to have people in the foreground. This girl fits perfectly into the landscape of the Dean Village, one of several diverse villages within Edinburgh. This was a milling community that supplied all the meal for the town and surrounding villages.

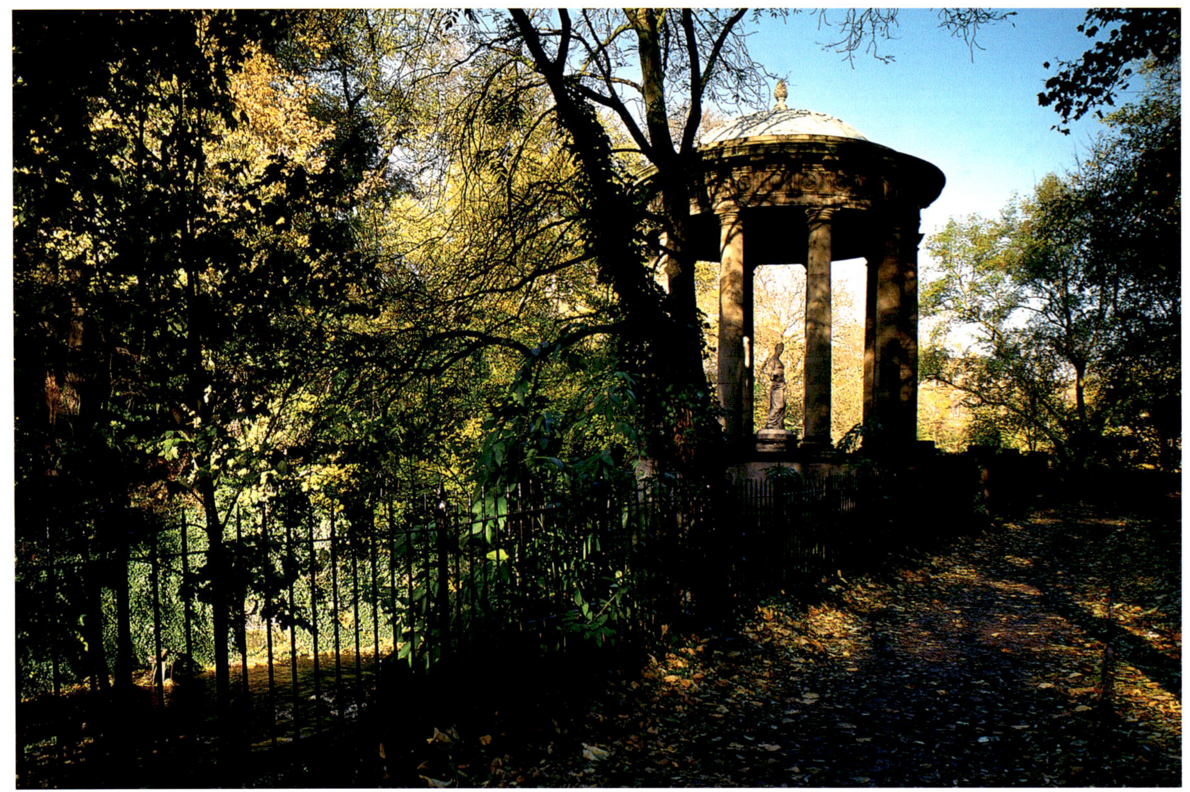

St Bernard's Well, with a statue of Hygieia, goddess of health, is a mineral spring and pump room near the Dean Village on the Water of Leith. It does what it is meant to do: it lifts your spirits and adds joy to your journey at any season. This idyll is particularly unexpected in the heart of the city and would not be out of place in the grounds of a stately home.

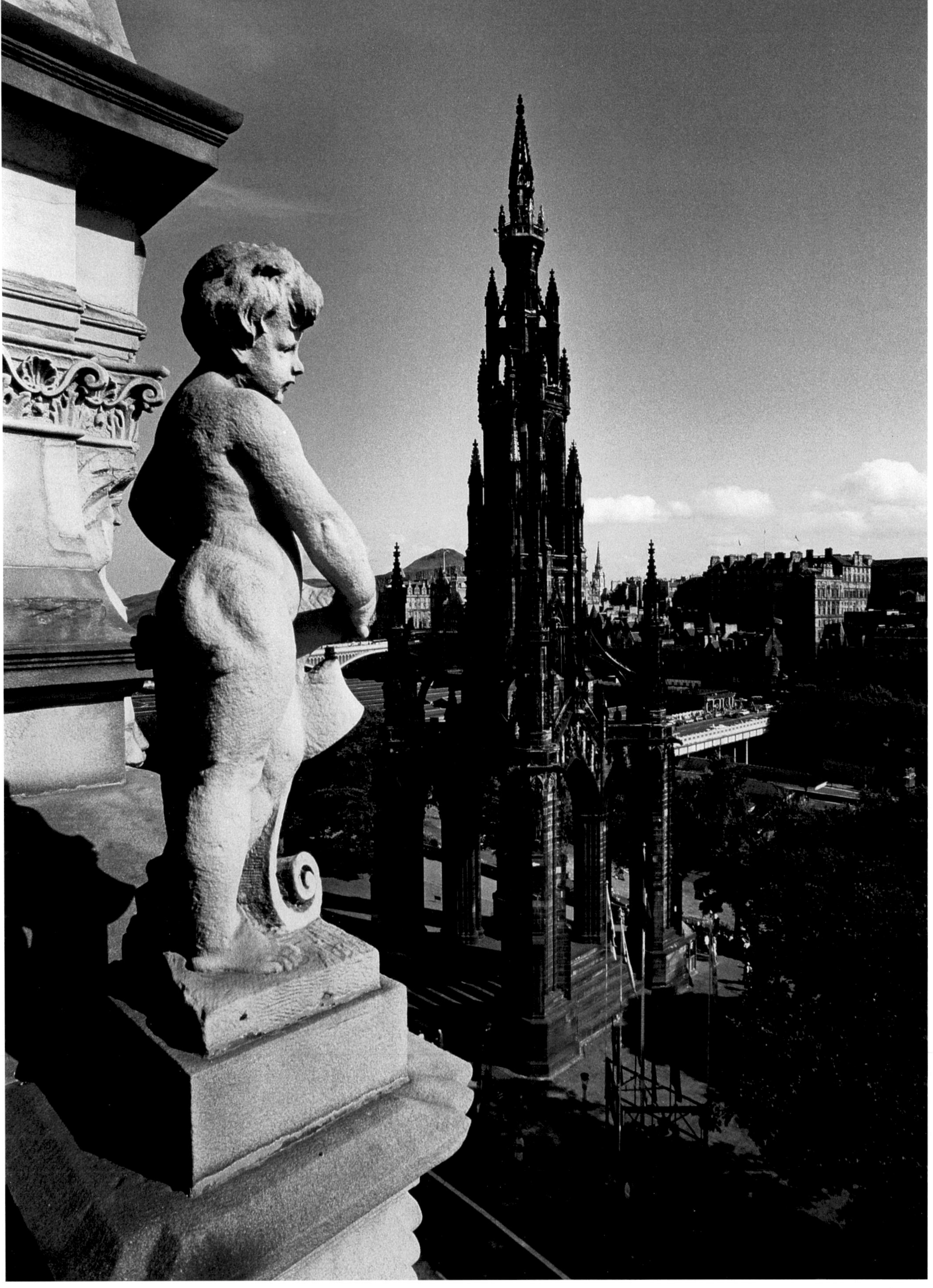

The days when I was allowed out on rooftops and had to hang by my fingernails to get a new angle on well-kent images are well and truly over thanks to health and safety legislation. This shot, taken in the 1970s from Jenner's department store, would now require scaffolding from the ground upwards or, at the very least, a cherry-picker. The monument to Sir Walter Scott is generally the first image you have of Edinburgh if you arrive by train. You could be excused if you thought this was a Victorian version of Thunderbird 3 from the popular 1960s' TV puppet show.

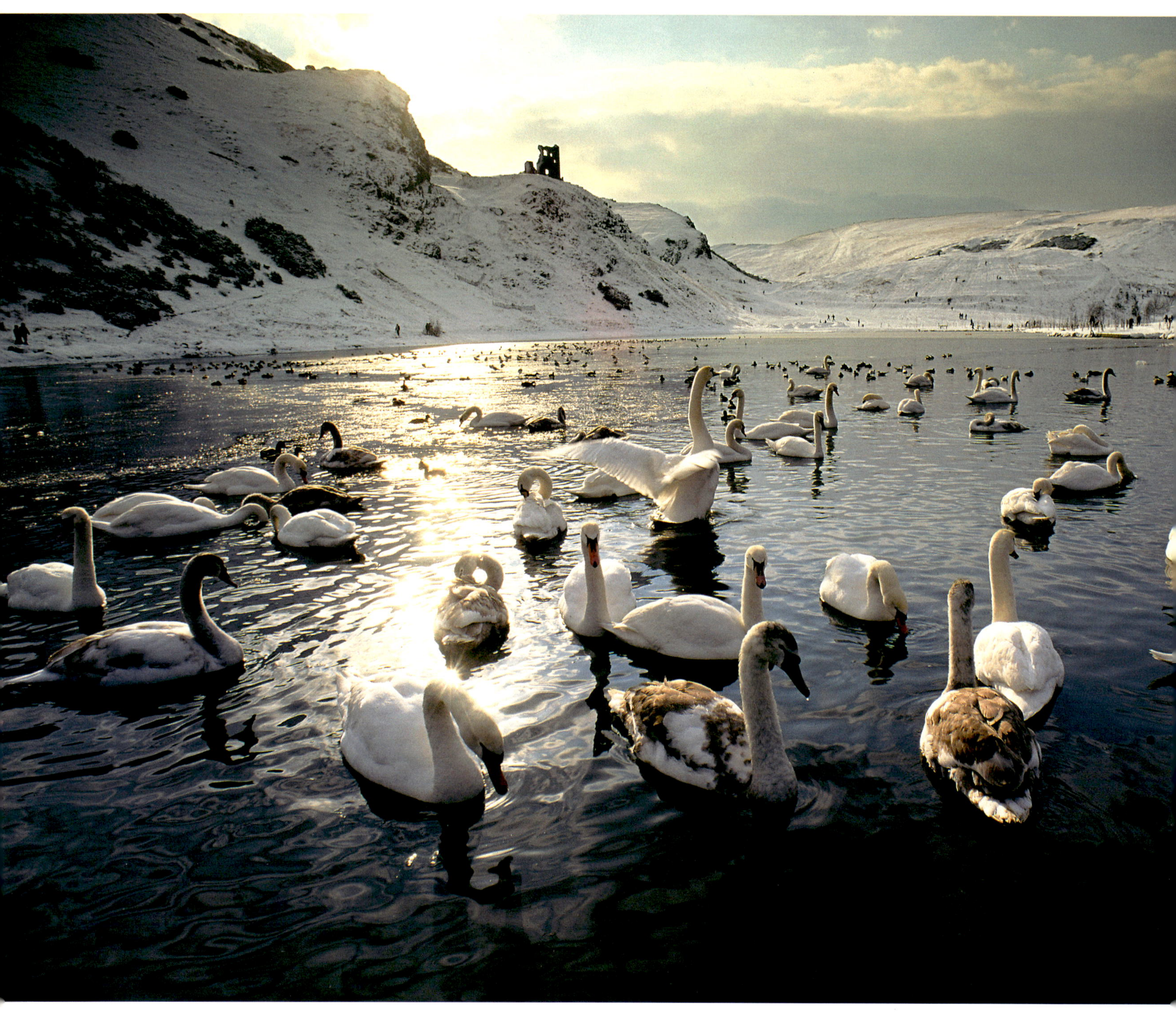

Seven Seas, a Japanese magazine for Members Elite (five-star travellers only), used this shot across a three-page foldout. It was titled Paradise View, but actually it is St Margaret's Loch, in Edinburgh's Holyrood Park, with the ruins of St Anthony's Chapel in the distance.

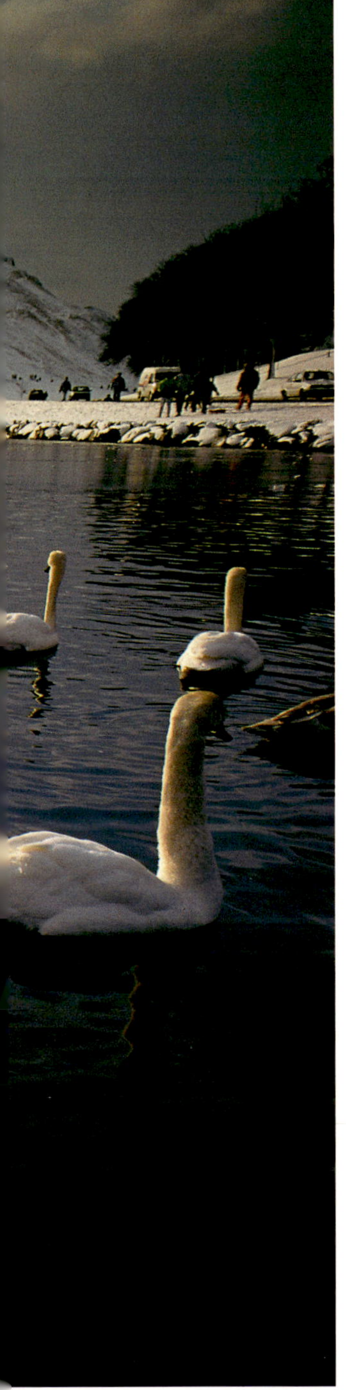

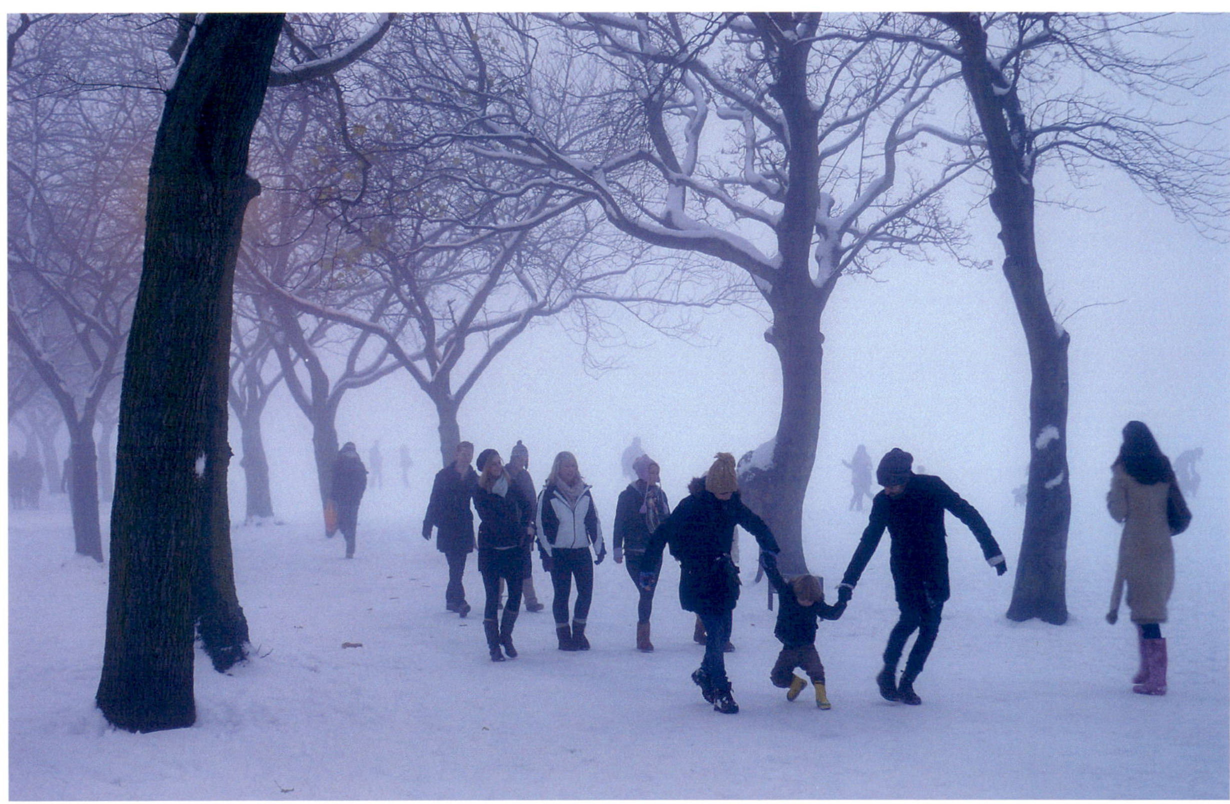

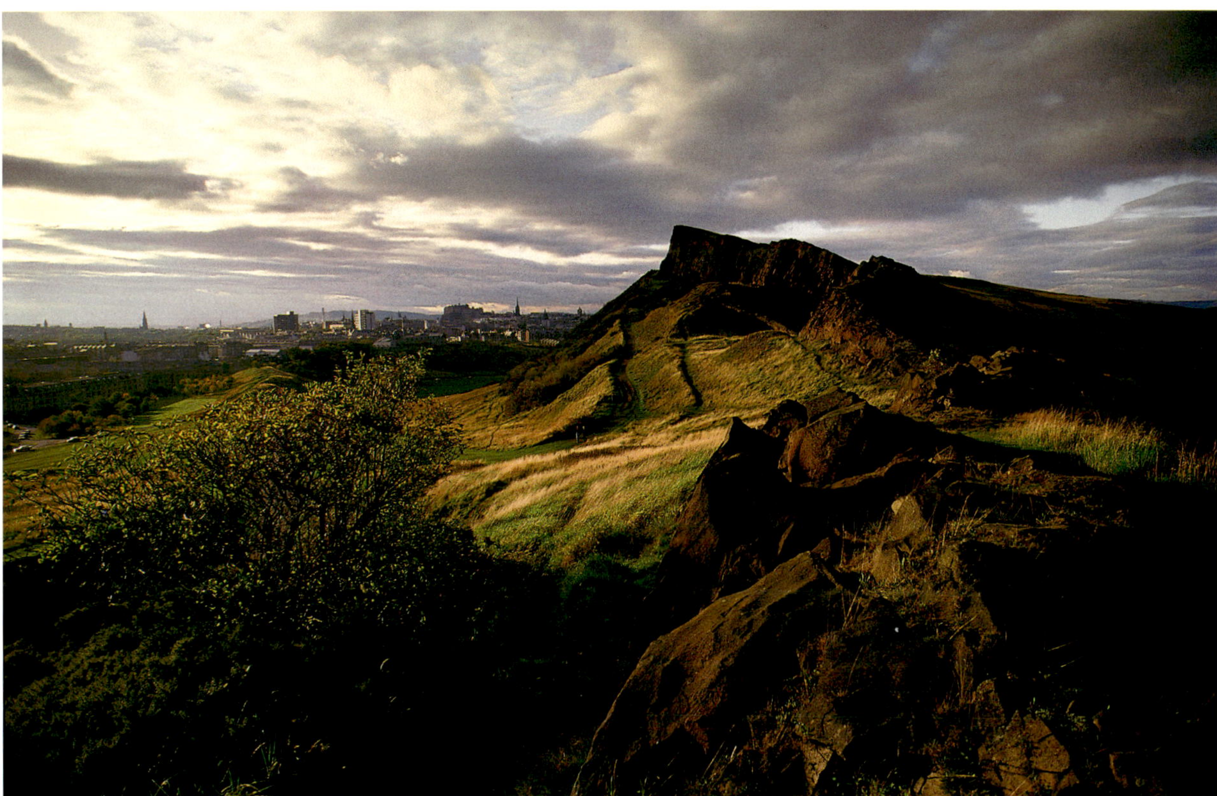

(Above) James Hutton, the father of modern geology, based his *Theory of the Earth* on his studies of Salisbury Crags in Holyrood Park. It is unique for a city to have such a wild and rugged space at its heart. Many of my favourite views are from here. When I first arrived in Edinburgh, sheep used to graze on the slopes of the Queen's Park, an alternative name for the park. The discovery here in 1836 of miniature coffins, complete with voodoo-like dolls, now in the National Museum of Scotland, never fail to delight the morbid curiosity of ghoulish adults and children alike.

(Top) There had been a heavy fall of snow on the Meadows in Edinburgh and a thick fog gave the city centre park an ethereal appearance. This strange atmosphere seems to echo the tales told to local children of the thousands of plague victims who were banished to the Burgh Muir area, at that time outside the city walls, and who were ultimately buried under what is now the innocuous Bruntsfield Links' pitch and putting course.

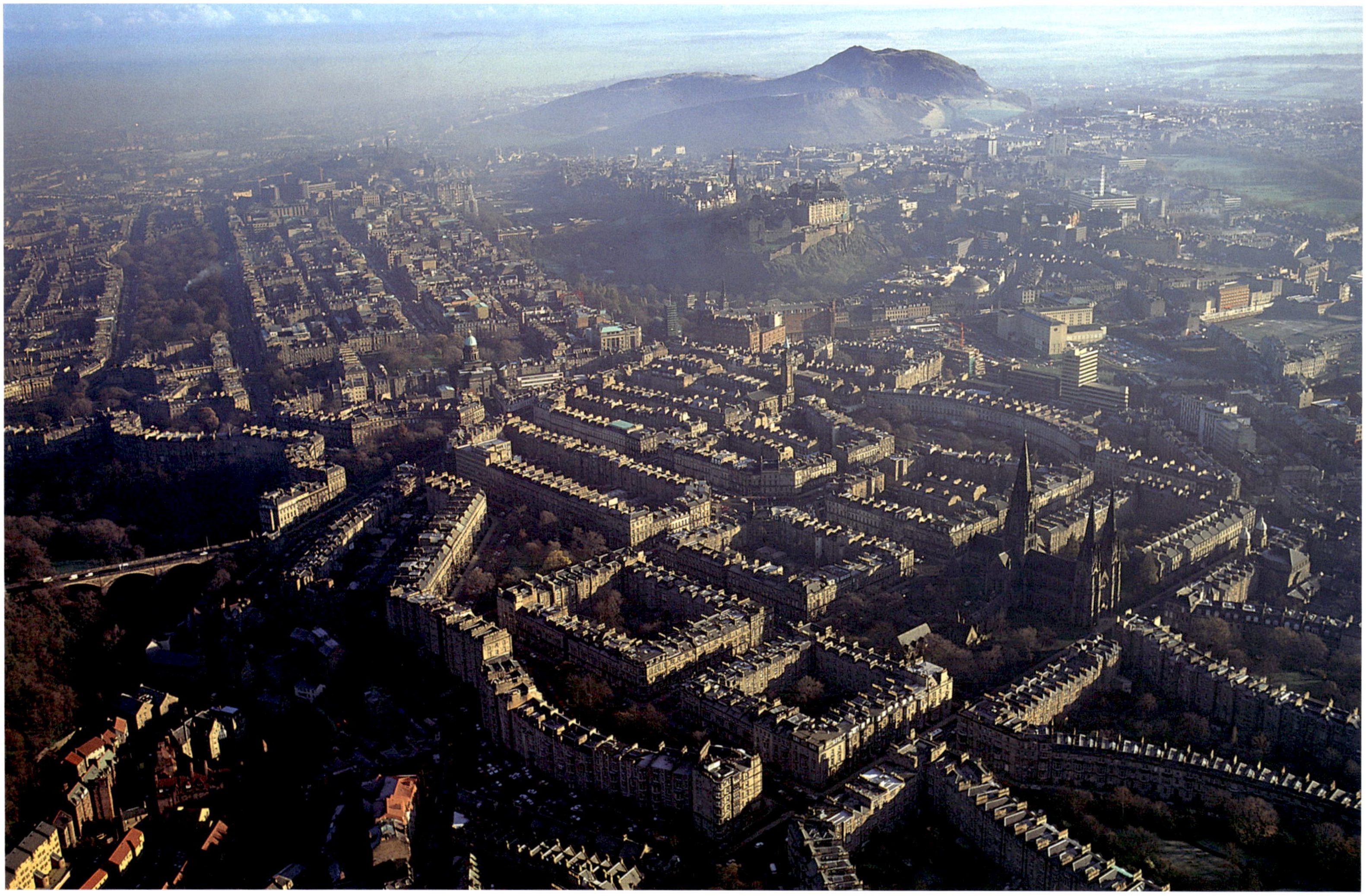

An Edinburgh haar (a mist that comes in from the Firth of Forth and engulfs certain parts of the city) can be seen in this picture, showing the New Town, the Castle and Arthur's Seat (an extinct volcano) in Holyrood Park. Aerial photography gives me so much stress as the cost of hiring a helicopter can be quite horrendous and success is all about weather, weather, weather. The Chinese travel writer Chiang Yee, in his 1948 book, *The Silent Traveller in Edinburgh*, describes Arthur's Seat as the Elephant Hill, whereas conventionally locals see it as a lion couchant – personally, I go along with the elephant.

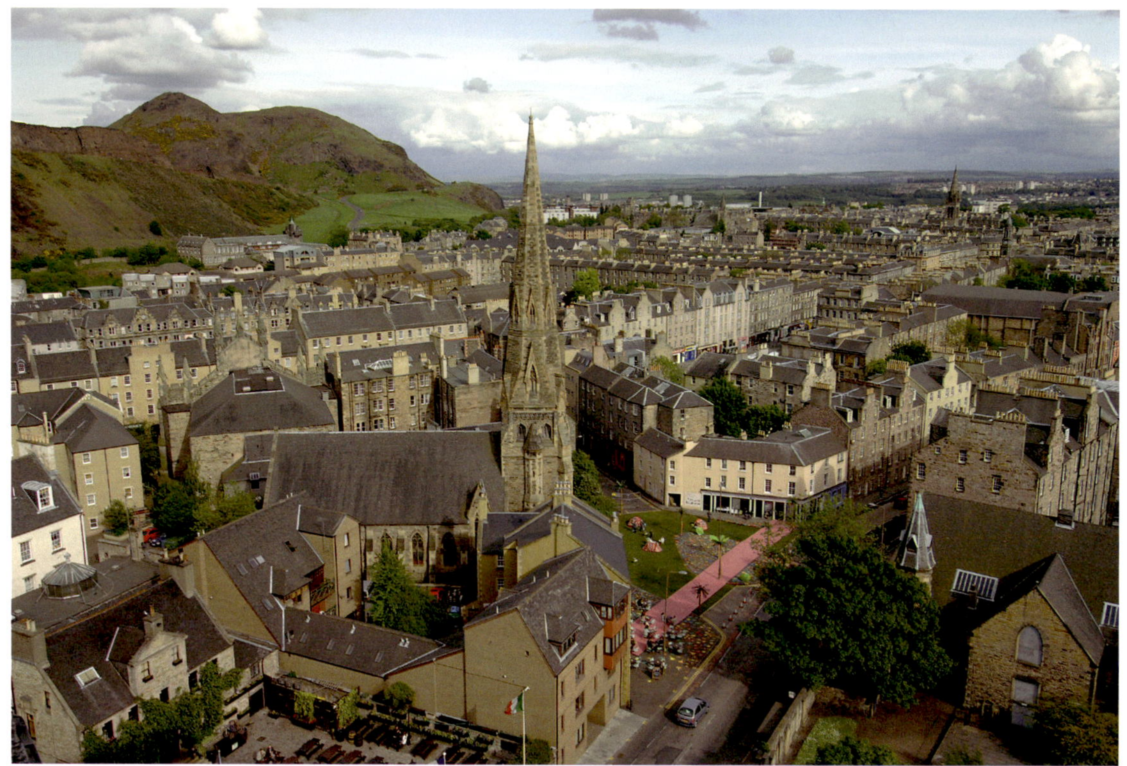

In front of their office in West Crosscauseway in 2008, Arcade Architects laid out a pink pavement with palm trees to show what, with a little imagination, can be done to an under-used urban landscape. Two days of street events involving the local community engaged all ages. I particularly enjoyed the piano accordionist as Will Starr was a childhood hero of mine.

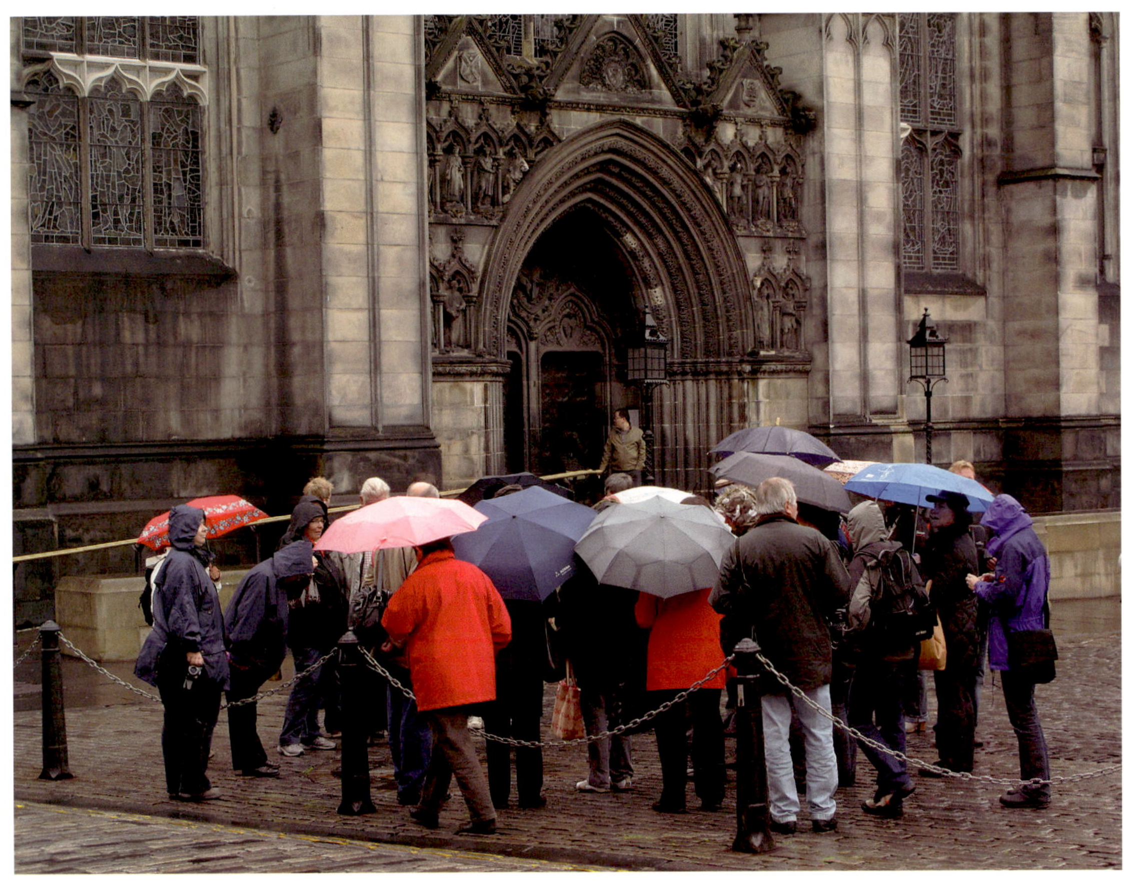

When I was commiserating once with American tourists about a spell of bad weather, they looked at me with surprise and said, 'We're from Texas and we get plenty of sun, and it's great to visit a place where the weather is happening.' This group of visitors outside St Giles Cathedral in Edinburgh didn't seem to be put off by the weather either. I wonder if they were conscious that they were standing at the Heart of Midlothian, indicated by a heart-shaped mosaic that marks what was once the administrative centre of the county of Midlothian. I also wonder if they are aware that a certain section of Edinburgh society has a superstition about spitting on the heart.

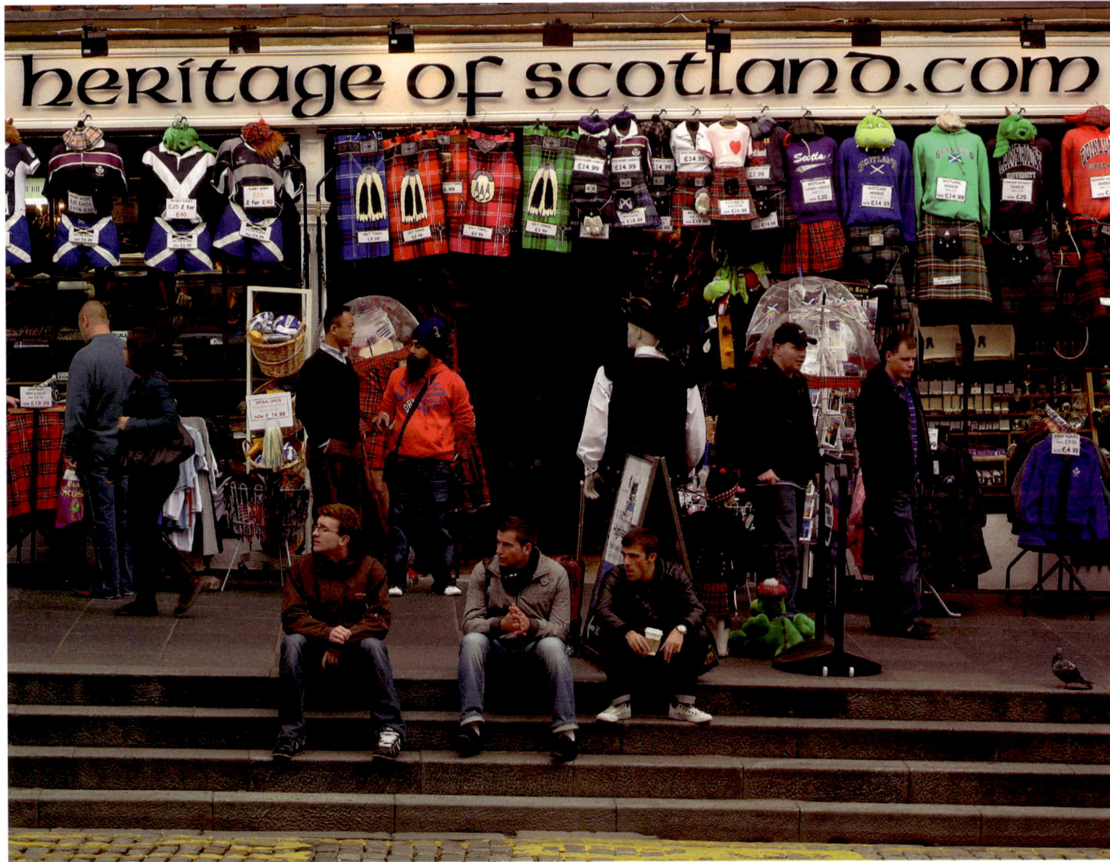

Is anyone proud of his or her country's tourist souvenirs? The argument is that they sell and are what the tourist wants. Taste should come into the equation, however, which is not always apparent in saltire-cross boxer shorts or 'See You, Jimmy!' hats on sale on the Royal Mile in Edinburgh. But at least we can be proud that none of it is produced in Scotland.

Edinburgh, showing the Victorian barracks of the Castle so hated by Lord Cockburn, an Edinburgh judge and early advocate of conserving the city's architecture. I still love this view, especially with the snow and Edinburgh's Christmas lights.

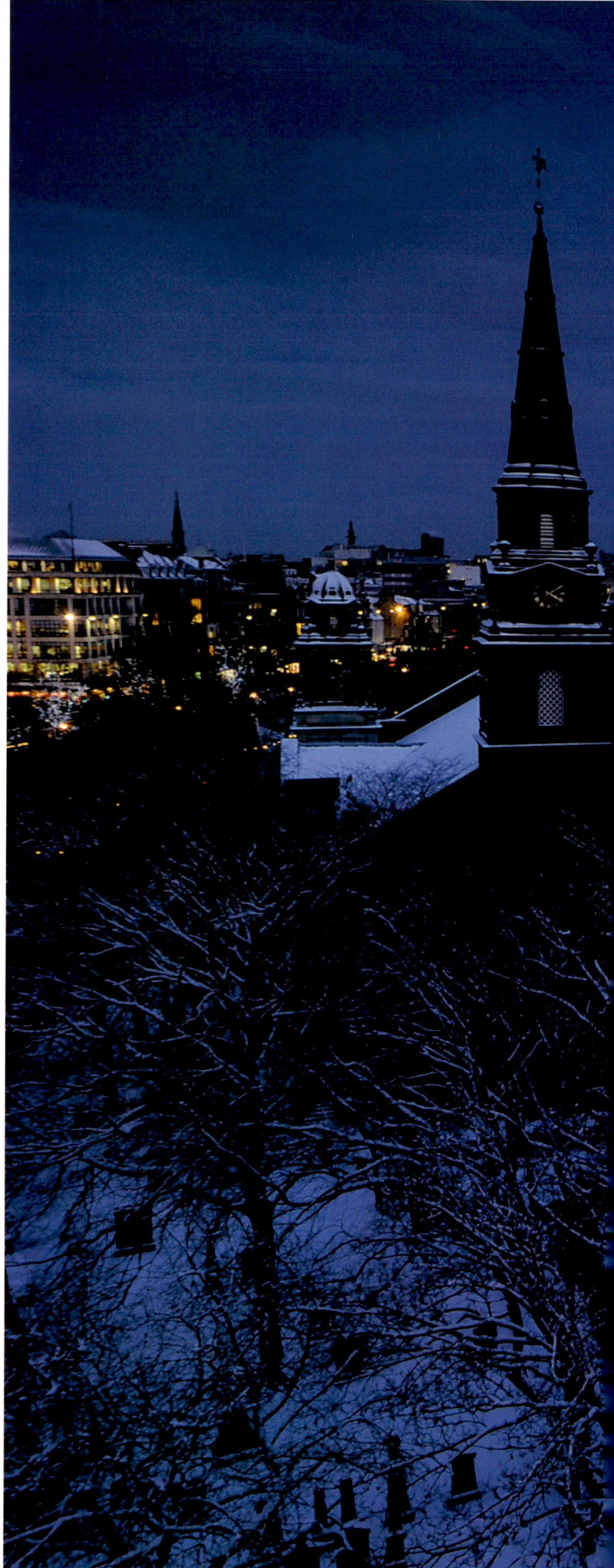

I hired a cherry-picker to shoot the Palace of Holyroodhouse, the official Scottish residence of Her Majesty the Queen. Permission had been given but the uninformed local constabulary appeared just as clouds threatened to spoil the picture. I was ordered down so they could check my credentials, but I managed to stall them, much to their annoyance, and finished shooting before the light failed. They were only doing their duty, but sometimes the needs of photographers and officialdom can be at odds.

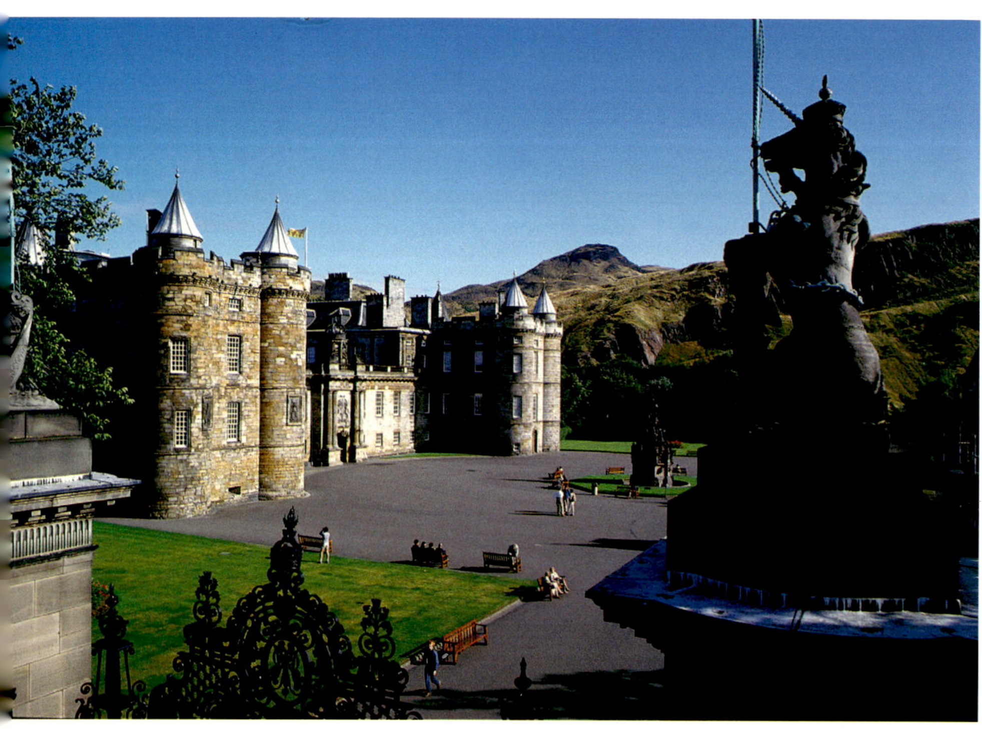

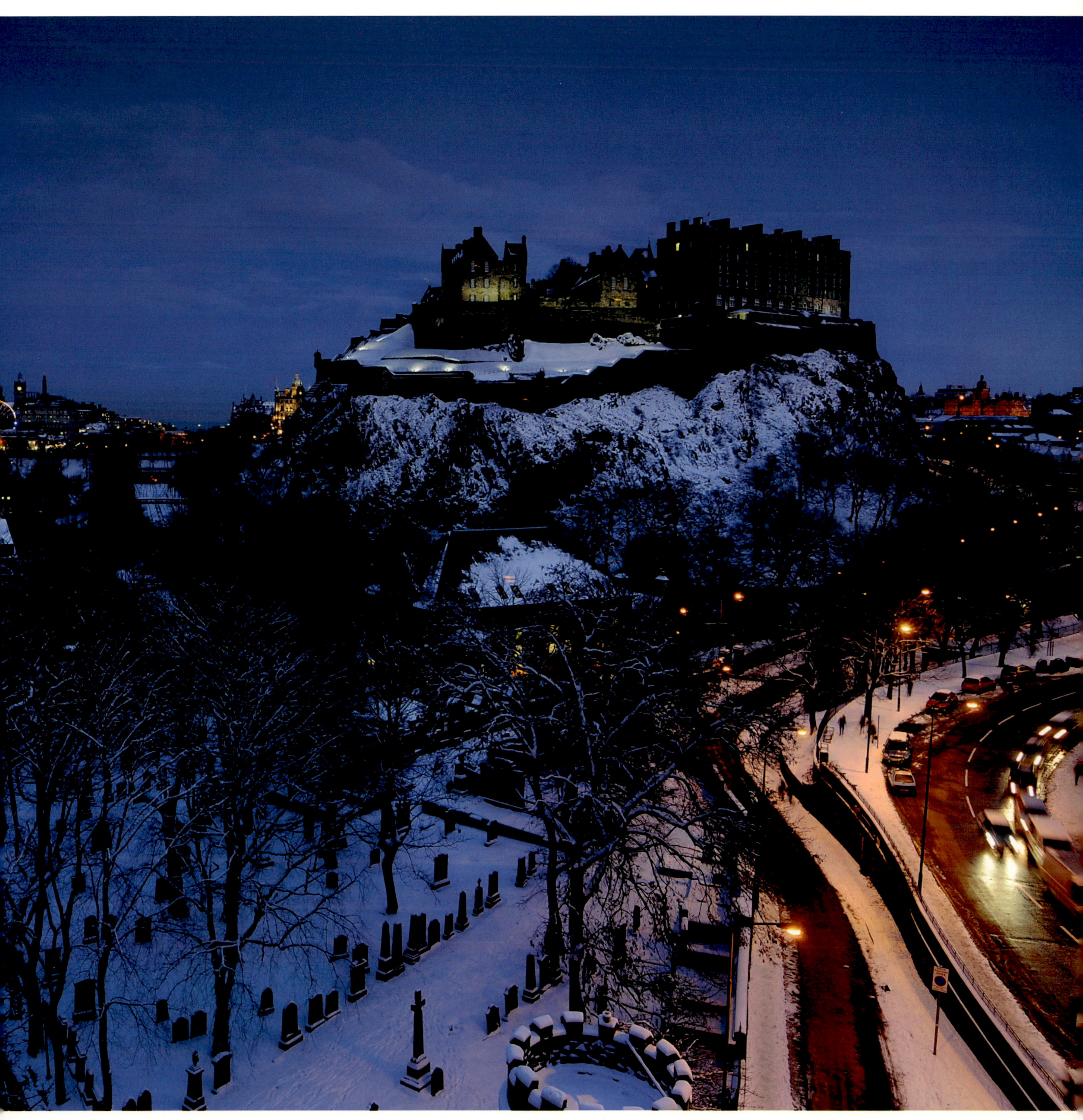

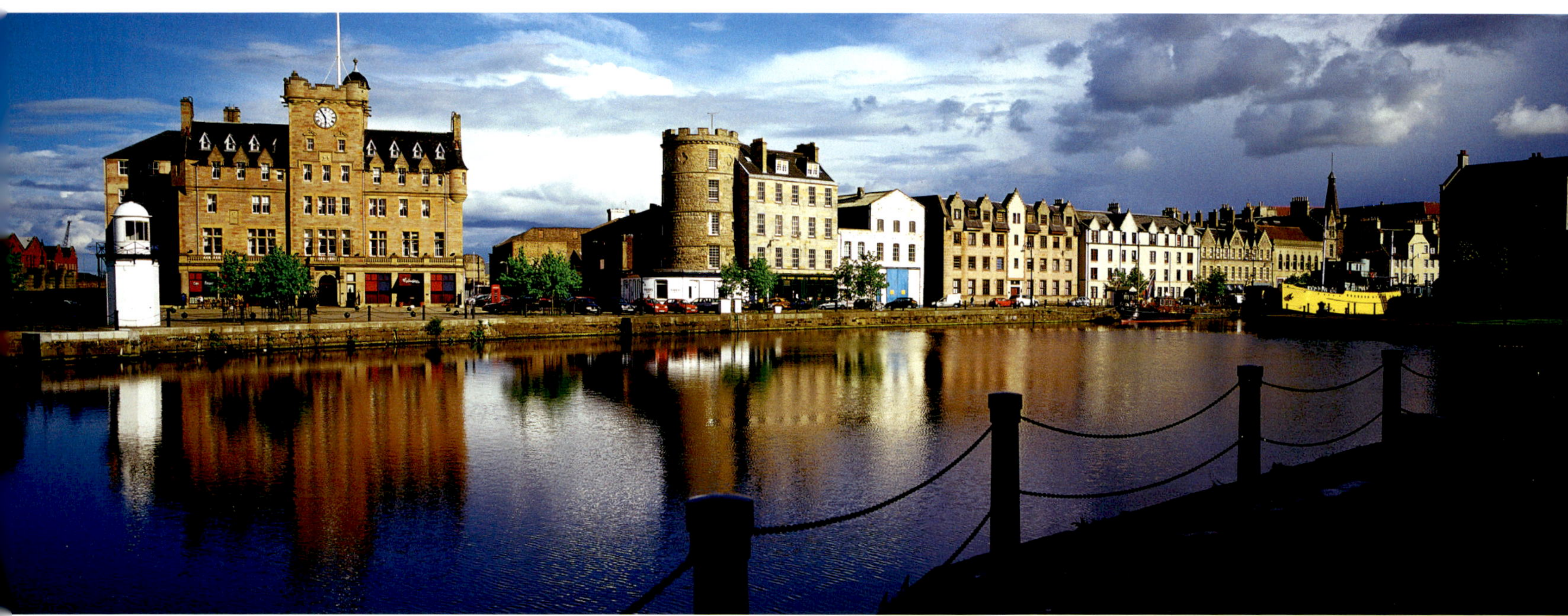

Leith waterfront, the port of Edinburgh, now a place of trendy (or whatever the latest buzzword is) bars, restaurants, shops and chic apartments.

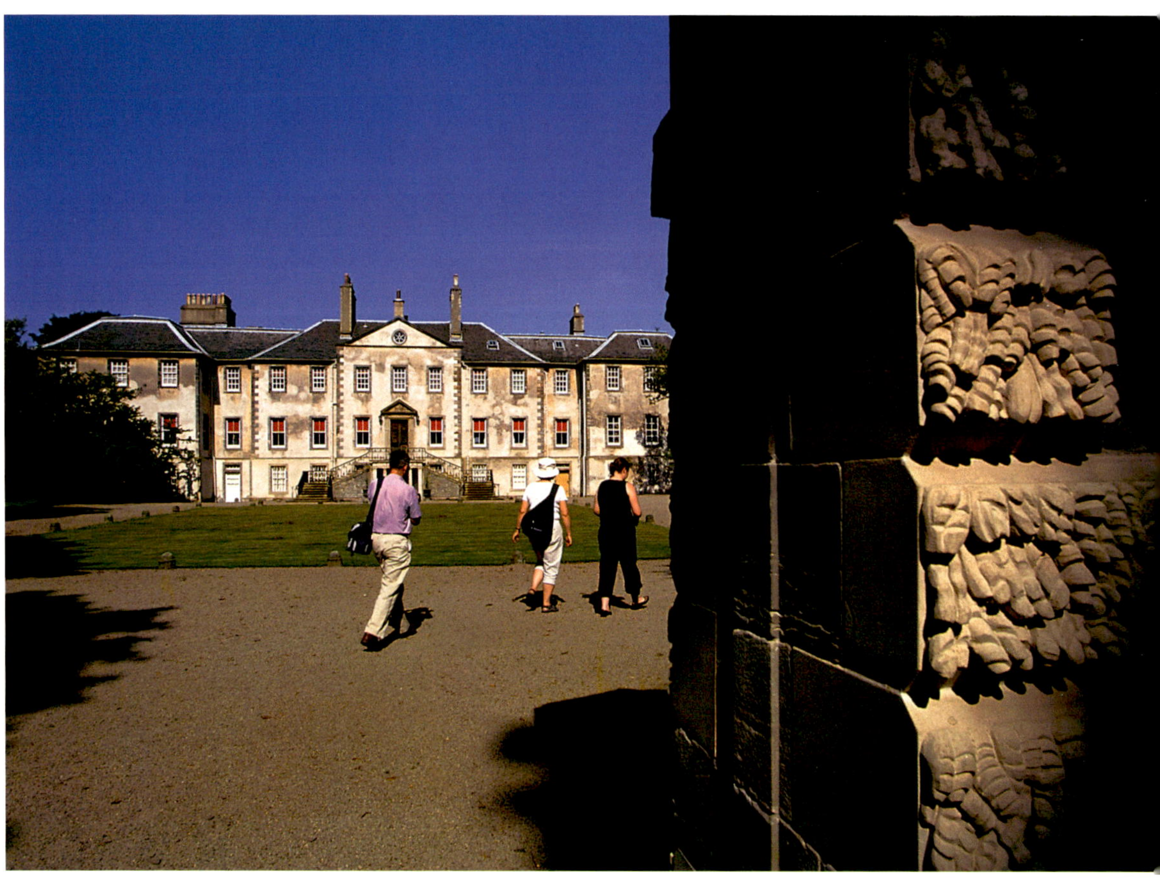

Newhailes, near Musselburgh, is an example of domestic Palladian architecture. The National Trust for Scotland has deliberately conserved the house as it was found rather than restoring it to its former glory. This includes furniture and fittings throughout from several periods going back to the 17th century, the original date of the house. While the rusty railings and distressed fabric may not suit everyone, some would expect Miss Haversham to be quite at home here.

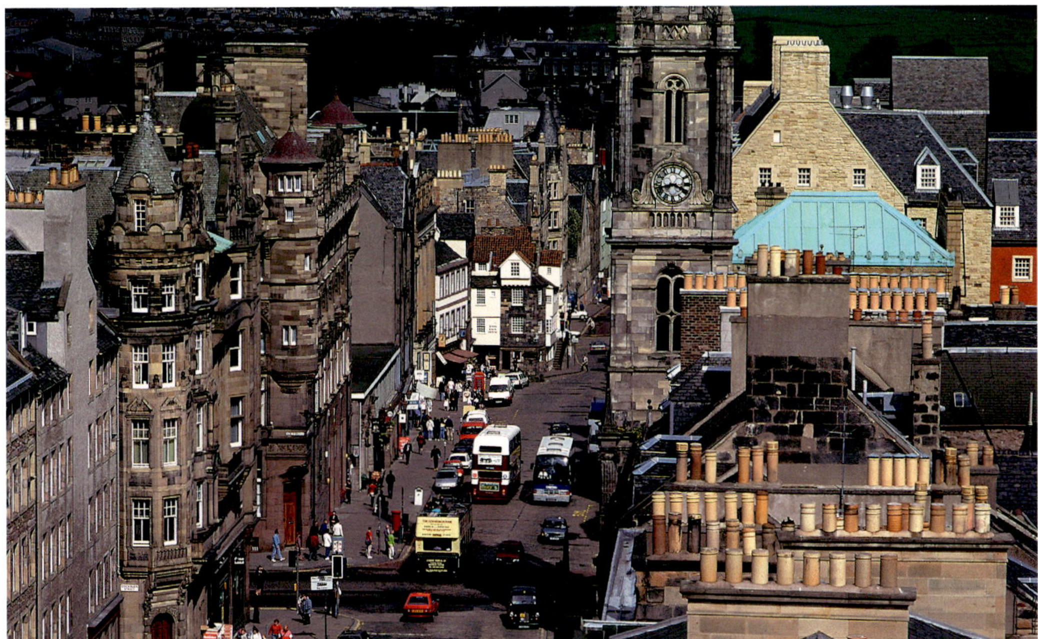

The Royal Mile, from the top of St Giles Cathedral's 15th-century lantern tower. St Giles is the patron saint of beggars and lepers. I witnessed an old Edinburgh vagrant regularly being given a cup of tea by a church warden. The red-roofed house of the Protestant reformer John Knox can be seen in the centre. He was installed as city minister in 1561 when the Catholic Mary Stuart became queen. The rest is history.

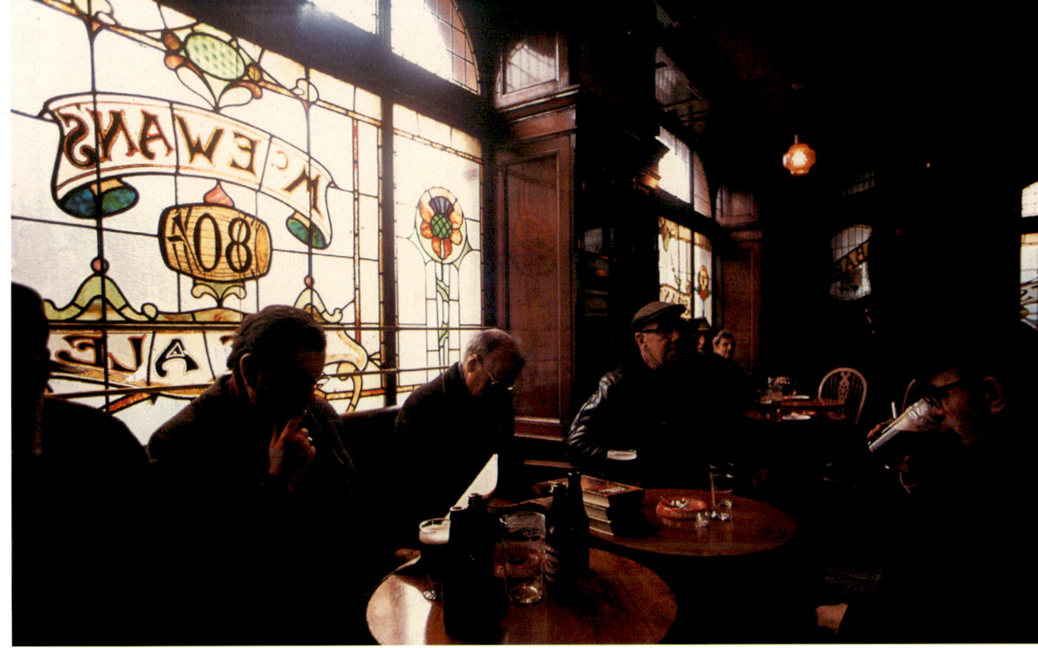

No shortage of ashtrays in Ryries Bar in Haymarket before the 2006 smoking ban in Scotland. It has an atmosphere that can't be created in the so-called theme pubs. If I were a pub-goer, this would be the type I would choose. New regulations can make the survival of public houses difficult.

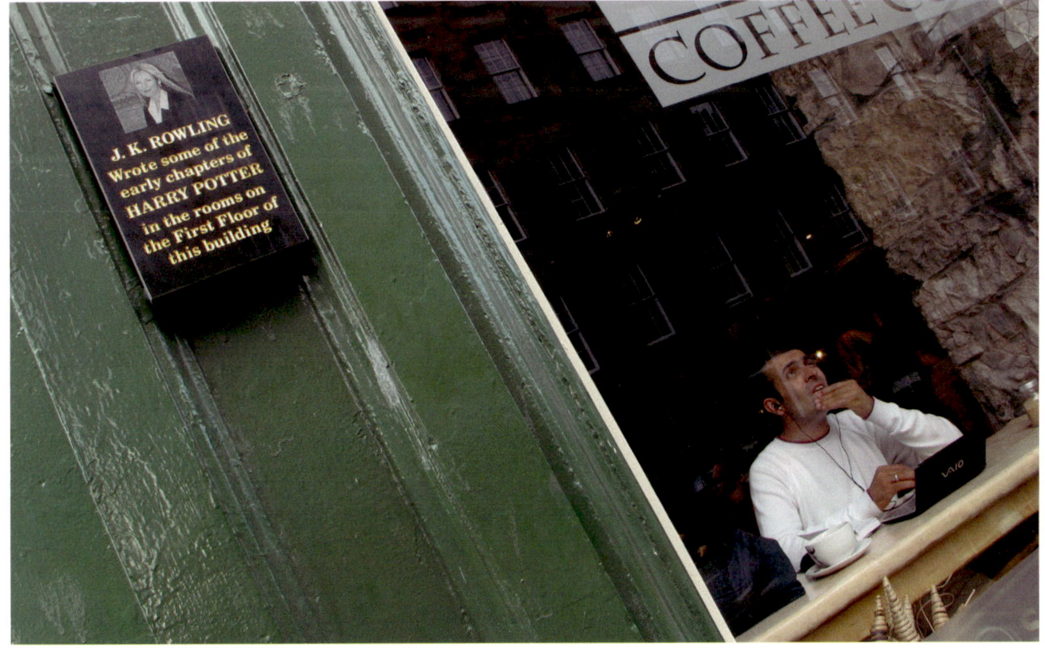

Sir Walter Scott, Robert Louis Stevenson, Sir Arthur Conan Doyle, J. K. Rowling and Alexander MacCall Smith represent the literary phenomena of Edinburgh. An American photographer friend was intrigued that I live in the same part of town as Ian Rankin's Rebus character and that Arthur Conan Doyle had lived three doors down from me.

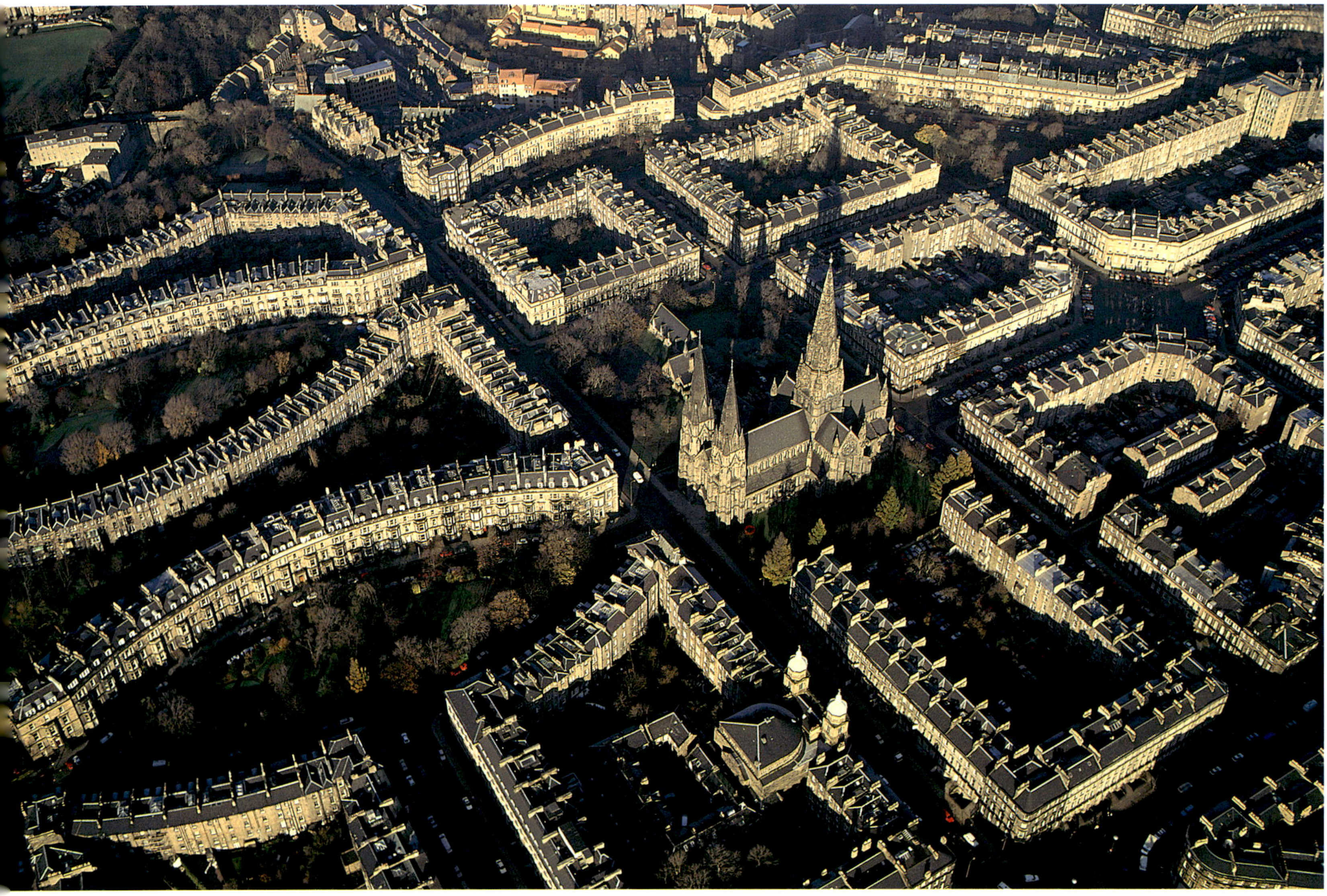

Edinburgh's West End is dominated by the largest church built in Scotland since the Reformation, St Mary's Episcopal Cathedral. The choristers come from neighbouring St Mary's Music School. The choir was the first in Britain to admit girl choristers, in 1978.

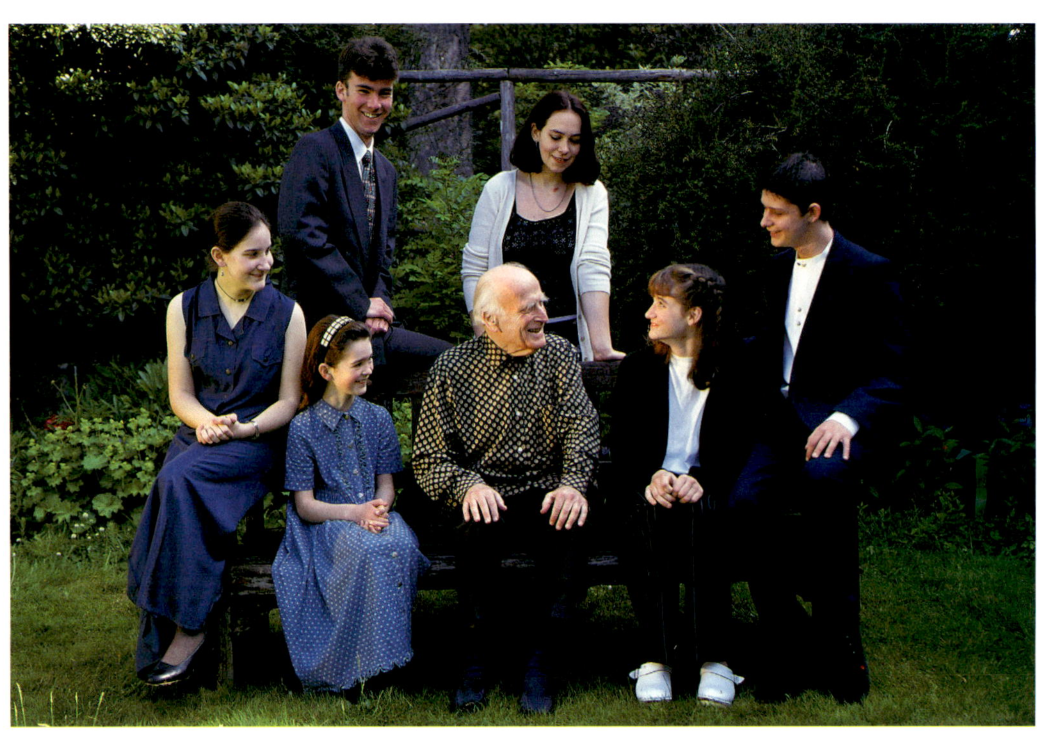

Lord Menuhin was patron and president of St Mary's Music School until his death in 1999. Here he is seen relaxing with pupils in the school grounds during a break in rehearsals for the school's 1997 Lamp of Lothian Concert, which he conducted.

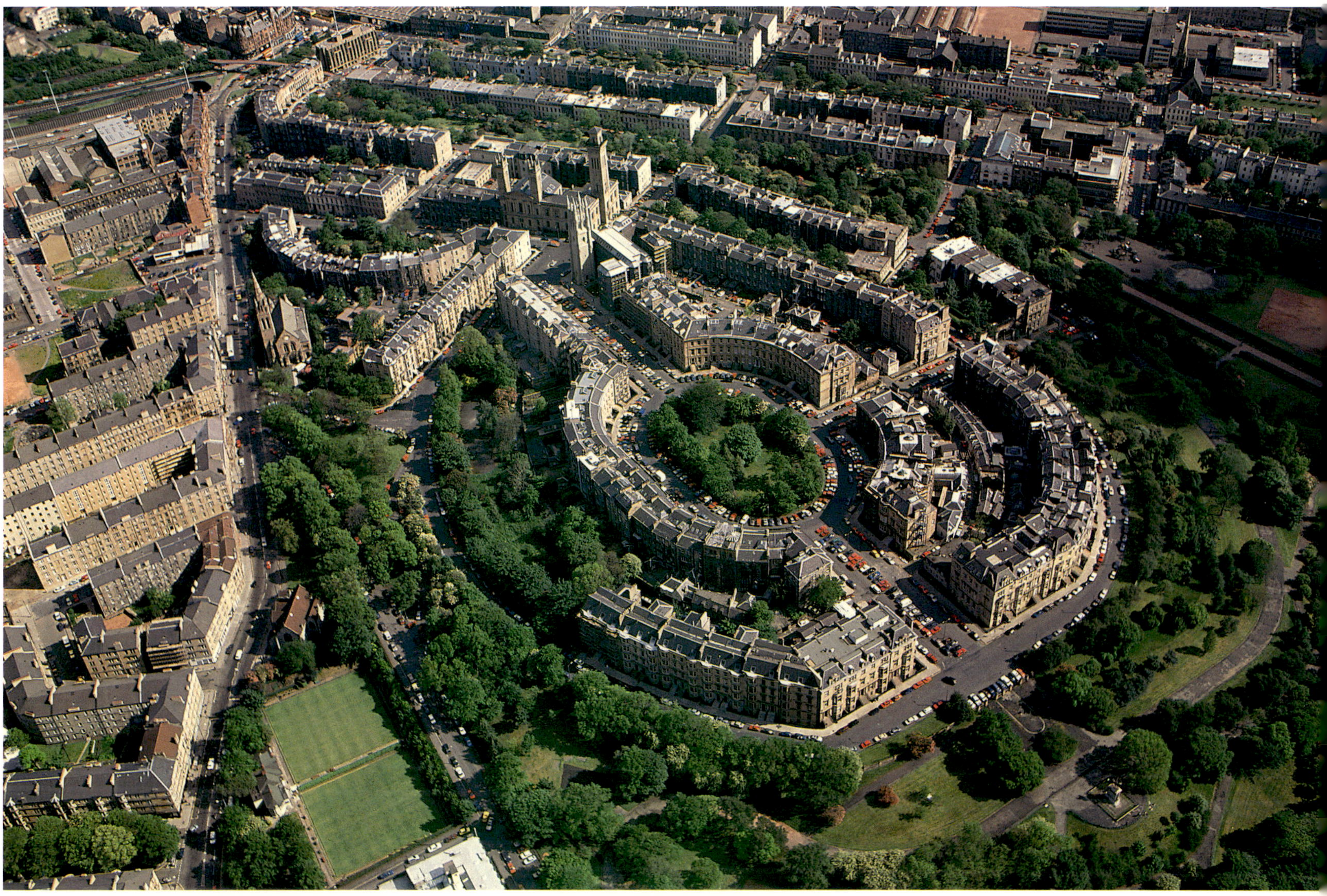

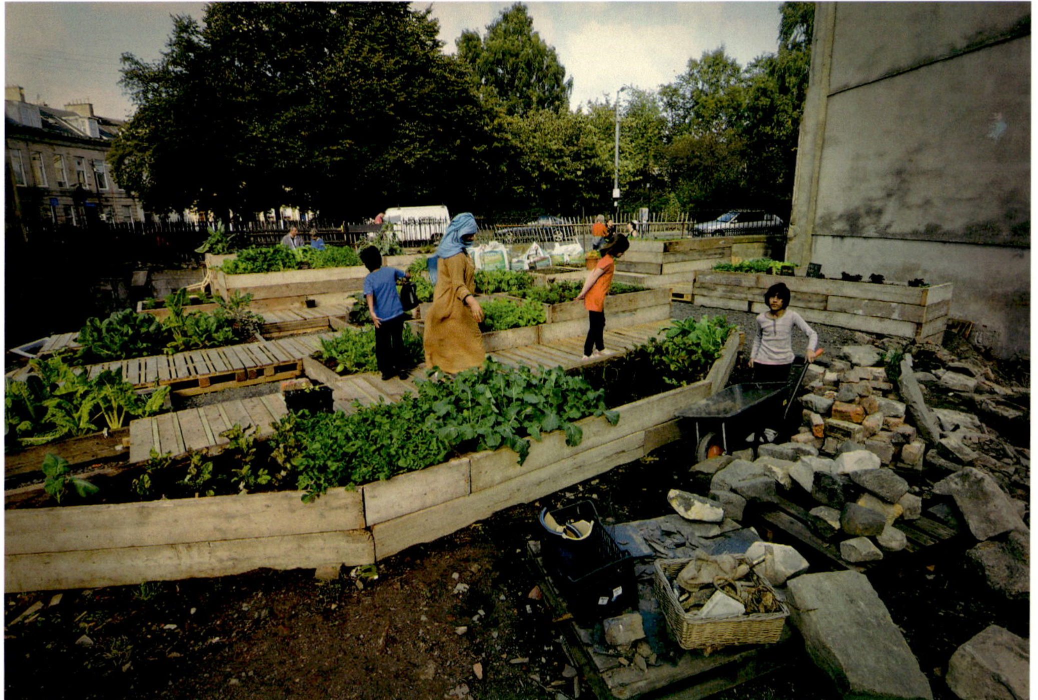

Park Circus in Glasgow was constructed between 1857 and 1858. This is urban Victorian housing at its grandest. Some of the spectacular interiors have been renovated to their former glory and attract creative businesses such as graphic designers and architects although private ownership is being encouraged. It also has one of the most beautiful and ornate marriage registry offices in Britain, number 22, the Casa d'Italia, a club that formerly housed the Italian consulate.

An Asian lady and her grandchildren are part of a community group who have transformed a gap site into a productive kitchen garden in just six months. Glasgow's Woodlands Community Garden is an example of citizens taking control of their environment, which it is hoped will inspire others to do the same.

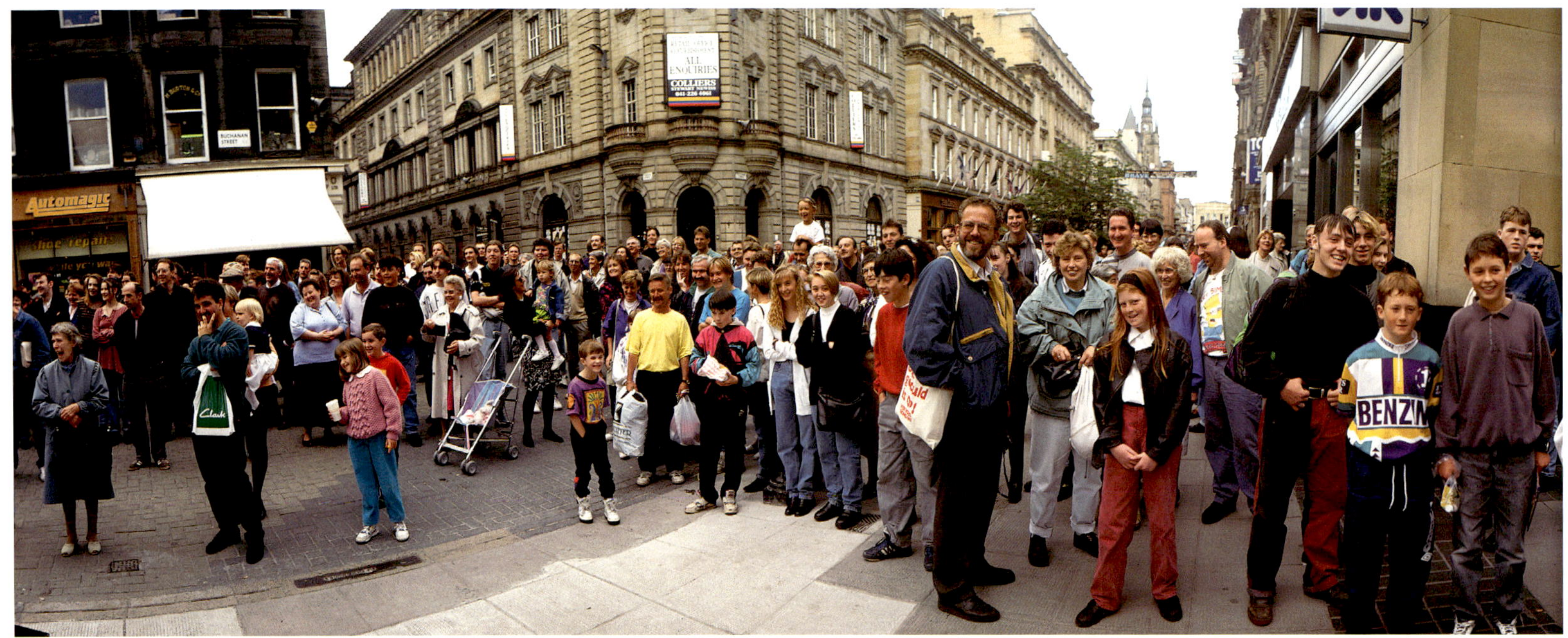

I'm invisible – they are looking through me and are all smiling, although one wee girl seems less amused. It was a busker on stilts holding their attention on a Saturday morning in Glasgow's Buchanan Street.

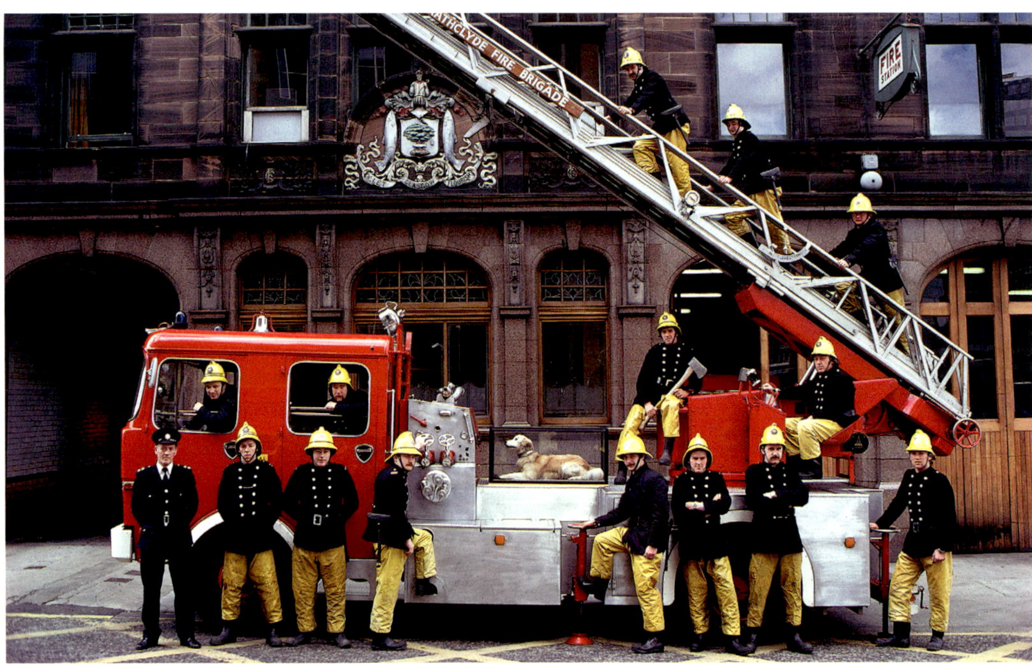

The Central Fire Station on Ingram Street became a restaurant. I deliberately posed this shot, taken in the 1970s, to echo an earlier era. The stuffed dog in the case was called Wallace. He wandered into the fire station one day and became their celebrated mascot until 1902.

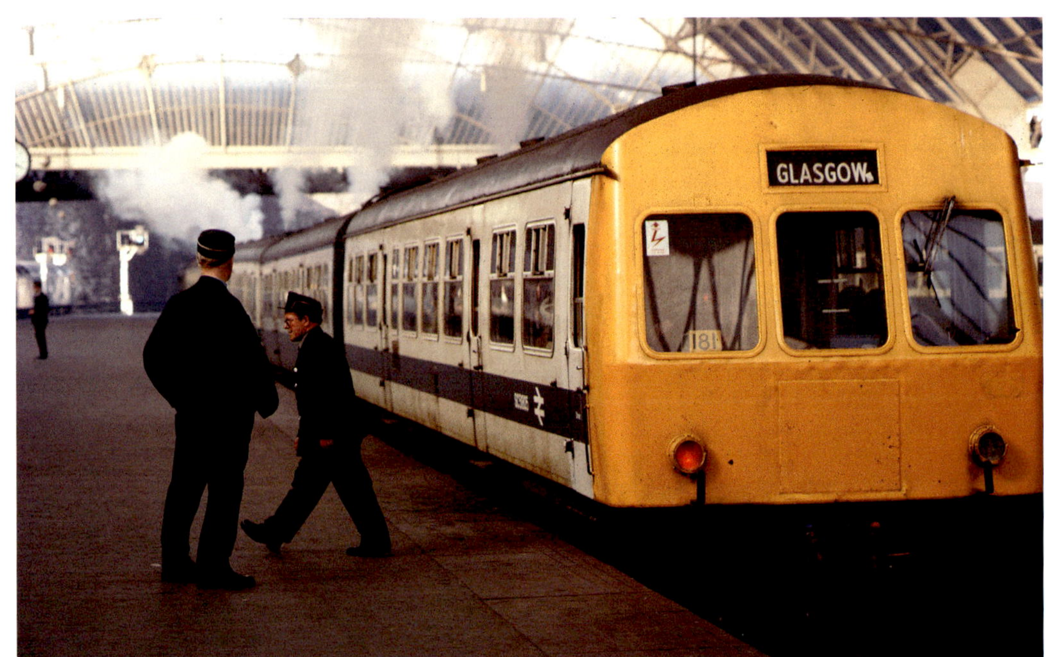

It is serendipitous when people strike just the right pose for a photograph. In my *Glasgow* book, Edward Boyd wrote: 'Queen Street Station is where trains leave to take Glaswegians into exile in the capital city, and here it should be explained that rabid Glaswegians regard any period exceeding 24 hours spent in Edinburgh as exile.'

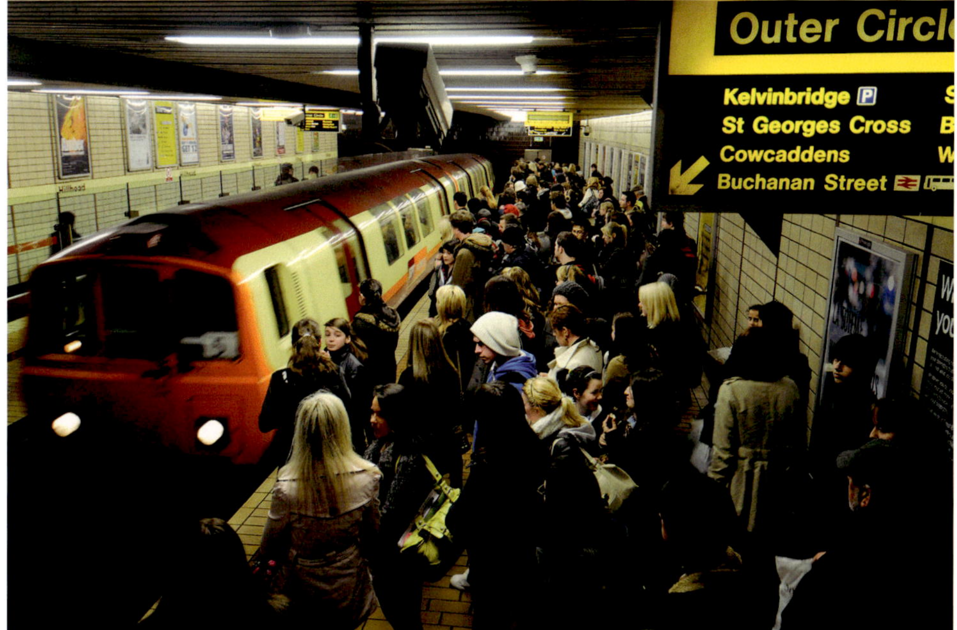

Glasgow's Subway opened in 1896 and is the third oldest underground rail system in the world after London and Budapest. Hillhead station is where students are the main passengers. It's known as the Clockwork Orange – don't you just love it when someone comes up with such a brilliant name. Glasgow has a tendency to rename places: for example, the Hielanman's Umbrella (a covered street beneath Central Station), the Armadillo (the Clyde Auditorium) and the Olive, the Lemon Wedge and the Cocktail Stick (the IMAX cinema, the Science Centre and its Glasgow Tower), not to mention the Squinty Bridge!

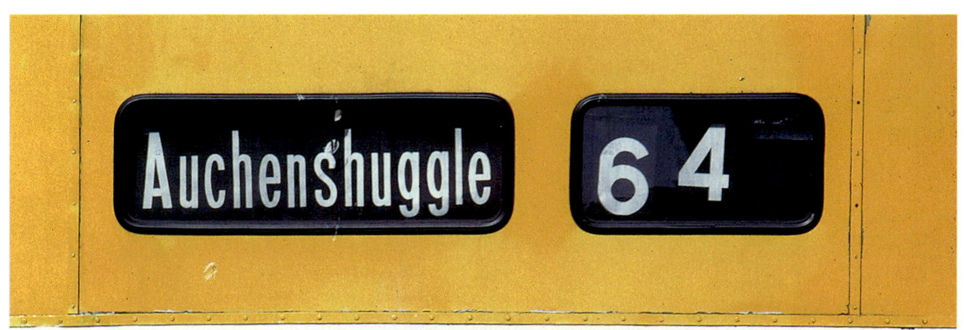

The name Auchenshuggle was made famous as the eastern terminus for the Number 9 tram from 1922 until 1962 when bus route Number 64 took over.

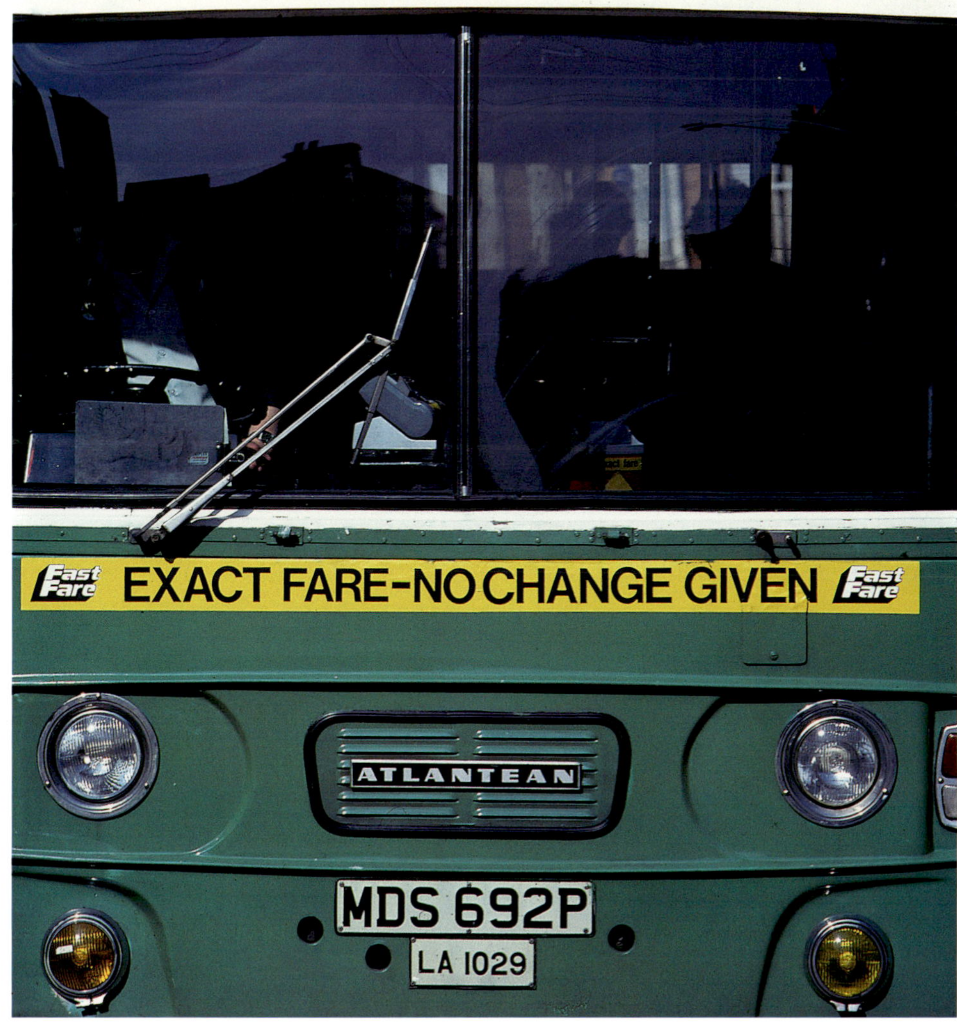

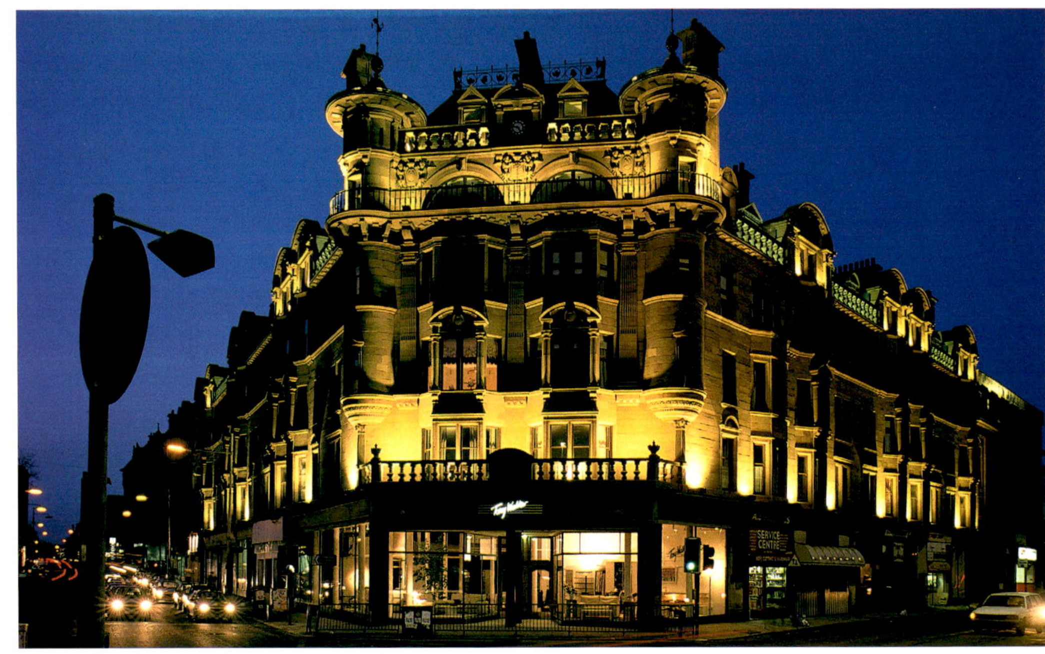

Poet Laureate John Betjeman, who was a great champion of preserving the British cityscape, described Glasgow as the greatest Victorian city in the world. I can't see any argument against this. (Right) St George's Cross Mansions. (Below) the Mitchell Library.

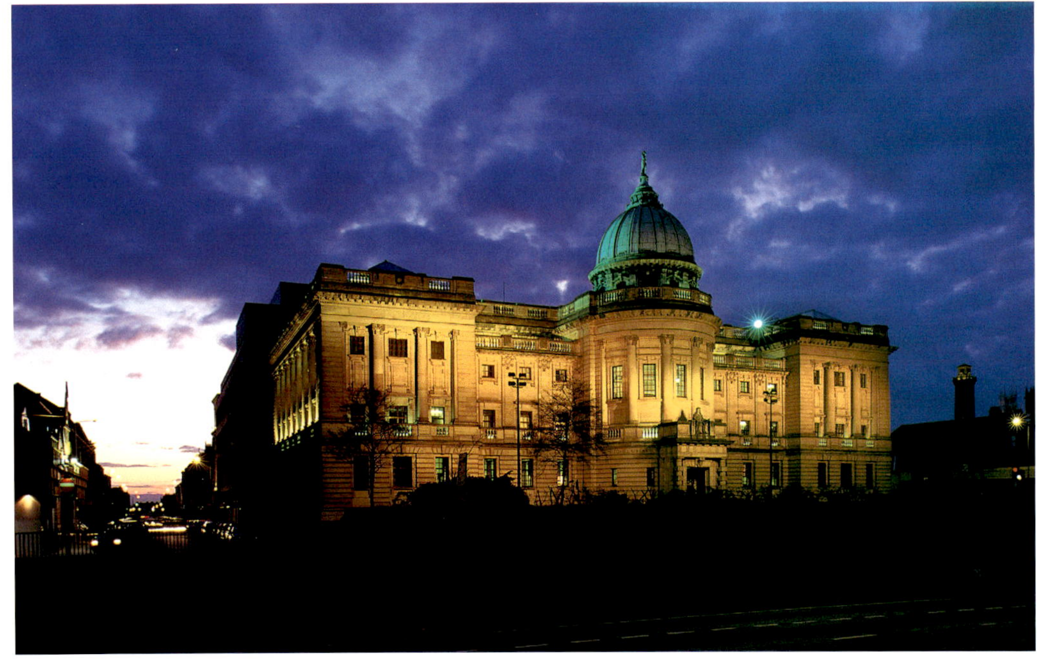

(Opposite) Glasgow's Cathedral dates back to the 12th-century. The public relations officer at the Royal Infirmary, from where I took this shot, asked, 'I hope you won't be climbing on Queen Victoria's statue?' I had worked with him in the past so he knew the lengths I'd go to for a shot. He left me in good faith, and what did I do immediately his back was turned?

(Right) Venice, what a joy of a city – apart from the cost of a coffee and a cake in Florian's cafe in St Mark's Square! James Templeton, the owner of Templeton's Carpet Factory, had been refused planning permission to build several designs on this site when he asked leading architect William Leiper to take on the task in the late 1880s. The result, with its ceramics, mosaics and painted brickwork, has been said to resemble the Palazzo Ducale (the Doge's Palace).

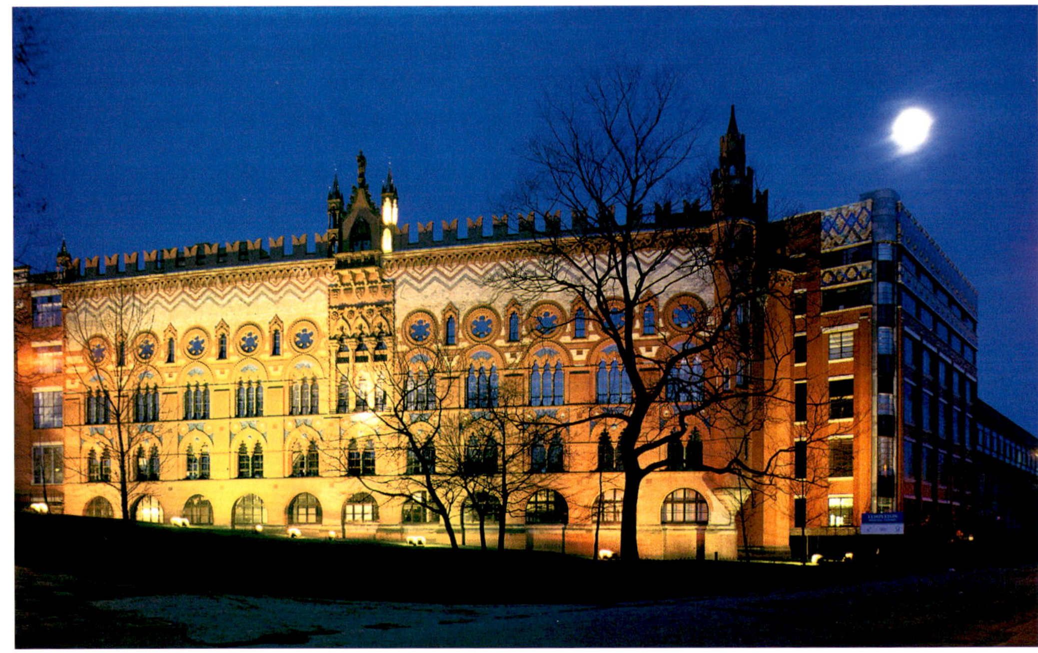

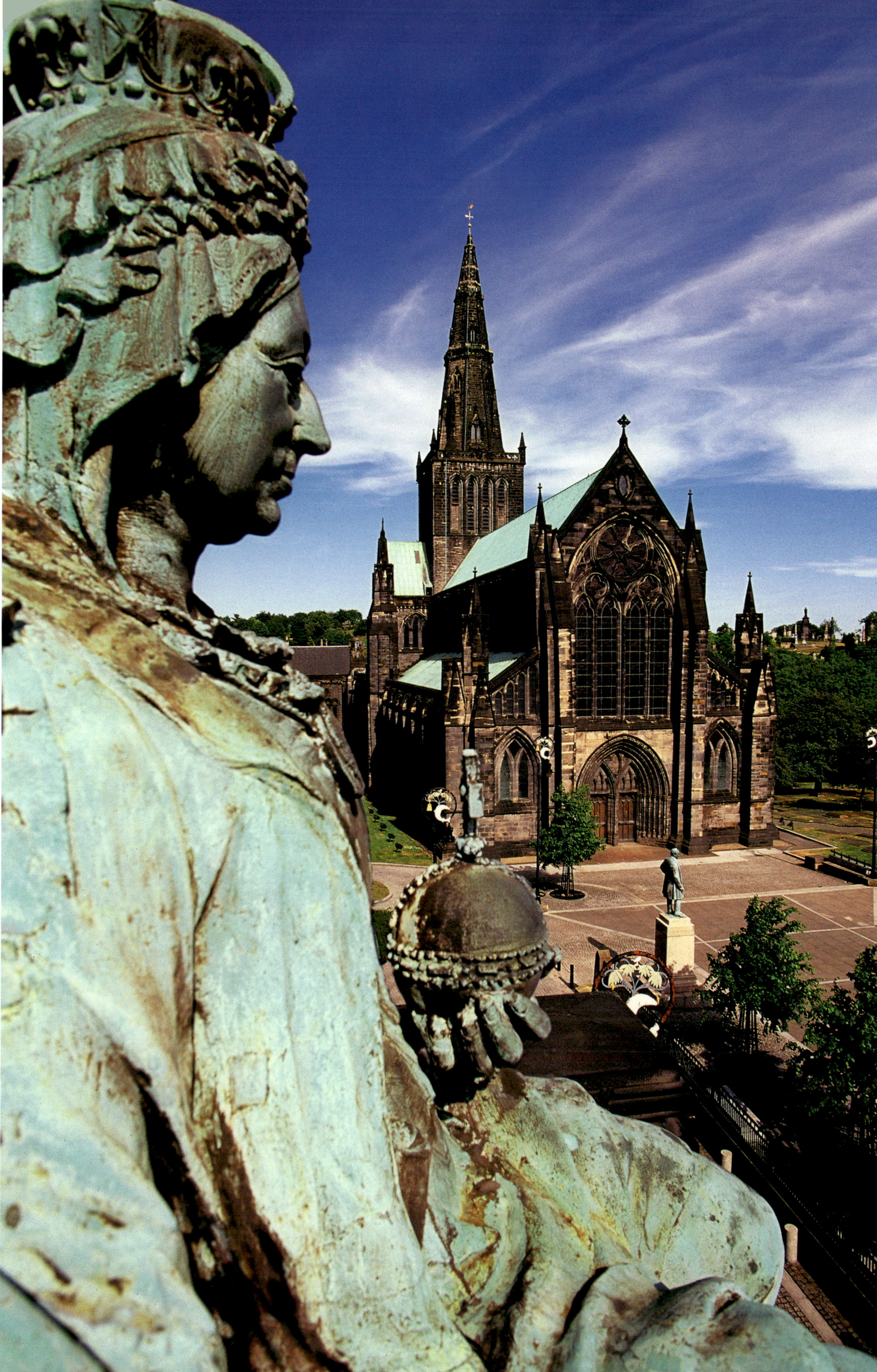

Originally designed by John Kibble in the 1860s for the grounds of his home in Coulport, Loch Long, this magnificent conservatory, now called the Kibble Palace, was dismantled in 1873 and sailed up the River Clyde by barge where it was reassembled at Glasgow Botanic Gardens. It recently underwent a £7 million restoration. From the air it bears a striking resemblance to the Starship *Enterprise* from the 1960s' series *Star Trek*.

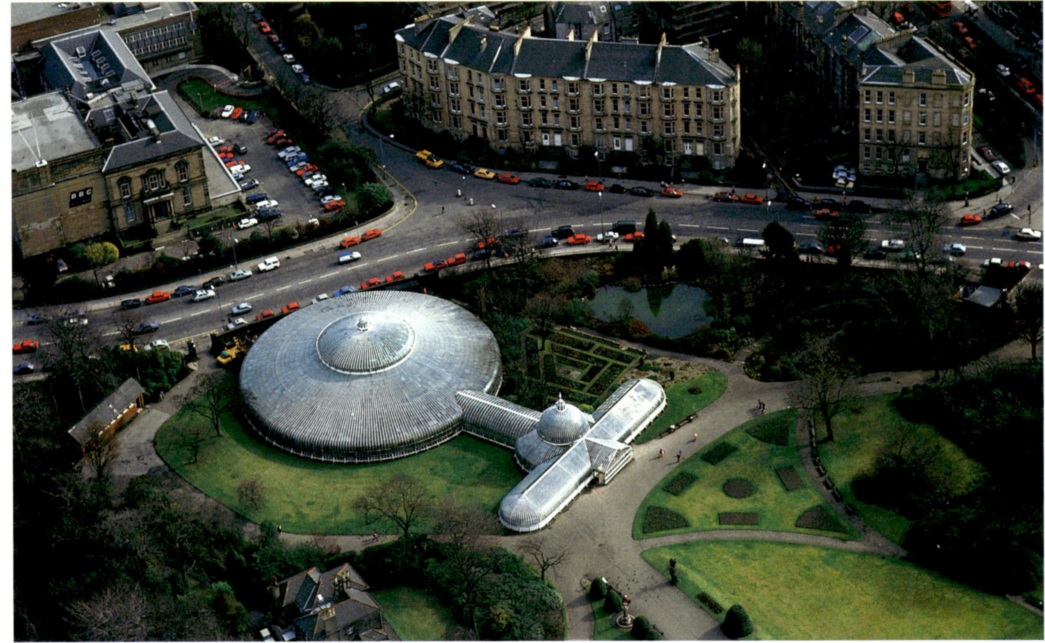

(Right) The Kibble Palace is a gift for wedding photographers.
(Far right) Sunday afternoon in the Kibble Palace.

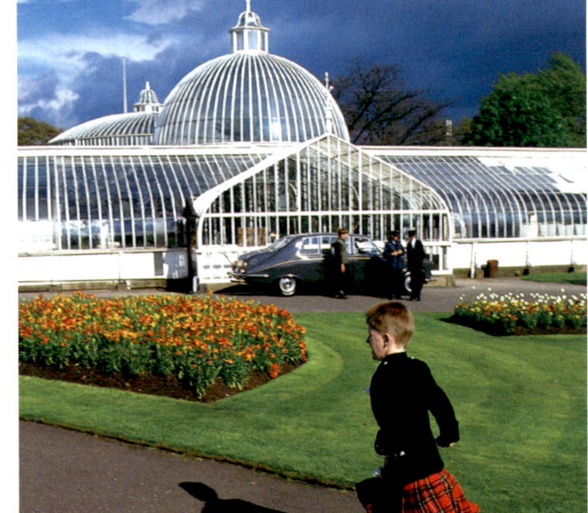

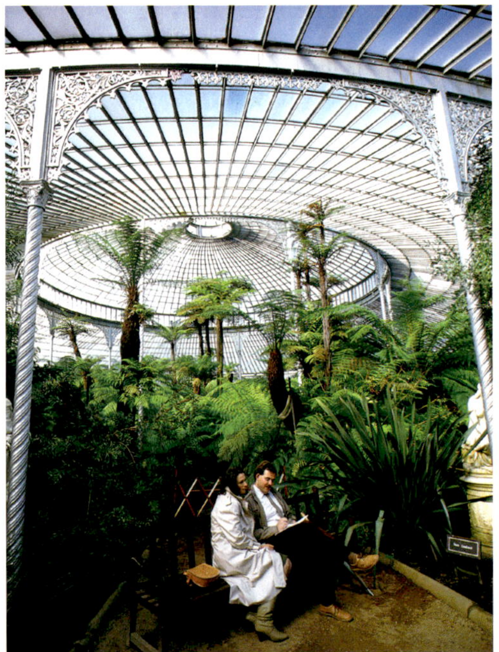

I chose to photograph Suzanne Bonnar, the jazz singer and actress, in the Kibble Palace. I enjoyed our photo session and was happy that I'd picked the right location.

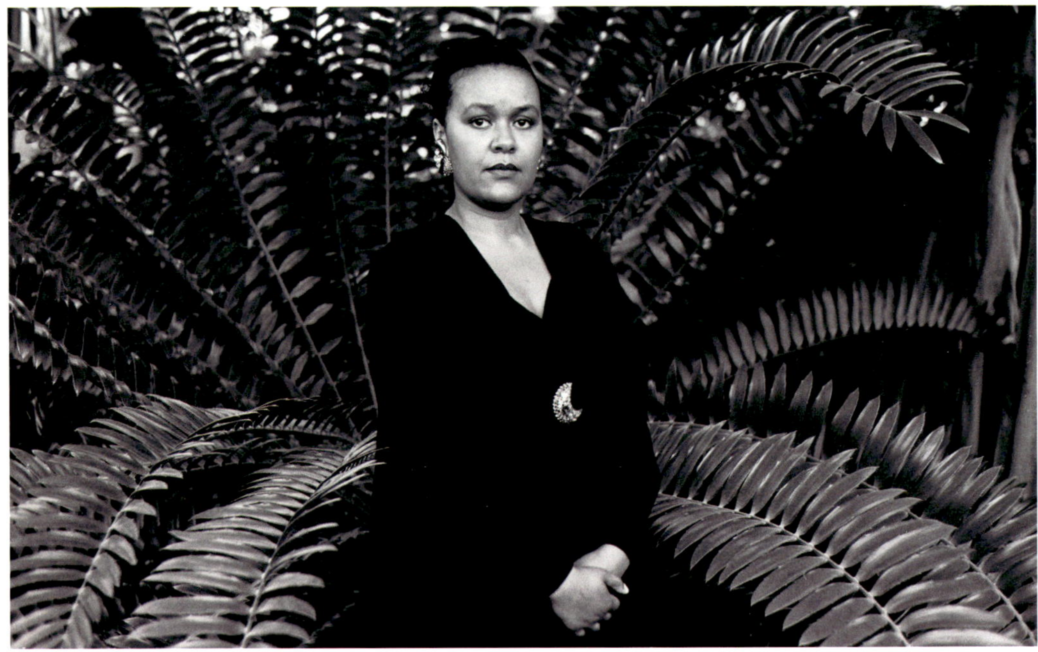

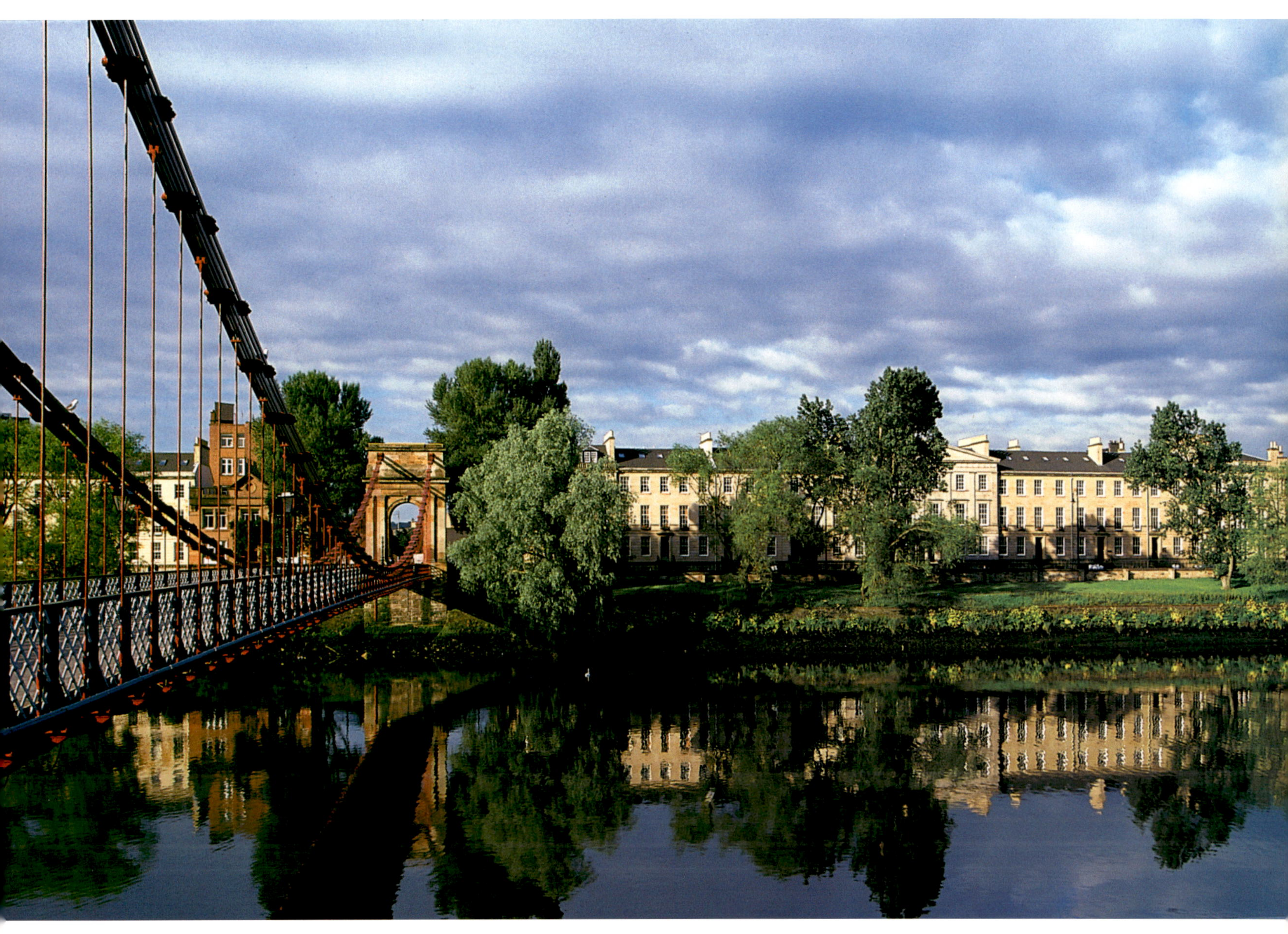

Carlton Place was Glasgow's original waterside living, and technically this is part of the Gorbals, which goes some way towards contradicting that area's prevalent stereotype. The magnificent Regency terrace reflects the city's wealth in the early 1800s. The suspension bridge featured at the end of John Schlesinger's brilliant 1983 TV drama *An Englishman Abroad*, standing in for Moscow in a flurry of snow. Another gem of the Gorbals is the Citizens Theatre, a unique haven for theatre.

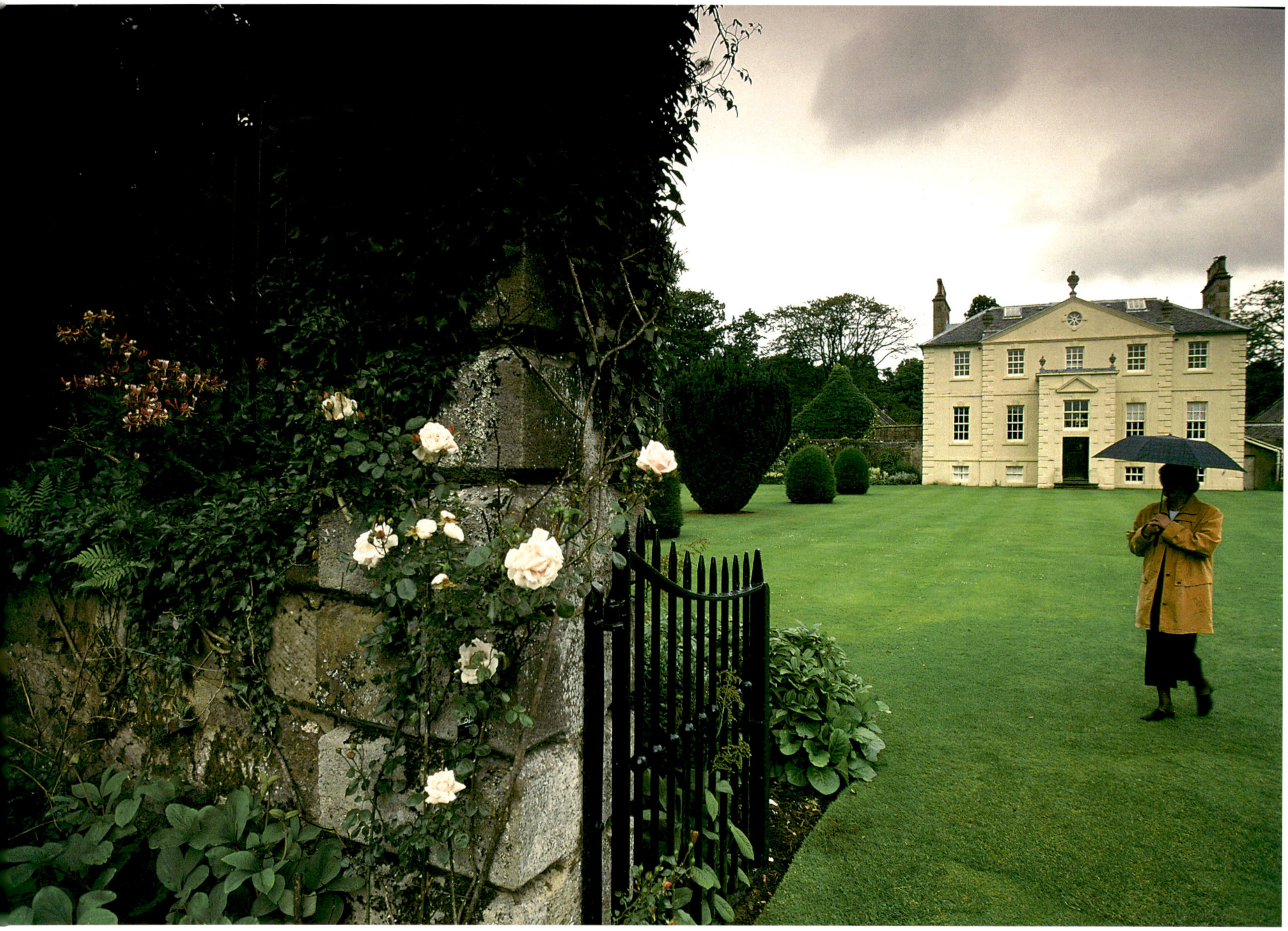

Greenbank Garden in Clarkston, on the outskirts of Glasgow, is really about its botanical collection. Great as it is, I would like to be able to enjoy the interior of this Glasgow merchant's house, dating from 1763, but it is open to the public only on rare occasions.

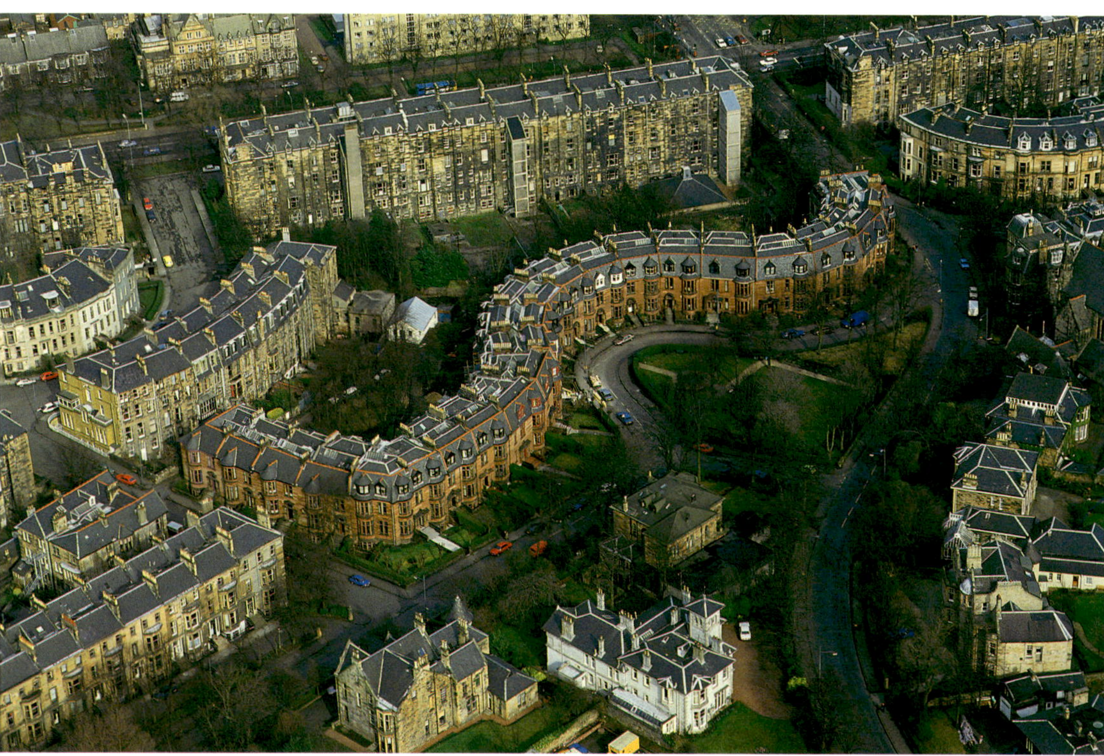

Kensington Gate, the serpentine-shaped townhouses in Glasgow's West End. One of the city's Victorian gems.

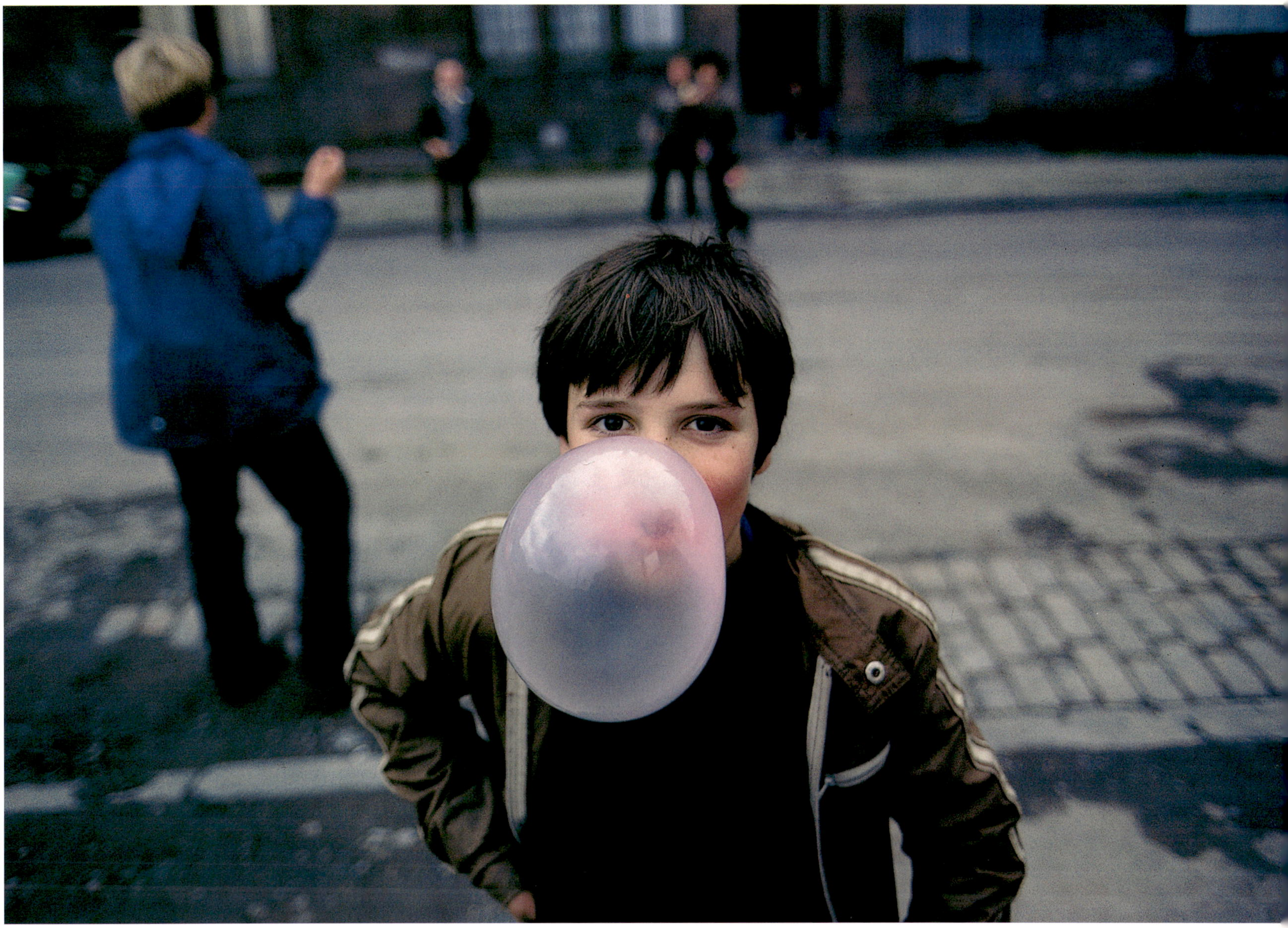

Sorry about this caption – straight from my local newspaper days: Nothing is going to burst his bubble! Maryhill in the 1970s.

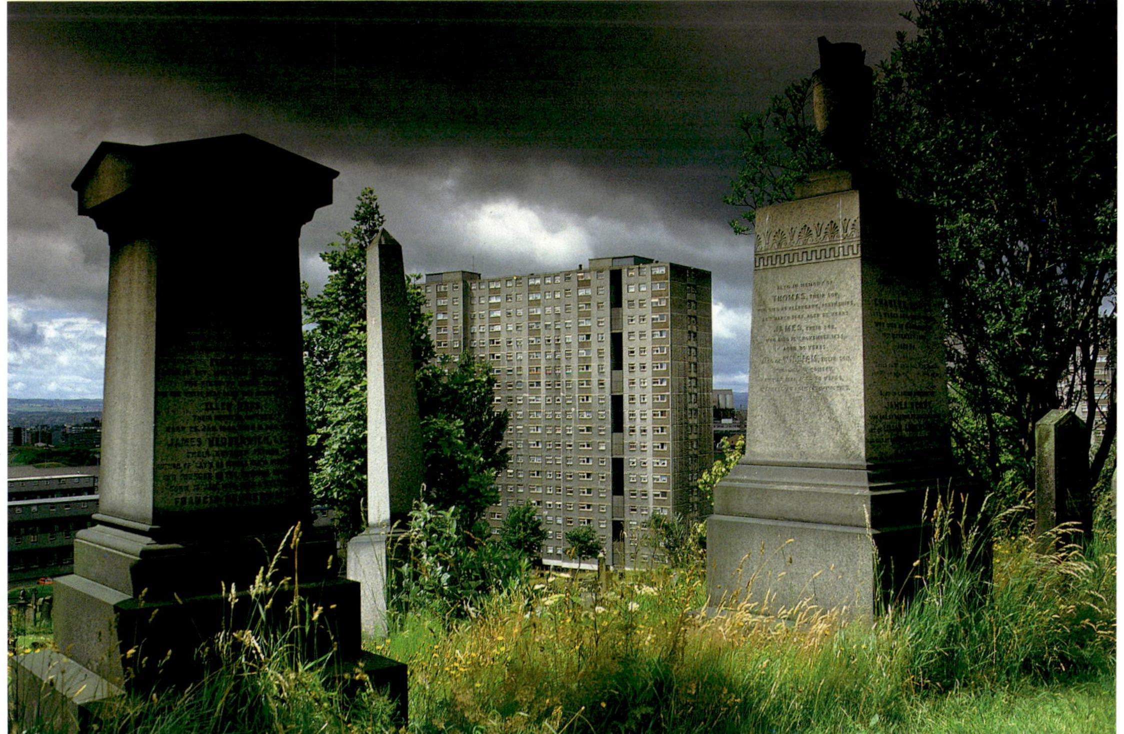

Here, the monolithic slab of high flats resembles a tombstone in nearby Sighthill Cemetery. Glasgow's cemeteries are often atmospheric places that can evoke many a strange tale. In 1954 there was a panic in and around the Southern Necropolis when children started a rumour that a vampire with metal teeth had already eaten two people in the graveyard. It was blamed on the influence of American horror comics of the day, which led to a question in parliament and a restriction on the imports.

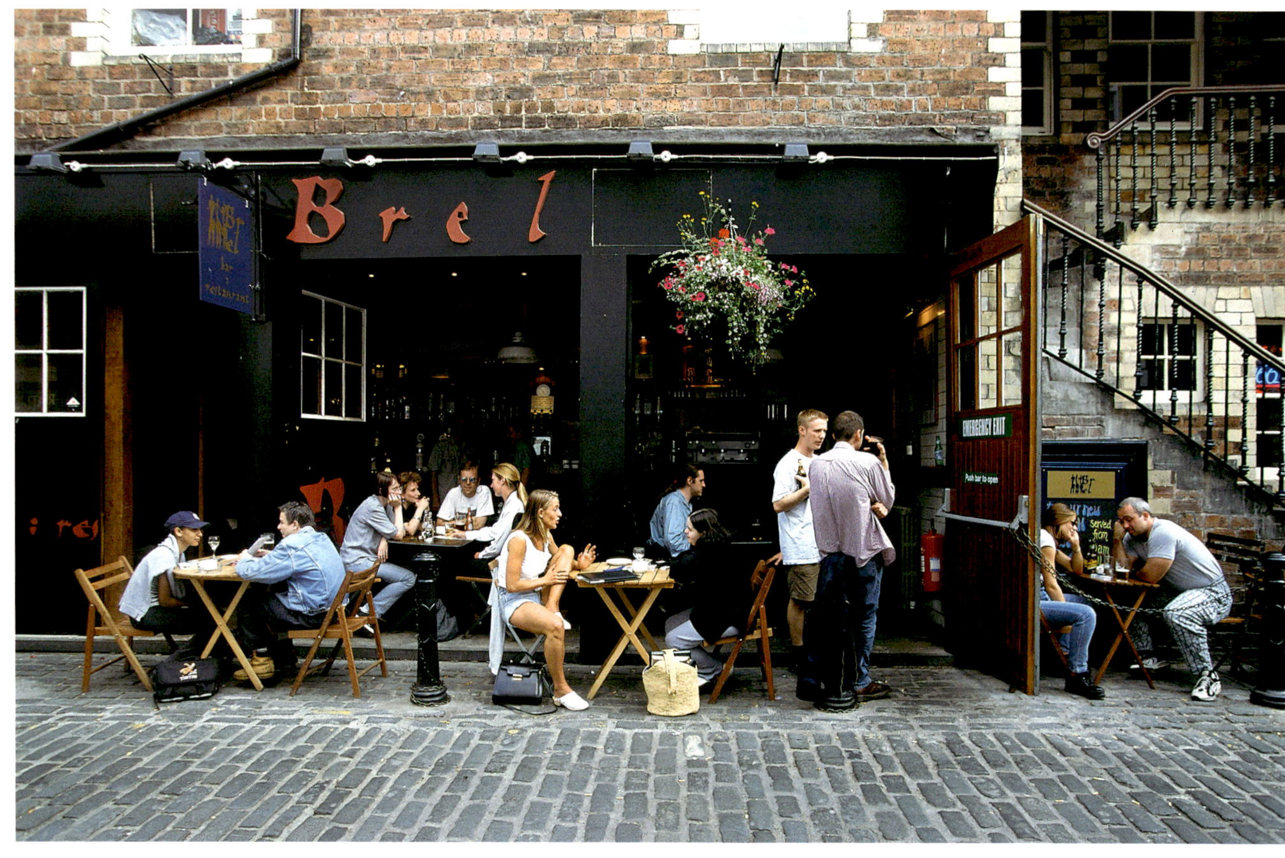

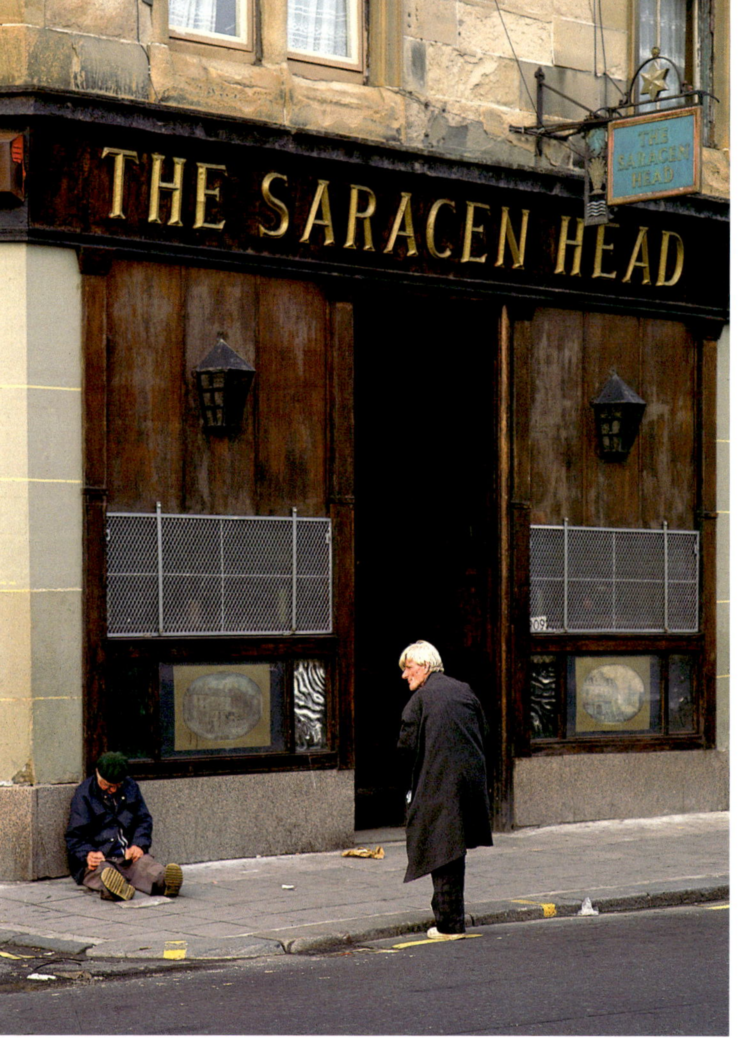

Glasgow's West End has a bohemian feel and a large student population. It has a different energy from the rest of the city. This is where I'd choose to live in Glasgow if I could avoid the noise of partying students through the walls at night.

The Saracen Head, known as the Sarry Heid to its regulars, originally dates from 1755 when it was a fashionable hotel on the other side of the Gallowgate. Customers included Robert Burns, Boswell and Dr Johnson. The skull of the last witch executed in Scotland is kept in a glass case in the bar.

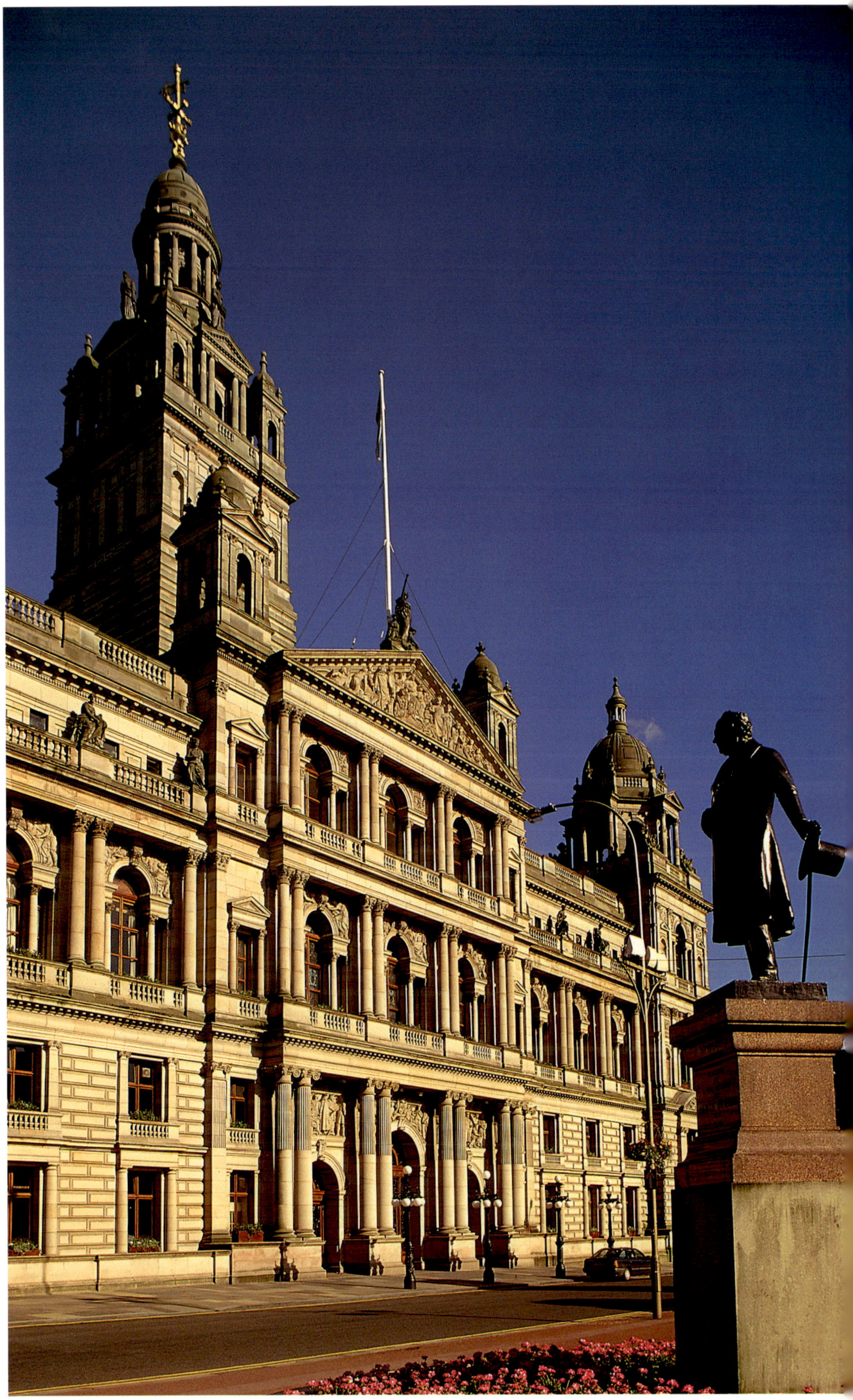

Glasgow City Chambers was opened by Queen Victoria in 1888. It is an Italian Renaissance palace with a wonderful marbled entrance and staircase. It has one of those interiors, like Durham Cathedral, that always surprises you, no matter how many times you visit. Perhaps that is a sign of a great building. While I was photographing the City Chambers, an elderly and proud citizen told me that C. R. Mackintosh had designed it. I chose not to inform him how wrong he was, but nonetheless it is a fine piece of municipal architecture.

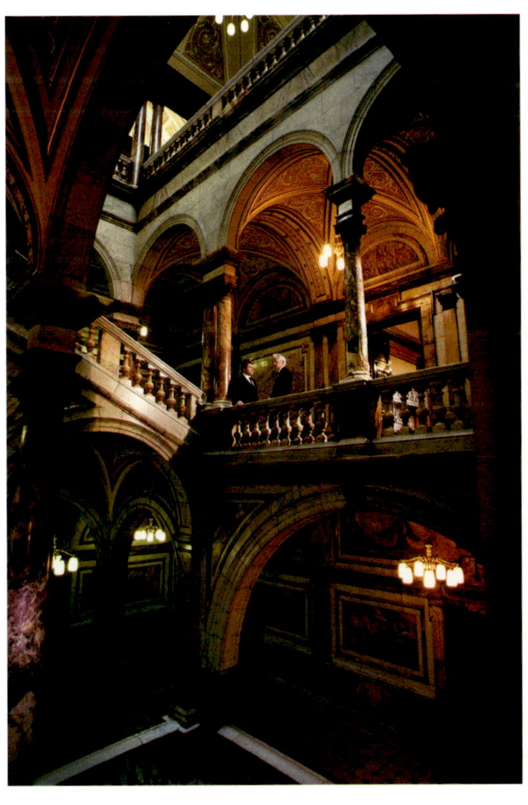

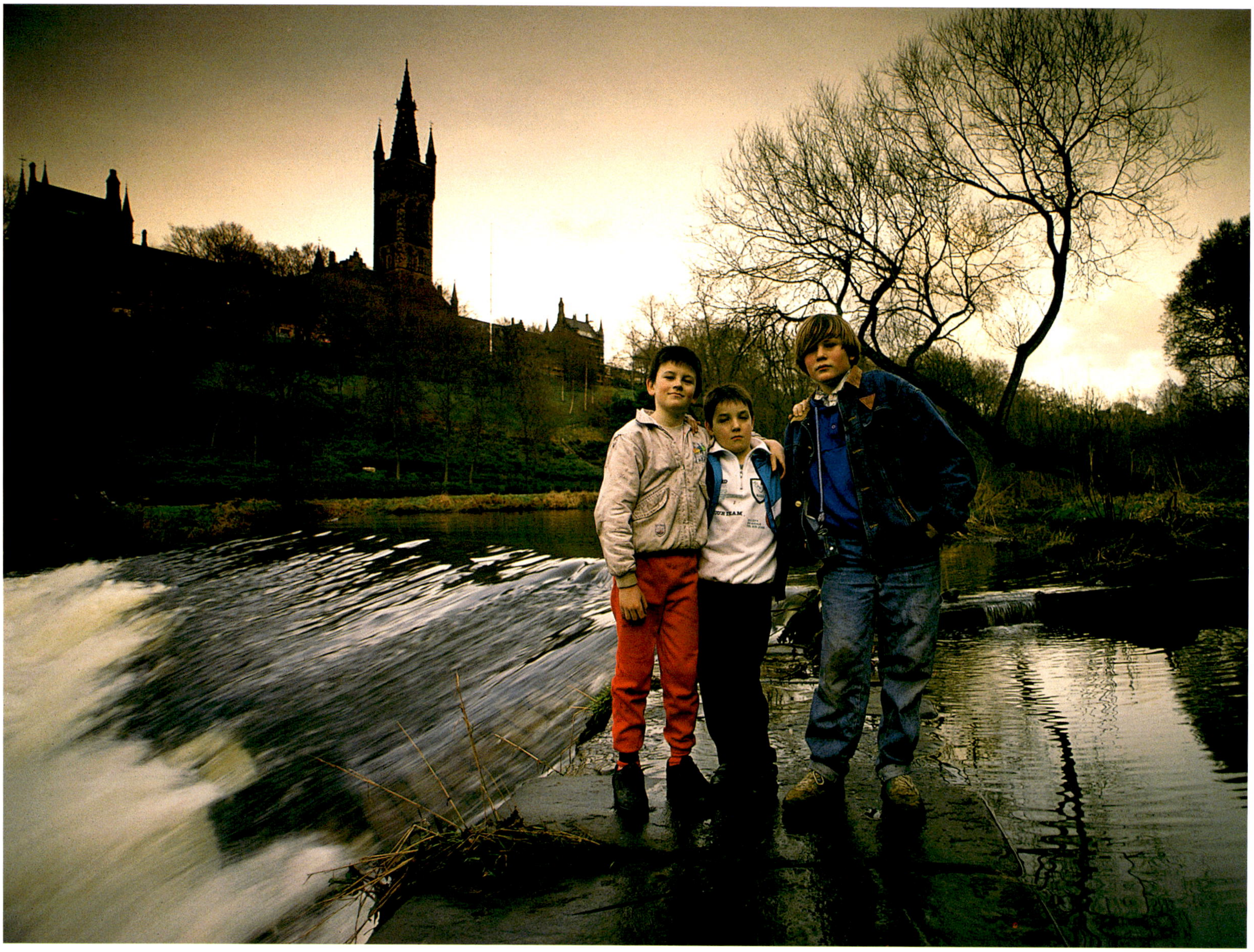

Glasgow's second river, the Kelvin, was once as polluted as the Clyde, but now salmon and brown trout can be seen leaping at the weirs of disused mills. At this point the river passes the University of Glasgow, whose tower still punctuates the Glasgow skyline in spite of competition from many high-rise buildings. These kids show a confidence that can be a sign of a self-assured city. In Argyle Street I was once approached by someone cadging, 'Have you got a spare £2,000, sur?' He got a quid for his inventiveness.

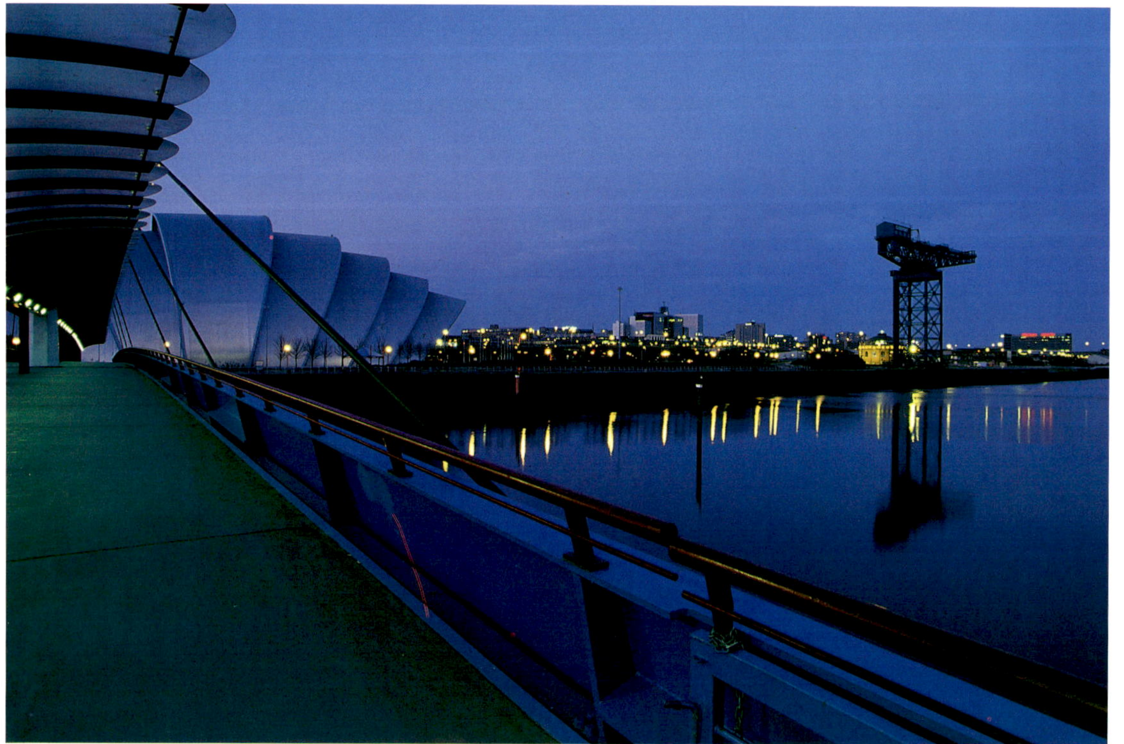

Many British cities have redeveloped their waterfronts or riversides for the aspirational or, to quote the outmoded phrase, the 'upwardly mobile'. In a TV documentary on Cardiff Bay, a long-time council house resident wryly asked where was she going to moor her yacht? This area of Glasgow is now the media hub of the city, reached by Bells' Bridge.

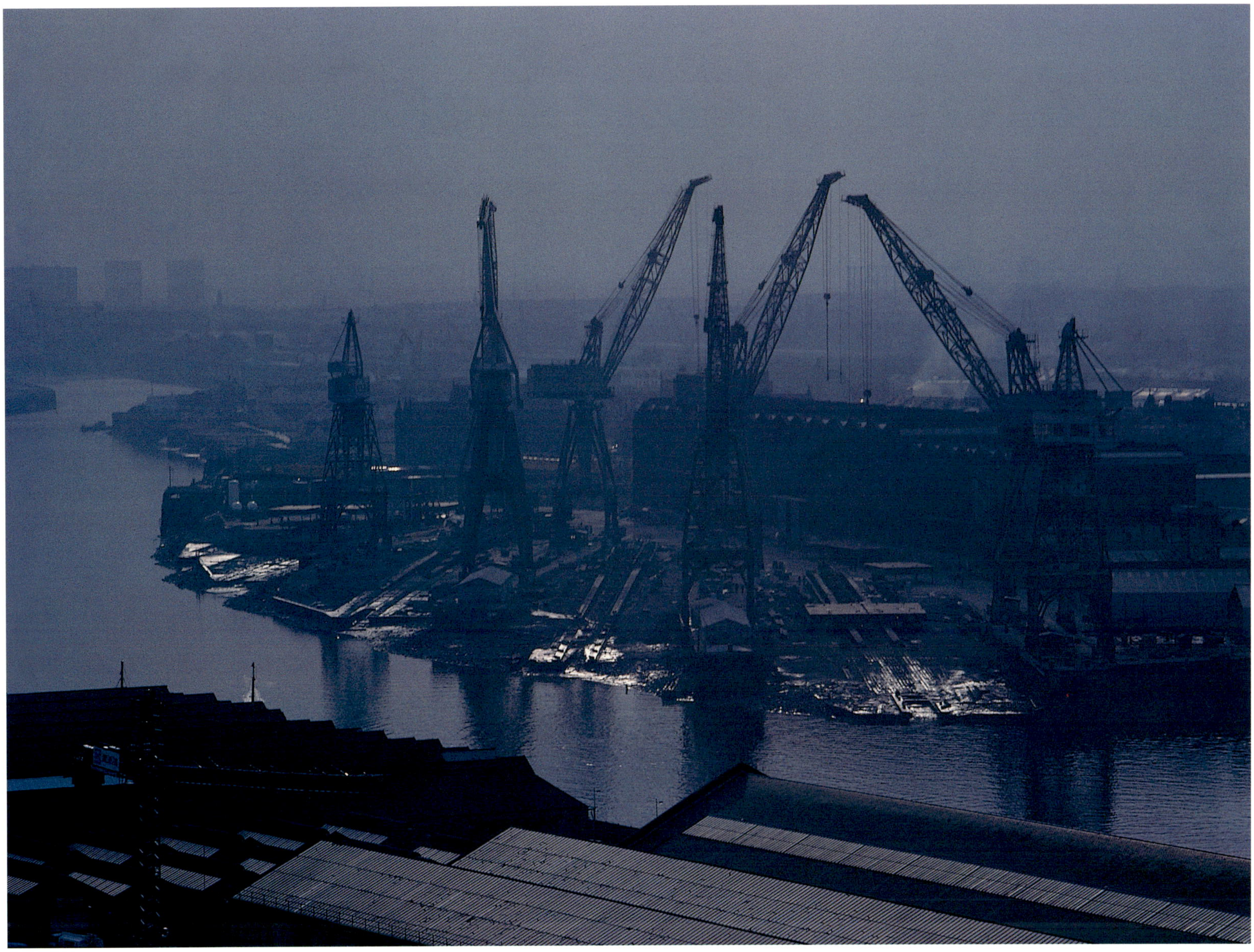

When I first worked in Glasgow in the 1970s, shipbuilding and heavy engineering were still part of the city. Glasgow has had to reinvent itself through events like the Garden Festival and European City of Culture year, which played a part in making it a tourism destination. The city has long been a major source of rock music, and in the visual arts boasts two Turner Prize-winners.

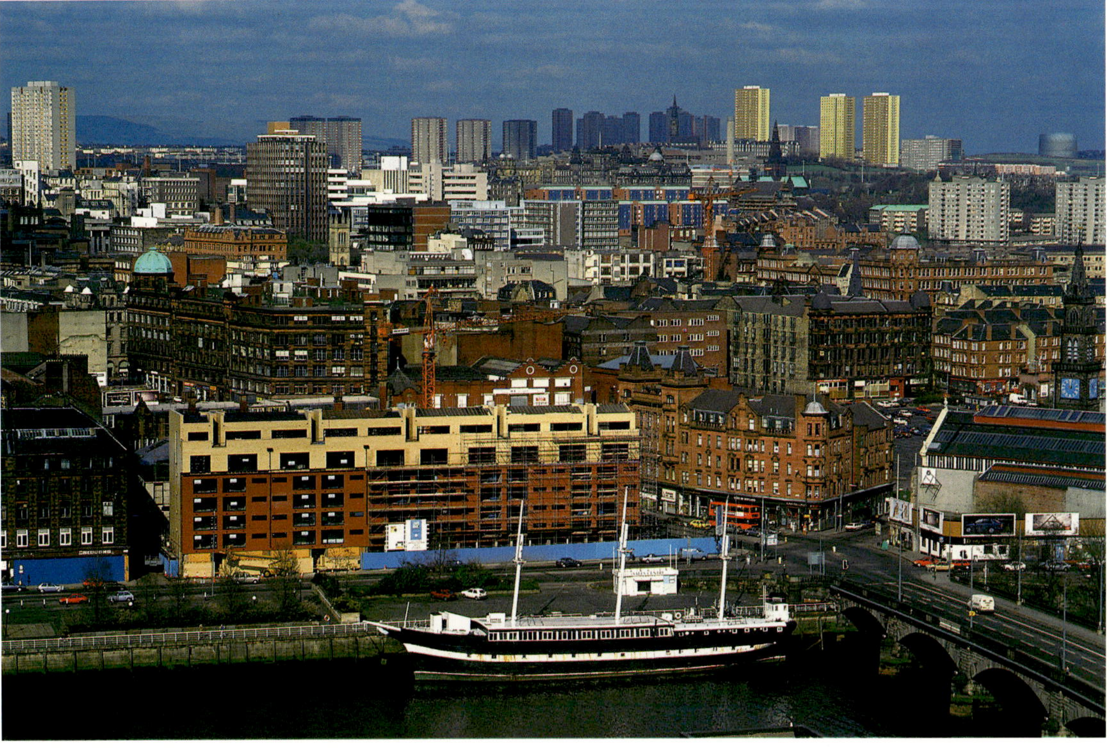

This was one of the new wave of apartment developments under construction on Clyde Street in the 1980s. In the foreground is the *SV Carrick*, also known as the *City of Adelaide*, which is the world's oldest surviving clipper ship and was a landmark on the River Clyde for many years. Currently it is awaiting restoration in Irvine, but its future is far from certain.

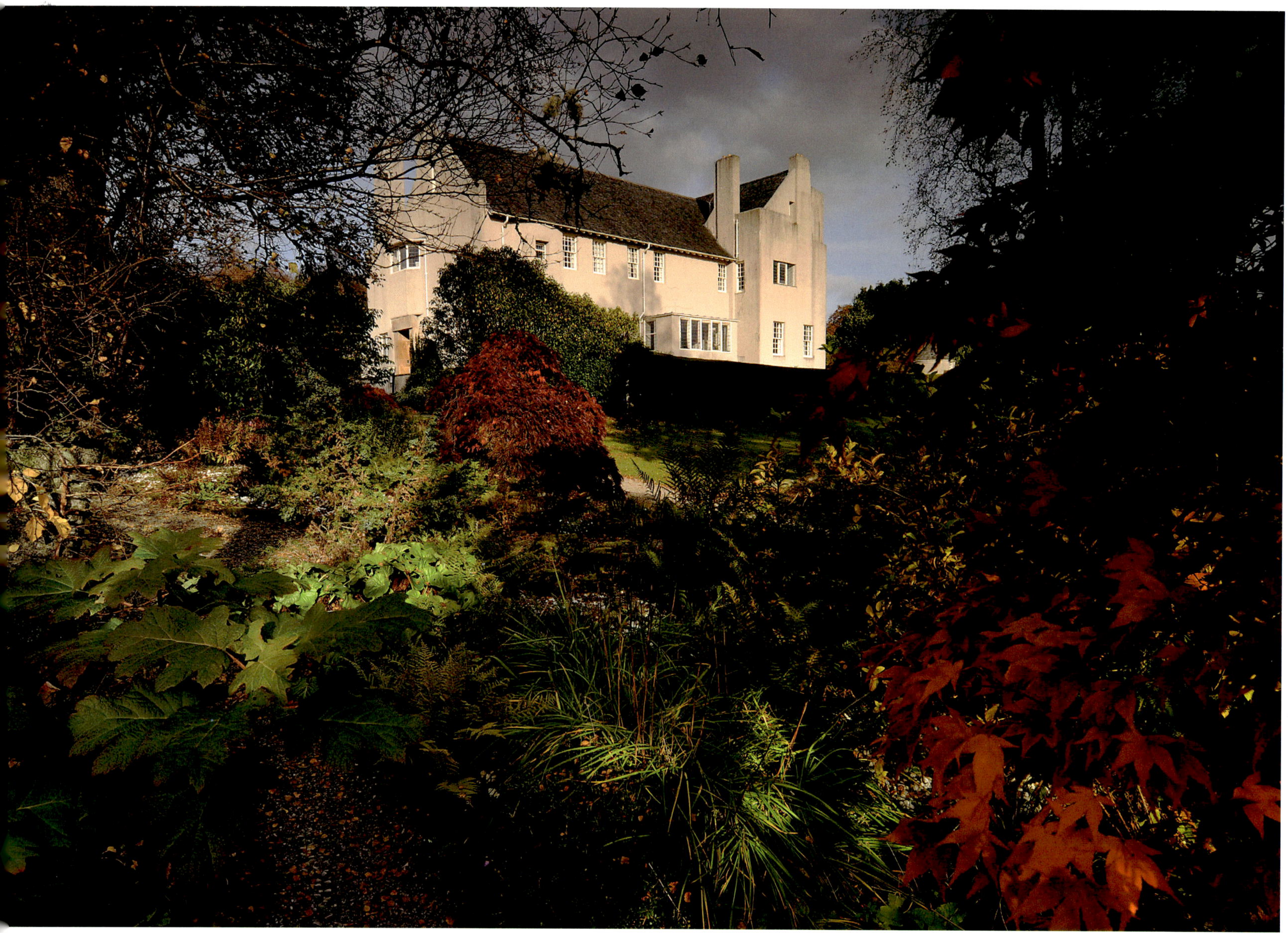

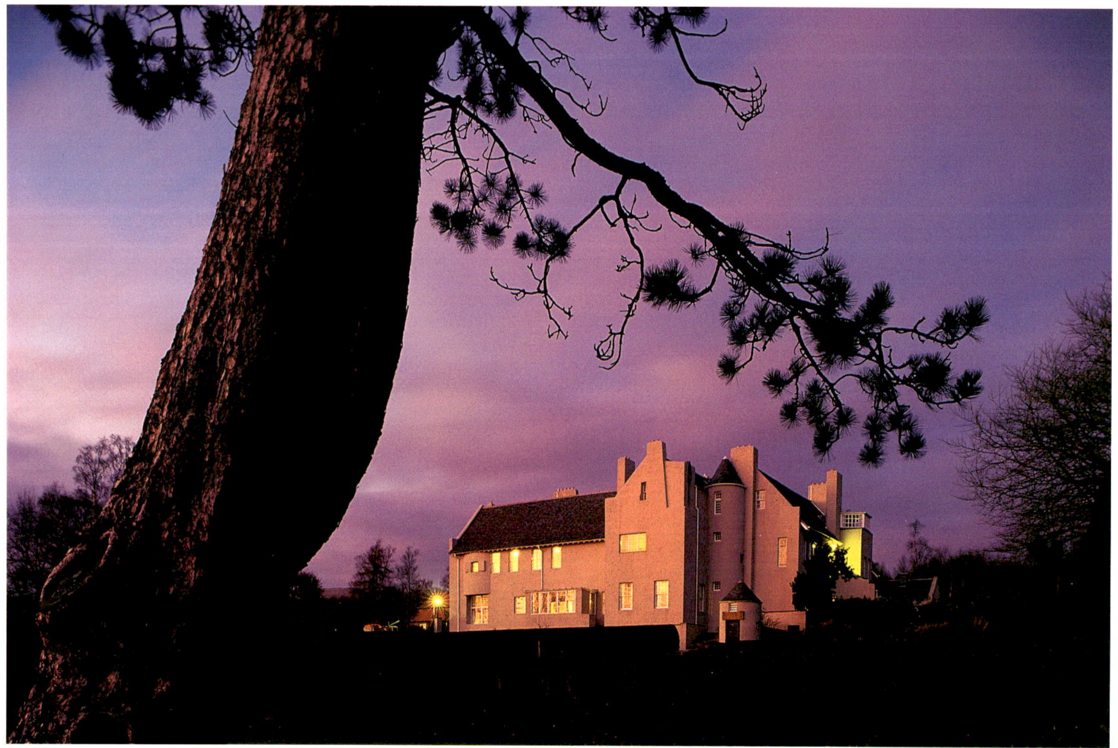

Charles Rennie Mackintosh designed The Hill House, Helensburgh, for the publisher Walter Blackie in the very early 20th century, and it is now in the care of the National Trust for Scotland. In the 1980s I met the then curator who had formerly been a pugilist and a warden at Barlinnie Prison. He said this job had opened up a new world of the arts for him and his wife. He told me, 'To the amazement of myself and our family we spend our holidays visiting other houses and art galleries.' This testifies that great architecture and a sympathetic environment can have a profound influence on people's lives. The great tragedy is that Mackintosh wasn't able to build more in his lifetime. Helensburgh was also the birthplace of John Logie Baird, the inventor of television.

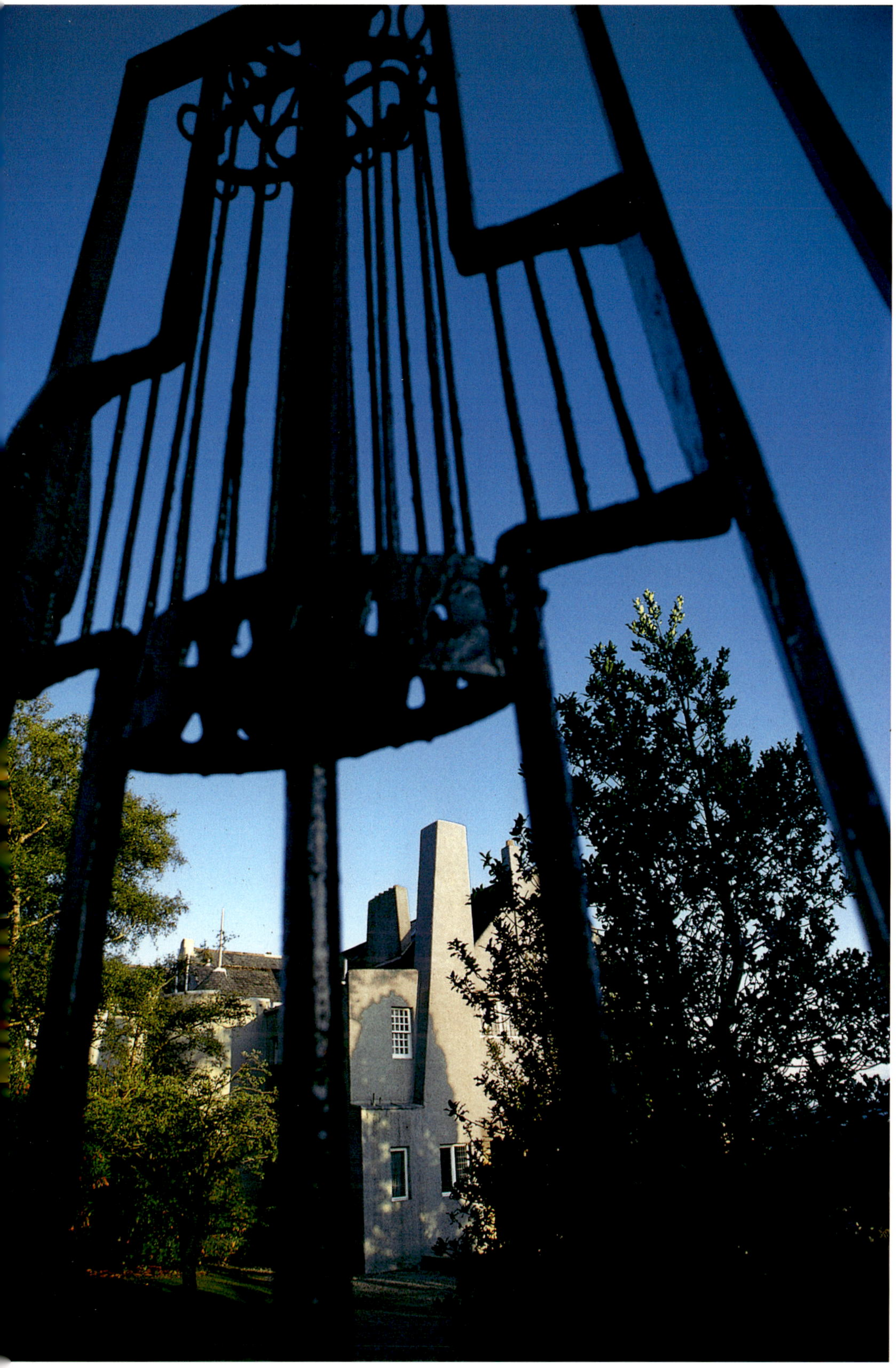

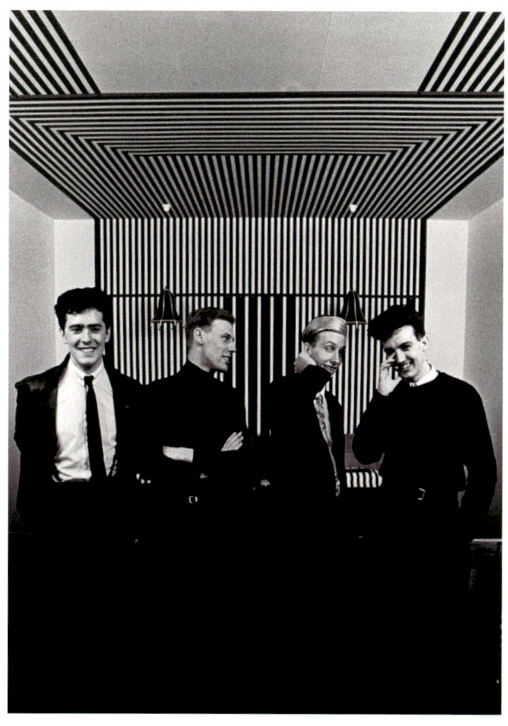

(Above) The reconstruction of a guest bedroom designed by C. R. Mackintosh for 78 Derngate in Northampton, the home of the engineer W. J. Bassett-Lowke in 1916, in the University of Glasgow's Hunterian Art Gallery. George Bernard Shaw, on being asked how he had managed to sleep in the room considering the boldness of the decoration, replied, 'I always sleep with my eyes closed.' I used it as the location for a shoot for the 1980s' band Baby Knives. The genius of Mackintosh is that his work is timeless.

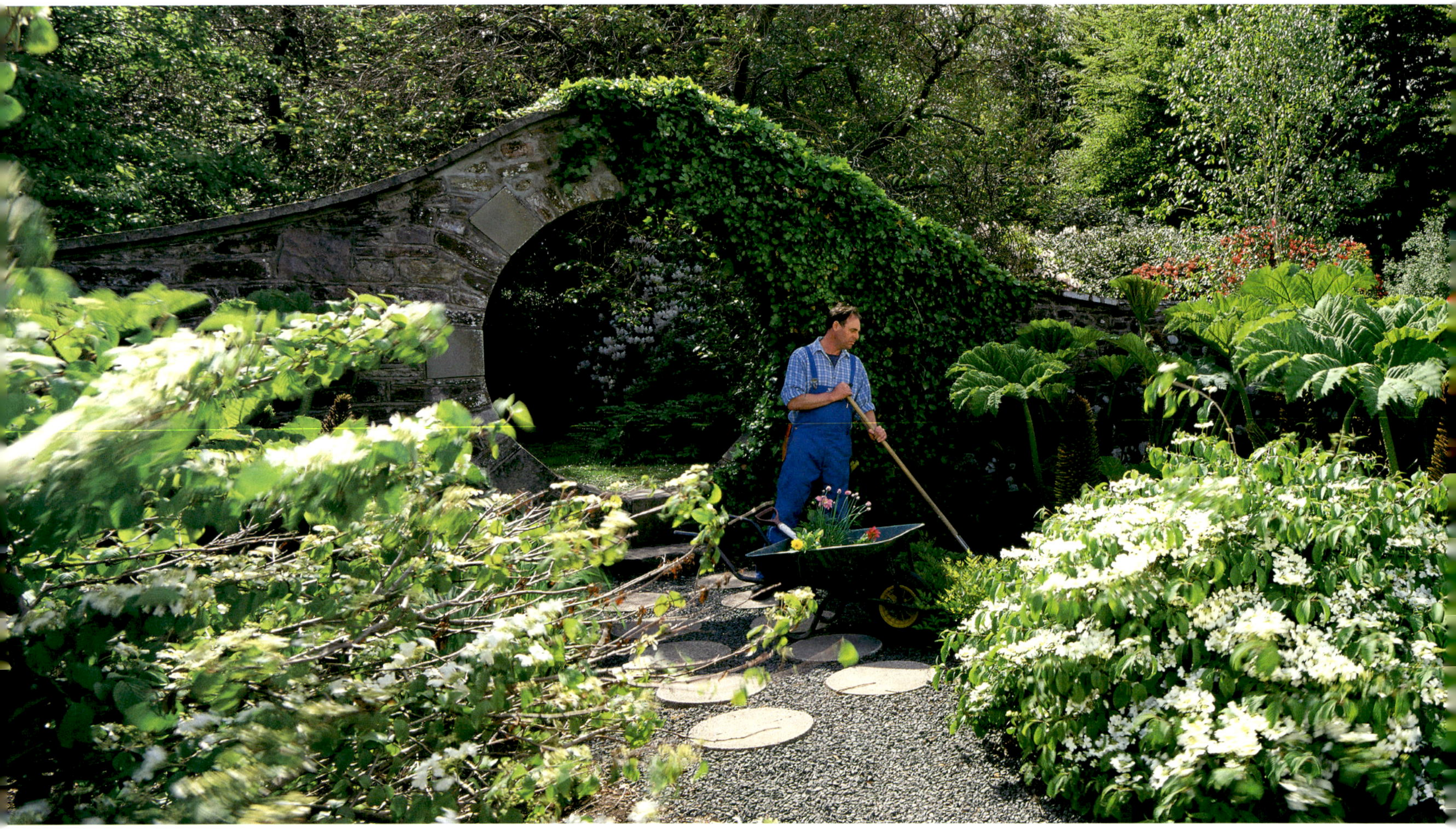

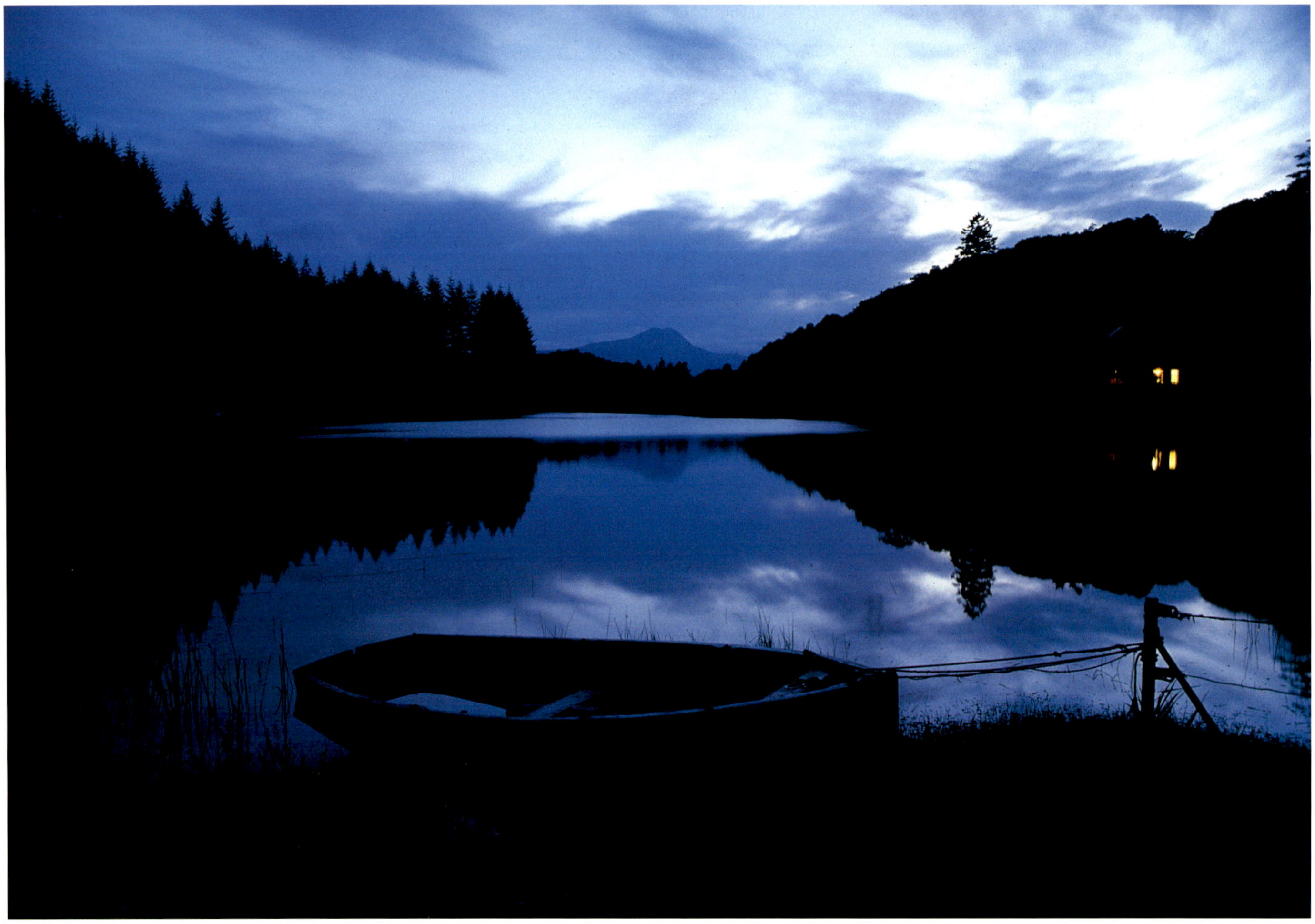

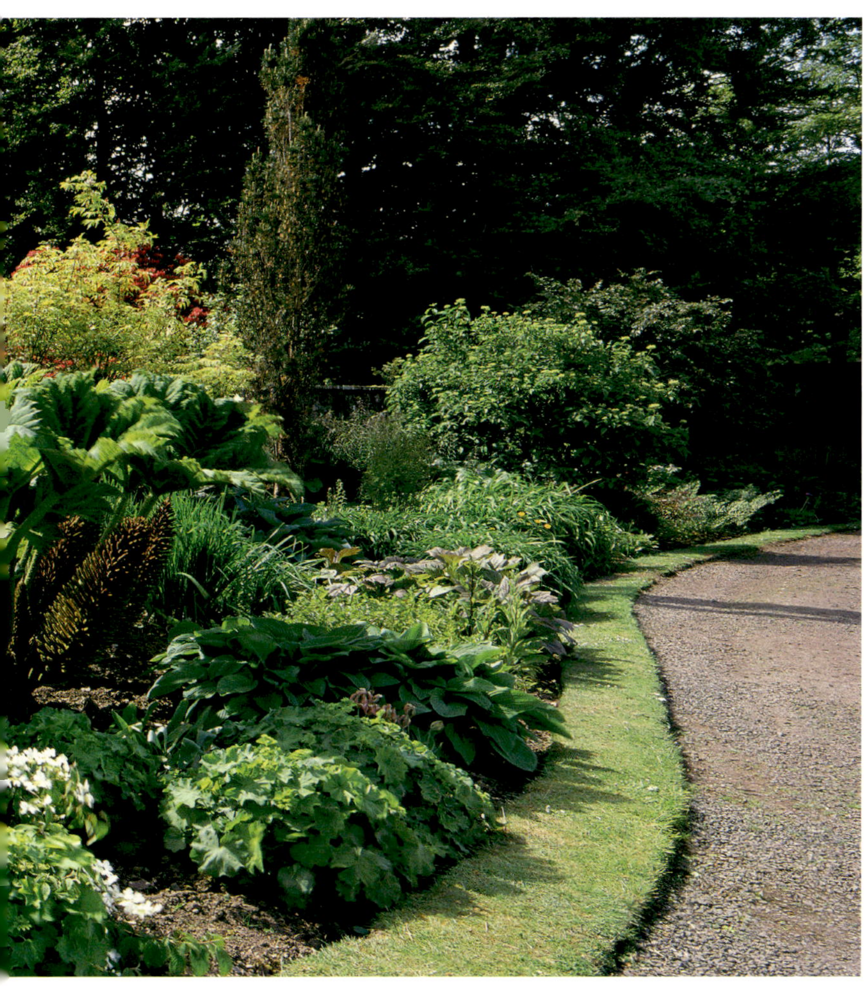

The Moongate in the Lady Curren Garden at Ross Priory on the shores of Loch Lomond. It is now owned by Strathclyde University but can be visited through Scotland's Garden Scheme. Sir Walter Scott is said to have gained inspiration for his *Waverley* novels during annual visits to the Priory. There has been a building on the site since 1693, but the present Gothic-style building, designed by James Gillespie Graham, dates from 1812.

(Below left) Ben Lomond reflected in Loch Ard, which is the source of the River Forth and is within the Loch Lomond and The Trossachs National Park, which was established in 2002 as Scotland's first national park.

(Below) The Scottish Tourist Board produced a poster from this picture, taken at Loch Lomond, which wasn't a set-up. I quickly asked the children's parents, 'Is it OK to snap your kids?' The saying 'Never work with children or animals' is very true most of the time.

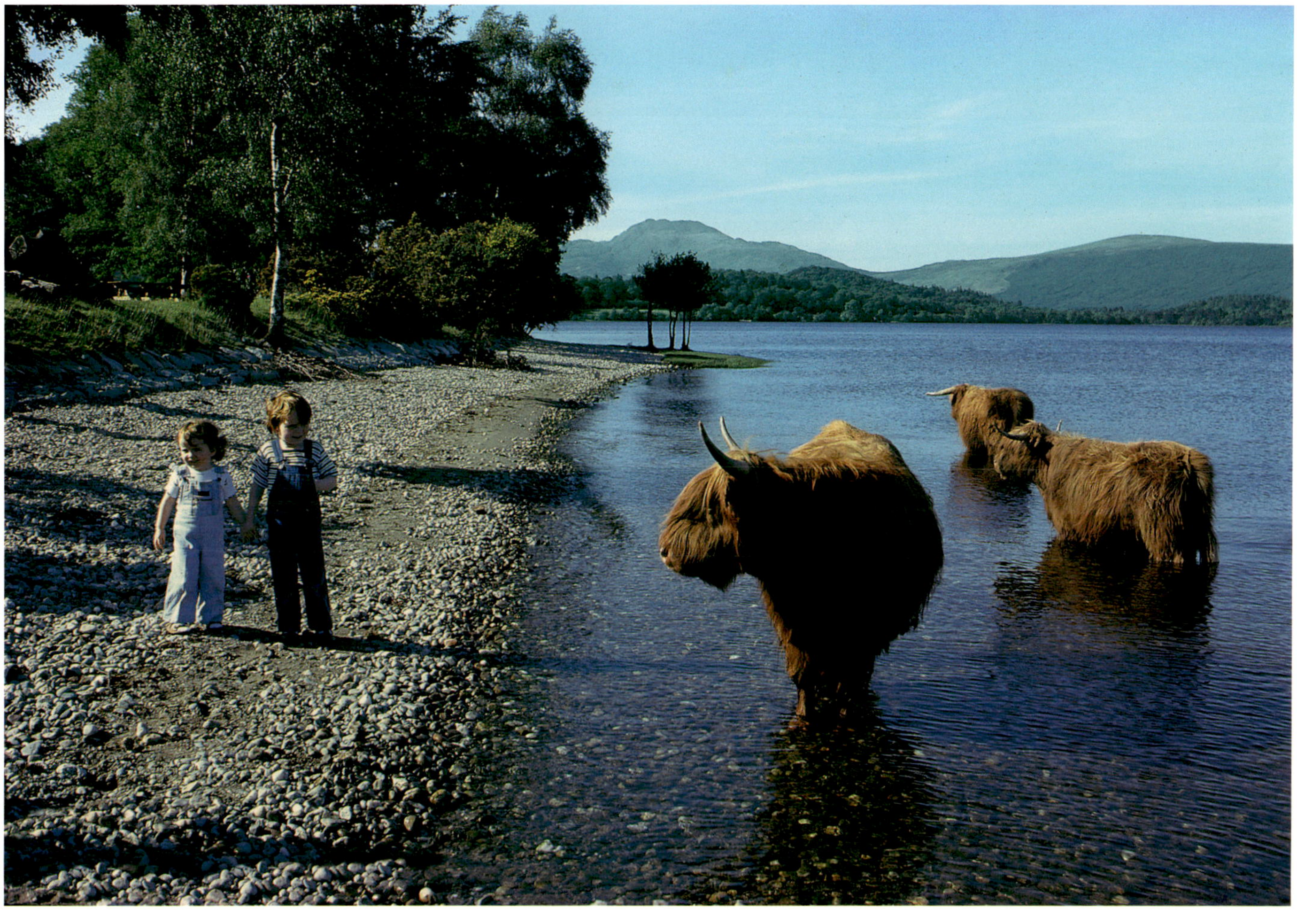

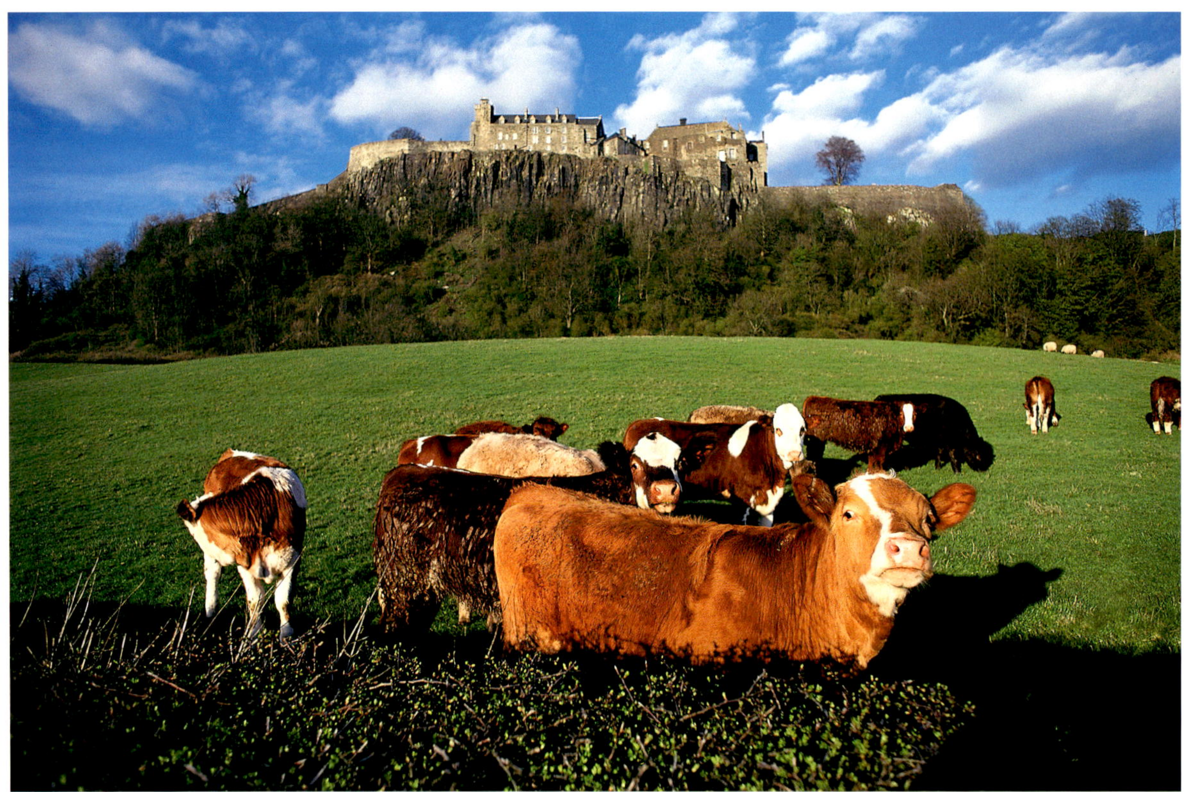

Stirling Castle, 250 feet above the plain, on an extinct volcano, is one of Britain's most magnificently sited castles and has way too much history to even attempt to put into this caption.

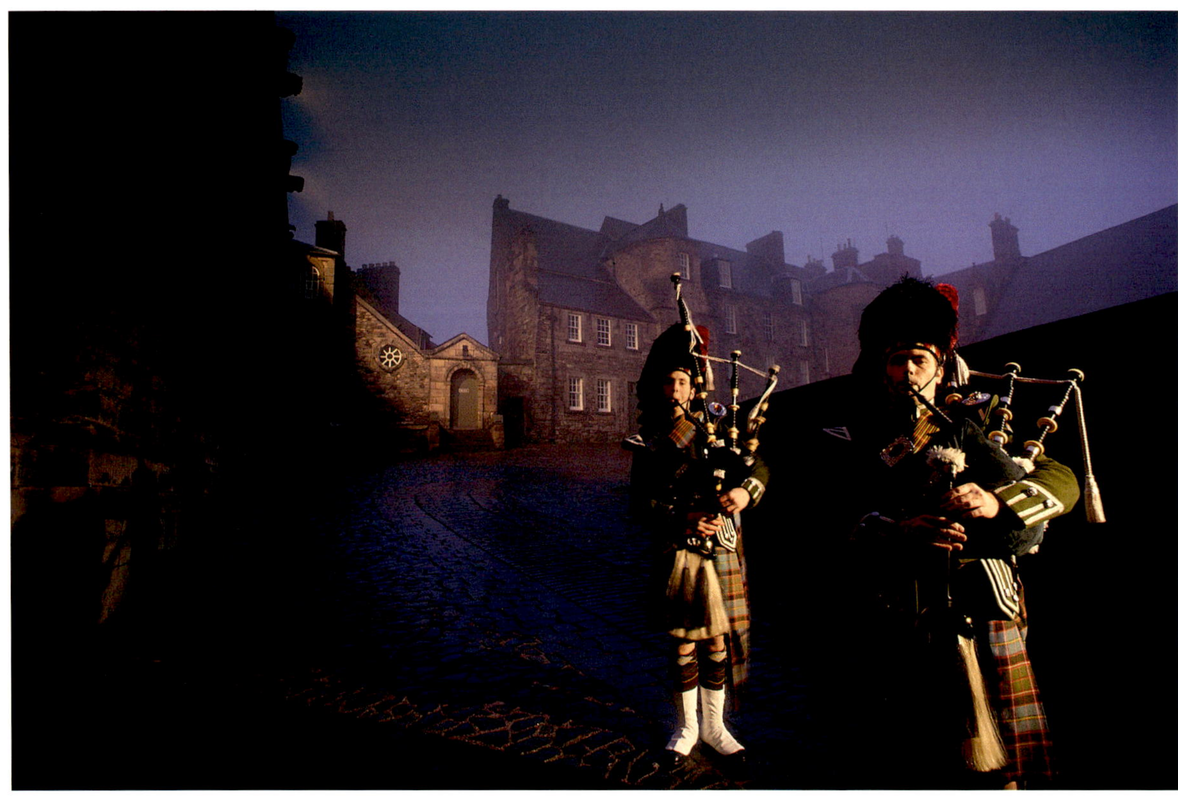

Neiman Marcus, the American store, commissioned me to photograph Stirling Castle for a Scottish travel promotion. I get a certain delight when I work for an international company and a brand name with cachet.

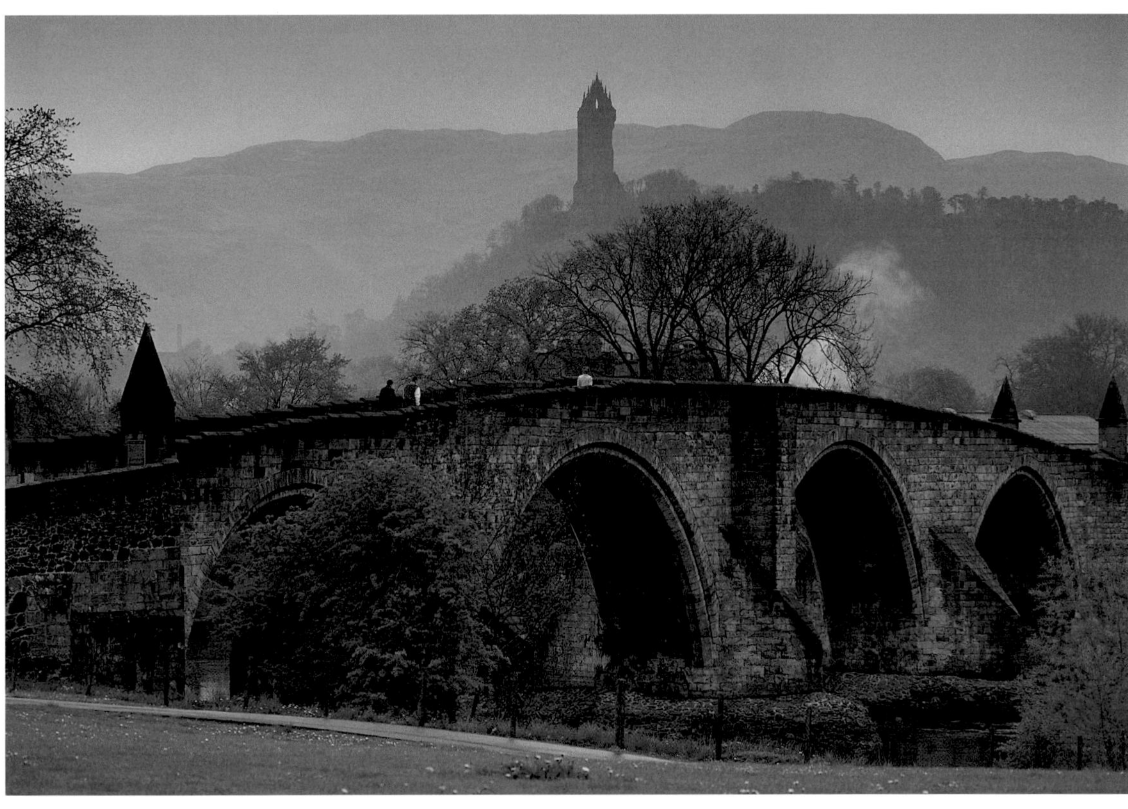

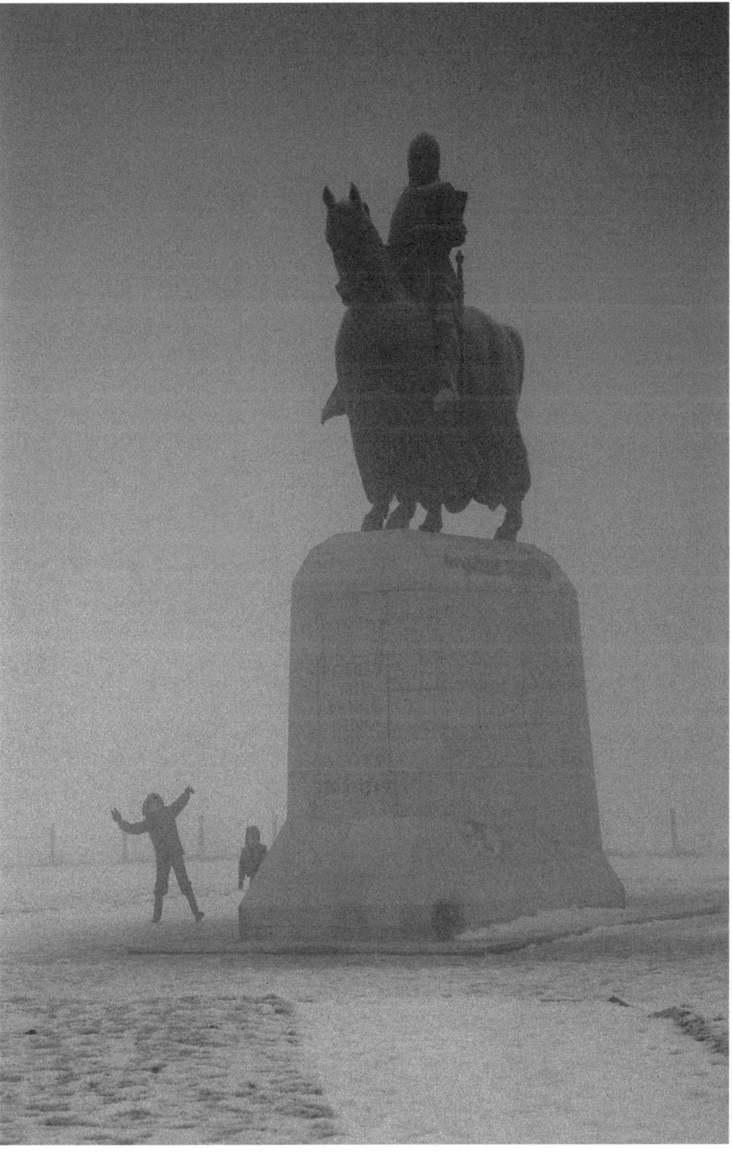

Built in 1400, the Old Bridge in Stirling, is one of several bridges that makes me marvel at its construction and its antiquity. The Wallace Monument (seen in the distance) was built in 1869 on the 360-foot Abbey Craig, which is 220 feet high and contains Sir William Wallace's sword. He is regarded as the founder of the Scottish nation. The Oscar-winning film *Braveheart* was inaccurate as it depicted him as an uneducated, uncultured warrior covered in woad (blue pigment) when he was in fact the second son of Sir Malcolm Wallace of Elderslie, part of the Scottish aristocracy.

The Battle of Bannockburn in 1314 loomed large in my history lessons at primary school. It did give Scotland four hundred years of fluctuating independence, during which time the Scottish aristocracy kept in with the English crown. This equestrian statue by Pilkington Jackson of Robert the Bruce, King of Scots, was erected at Bannockburn in 1964. What does it say to us today?

The Atholl Highlanders are Europe's only private army. It is now purely a ceremonial regiment, comprising 100 men including the pipe band, but has a formal duty to defend Blair Castle in Highland Perthshire. It was formed in 1777 by the 4th Duke of Atholl to relieve other regiments serving in the American War of Independence, although it never got any farther than Ireland.

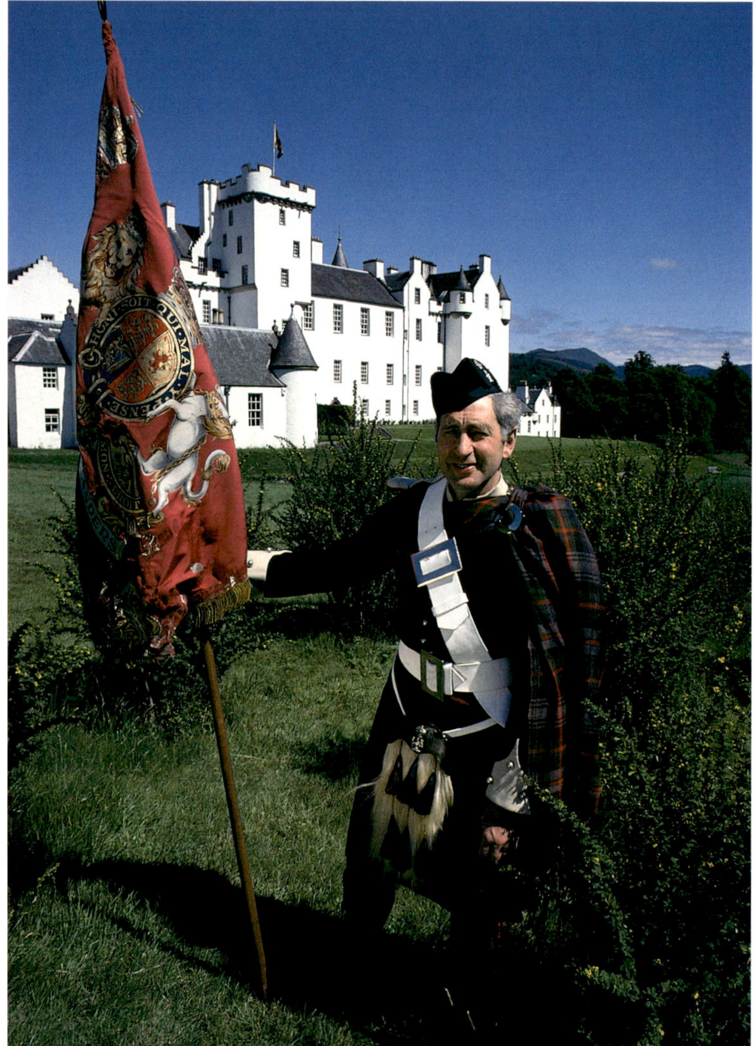

The curling bonspiel (outdoor tournament) at the Lake of Menteith near Stirling is a rare event on Scotland's only 'lake'. About every twenty years or so the ice grows thick enough to hold the many players and their heavy granite stones. Curling games now are usually held in sterile indoor ice rinks, which makes it difficult to get atmospheric action shots like this one, taken in 1979.

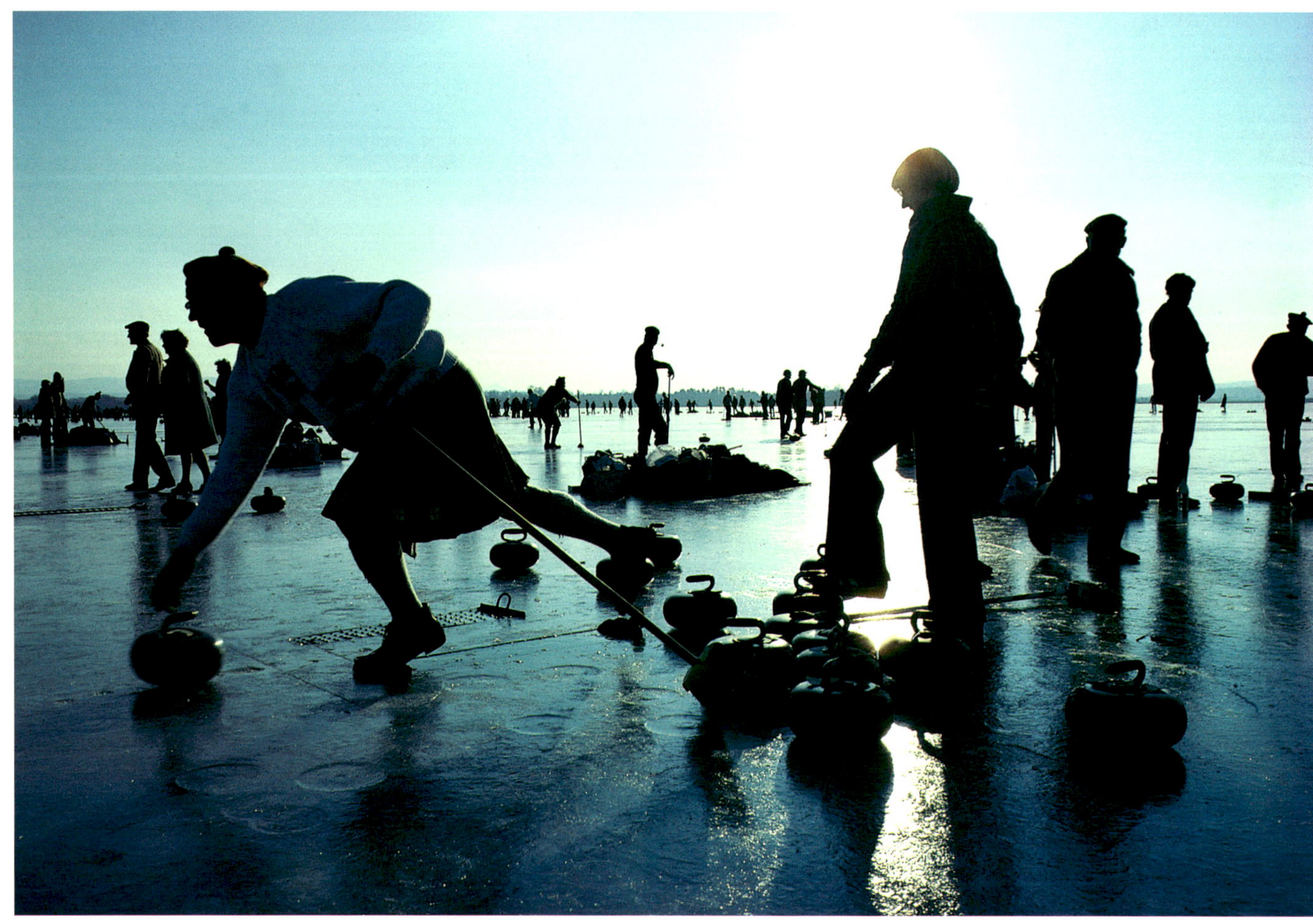

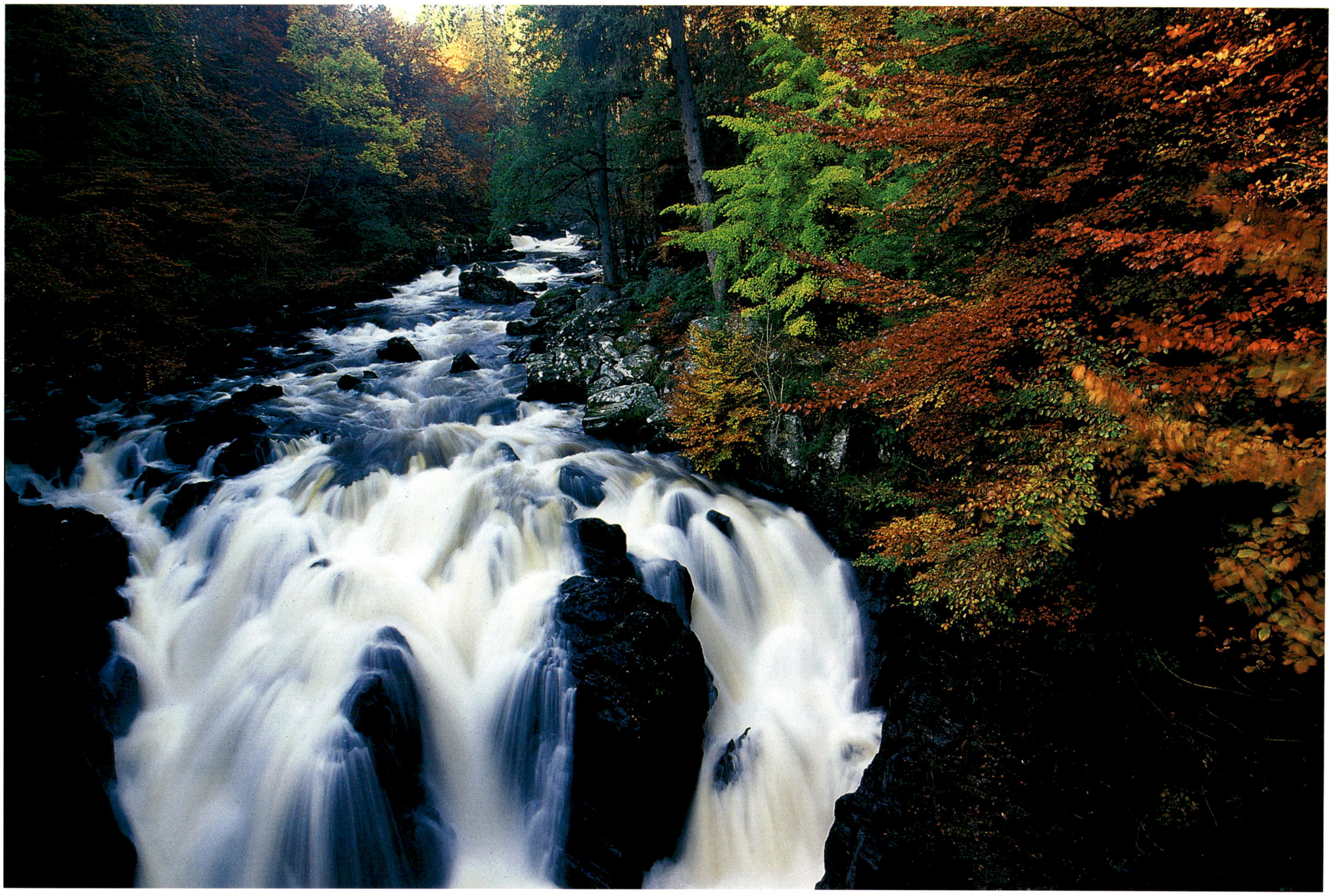

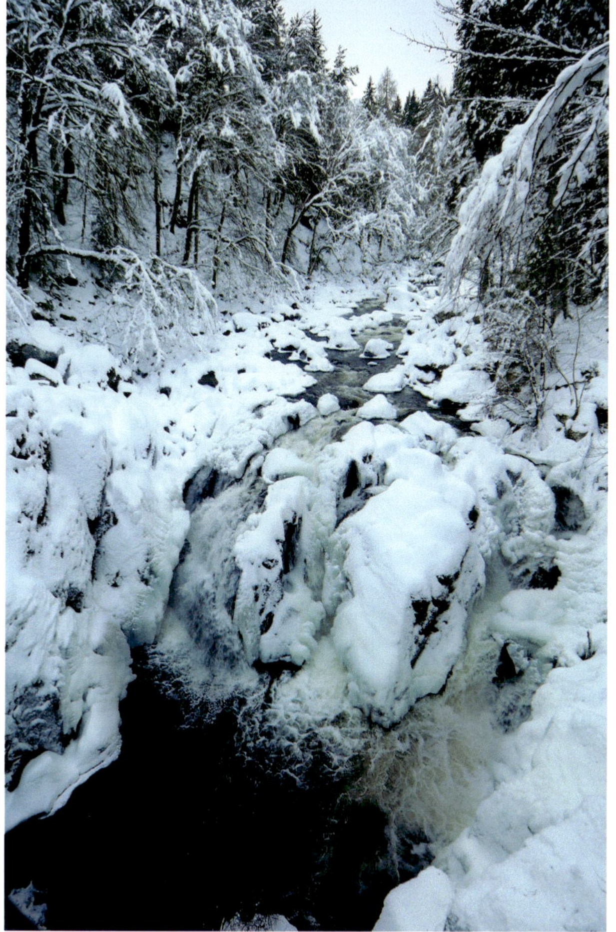

Half a mile north of Dunkeld in Perthshire a woodland walk takes you to the Hermitage, an area of woodland with two 18th-century follies, Ossian's Hall and the Hermit's Cave, built to honour the Gaelic poet Ossian, the invention of the poet James Macpherson, whose works made a great impression on European Romantics. A short stop en route to or from the Highlands gives such dramatic rewards at any time of the year.

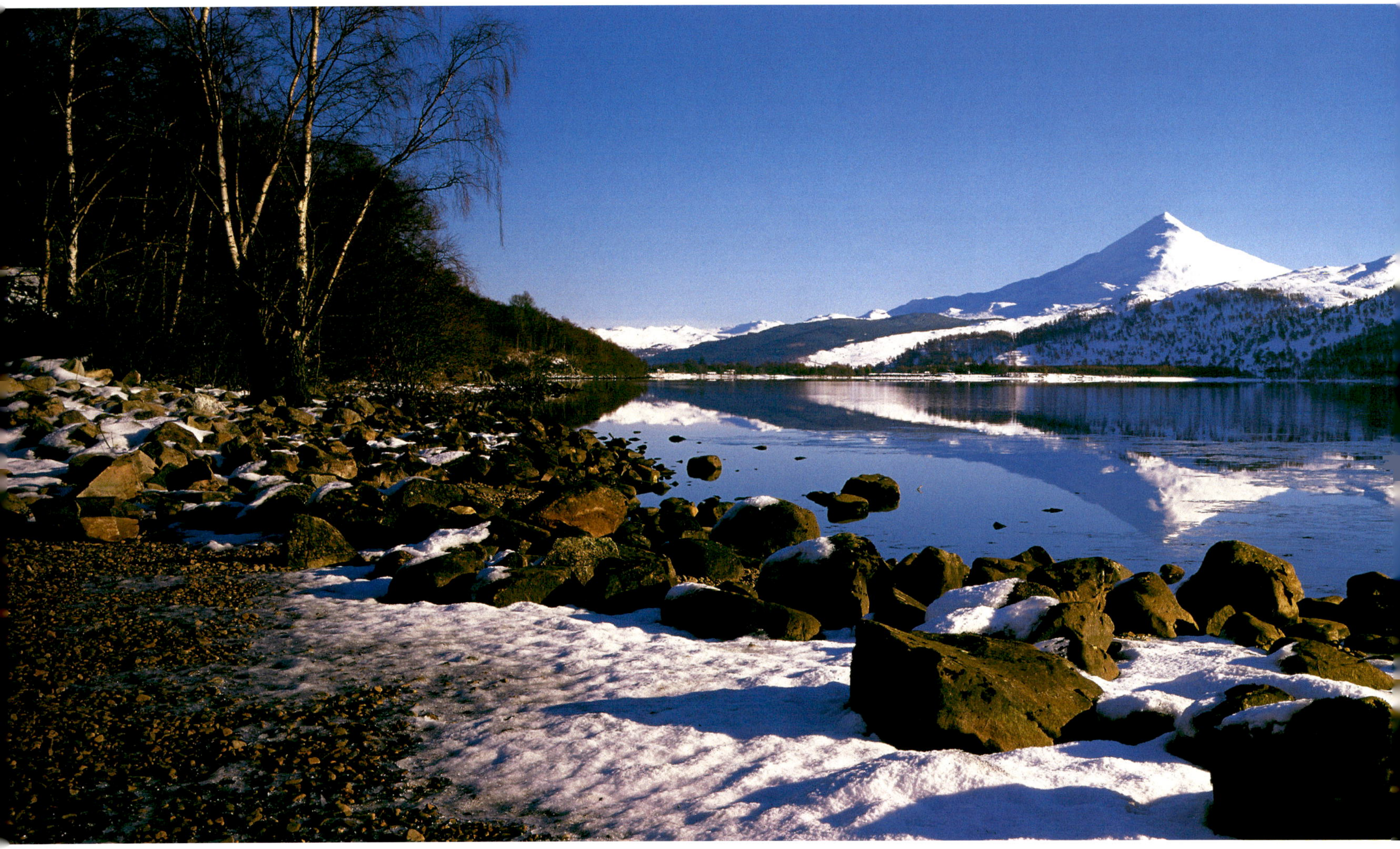

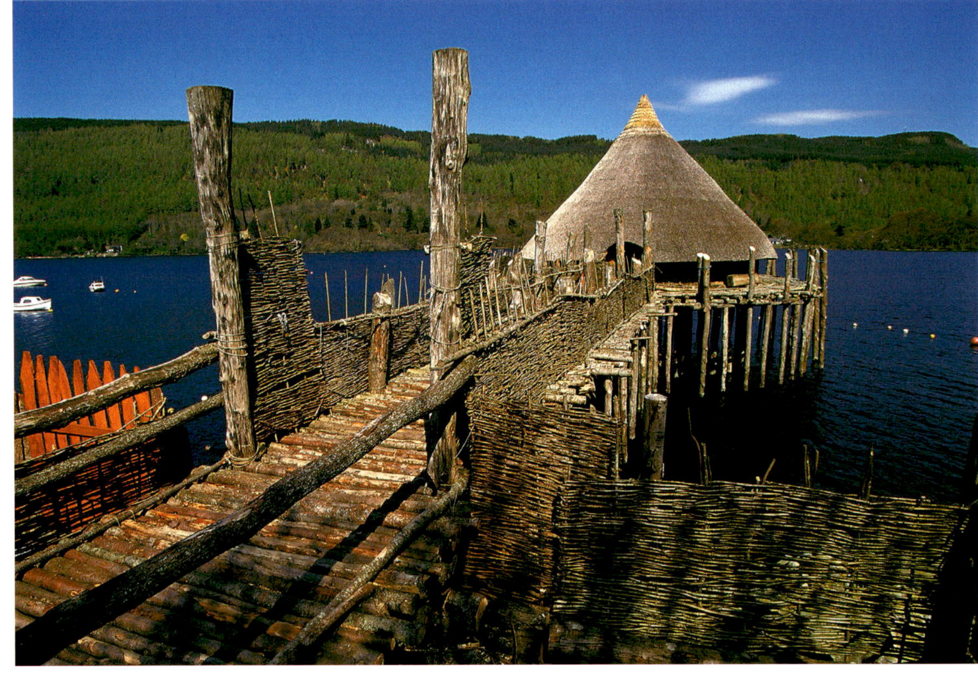

A reconstruction of a crannog on Loch Tay. Such lake dwellings were used from prehistoric times to the 16th century, giving the inhabitants protection from wild animals, such as wolves and bears, and from human enemies. This is a more evocative way of communicating history than a dry book or an overproduced documentary, with presenters forced to walk backwards while addressing the camera.

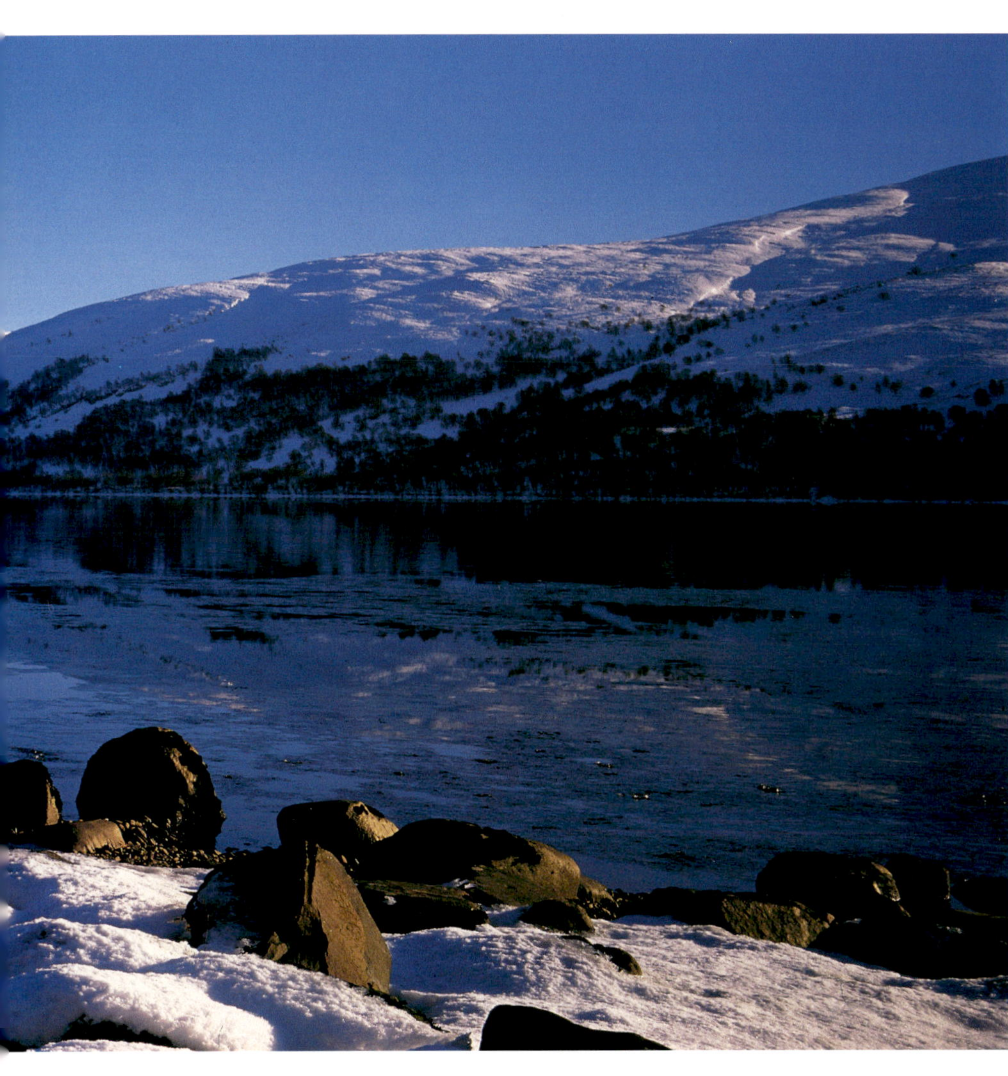

I usually go with the maxim that cloud is essential to good landscape photography, but the 3547-foot-high Schiehallion reflected in Loch Rannoch on a beautiful crisp winter's day more than makes up for the lack of cumulonimbus.

(Below) Autumn colours near the Queen's View on Loch Tummel. In 1777 the Astronomer Royal, Nevil Maskelyne, used Schiehallion in Perthshire in experiments to determine the Earth's mass – important and clever stuff. Maybe we should change it to Maskelyne's View; after all, Queen Victoria just paid a visit and was hopefully amused.

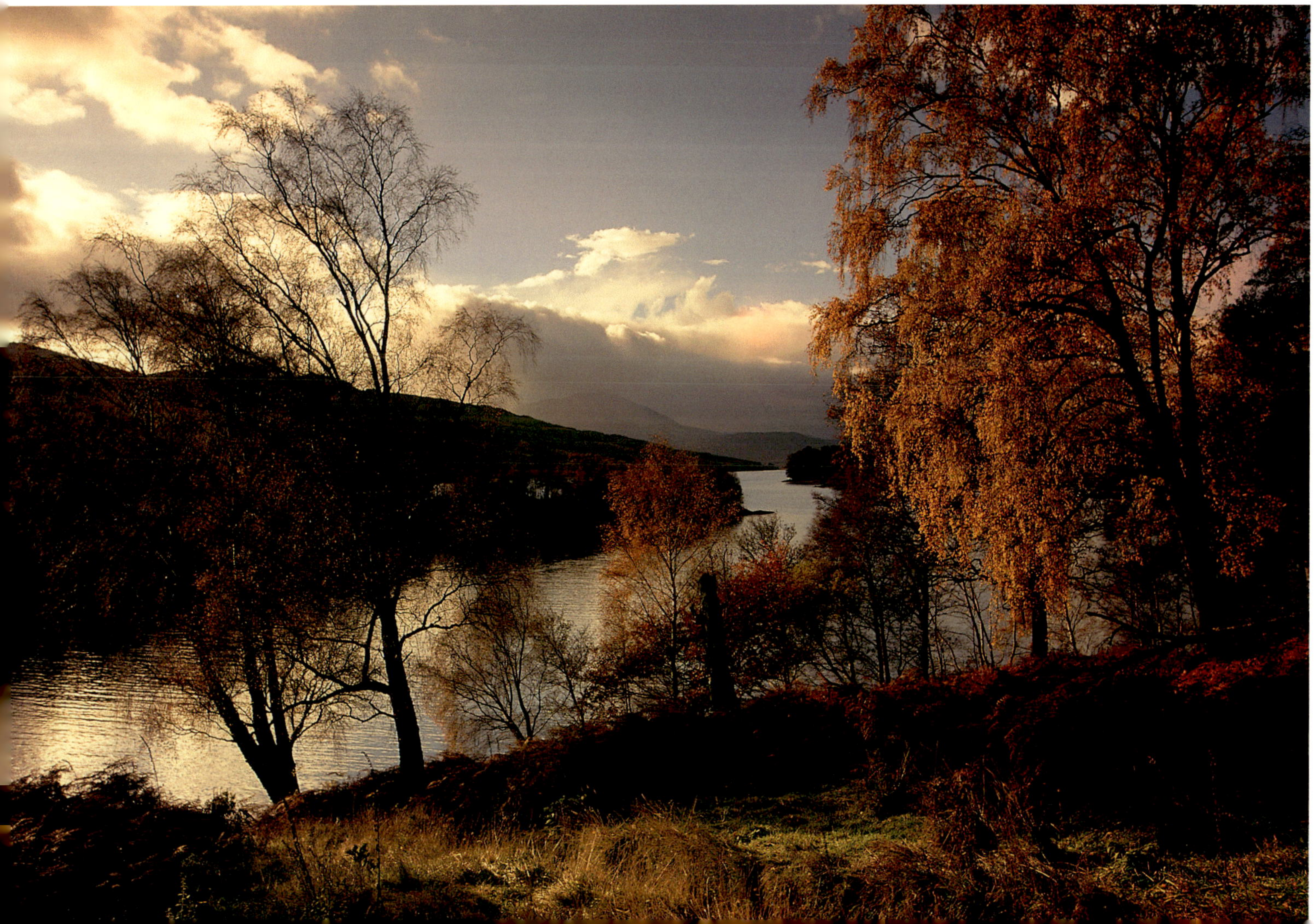

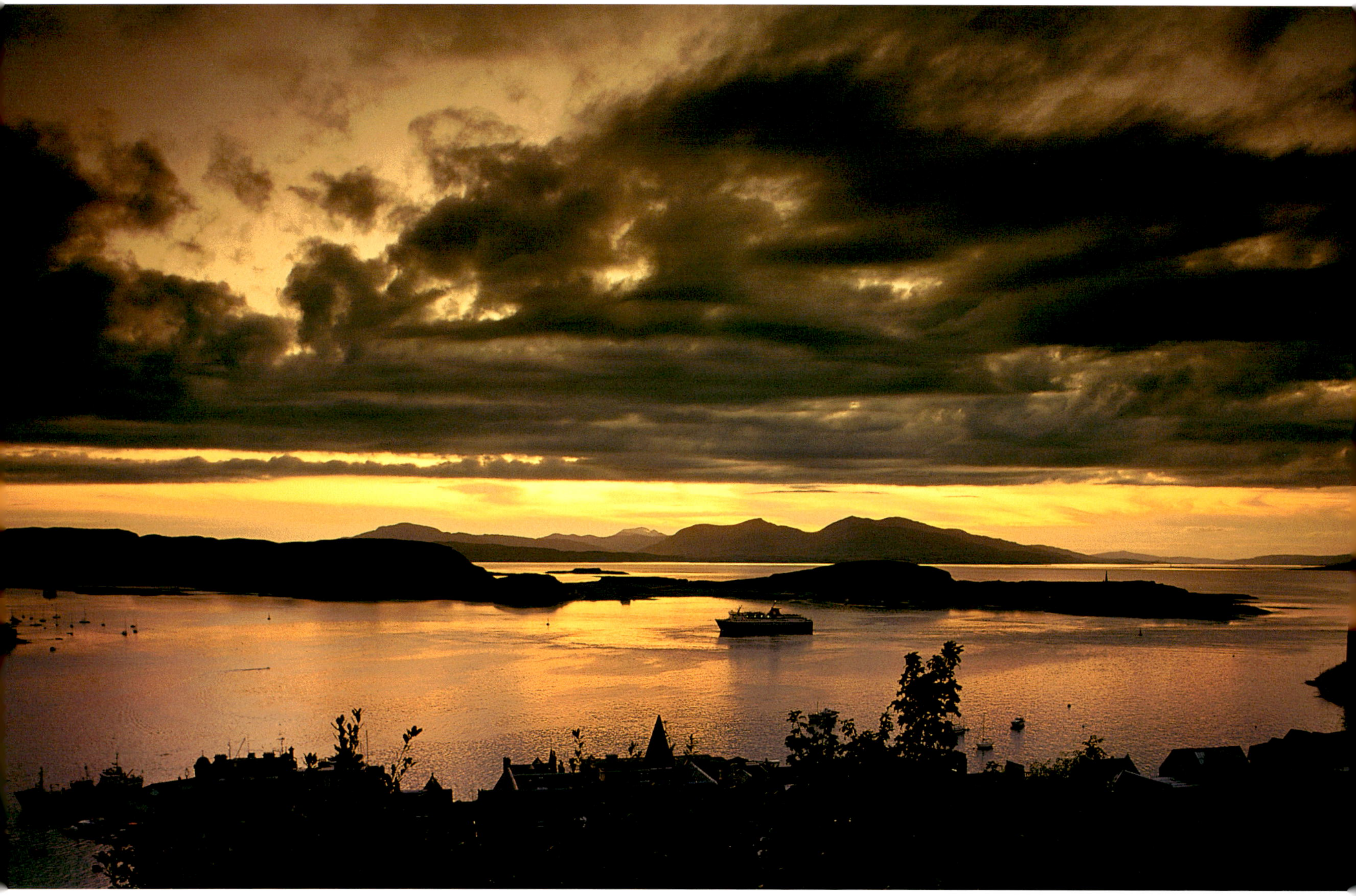

When on holiday in Oban, in Argyll, everyone goes up to McCaig's Tower to watch the sunset over the islands of Kerrera and Mull in the distance. If you don't, your hosts will want to know why. You have to nudge your way through a forest of tripods to get the best viewpoint, so get there early.

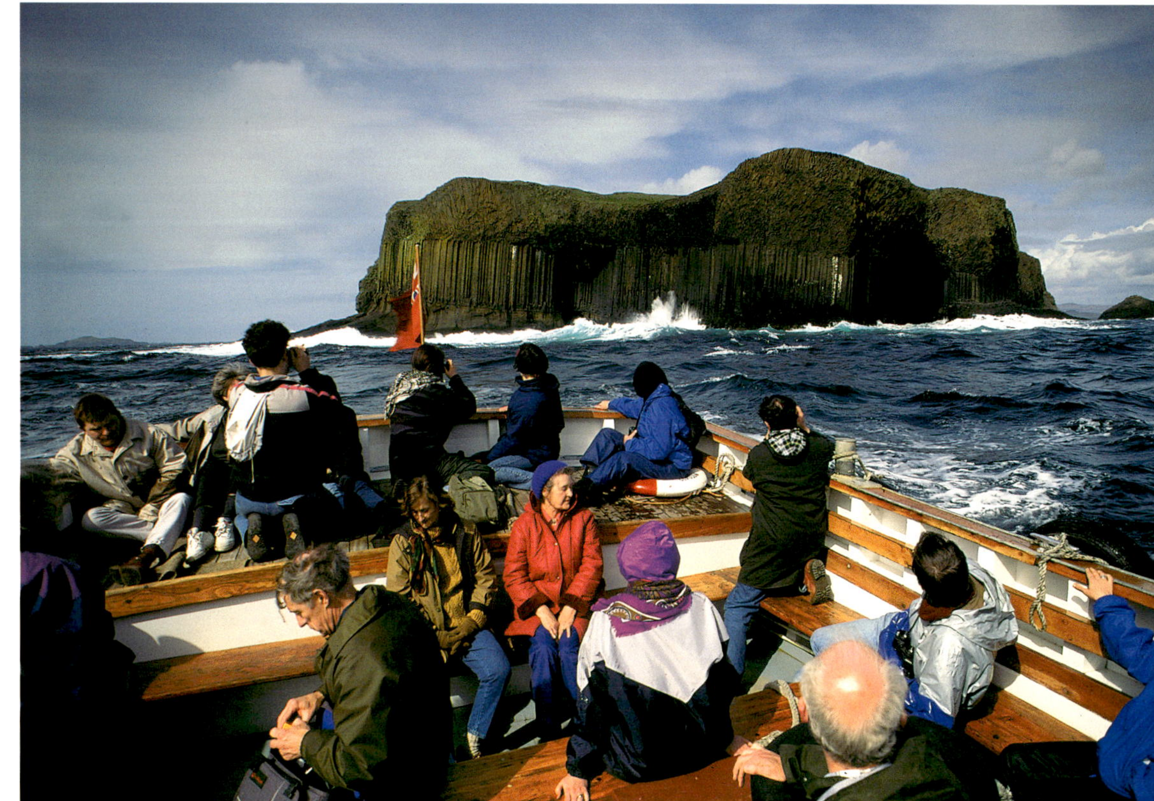

Mendelssohn's *Hebridean Overture* was inspired by the isle of Staffa, west of Mull. Fingal's Cave is named after Fionn mac Cumhaill, the giant who, legend says, built both Staffa and the Giant's Causeway in Northern Ireland. I have my reservations.

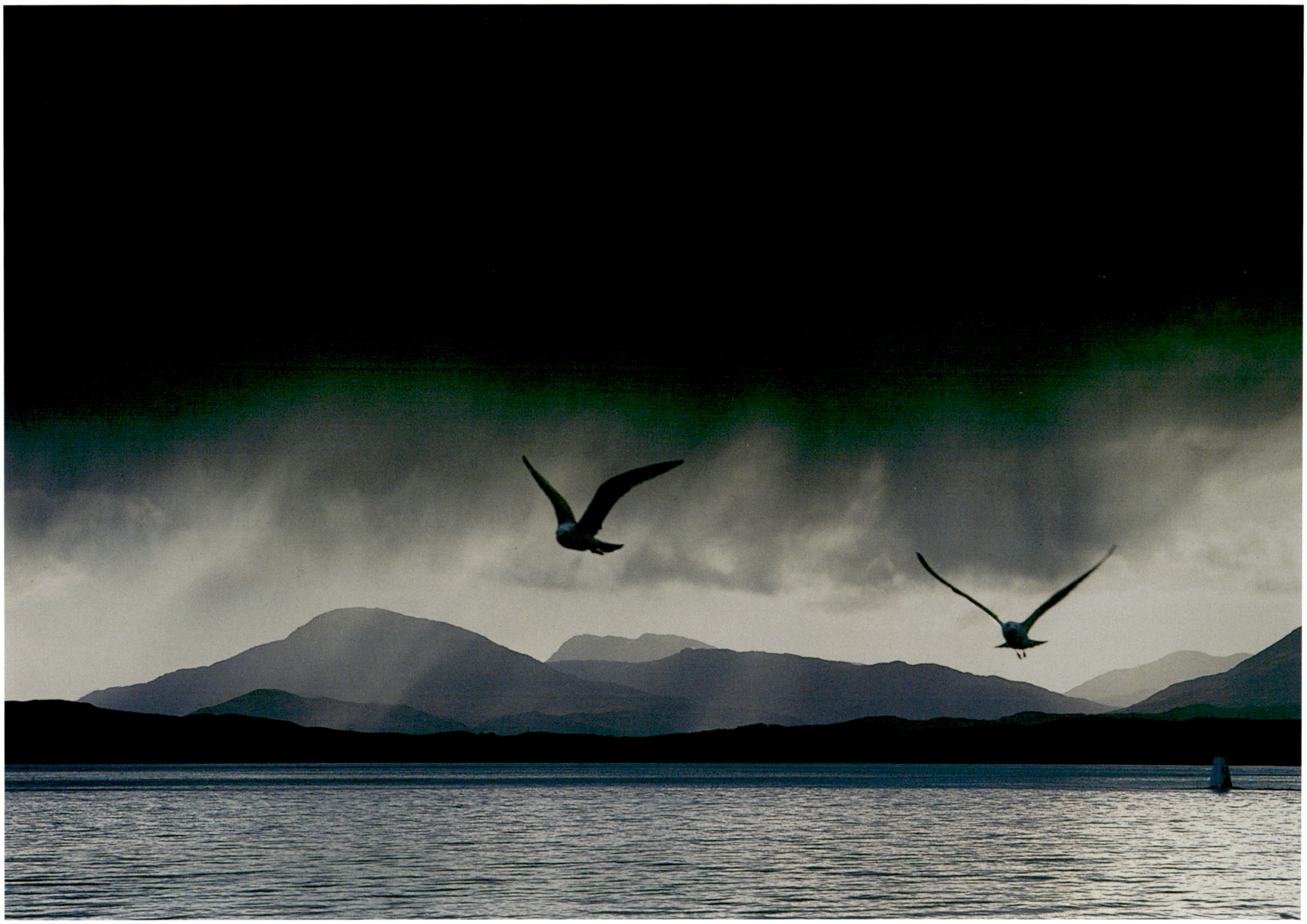

The island of Mull is picturesque and hilly, situated in the Inner Hebrides, and is ideal for family holidays with its beautiful beaches. Dr Johnson was an early visitor, in 1773. He commented, 'Oh sir, a most dolorous country.' It must have been a rainy day and he can't have seen the delightful town of Tobermory.

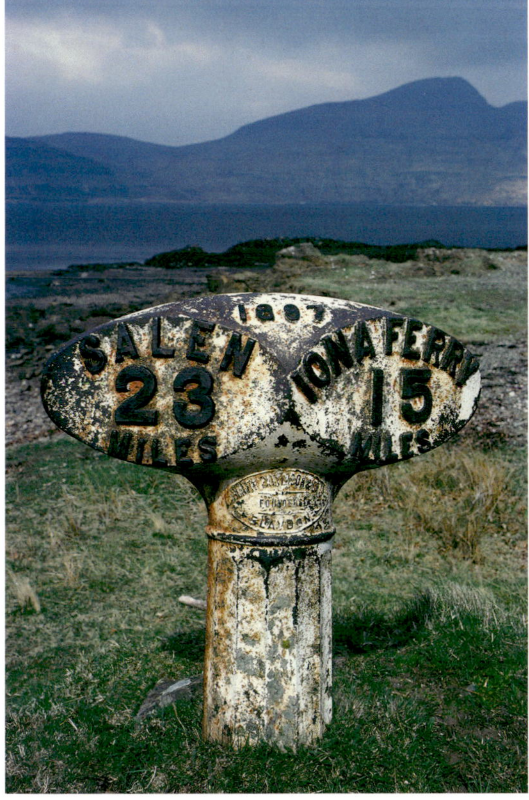

The date when this very fine cast-iron road sign was put up on Mull is 1897. Like our remaining red telephone kiosks, is it in danger of being neglected and rusting away? Please preserve these objects from our past, even when they don't conform to the designated size of lettering. It reminds me a bit of Spielberg's *ET*.

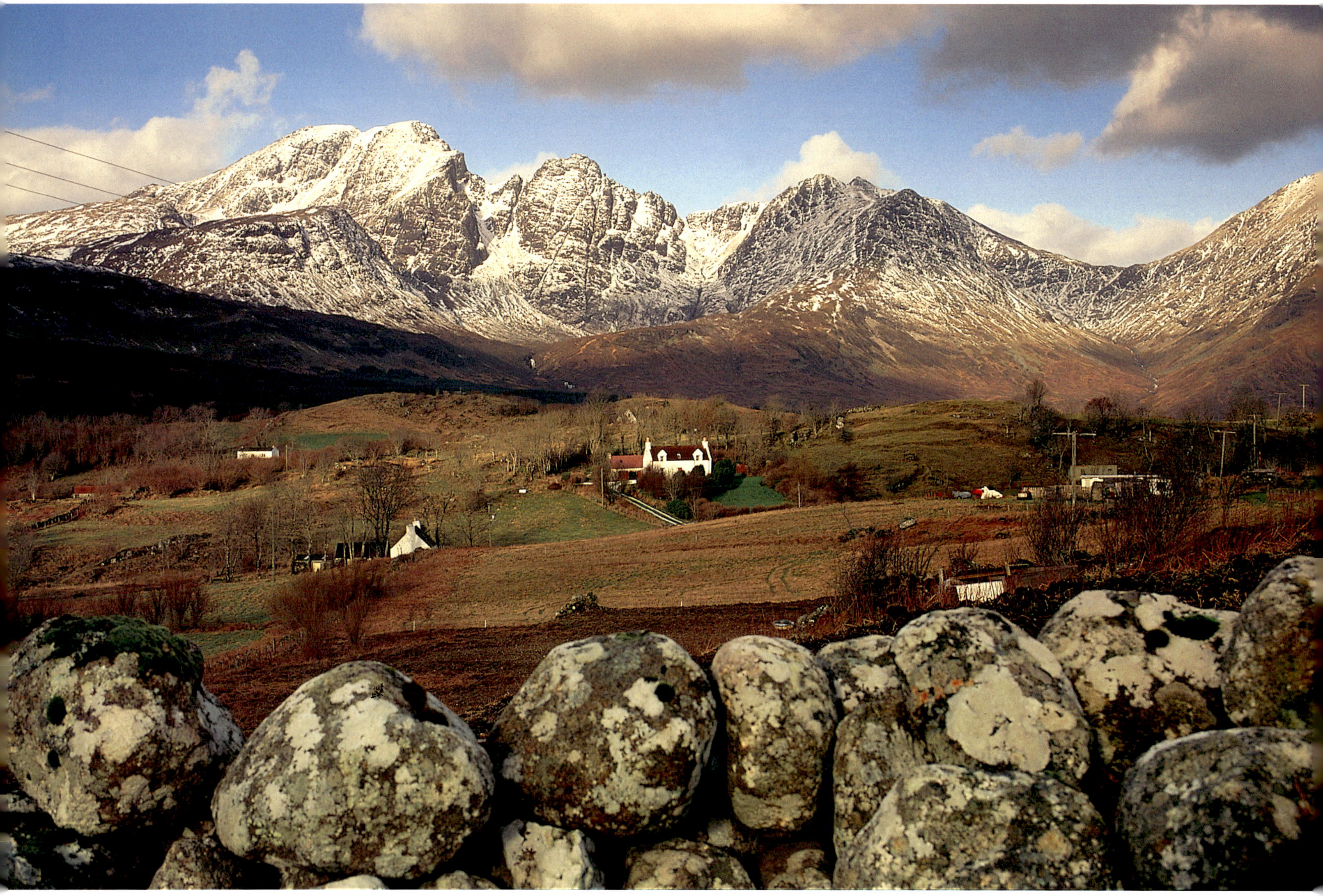

The road to Elgol on the Isle of Skye is one of the most varied and dramatic drives in Scotland. This view from the village of Torrin shows the beautiful mountain of Blaven, an outlier of the Black Cuillin range.

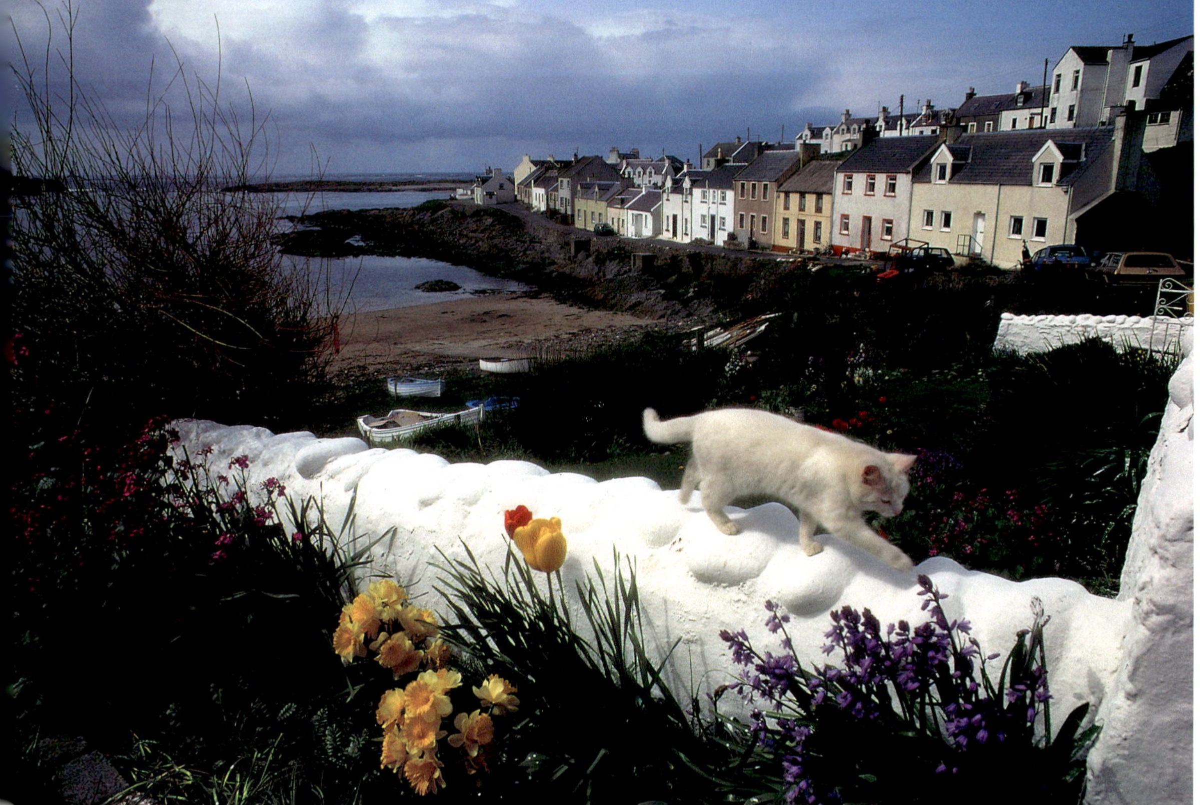

Mrs Cooper, the postmistress at Portnahaven on the Isle of Islay in the mid-1990s, told me that she and a preservation group had bought a copy of my book on rural post offices for each of the Scottish members of parliament at Westminster as part of a powerful argument for keeping this vital lifeline to rural communities. Here is Mrs Cooper's cat in her garden.

Would this 1970s' postbus be called vintage now? The postie's uniform has gone through several transformations since then too. The shot was taken at Port Askaig on Islay, which is one of the island's smaller communities but is an important ferry port.

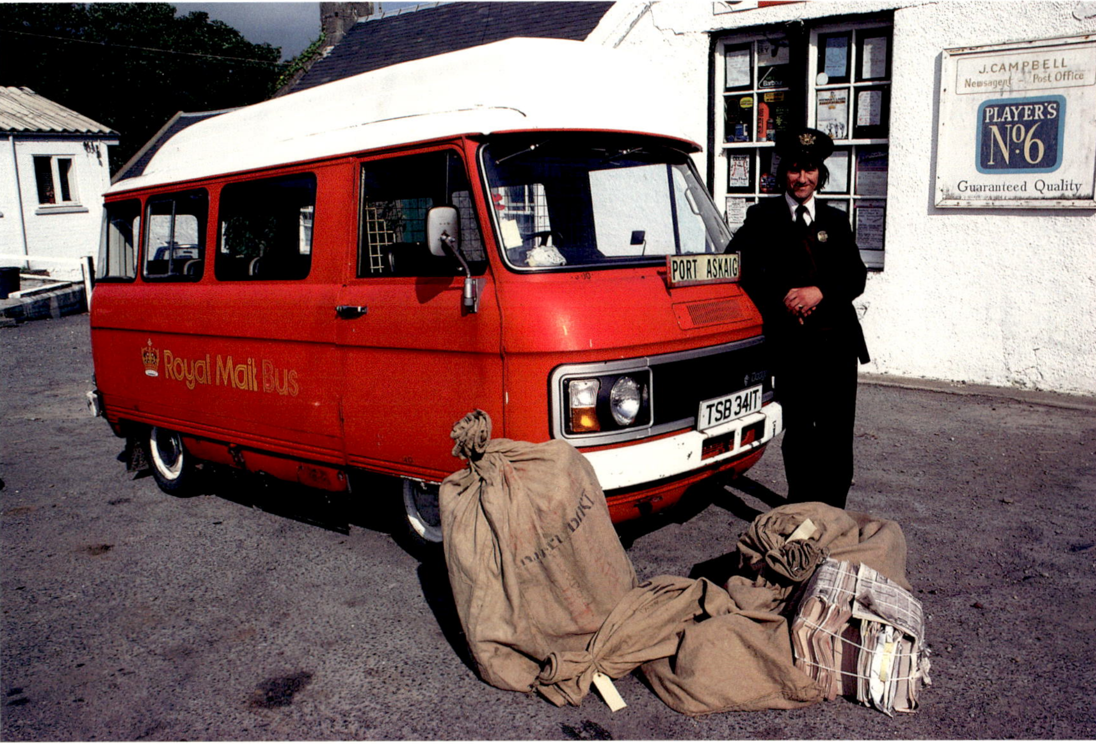

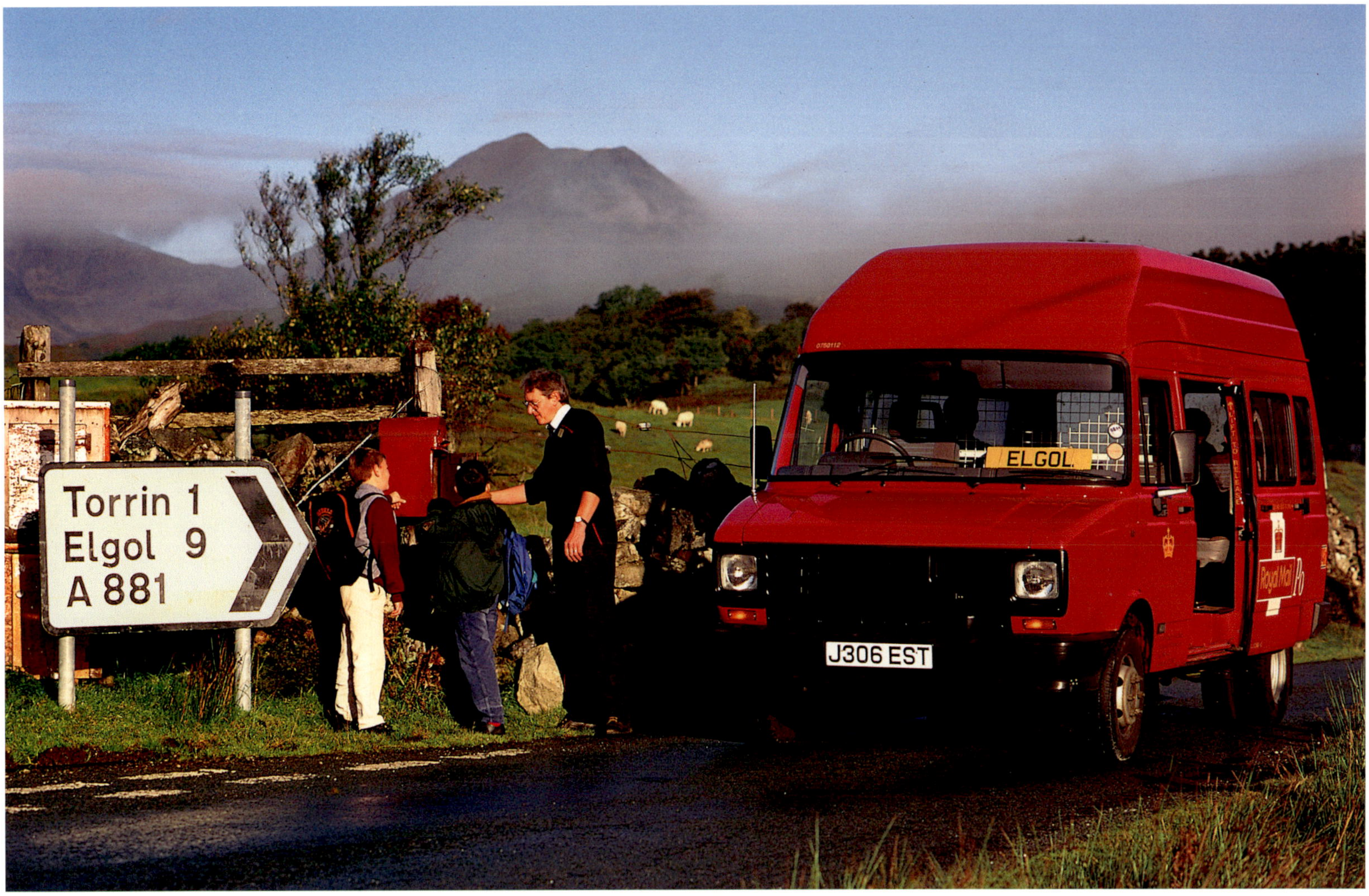

The Broadford to Elgol postal route on Skye. Nigel Nice had the busiest run I experienced while shooting for the *Postbus Country* book, commissioned by Royal Mail, in the 1990s. Delivering people, prescriptions, parcels, papers and post, his compensation was that he had one of the most scenic routes in Britain.

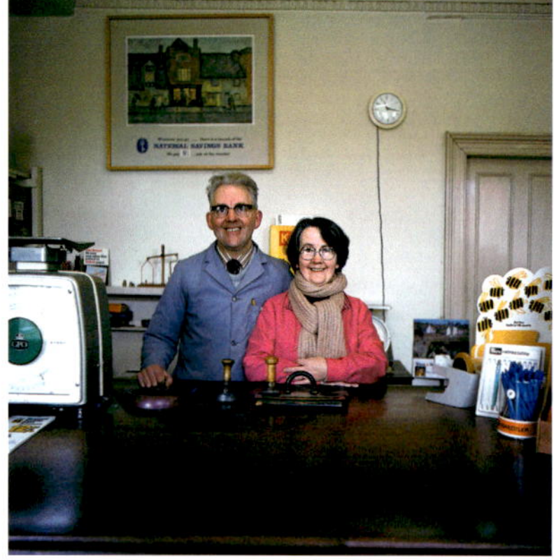

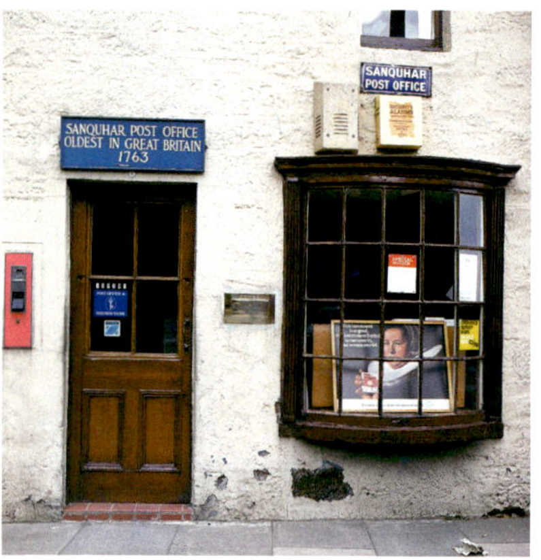

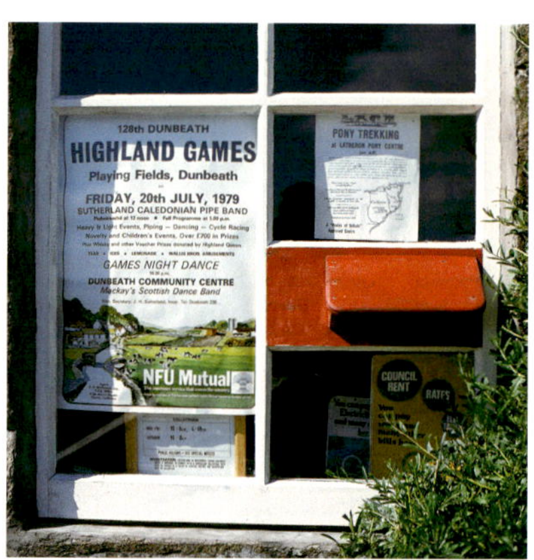

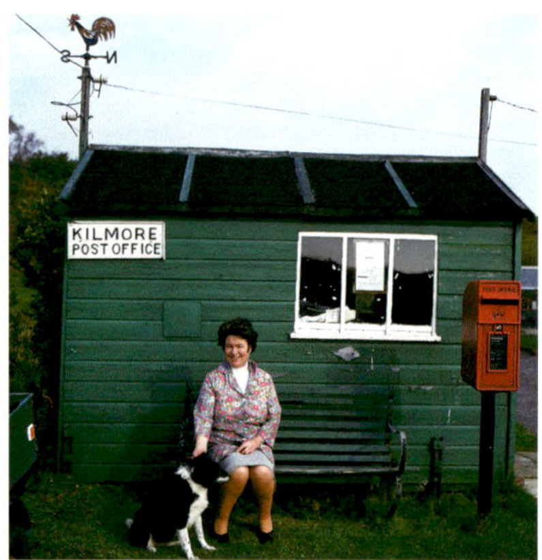

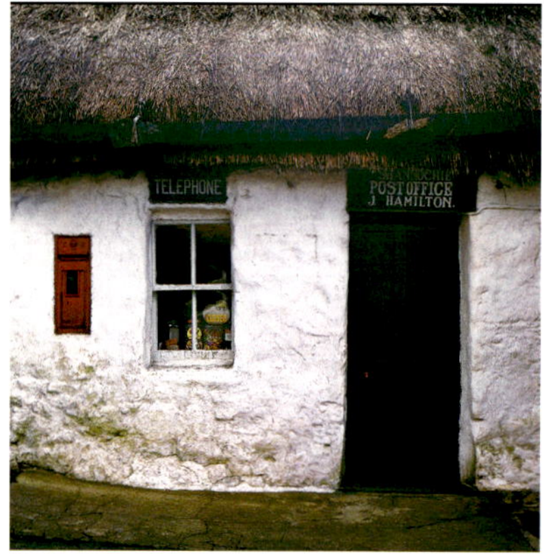

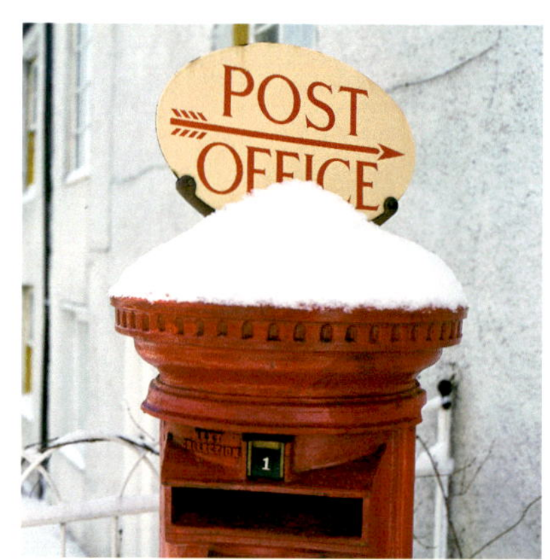

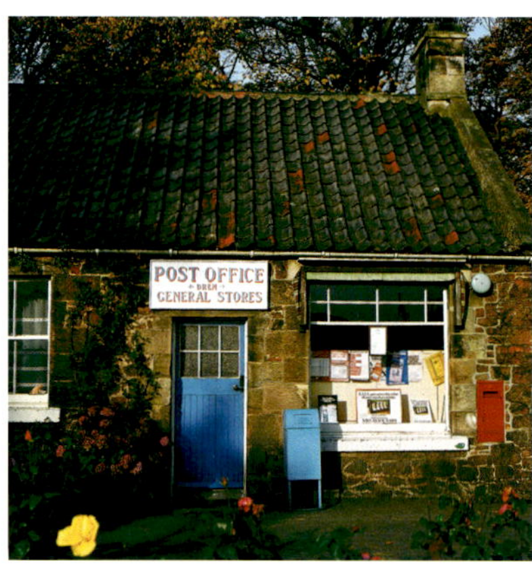

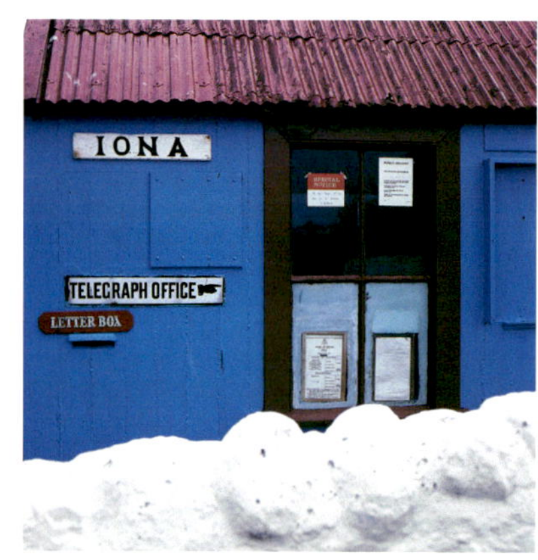

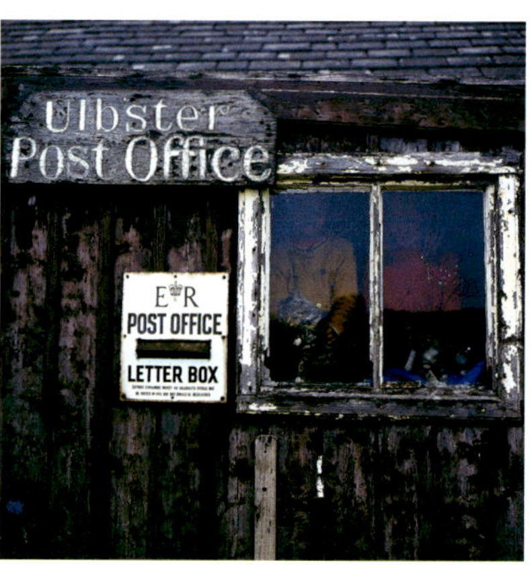

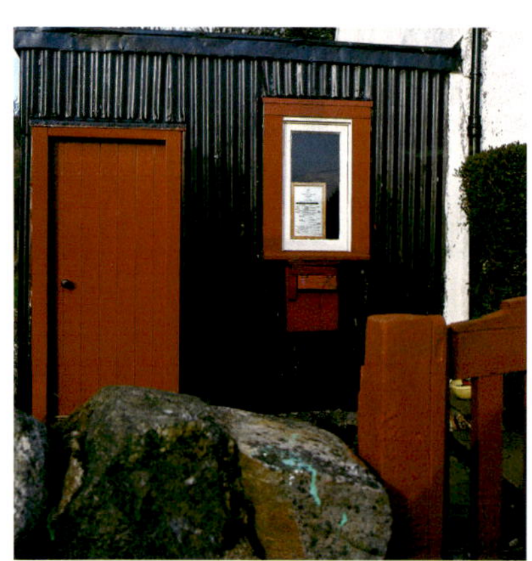

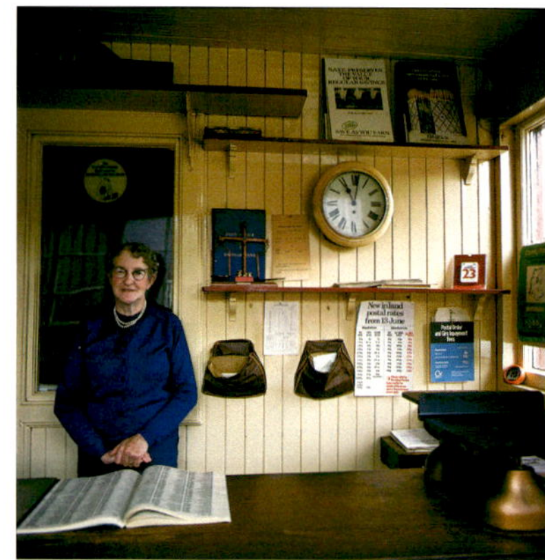

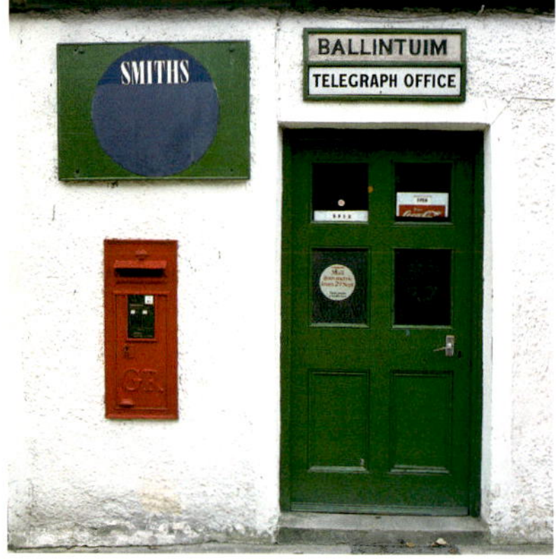

Feeling strongly that sub-post offices have an important role to play in the community, whether in the town or country, and are well worth preserving, I made a montage of some of these images, which then became a best-selling poster for the Scottish Tourist Board. I was forever hearing people say, 'We have that in our kitchen – did you do it?' The lack of uniformity gave these post offices an individual charm. I followed this up with a book of post offices published in 1988. Sadly, many of these establishments no longer exist.

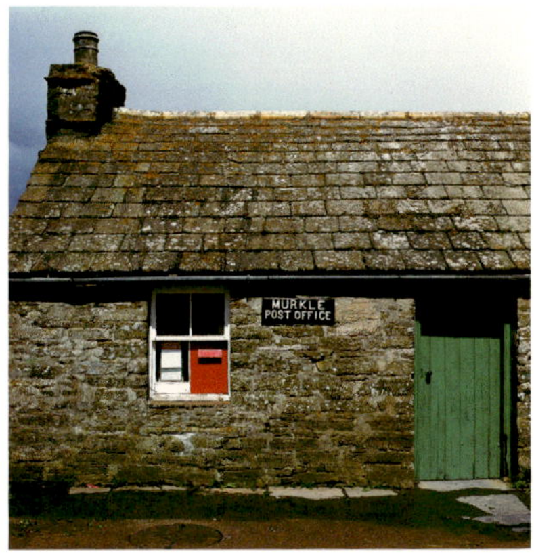

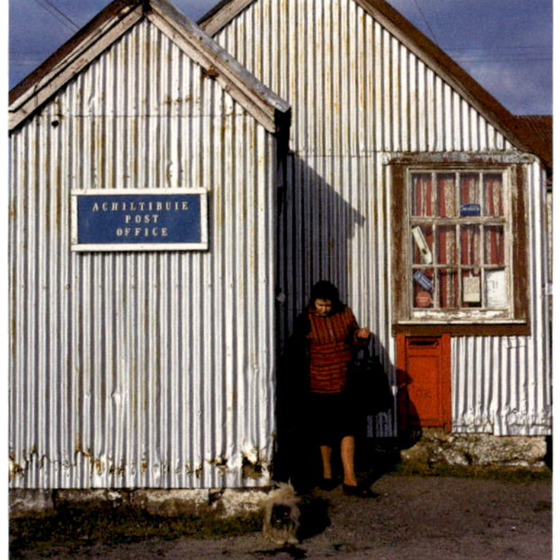

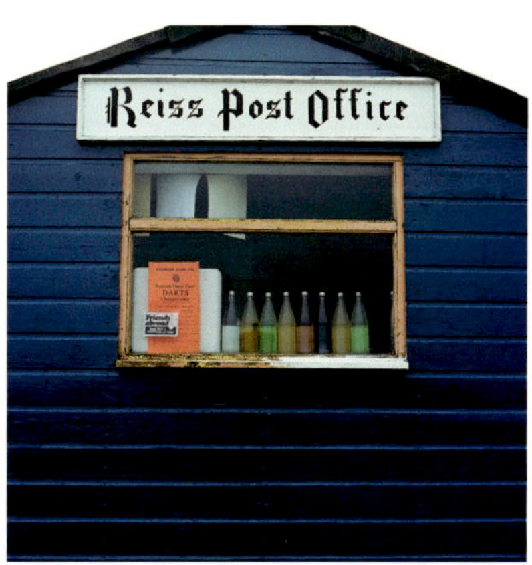

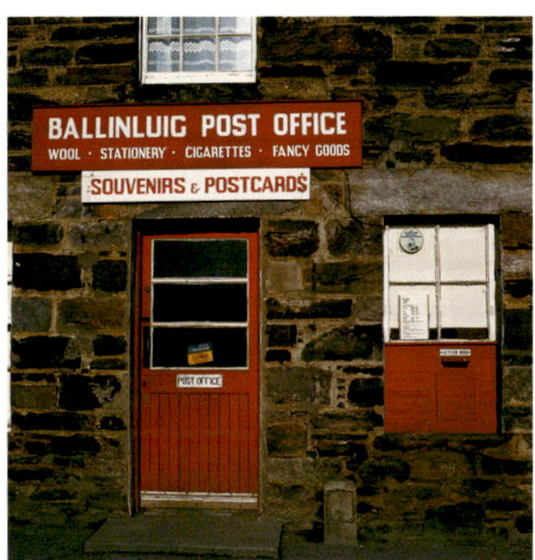

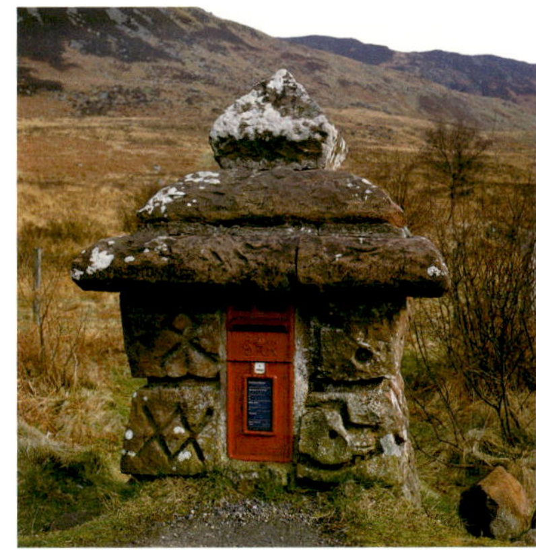

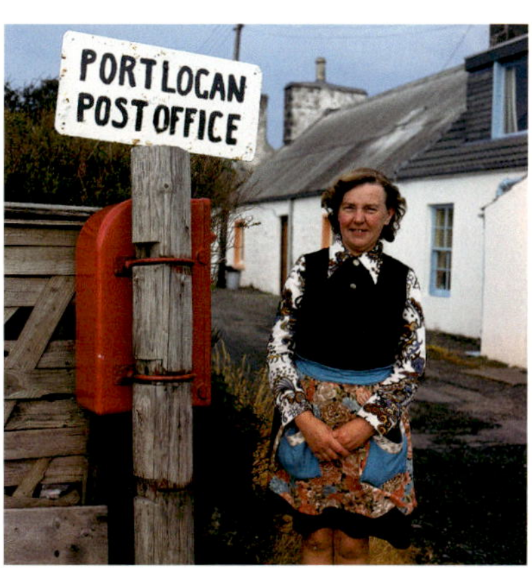

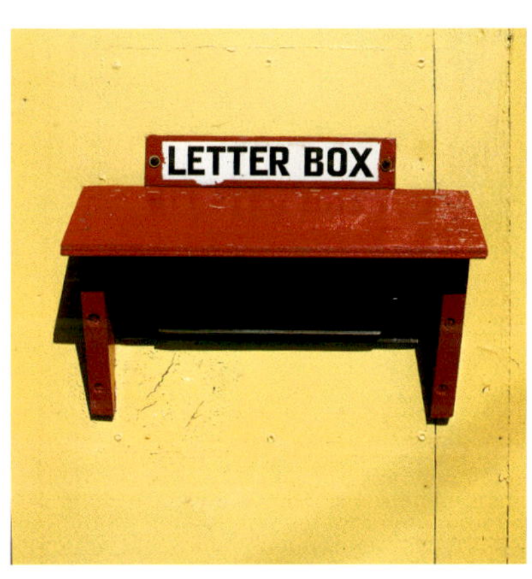

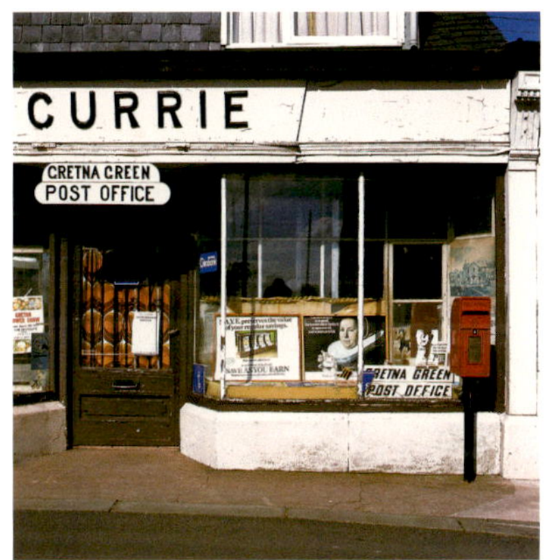

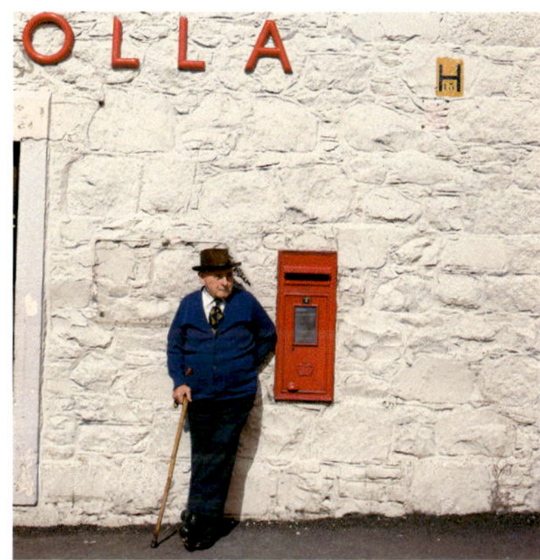

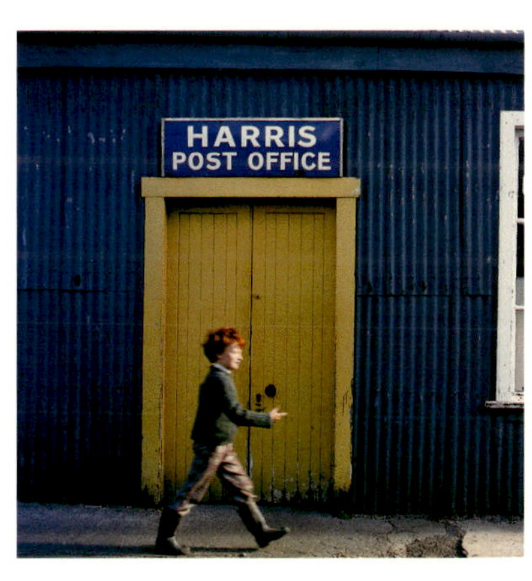

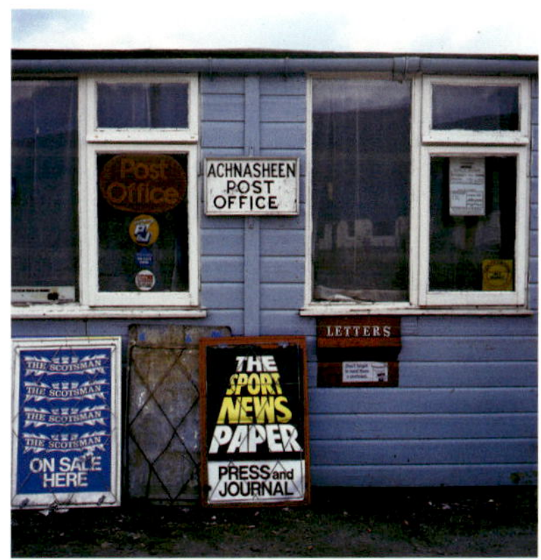

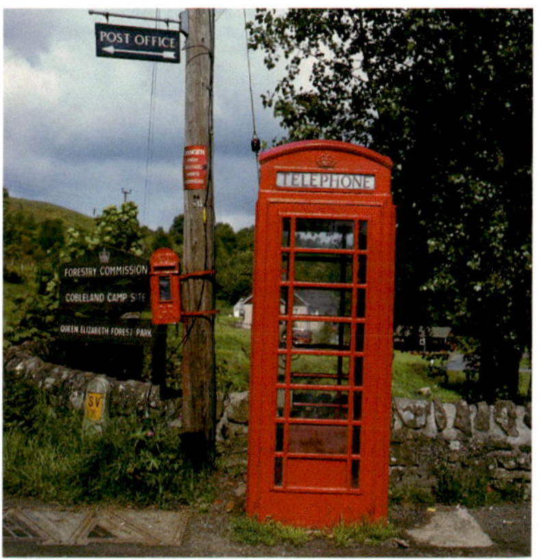

Opposite page, from left to right and top to bottom: Fettercairn, Kincardine; Sanquhar, Lanarkshire; Dunbeath, Caithness; Kilmore, Argyll; Shannochie, Ayrshire; Carrbridge, Inverness-shire; Drem, East Lothian; Iona; Ulbster, Caithness; Dornie, Wester Ross; Glenlivet, Banffshire; Ballintuim, Perthshire. This page: Murkle, Caithness; Achiltiebuie, Wester Ross; Reiss, Caithness; Ballinluig, Perthshire; on the String Road on the Isle of Arran; Port Logan, Wigtonshire; Dunbeath; Gretna Green; Newton Stewart; Tarbert on the Isle of Harris; Achnasheen, Ross and Cromarty; in the Trossachs.

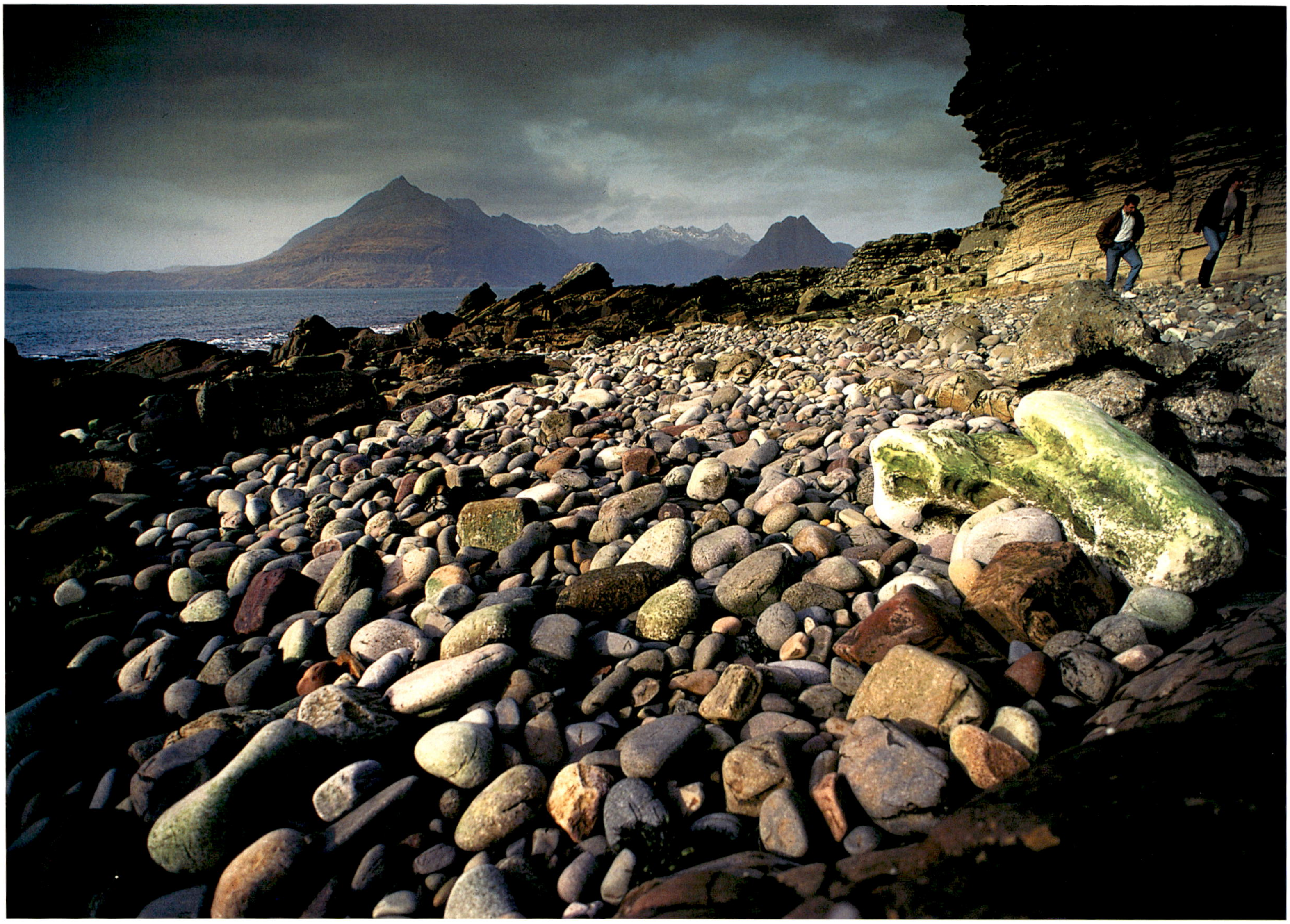

From Elgol on Skye, one of Scotland's classic views of the Cuillin Hills above Loch Coruisk. I'm always trying to find a new angle and feel that in this case the figures add scale to the foreground.

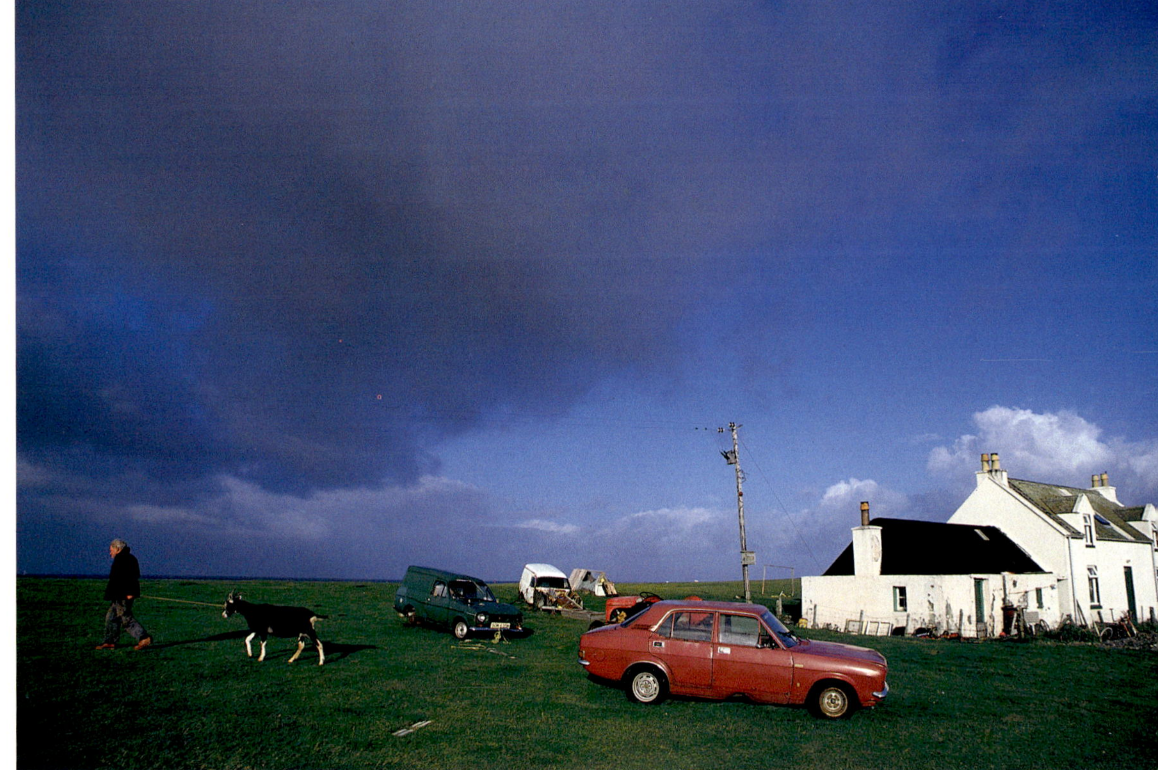

Dumping cars and fridges is a problem common to small islands, the cost of shipping waste to the mainland being the reason. Tiree is no exception.

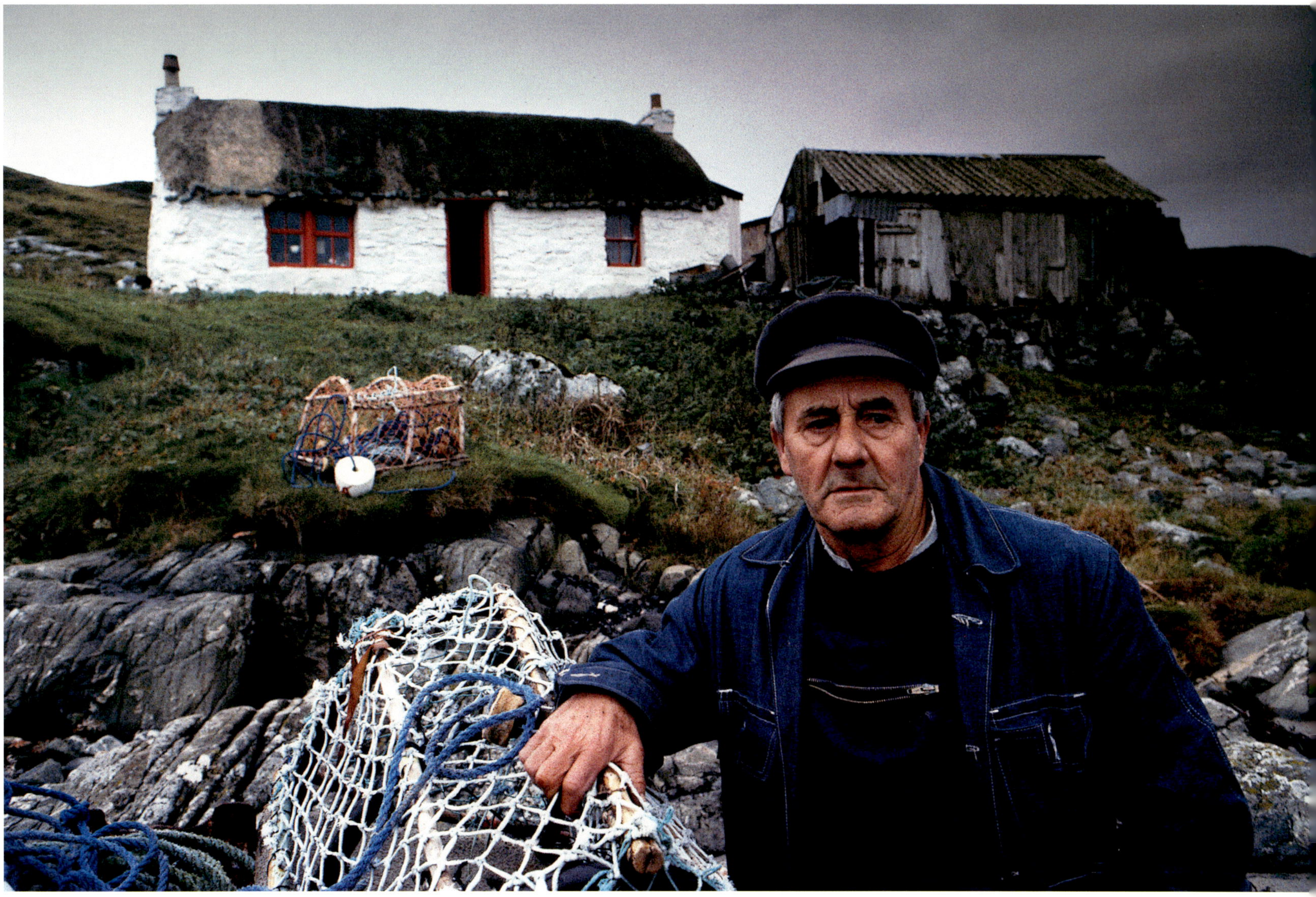

The Isle of Coll has a population of around 164. When I took this shot in the early 1980s, the crofter gave the impression of self-sufficiency. The creels are for lobsters, which may have been destined for the best continental restaurants.

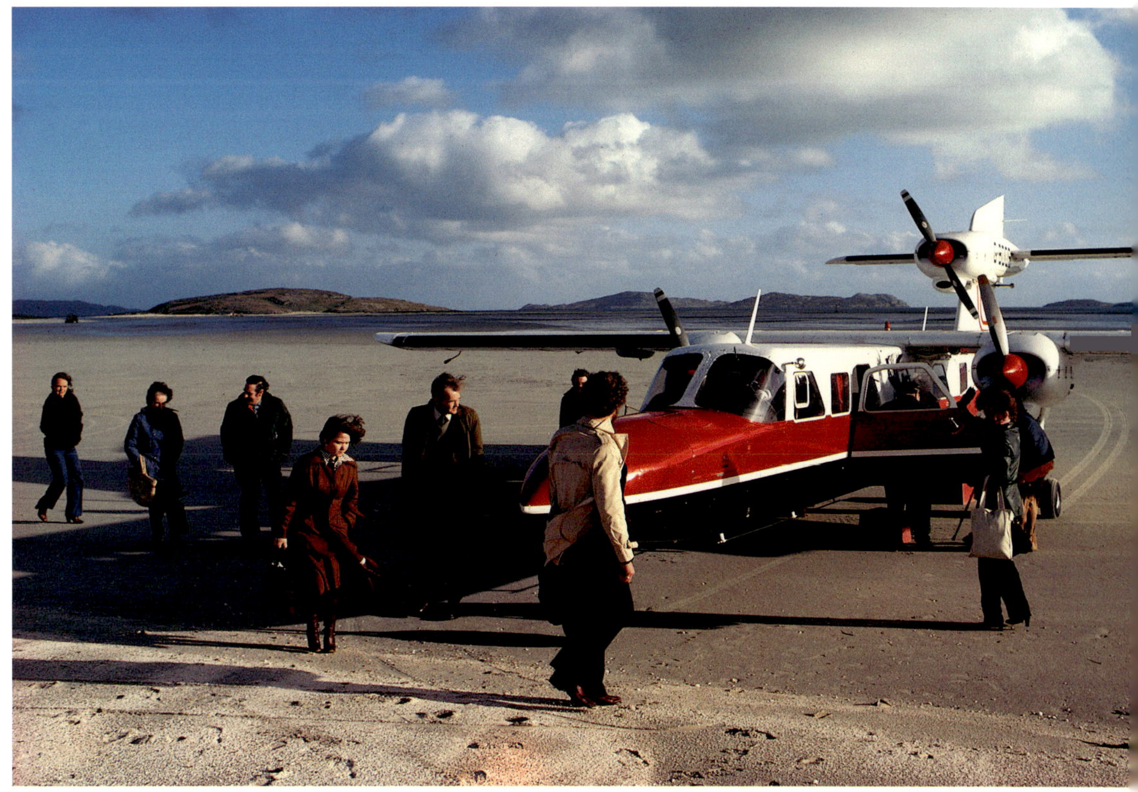

I have had several memorable flights on Loganair, which was set up in 1962 to serve the islands. The most spectacular landing is on the beach at Barra. Having landed here once in gale force winds, my fellow passengers and I were stuck in a guest house for three days. At dinner one night an American lady said, 'Isn't this just like an Agatha Christie novel?'

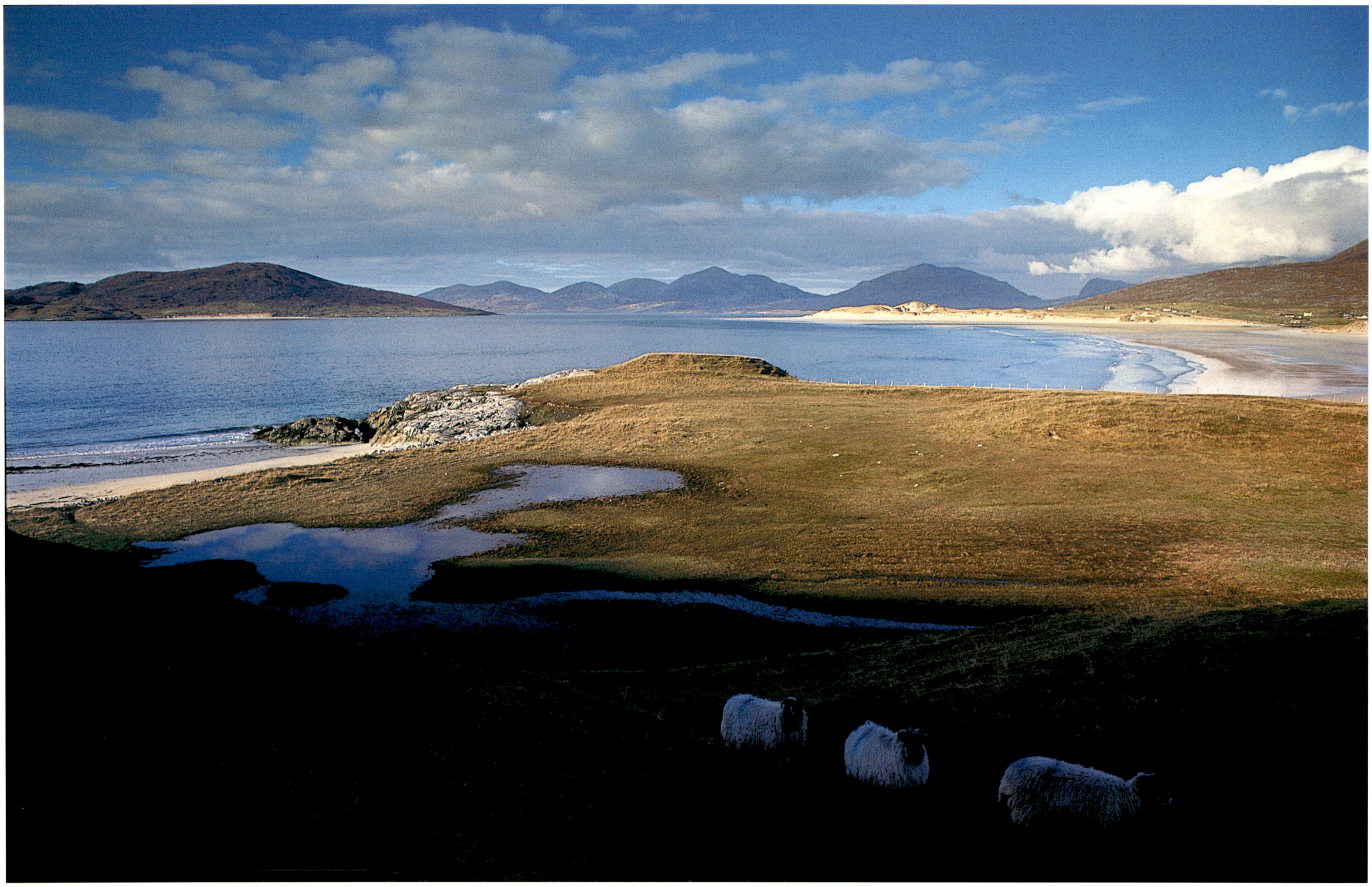

Luskentyre Bay on the island of Harris has been voted one of the world's top beaches. Offshore is the now uninhabited island of Taransay, which was used by the BBC in 2000 for its reality show *Castaway*.

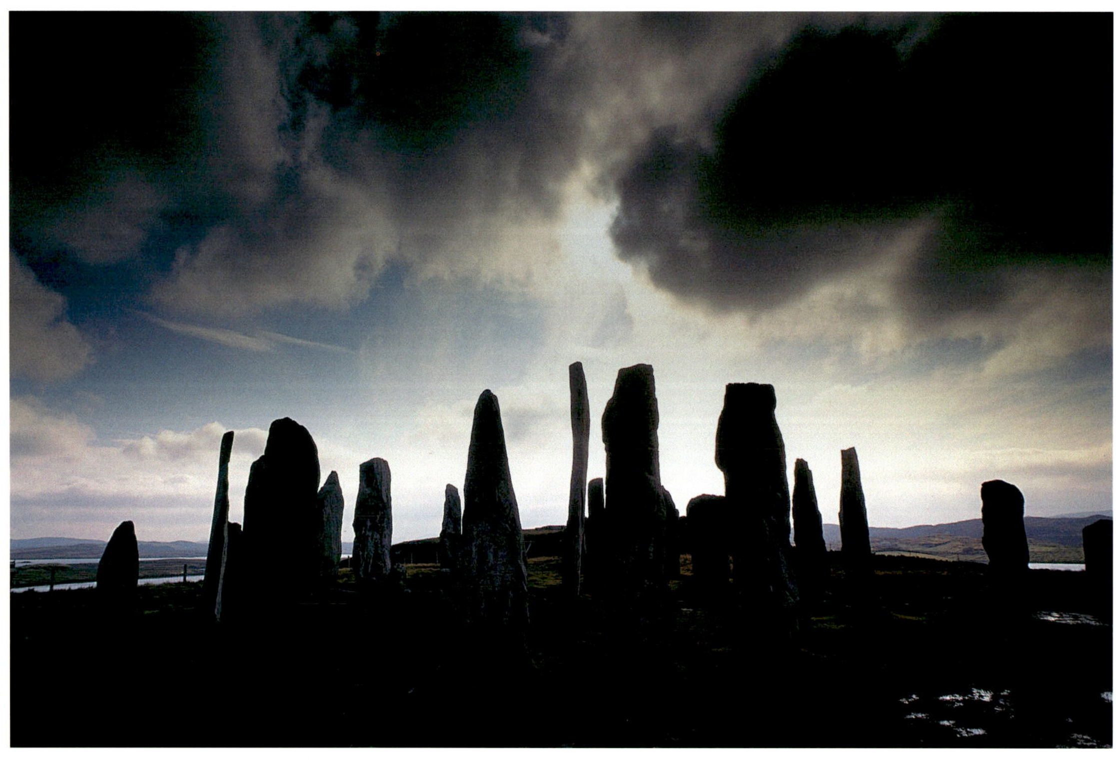

The first time I arrived at Calanais (or Callanish) on the Isle of Lewis in the 1970s, Scottish country dancers were prancing to the tune of 'Mairi's Wedding' while being filmed for TV. It did somewhat lessen my experience of the standing stones, which consist of thirteen stones surrounding a monolith. There are many theories abounding as to their purpose, but I doubt we'll ever know. Were there maybe Bronze Age NIMBYs saying, 'Not another henge ruining our outlook!'

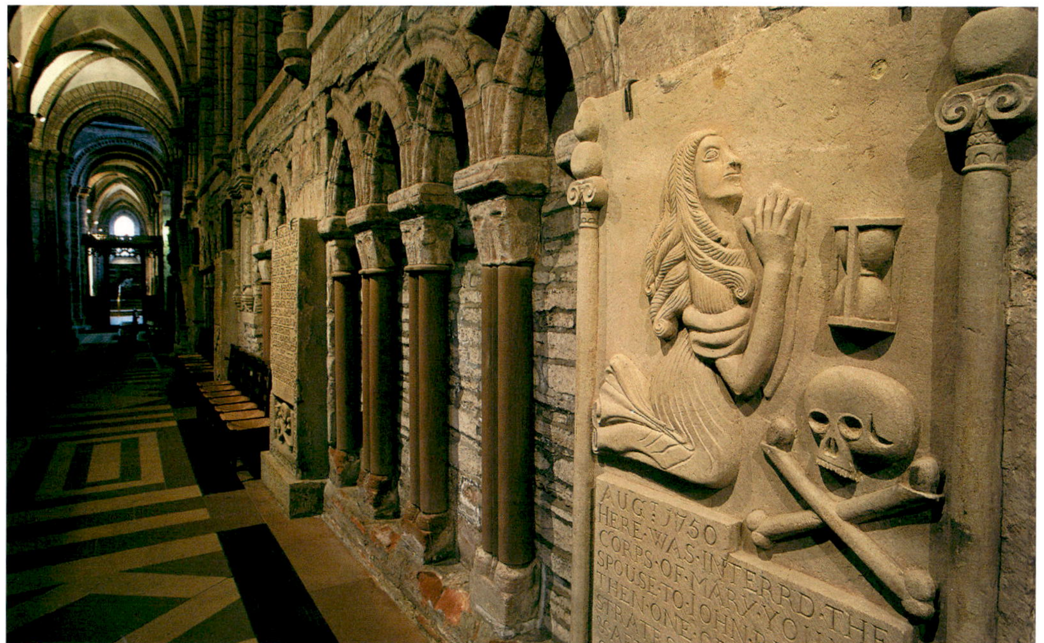

St Magnus Cathedral in Kirkwall – and Orkney in general with its palaces and the oldest public library in Scotland (founded in 1683) – makes me question a lot of my preconceived ideas about Scottish history, particularly in relation to the Highlands and Islands. These 18th-century memorials appear to predate a more modernist aesthetic.

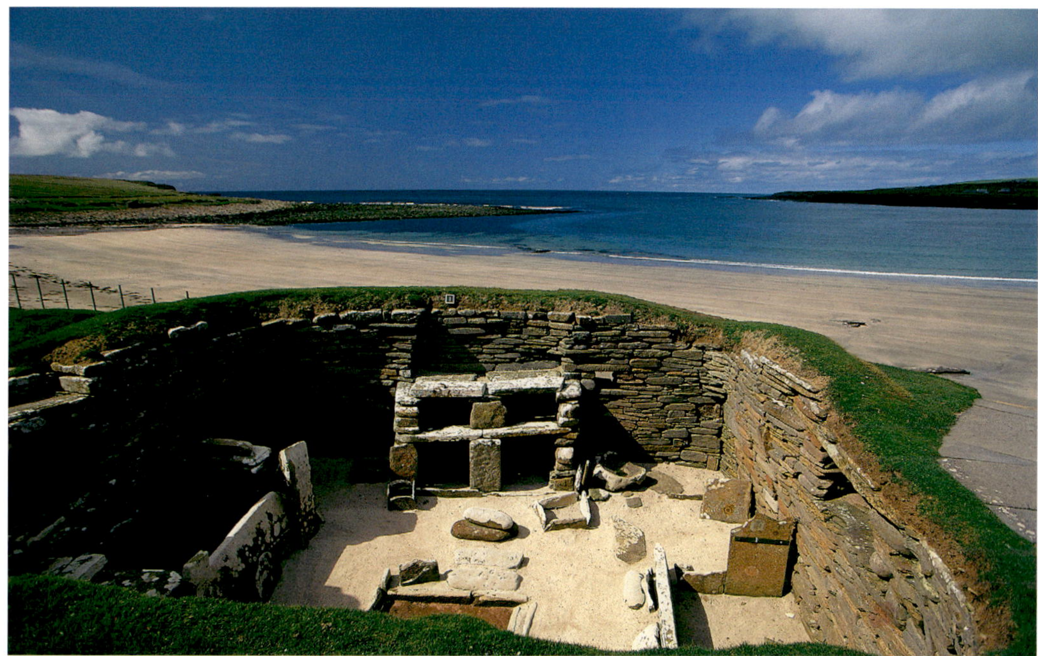

On Orkney, Skara Brae, a neolithic settlement that was occupied from 3000 BC until a great storm around 2200 BC caused the population of perhaps fifty to flee. The site remained undiscovered until another storm in 1850 revealed it again.

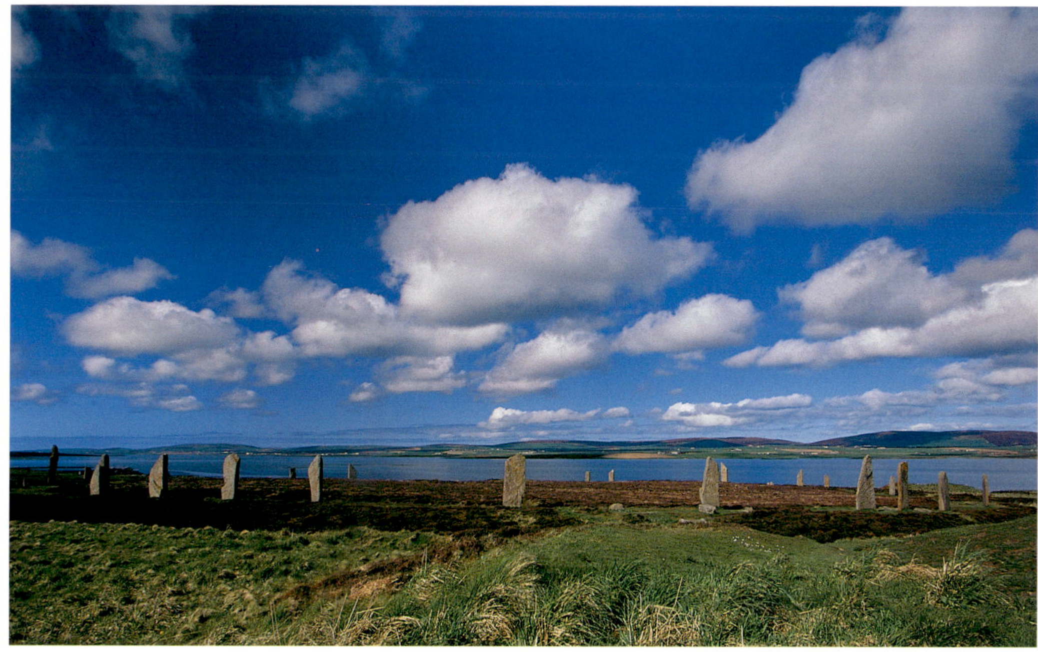

The islands of Orkney have the highest concentration of prehistoric monuments in northern Europe. Twenty-seven of what were probably sixty standing stones make up the Ring of Brodgar. Orkney is the most historically diverse of all the Scottish islands.

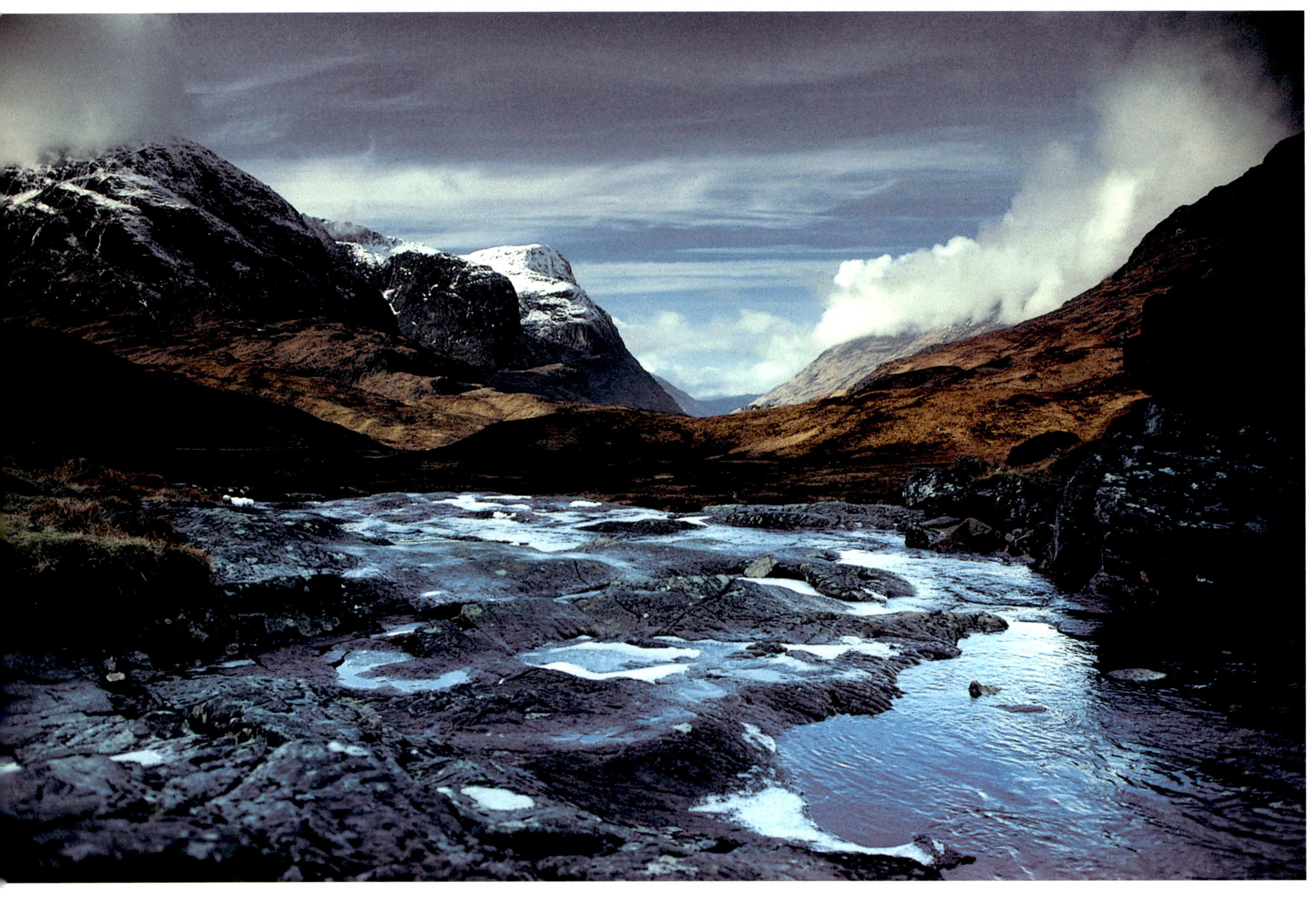

Glencoe is where I feel I've reached the Highlands. This is one of my stops, just a few feet from the lay-by. While driving in other scenic areas, for example in the English Lake District, I have been frustrated by seeing a potential shot but having nowhere to pull over. In Scotland many of our best viewpoints are easily accessible. Here we see the Three Sisters, all around 2,500 to 3,000 feet high.

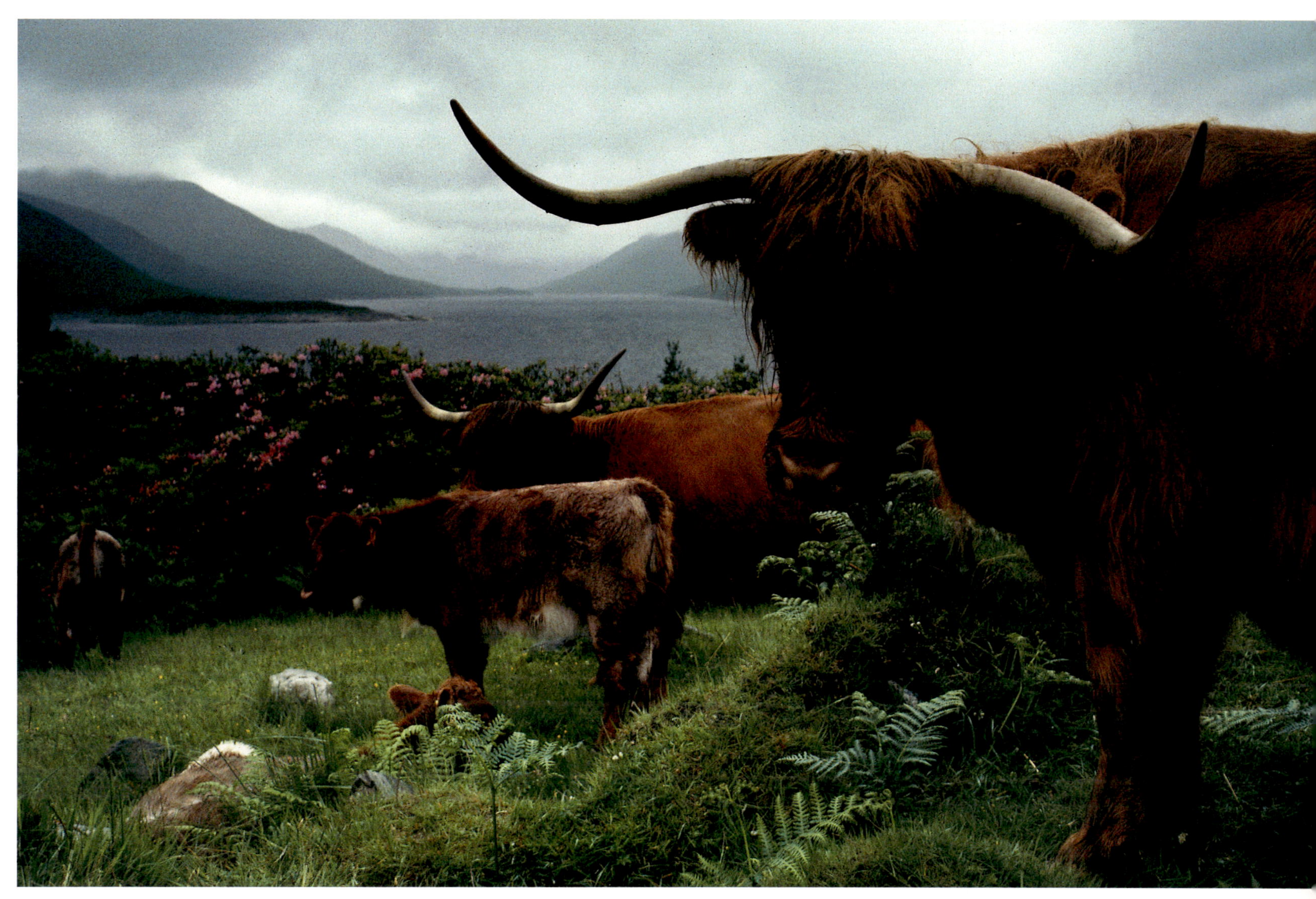

I find Highland cattle quite easy to persuade to move into position for a snap, by making various noises that would have any onlooker doubt my sanity. I was on Jimmy MacGregor's Radio Scotland show, 'MacGregor's Gathering', in the 1980s and stupidly mentioned this. 'Give me an example,' he said. Thankfully, I managed not to make a complete fool of myself on national radio. These bovine beauties were on the banks of Loch Hourn, north of the Knoydart peninsula.

Castle Stalker, dating from the 13th-century, an ancient home of the Stewarts of Appin. It fell into disuse in the mid-19th century but was restored in the 1960s and is occasionally open to the public. It was used in the film *Monty Python and the Holy Grail* as Castle Aaaaarrrrrggghhh. It stands on a tidal rock in Loch Laich, an inlet of Loch Linnhe.

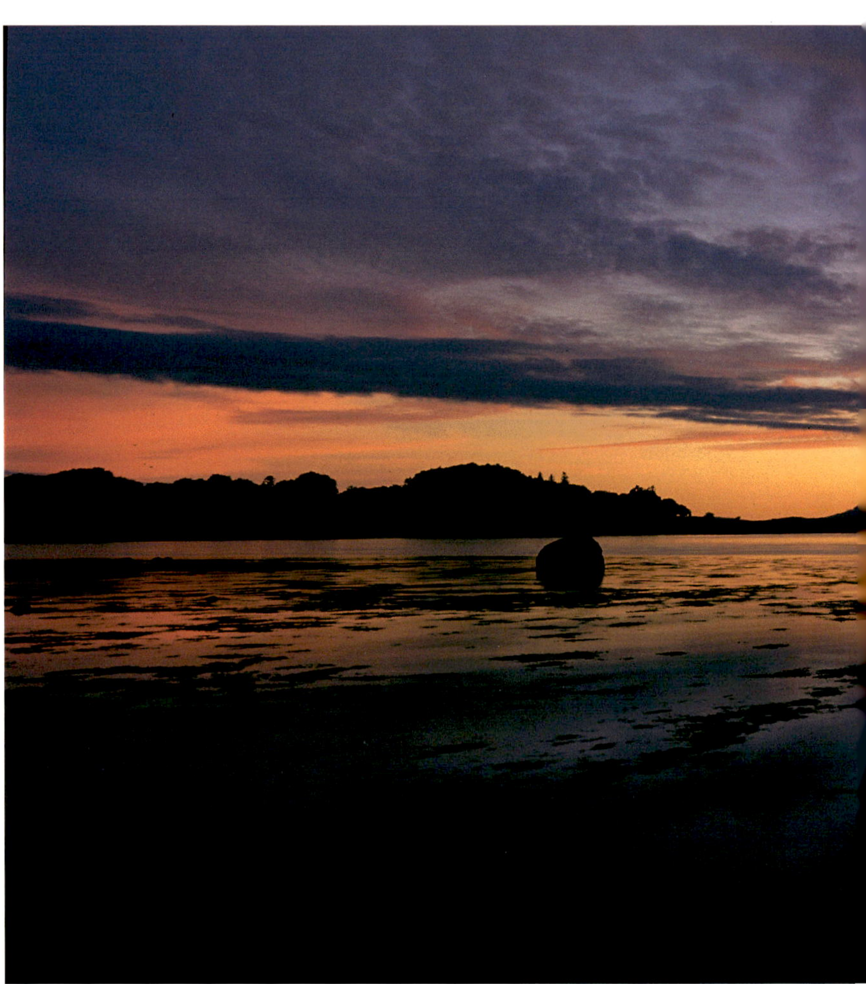

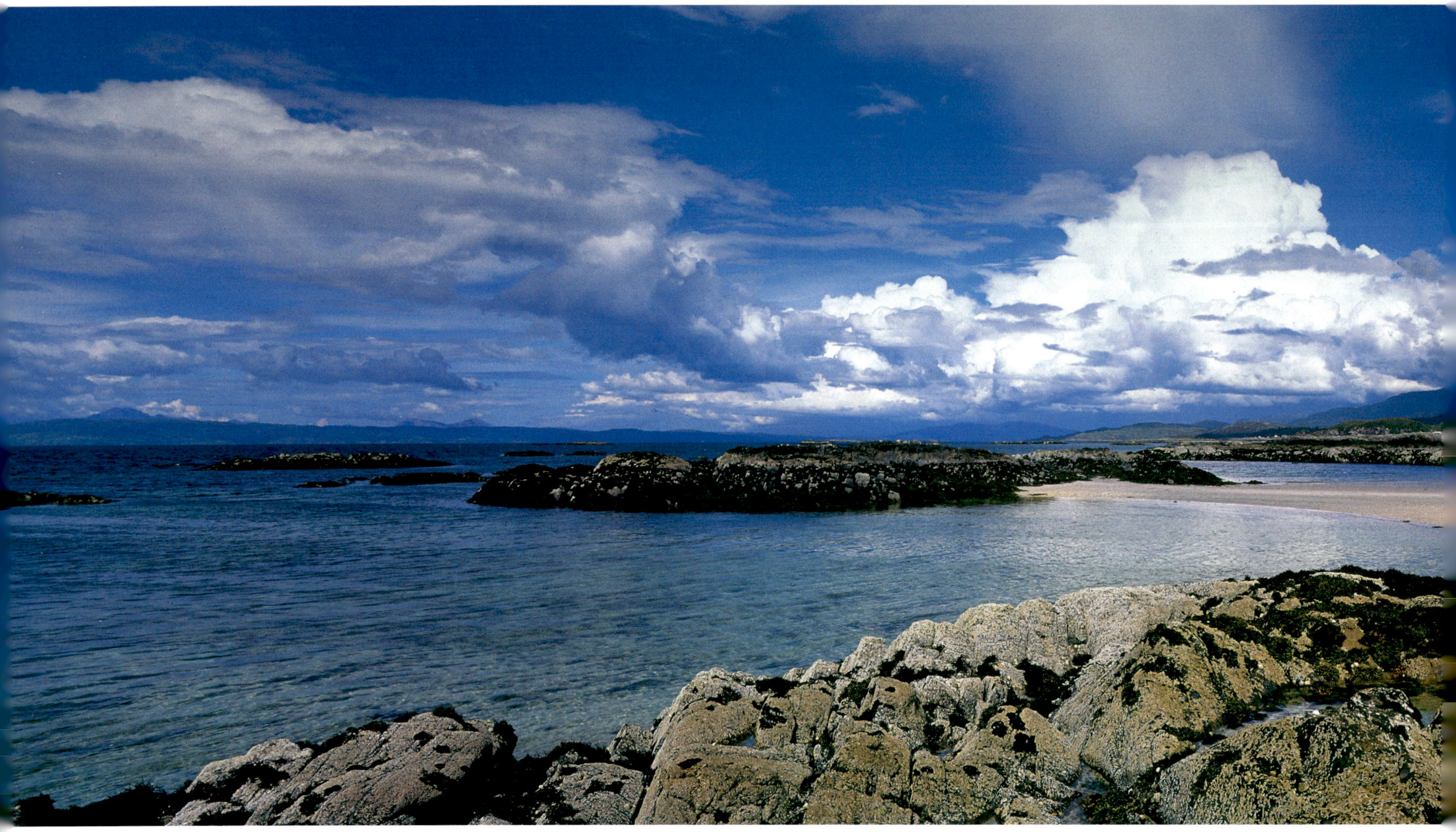

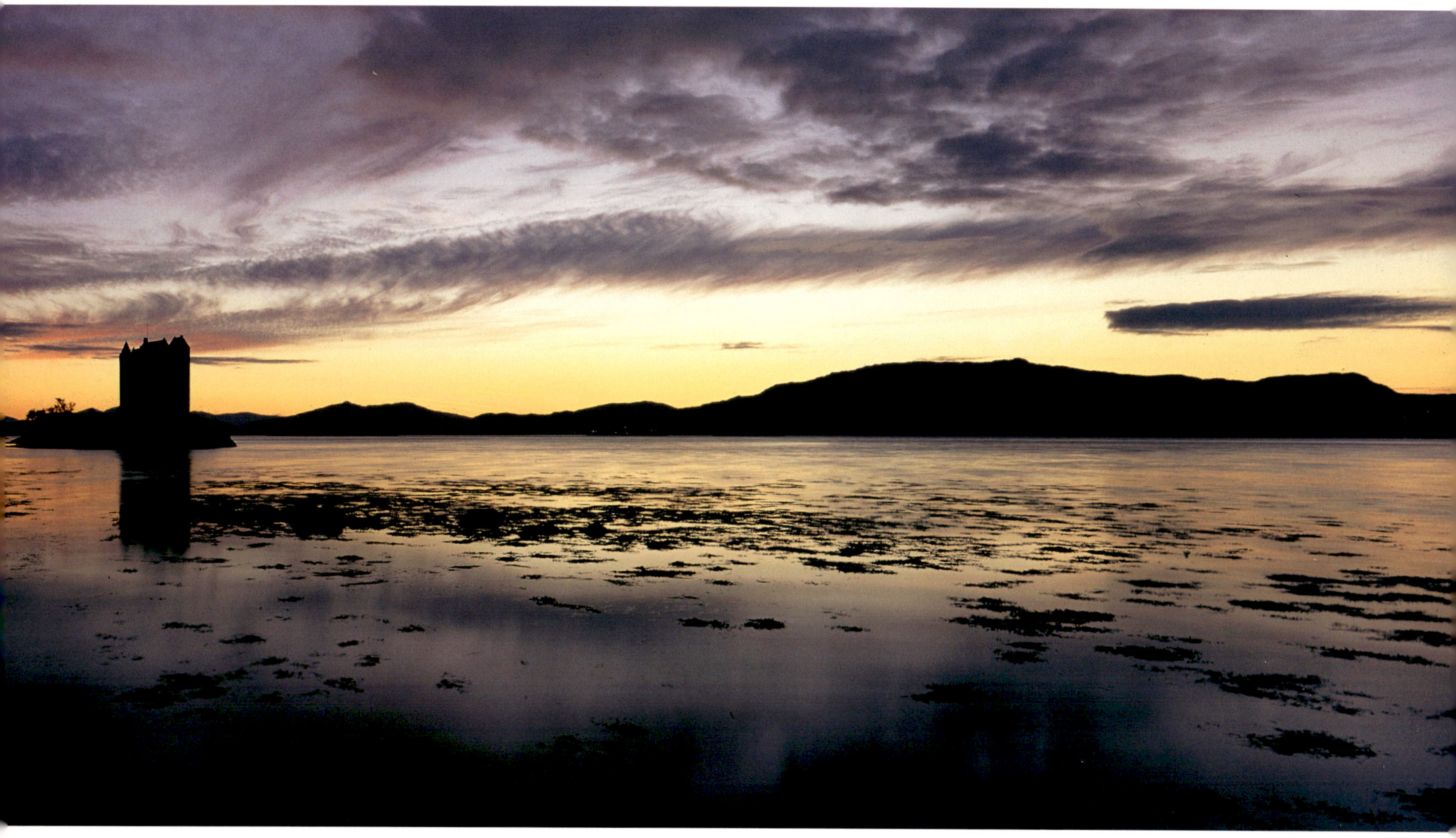

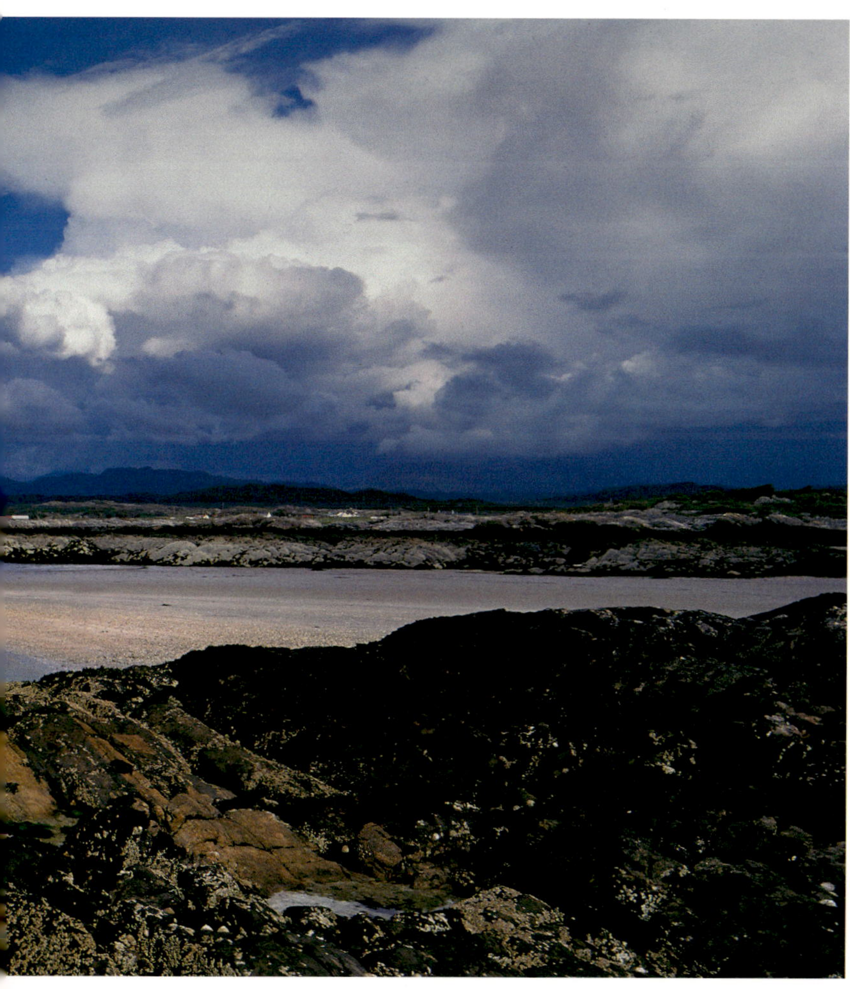

The beautiful beach at Arisaig. After a few days of sunshine, the sea pools on the west coast can rise in temperature and are very pleasant for swimming (honest!). Capturing the image of the view from this spot of the small isles of Eigg, Rum, Muck and Canna has always eluded me. The great American landscape photographer Ansel Adams' diktat was, 'Don't wait around too long as you'll miss what's going on around the corner.'

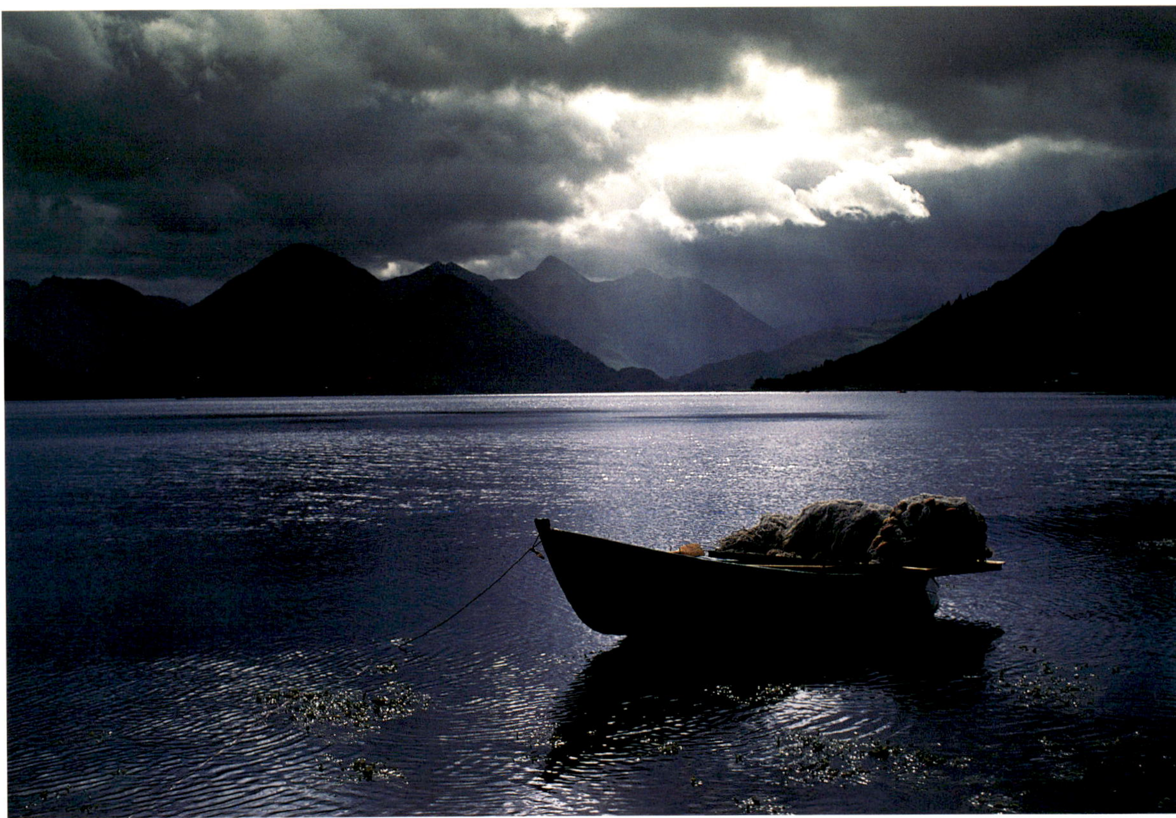

The Five Sisters of Kintail from Loch Duich with heavy rainclouds. Yes, we do have 'happening' weather in Scotland. Kintail is now in the care of the National Trust for Scotland.

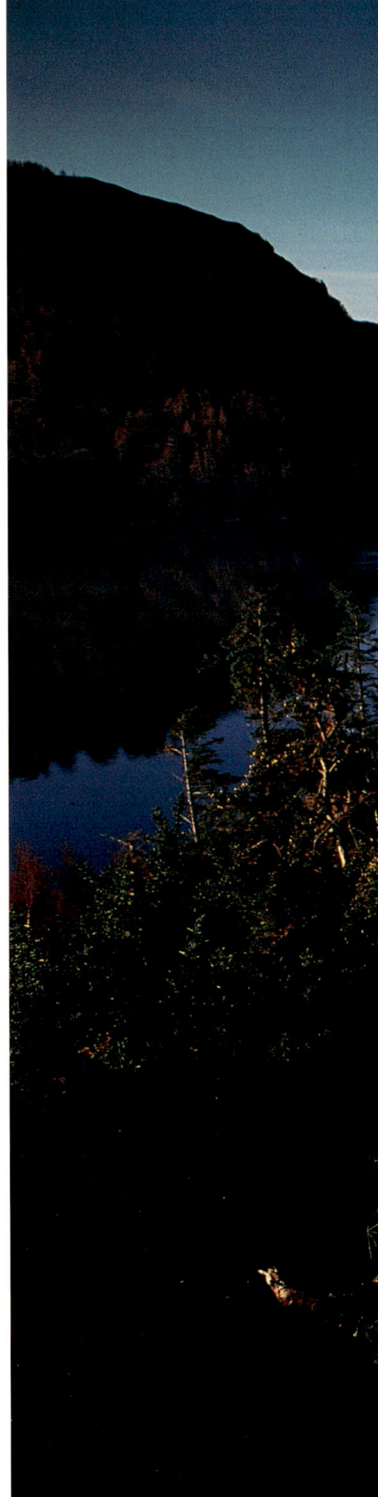

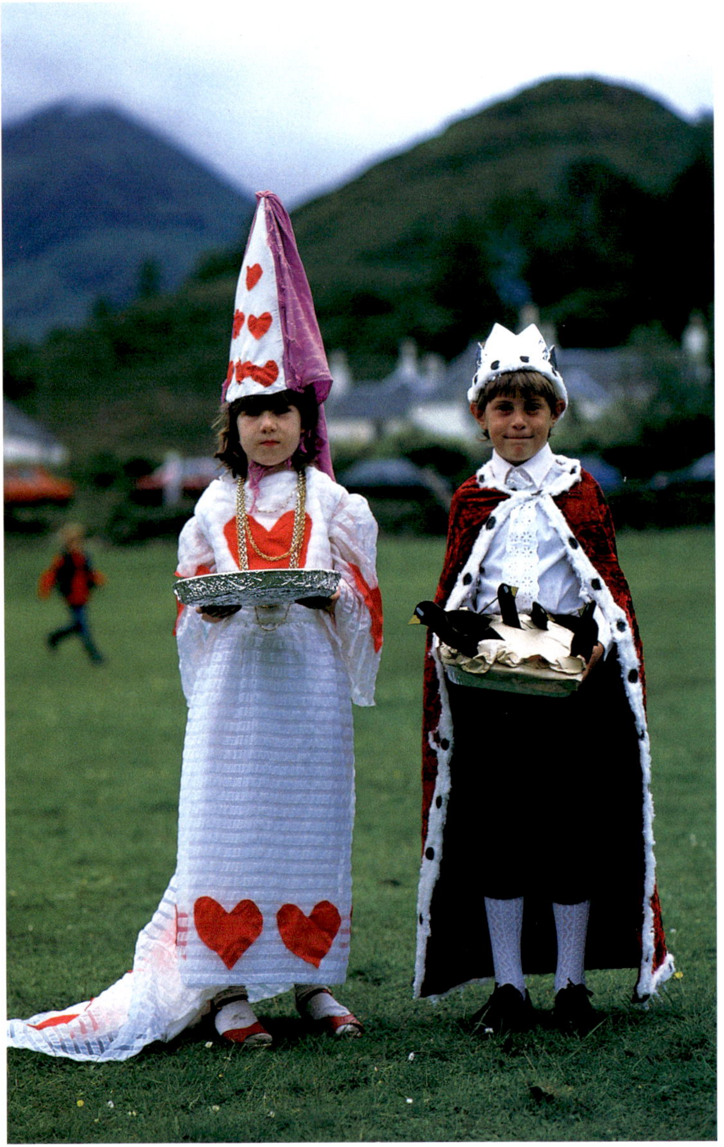

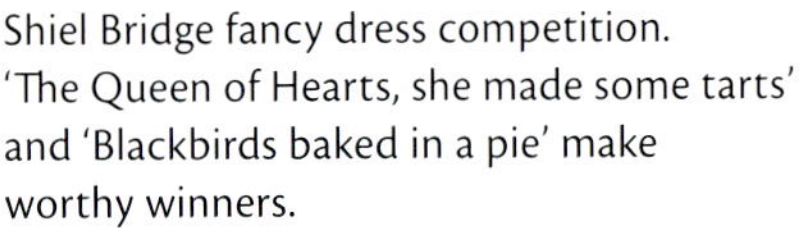

Shiel Bridge fancy dress competition. 'The Queen of Hearts, she made some tarts' and 'Blackbirds baked in a pie' make worthy winners.

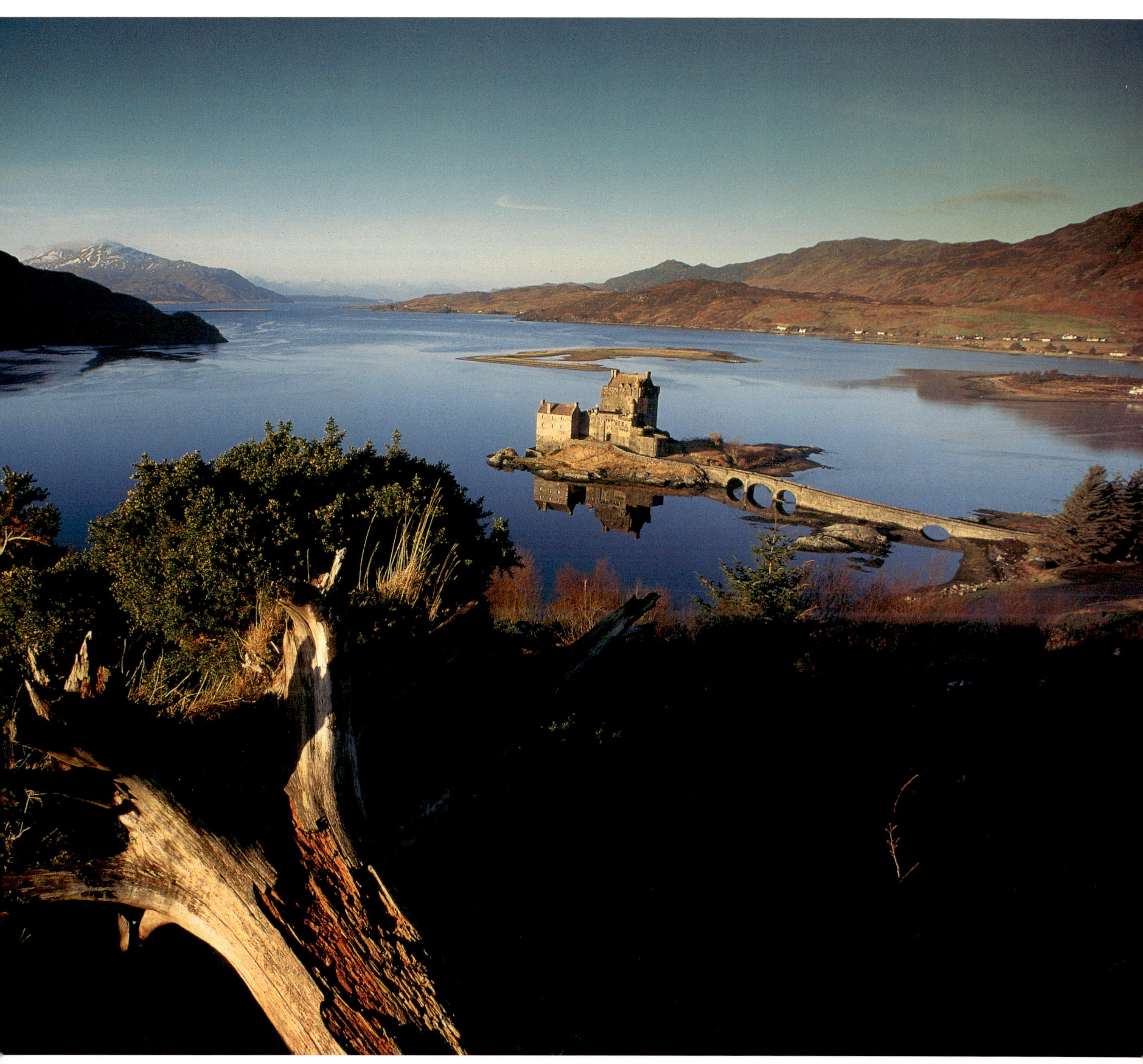

Eilean Donan, the shortbread tin image of Scotland. I don't care as it is wonderful and sums up all that is romantic about the Highlands. An apocryphal story says that a well-known scenic photographer took a classic view, framed it with a beautiful rowan tree that he then chopped down to make his image unique. I can't believe that anyone in our trade would stoop to such depths.

Loch Sunart, Ardnamurchan. The road alongside is a spectacular drive with almost continuous blind summits and hairpin bends. You most definitely wouldn't want to be behind me on this road, especially if I am pulling my caravan. Caravanning – the new rock 'n' roll or for sad people? Mine is a beautiful French retro 1950s' number called Toby, with 'Born to Tow' on the rear.

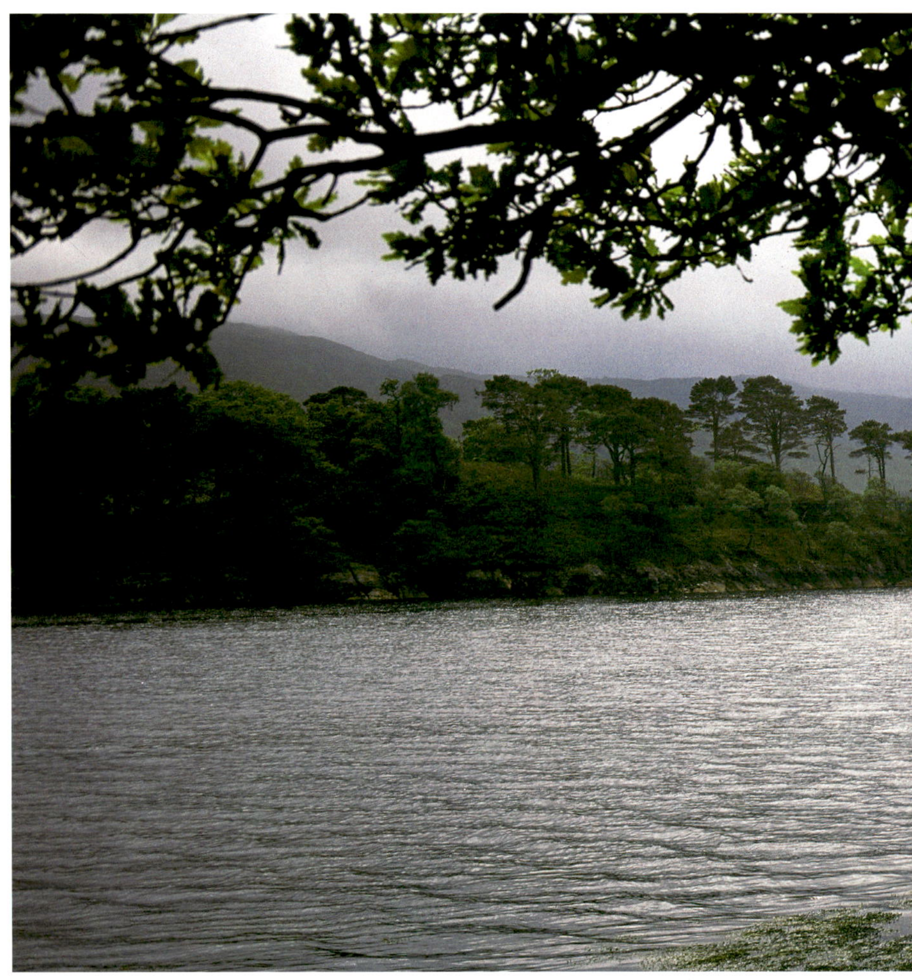

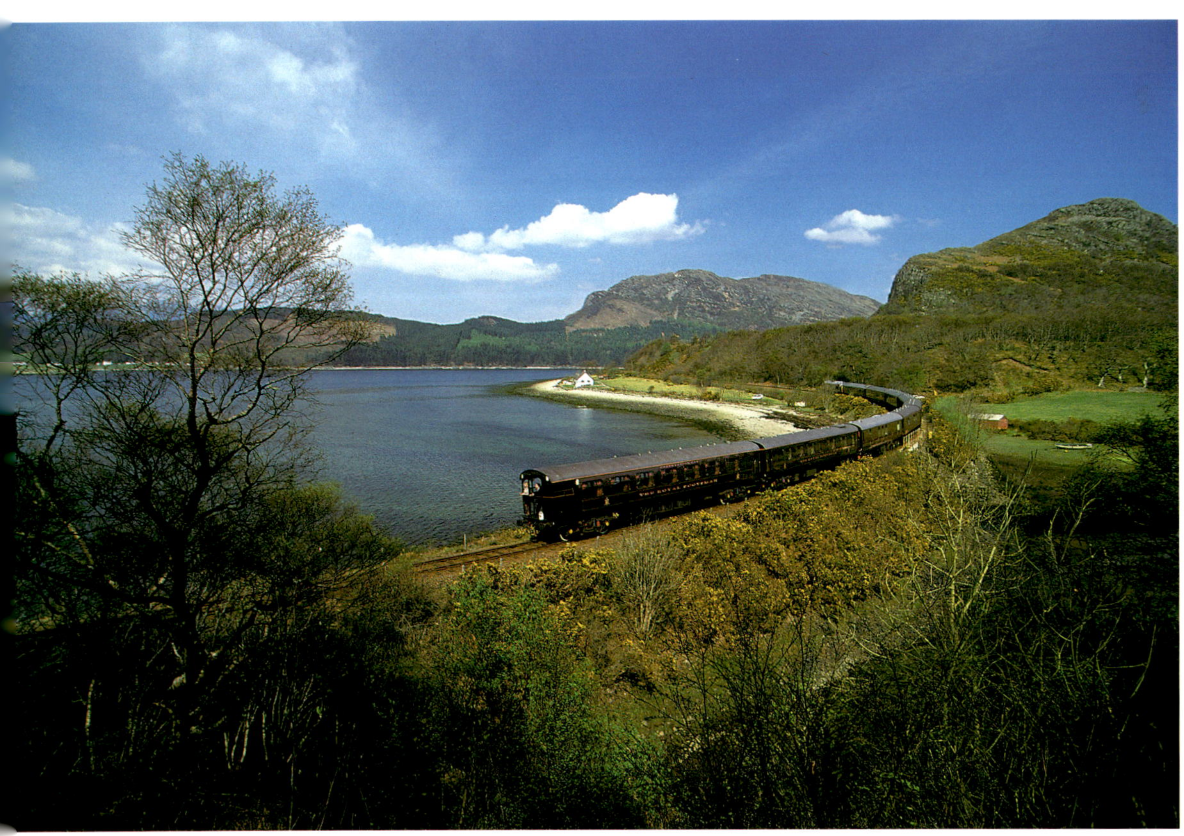

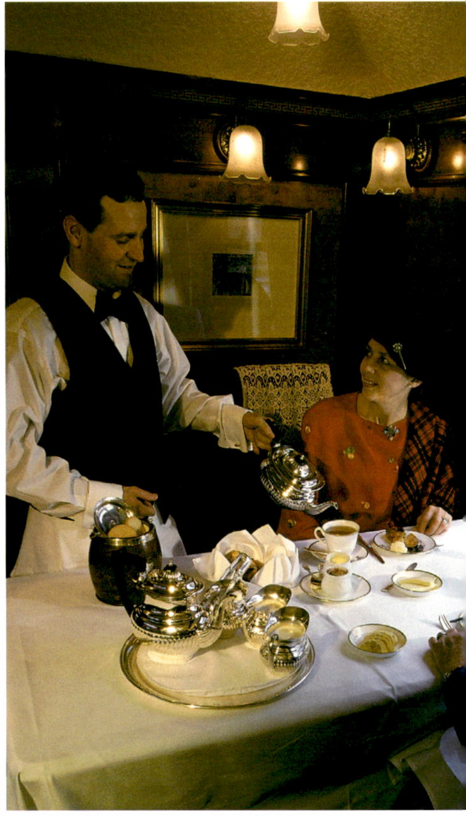

The Royal Scotsman offers five-star accommodation while taking in some of Scotland's finest scenery. Guests are requested to don black tie on several evenings. This was a most enjoyable assignment in the 1990s. The photographer sometimes gets to sample a champagne lifestyle on beer wages. On one occasion a guest, who was the proprietor of a three-Michelin-starred restaurant in Belgium, made a point of giving praise to the young talented Scottish chef. A couple on the open deck of the observation car while travelling alongside Loch Carron in Wester Ross.

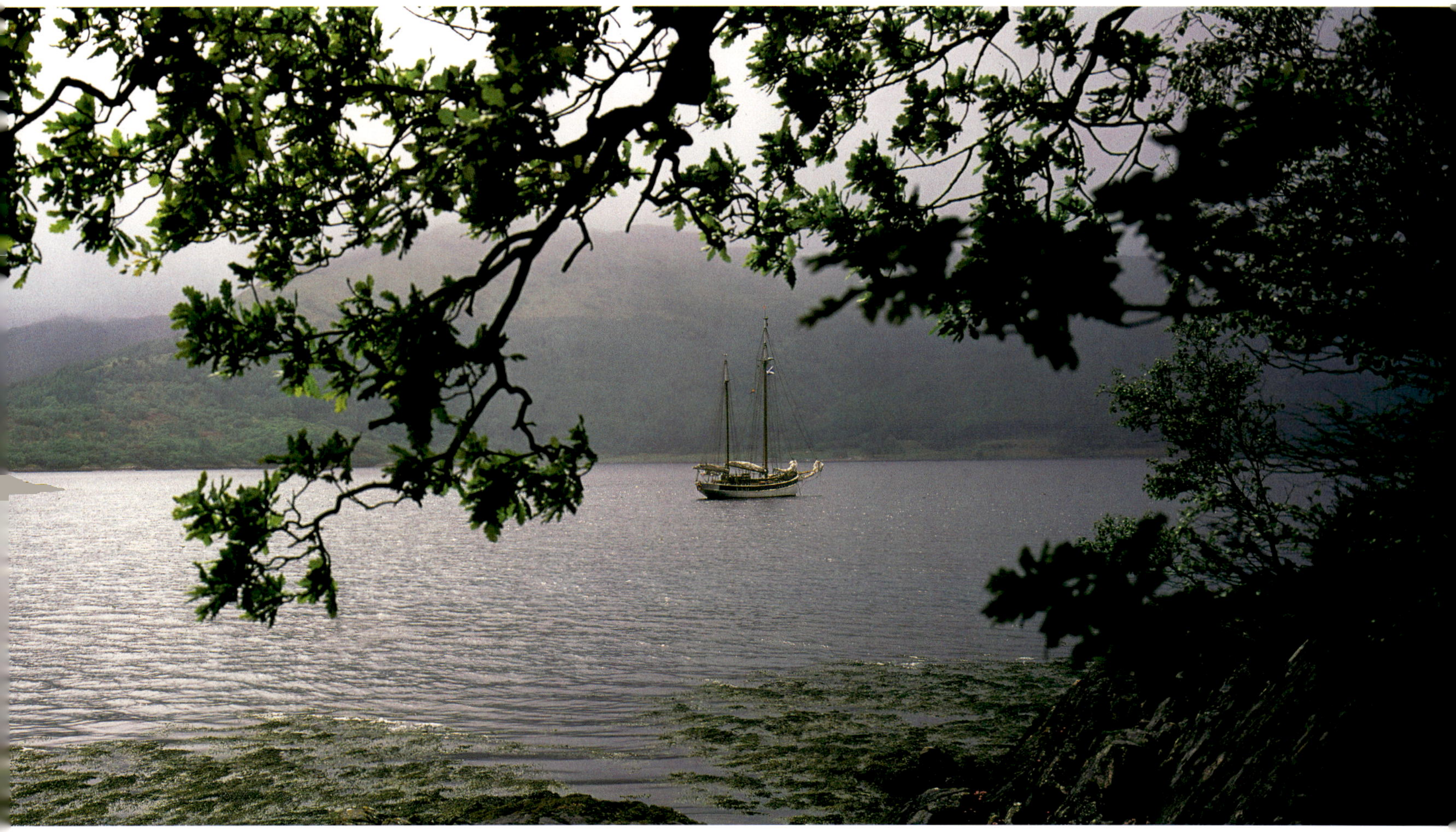

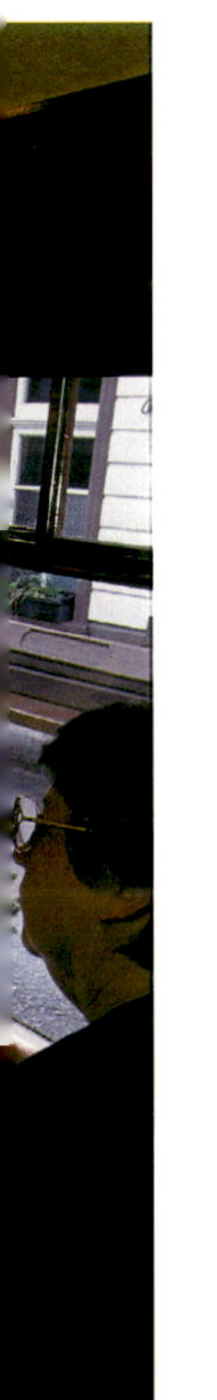

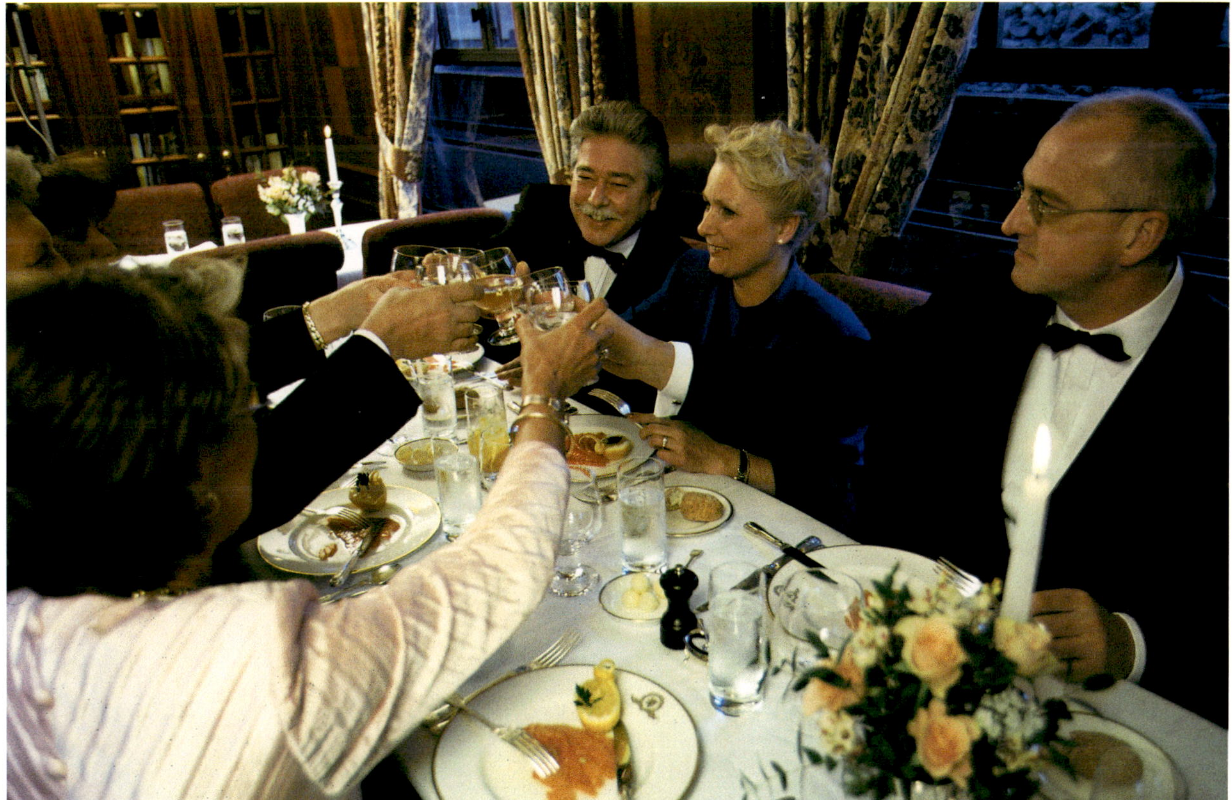

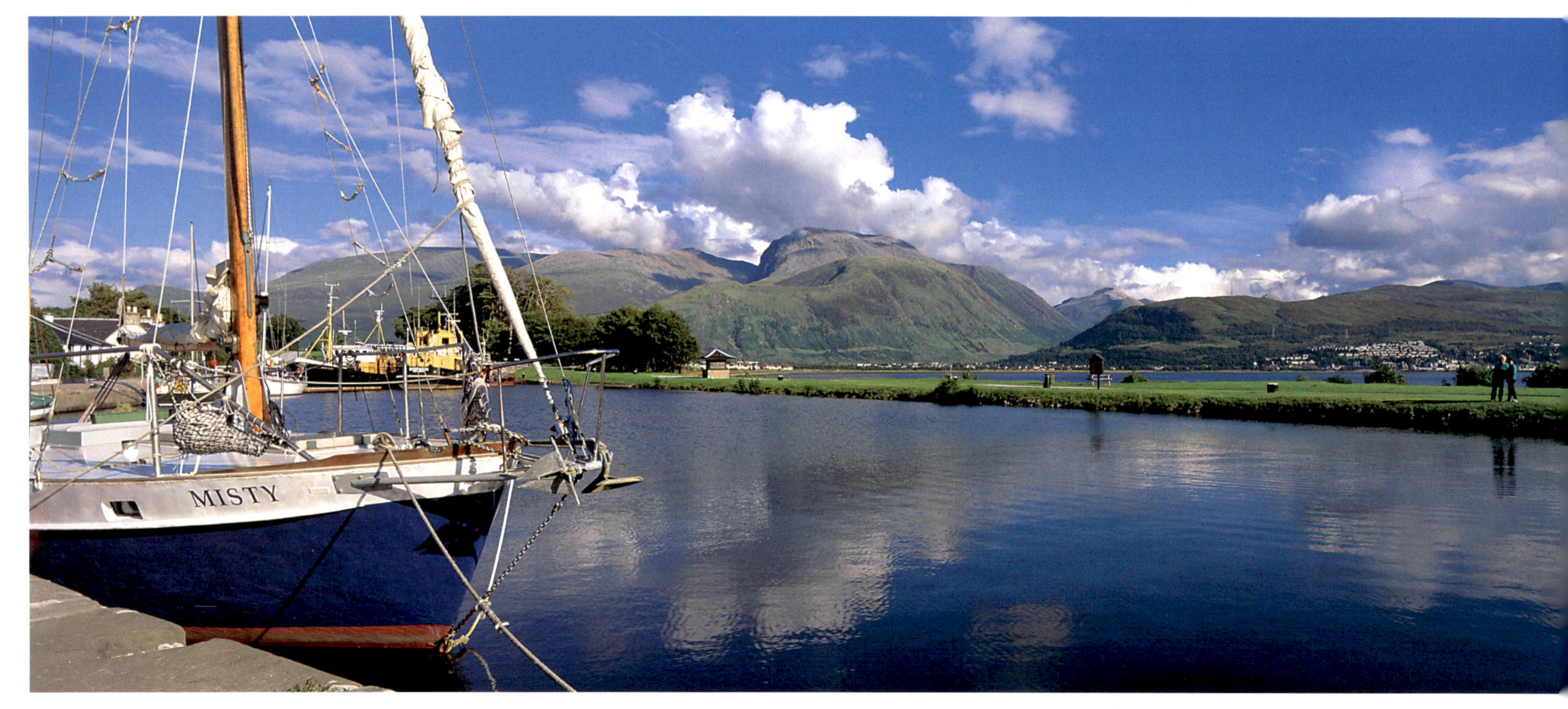
MISTY

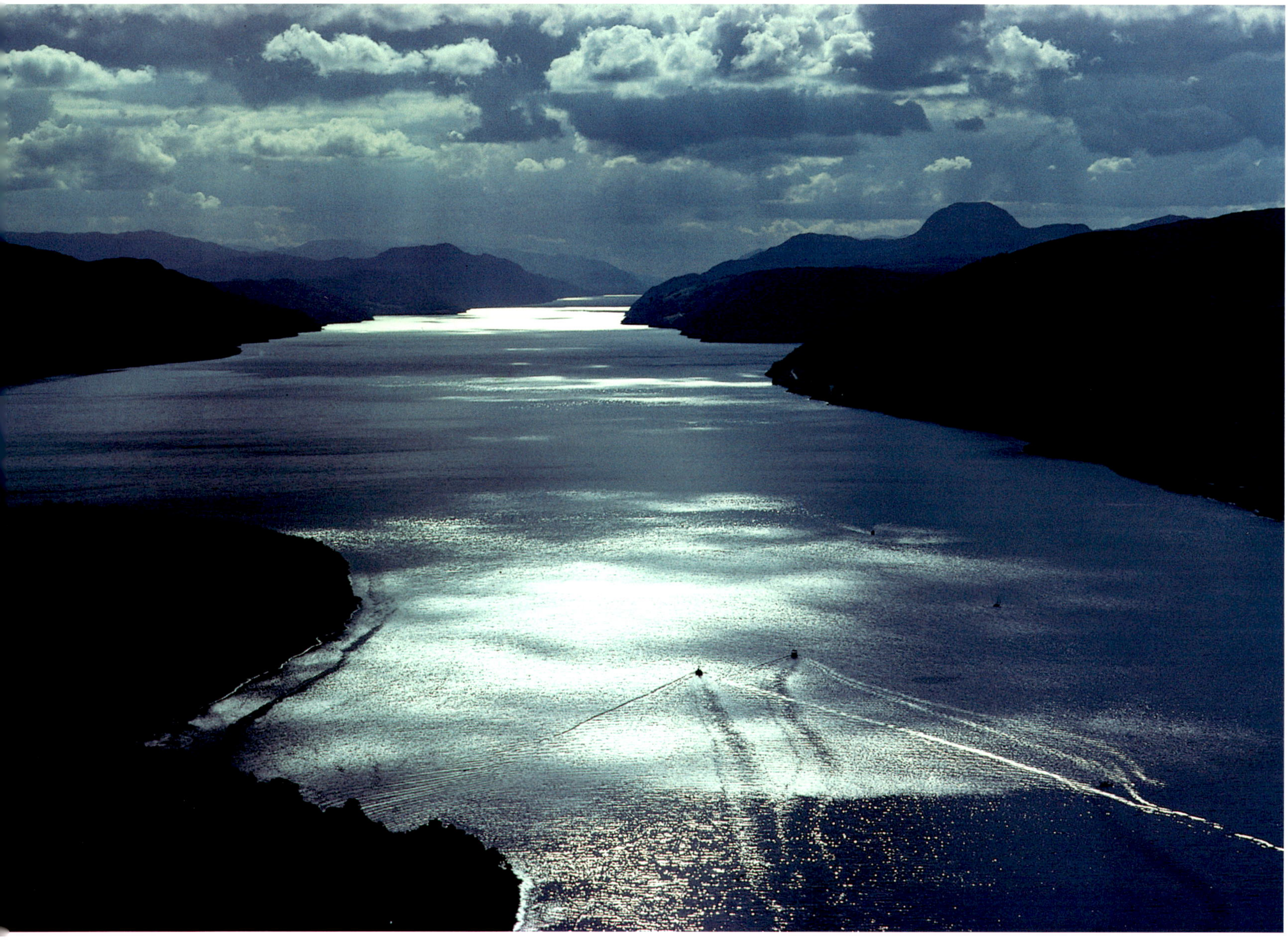

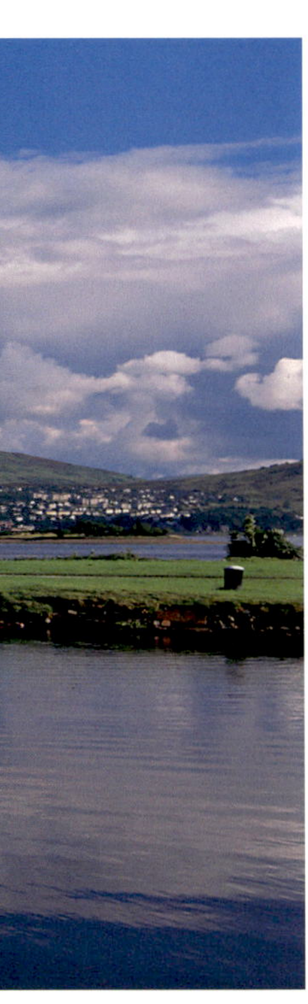

Ben Nevis, the highest mountain in Great Britain at 4,406 feet. The shape of the summit diminishes its impressive height. Shot from the Caledonian Canal at Corpach, this panorama shows how the ben dominates Fort William.

This aerial view of Loch Ness shows Mealfuarvonie, 'Mountain of the Cold Moor', on the right. Living at the foot of the mountain is Neil Oram, author of *The Warp*, the longest play in the world (a running time of around twenty-two hours), which was directed by the actor Ken Campbell. On the opposite shore is Boleskine House, the former home of Aleister Crowley, magician, poet, artist and adventurer. In between lies one of the world's great unsolved mysteries.

As a child, I thought that the Greig Street Bridge in Inverness was elegant and beautiful – and I still do. It was common practice for a group of kids to jump up and down in unison to cause an unnerving wave motion that was not appreciated by everyone.

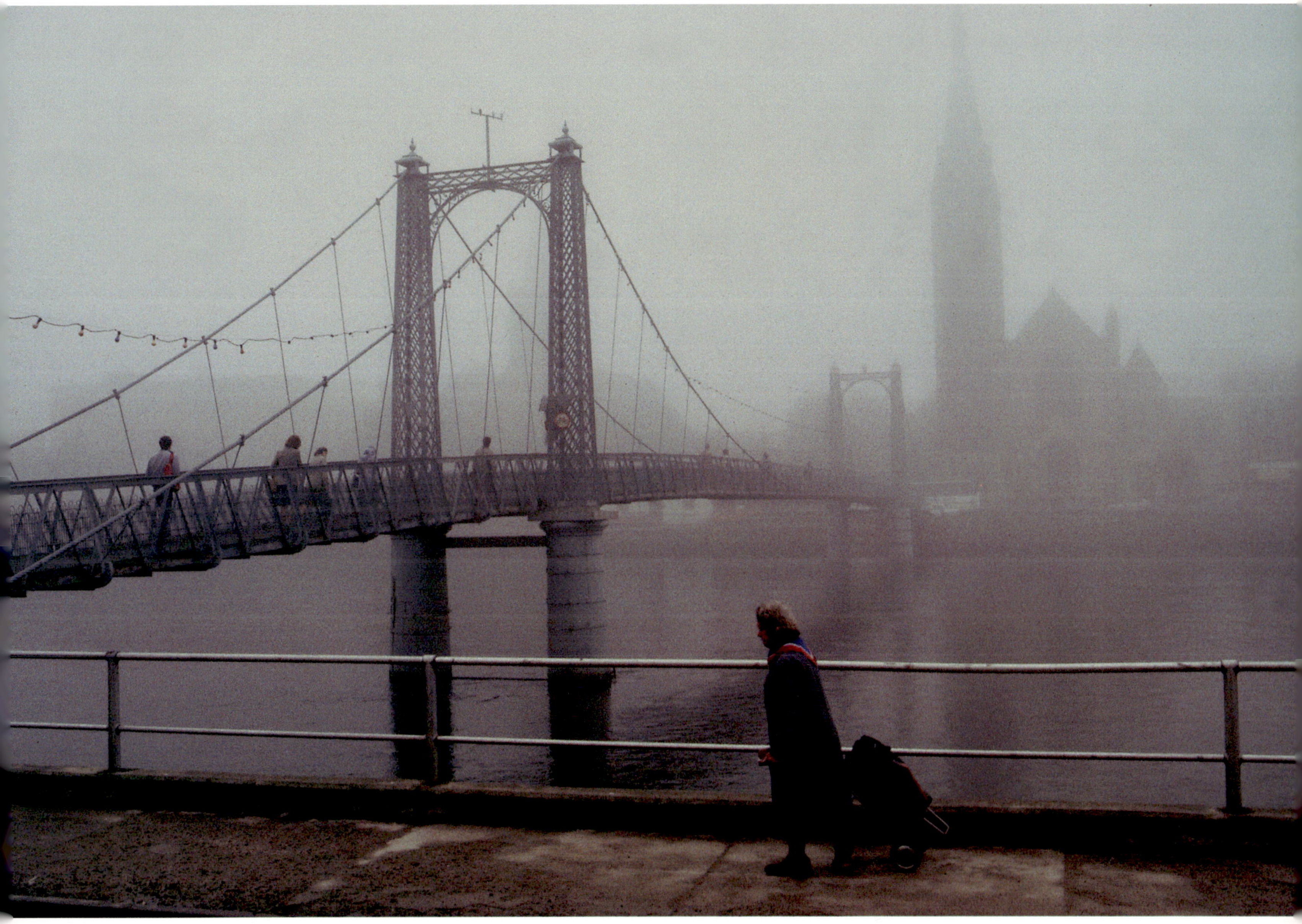

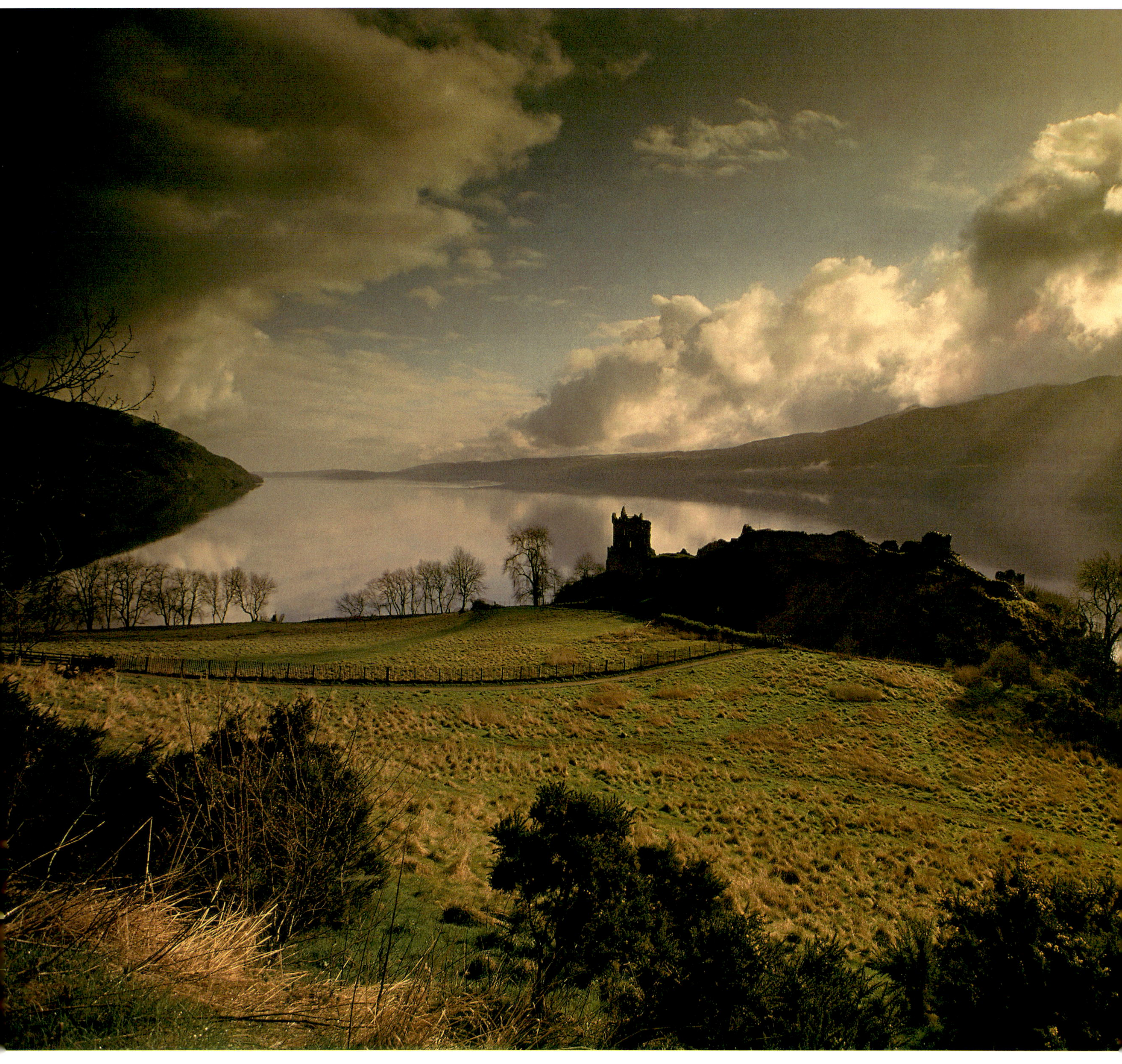

The ruins of Urquhart Castle, blown up to prevent its occupation by Jacobite forces in 1692. I have passed it so many times when it was shrouded in mist or the light was just too flat to achieve a successful photograph. This was taken at 6.30 on a summer's morning after a mad dash from the lay-by, laden with gear, with a hazardous climb over the perimeter fence and just managing to catch the drama.

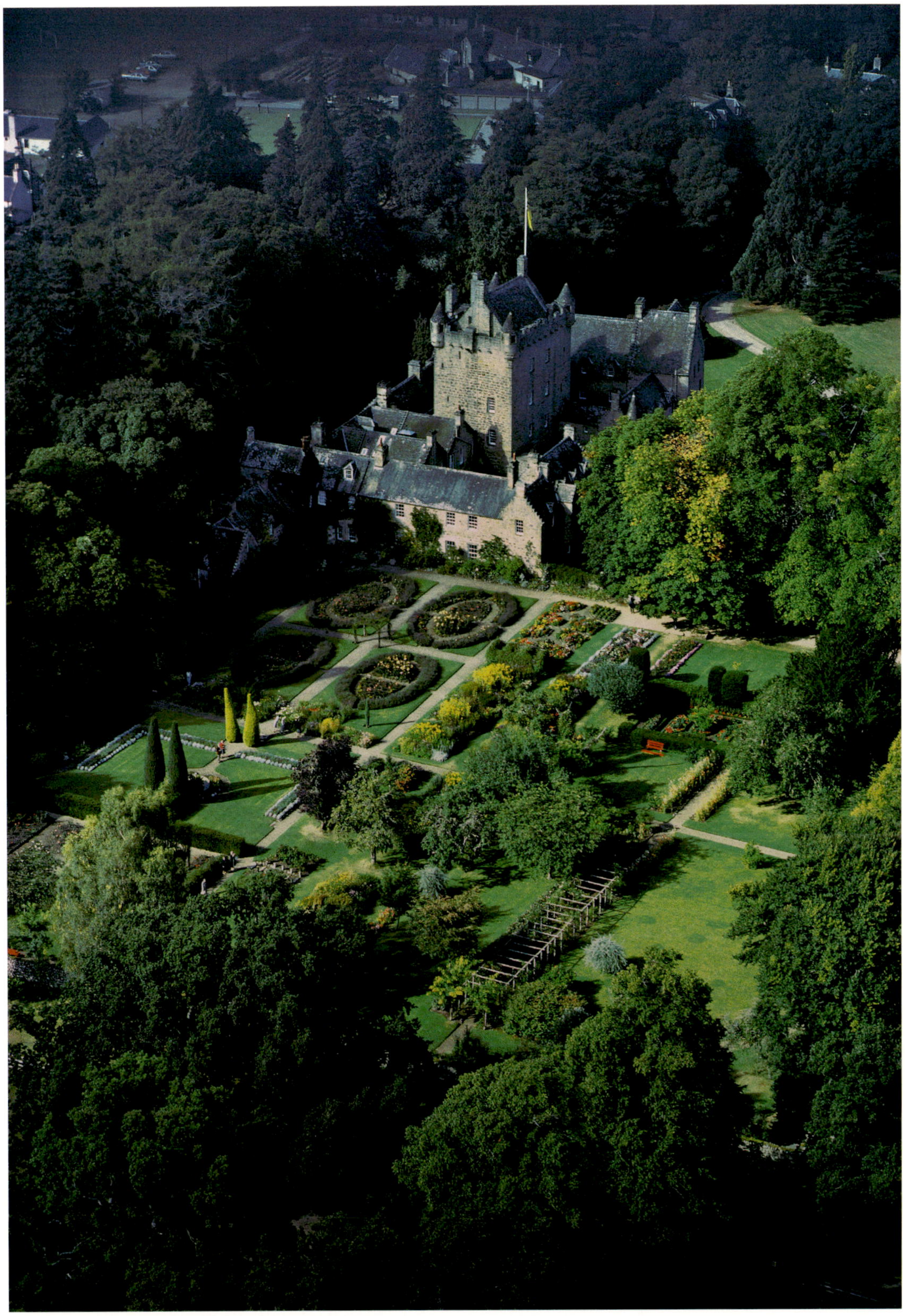

Cawdor Castle, near Nairn, dating from the 14th and 15th centuries, is everyone's idea of what a castle should be. Shakespeare's *Macbeth* was the Thane of Cawdor, but the plot is almost completely fictitious. The castle's guide book has the 5th Earl of Cawdor quoted as saying, 'I wish the Bard had never written his damned play!'

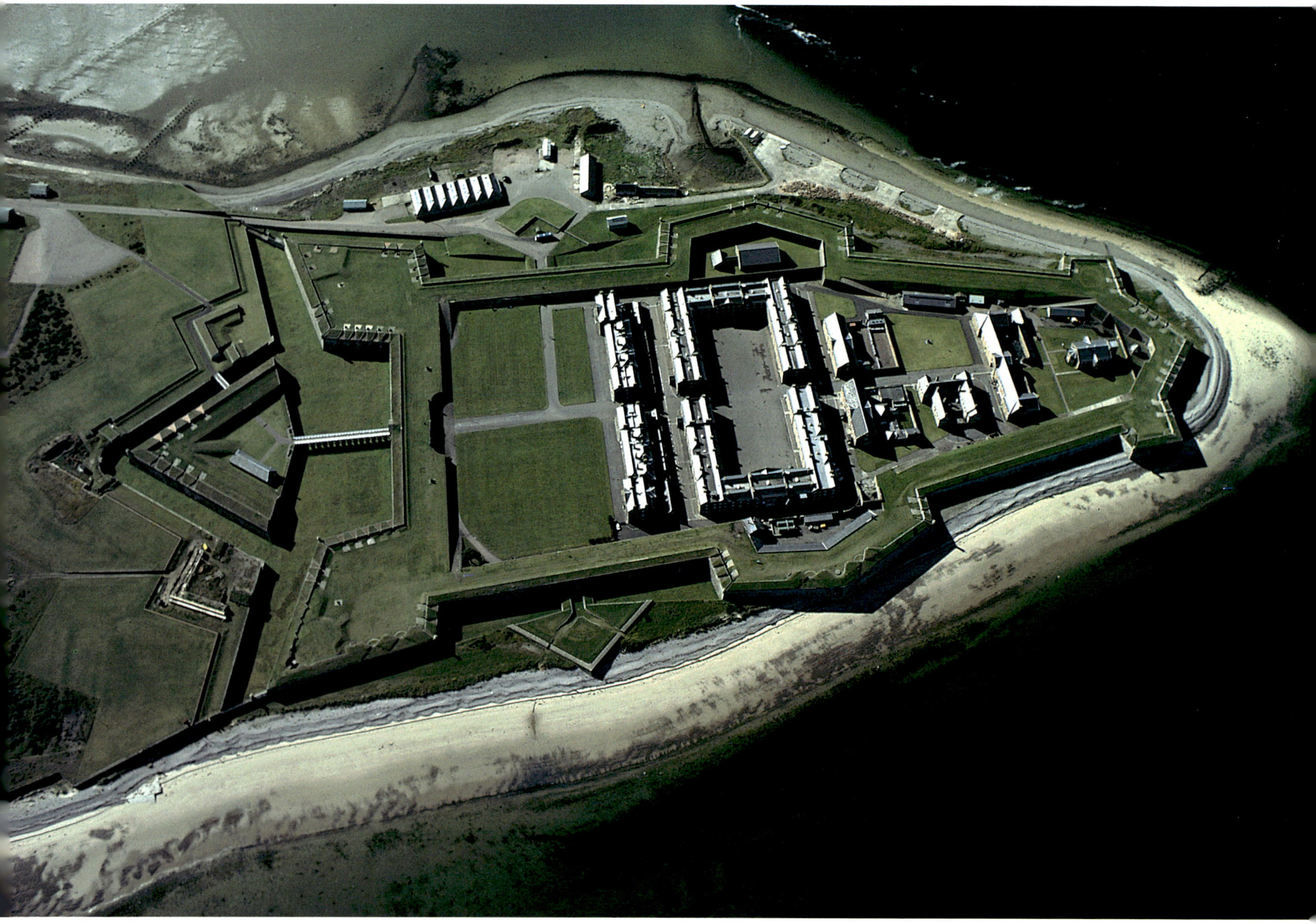

It is to be hoped you get this great view of Fort George when flying into Inverness airport. The designer, Lieutenant General William Skinner, had obviously studied the great French military architect Vauban. It was built to contain the Highlands after the events leading up to the battle of Culloden in 1746. As it never saw any action it is one of the most pristine of our military structures.

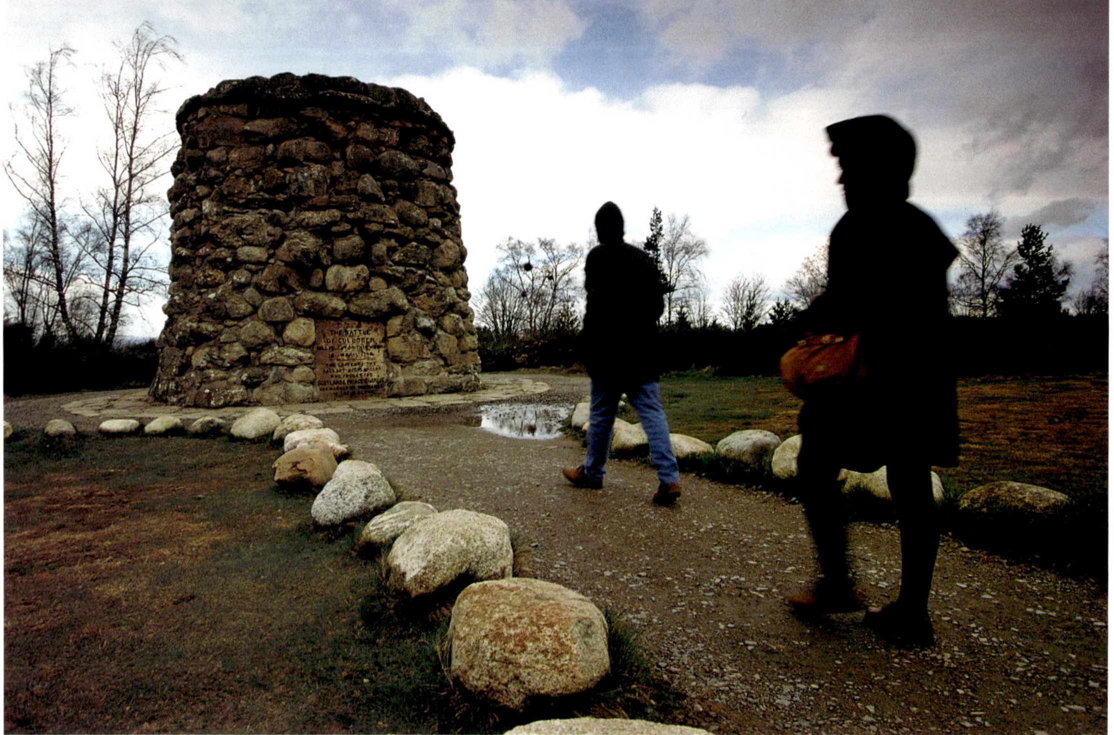

Even on a bright summer day Culloden battlefield, the site of the last pitched battle on British soil, has a tragic air. The stark moorland with small stones marking the mass clan graves can prove to be a moving experience for the visitor. This was the end of Prince Charles Edward Stewart's ambition to regain the crown for the Stewarts and the beginning of many romanticised versions of its history.

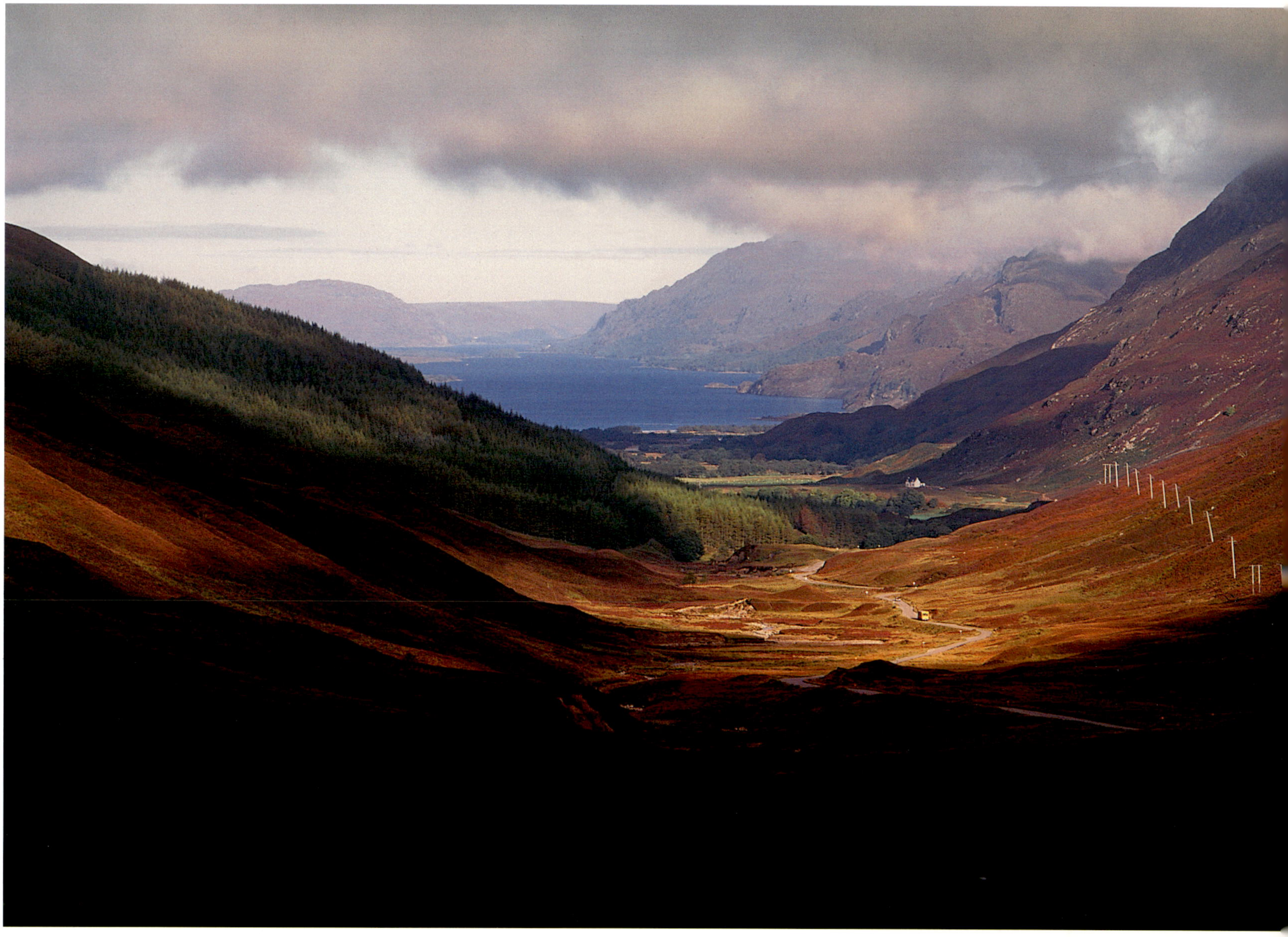

This shot was used for the cover of the book *Postbus Country* in the 1990s. It was taken from Glen Docherty looking towards Loch Maree. It was decided that the yellow van should become red, giving the illusion of a postbus. This level of deception is as far as I would ever like to go with image manipulation of scenic photography.

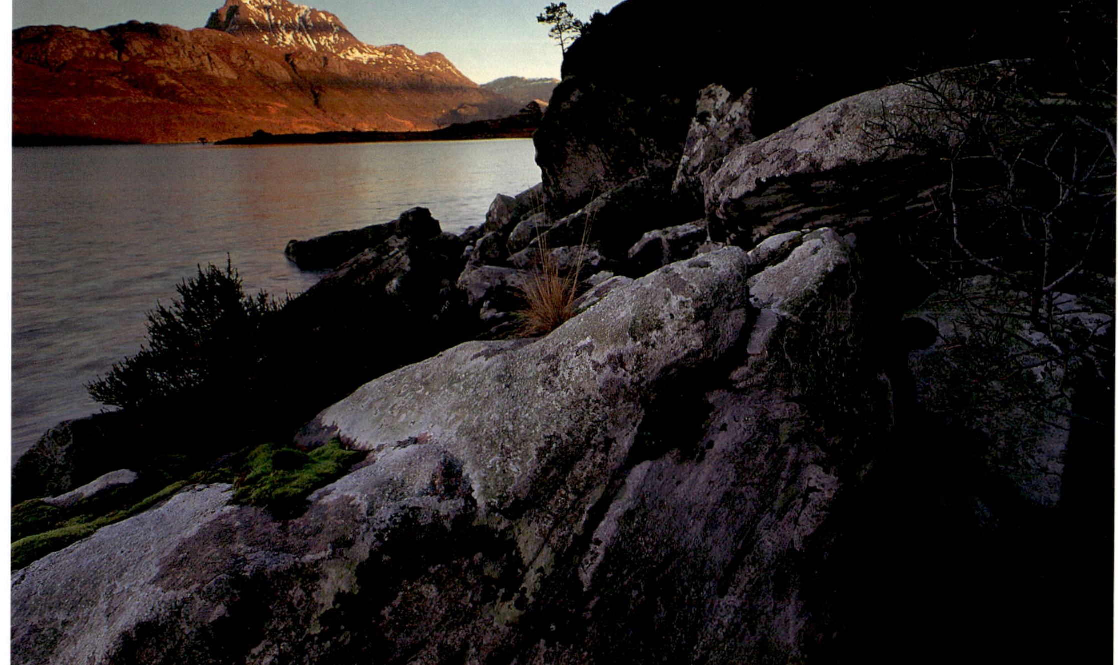

Loch Maree and Slioch (3,217 feet). I had just returned from shooting a guidebook on Japan and had the rock gardens I had photographed there in mind when I took this shot for a Bank of Scotland calendar in the early 1990s.

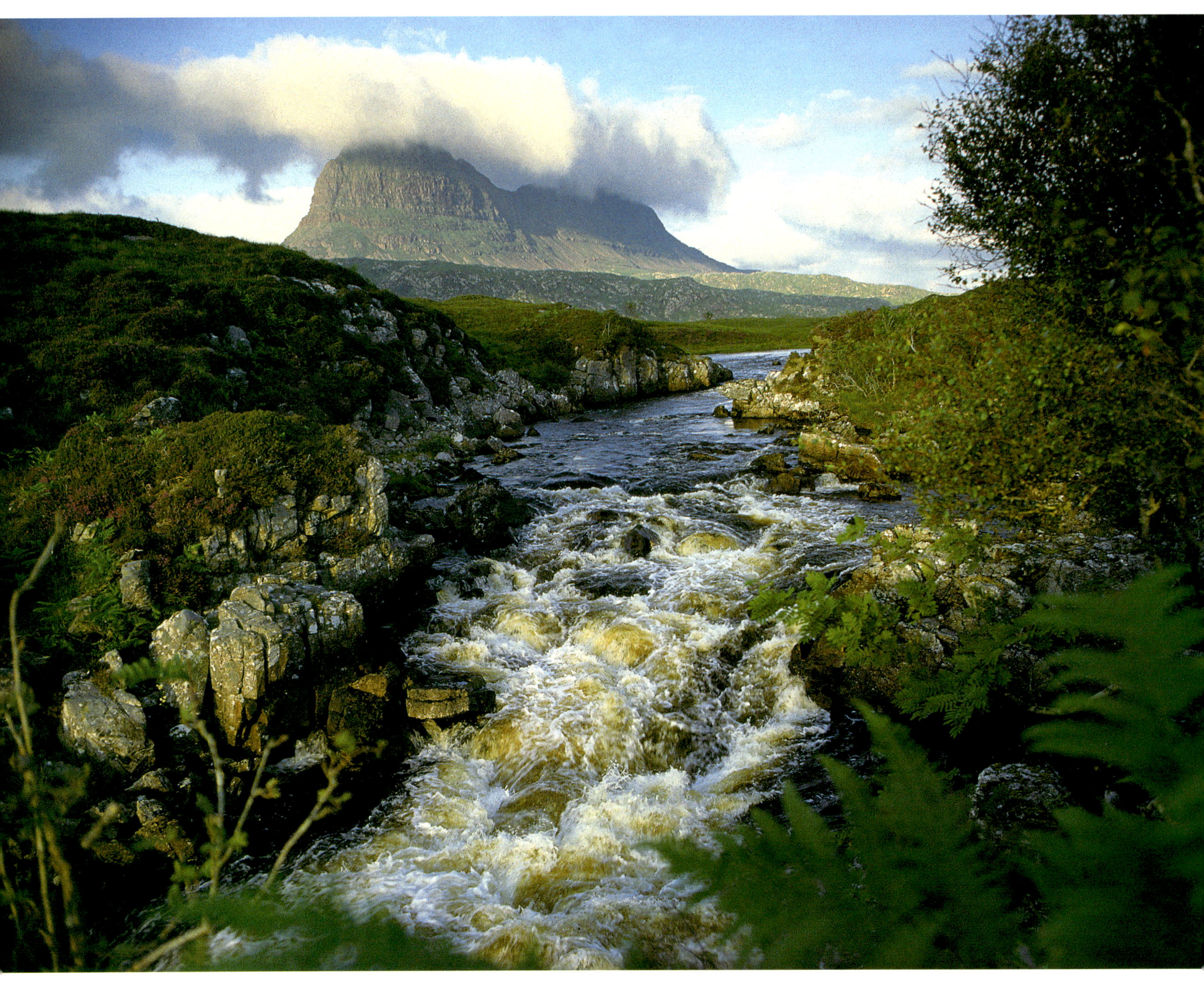

(Above) This view of Suilven (2,399 feet) from the River Kirkaig was used on the cover of *American Popular Photography* with an article on how I'd shot it. This to me was quite an accolade. I failed to mention, however, that I was trouserless and up to my thighs in freezing water and being bitten by a swarm of clegs.

(Above right) Loch Inchard, Sutherland. Only the Velux windows tell us that this is a contemporary picture, taken in 2009. The northwest coast of Scotland is glorious in any weather except whenever the mist obscures everything. *National Geographic* photographer Jim Richardson phoned me while on a shoot in the northwest: 'Doug, I'm seeing the most amazing light but every time I pull over to photograph it has disappeared.' I replied in mock disbelief, 'Really!'

(Right) Durness is still one of the last remaining sizeable villages in mainland Scotland that can be accessed only by single track road and is also the most northwesterly village on the British mainland, being only nine miles from Cape Wrath. John Lennon spent long summer holidays in Durness from the ages of nine to fourteen. A memorial garden has been created with the help of BBC's Beechgrove Garden. I'm sure John would have been knocked out by the ceilidh that was held to celebrate the opening of the garden. I did a shot of Strawberry Fields in New York, which captured the essence of the other memorial. On receiving a copy, Yoko Ono sent me a drawing by John as a thank-you.

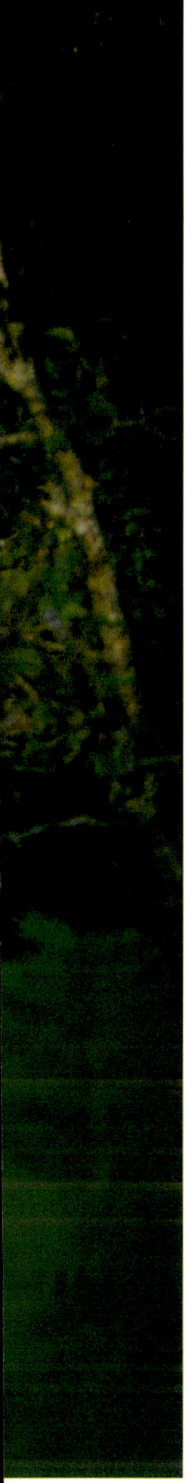

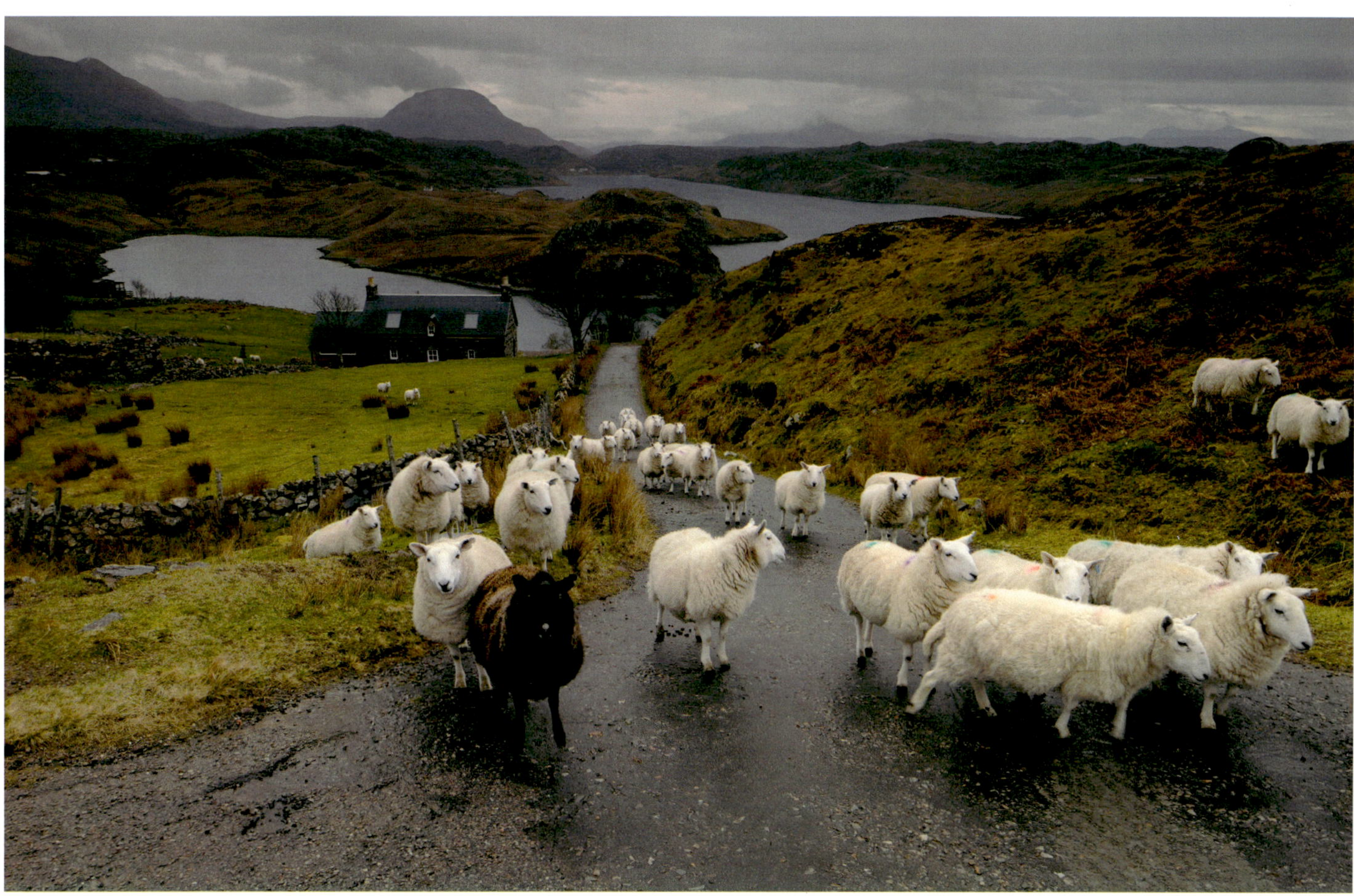

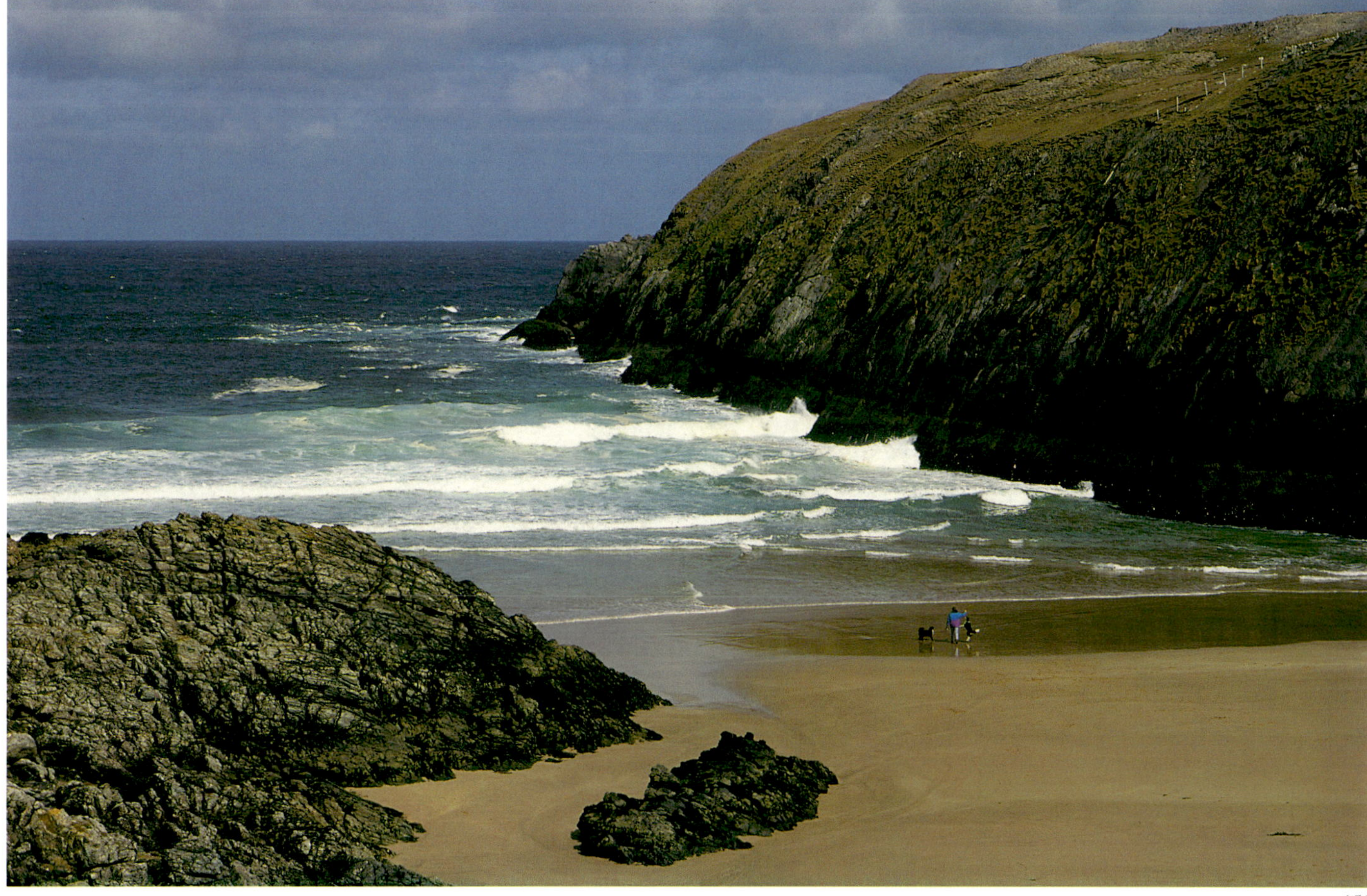

The cottage of Hugh Miller, the geologist and writer, born in Cromarty on the Black Isle in 1802. These skilful craftsmen are rethatching his birthplace, now in the care of the National Trust for Scotland. The burgh has thankfully escaped major development during the last 200 years. Perhaps Highland region could see it as their Culross.

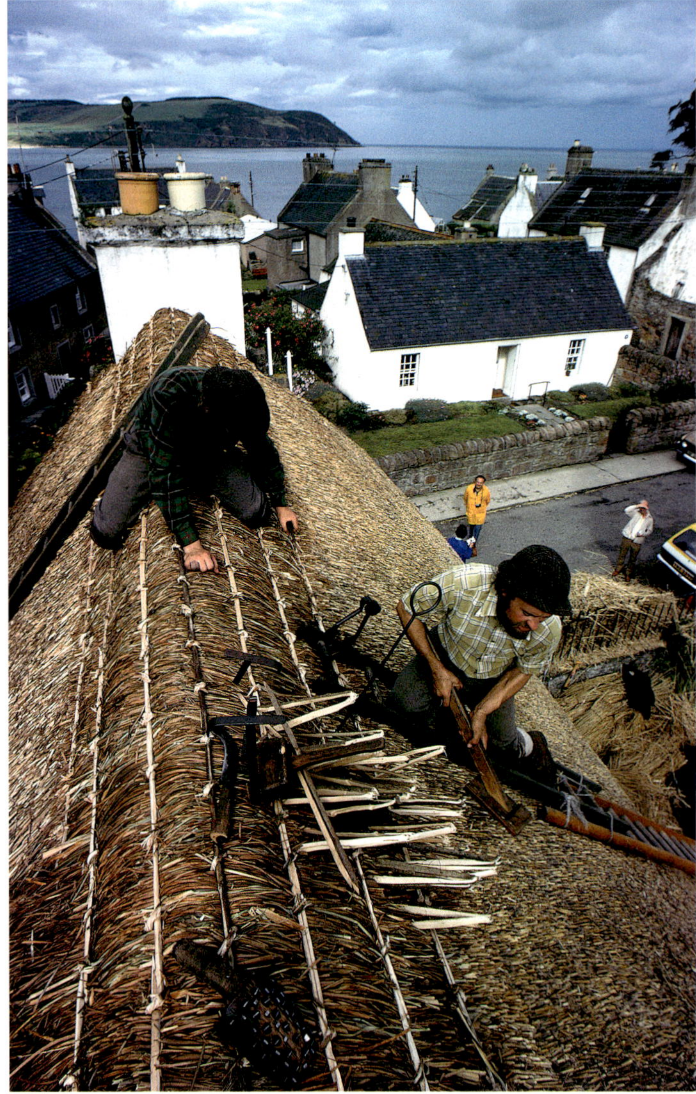

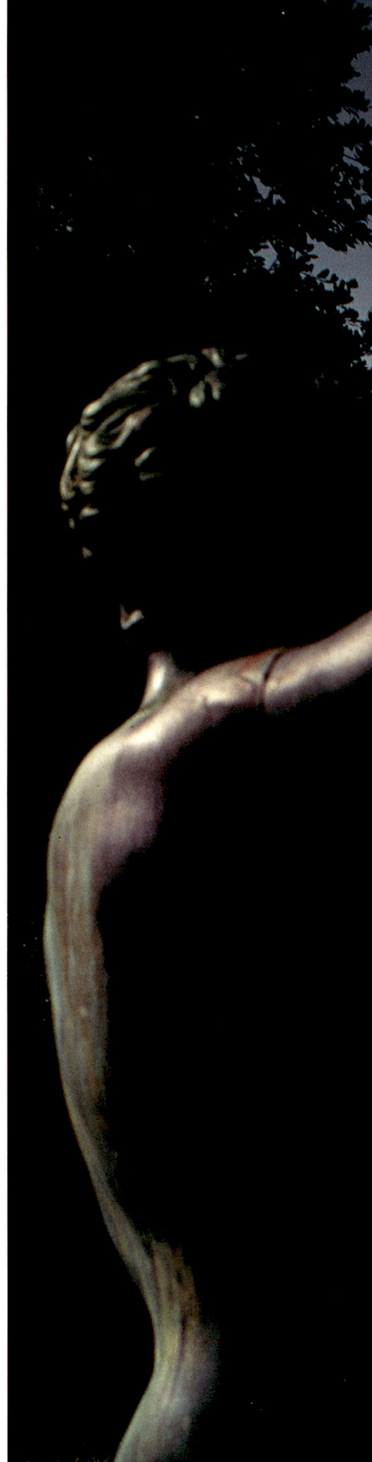

This stained glass depicts a rural idyll with the rich diversity of wildlife native to Scotland, the stag echoing Landseer's painting *Monarch of the Glen*.

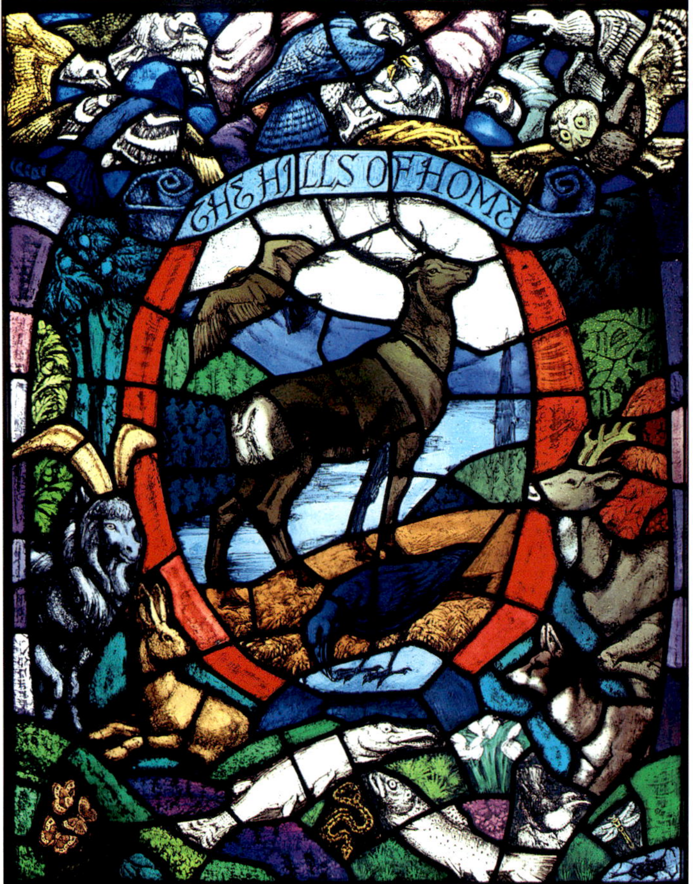

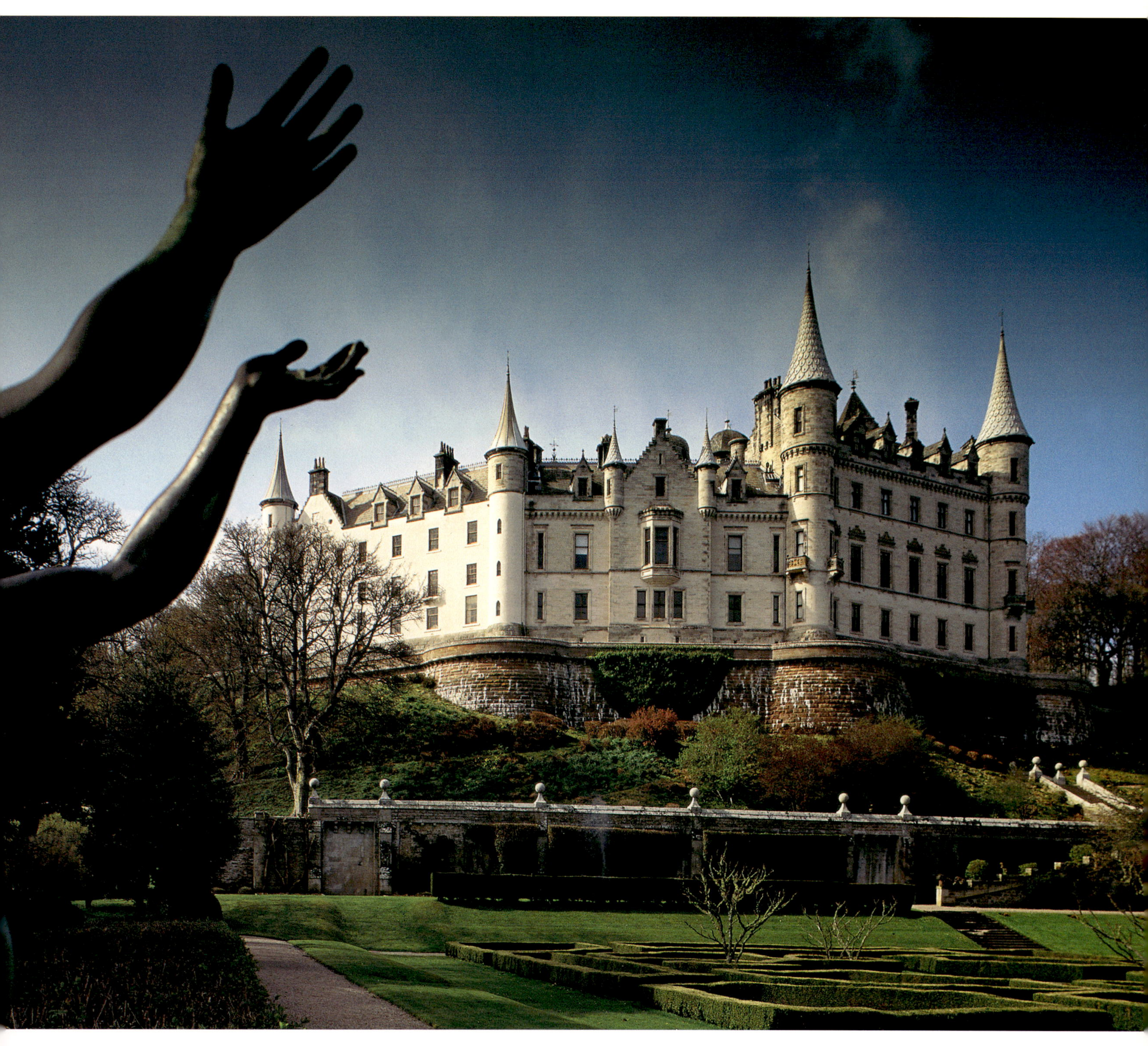

Dunrobin Castle, Golspie, rebuilt in the mid-19th century by the second Duke of Sutherland in the style of a French chateau. His father, the first duke, was a controversial figure in the infamous Highland Clearances. The original castle was built in 1275.

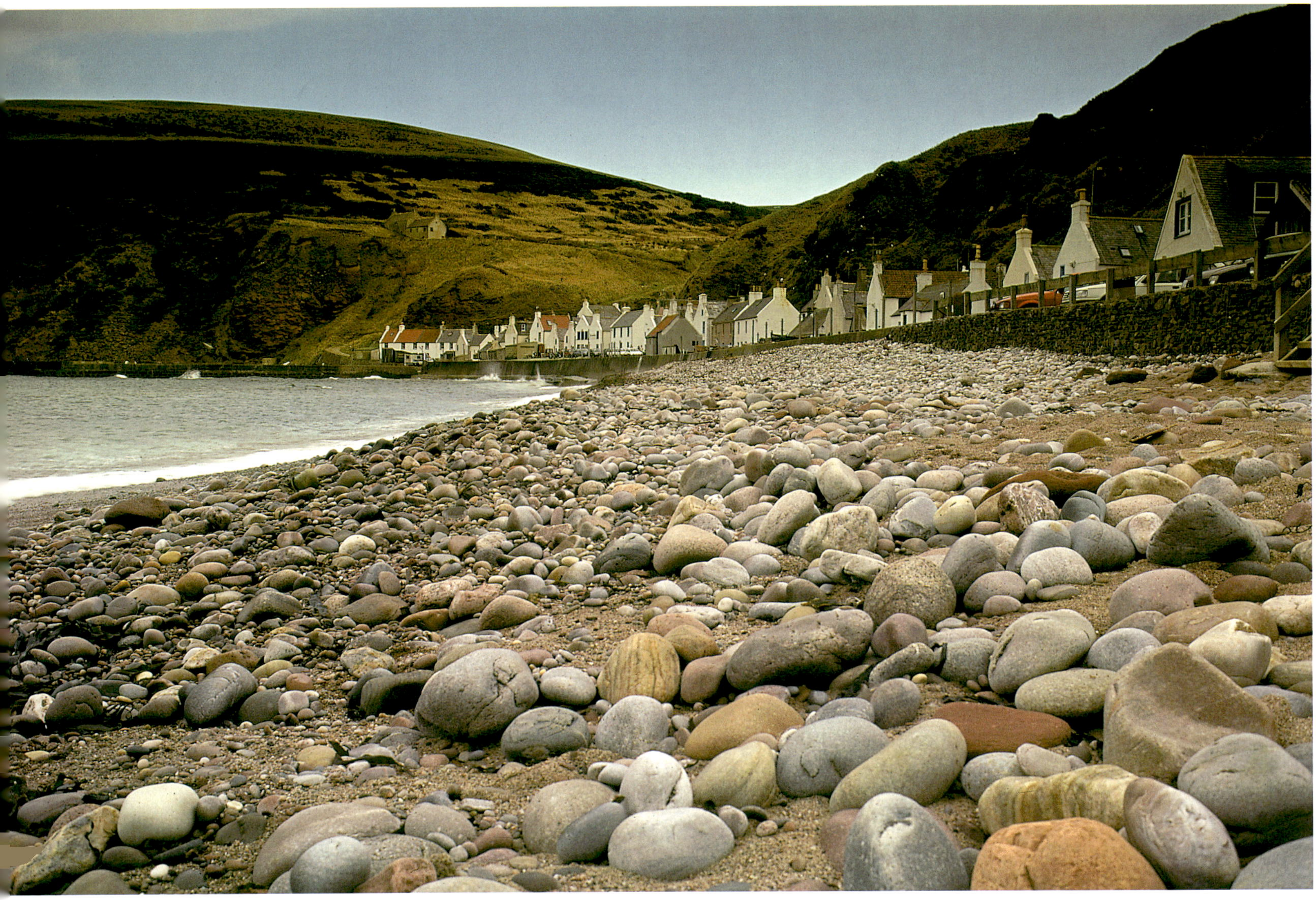

Pennan in Aberdeenshire was once a smugglers' paradise, then a fishing village but now mostly holiday homes. A more recent claim to fame was that it was the main location in Bill Forsyth's wry 1983 comedy, *Local Hero*, starring Burt Lancaster.

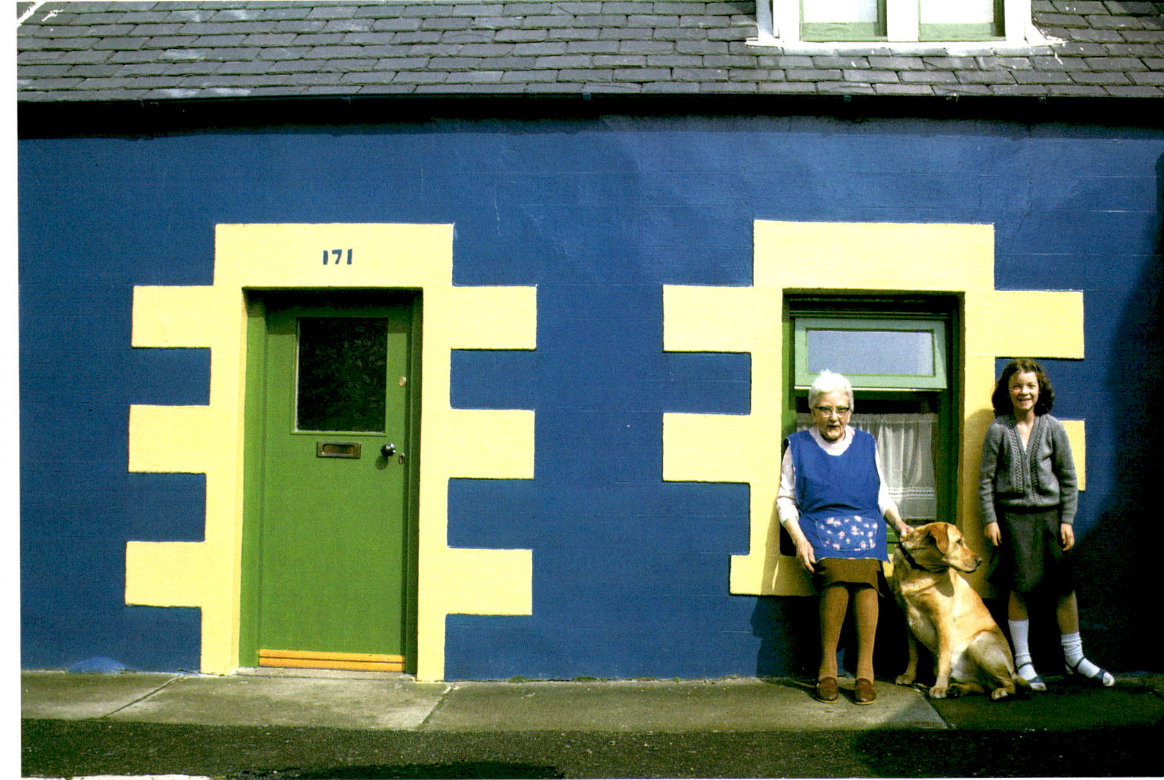

Cullen, a former fishing town and holiday resort on the northeast coast. Originally, its cottages would have been painted with left-over paint from the fishing boats, but now it has become such an attractive feature that the tradition carries on.

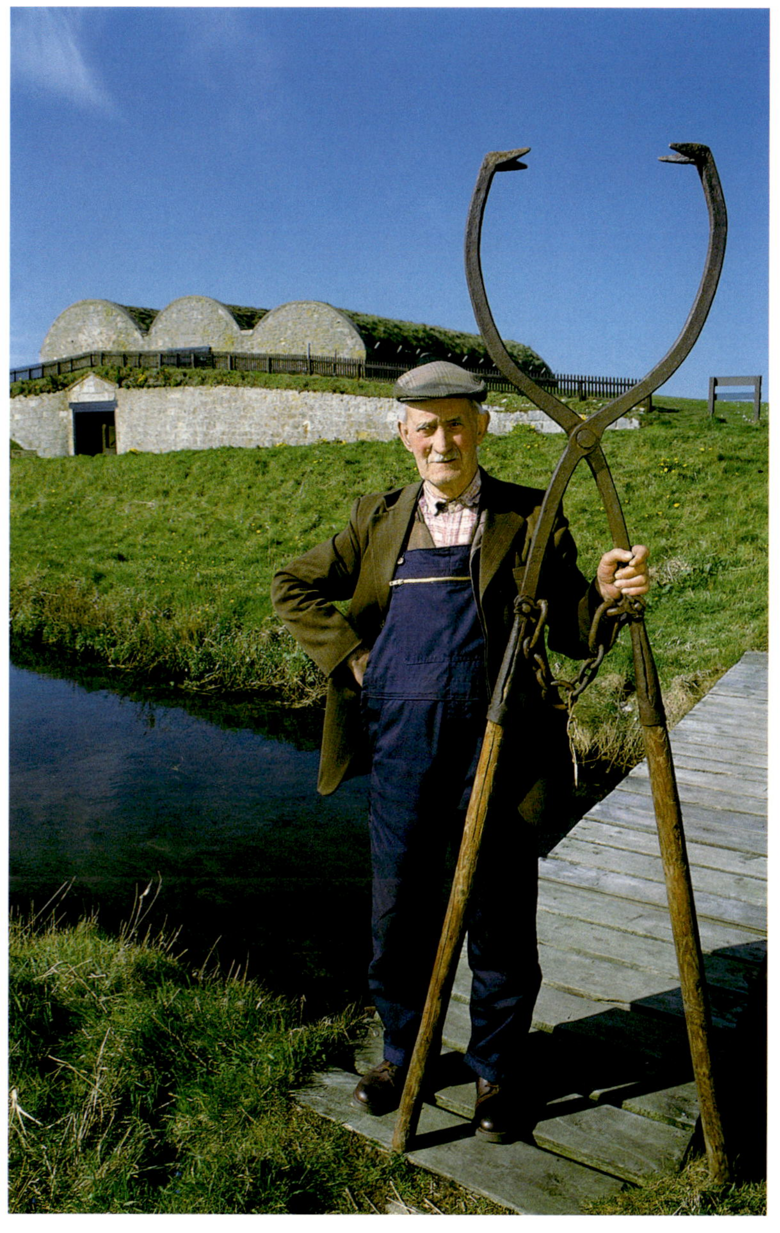

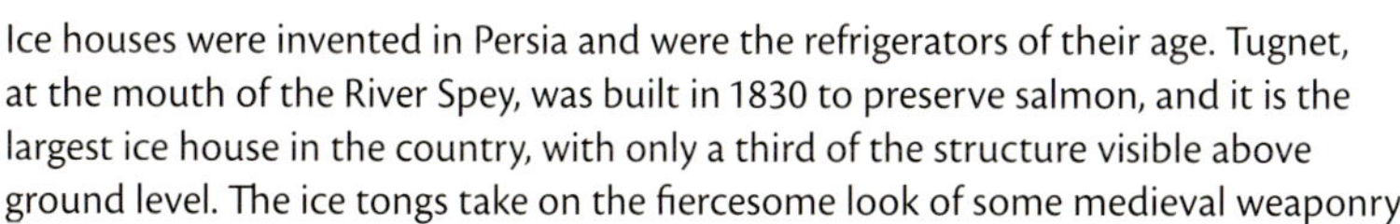

Ice houses were invented in Persia and were the refrigerators of their age. Tugnet, at the mouth of the River Spey, was built in 1830 to preserve salmon, and it is the largest ice house in the country, with only a third of the structure visible above ground level. The ice tongs take on the fiercesome look of some medieval weaponry.

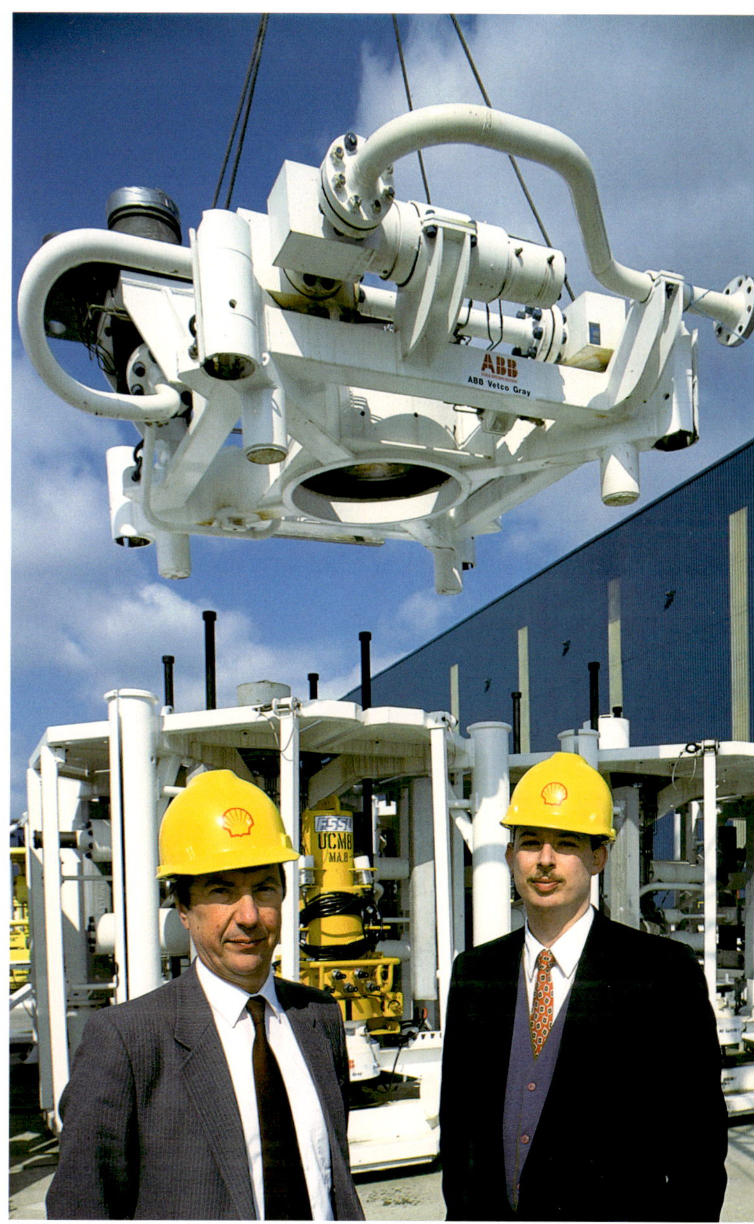

The North Sea oil industry of the 1970s called for innovations in technology. I had this piece of gear lifted by crane over the heads of the engineers for dramatic effect in the 1990s. Aberdeen was transformed from having a thriving tourism and fishing economy to being a major player in the petroleum and gas industry.

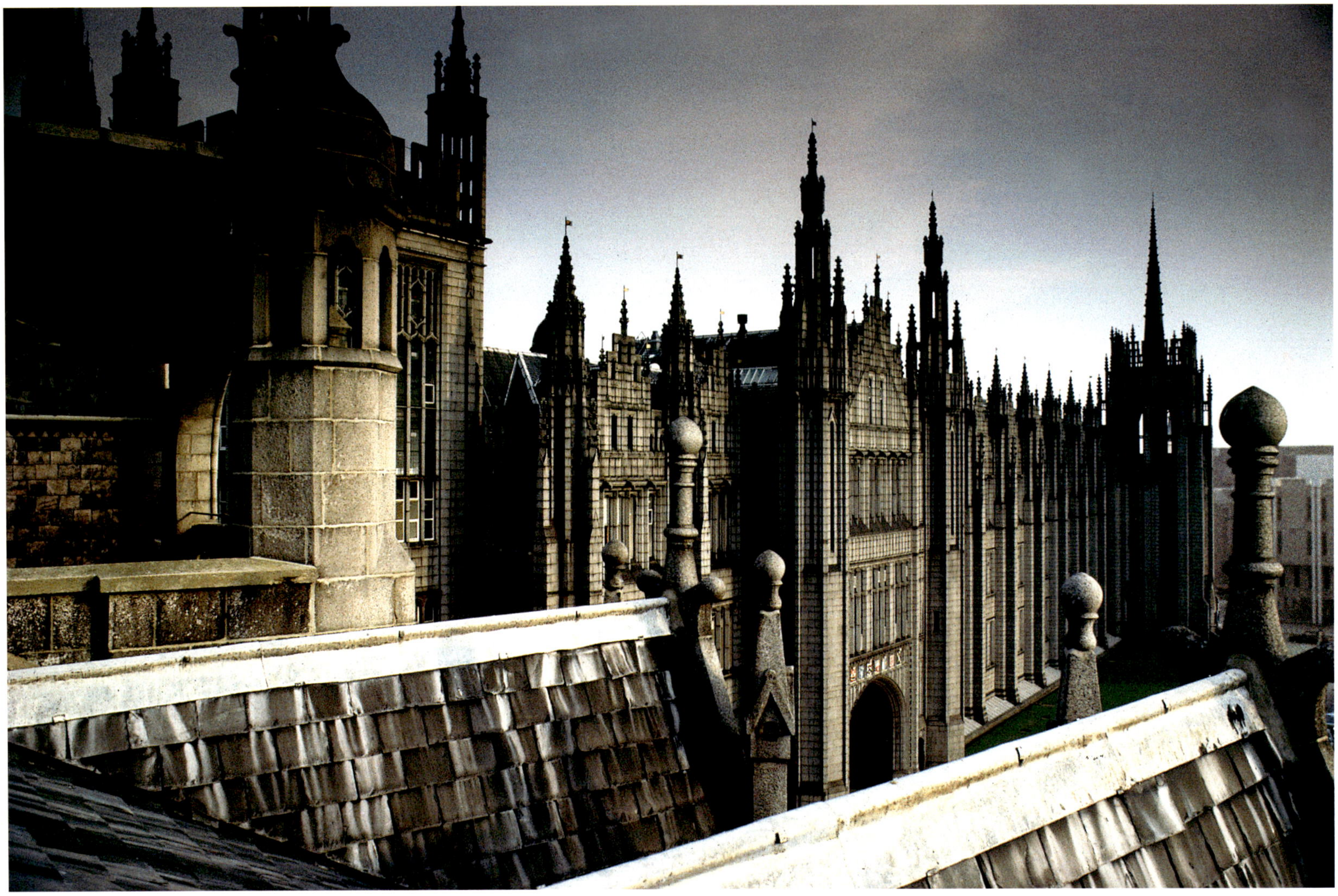

Marischal College was given its charter as a university in 1593 and merged with King's College in 1860 to form the University of Aberdeen. The present building was completed in 1891 and is the second largest granite building in the world, after the Escorial Palace near Madrid in Spain. One of the qualities of granite is that it shows little sign of wear, so, unlike the sandstone buildings of Edinburgh and Glasgow, Aberdeen's historic buildings are almost as pristine as when they were erected.

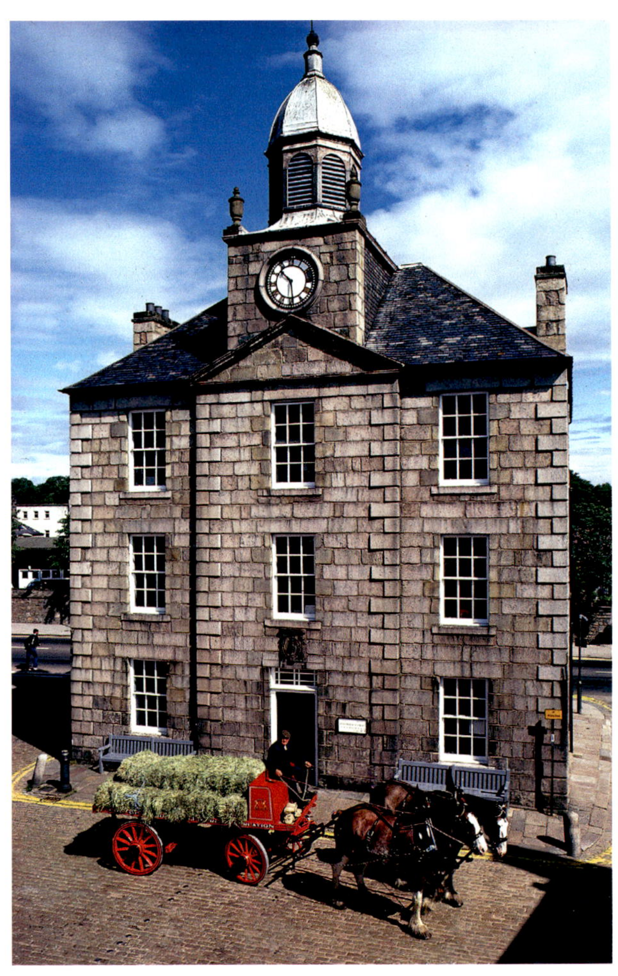

The Aberdeen Parks Department's horse and cart makes a beautiful sound on the granite cobbled streets of Old Aberdeen. When this was the norm, straw would be put down on the streets to deaden the noise, for example when someone was ill. The Georgian Old Town House is now part of the University of Aberdeen.

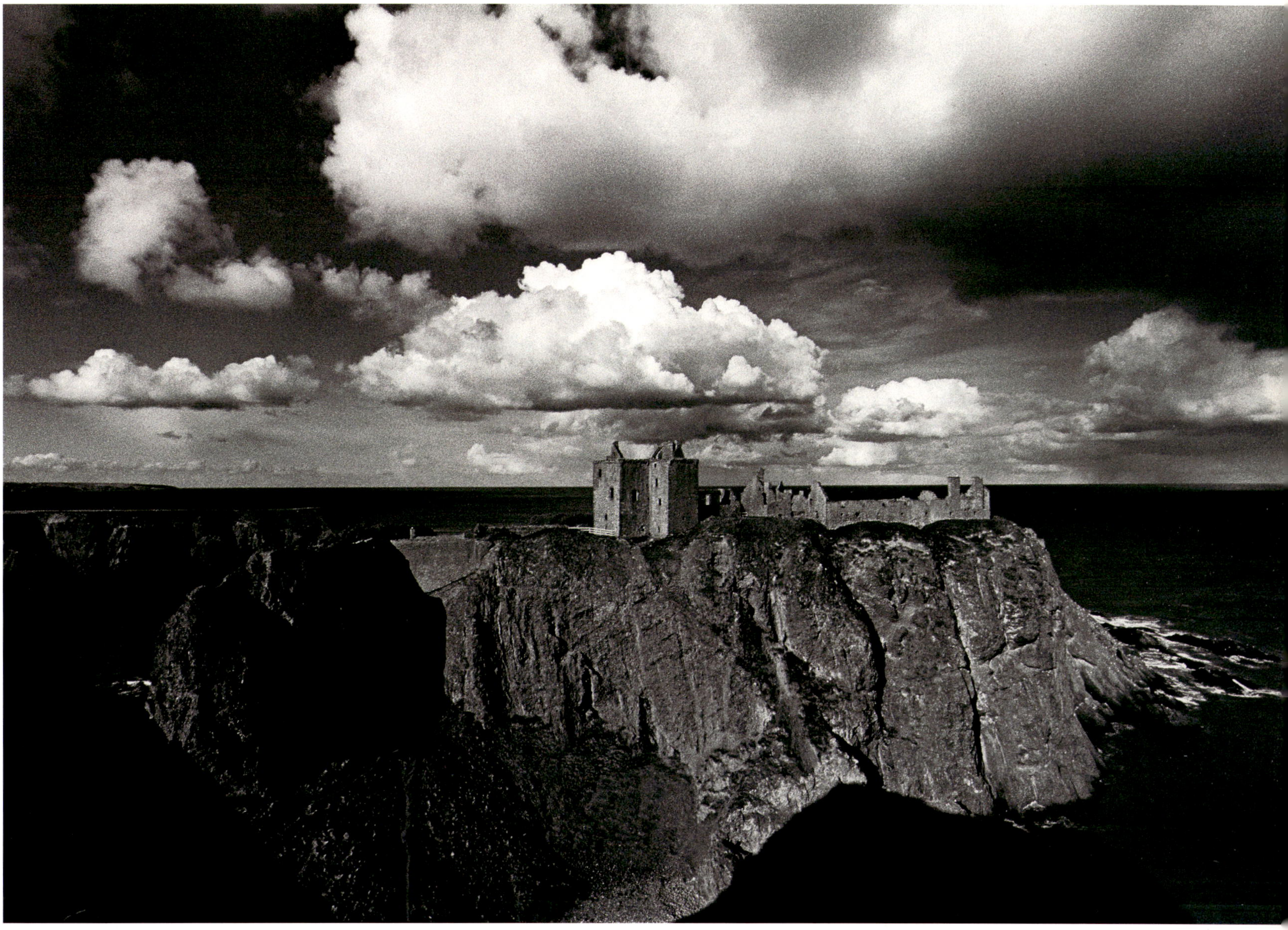

Sitting on a rocky outcrop, Dunnottar Castle near Stonehaven looks impregnable but in the event proved not to be so. In 1651, during the Commonwealth Wars, the Scottish regalia were kept here but were removed when it became apparent that Oliver Cromwell's siege could not be resisted. This is one of the places I always stop at in the hope of getting a new angle or an even more dramatic sky.

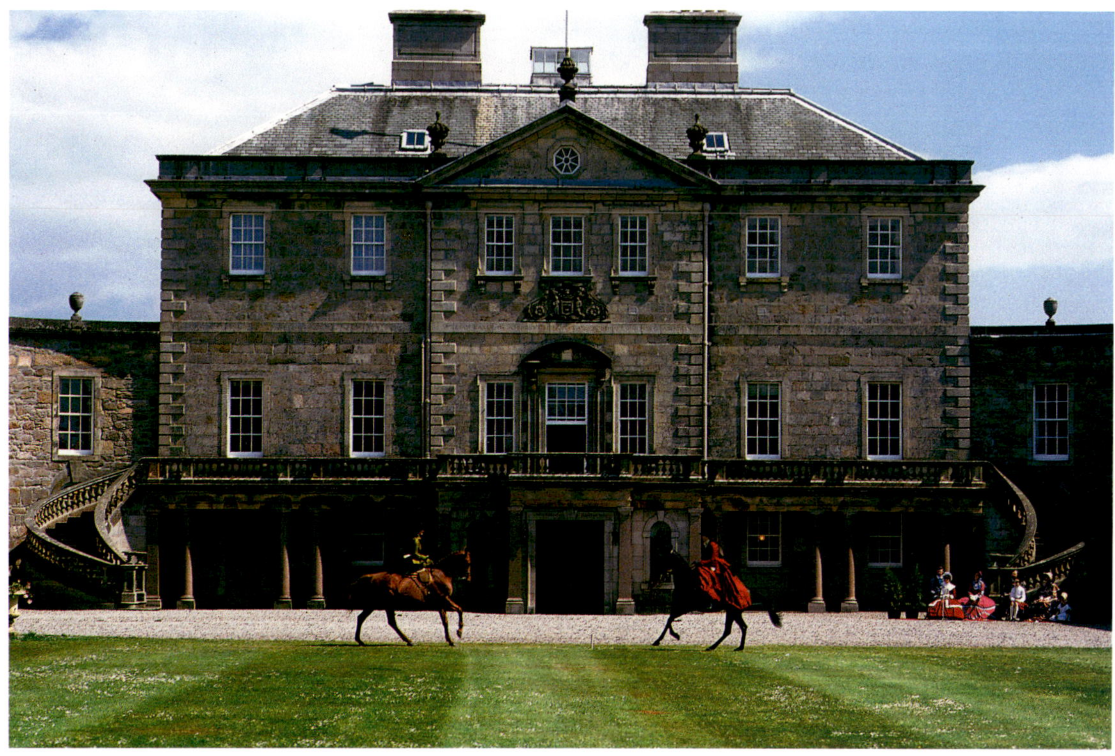

Haddo House, Ellon, was designed by William Adam in 1732. The restrained Georgian exterior contrasts with the over-the-top Victorian interior. This equestrian event brings a bit of life and fits in to the rather cool, classical façade.

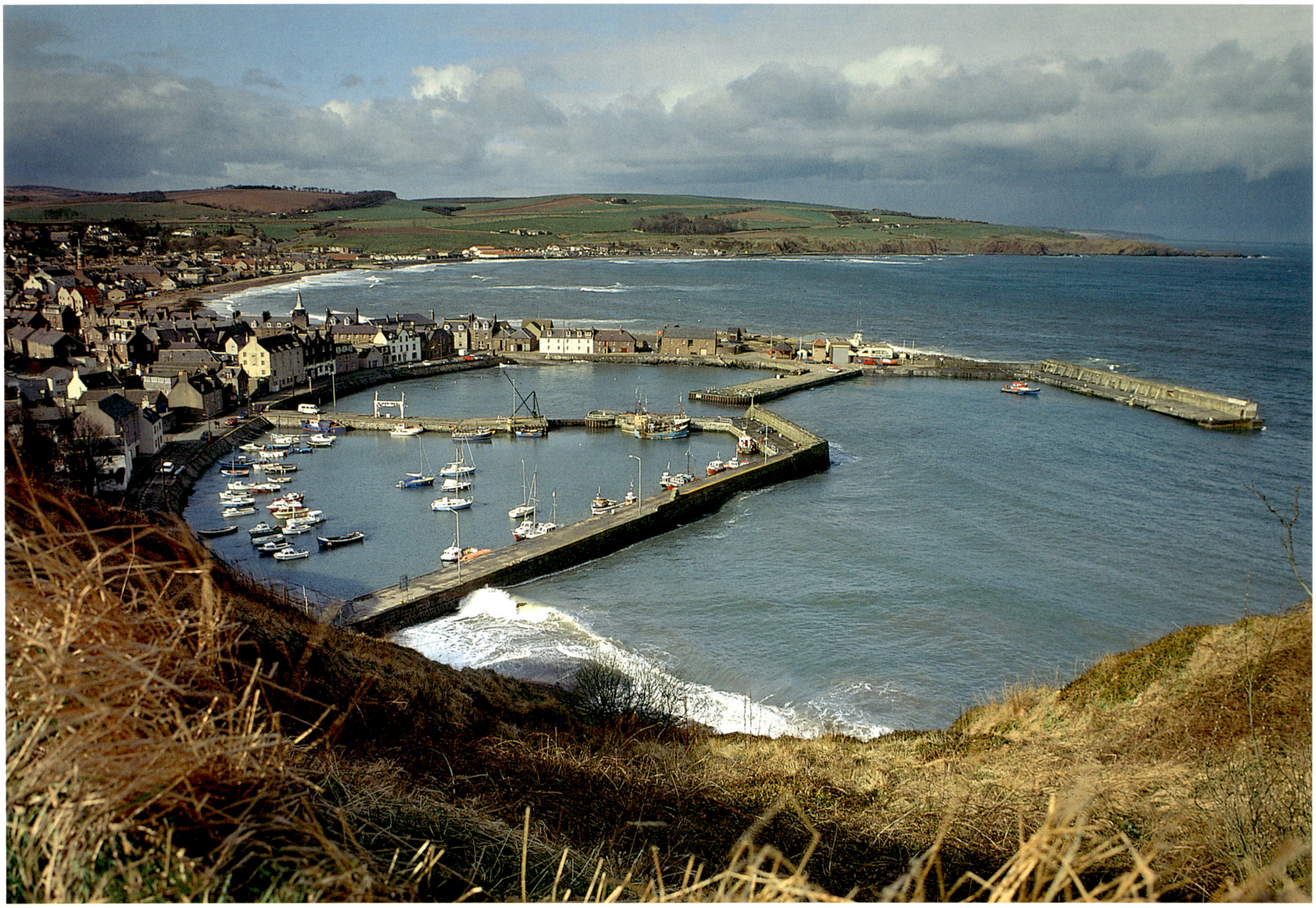

From this viewpoint, Stonehaven looks as if it hasn't changed in the last century. On the quay is a 16th-century tollbooth. On Hogmanay, fireballs of tallow rope are swung throughout the streets. Famous sons include Robert William Thomson, inventor of the pneumatic tyre and the fountain pen, and Lord Reith of Stonehaven, first Director-General of the BBC.

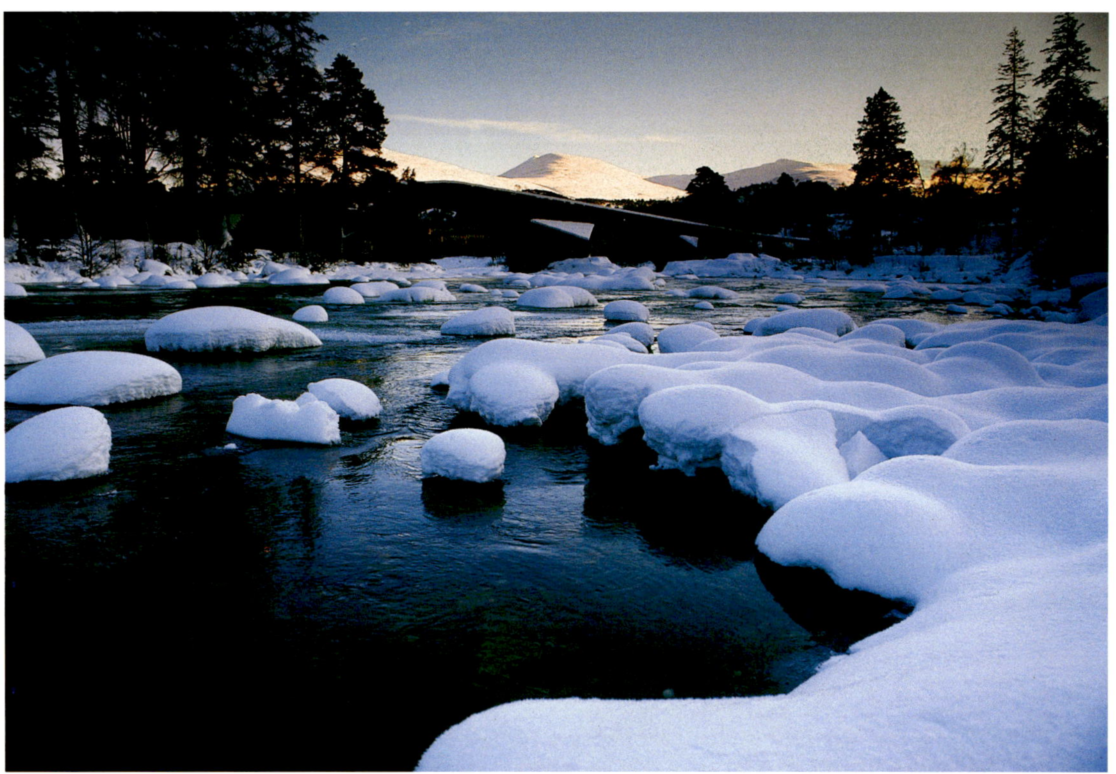

It was −15°C when I photographed the Brig o' Dee between Balmoral and Braemar. The cold gave the late afternoon light a crispness I have rarely witnessed.

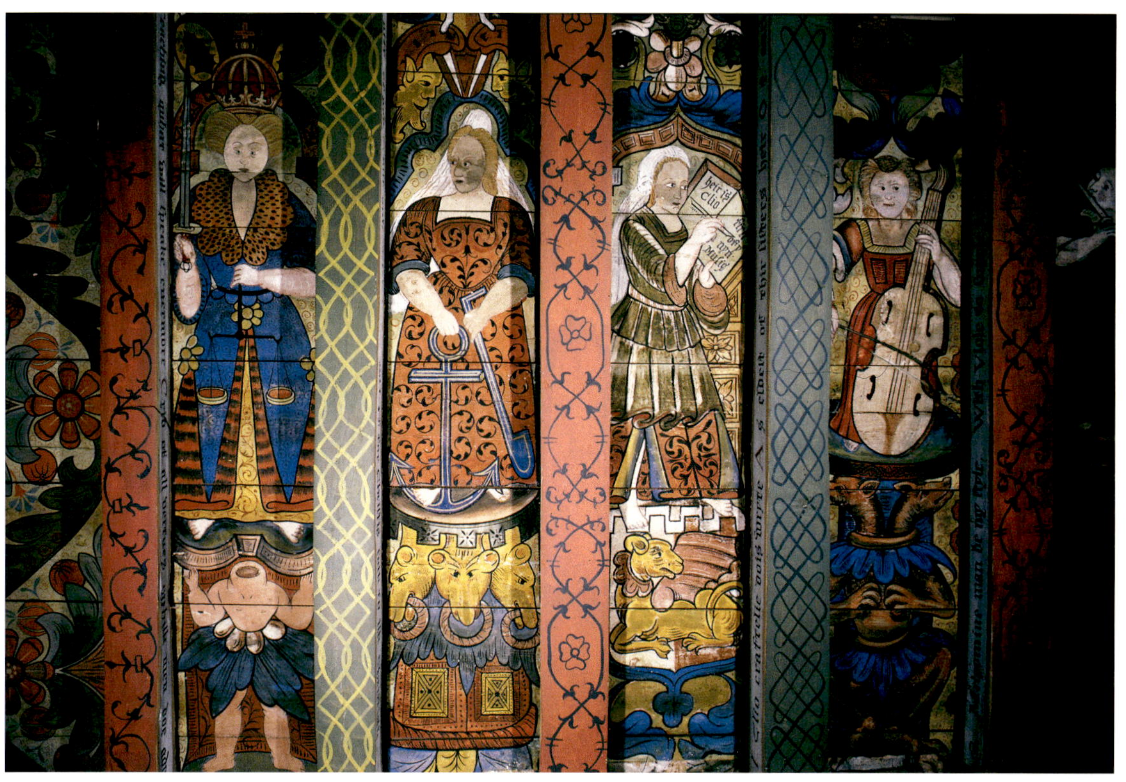

The painted ceilings of Crathes Castle, near Banchory, date from 1599 and are some of the finest in Scotland. To me, such examples open a whole new aspect to our past and make it even more romantic and cultured than I had imagined.

Craigievar near Alford is my favourite Scottish building. It was built to an L-plan in the Baronial style from 1610 to 1624. On a break from shooting while on an assignment with a London film crew, I took everyone to visit and they were all utterly enchanted. Any other reaction would have met with my great disappointment. Over the fireplace is the inscription 'Doe not vaiken sleeping dogs'.

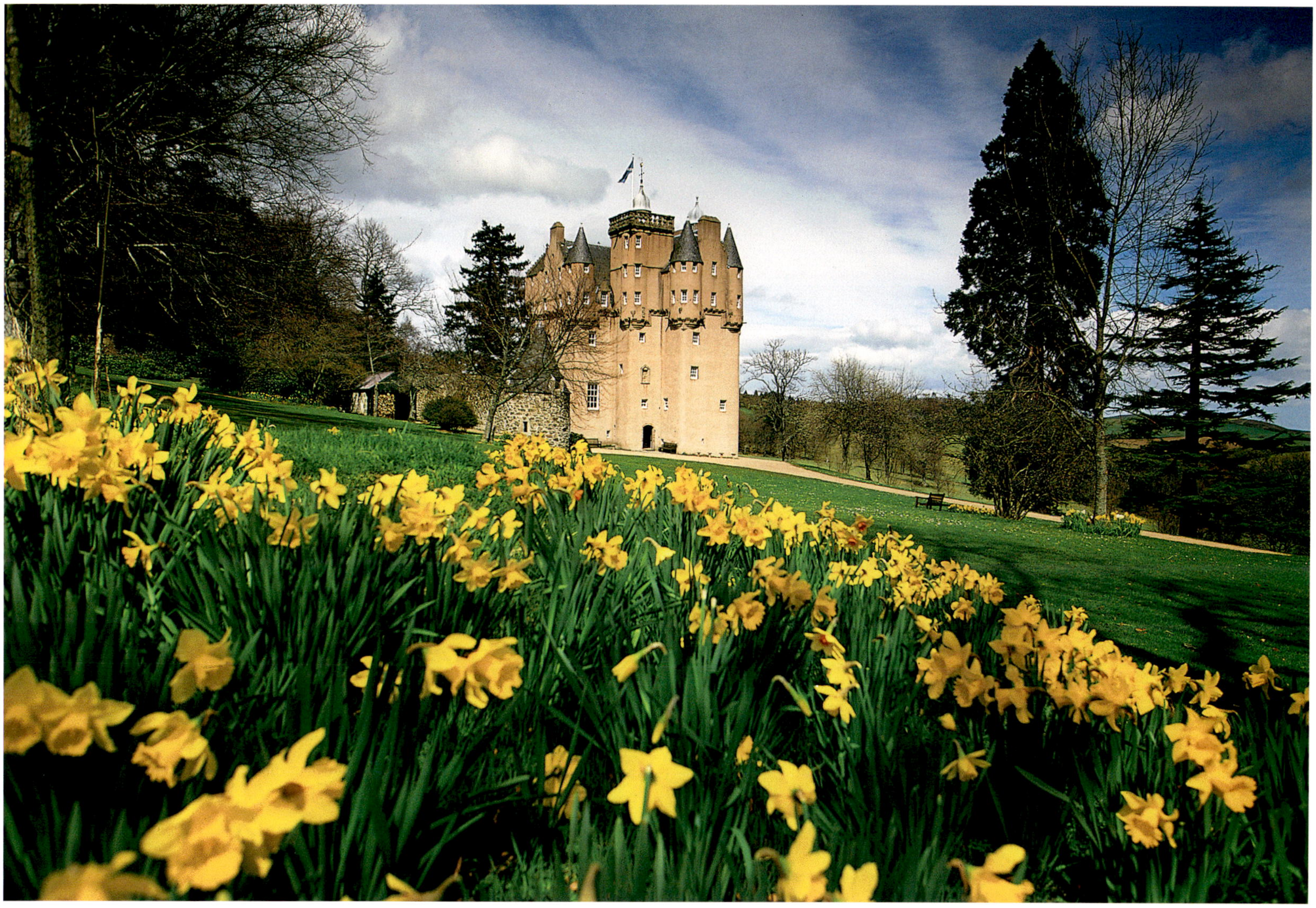

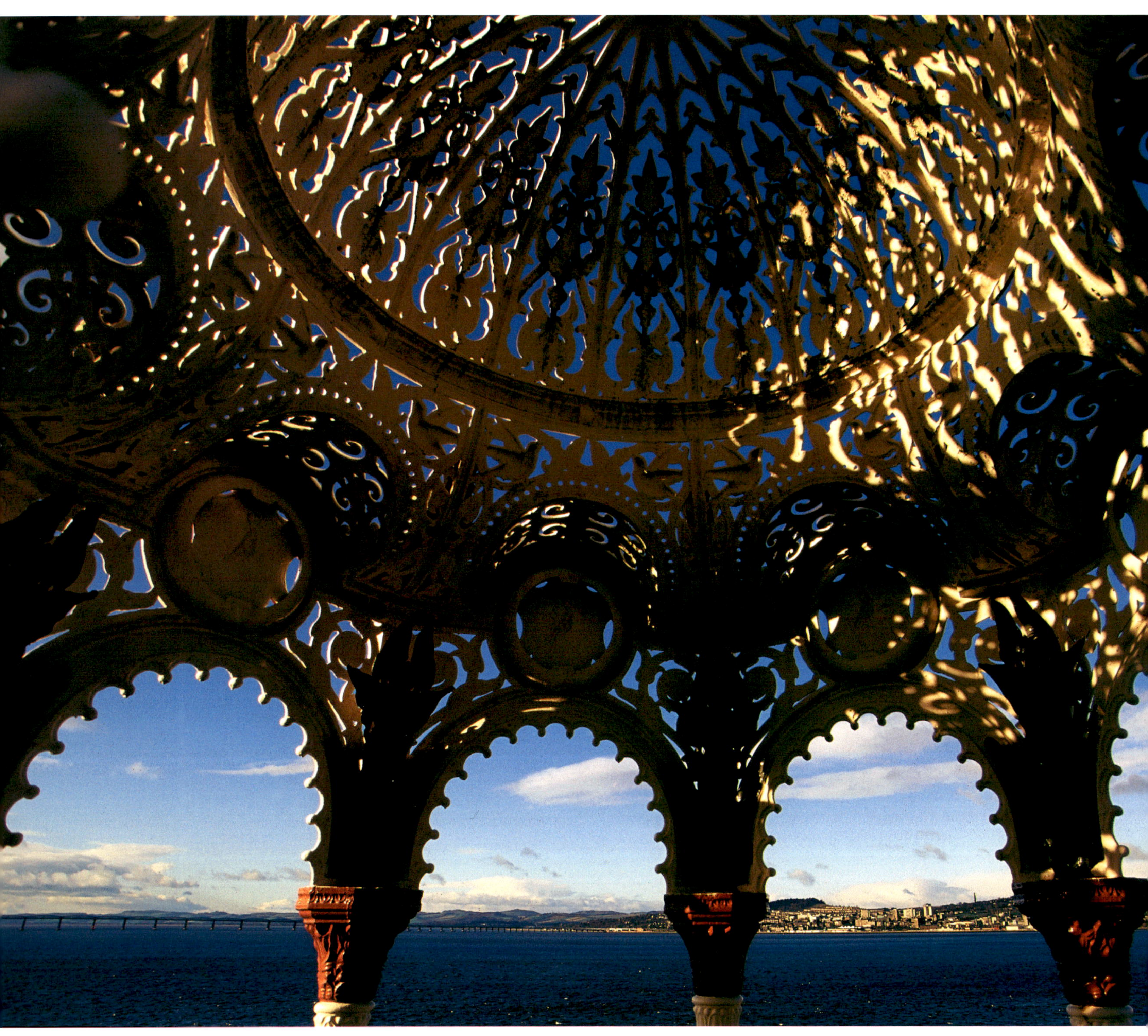

An elaborate drinking fountain in Tayport, Fife, frames the city of Dundee across the River Tay. I remember such fountains in school playgrounds, parks and elsewhere. They have since been blocked up as Health and Safety would not allow them. We now pay for inferior bottled water – how gullible can we get? The city's skyline will be changed when the proposed outpost for the Victoria and Albert Museum is built. Let's hope it does for Dundee what the Guggenheim Museum did for Bilbao in Spain.

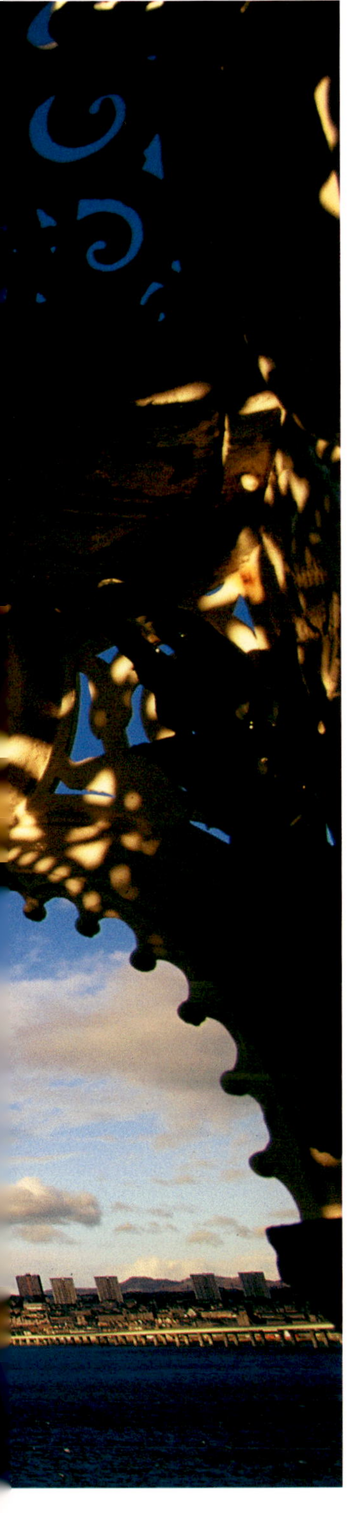

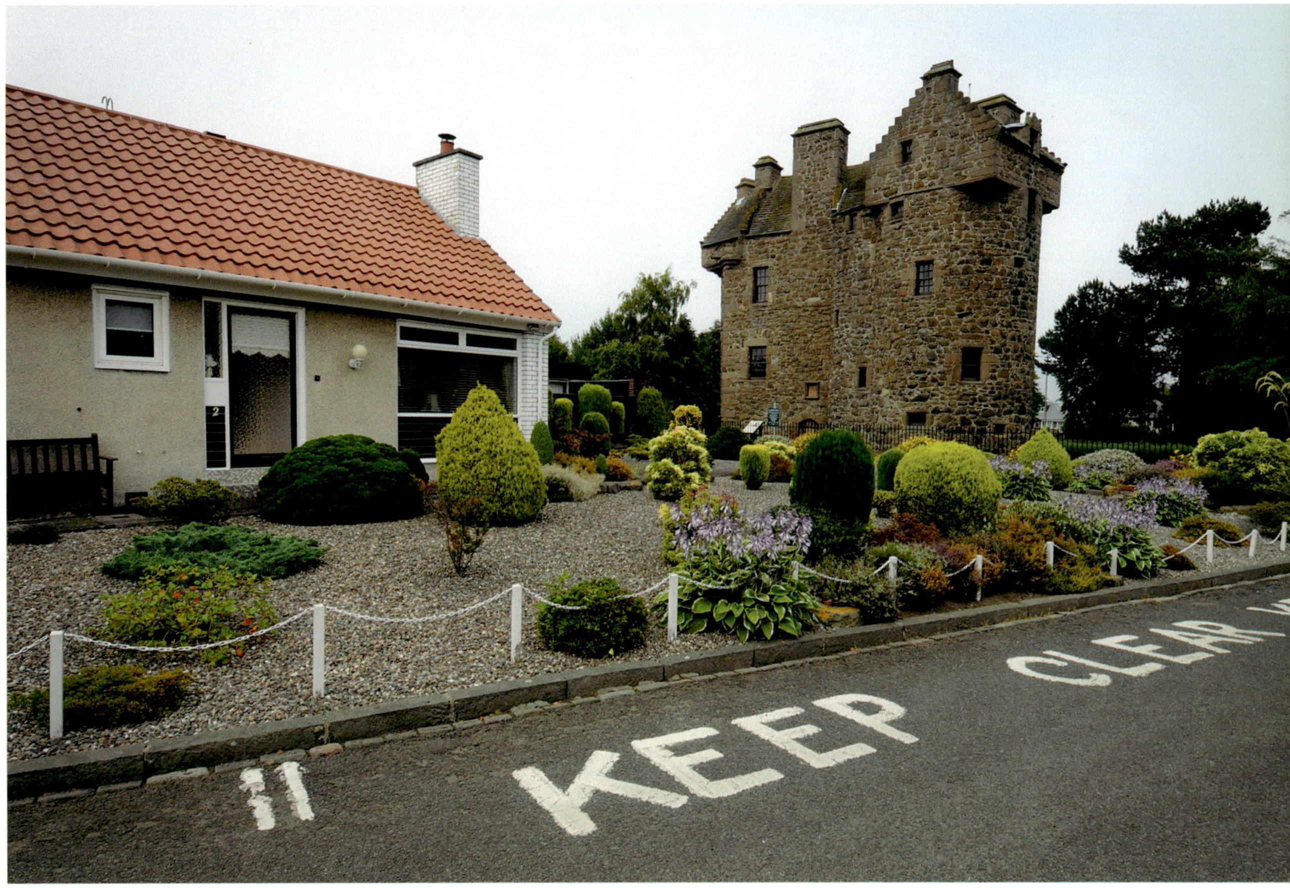

This family's niminy-piminy house looks like it has a castle in its garden. Claypotts, Broughty Ferry, is a 16th-century Z-plan tower house.

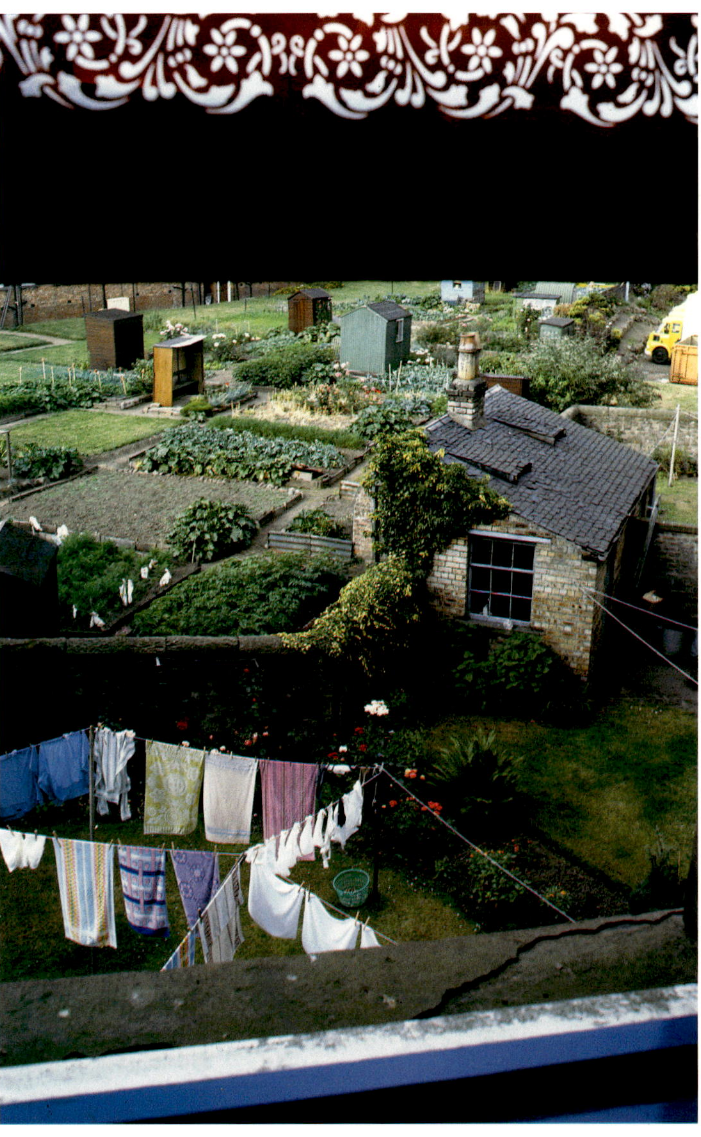

A Dundee tenement garden, a clothes-drying green, an original wash-house and a productive vegetable patch – a fine example of sensible and ecologically sound city living. Some of the more trendy, self-righteous environmentalists could learn from our past.

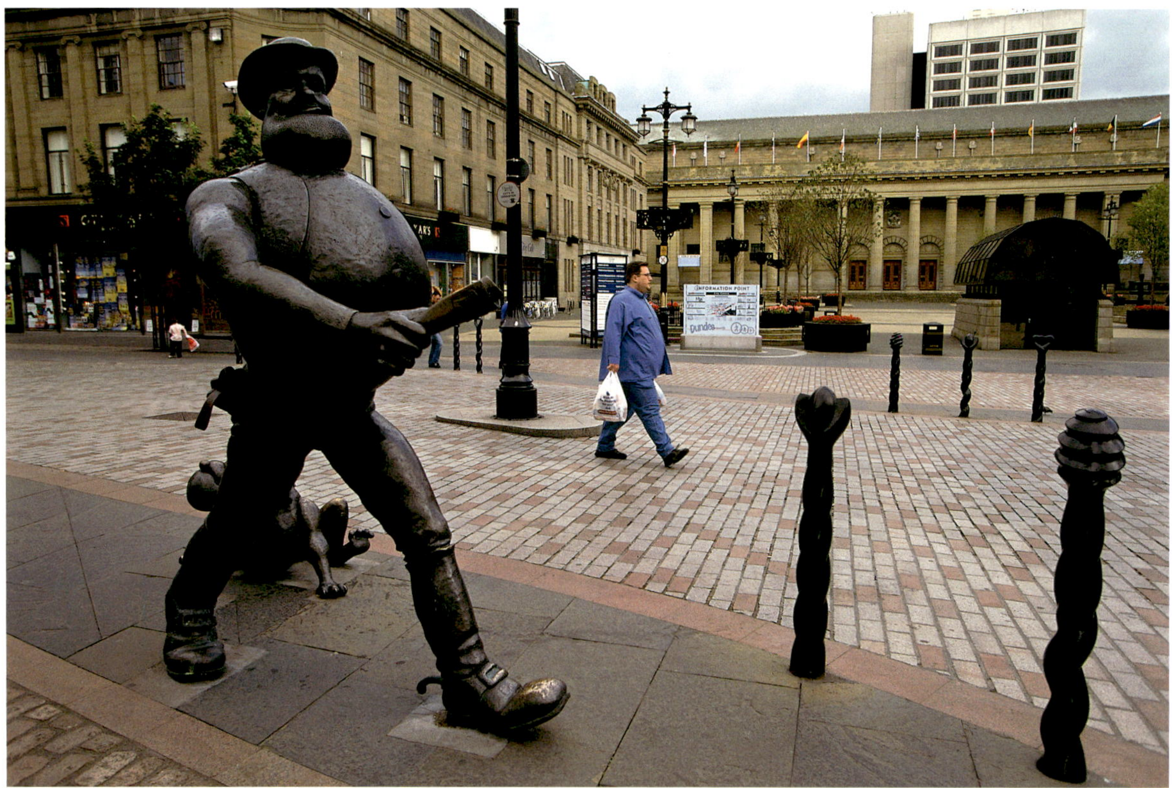

We were all brought up on *The Dandy* and *The Beano*. The publisher, D. C. Thomson, produces more than 200 million comic books, magazines and newspapers every year, making it one of the most successful UK companies. Desperate Dan's cow pie helped in my conversion to vegetarianism.

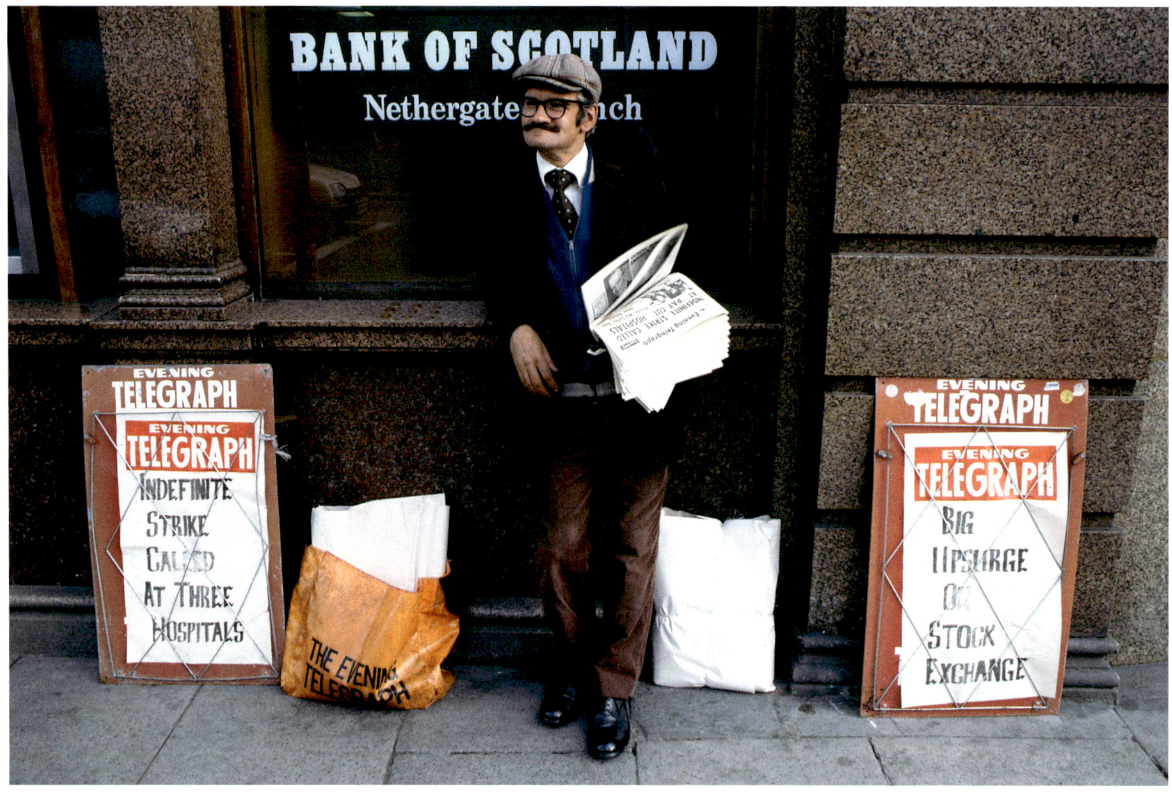

Dundee was once known for its jam, jute and journalism. This newspaper vendor sits comfortably in his city centre pitch. When the Beatles played Dundee's Caird Hall in 1964 they were asked by a journalist did they know where they were, to which they replied, 'Cake'.

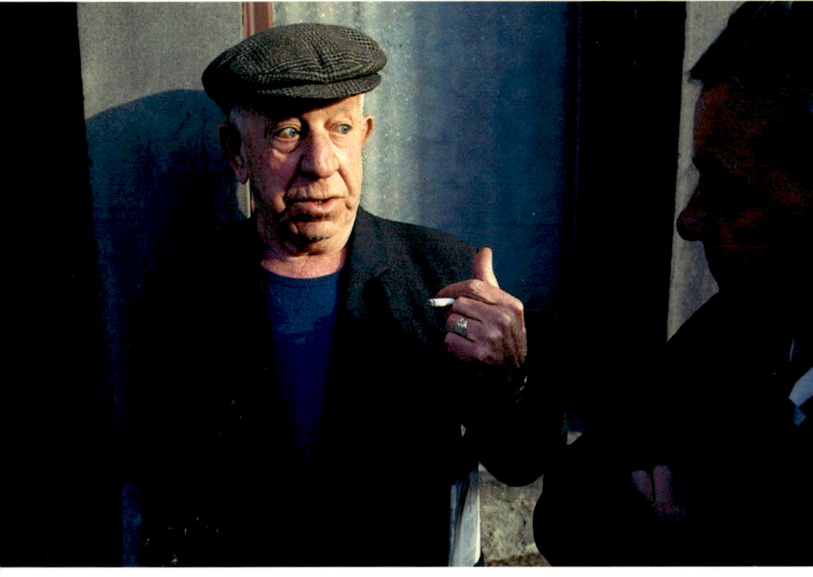

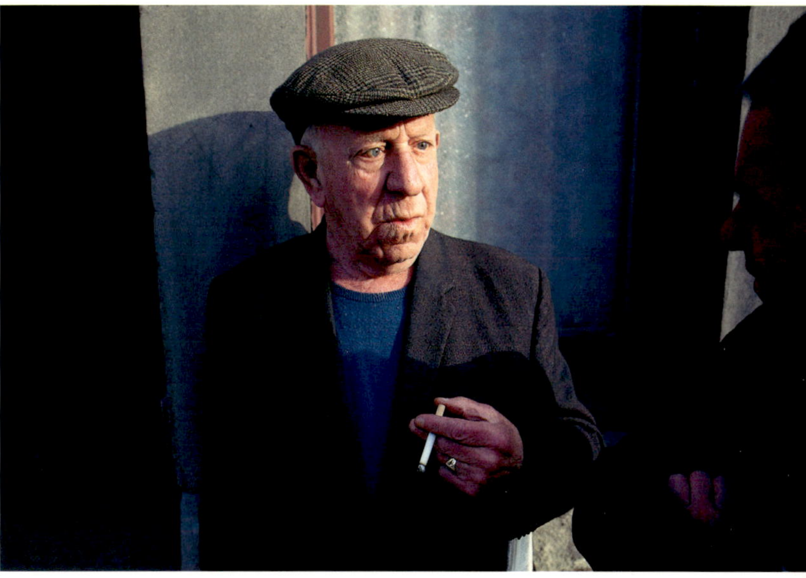

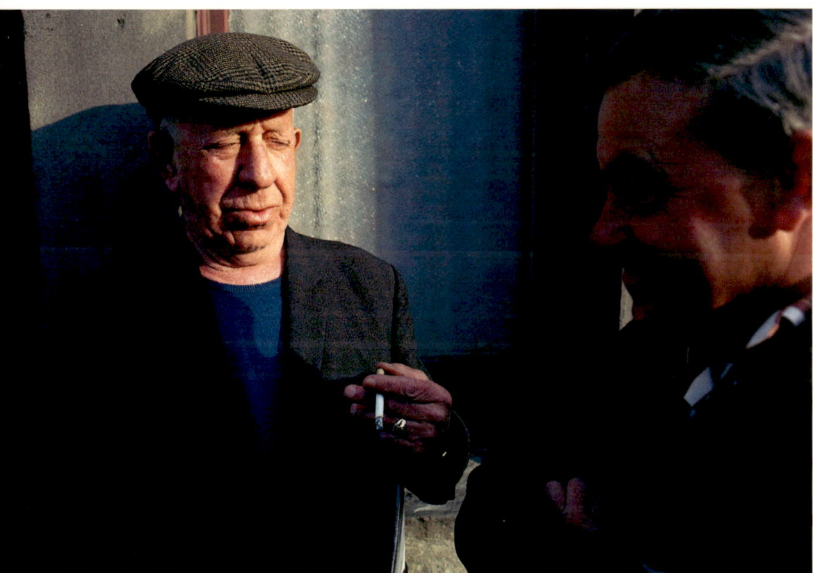

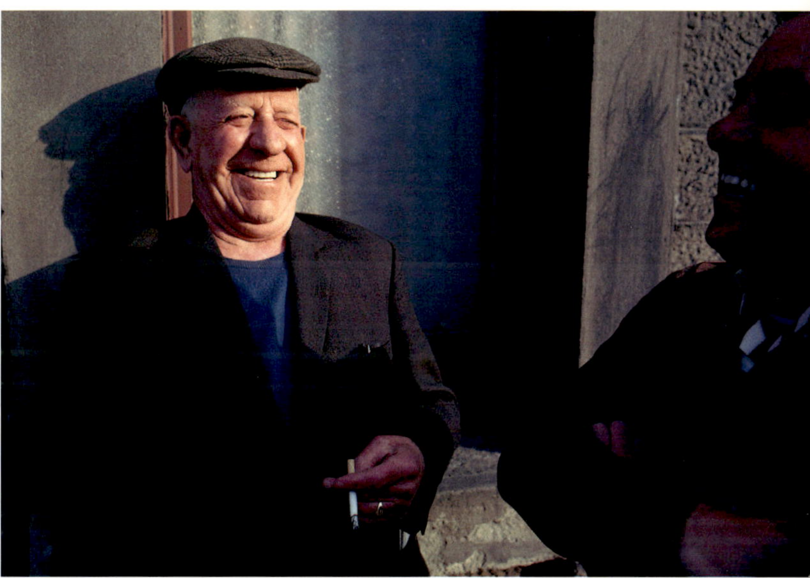

This Dundonian is how I remember some of the older folk of my childhood, true to himself, with contentment and a sense of humour.

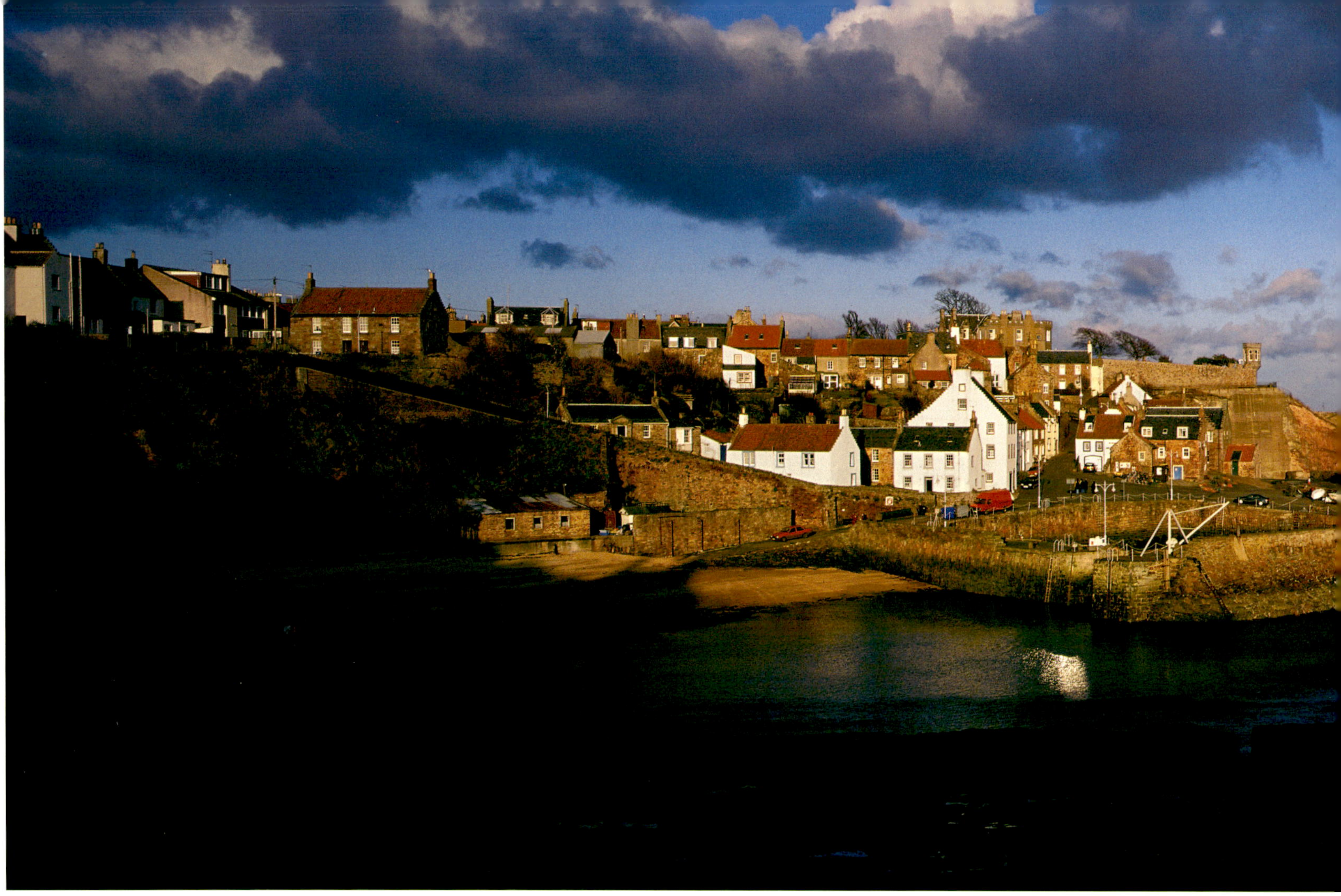

(Above) Crail, a fishing village in the East Neuk of Fife, shows how diverse the architecture of a small country can be. I am fortunate that my job has given me time to enjoy such gems, with its pantiled roofs, crow-stepped gables and houses dating from the 16th century.

(Below) Tentsmuir is a great expanse of beach in northeast Fife, near Leuchars. The area is a National Natural Reserve and has abundant wildlife, including roe deer, red squirrels, waterfowl and seals. I enjoyed this honest sculpture created from flotsam and jetsam. Contemporary conceptual artists exhibit in the world's top galleries with not dissimilar works.

(Right) The 14th-century church in St Monans says it'll always be here. The building's solidity and balance as well as its location give an appearance of perfection despite it being an unfinished cruciform (T-shaped) structure.

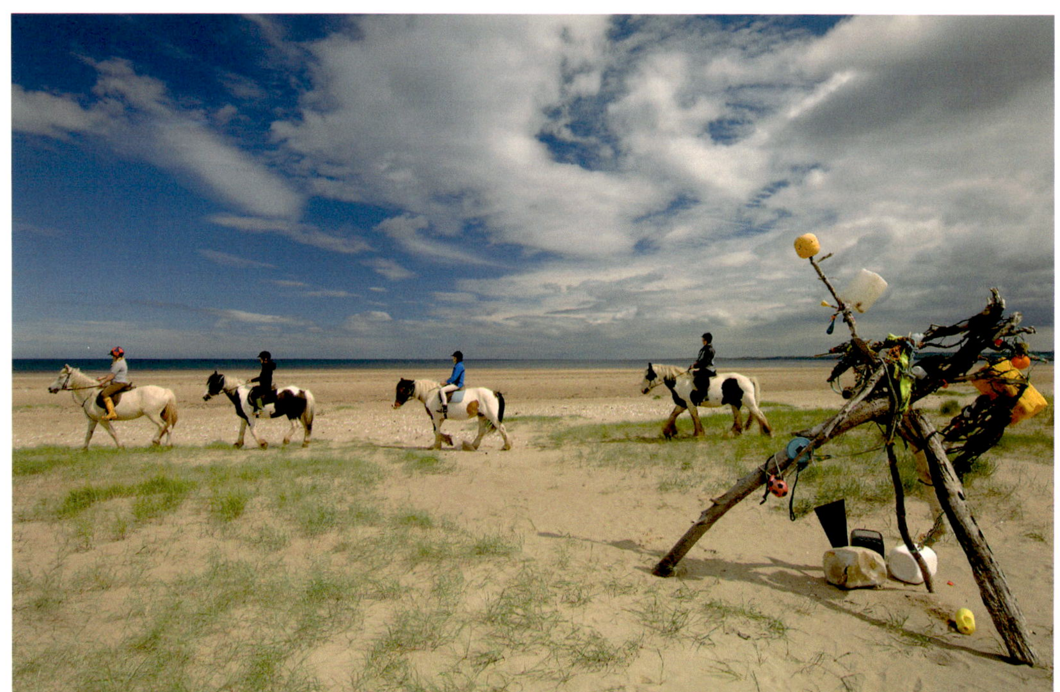

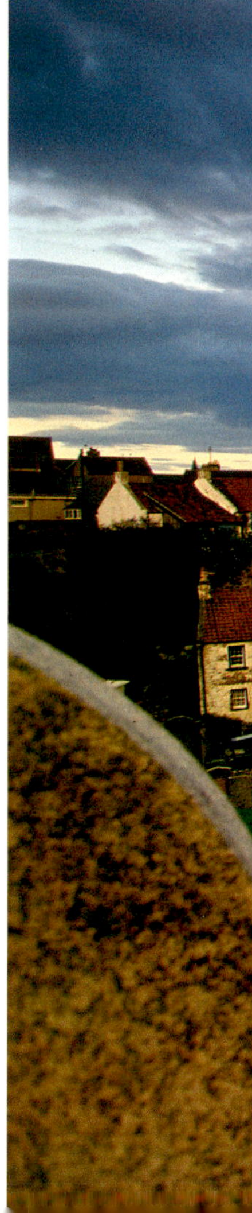

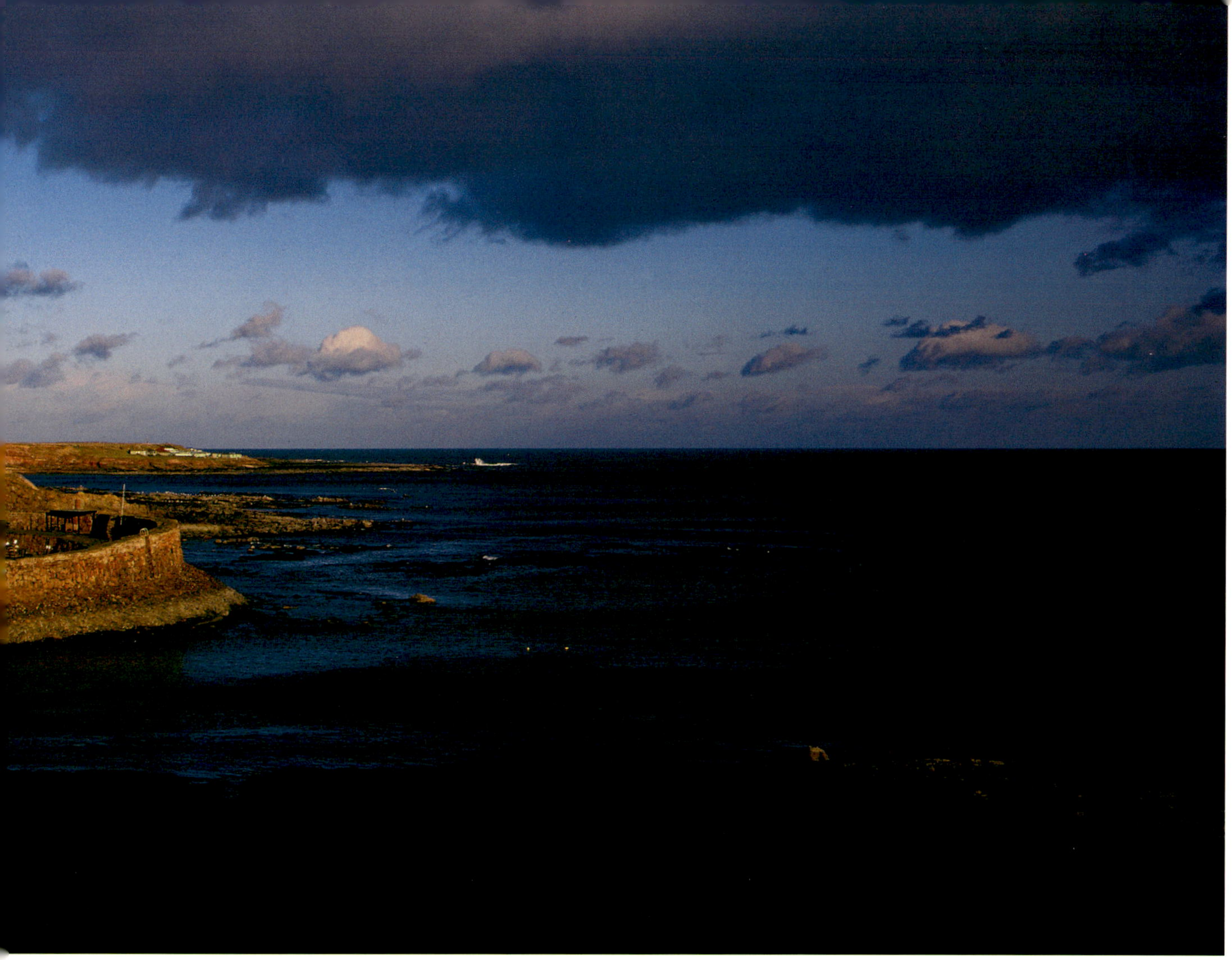

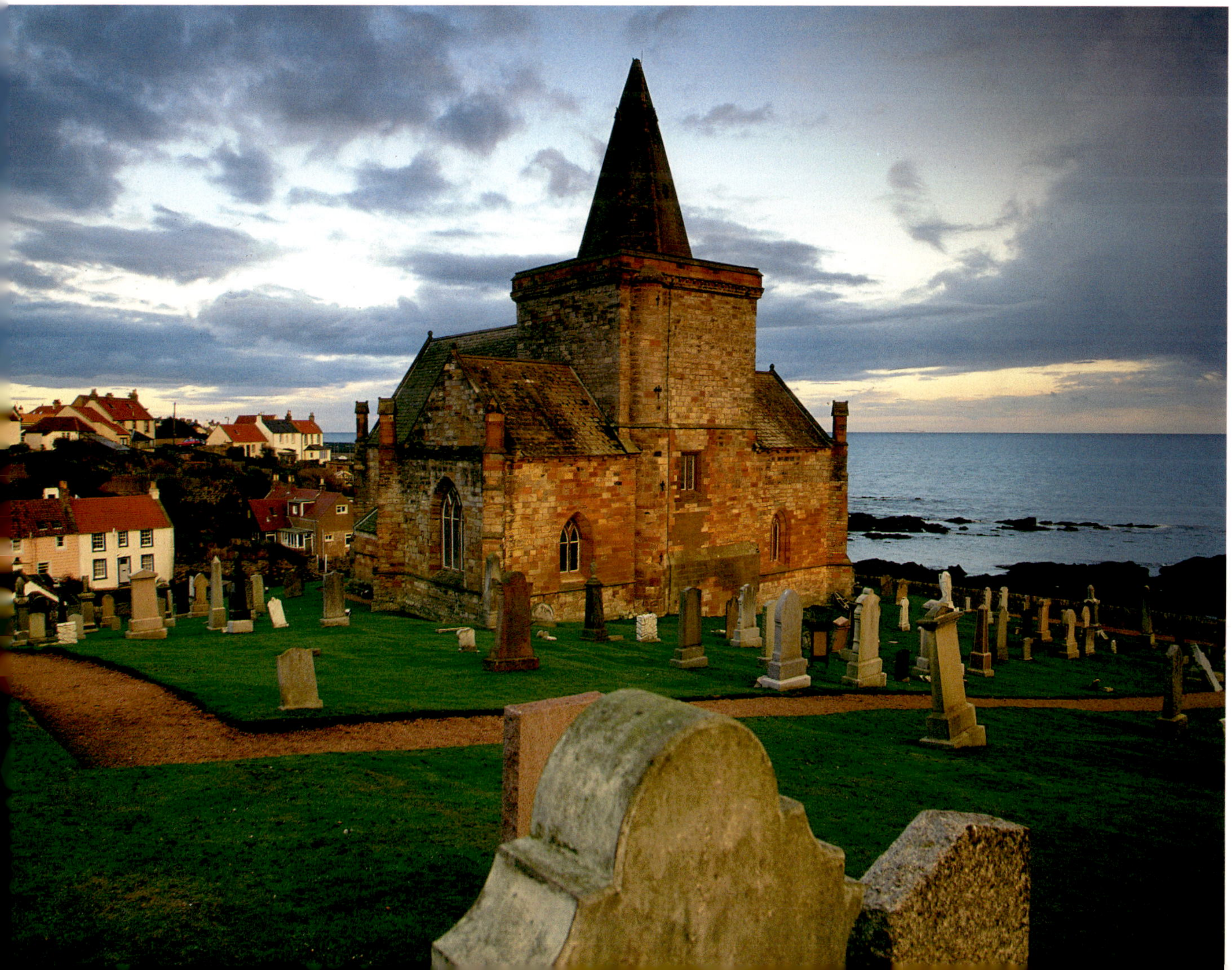

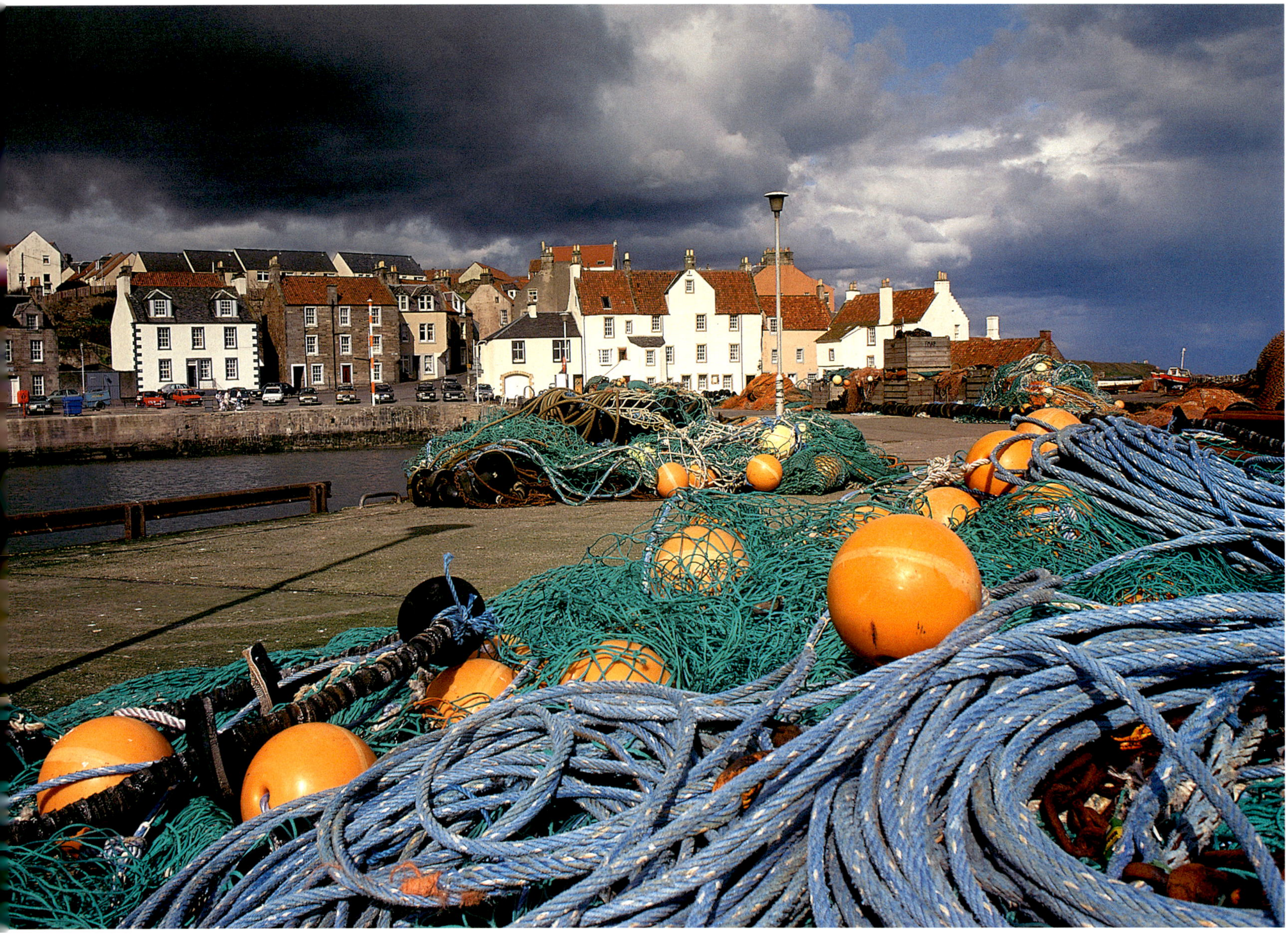

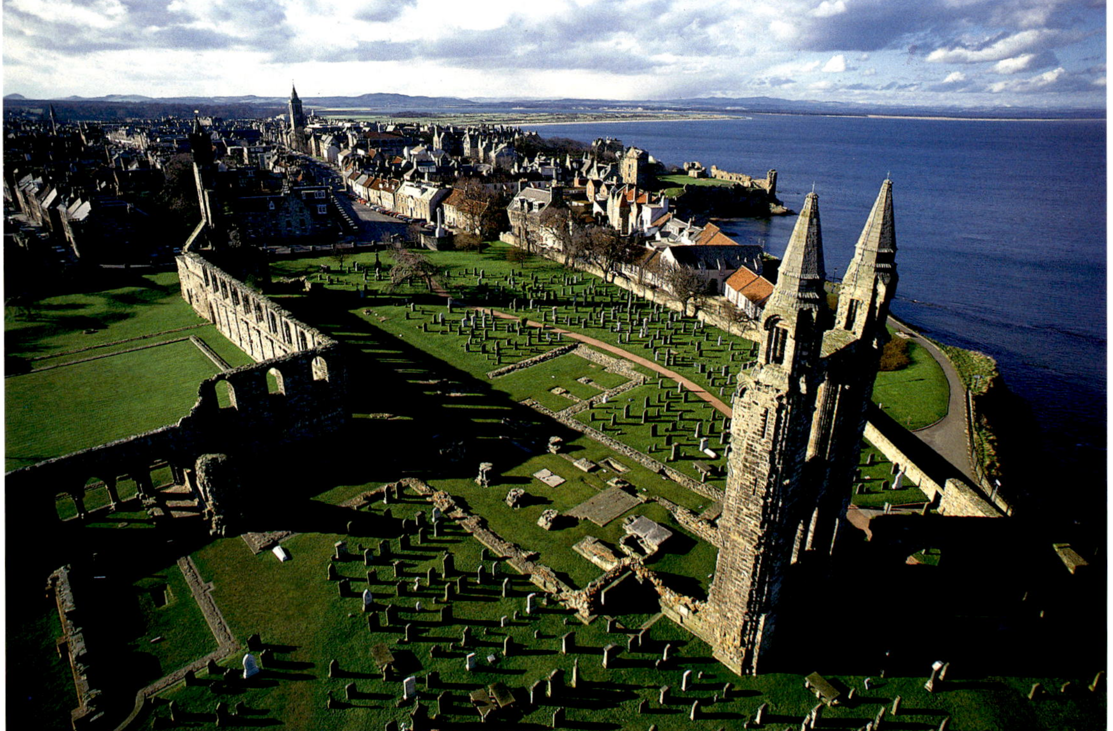

The East Neuk of Fife is a string of delightful fishing villages that still manage to preserve their identity despite the shrinking fishing industry. Pittenweem holds an annual arts festival where artists and crafts people exhibit in private houses throughout the village.

St Andrews Cathedral from St Rule's Tower. Built in the 12th-century, the 108-foot-tall tower is the town's highest viewpoint. From here you look towards the castle, which has a contrasting 24-foot-deep bottle dungeon. Beyond that is the Royal and Ancient Golf Club, which is the home of golf. I find it very difficult to get a picture that identifies the course, except for the club house and the tiny Swilcan Bridge.

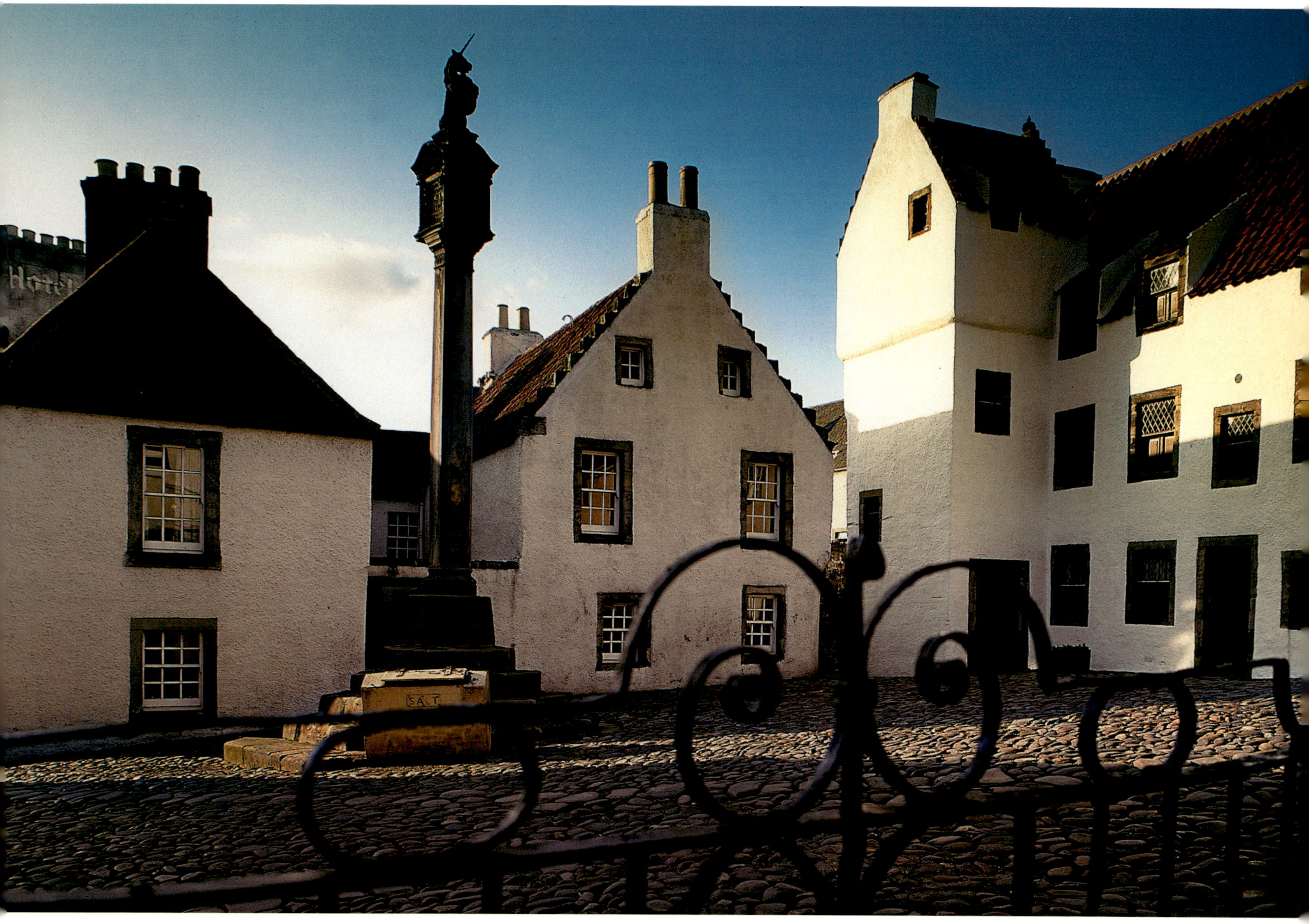

A remarkable example of a 16th-century Scottish burgh, Culross is an absolute gem. It has the benefit of being mostly controlled by the National Trust for Scotland, who have preserved many of the old buildings with crow-stepped gables and pantiled roofs. The snuff-maker's house (circa 1673) has an inscription, 'Who would have thocht it, Noses would have bocht it.'
(Above) Market Cross. (Right) Culross Palace.

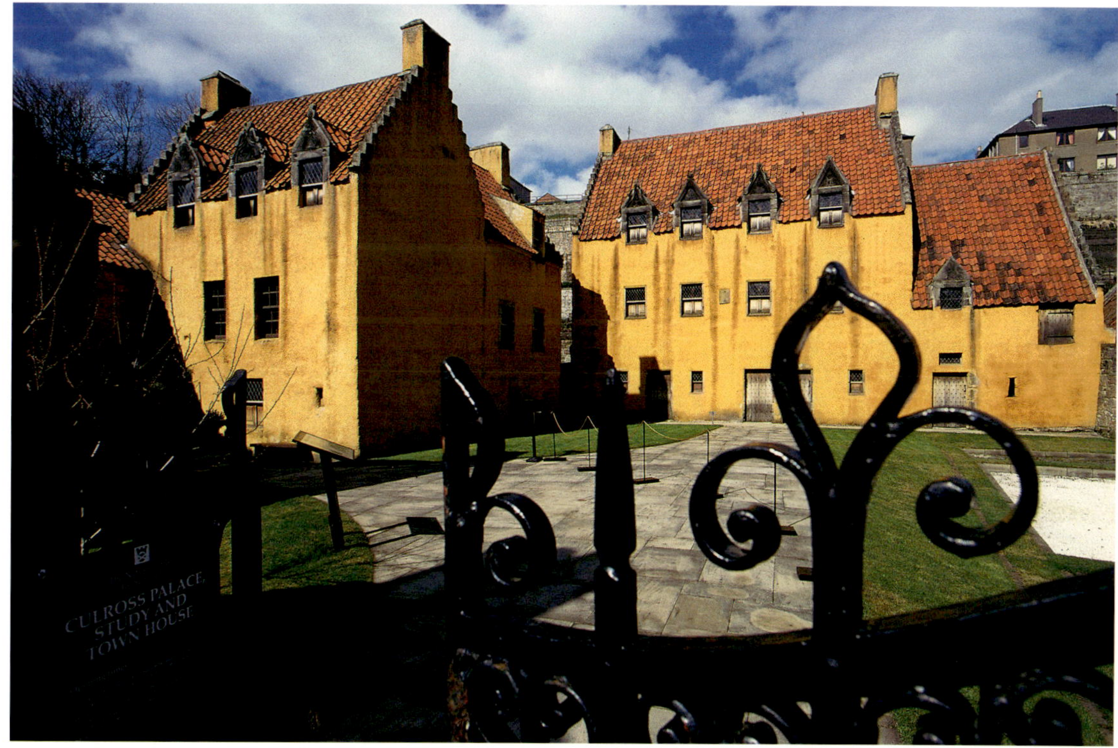

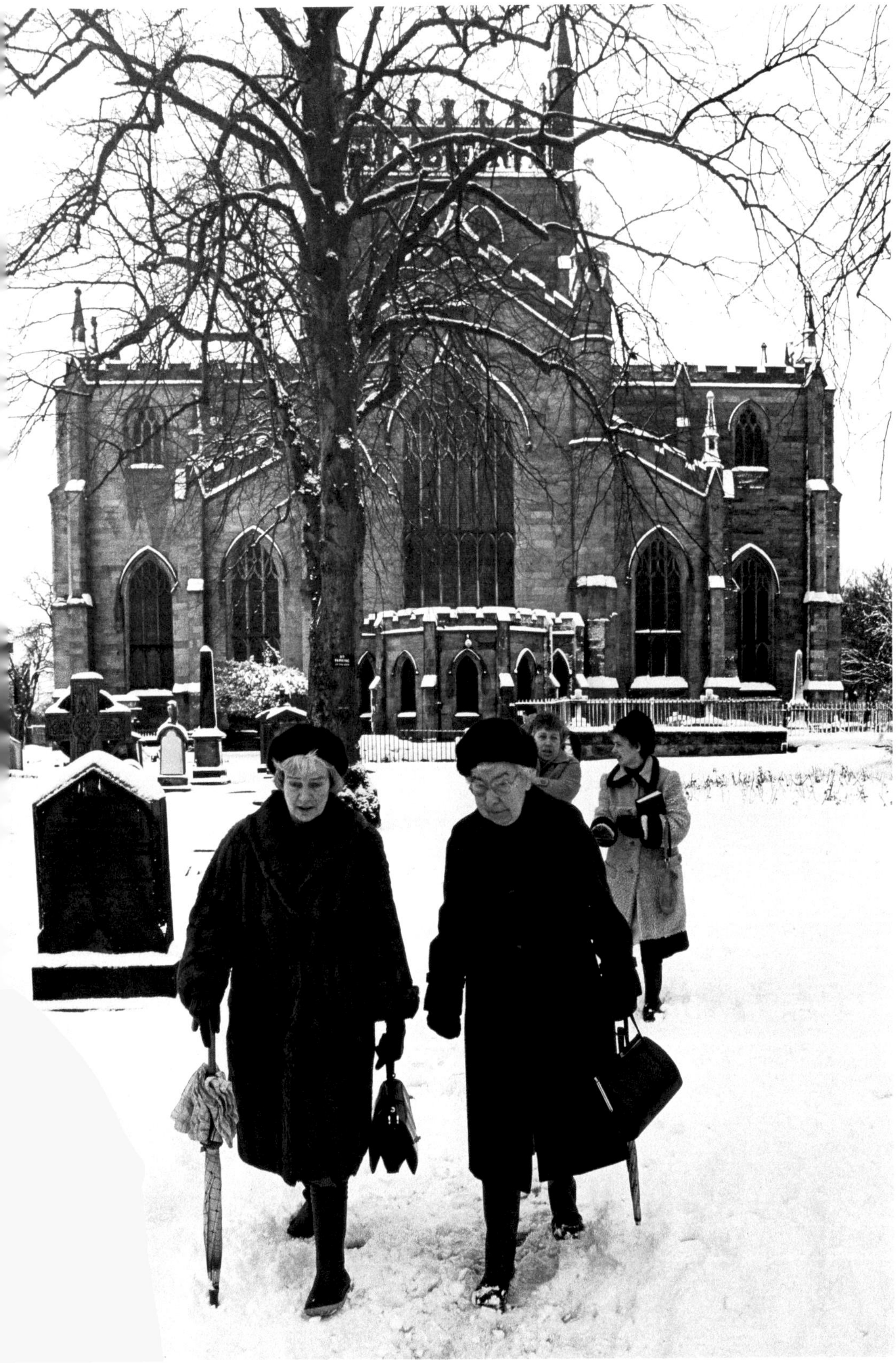

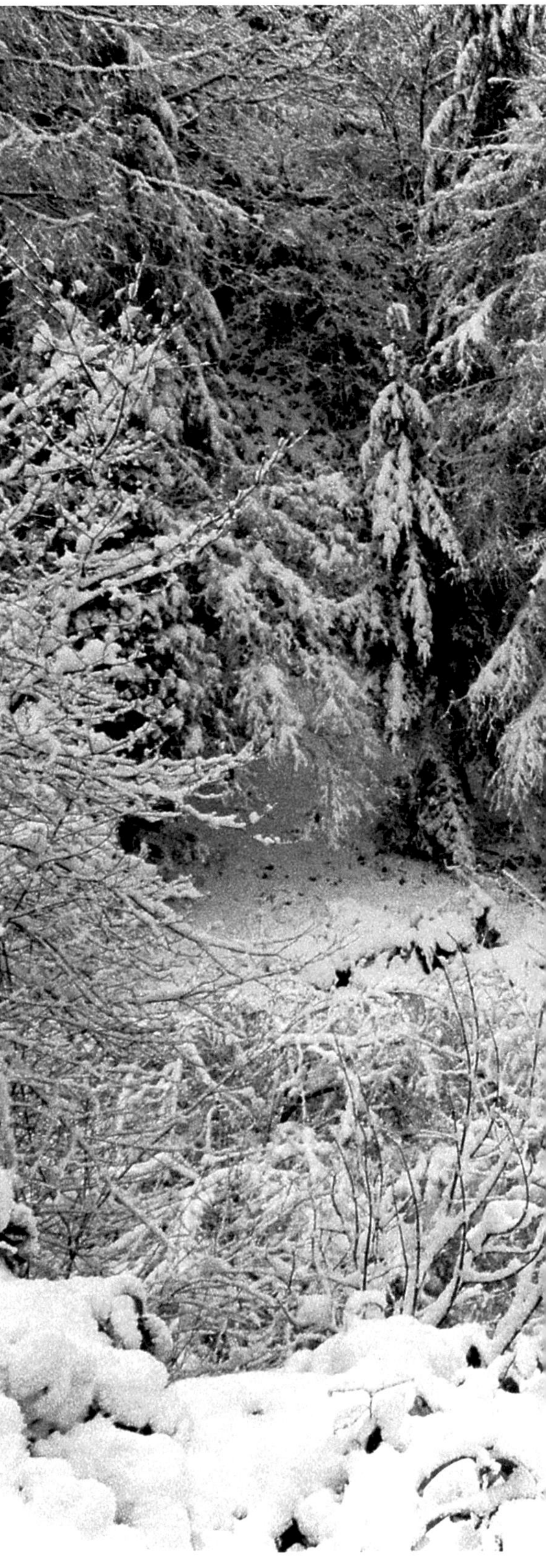

Dunfermline ladies brave the winter snow in the 1980s. My granny walked to church every Sunday, whatever the weather. It was a sin to use a car or public transport. She gave us Roy Rogers books as he was a chum of the evangelist Billy Graham. Sundays were not for fun.

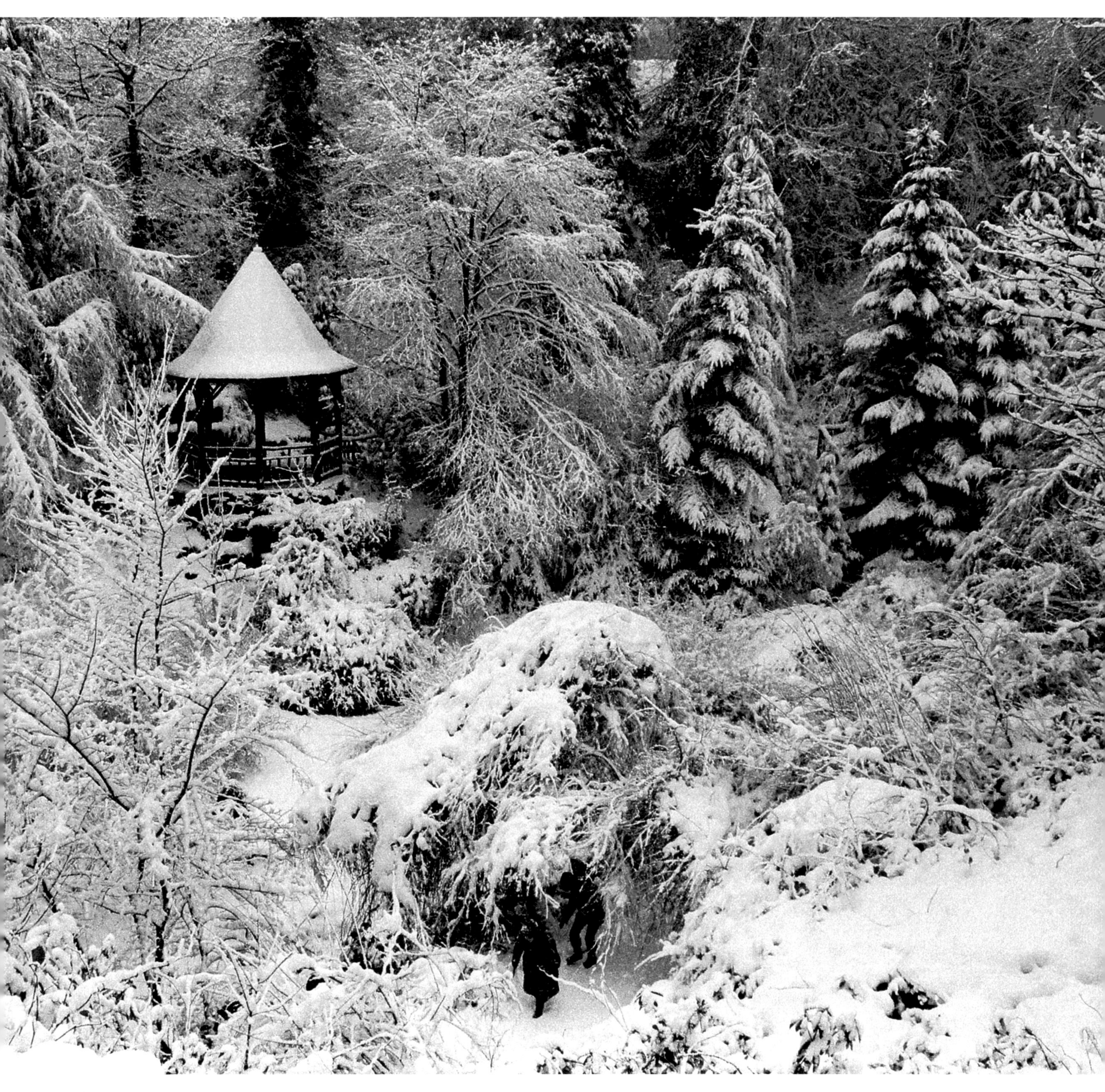

Pittencrieff Glen was presented to Dunfermline by Andrew Carnegie in 1903. It also contains a 17th-century mansion. I was pleased enough with this image, and then the two Bruegel-like figures appeared. To me, this is what I think photography is about: spontaneity and catching the unexpected. Luck happens to the prepared mind.

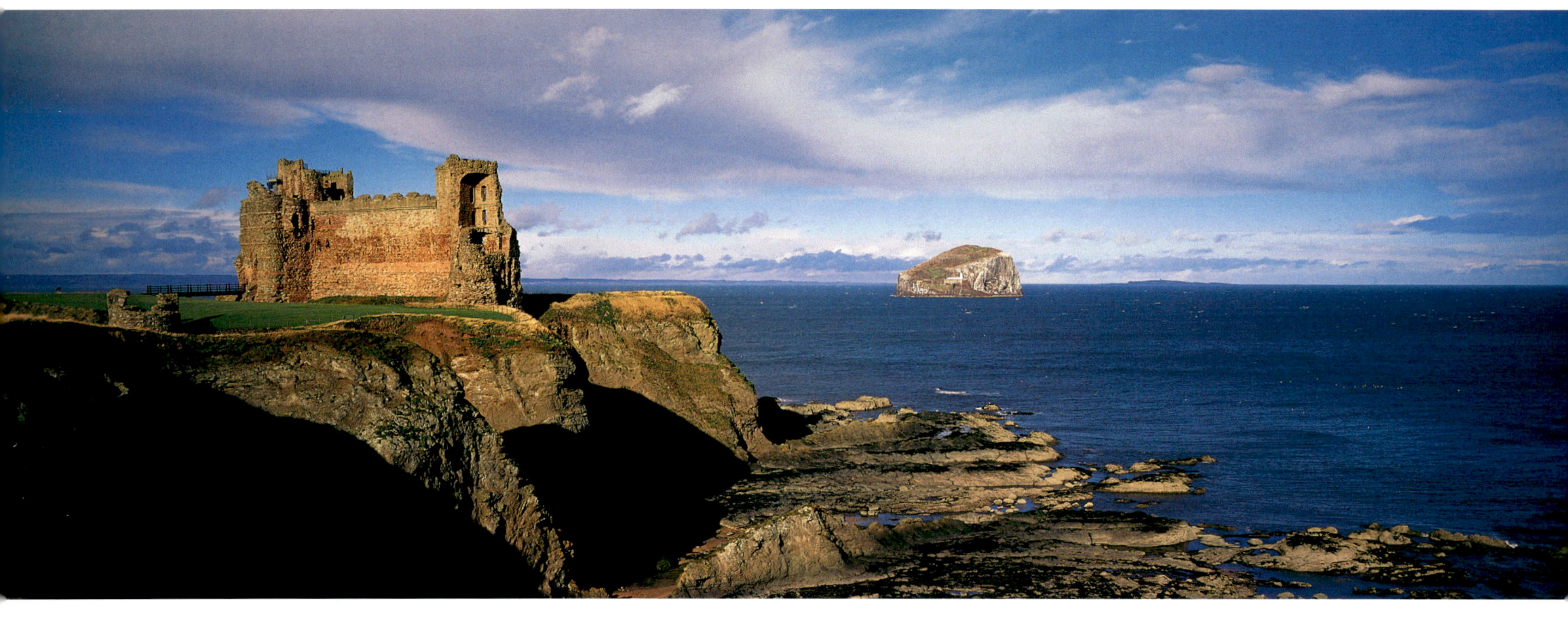

Sir Walter Scott immortalised Tantallon Castle and the Bass Rock in his epic ballad *Marmion*:
Broad massive, high and stretching far,
And held impregnable in war,
On a projecting rock they rose,
And round three sides the ocean flows.
The fourth did battled walls enclose
And double mound and fosse . . .

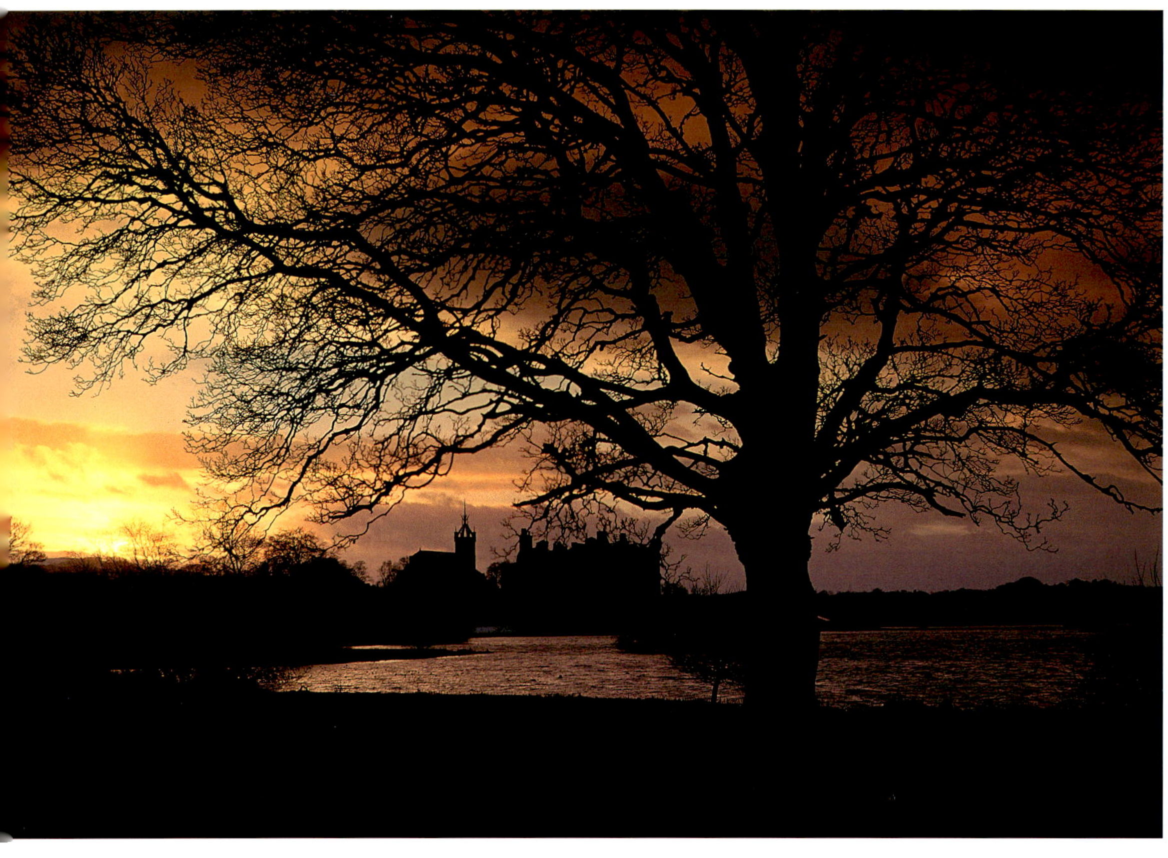

Mary, Queen of Scots, was born in Linlithgow Palace, and even though it is in a ruined state it is still a great place to take those with the imagination to realise how magnificent this renaissance palace would once have looked.

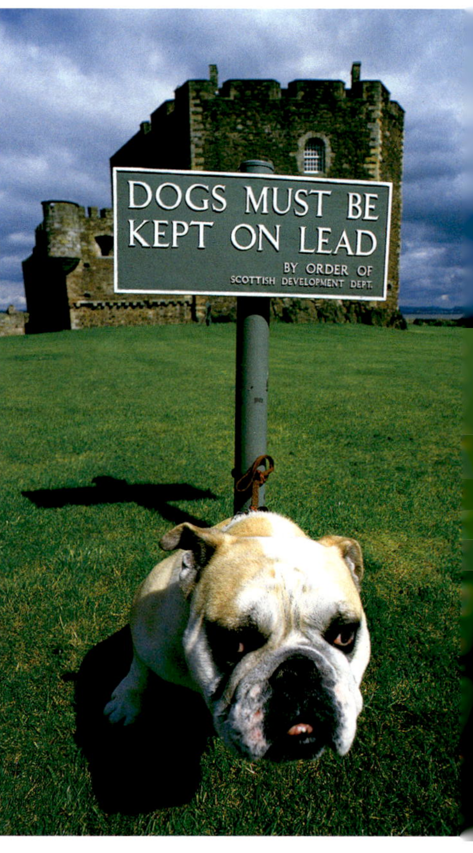

I have sometimes looked upon figures of authority as jobsworths when they didn't agree with my photo requests, even when these might have been a bit extreme. The dog at Blackness Castle on the banks of the Firth of Forth reflects my frustration at such obstacles. The 15th-century castle was used by Franco Zeffirelli in his film of *Hamlet*.

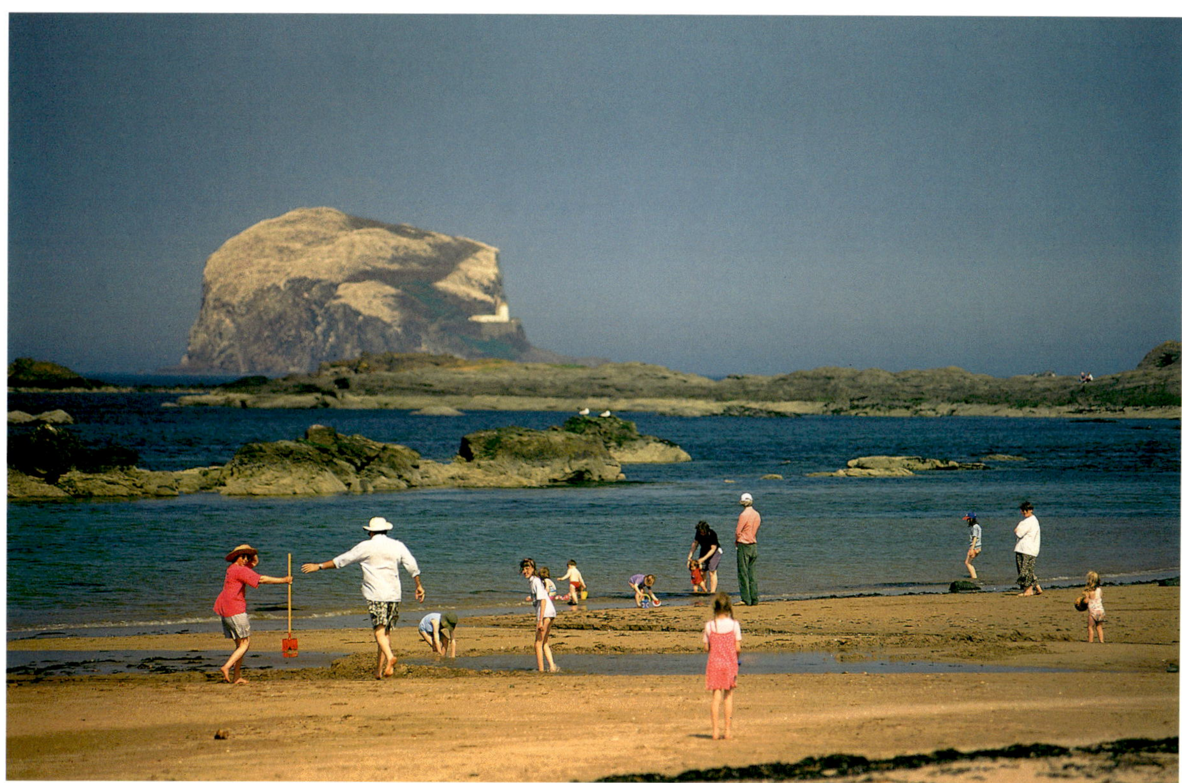

The 351-foot Bass Rock was once used as a Covenanters' prison and features in Robert Louis Stevenson's novel *Catriona*. It is the world's largest single rock gannetry. This was a frequent, weather-permitting tourist trip from North Berwick but it can now be viewed via ten cameras at the Scottish Seabird Centre in the town. The rock is the most prominent natural landmark in the Firth of Forth, and its many different faces can be appreciated from many different East Lothian beaches.

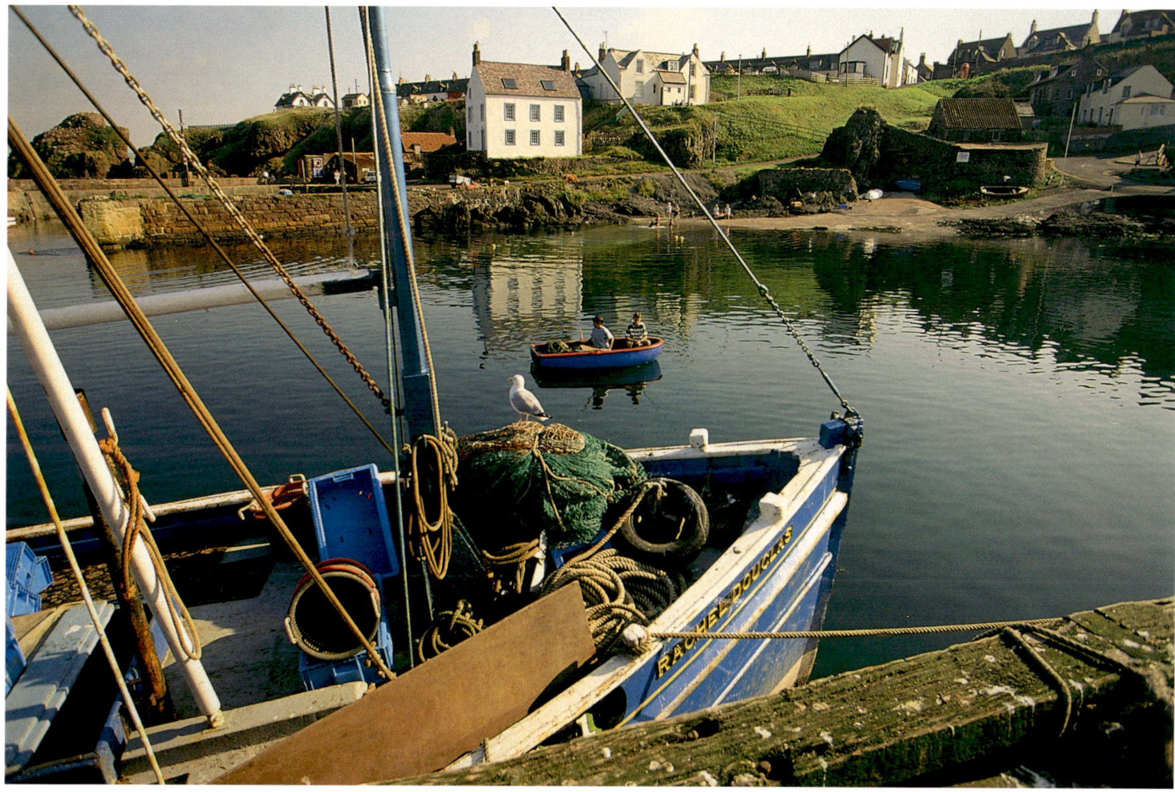

Two boys in a boat in a safe harbour, with a fishing rod and a tin of bait – paradise when you are ten years old and on holiday. St Abbs still reminds me of my own childhood holidays in Arran, Nairn and Ullapool, where freedom and independence were the norm. We tend to romanticise some of these times and carefully forget about the sand in the sandwiches, rainy days stuck inside with boring board games and calomine lotion to put on our sunburn. We didn't know about factor 25.

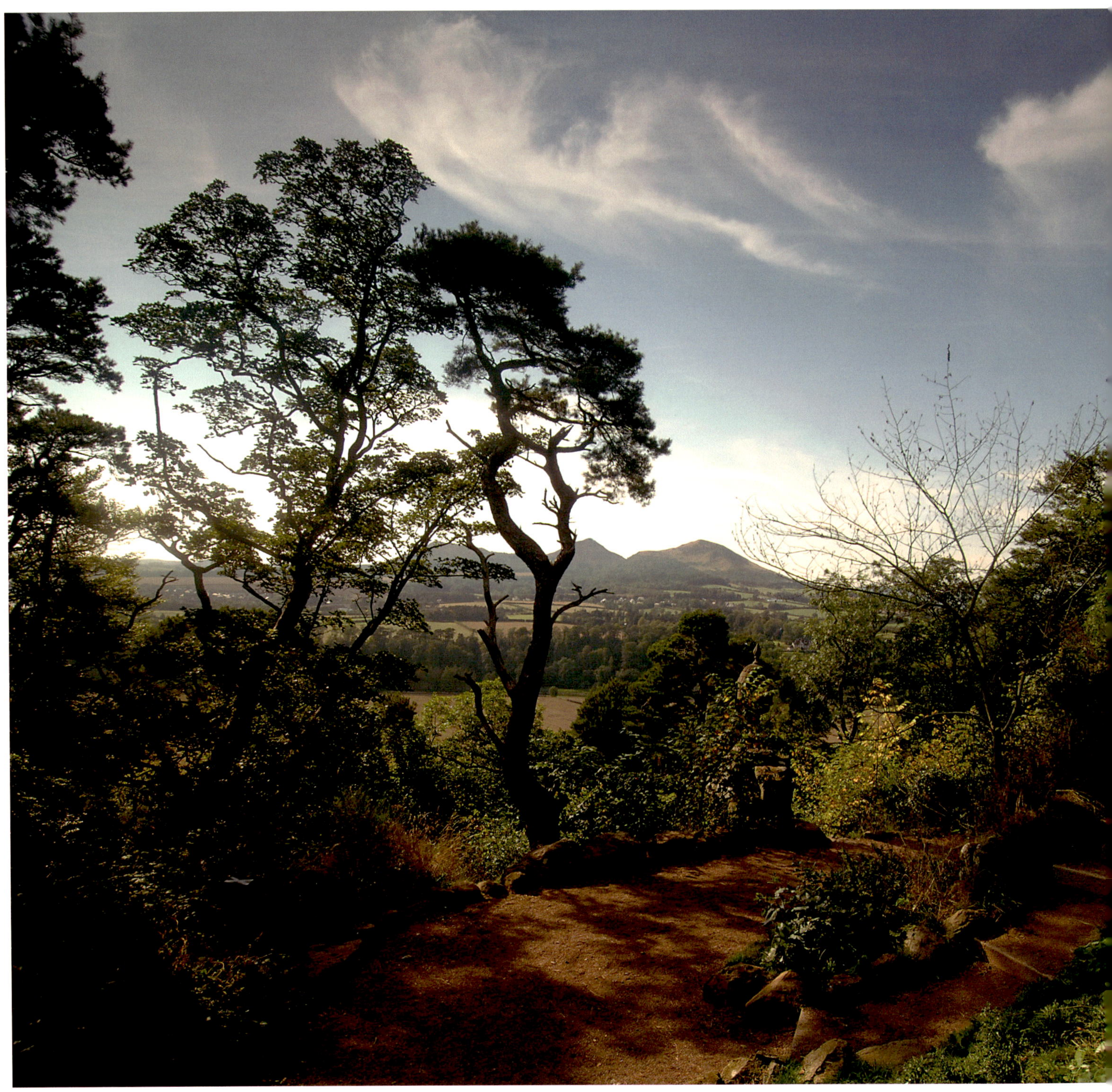

This 31-foot-tall statue of William Wallace was raised above the River Tweed at Bemersyde in around 1814. The natural beauty of the scene is in stark contrast with the harshness of the red sandstone giant. Like the Scottish Borders region in general, the site is somewhat undiscovered, which is also part of its attraction.

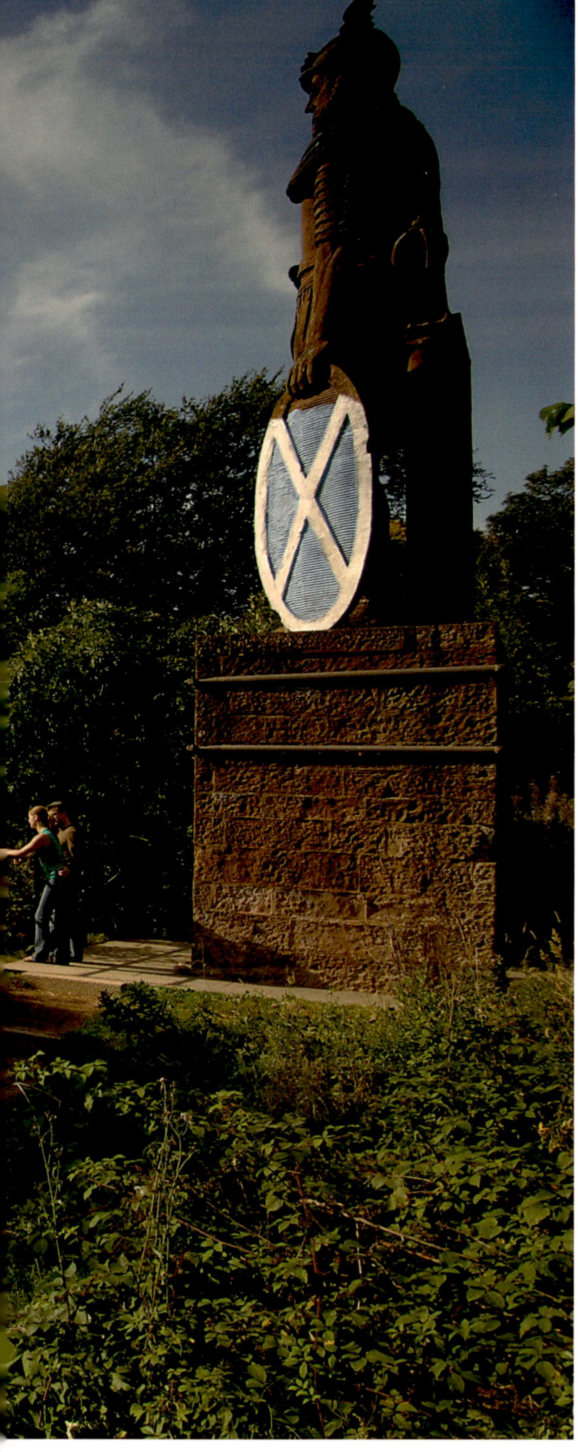

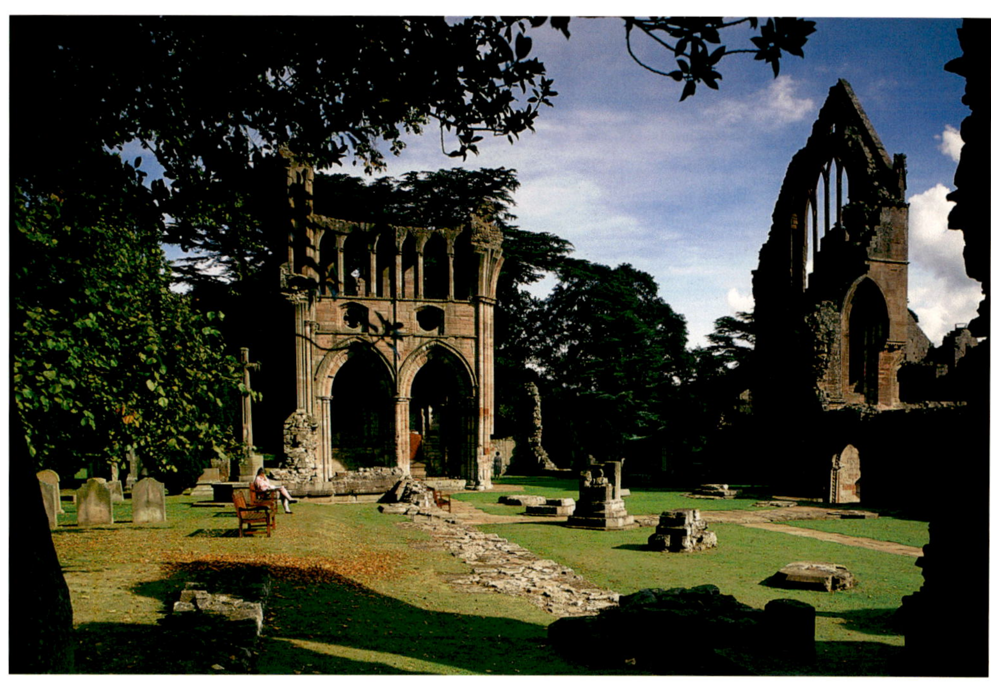

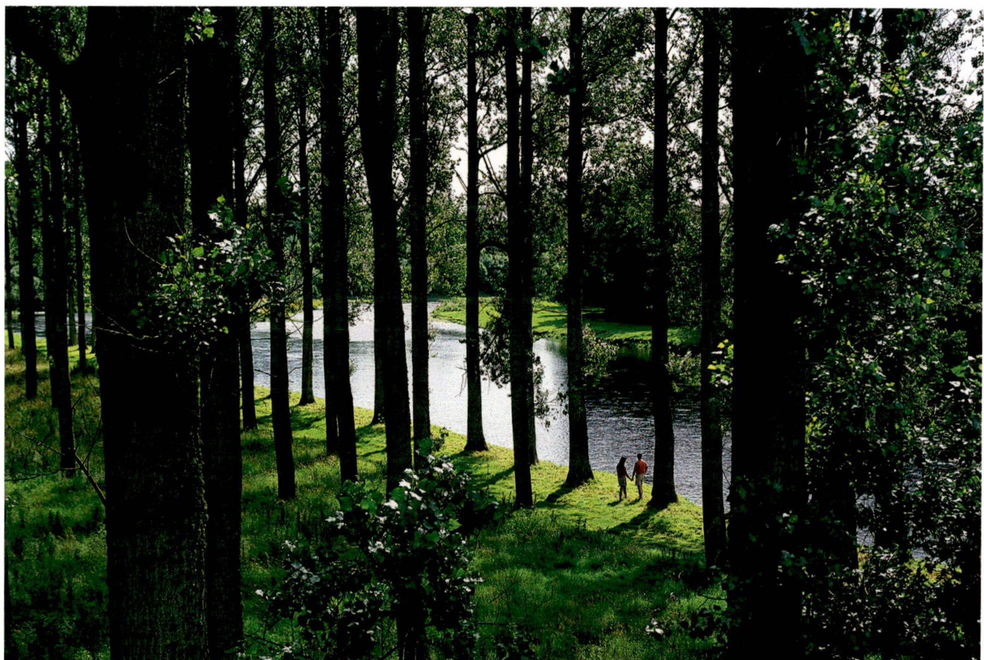

(Top) Dryburgh Abbey is surely the most romantic of all the Border abbeys. It is the burial place of Sir Walter Scott and also of Field Marshal Earl Haig. It was damaged by English forces in 1544. In early prints of the abbey there is no evidence of the trimmed and perfect lawns that seem to be the current vogue.

(Above) Crossing the River Tweed at Mertoun Bridge near St Boswells you could easily miss this line of beautiful poplar trees. The nearby Mertoun House Gardens could be up to 350 years old, with an arboretum, walled garden and ancient dovecote.

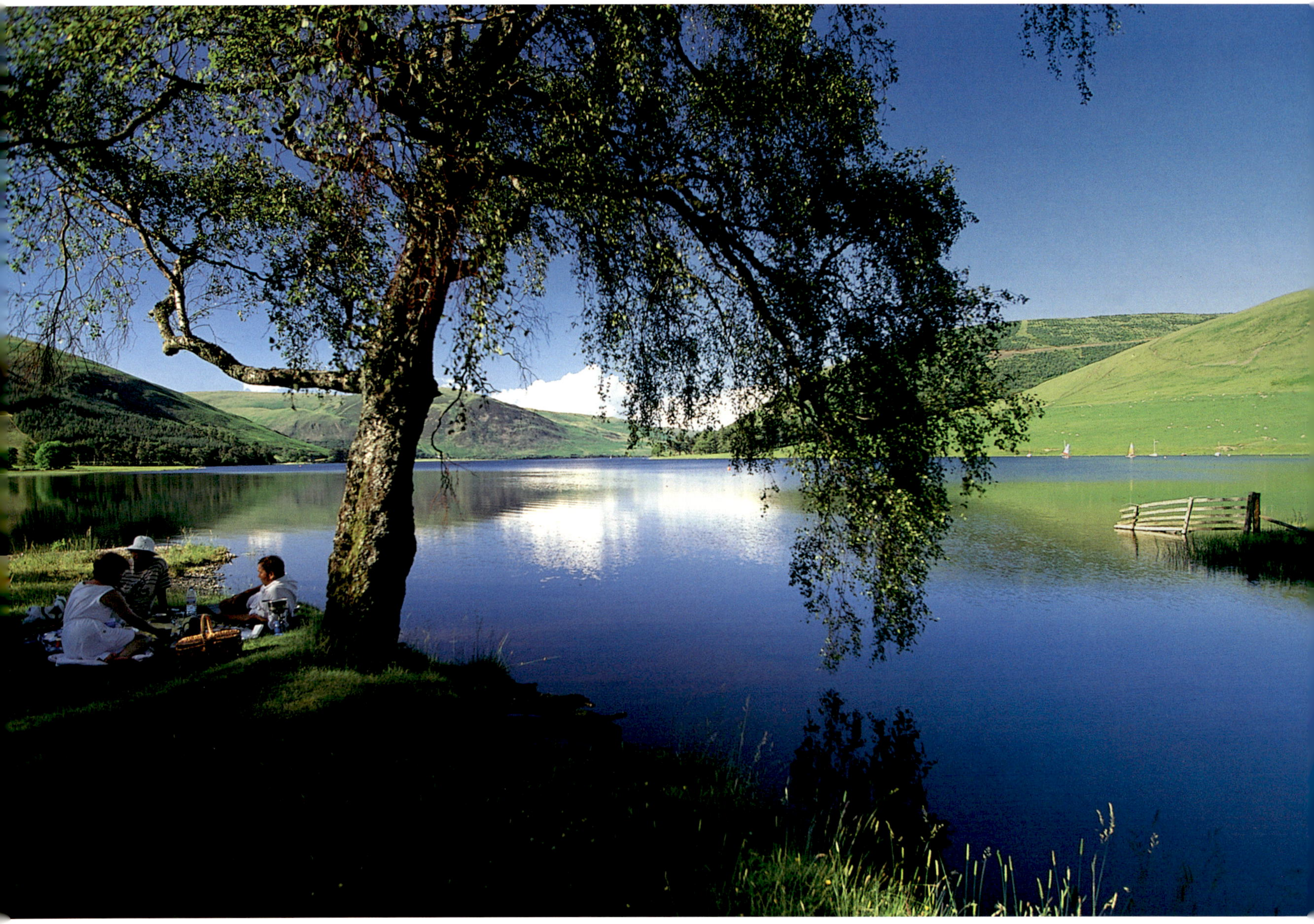

St Mary's Loch, whose praises have been sung by William Wordsworth in *Yarrow Visited* and Walter Scott in his *Marmion*. Surrounded by green, lowland hills at the head of the Yarrow valley, it must be one of my favourite picnic spots and I am a bit loathe to share it.

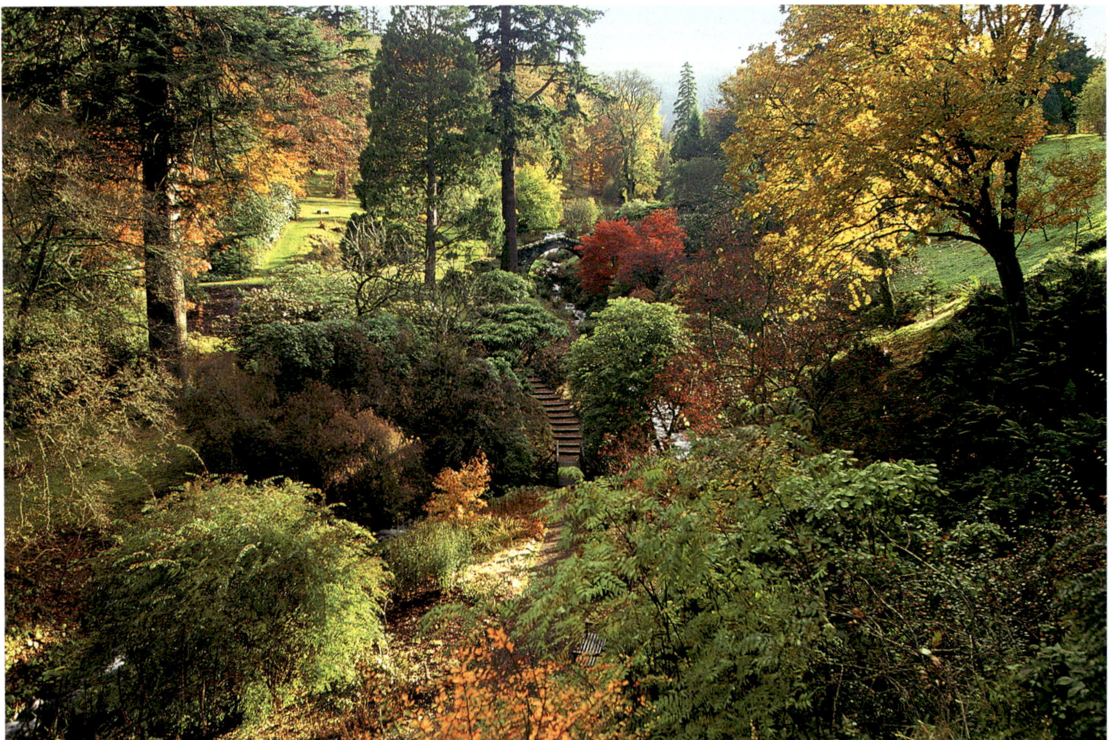

Dawyck Gardens in the Borders is one of the world's finest arboreta. It is now an offshoot of the Royal Botanic Gardens in Edinburgh. The shot I would like here would be taken *contrejour*, with the autumn colours and an early morning frost. I just missed the frost on this morning.

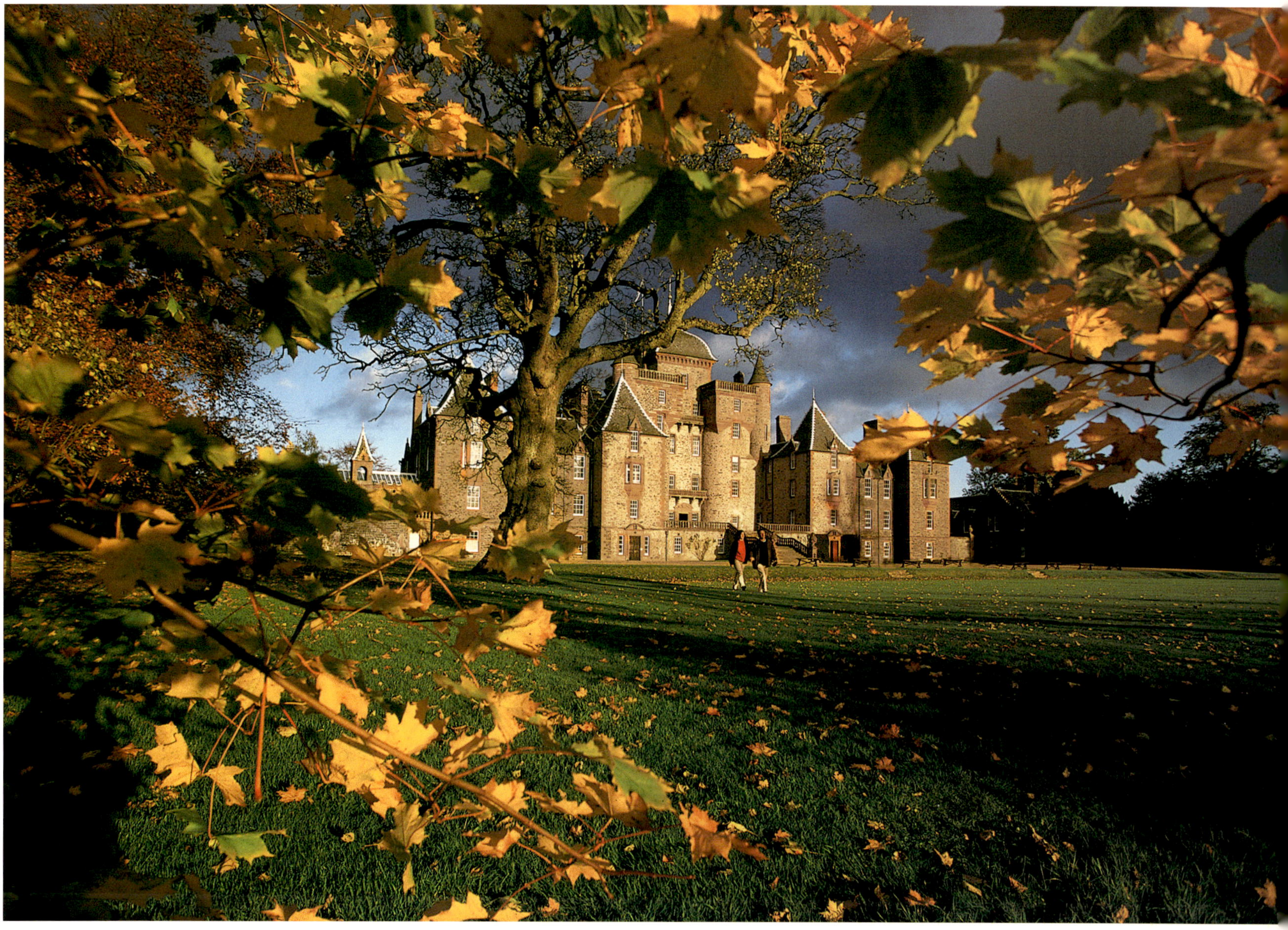

I was on an autumn shoot for the Borders Tourist Board and it had been overcast all day until a late afternoon burst of light gave Thirlestane Castle this magical appearance. A castle has been on this site from the 13th century, and it is particularly notable for its rich plasterwork, created by Italian craftsmen.

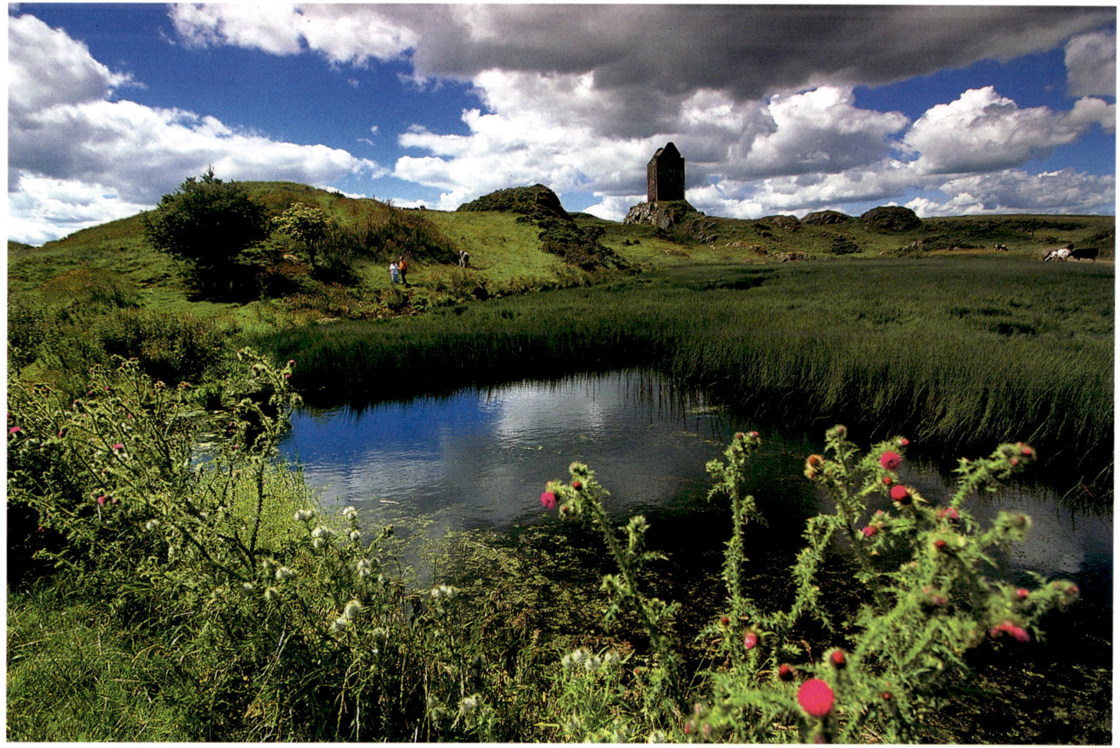

A classic Borders peel tower from the early 15th century, Smailholm Tower is well situated for security, with commanding views of the surrounding area. The painter J. M. W. Turner made a sketch of the tower in 1831 while visiting Sir Walter Scott. The image was used to illustrate Scott's *Poetical Works*.

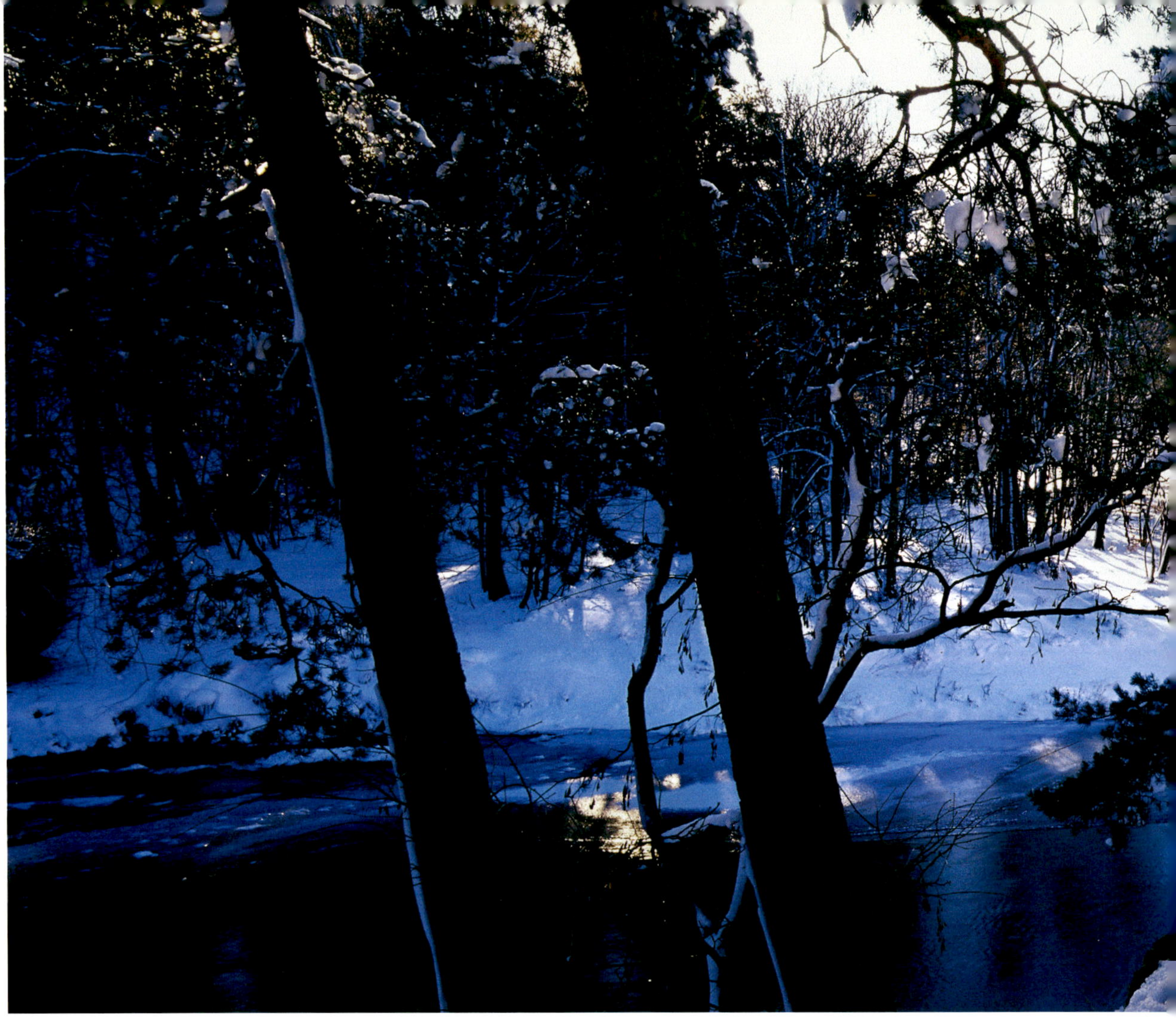

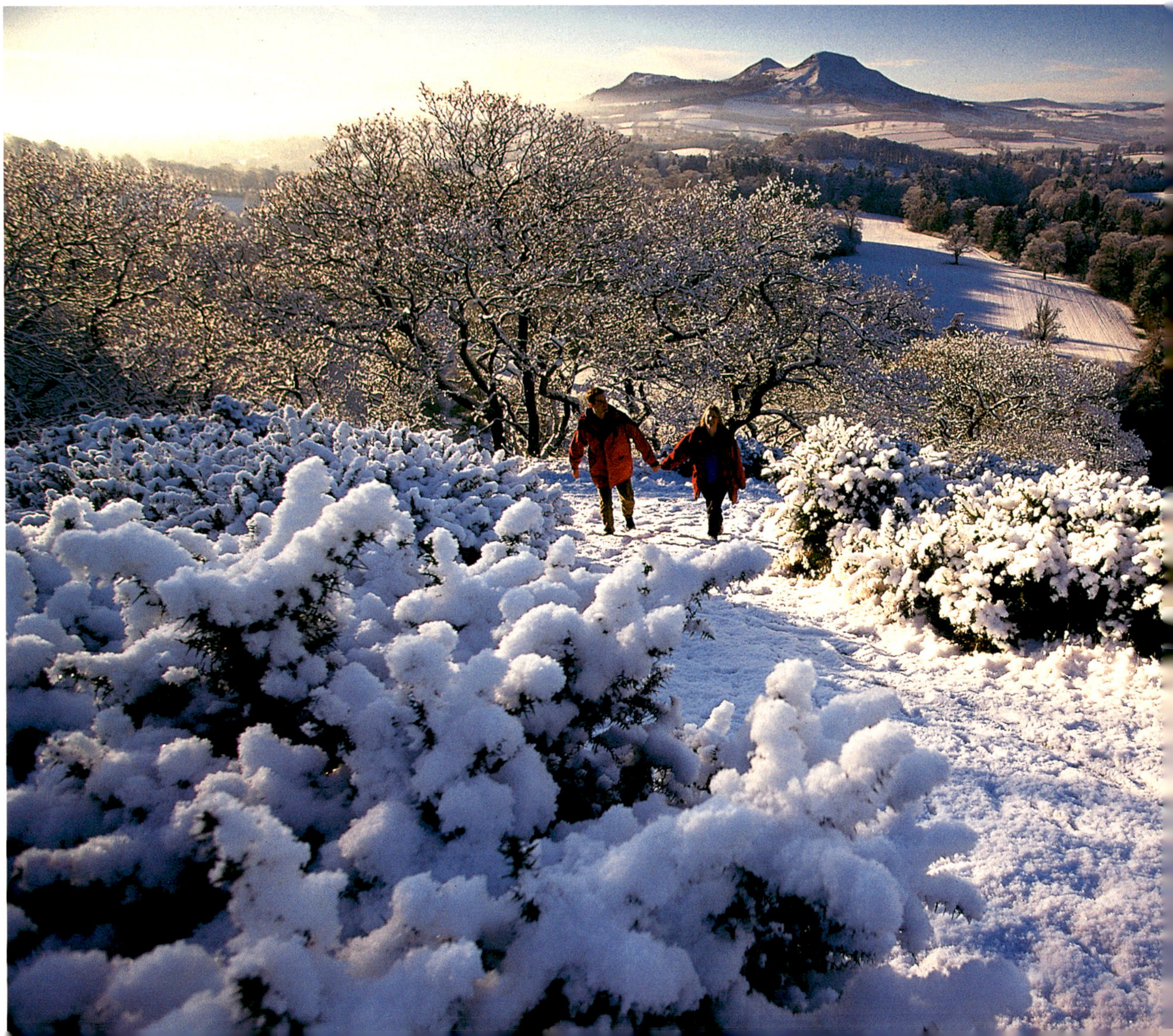

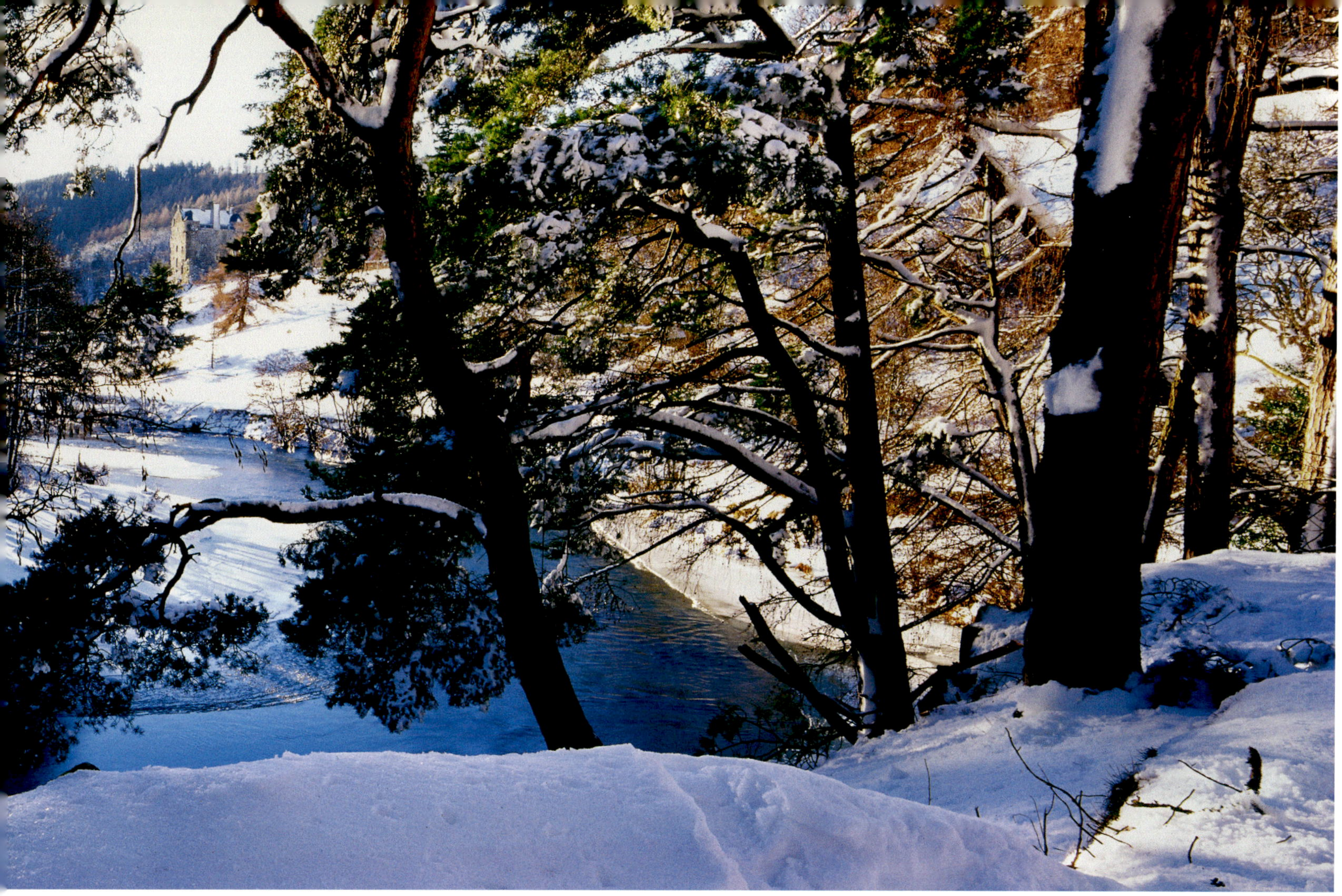

This view of Neidpath Castle on the River Tweed is a ten minute walk along the riverside from Peebles. The castle has 11-foot-thick walls, and this early Fraser stronghold has a commanding position, but it still suffered badly from Cromwell's artillery.

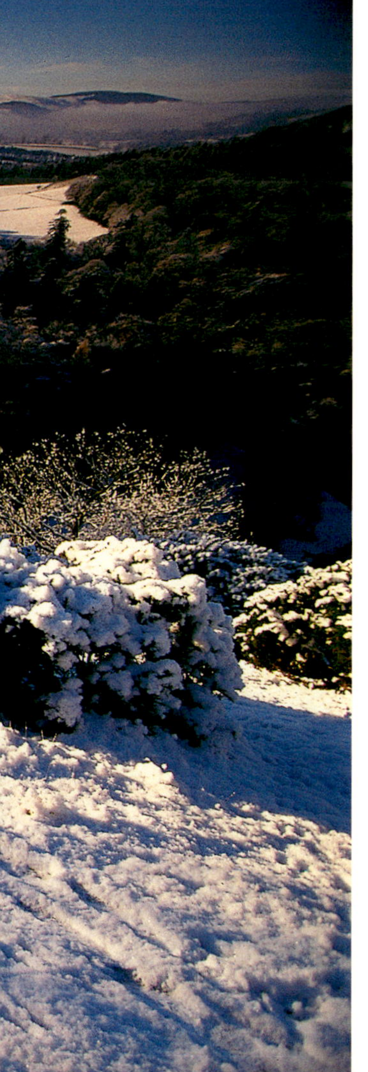

Snow can make an already great scene even more beautiful. Scott's View in the Borders was Sir Walter Scott's favourite vista of the Eildon Hills. When his funeral cortège came to this point, his horse stopped out of habit and, without its master's command, the procession was stalled.

Early morning riders on Coldingham Bay near Eyemouth. Inland is a priory first built in the 7th century on land granted by a Northumbrian princess, Ebba, who was shipwrecked nearby.

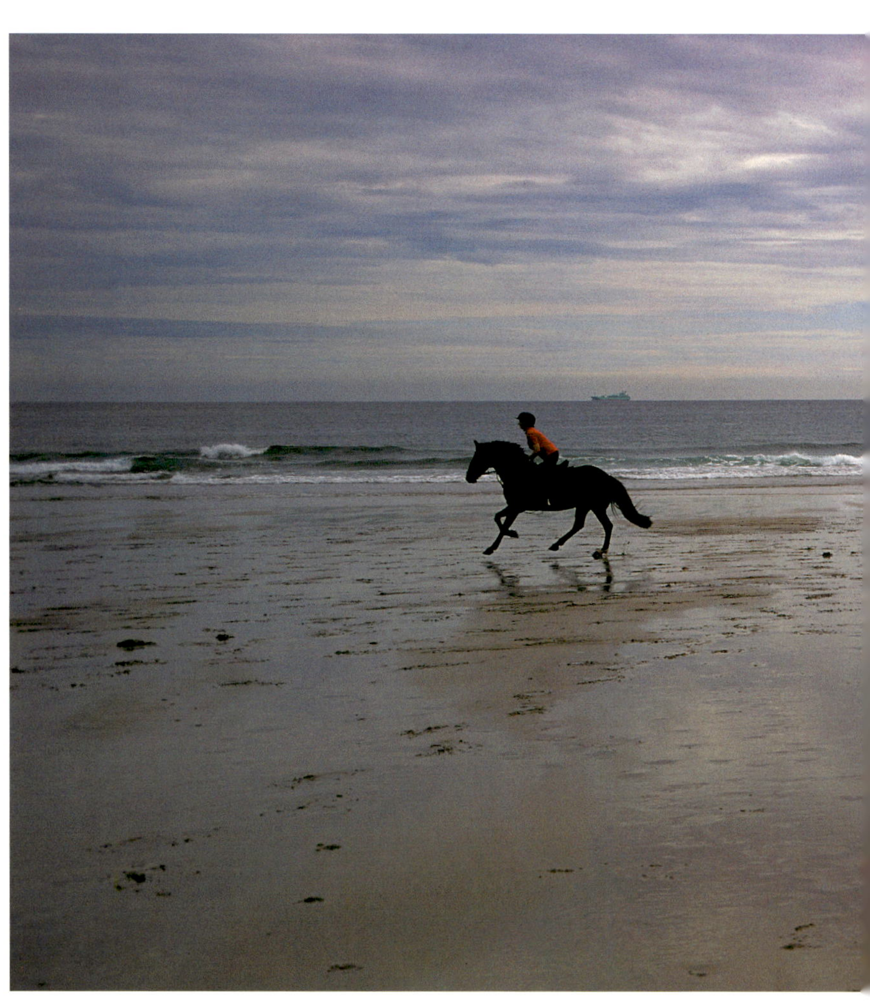

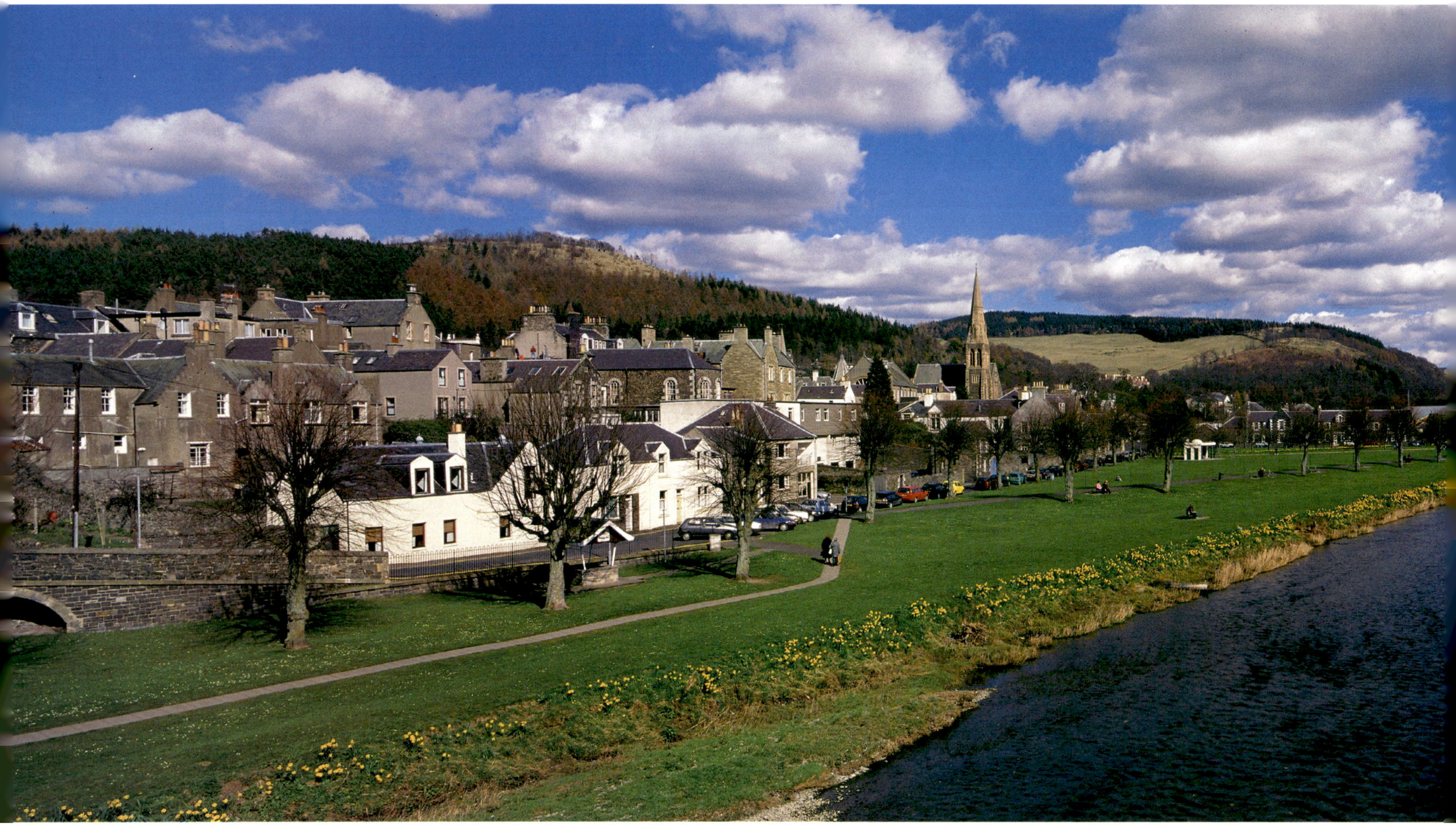

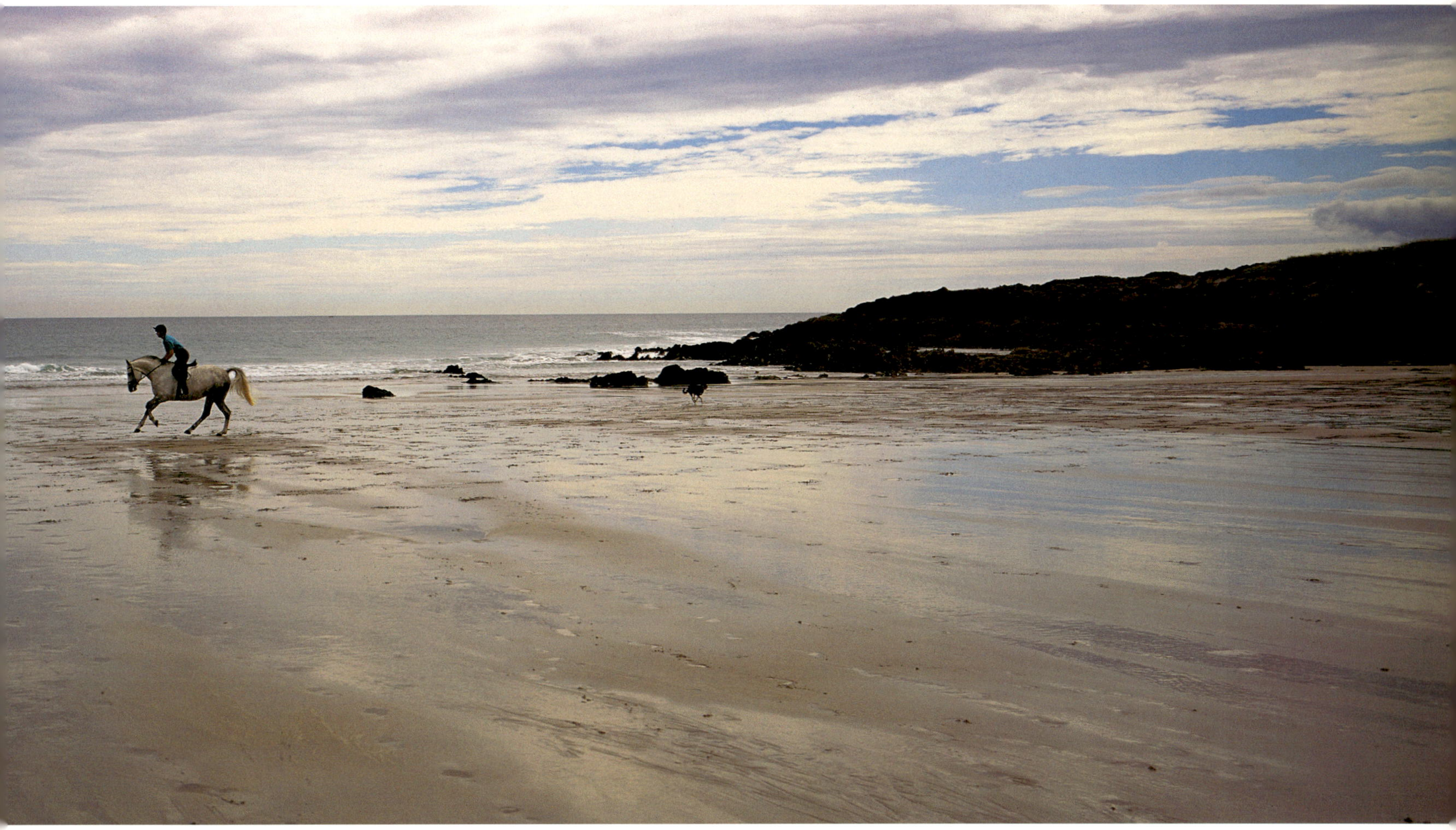

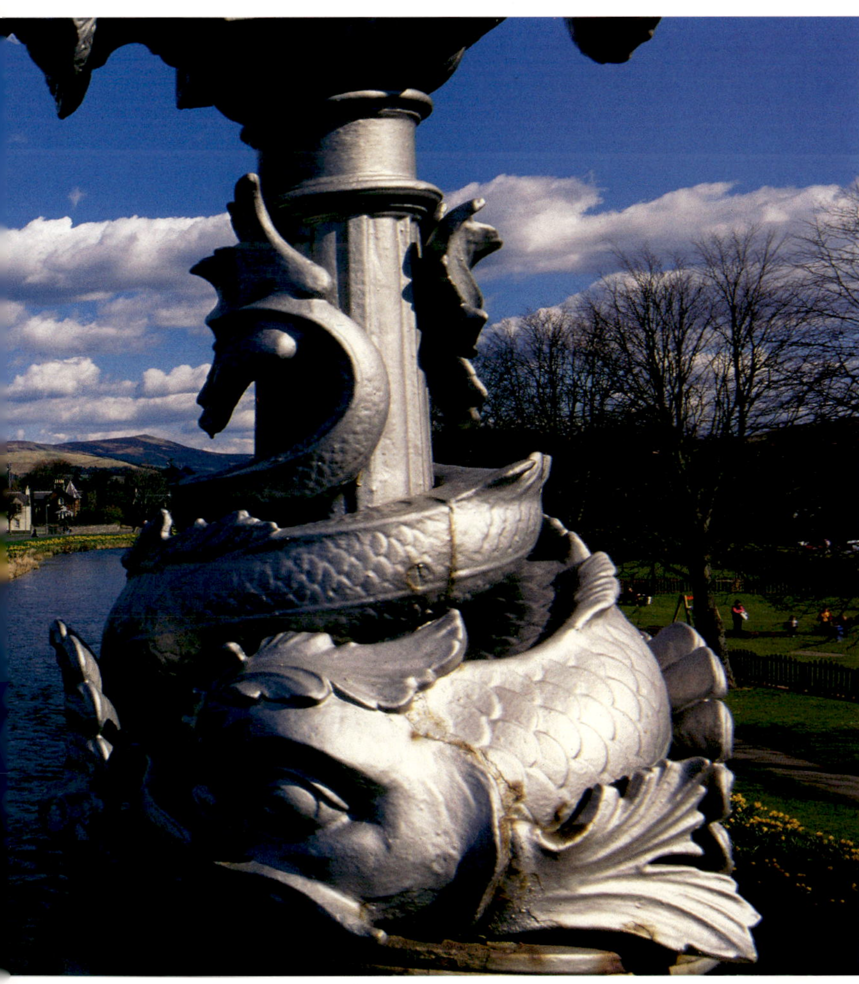

The usually quiet and reserved town of Peebles comes alive during the Beltane Festival in June. This pagan ceremony celebrates the return of summer and is symbolised by fire. The town has a most delightful setting on the banks of the River Tweed. These magnificent lamp standards always give me pleasure, unlike the concrete horrors in my own street in Edinburgh.

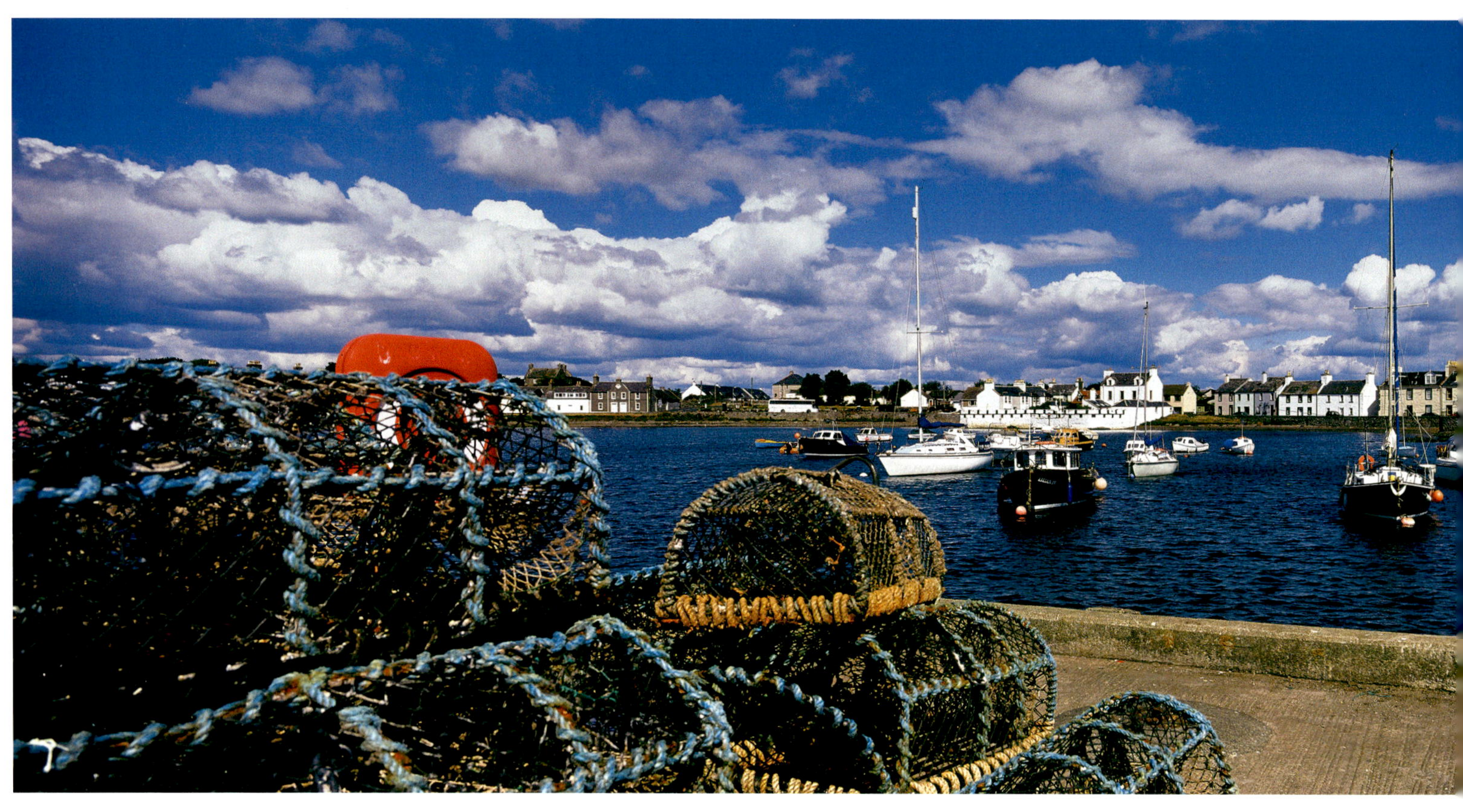

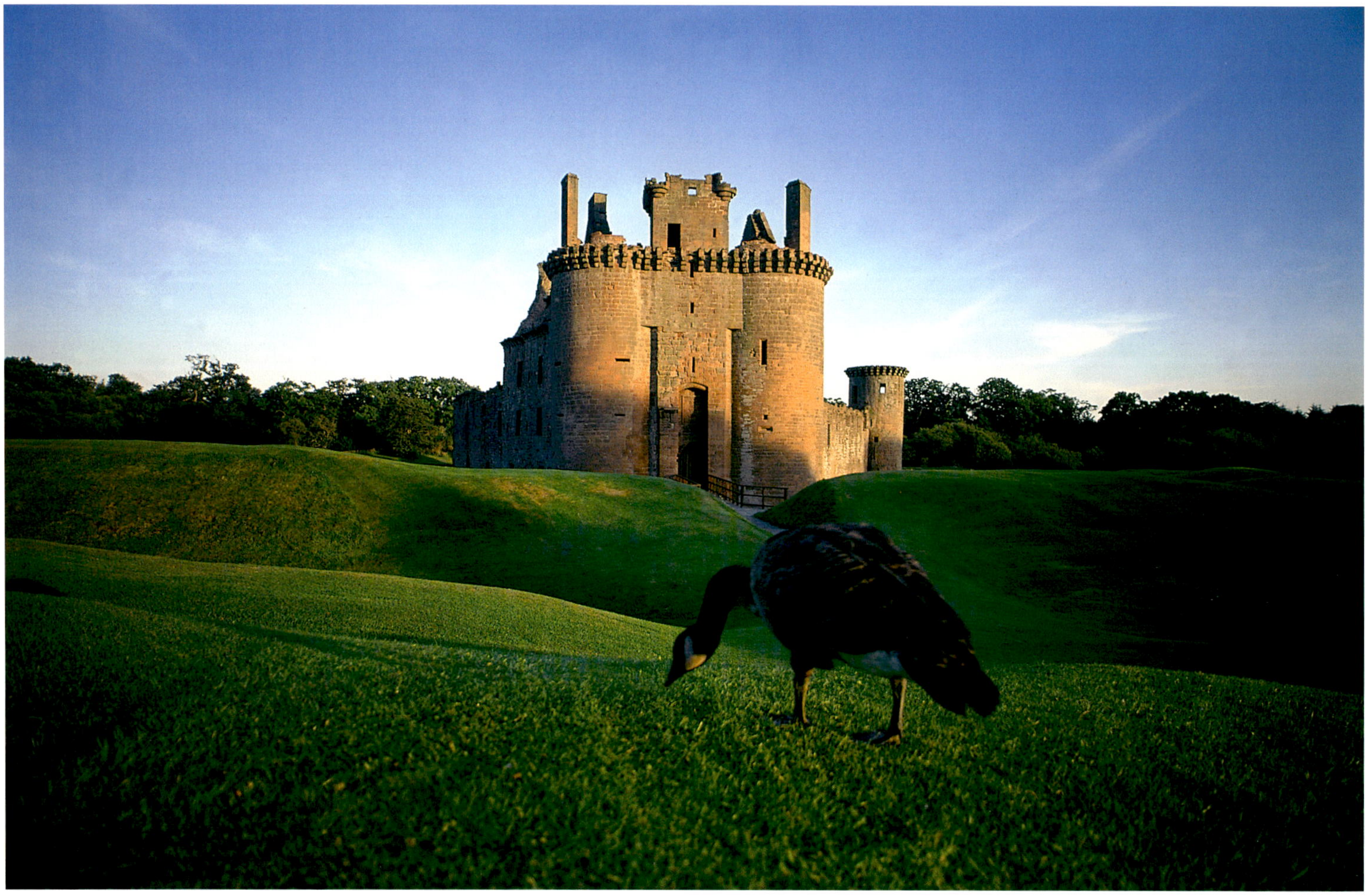

Caerlaverock Castle, complete with moat and a unique triangular shape, is a formidable medieval stronghold. This satisfies every childhood fantasy of what a castle should be, and the toy castle my father made for me when I was six years old could have had this as its inspiration.

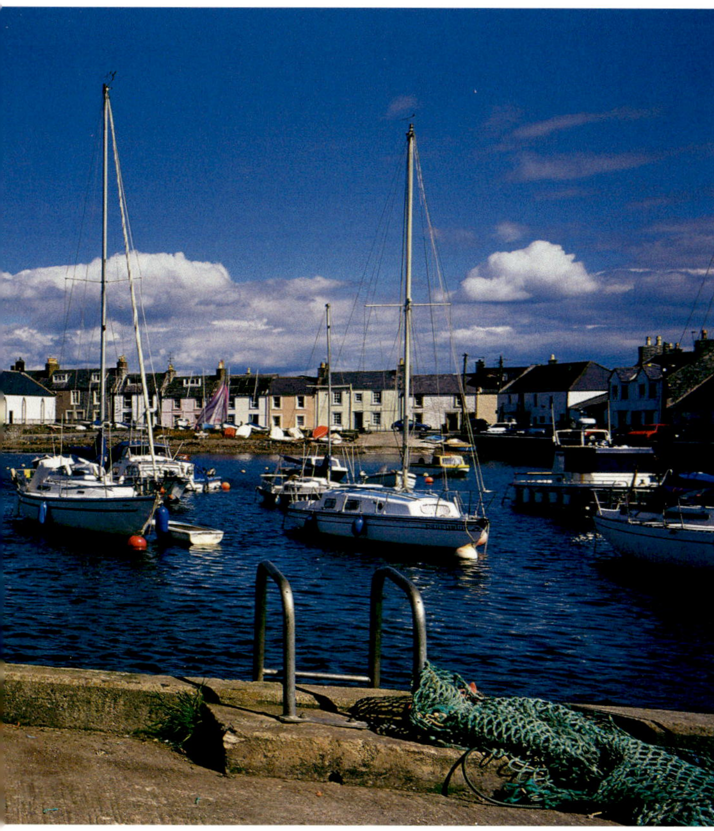

(Above) I was photographing the Isle of Whithorn in the southwest for the Tourist Board. A picnicking family said, in a good-natured way, 'Go away, we want no-one else to know about this area.' The British Tourist Authority photographer Barry Hicks said his dilemma was whether he should bypass some places to preserve them from overexposure and unsympathetic development or promote them in the hope that they benefit in a positive way.

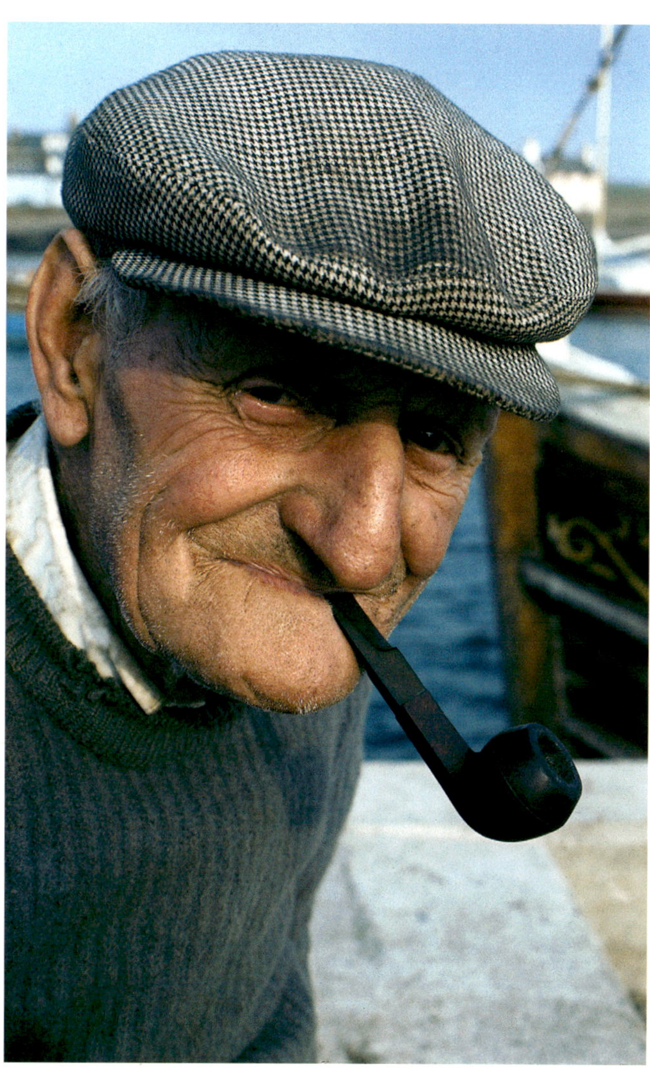

(Above) The face of this resident of the Isle of Whithorn in the 1970s reflects a life at sea. The bow of the fishing boat showing on the right is a contrast to the pleasure craft now occupying the harbour.

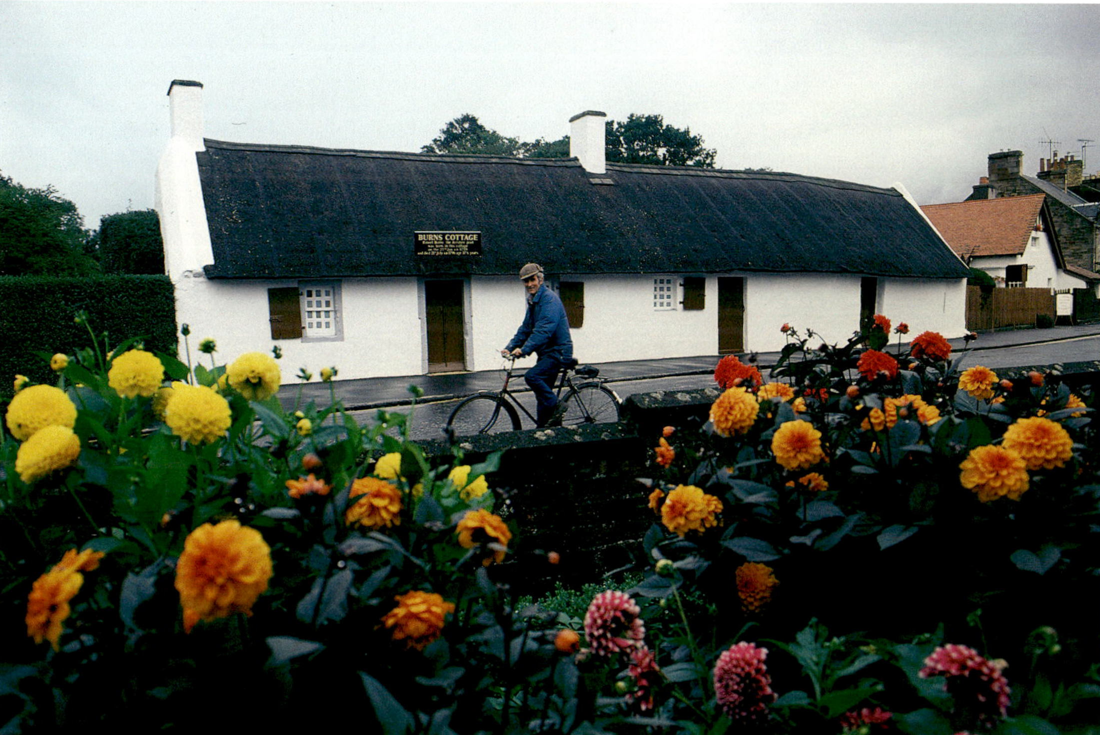

'O would some power the giftie gie us to see ourselves as others see us.' From 'To a Louse' by Robert Burns. It is a pity that we don't follow more of Burns' philosophy. He was the Beatles of his day. His birthplace in Alloway is part of the Burns' industry, much of which would not have pleased the bard. Sadly, we too often opt for the corny side when promoting our heritage.

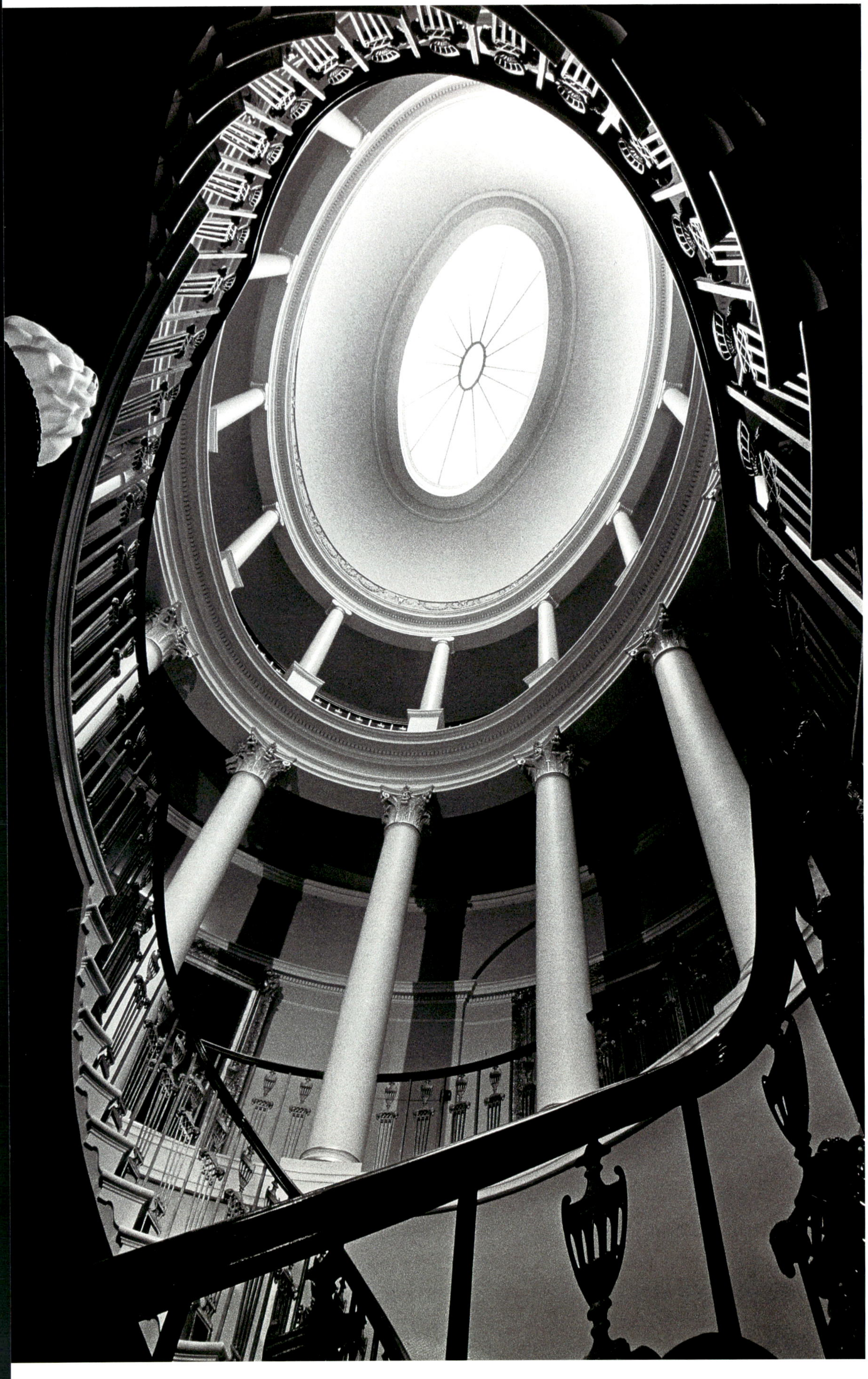

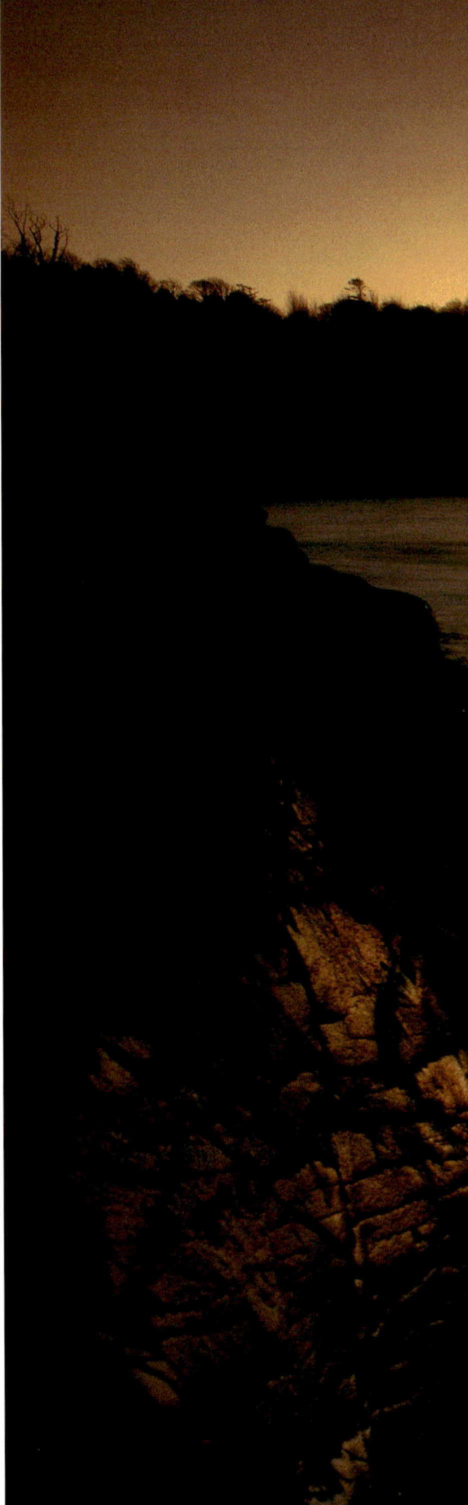

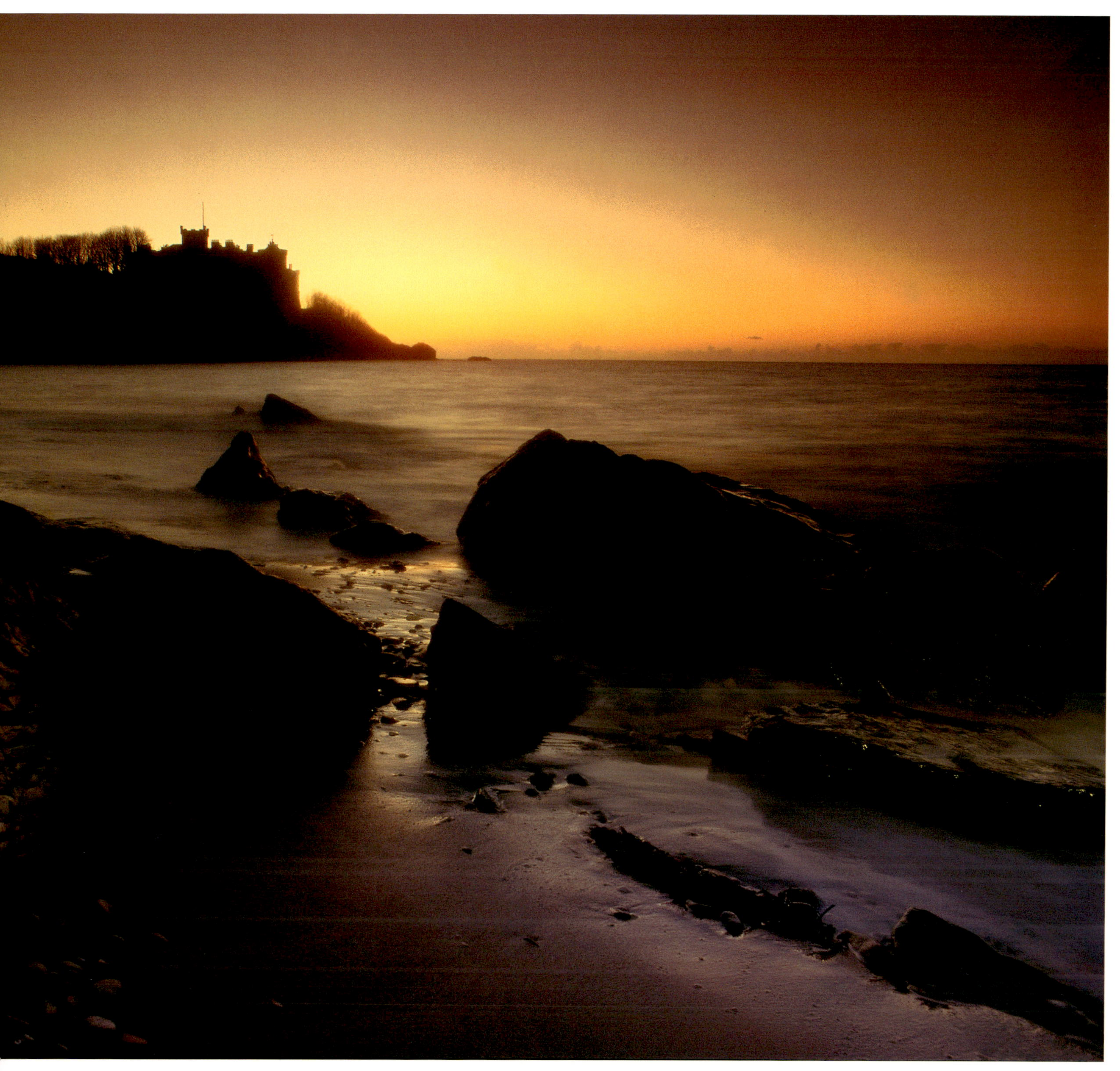

Culzean Castle, an italianate creation built by Robert Adam in 1777. When gifted to the National Trust for Scotland by the Kennedy family in 1945, they asked that an apartment be given over for the exclusive use of General Eisenhower in recognition of his services to Britain during the Second World War. In the entrance hall to the castle, as in many other grand houses, there is an excessive display of bayonets, muskets, swords and other gruesome weapons.

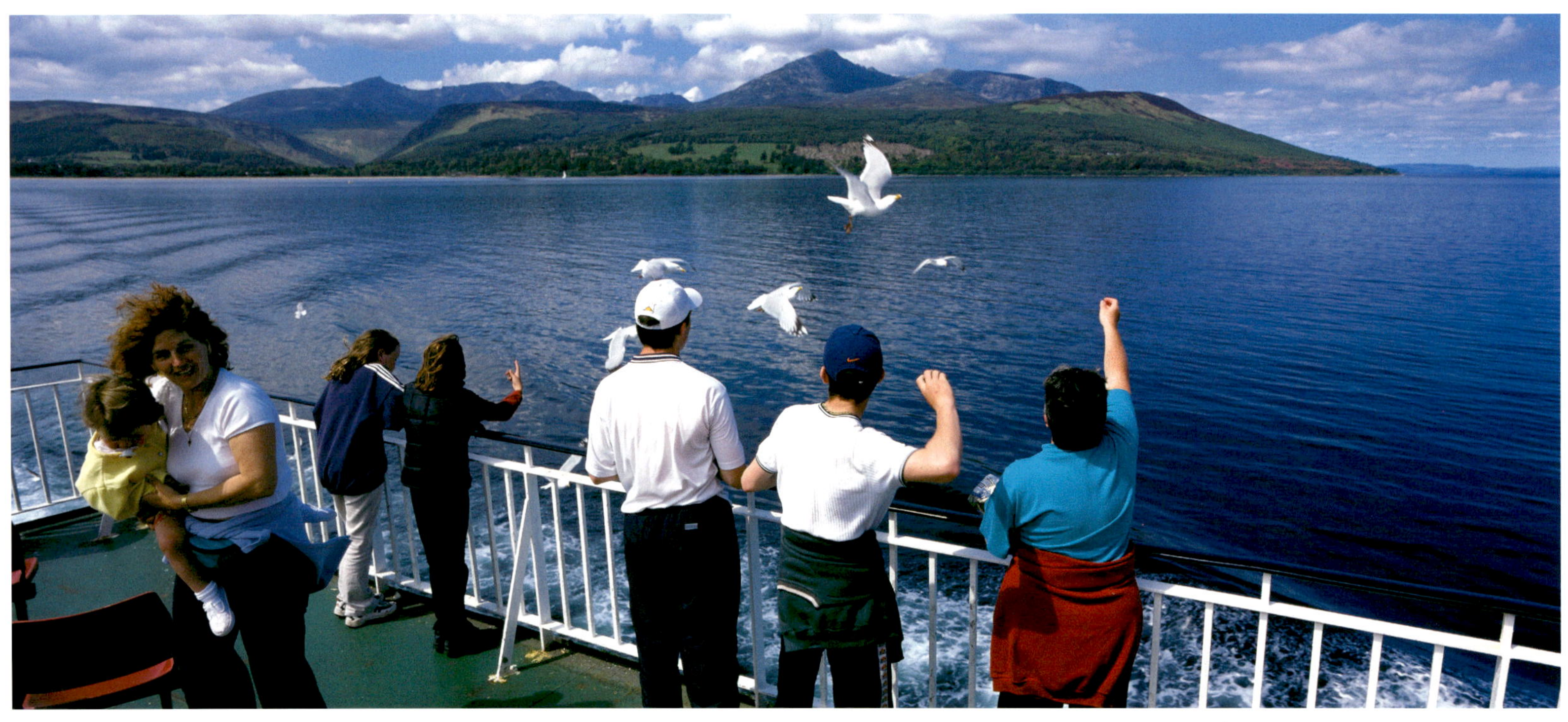

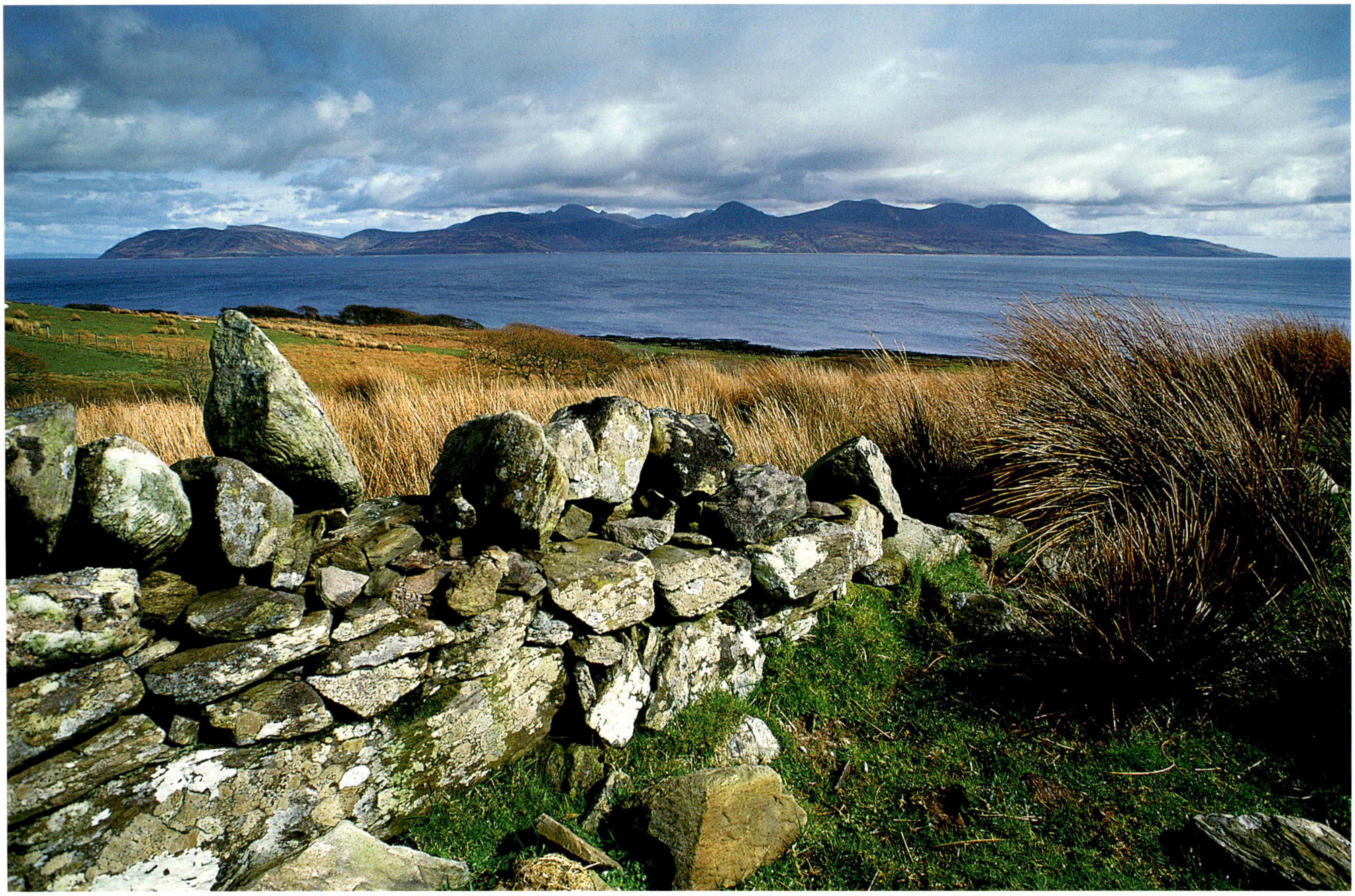

When you get off the ferry in Brodick, Isle of Arran, the water is remarkably clear. I remember this from childhood holidays. I have a family snap of myself, taken on the beach at Blackwaterfoot. I was in the 'bare scuddy' (naked) aged four. My father's caption in the album was *What will he think of this when he is 21?*

My brother and I were sent to the farm with brown jugs to collect fresh milk every morning. We would feed the donkeys on the way with stale bread.
(Top) Goatfell from the Ardrossan-Brodick ferry.
(Bottom) Arran from Kintyre.

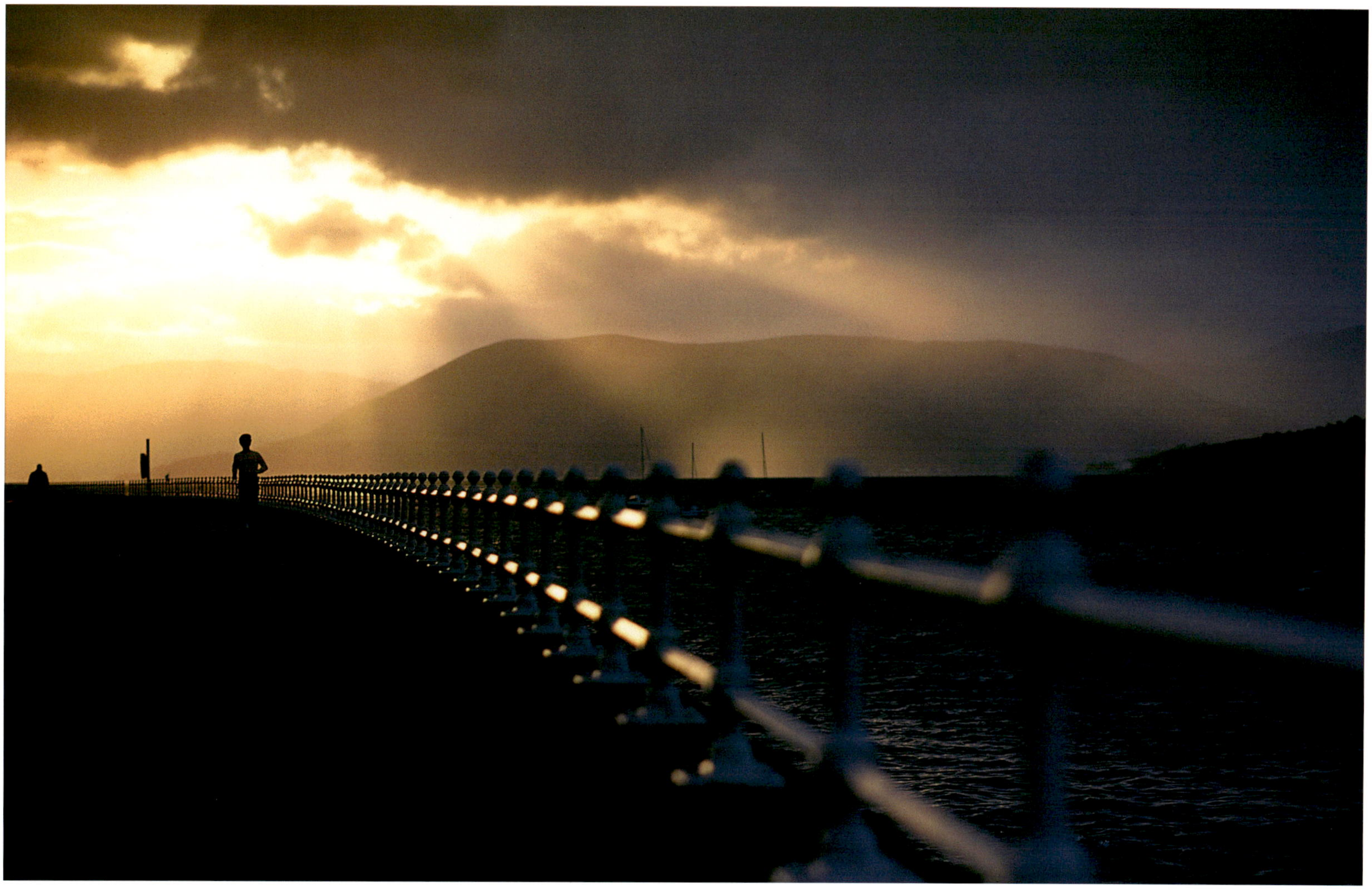

Greenock has some of the most extravagant public buildings anywhere in Scotland. The Esplanade – this mile-long sweep lined with elegant villas with views across the Firth of Clyde – is visually far removed from the industry that created its wealth. James Watt, the 18th-century inventor and a father of the Industrial Revolution, is the town's most famous son.

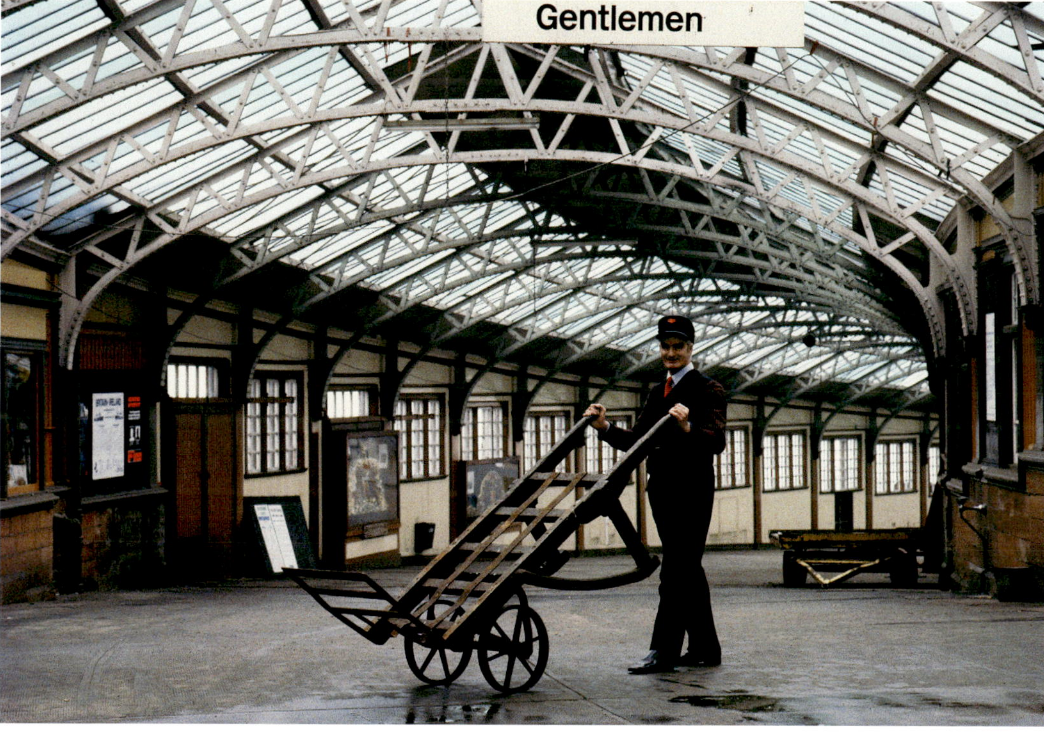

Many Victorian and Edwardian station frontages have been pulled down and replaced by featureless concrete structures. Thankfully, many interiors are still intact but too often are filled with garish fast food outlets that mask the wonderful architecture. Wemyss Bay walkway to the steamer pier is a good example of a structure that has survived.

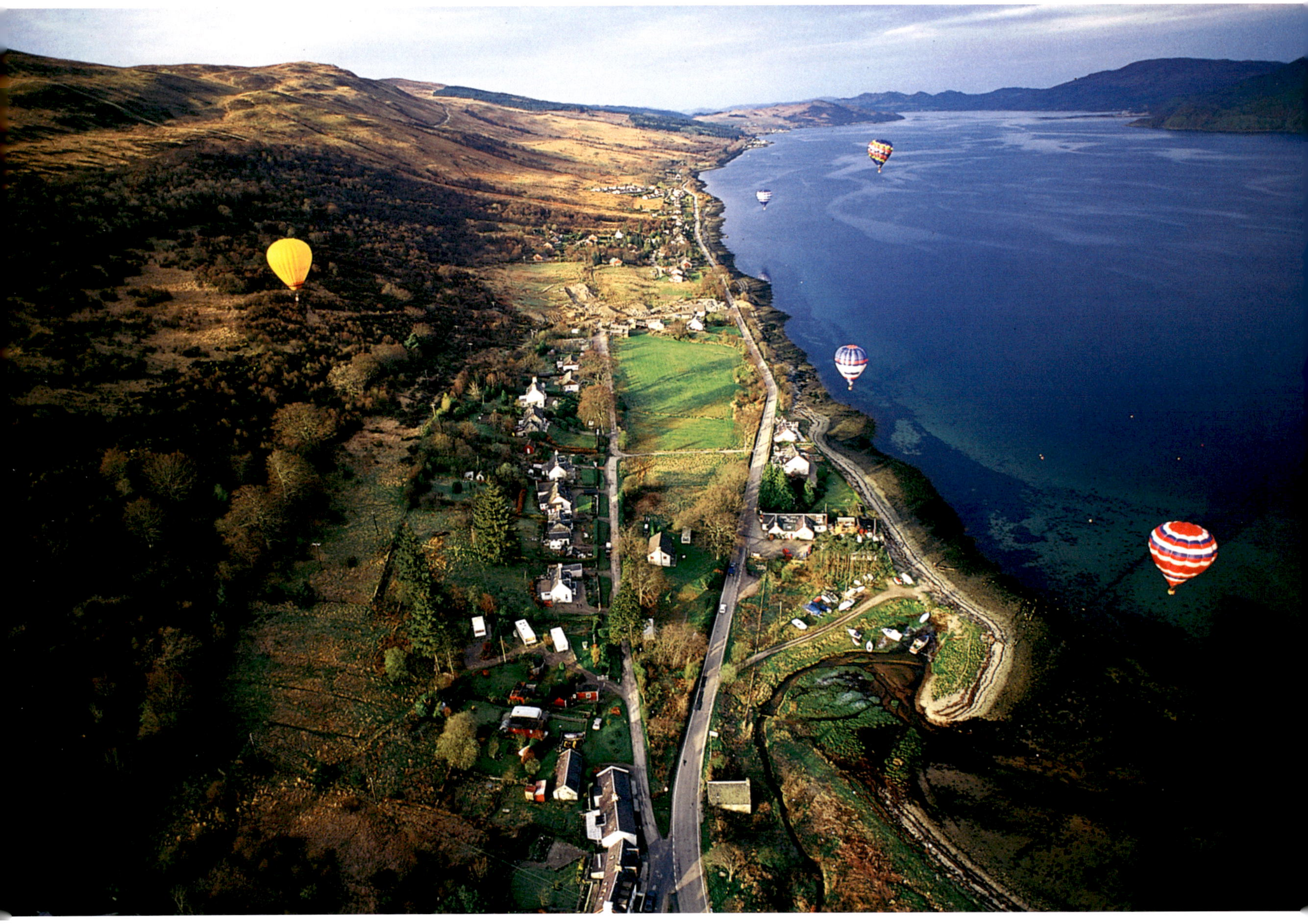

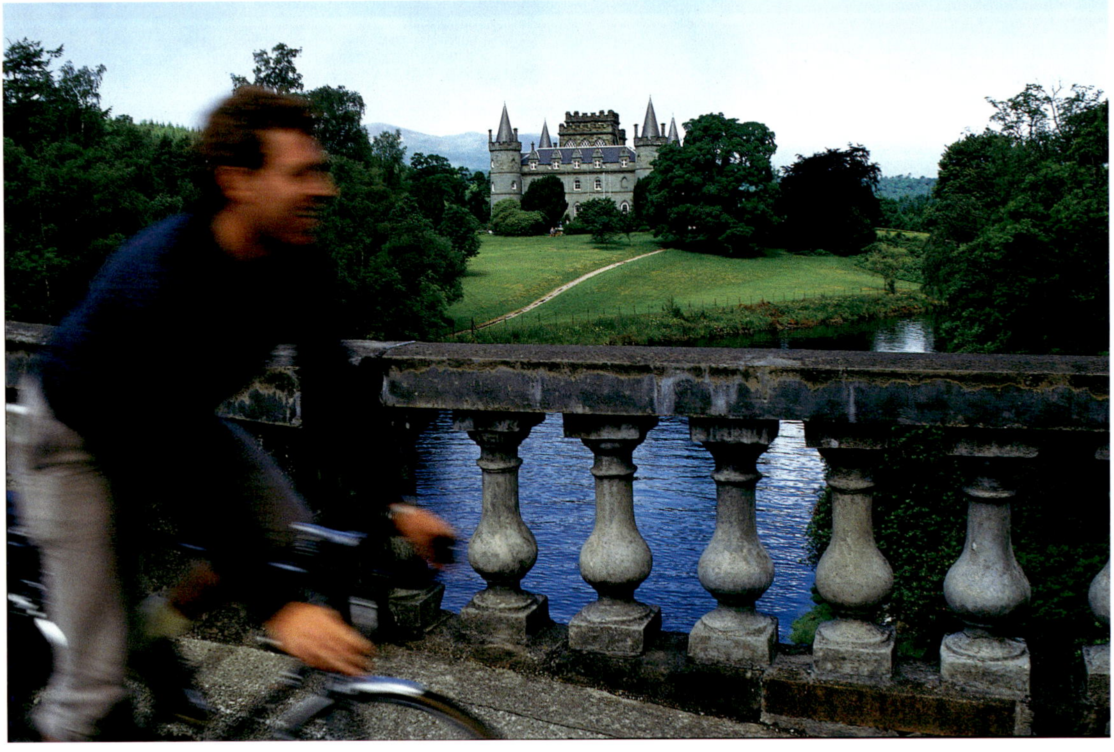

(Above) My second time photographing from a hot air balloon was above Loch Fyne in the 1990s. When we landed, I had to jump out and grab an anchor line; a gust of wind twisted the rope around my leg and I was lifted several feet off the ground. Later I recognised something of this in the opening chapter of Ian McEwan's novel *Enduring Love*.

(Right) The Highlanders march on their way to the Lonach Games in Strathdon, Aberdeenshire, and stop at seven big houses for a dram. Billy Connolly owns one of the houses, and on occasion a houseful of celebrities, such as fellow comedian and actor Robin Williams, has been known to greet the marchers.

(Left) The 18th-century Inveraray Castle is the home of the Duke of Argyll, head of the Clan Campbell. Its architecture is Gothic meets Adam. That said, the neoclassical interior's tapestries, period furniture and porcelain (not to mention Rob Roy's sporran and dirk handle) make for an interesting visit.

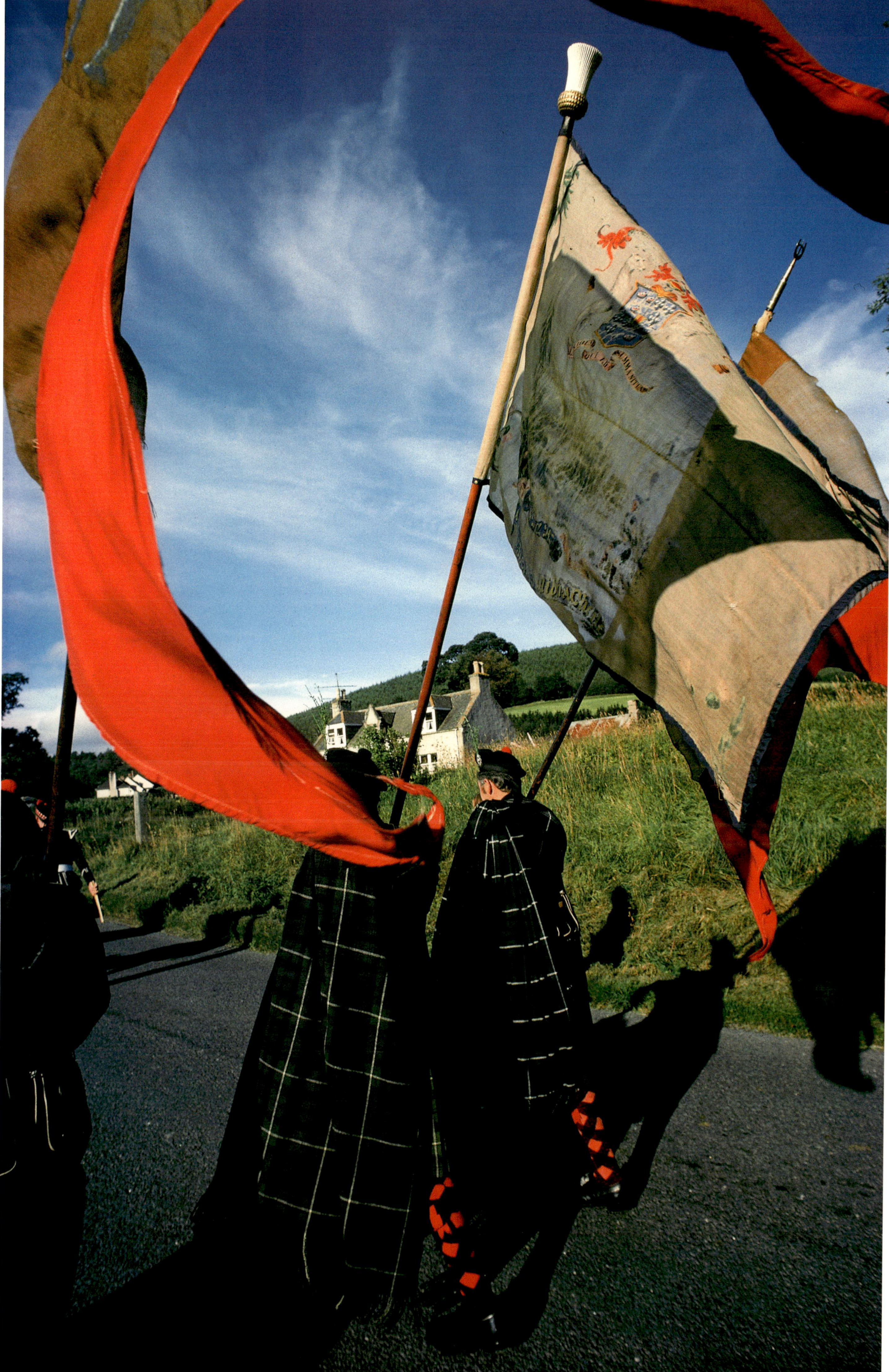

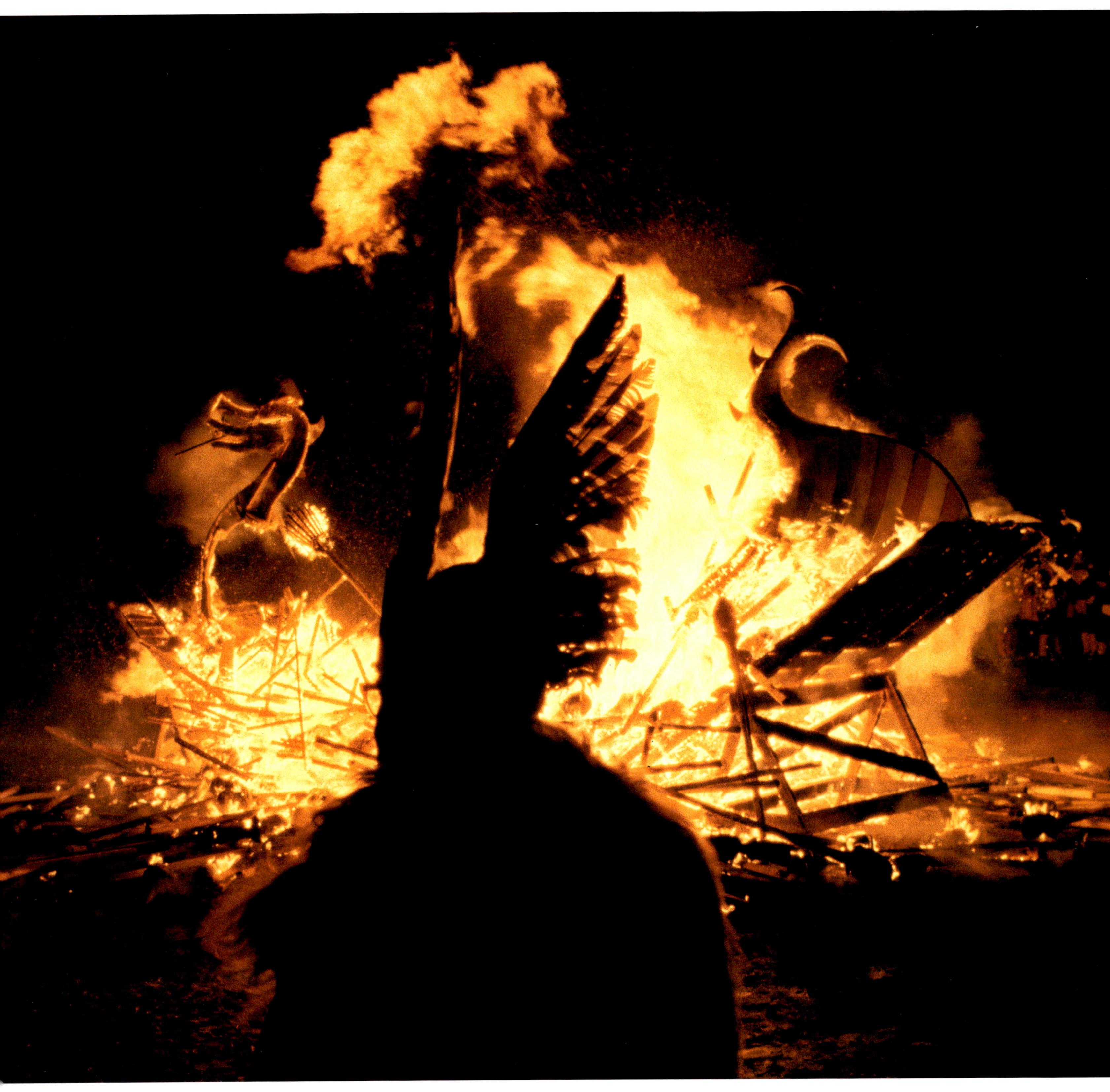

Up Helly A is a Viking midwinter festival in Shetland where a full-size replica long boat is burned. I felt it was more of a local event than for tourists, even though it is one of the most spectacular events in Scotland. The gangs of guisers who follow the long boat on the procession through Lerwick compete to have the best costumes and theme, and the standard is exceptionally high.

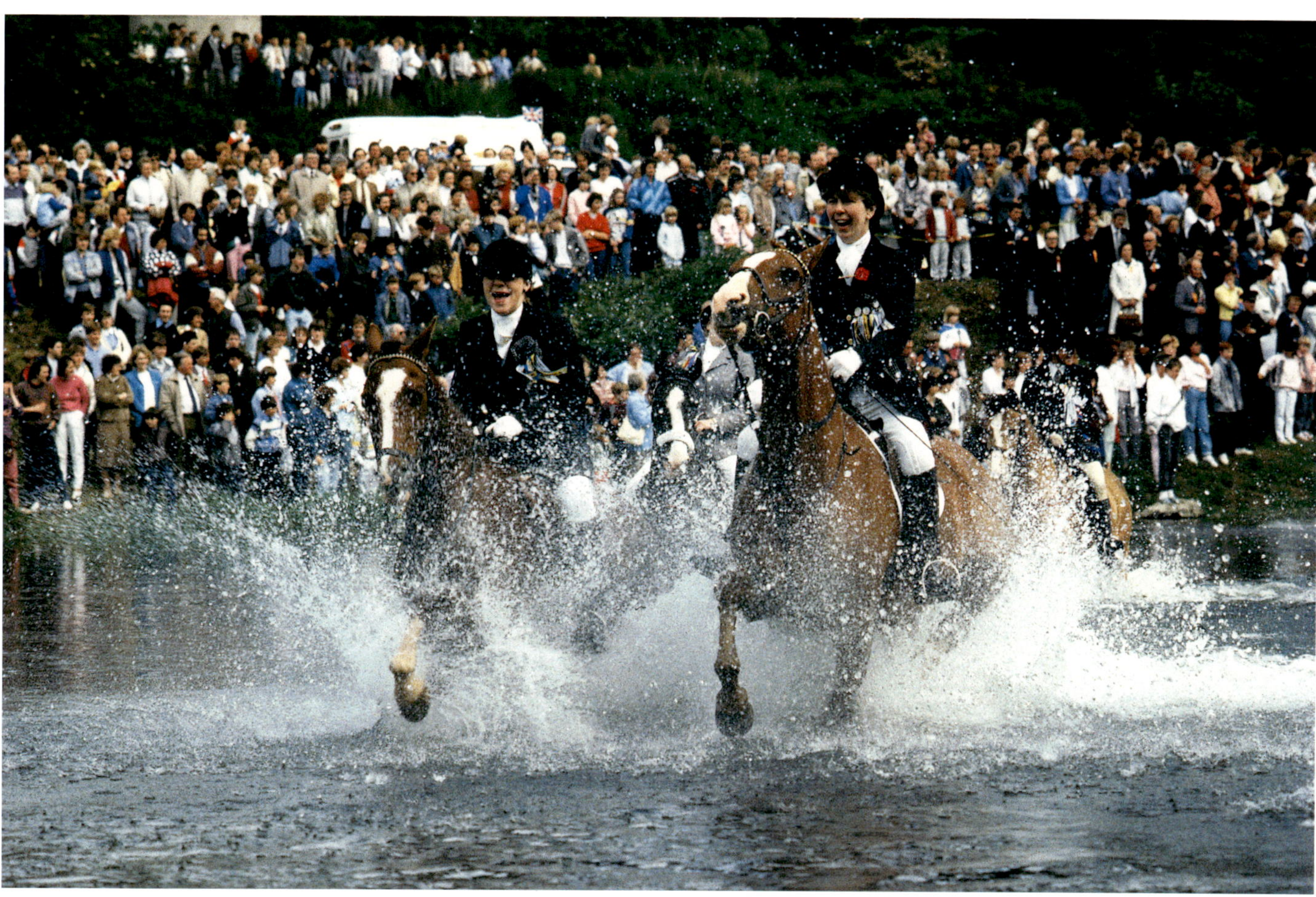

I had no idea what Riding the Marches was about, having had no experience of the Scottish Borders, until I had to photograph it for the Tourist Board. It is so much a part of Borders' life, now symbolic rather than an essential duty to perform every year, to claim the ancient boundaries. Along with rugby, the 'ride-outs' give the Borders a strong and individual identity.

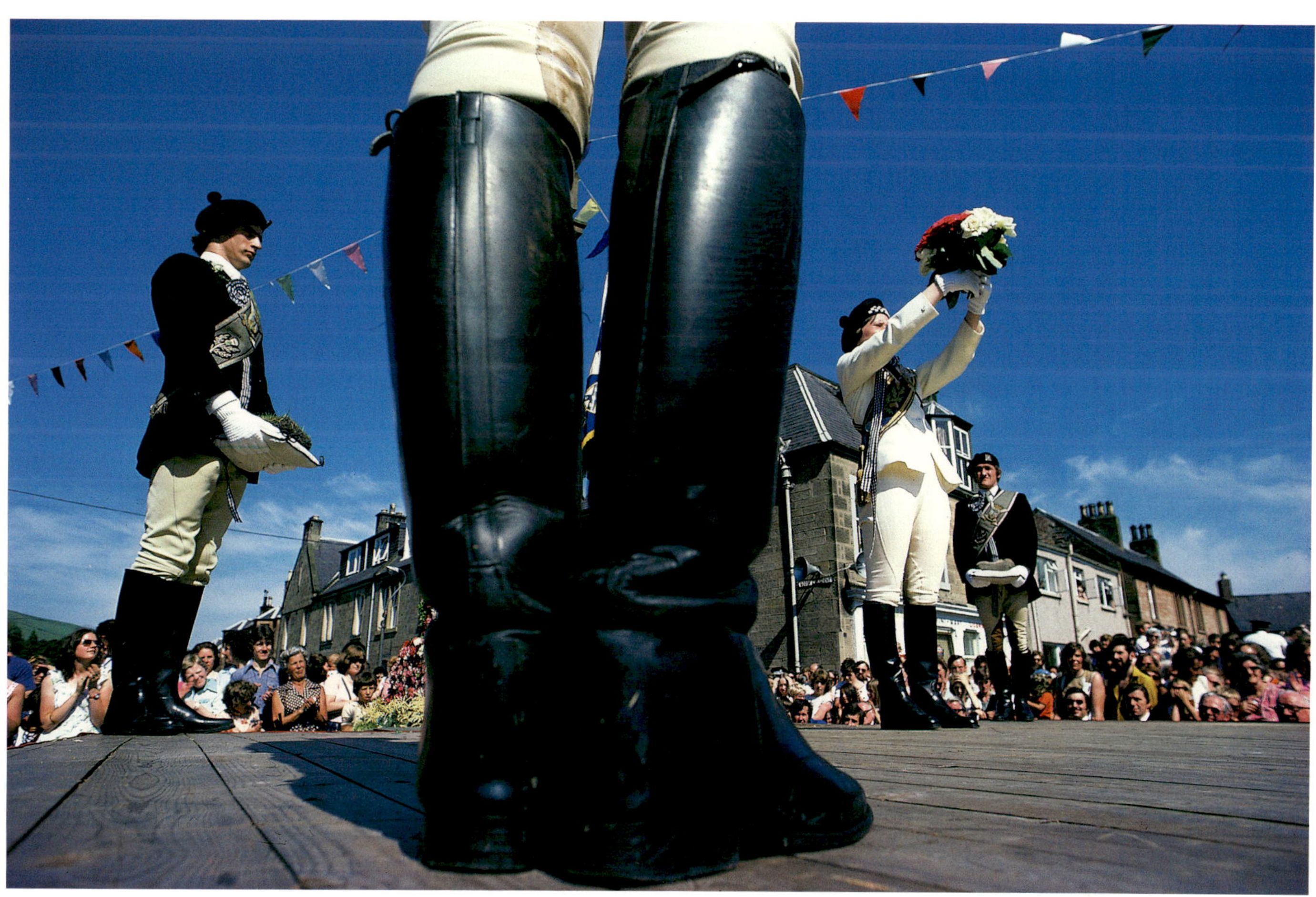

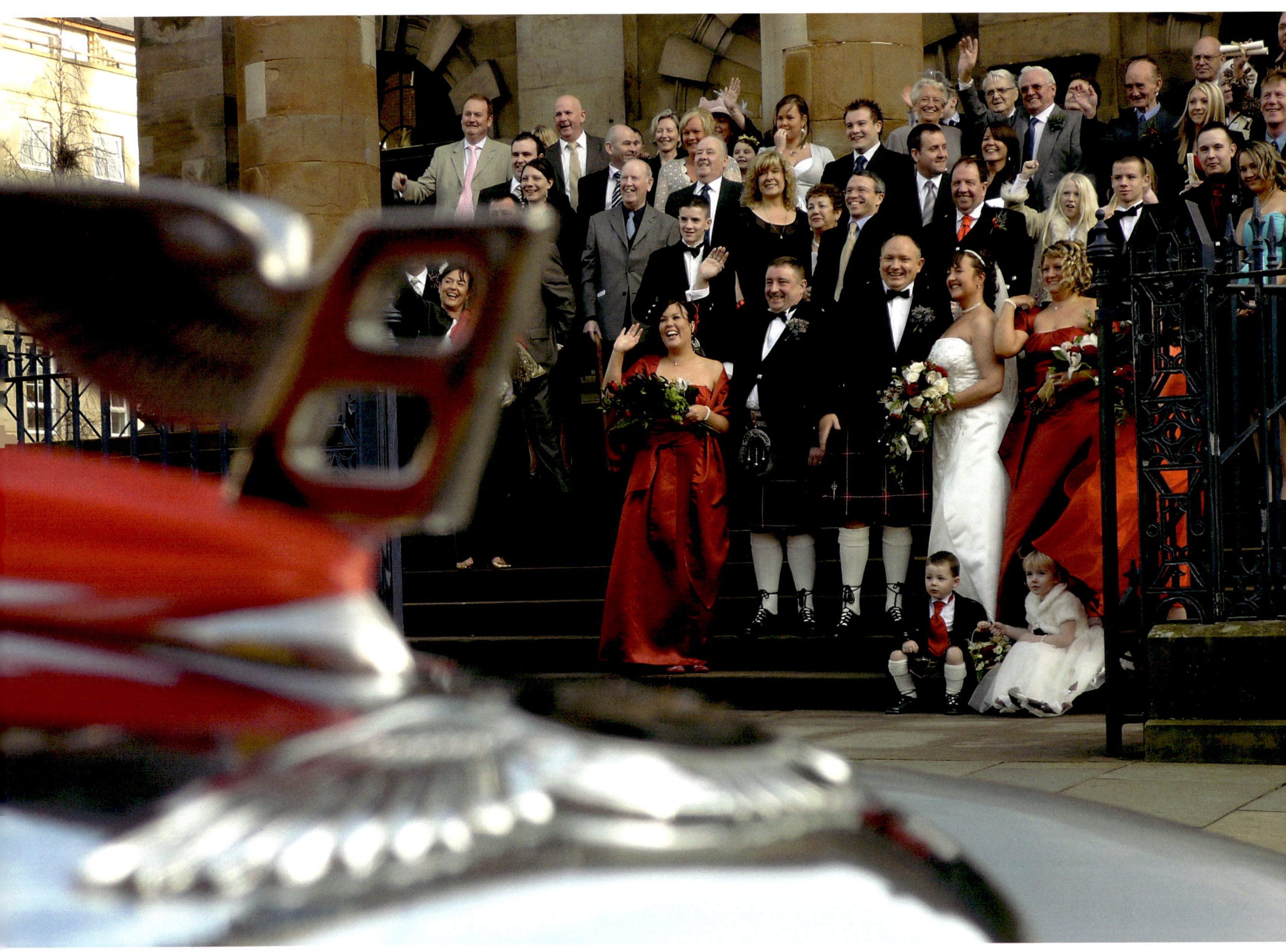

Being a wedding photographer can be a difficult and stressful job, but a wedding makes a great subject to shoot from the sidelines. Here we see a Glasgow couple who want their day to be the best – from the venue, St Andrews in the Square, a Georgian former church the design of which is based on London's St Martin in the Fields, to the vintage Bentley car. The waves from well-wishers on a passing open-topped tour bus added a nice spontaneity to an all too often formal set-up.

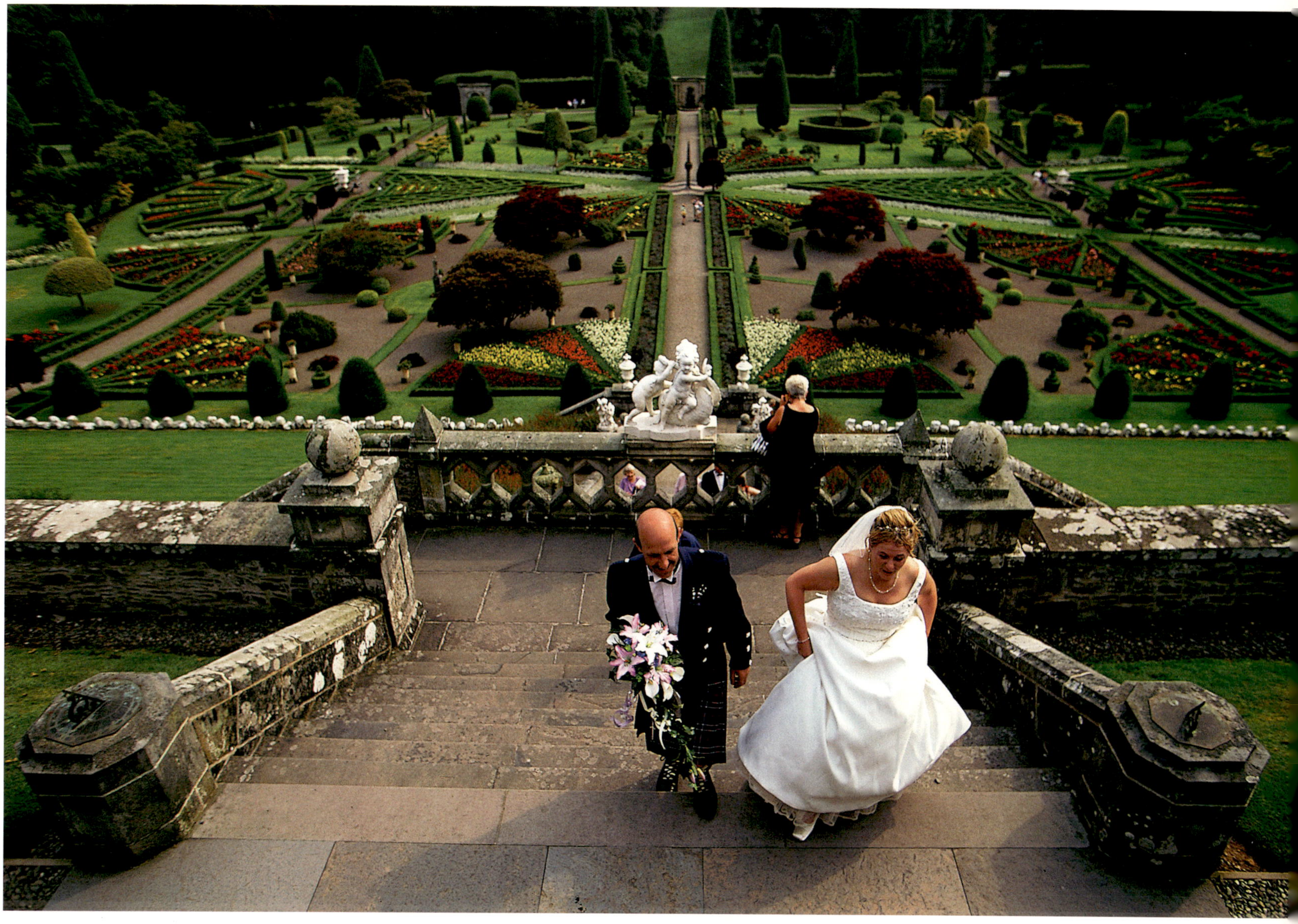

The elaborate terraces, parterres and statuary at Drummond Castle, near Crieff, make a great setting for a wedding. The formal garden was also used as a location for the film *Rob Roy*. The entrance price tariff board for the castle and gardens lists Adults, Children and, much to my approval, Super Adults (concessions for over 60s).

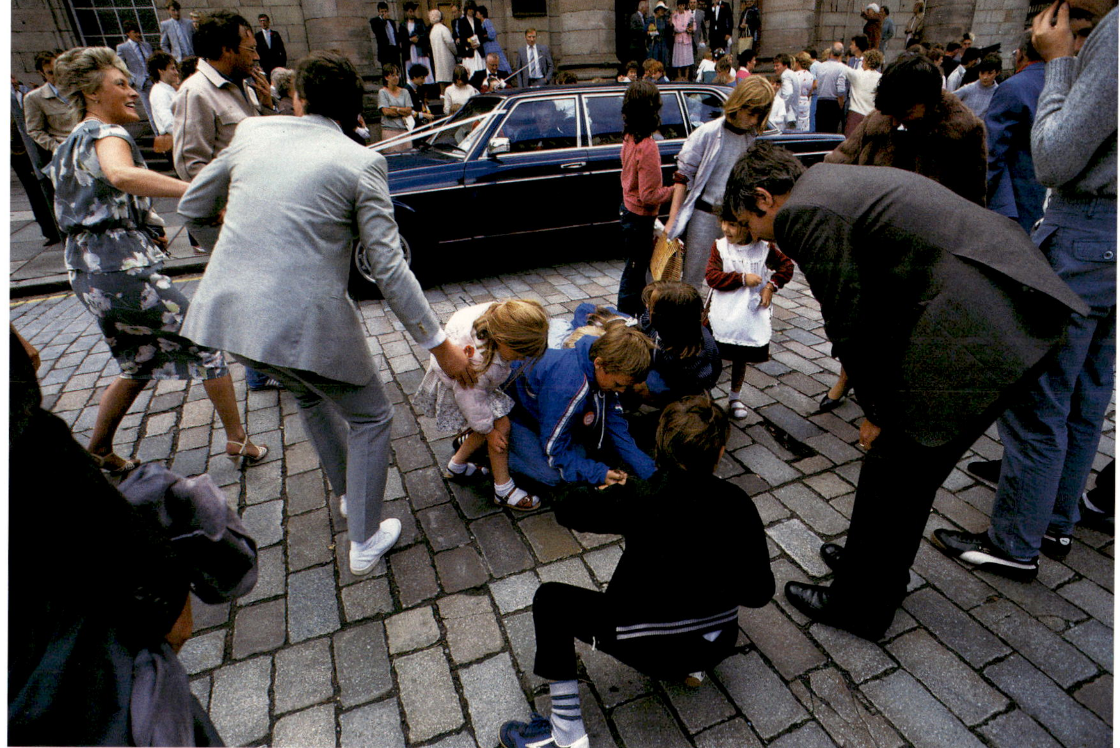

At weddings, children used to gather for a 'scramble', when the bridegroom would throw from the window of the bridal car coins ranging from pennies to half crowns. I took this shot in the 1980s in Greenock where this tradition still continued. The boy in the blue anorak seems to be doing pretty well. I wonder if they throw pound coins now.

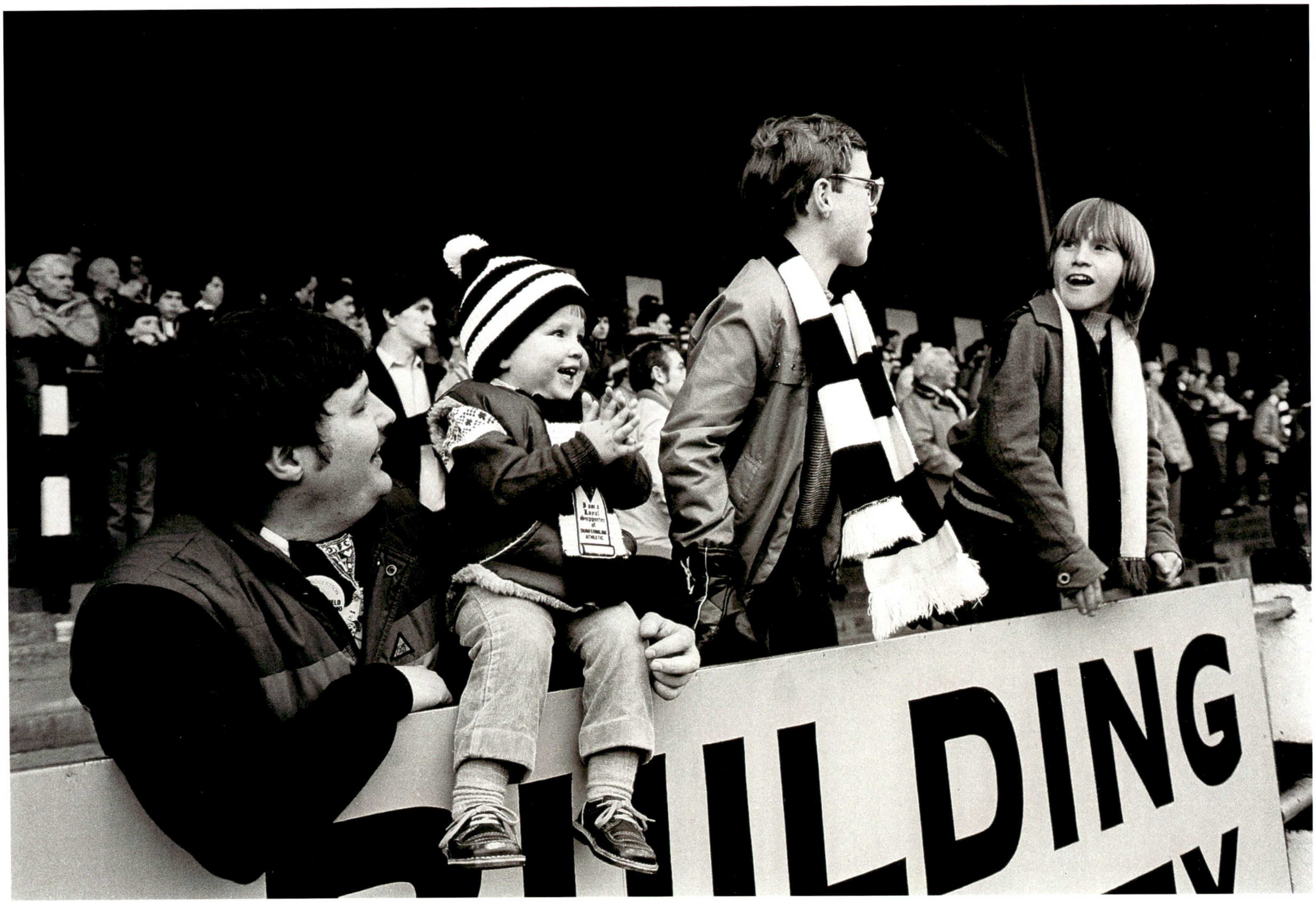

Surely this is how football should be: Dunfermline supporters in the early 1980s, a far cry from the histrionics we see today from players and fans, which add nothing to the game.

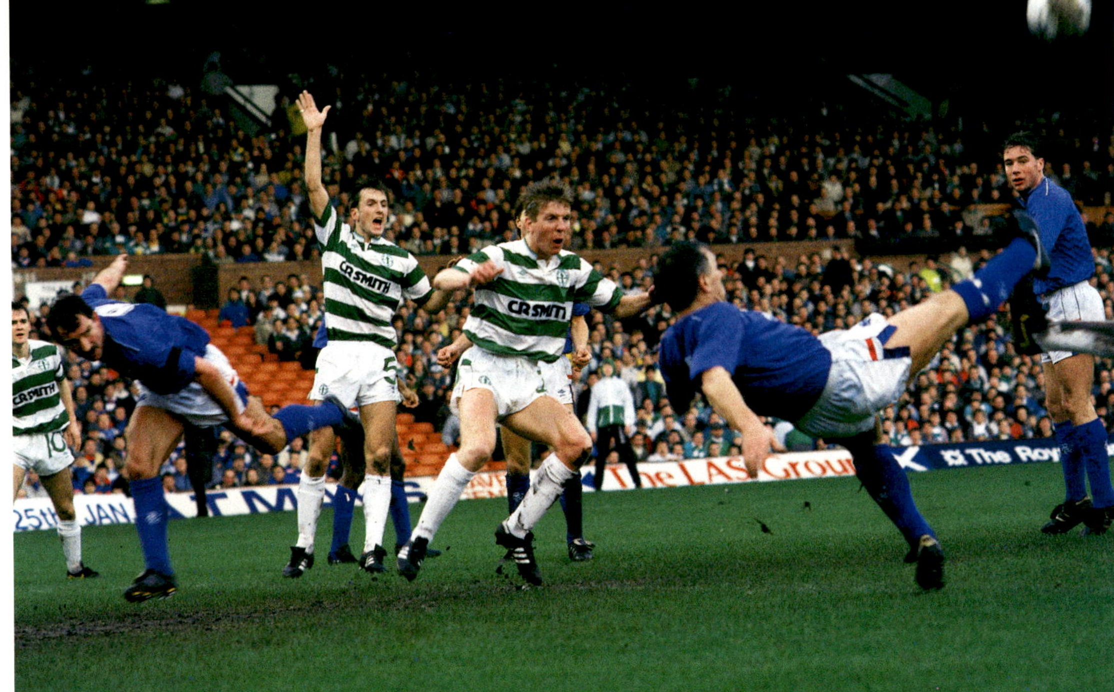

Naming the footballers for newspaper captions I found impossible and always had to rely on the knowledge of others back in the office. This Old Firm Derby on 2 January 1988 has, from left to right, Anton Rogan, Graeme Souness, Lex Baillie, Andy Walker, Graham Roberts and Ally McCoist.

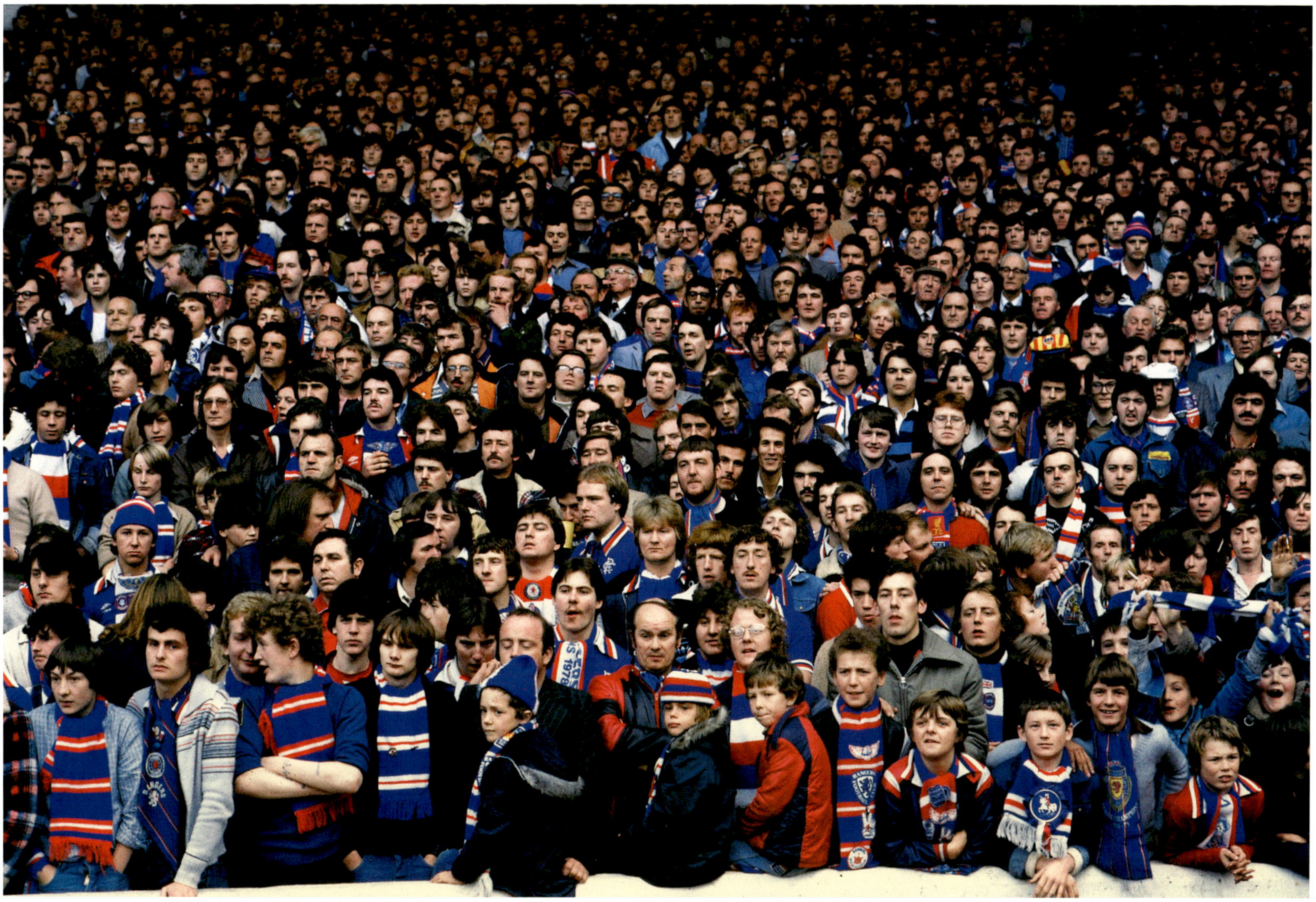

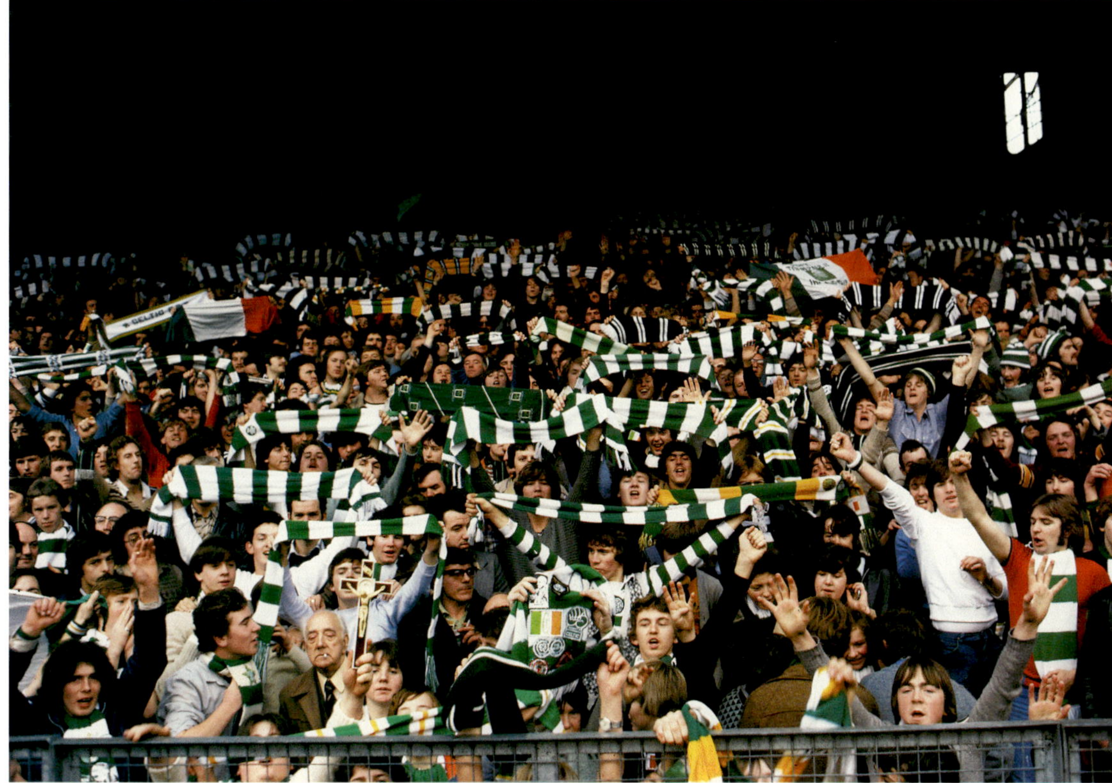

'Scotland is north and south, east and west, Rangers and Celtic,' as said by Douglas Gordon, the Glasgow-born Turner Prize-winning artist, in a television interview.

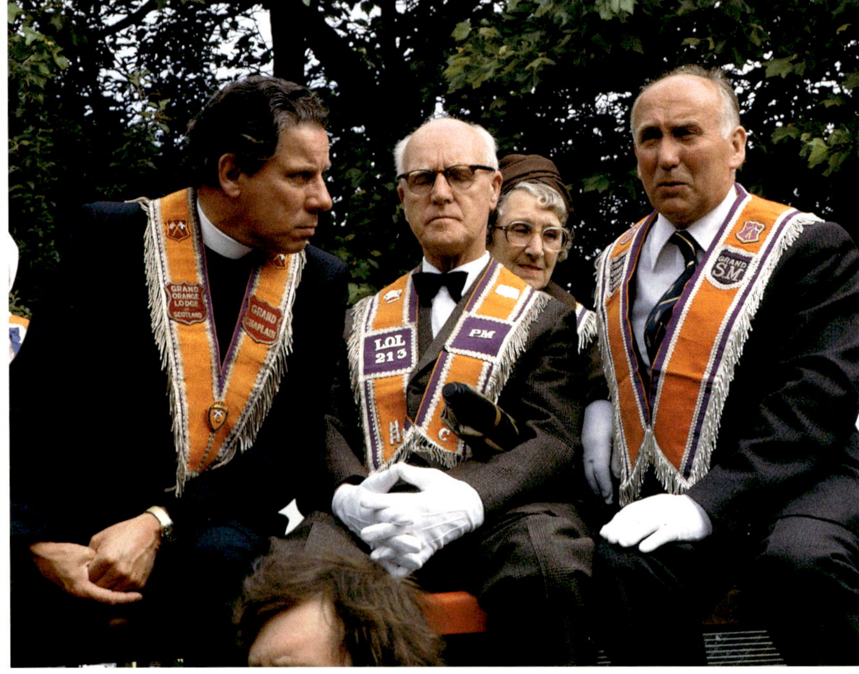

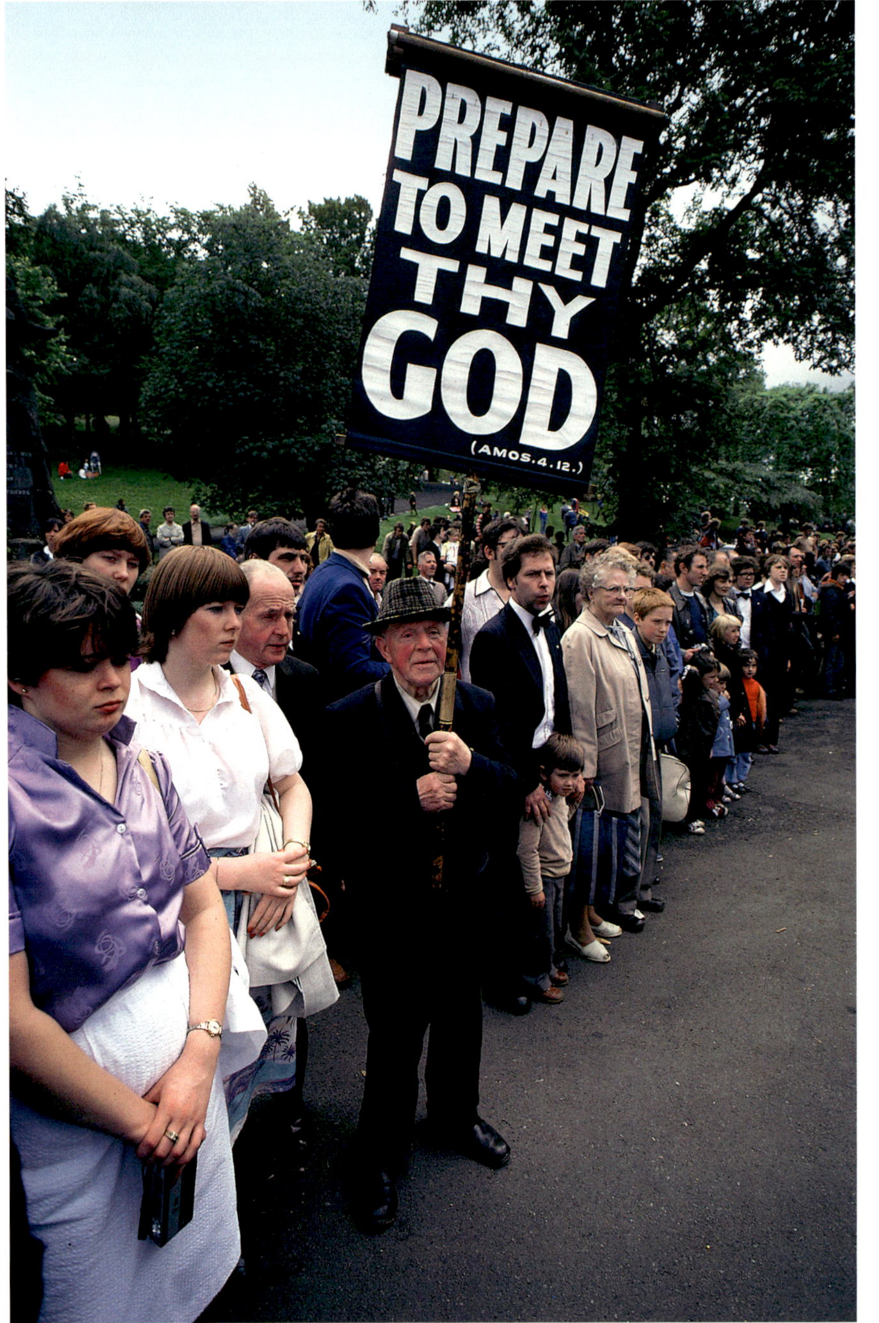

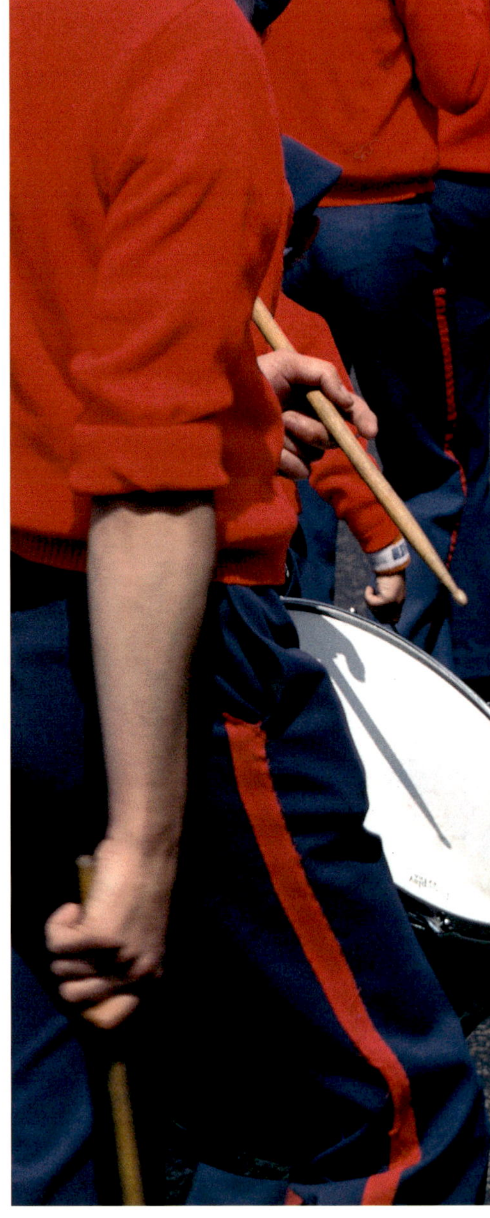

The depressing sectarian divide with all its intolerance still pervades parts of Scotland and is evident in Glasgow's annual Orange Walks. Both sides seem to rejoice in the bigotry.

(Opposite) Pope Benedict XVI, on his state visit to Britain in September 2010, passed through the neighbourhood where I have lived for thirty years. I have a very pleasant view on to the Meadows, Edinburgh's Central Park, but just two blocks down the area is less salubrious and that is what the Pope saw. The Popemobile is surrounded by establishments for gambling, exotic dancers and the 'bling' shop, appropriately named Rockman, as the first Pope was Peter, which means 'rock', and the pontiff is seen as the rock on which the church is built.

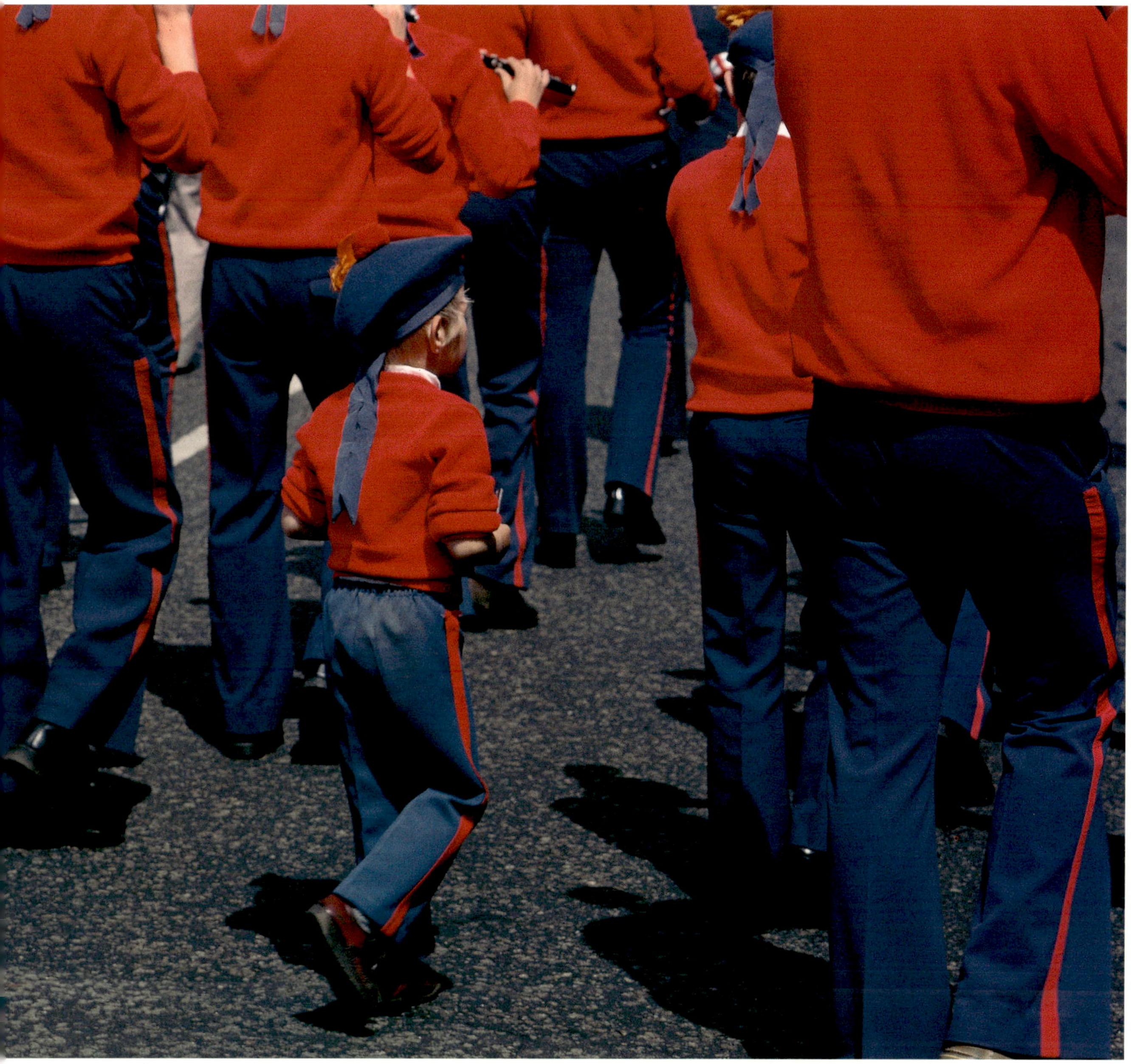

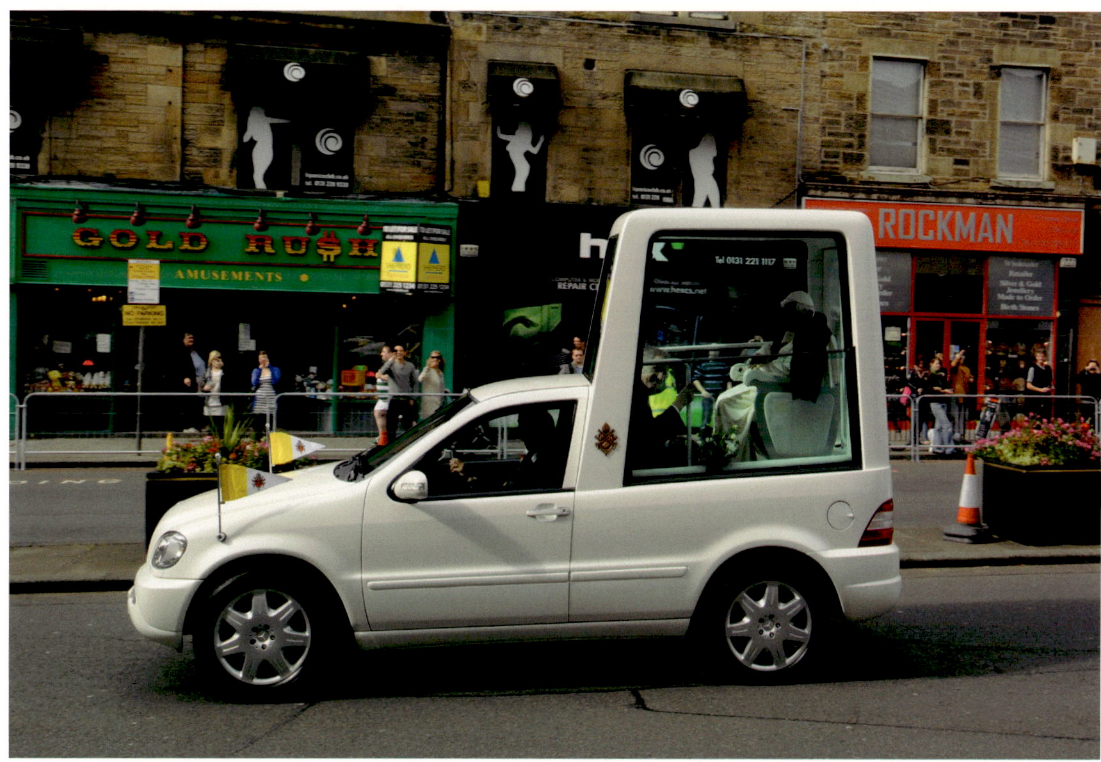
GOLD RUSH
AMUSEMENTS
ROCKMAN

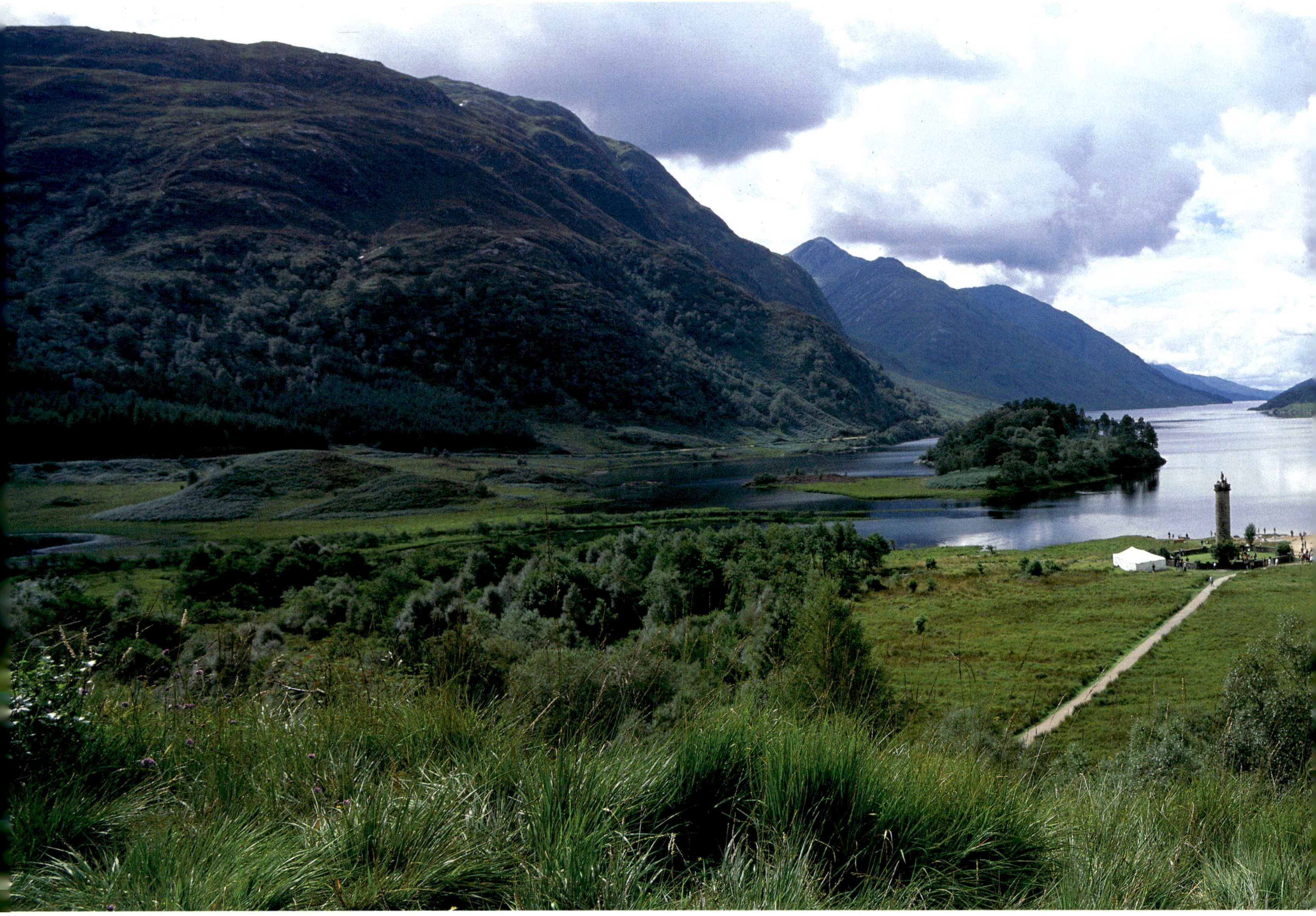

(Above) Glenfinnan is an incomparable site for holding a Highland Games. Hasselblad, the maker of the Rolls Royce of cameras and of the one taken to the Moon, used this as part of an international advertising campaign. I had taken this picture using their latest panoramic model in the 1990s. While on a job in New York it was good to see my image displayed prominently as a poster in a camera shop that I had hired my lighting from.

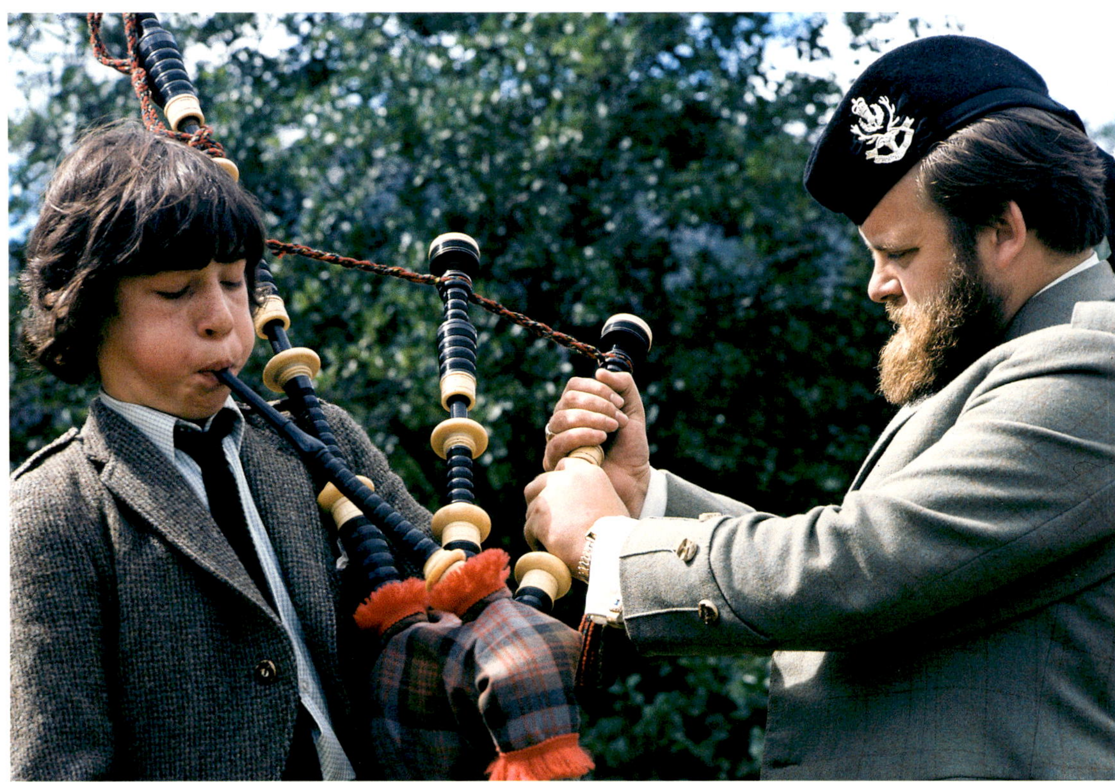

(Right) Tuning up (is this my shortest caption?)

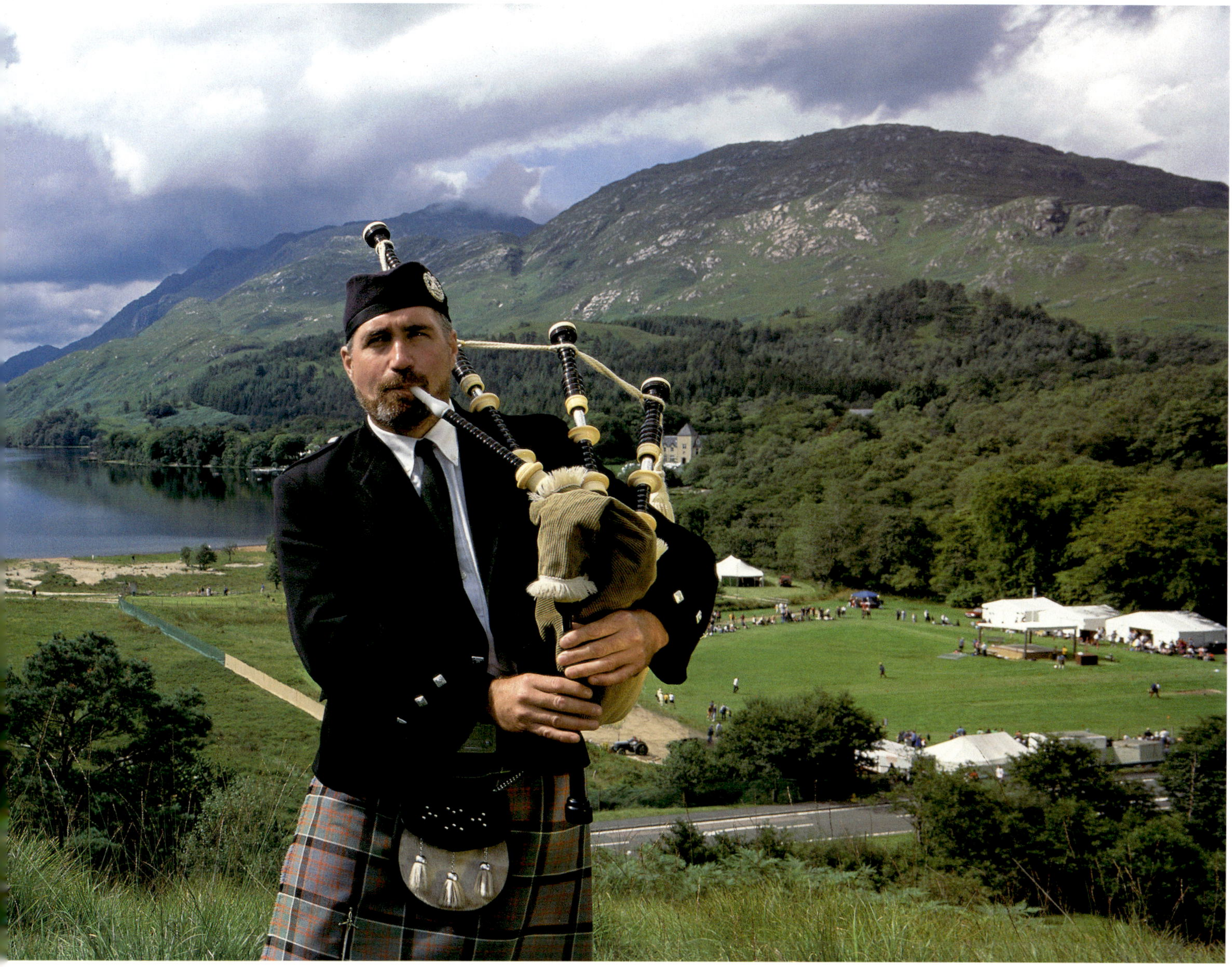

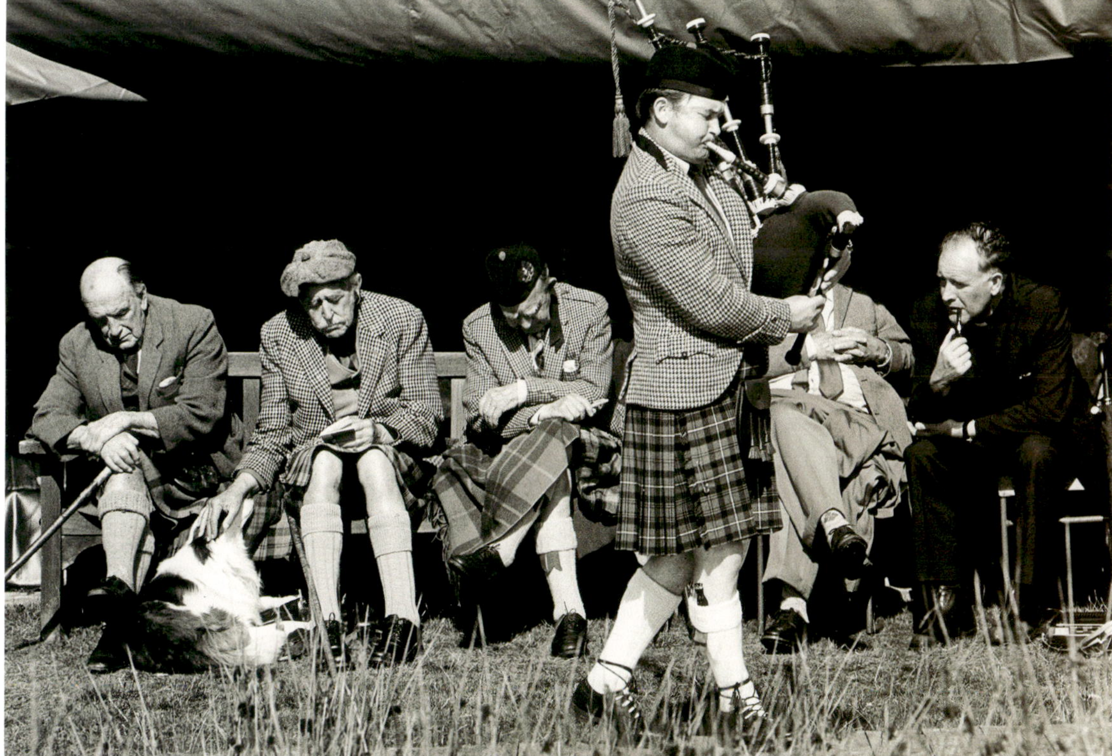

(Left) The pibroch is a complex form of bagpipe music that is difficult for the average person to follow. It can be a contemplative sound and it may enable you to get in touch with a deeper part of yourself. The judges in this competition have a sympathetic respect for the melancholic air of the piece.

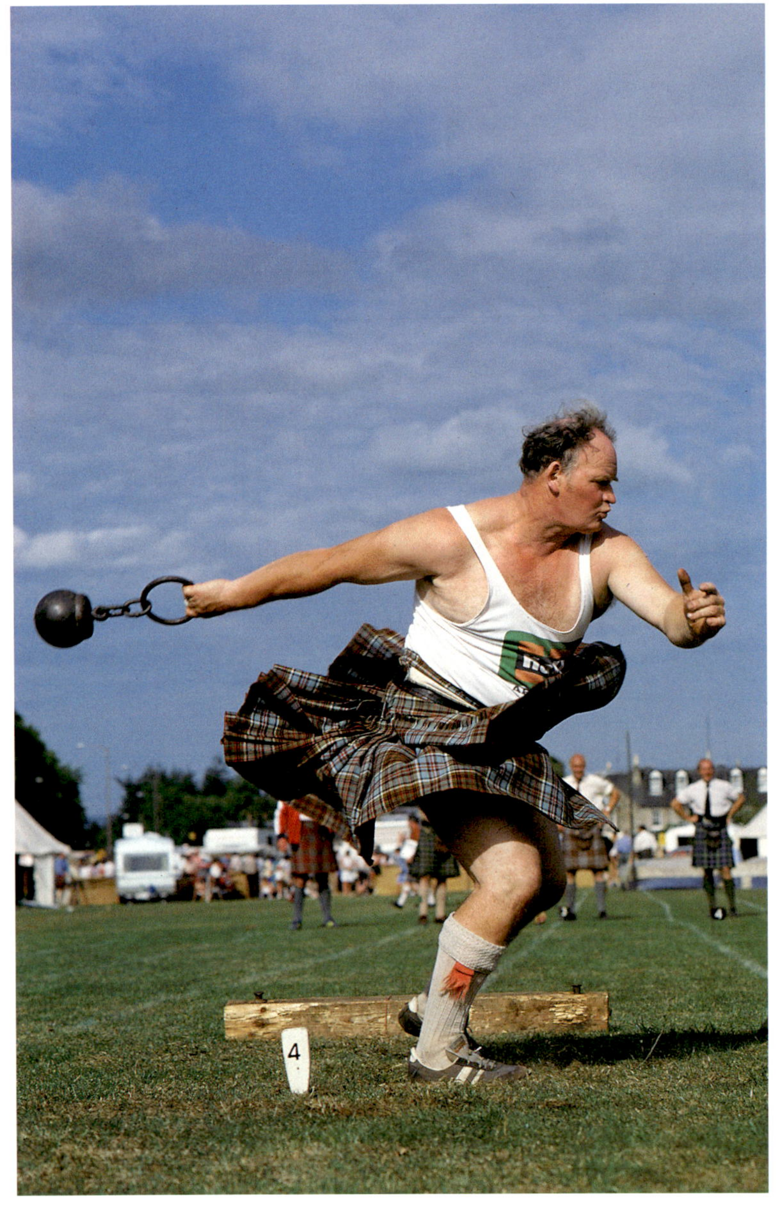

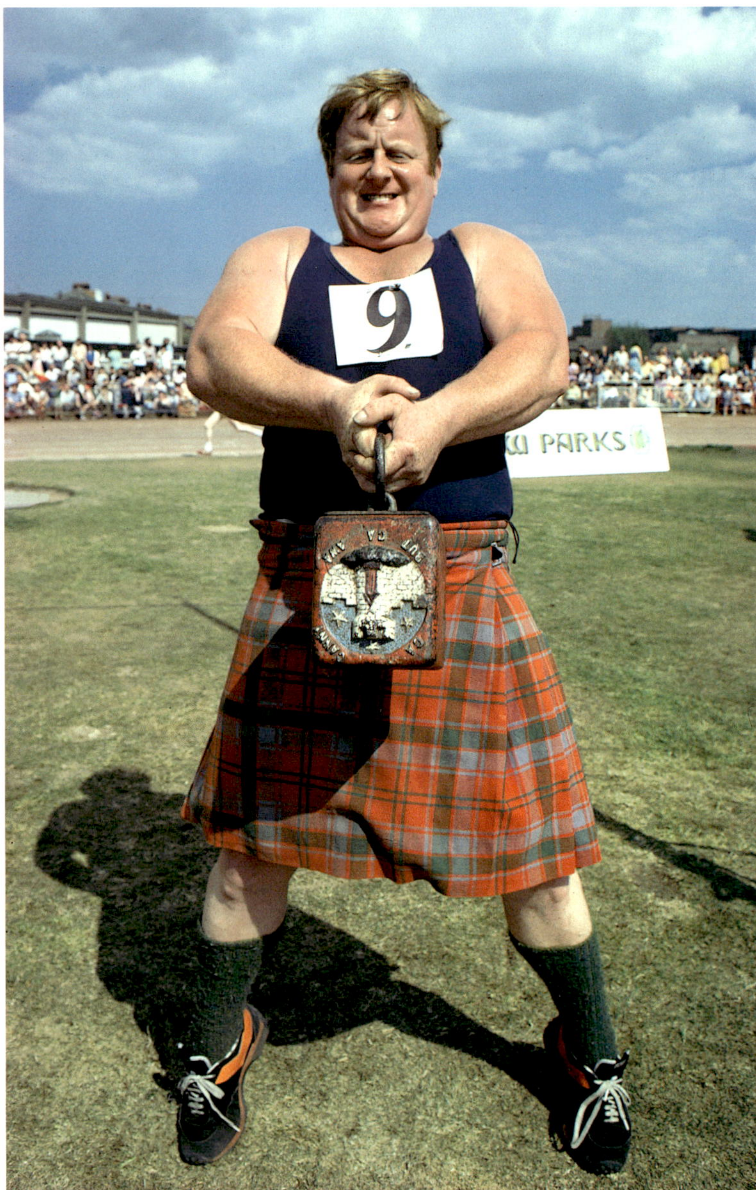

Highland Games are a great source of pictures. I have photographed many events but have never attended solely as a spectator. I often wonder how much pleasure people derive from these events, which can range from the highly commercial and tightly organised to the more homespun where the public address system goes haywire and the competition is unevenly pitched. On one occasion while I was watching a weight-throwing competition the weight came off its chain and missed my head by inches. My leap to safety brought a round of applause from the crowd.

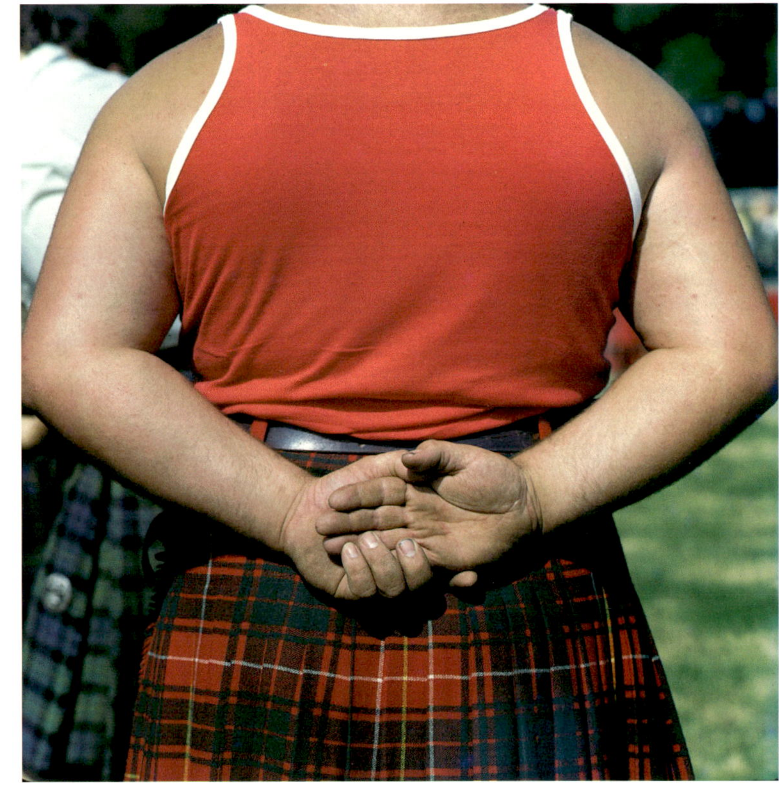

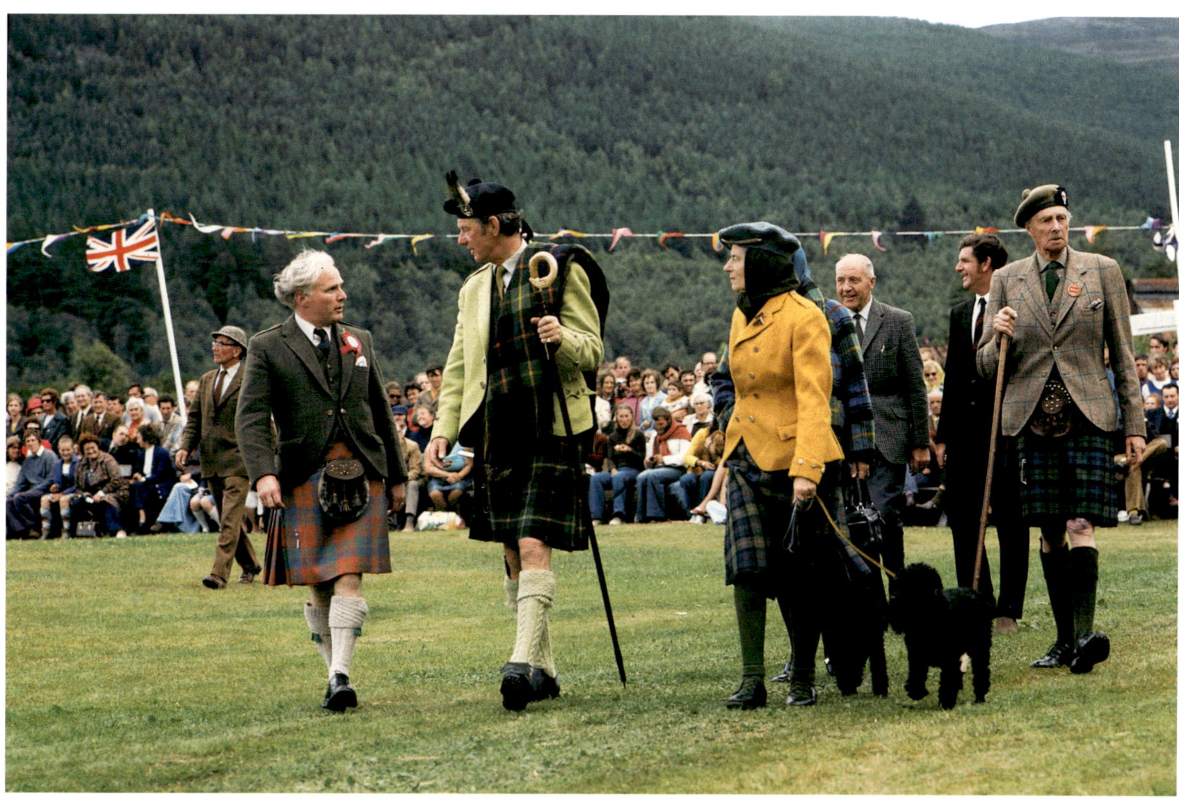

Sir Walter Scott's Highlandism and 'tartanry' is the order of the day, which can look good when it is done properly and I still unashamedly fall for the whole invention. Isn't every human activity an invention?

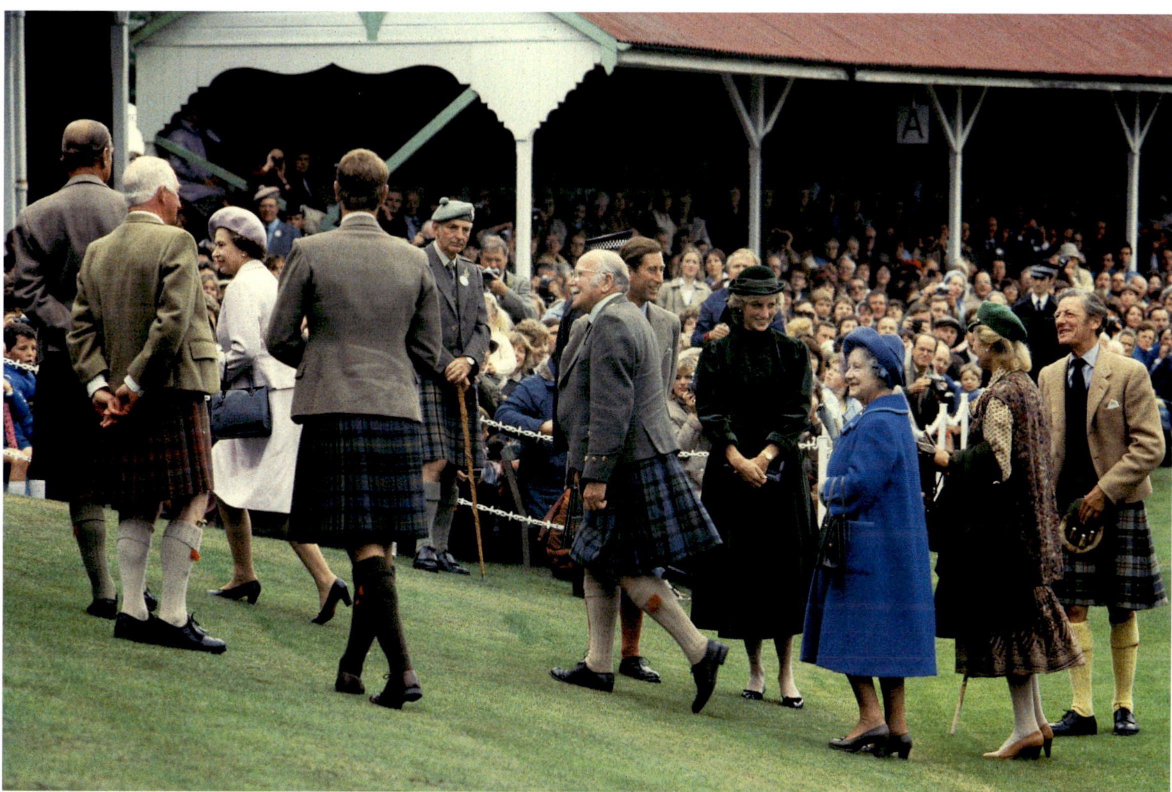

It has been said that Her Majesty the Queen is never happier than when she is on holiday in Balmoral, and Prince Charles says it is his favourite place on Earth. The royal party attends the Braemar Highland Games in the afternoon – in this case in the 1980s – when the main activity is saved for the period between their arrival and departure. Similarly, the smell of fresh paint is prominent at a lot of Her Majesty's engagements.

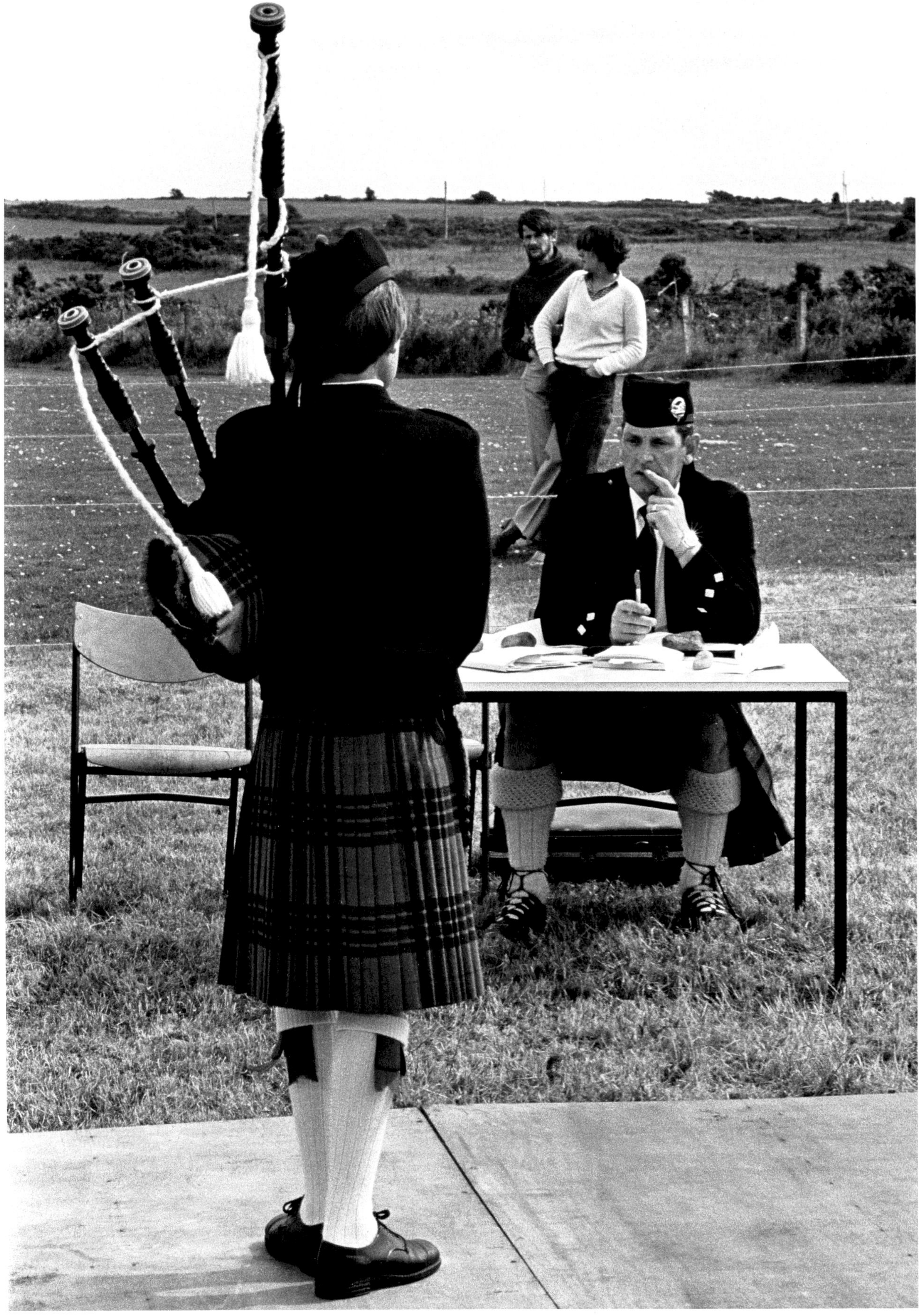

This competitor in the 1980s does not have a large audience and the judge's papers are held down by a stone as it was obviously windy. If this young piper was judged for being perjink (smartly turned out) he would score highly.

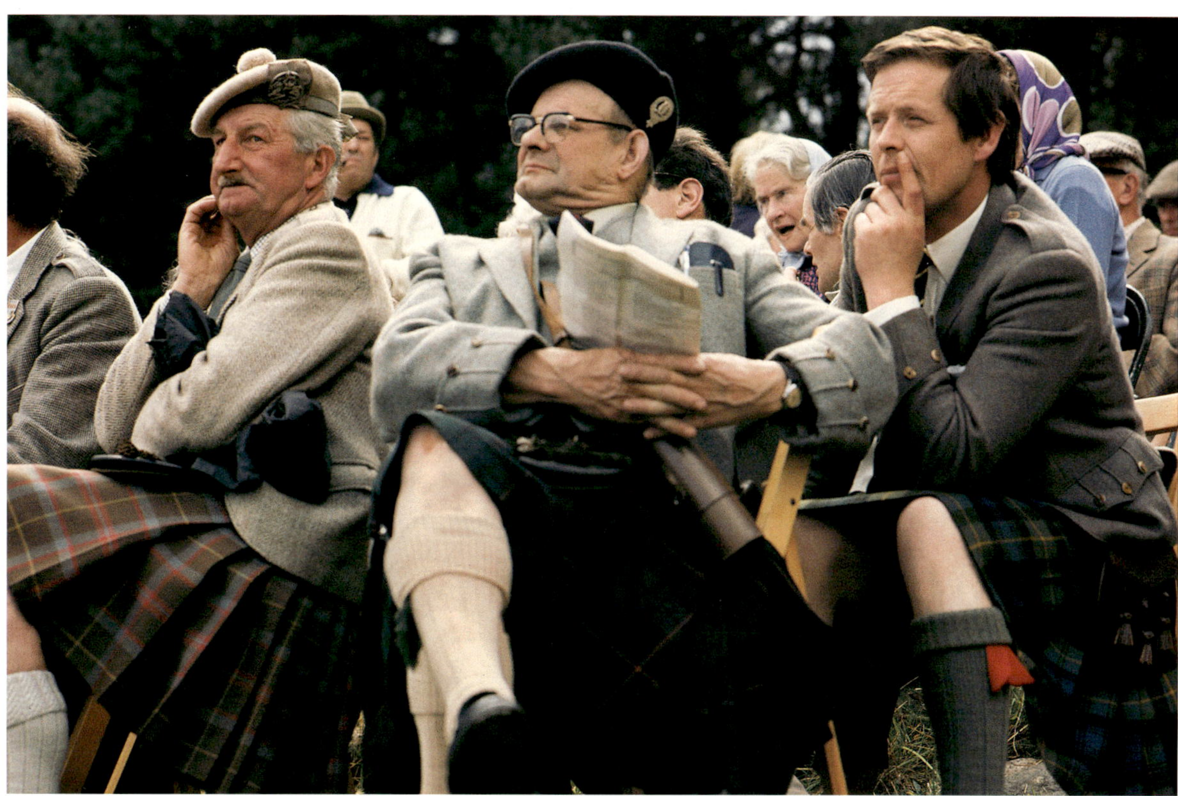

The intensity on the faces of these gentlemen emphasises a knowledge and expertise of the games.

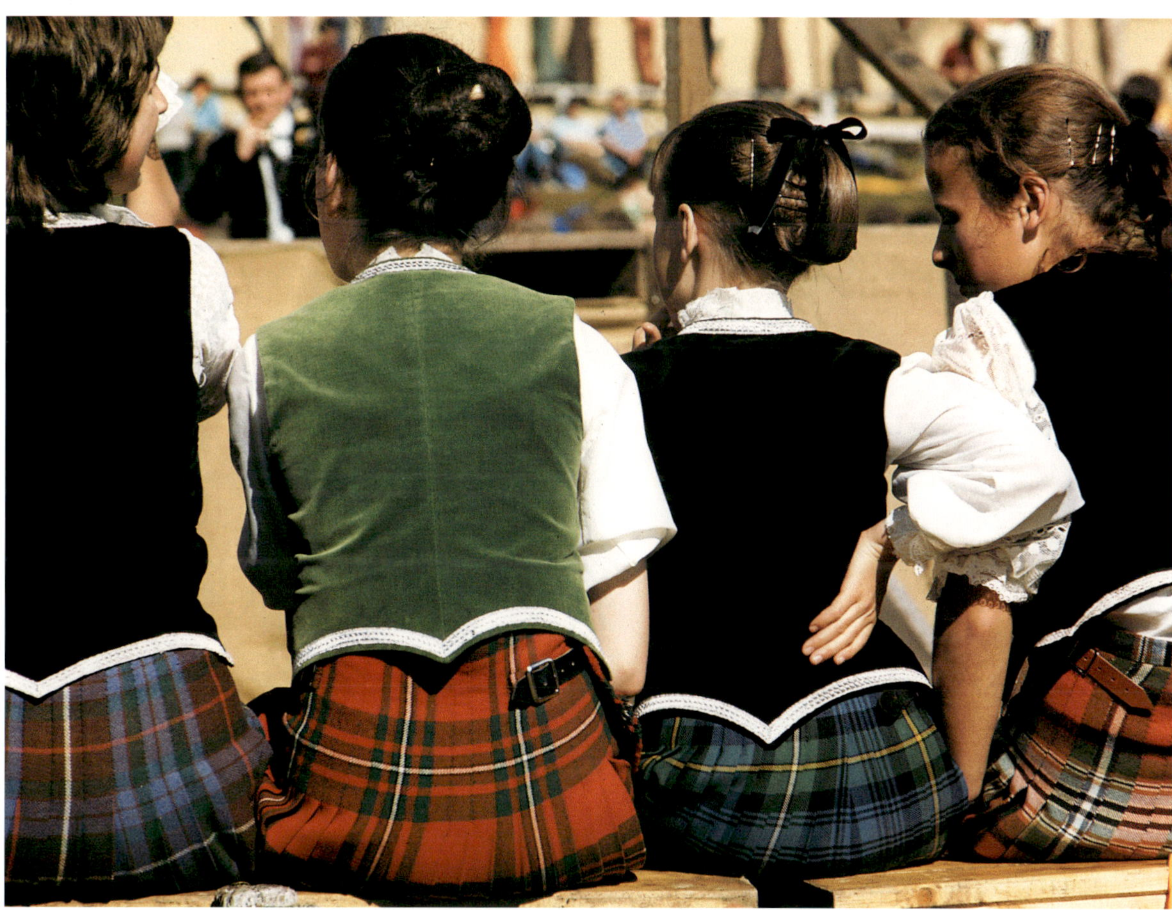

Looking at the competition, these young Highland dancers at Glenfinnan size up their rivals in the Highland fling, the sword dance or the hornpipe. They sometimes display more medals than certain nations' military top brass.

These young boys have various ideas about the length of their kilts, but when you give off signals of a more urgent need, like the boy on the right, what's his priority?

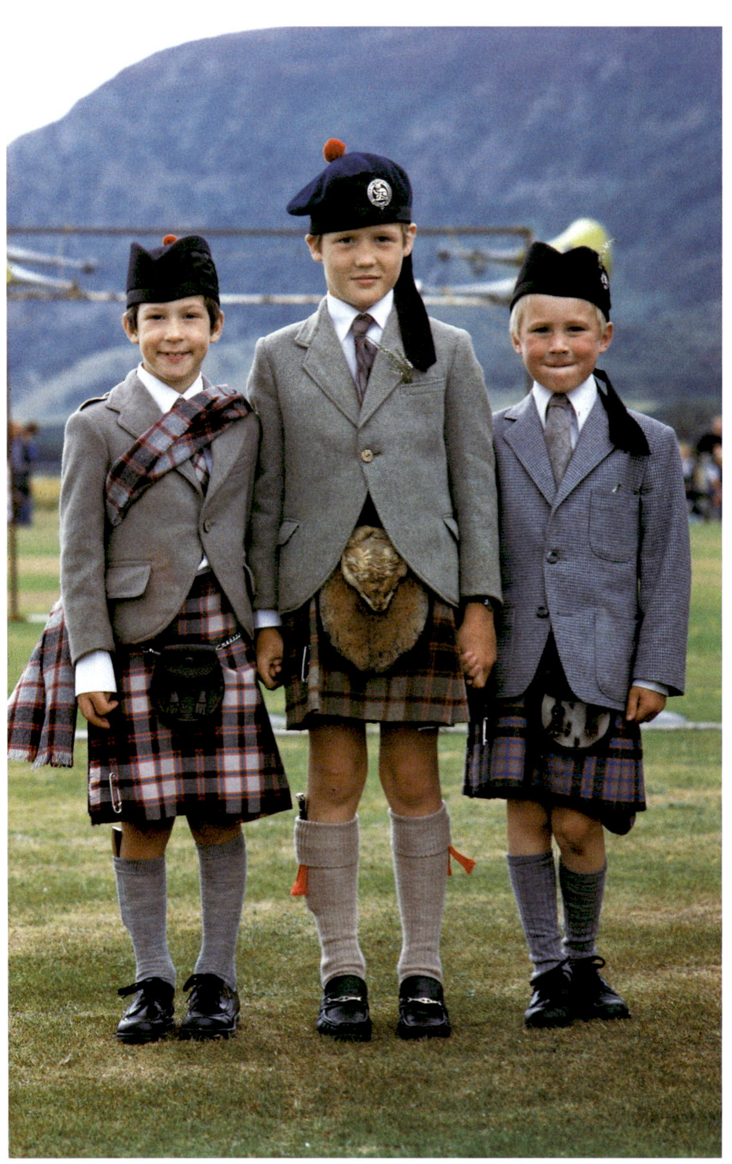

Lisle-style stockings are de rigueur for this lady at Inveraray Highland Games.

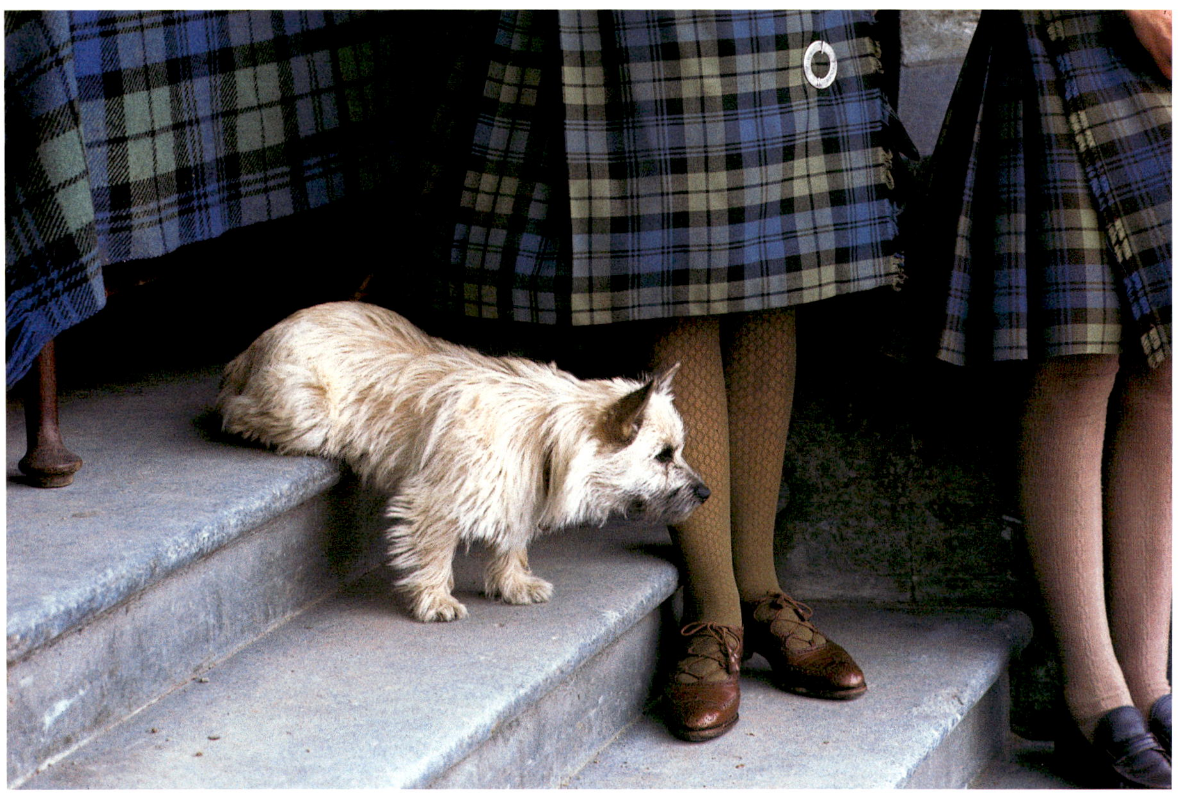

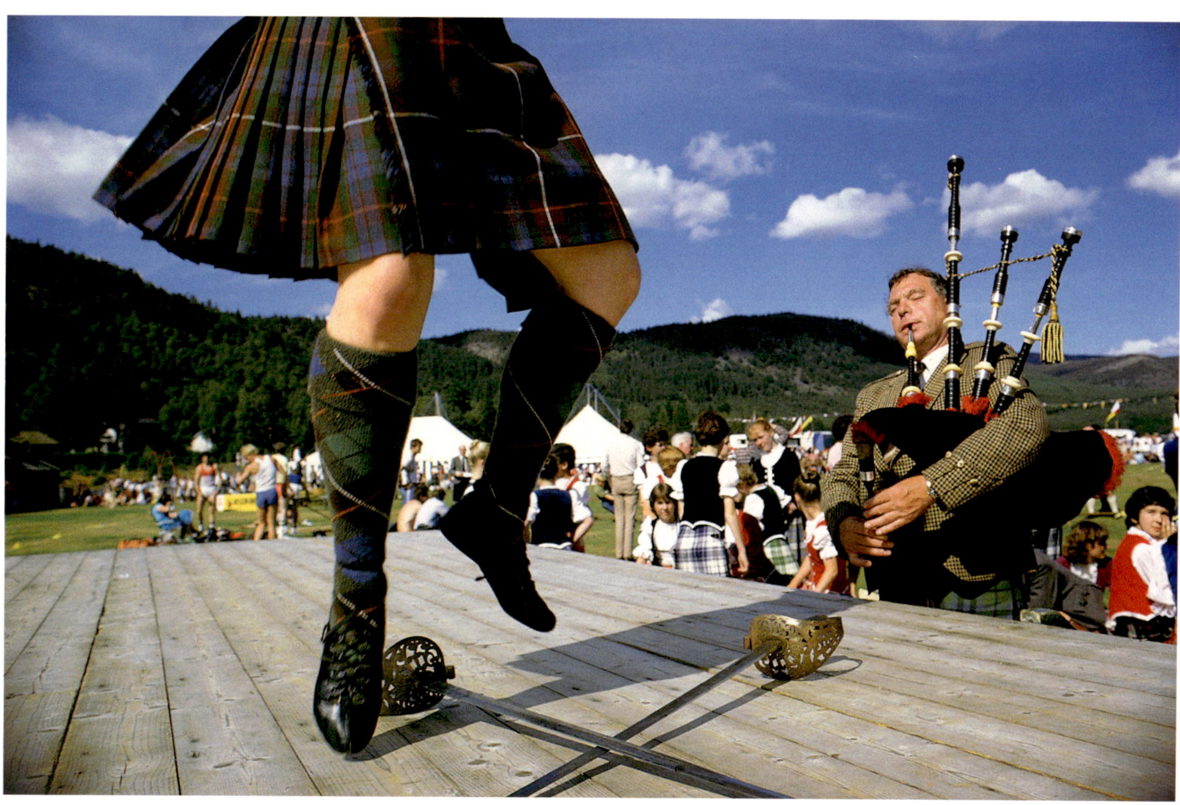

Solo Highland dancing goes back to antiquity but until 1900 it was only boys who entered dance competitions. Now the girls far outnumber the boys.

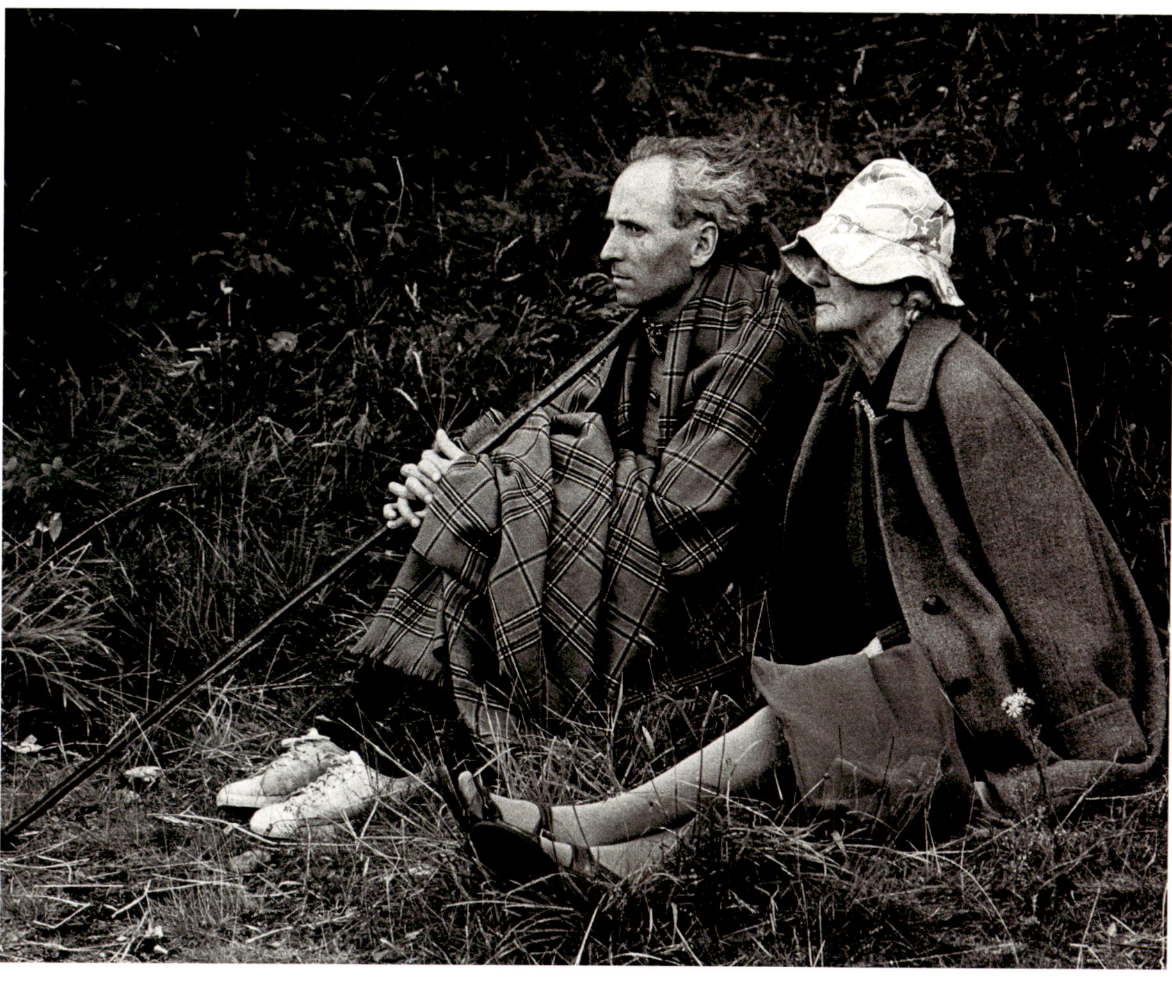

These folk photographed in the 1970s look as if they have been regulars of Highland Games over the years. The tweedy look is good and even in summer can be essential wear for the sudden squalls that our weather can bring.

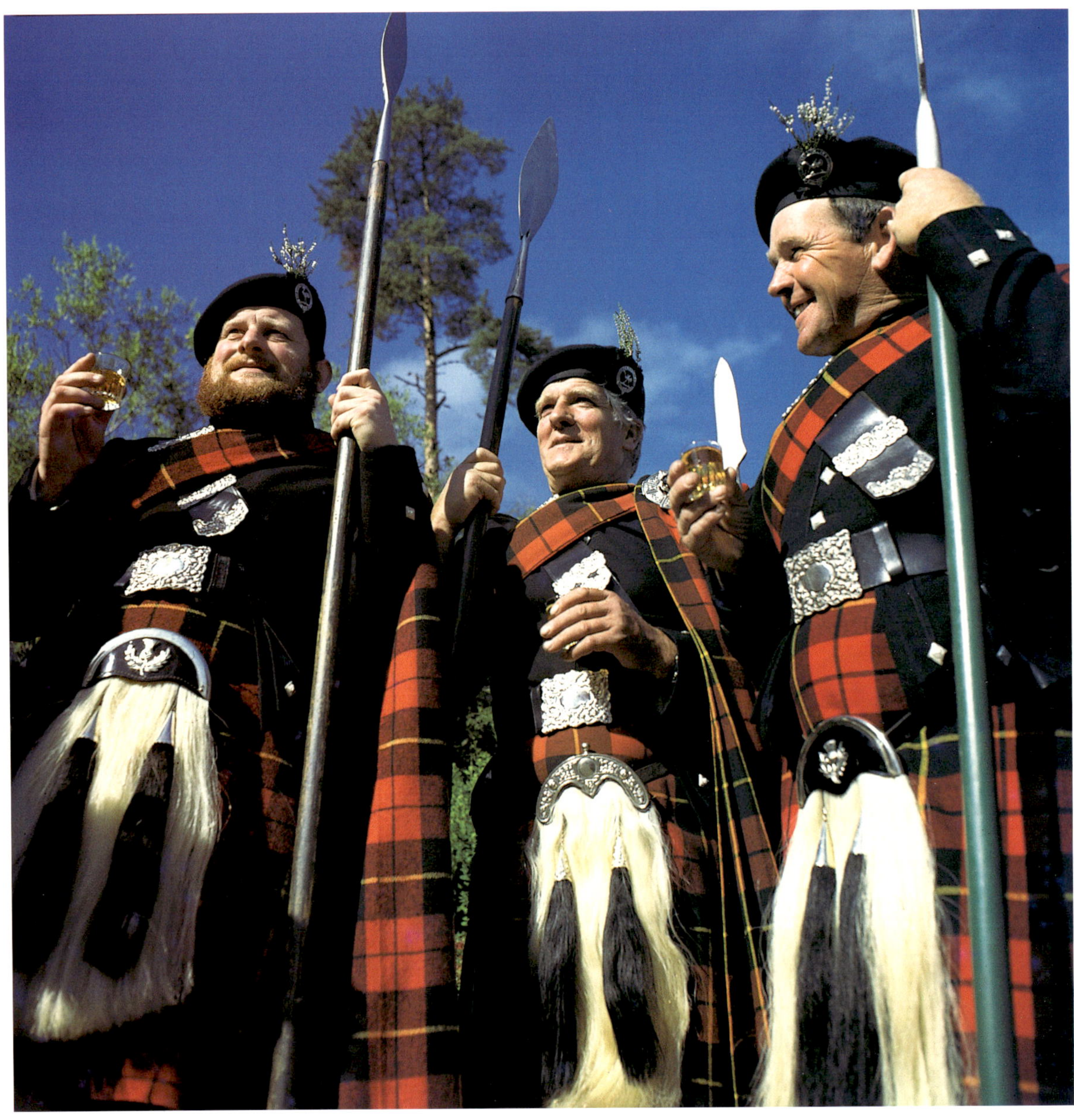

The Lonach Highlanders, Strathdon, Aberdeenshire, are a friendly society formed in 1823 to preserve Highland dress and the Gaelic language. They also promote benevolent feelings among the inhabitants of the district along with 'supporting loyal, peaceful and manly conduct'.

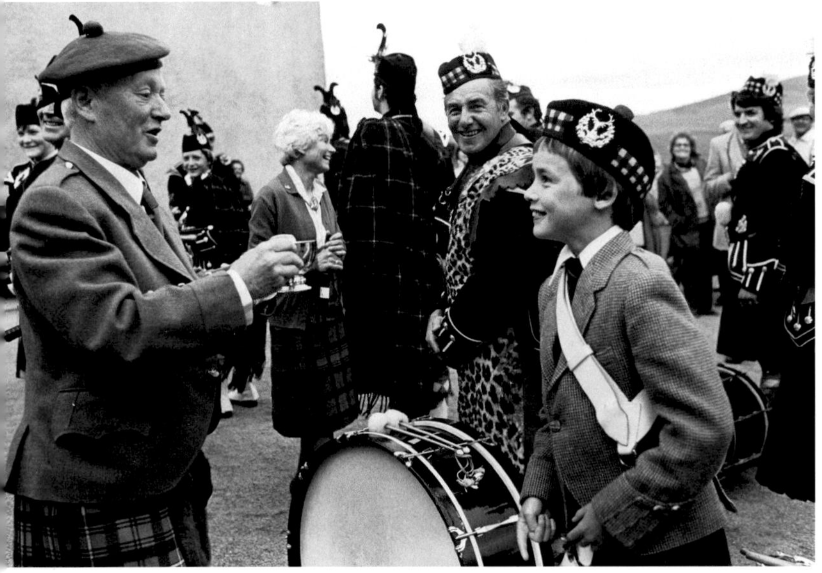

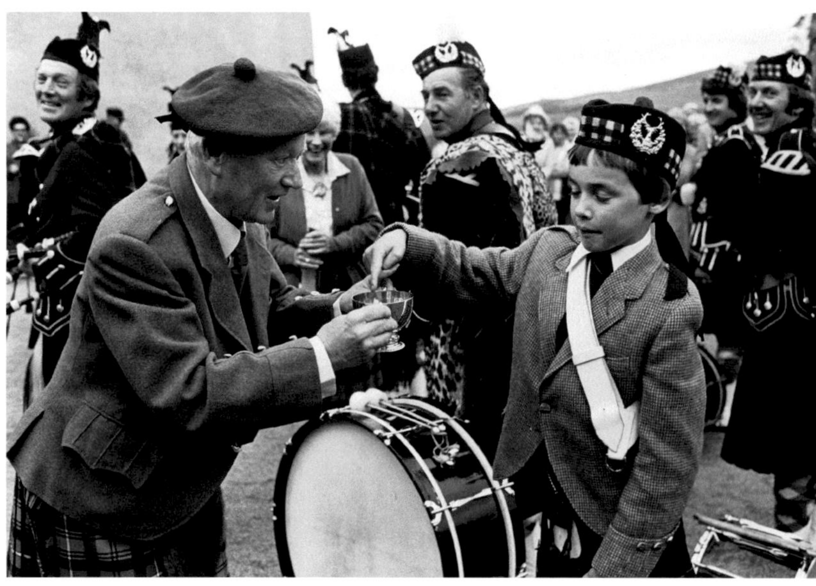

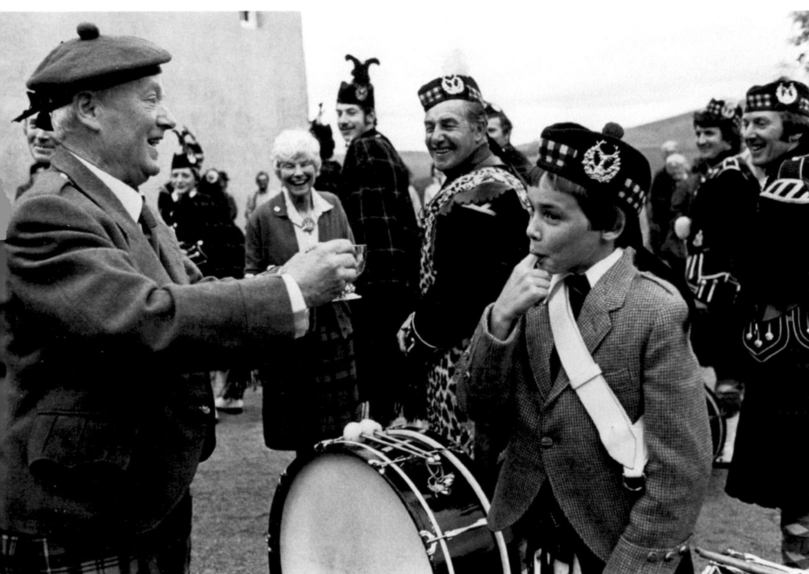

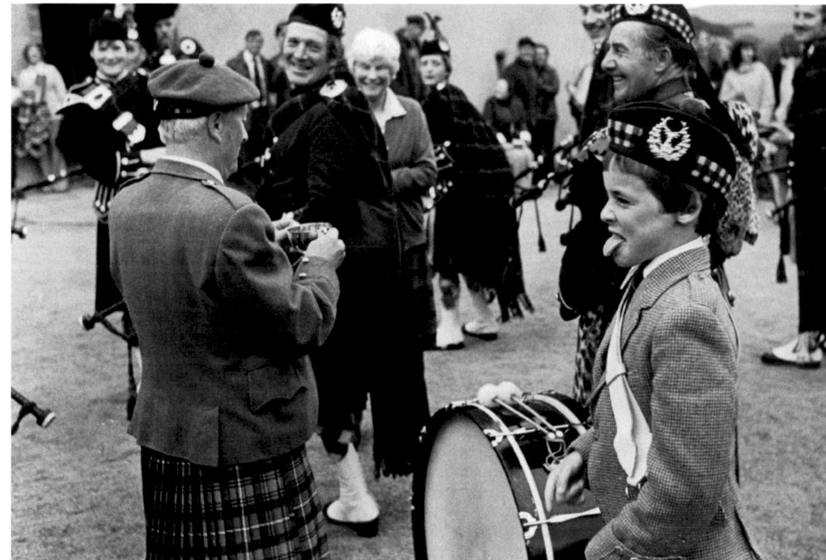

The silver quaich, filled with the best malt whisky, is passed around the pipers at Craigievar Castle in the 1980s and reminds me of my first reaction to the amber nectar – it is very much an adult taste.

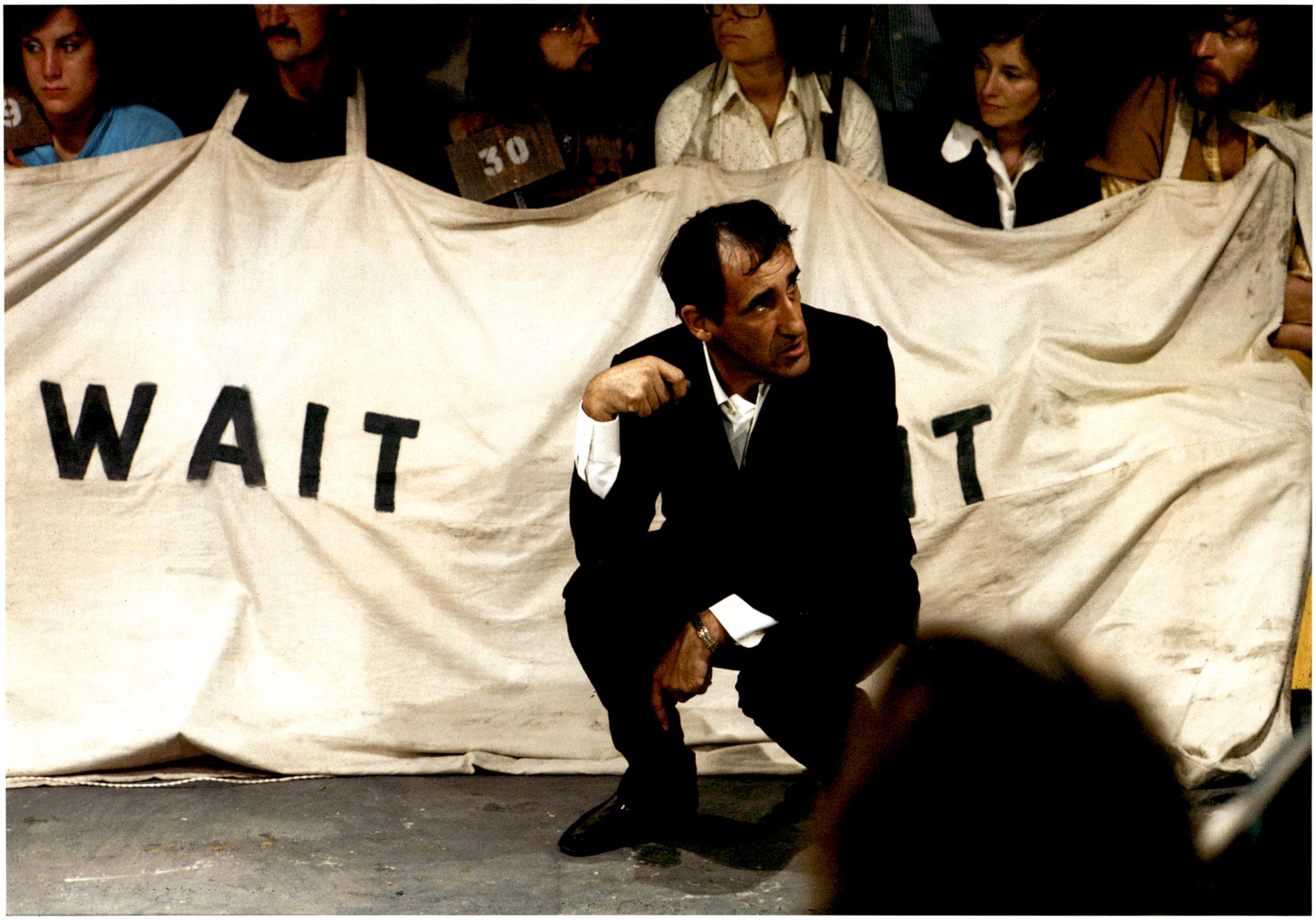

The innovative Polish actor and artist Tadeusz Kantor directing as part of the performance of his Edinburgh Festival Fringe production of *Lovelies and Dowdies* at the Forrest Hill Theatre in 1973. The strong and brilliant visual staging made translation unnecessary.

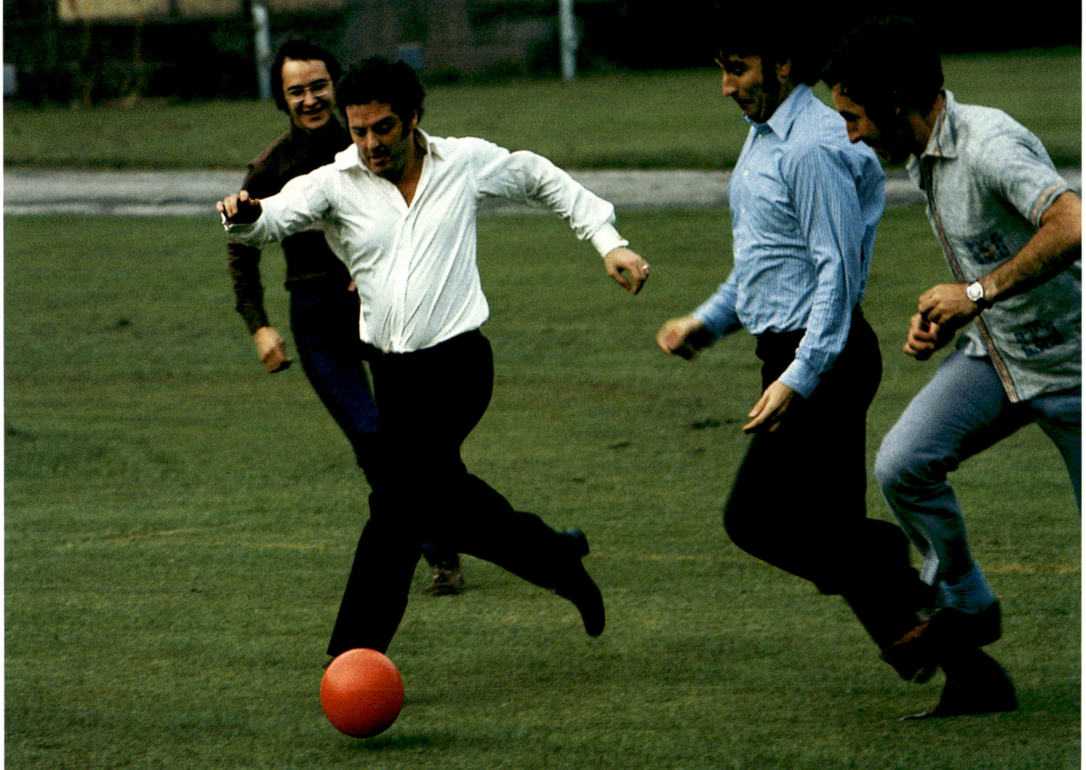

The Argentinian-Israeli musician Daniel Barenboim catches a game of football in the grounds of George Watson's College while rehearsing his operatic début as conductor of the 1973 production of Mozart's *Don Giovanni* at the Edinburgh International Festival.

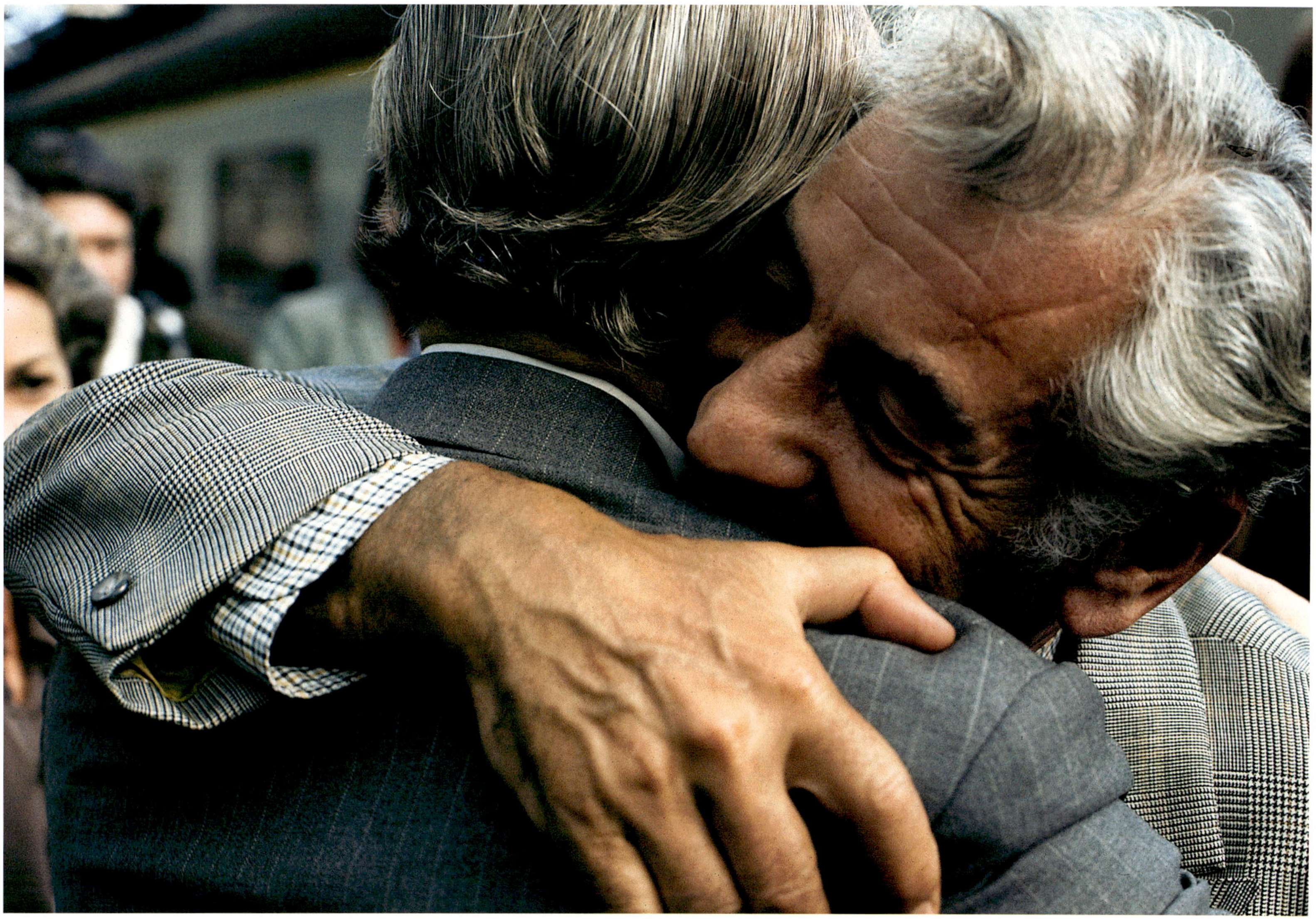

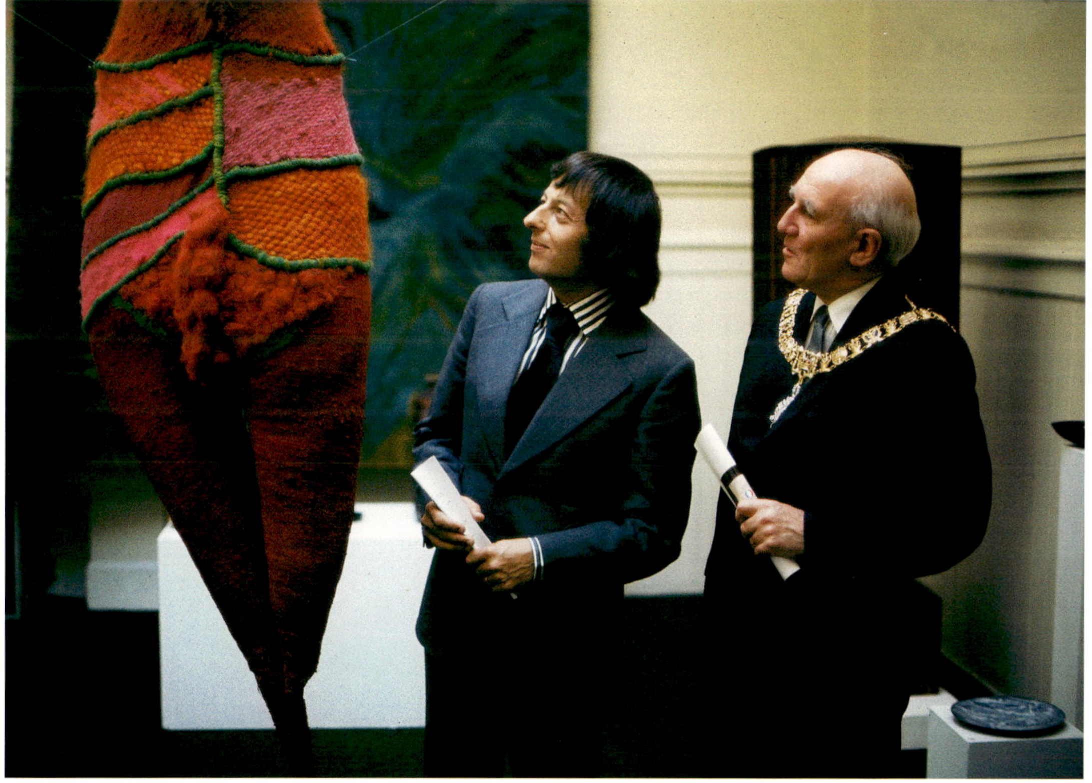

Arriving at Waverley Station, the American composer and conductor Leonard Bernstein embraces Peter Diamand, director of the Edinburgh International Festival from 1965 to 1978. As the official photographer at Mr Bernstein's 55th birthday celebrations at Hopetoun House, I had to arrange a group that included Peter Ustinov, Daniel Barenboim and Issac Stern, to name but a few. The usually disciplined performers were larking about in front of the camera, making my life difficult, and Mr Ustinov was particularly troublesome.

The American conductor André Previn and the Lord Provost of Edinburgh admire a suggestive woven sculpture at a Festival exhibition. What are they really thinking or are they just going through the motions? Having photographed so many of these, I wonder if the public realise how much time is spent by officials on 'Grip and Grin' (Meet and Greet).

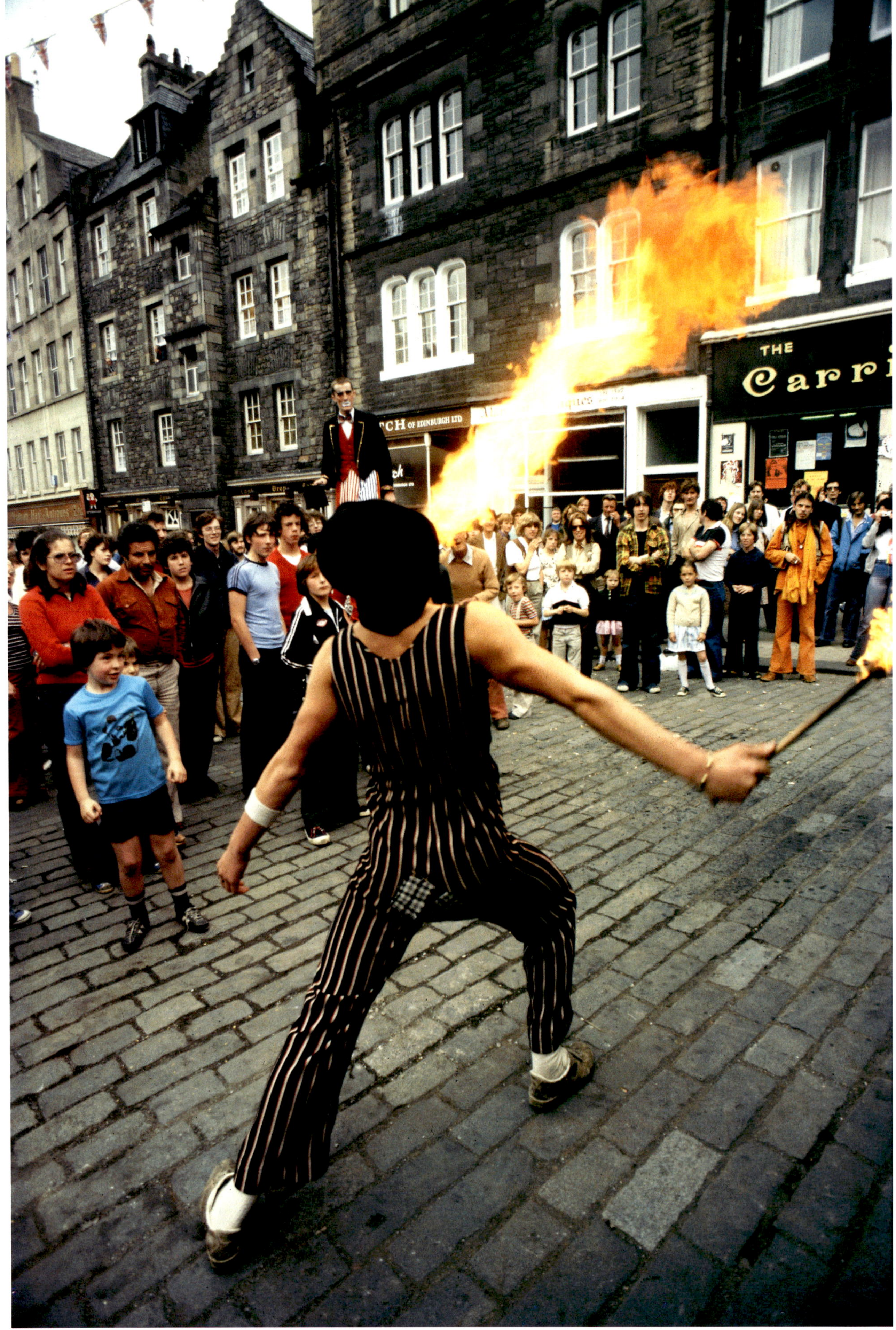

My first year in Edinburgh and my first Festival, in 1973. Buskers, like this one in the Grassmarket, were much more relaxed about photographers. Nowadays we sometimes find ourselves on the receiving end as the butt of their jokes. I am particularly prone to this, being follically challenged.

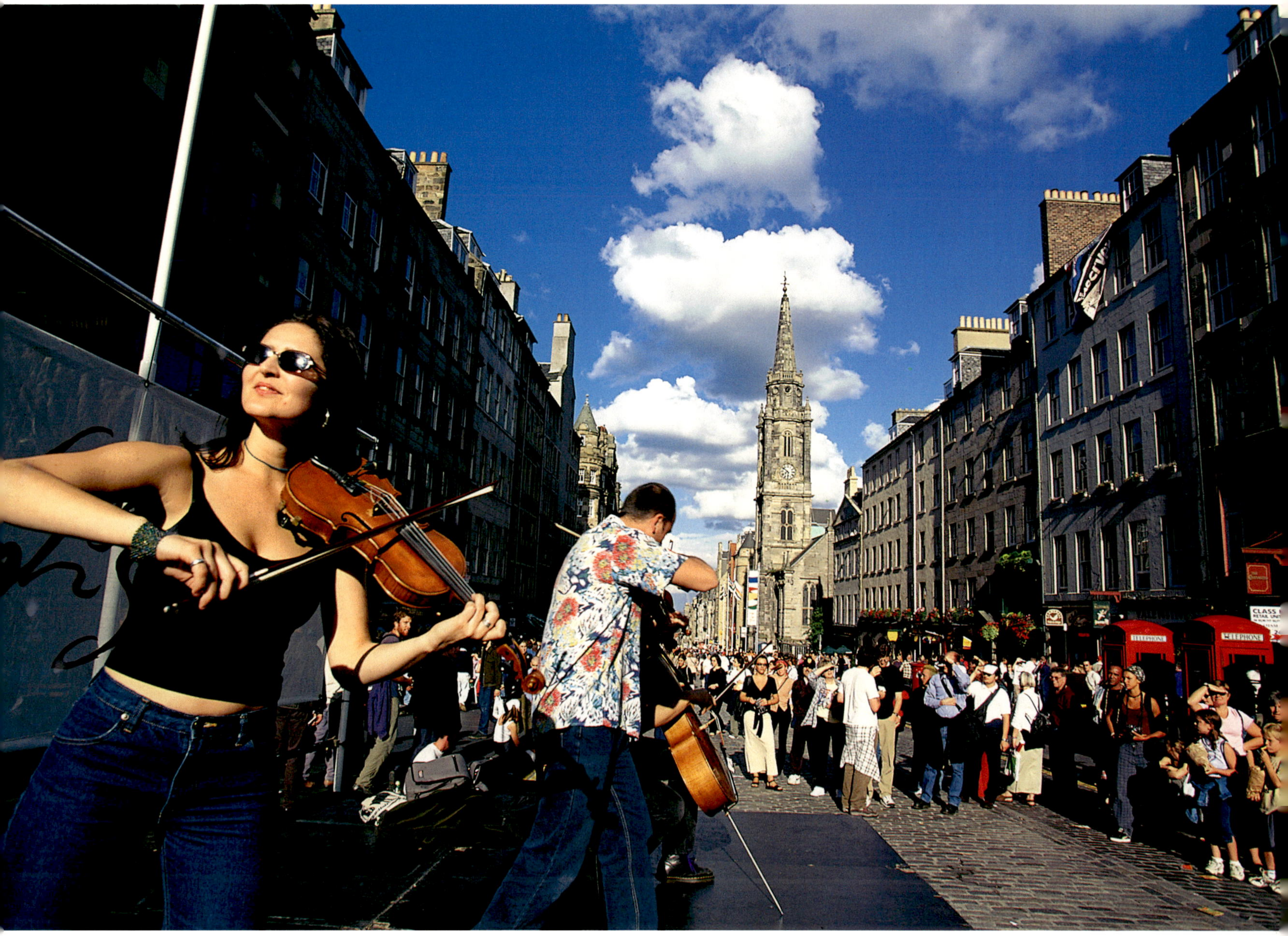

After I had photographed this excellent Australian fusion group in 2000, I asked them if they knew my friend, composer and musician Rik Rue. I was pleased when they said, 'He's the main man.' I've known Rik from the 1960s when he was 18 and mixing tapes in his mother's converted wash-house in an inner Sydney suburb. Check him out.

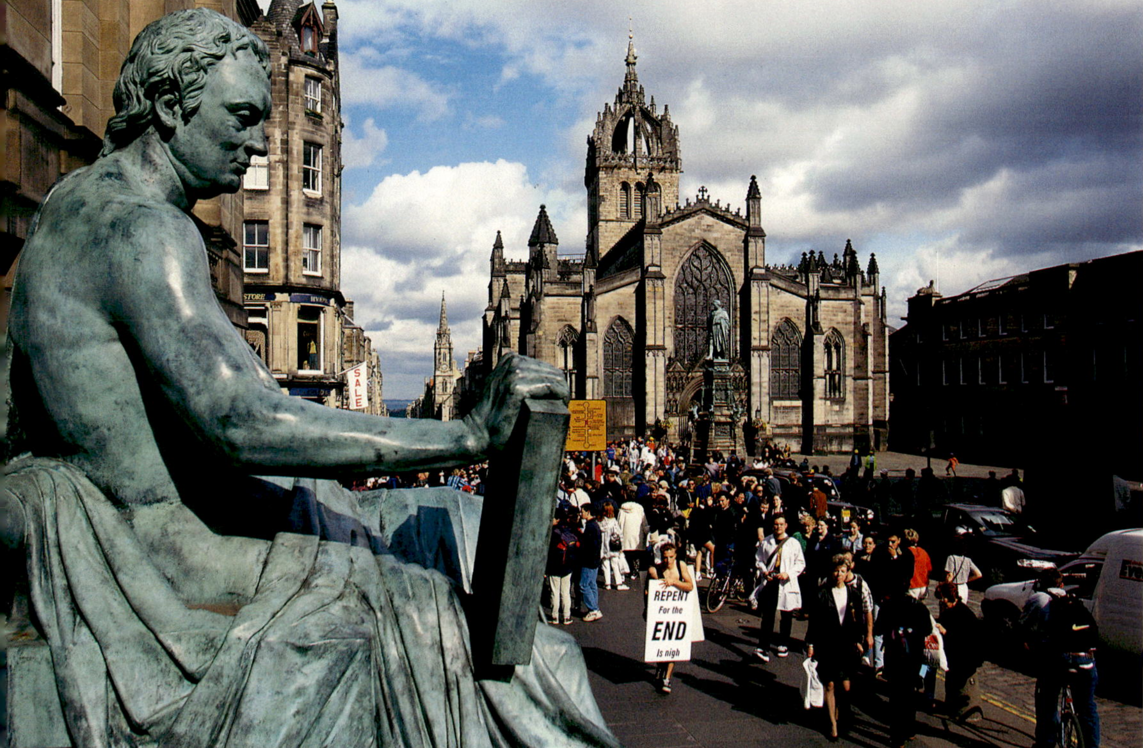

You can imagine words from the pulpit of St Giles echoing the sentiment of the sandwich board. Both the bearer and the philosopher David Hume appear to share a fashion for being under-dressed (at least according to sculptor Alexander Stoddart's interpretation).

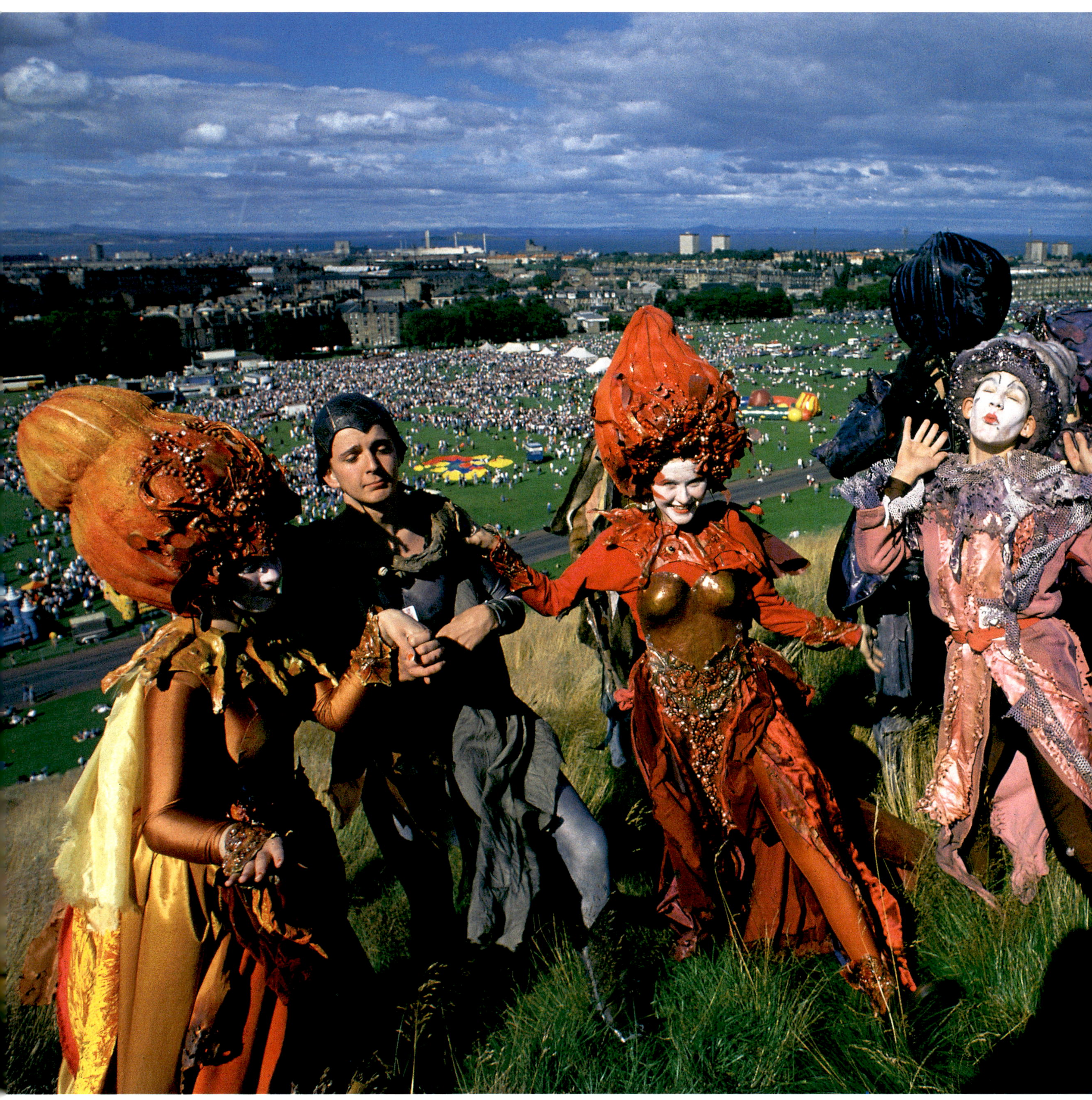

The Fringe Sunday event used to be held in Holyrood Park. This lively bunch in great costumes sums up the best of the Fringe performers. I'm always impressed by the boundless energy and enthusiasm that an endless stream of amateur and student performers bring to the Fringe year after year. For many of the individuals involved, however, it may be the only time they ever tread the boards before settling down to a future out of the spotlight.

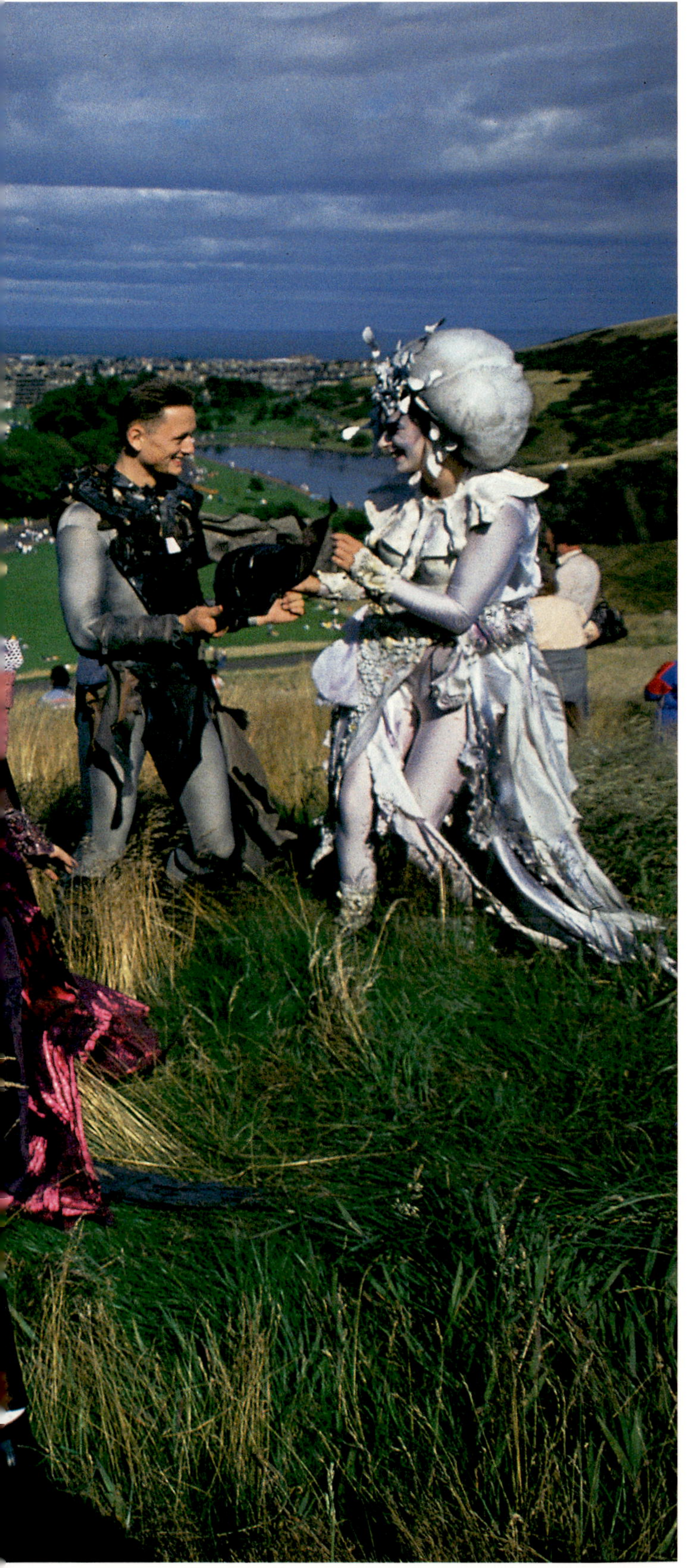

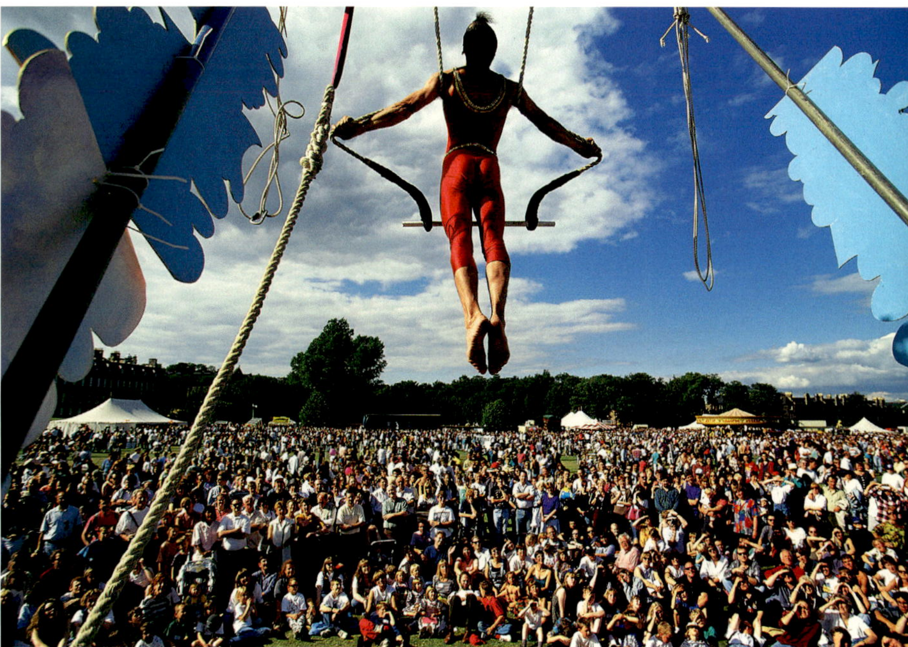

Fringe Sunday is a free event that gives a platform for many acts to promote their productions. Weather permitting, they are assured of a large audience. The venue has since changed to the Meadows.

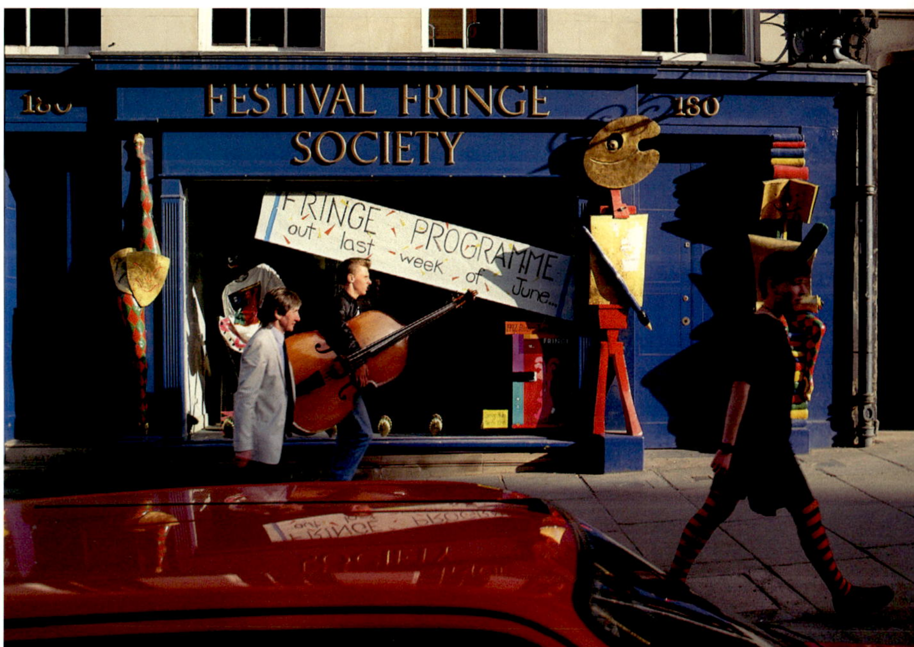

A nice addition to the High Street with the Miró-like figures on the Fringe shop. It was fortuitous that I caught the musician passing, which adds to the shot, but it is a pity that the atmosphere created by the Festival and its visitors can't last all year.

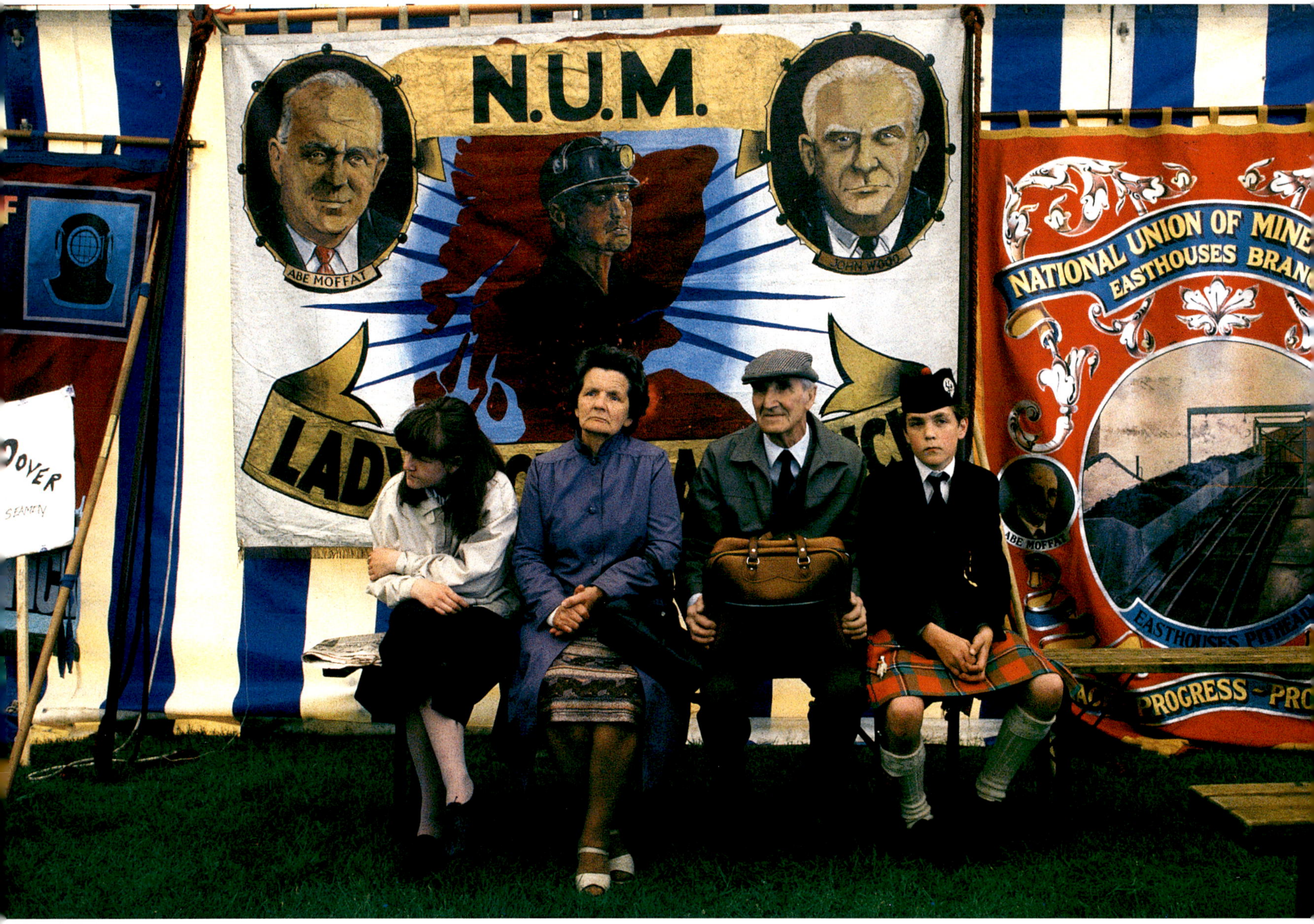

A miners' rally in Edinburgh during the 1970s. The lady echoes the strength and solidarity that I associated with mining communities.

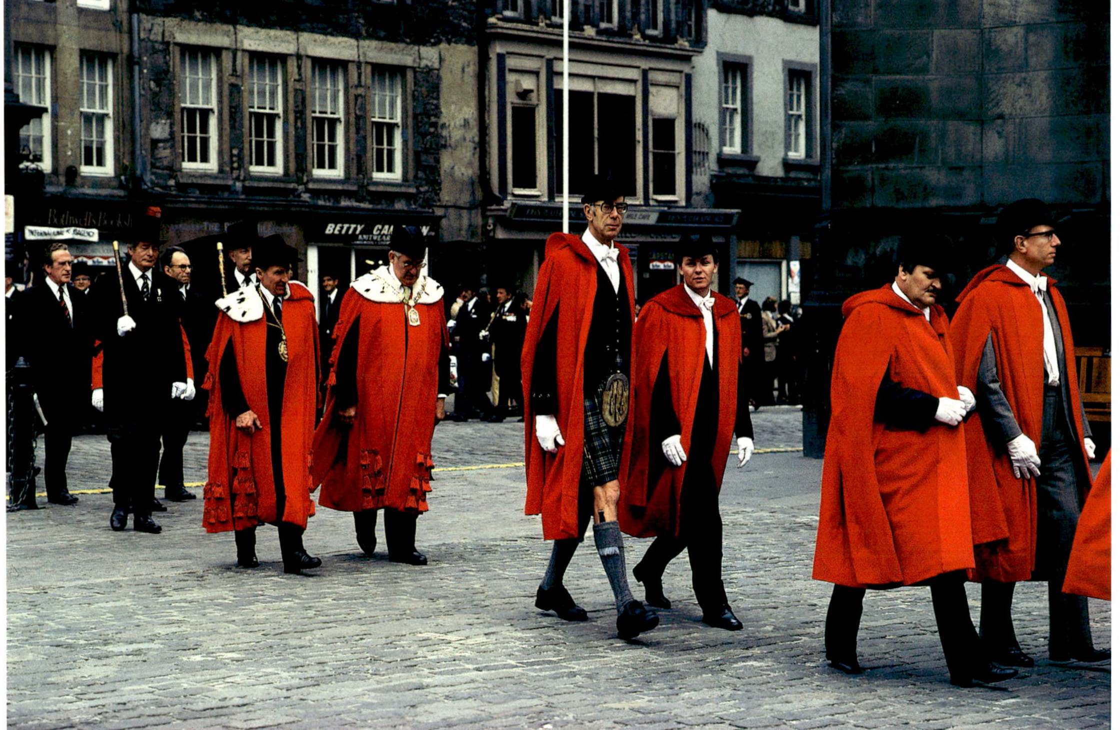

The annual Kirking of the Council at St Giles Cathedral, Edinburgh, in the 1970s. The kilt is a bit incongruous with robes and a cocked hat. Let's hope that some divine intervention can stop a large council tax increase.

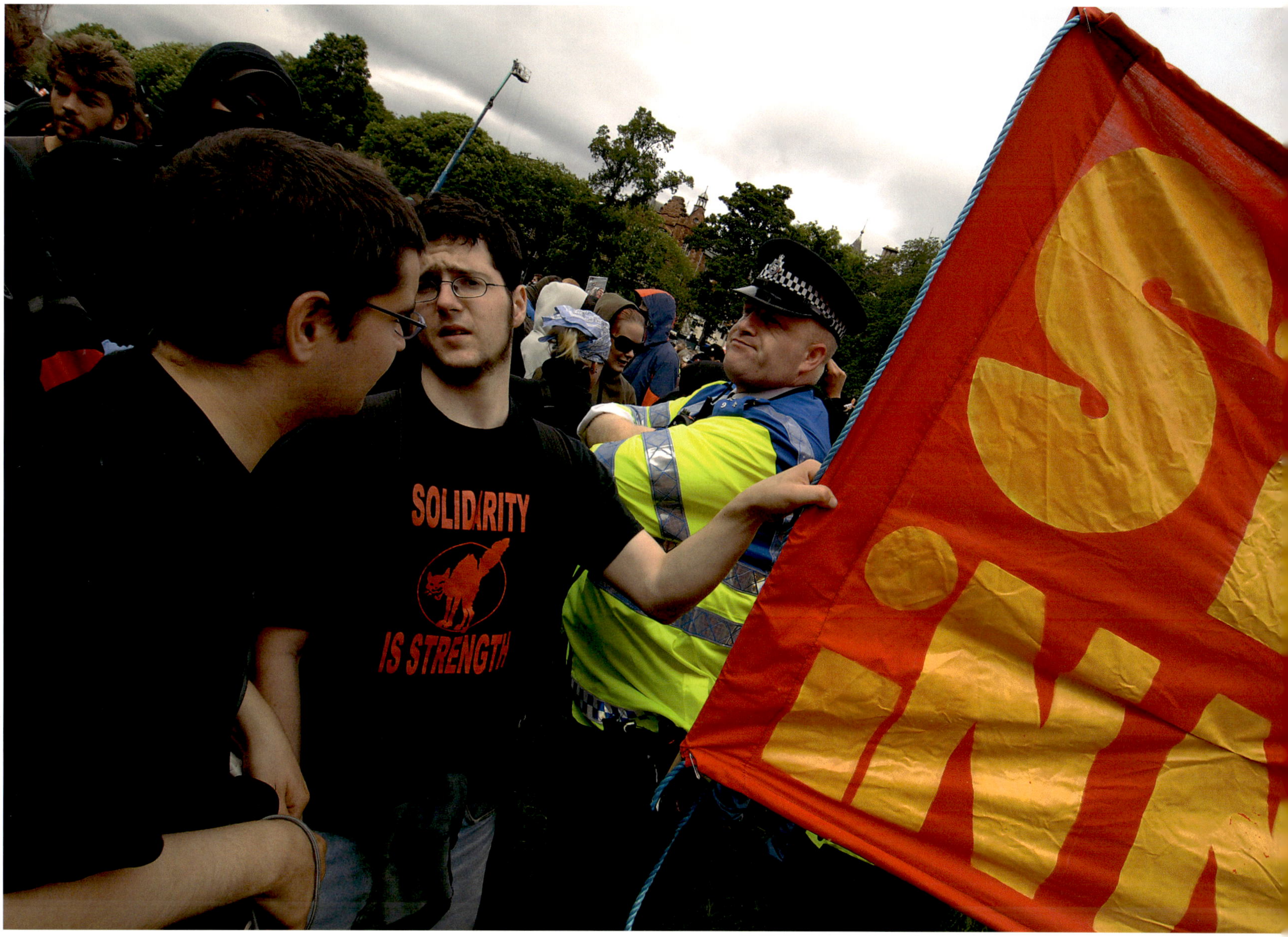

The Make Poverty History campaign attracted almost a quarter of a million people to Edinburgh's Meadows to demonstrate at the G8 summit in July 2005, with groups as diverse as Anarchists and Church Women's Guilds.

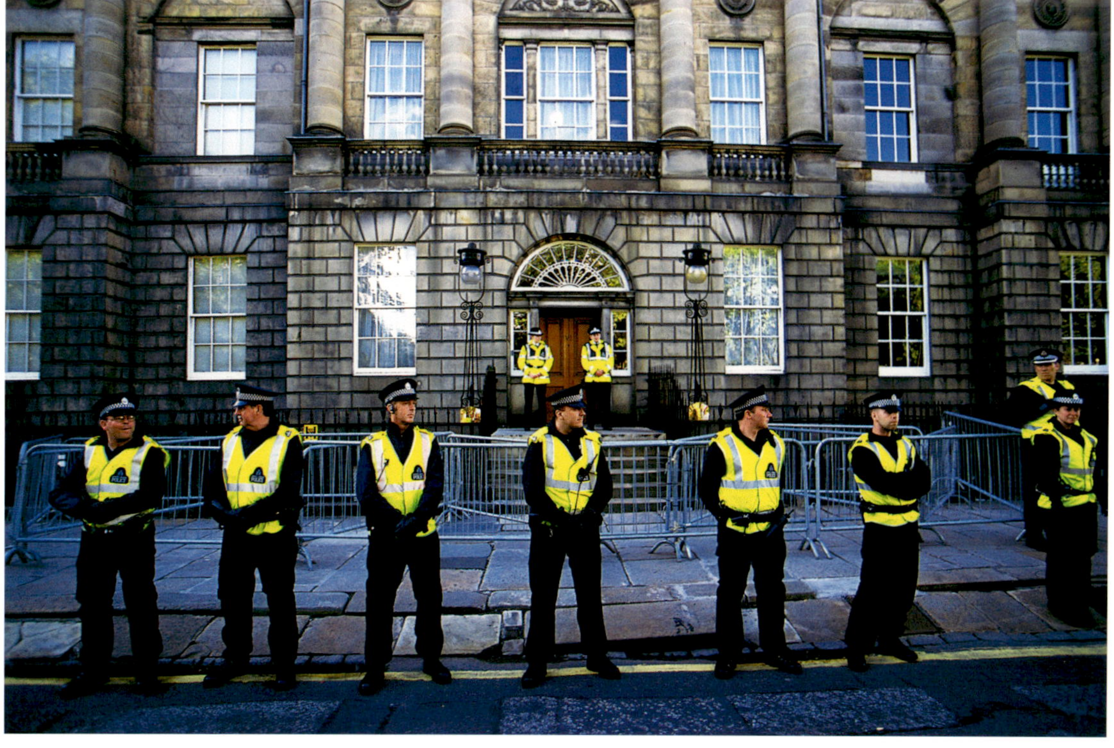

The First Minister's residence in Charlotte Square was being protected from a group of people demonstrating for peace in 2004. They were the least aggressive-looking folk you could imagine. Is a bit of idealism really that dangerous?

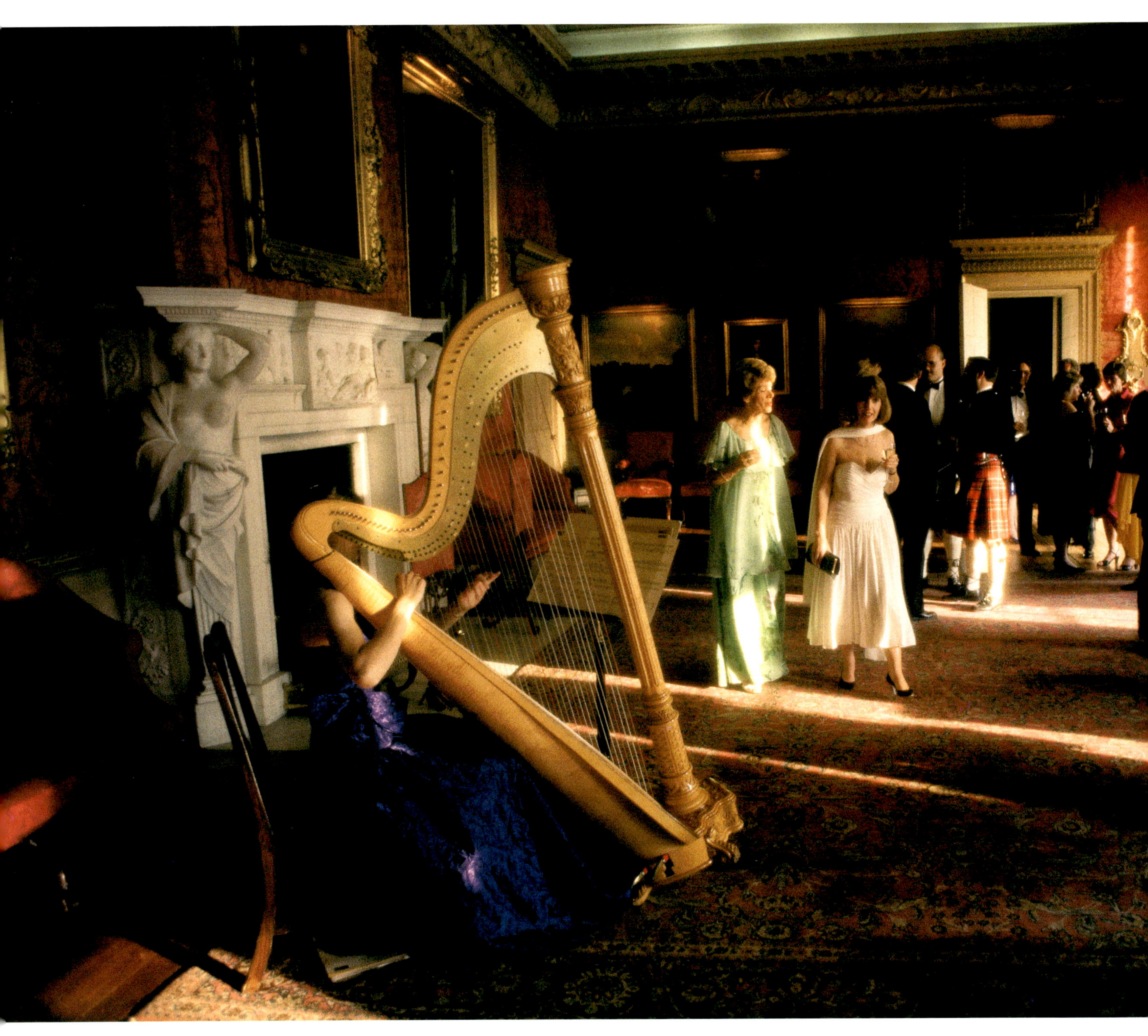

A swanky corporate do in the 1990s to give the hoi polloi a few hours of aristocratic living. Built in 1721, Hopetoun House on the edge of Edinburgh is William Adam's grandest Scottish mansion.

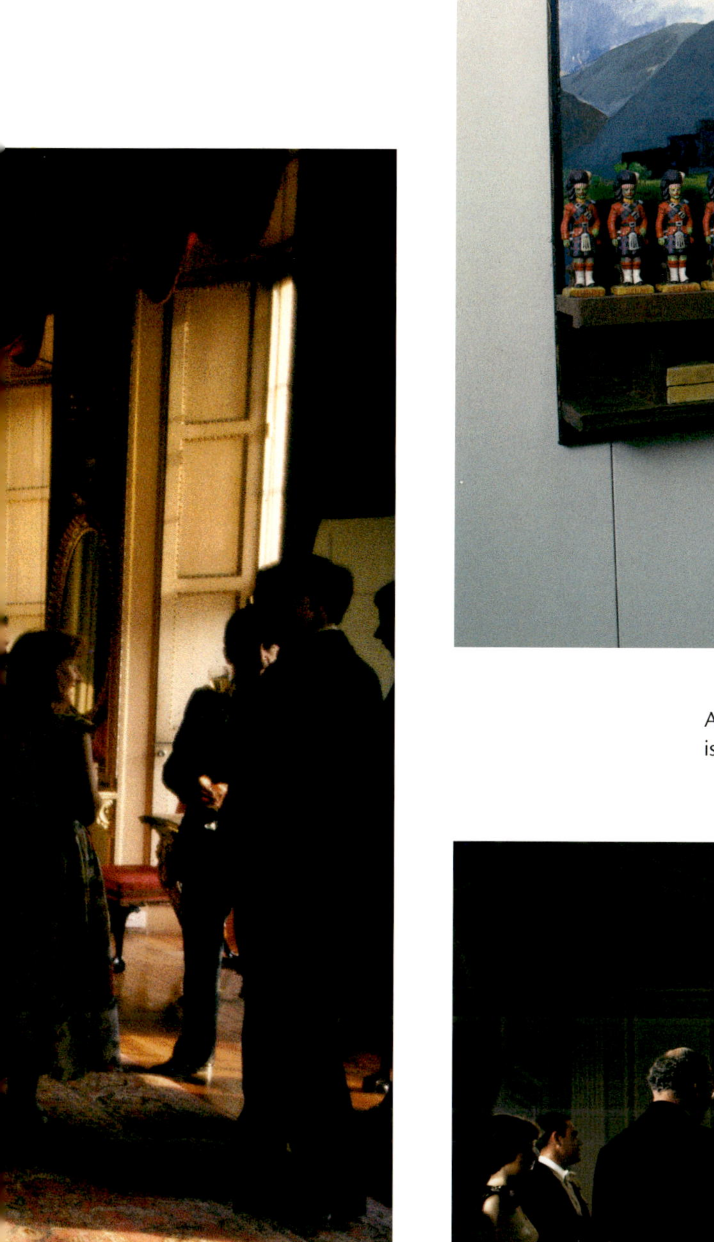

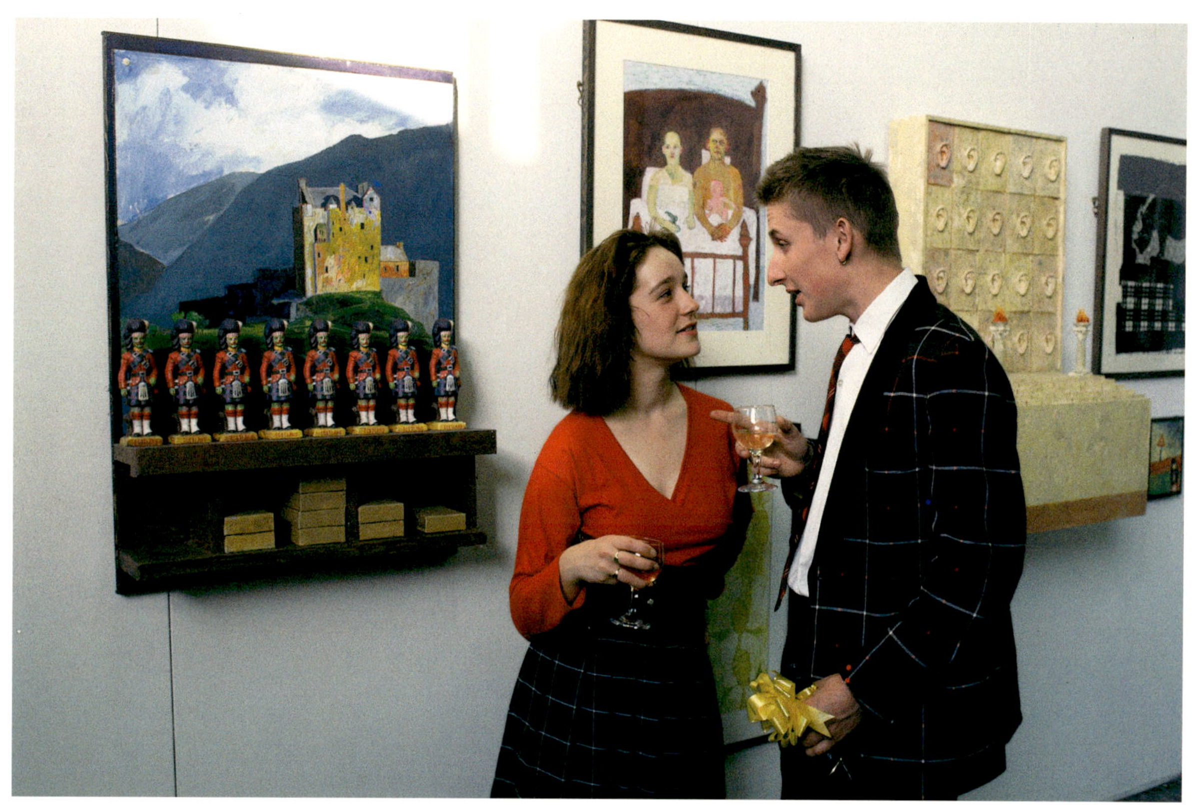

An Edinburgh College of Art Degree Show in the 1990s. The artist's jacket is in keeping with his tartan Pop Art construction.

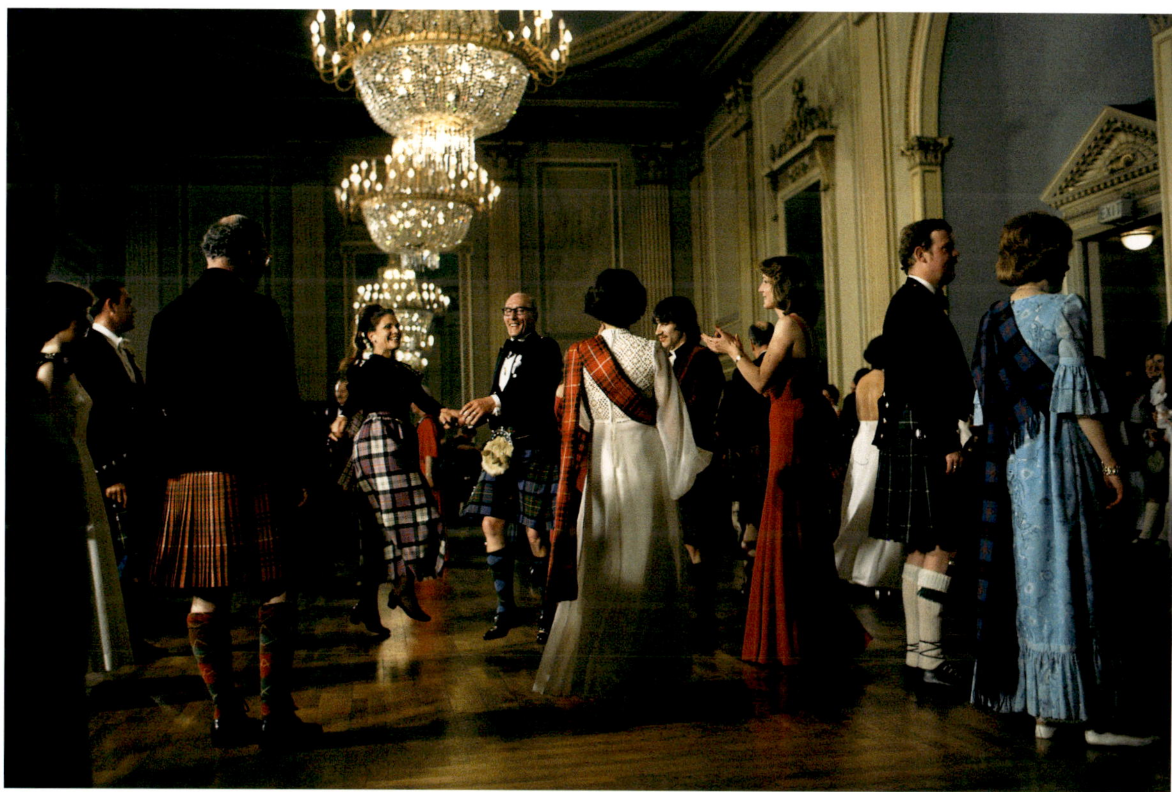

A posh Highland Ball in the Assembly Rooms in Edinburgh in the 1970s. The gentleman on the far left with his back to camera is Andrew Douglas Alexander Thomas Bruce, 11th Earl of Elgin and 15th Earl of Kincardine, KT, CD, JP, DL. He is a descendant of the Lord Elgin who took the marbles from the Parthenon in Athens, now housed in the British Museum.

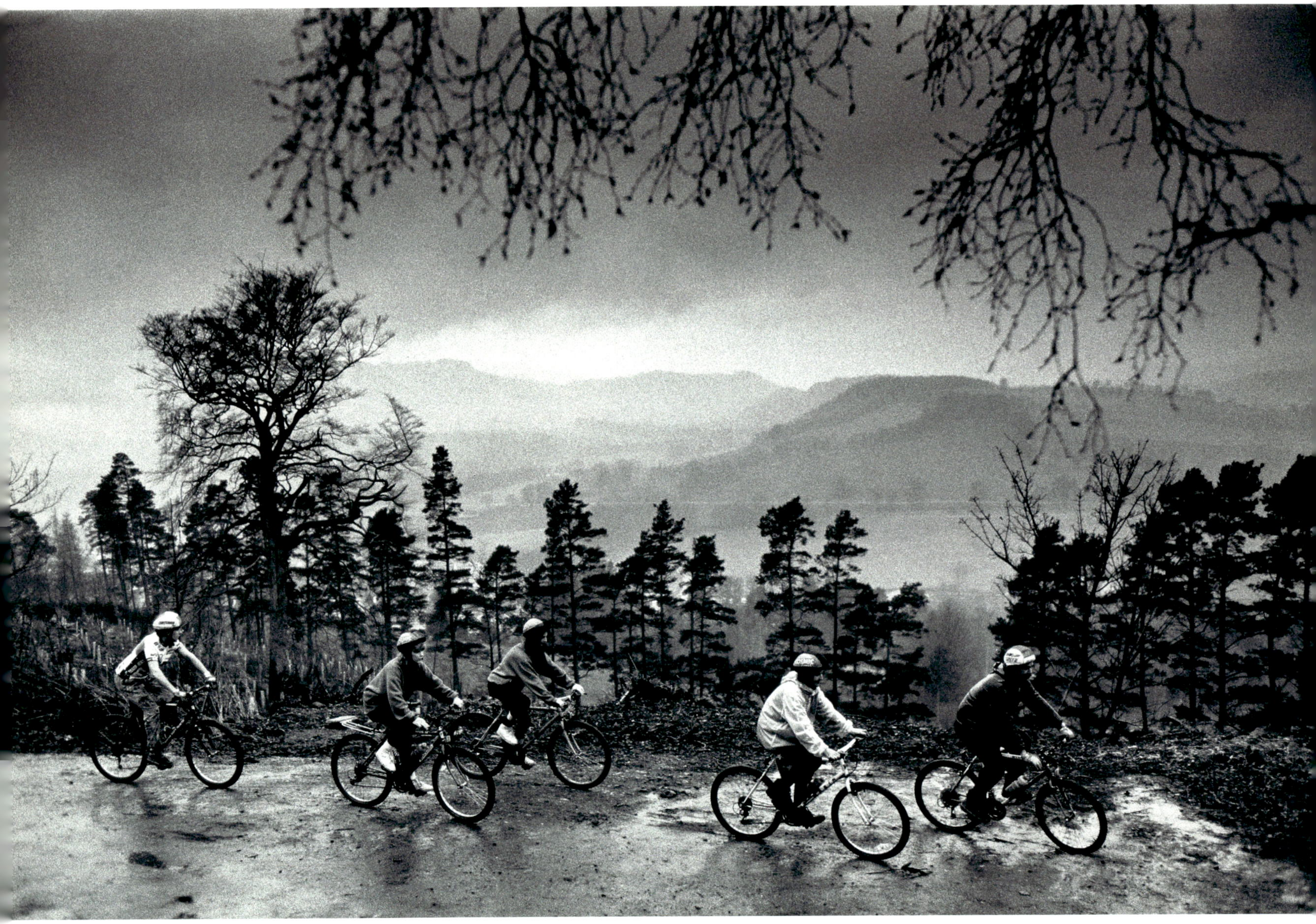

In the 1950s everyone cycled, more out of necessity than for pleasure (or for political correctness). I shot this above Crieff in the early 1990s when cycling had undergone a rebirth as a major leisure activity. This sedate image contrasts with the more extreme forms of mountain biking. The setting is imbued with some of the delicacy of a Chinese painting.

Fort William plays host to an international event, the Scottish Six Day Trials. This extreme sport has riders going up mountain streams and manoeuvring from rock to rock. My uncle, Gordon Morrell, was one of Scotland's top riders when it was a purely amateur sport. As a kid I remember accompanying him to a trial. I was waiting at a very difficult stage when I overheard a spectator comment,'This is Morrell coming – he's worth watching'.

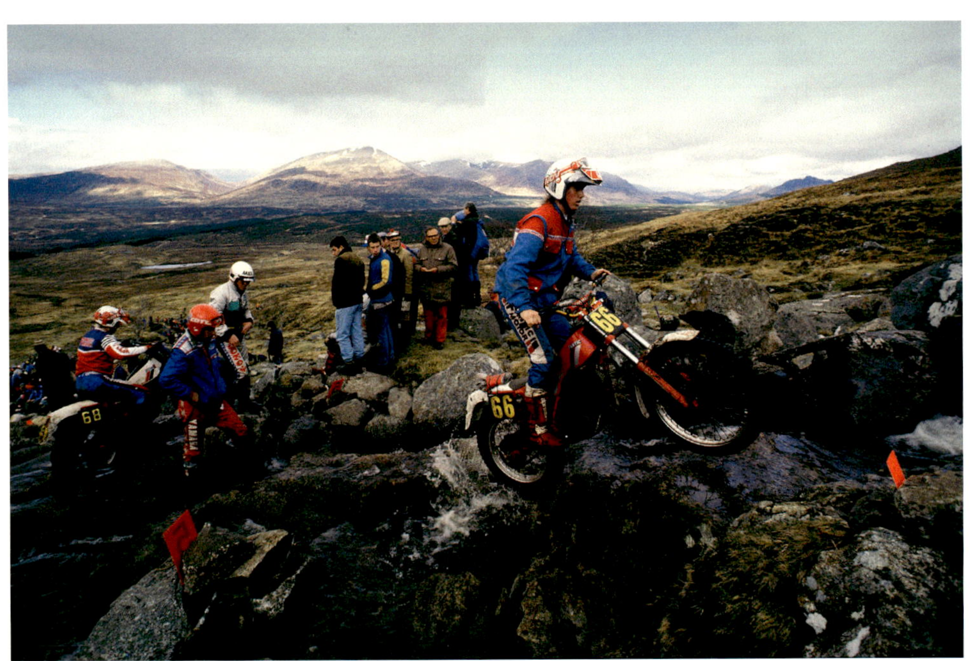

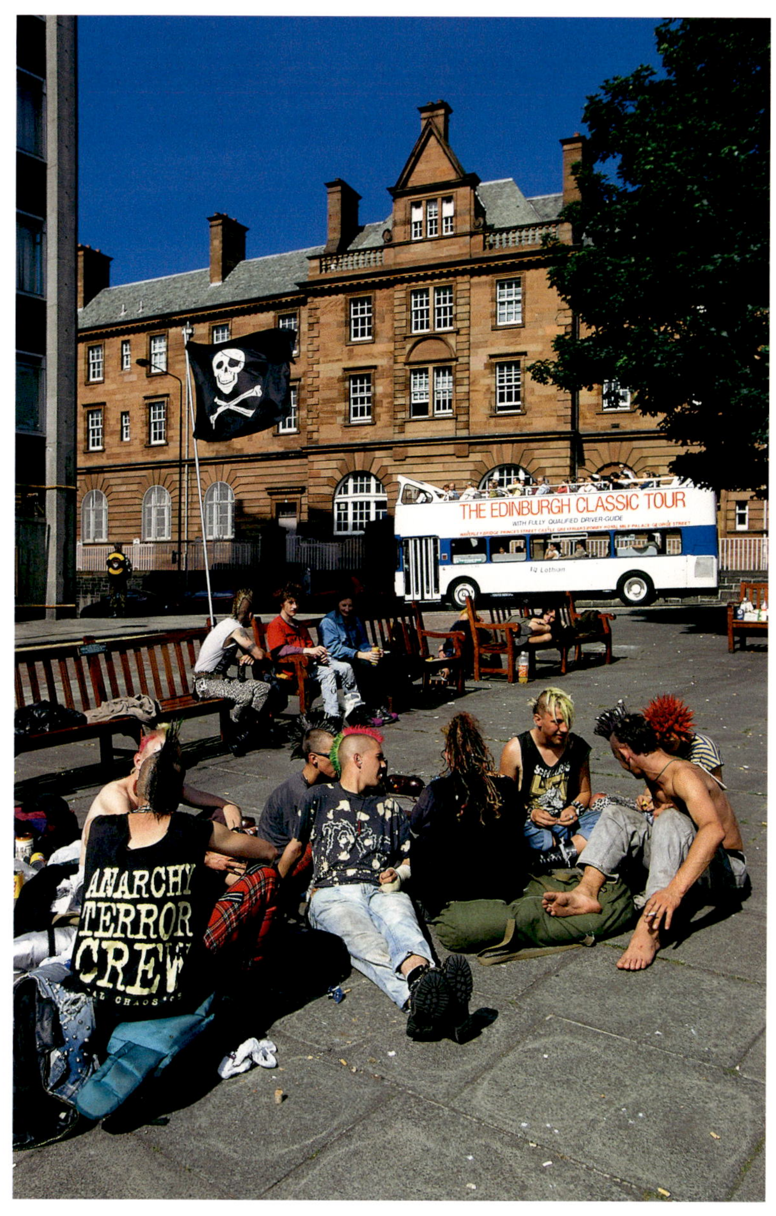

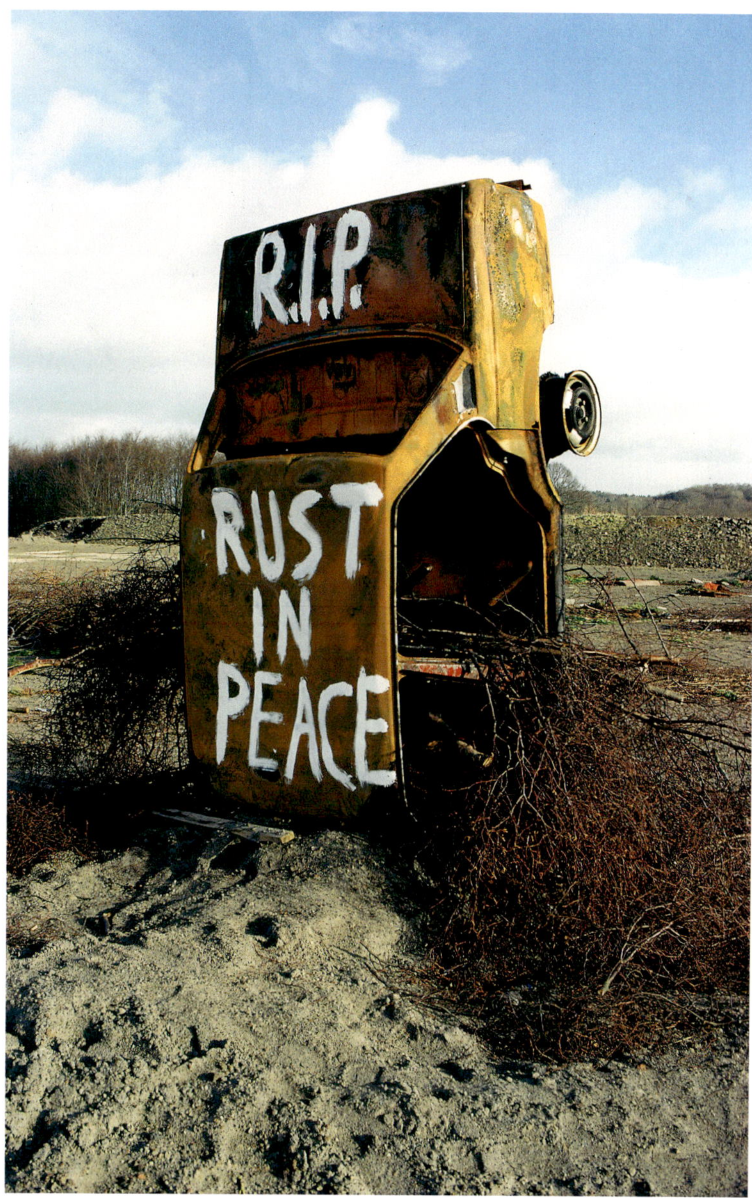

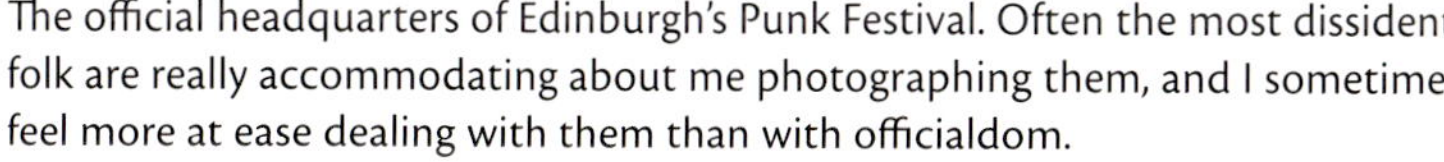

The official headquarters of Edinburgh's Punk Festival. Often the most dissident folk are really accommodating about me photographing them, and I sometimes feel more at ease dealing with them than with officialdom.

A work of protest art (along with tree-top protesters) on the outskirts of Glasgow, which was against a new road that threatened to encroach on a public park and displace a school.

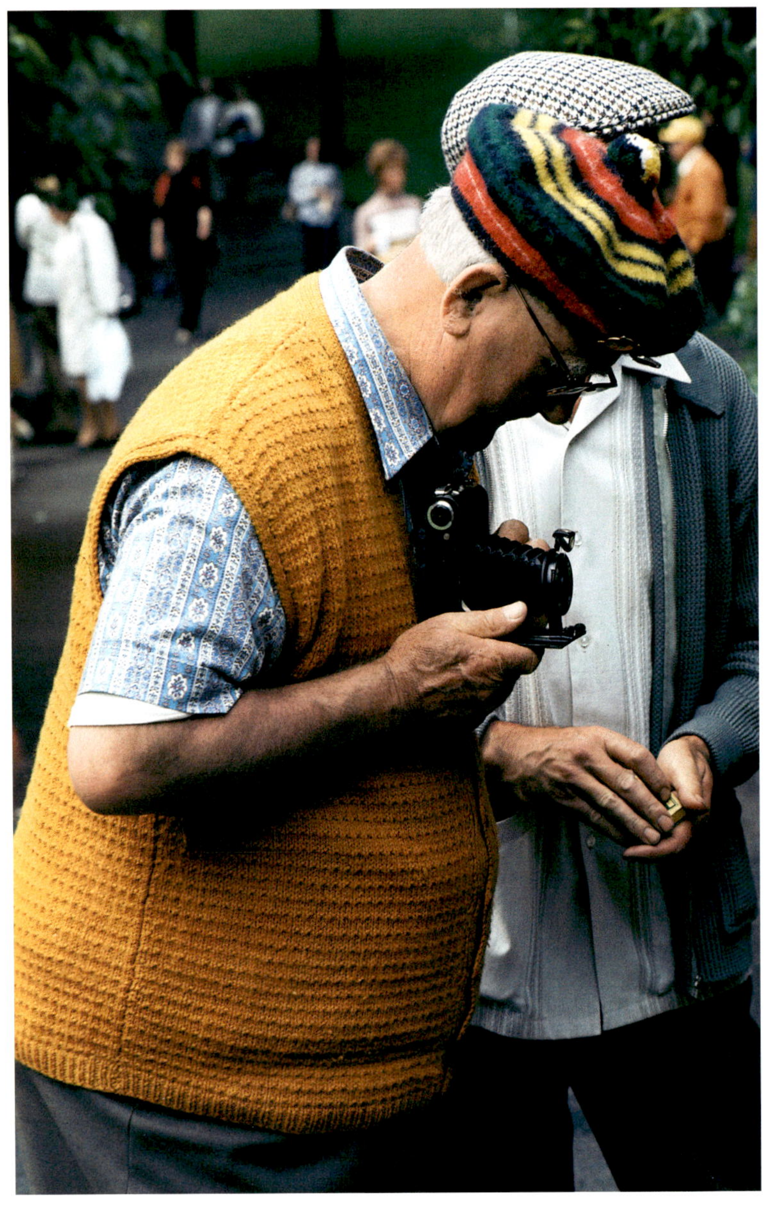

A pre-digital snapper in Princes Street Gardens, Edinburgh, in the early 1970s. Recently, a former assistant introduced me to one of his contemporaries as 'a photographer of the old school', whatever that means. I'd be happy to belong to any school.

Index of Photographs